History of Ethics

HISTORY OF ETHICS

by Vernon J. Bourke

DOUBLEDAY & COMPANY, INC.

Garden City, New York

1968

Library of Congress Catalog Card Number 67–19089
Copyright © 1968 by Vernon J. Bourke
All Rights Reserved
Printed in the United States of America

Contents

Introduction   7

PART ONE: GRAECO-ROMAN THEORIES

  I. Early Greek Eudaimonism   11
  II. Teleological Eudaimonism: Aristotle   23
  III. Hellenistic Ethics: Stoic, Epicurean, and Neoplatonic   32

PART TWO: PATRISTIC AND MEDIEVAL THEORIES

  IV. Patristic and Early Medieval Ethics   47
  V. Medieval Jewish and Moslem Ethics   65
  VI. Right Reason Theories   87

PART THREE: EARLY MODERN ETHICS: 1450–1750

  VII. Humanist Ethics in the Renaissance   111
  VIII. British Egoism and Its Reactions   131
  IX. Rationalistic Ethics on the Continent   151

PART FOUR: MODERN THEORIES

  X. Utilitarian and Subjectivist Ethics in Britain   175
  XI. German Idealistic Ethics   190
  XII. Franco-Latin Spiritistic Ethics   203
  XIII. Societal Ethics in Europe   218

PART FIVE: CONTEMPORARY ETHICS

  XIV. Axiological Ethics   237
  XV. Self-Realization and Utilitarian Ethics   249
  XVI. Naturalistic Ethics   263
  XVII. Analytic Ethics   279
  XVIII. Existential and Phenomenological Ethics   295

Notes   311

Bibliography   353

Index   419

Introduction

THE PRESENT HISTORY attempts to provide an account of the ethical theories of Western philosophers from the beginnings, five hundred years before Christ, to the present. All the writers on ethics that I know to have any importance are included, with the exception of strictly contemporary ethicians. There are simply too many of them for one volume, so key members of different contemporary schools have been selected. Such broad scope means that lengthy expositions of the individual views of these thinkers cannot be given. However, I have tried to emphasize the key contributions of each thinker, in the field of ethics only. In cases where the ethical theory depends rather directly on a writer's epistemology, psychology, metaphysics, or other such position, this speculative background is sketched briefly.

This is not a "critical" history; that is to say, I have not attempted to offer my own evaluations of the theories covered. My intention has been to give an open and fair-minded presentation to each type of ethics. There are some that I like better than others but my preferences are not permitted consciously to intrude. In teaching courses on all periods of the history of philosophy for almost forty years, first at the University of Toronto and later at St. Louis University, I have come to feel that the best criticism is found in philosophy's own story. Sometimes earlier thinkers are neglected, or unfairly appraised, in subsequent centuries, but good thoughts have a way of rising to the surface and eventually making themselves evident again.

Ancient and medieval ethical theory centers on the problem of how man in general is to achieve well-being. Before the Renaissance it was generally assumed that all men are by nature ordered toward the attainment of one ultimate end. In different writers this over-all goal is described diversely but the orientation of all premodern ethical thought is teleological. This means that the focal point of nearly all the ethics covered in the first two parts of this history is the question: How may man best live and act, so that he will reach his final objective as a man?

On the other hand, modern and contemporary ethical theories focus on the problem of practical judgment: How can one explain and justify "oughtness" in human experience? This contrast between the older and the modern viewpoints is a matter of different emphases and not an absolute shift in the meaning of ethics. The ancient or medieval thinker was, of course, aware of the importance of moral obligation and judgment; he was certainly not unacquainted with the importance of the "ought-to-be-done." Similarly, although they do not stress ultimate ends and final causes, nearly all modern ethicians recognize that the results of human actions and attitudes are implied in the awareness of every ought.

Thus, from the time of the first Greek philosophers, ethics has had but one meaning: it is the reflective study of what is good or bad in that part of human conduct for which man has some personal responsibility. The variety of meanings given to "good or bad" (or other evaluative terms) in this moral context is what makes the diversities of position in the history of ethics. Religious moralities with no reflective or theoretical base are not included in this history, unless they have had some important influence on ethical thinking.

Always a problem in a work such as this is terminology. I have tried to avoid jargon peculiar to but one minor thinker or one narrow school but where specialized terms occur they are explained. Often it has been convenient to use the classifications developed by Thomas E. Hill in his excellent book *Contemporary Ethical Theories*. There, six self-explanatory categories are used: ethical theories may be skeptical, approbative, process, psychological value, metaphysical, or intuitive, in their types. These classifications cover most of the possibilities of variation in the field. Incidentally, English writers have not been able to agree on what to call a person who works at ethics: I usually write "ethician" but have no objection to "ethicist." "Moral philosopher" is an older term and I use it as equivalent to ethician. The name "moralist," however, has a different meaning: it suggests one who moralizes, rather than a person interested in the theory of ethics.

As far as geographical scope is concerned, no effort is made here to treat Oriental ethics; not that it is unimportant, but its study requires a background and linguistic equipment that are not mine. Most theories presented in this history have some direct relation to, or impact on, the cultural development of Western man. Perhaps they will not tell us clearly what is the best way to live, or even what is an unassailable ground for moral judgment, but they do provide a wide variety of important suggestions as to how we might think on these human problems.

PART ONE

GRAECO-ROMAN THEORIES

CHAPTER I

Early Greek Eudaimonism

THE FIRST Greek philosophers were not primarily interested in ethics but in speculation concerning the constitution of the physical universe. However, some of the predecessors of Socrates made fragmentary contributions to moral theory. Among the first were the Pythagoreans, who were organized into a religious brotherhood during the sixth century B.C. and continued as a school of practical philosophy into the first centuries of the Christian era. Their founder was Pythagoras of Samos (fl. 530 B.C.), who remains an obscure figure, despite biographical sketches by Iamblichus, Porphyry, and Diogenes Laërtius. It is impossible to distinguish his personal views from the ethical thinking of his immediate followers, because our only sources of information are fragmentary quotations and summaries found in much later Greek writings.[1]

Mathematics and music were central studies in Pythagorean schools. That numbers and harmonious proportions constitute all reality was the basic conviction of the Pythagoreans. They saw the human soul as the life spirit which endures after the death of its first body and may take up its abode subsequently in another human or animal body. This theory of metempsychosis, or transmigration of souls, is ethically significant since it provides for the rewarding of good action and the punishment of evil in these subsequent reincarnations.[2] Possibly the most important Pythagorean contribution to ethics stemmed from their study of mathematical means. Mathematically, the "mean" was a function midway between two extremes, combining and harmonizing the best features of each. In practice, the Pythagoreans used the idea of the mean to locate good health as a medium condition between excess and defect in temperature, in the amount of liquid in the body, in the taking of exercise, and so on. It was but logical for the Pythagoreans to think of good moral behavior as a mean between extremes. When Aristotle later developed his sophisticated theory of moral virtue as a golden mean between extremes of vice, he gave full credit for the basic idea to the Pythagoreans.[3]

The Pythagoreans also developed a theory of opposites in which the "limiting" and the "non-limiting" were the chief pair. They understood limit as a definite and measurable characteristic of anything, and the non-limited as that which defied attempts at definition and measurement. Their standard geometrical example of the latter was, of course, the diagonal of any rectangle: it is impossible to express its length simply in terms of the sides. The diagonal is then a surd, an irrational number. Falsehood and envy are thus identified by the Pythagoreans with the non-limited and irrational.[4] This is the beginning of one very important approach to ethical problems, the view that good means what is rational and intelligible. Thus, in the fourth century B.C., a later Pythagorean, Archytas of Tarentum, first enunciated the principle of "right reasoning" as the key to good behavior: "Right Reckoning, when discovered, checks civil strife and increases concord . . . (it is) the standard and deterrent of wrong doers."[5] It is quite possible that Aristotelian and medieval theories of right reason (recta ratio) as the norm of ethical judgment are directly indebted to Pythagorean intellectualism. The classic Greek respect for the life of reason (logos) is already evident in the early Pythagorean teachings.

Contemporary with the early Pythagoreans but not members of that school were certain individual philosophers who made minor contributions to moral theory: Heraclitus, Democritus, and Anaxagoras. The first of these, Heraclitus of Ephesus (fl. 500 B.C.) is best known for his cosmological teaching that all things are in constant flux or change. Actually, many Heraclitean fragments suggest that there is an ever present rational pattern (logos) in this process.[6] Heraclitus had the notion of "law" as a principle of regularity in natural processes but he was also well aware of the importance of law (nomos) in the political sense. Associated with his respect for law and order is Heraclitus' view that the strife between opposites (such as love and hate) is to be resolved according to a measure (metron). The Heraclitean measure is close in meaning to the Pythagorean mean. Some recent studies of Heraclitus suggest that his moral views are of primary importance in his teaching.[7]

In Democritus of Abdera (fl. 420 B.C.) we have the first appearance of one of the key themes in Greek ethics: eudaimonia as the condition of man's "well-being." Democritus' ethical treatise On Cheerfulness has been lost but we have reports on it in Seneca and Plutarch.[8] Though usually classified as a materialistic atomist, Democritus in fact stressed the soul as the locus of human well-being. His concept of eudaimonia includes both the notion of "good existence" (eu—esto) and "good feeling" (eu—thumiē).[9] Indeed, his emphasis on serenity of spirit or undismay (athambiē) is now regarded as an anticipation of the Epicurean condition of ataraxia, the poised attitude of the moral sage. One fragment reads like a Stoic maxim: "Medical science heals diseases of the body but wisdom rids soul of passions."[10] Quite evident in Democritus is the recognition that virtue consists in moderation, or in measured activity.

The first philosopher to teach his subject in Athens was Anaxagoras of Clazomenae (500–428 B.C.). He had no formal ethical teaching but he did introduce the notion of Mind or Intelligence (nous) into Greek philosophical speculation. Anaxagoras suggested that "Mind is infinite and self-ruling, and is mixed with no thing, but is alone by itself."[11] Aristotle gave Anaxagoras credit for the soberness of his thought but criticized him for failing to use nous consistently in explaining cosmic events.[12] In any case, it was Anaxagoras who provided the Greeks with a term which enabled later thinkers to discuss the mental aspects of human conduct and world order.

From the fifth into the fourth century B.C, the Sophists constituted an ill-defined group of Greek teachers. The name meant "wise man" but Aristotle claimed that "the art of the Sophist is the semblance of wisdom without the reality, and the Sophist is one who makes money from an apparent but unreal wisdom."[13] Plato liked them no better, calling the Sophist "a paid hunter after wealth and youth."[14] Sophistry was not really a school of philosophy. The Sophists (1) taught for money, (2) taught mostly practical subjects, and (3) were inclined toward skepticism, subjectivism, and practical relativism.

The most important of the Sophists for the history of ethics was Protagoras of Abdera (fl. 440 B.C.). We know his views through the unfriendly reports of Plato, Aristotle, and later writers. Protagoras probably shared the general sophistic attitude of skepticism toward absolute judgments on truth and rightness. He was a religious agnostic in a period when most Greeks professed some sort of faith in the gods: "As to the gods, I have no means of knowing either that they exist or that they do not exist."[15] Protagoras took a relativistic position on ethical judgments. Plato's dialogue *Protagoras* depicts him, at the start, as defending against Socrates' professed skepticism the view that virtue can be taught. At the end of the dialogue, however, the disputants have reversed positions and Protagoras is denying that virtue is teachable.[16]

Protagoras' most famous teaching was that man is the measure of all things.[17] Whatever this means precisely, it is the first noteworthy assertion of the philosophy of humanism. Some interpreters think that Protagoras understood "man" in terms of the species and was simply saying that we are bound to view reality and action from the standpoint of humanity. Such an interpretation would closely align him with the common Greek respect for the judgment of rational beings. In fact, Protagoras did advocate the practical virtue of good judgment.[18] On the other hand, it is more probable that Protagoras meant that each *individual* man is the sole judge of what is true or right for himself. This is the interpretation suffered by Sextus Empiricus: "he posits only what appears to each individual, and thus he introduces relativity."[19] In the sphere of ethics this would imply that there are no fixed laws, rules, or judgments— and that in the final analysis all opinions are equally valid. As Aristotle says in discussing the teaching of Protagoras: "If, then, reality is such as the view in question supposes, all will be right in their beliefs."[20] This, of course, appears to Aristotle to offend the principle of non-contradiction and would be equivalent to the statement that there can be no scientific knowledge of ethics.

Of the other Sophists, Thrasymachus of Chalcedon (fifth century B.C.) is alleged to have taught that "might is right." In the first book of his *Republic* Plato introduces "Thrasymachus" as a character who claims that "just or right means nothing but what is to the interest of the stronger party."[21] Later, Plato (without mentioning Thrasymachus) suggests that this teaching is the conclusion of an attack on a natural-law approach to justice: the Sophists say "that the honourable is one thing by nature and another by law, and that the principles of justice have no existence at all in nature, but that mankind are always disputing about them and altering them. . . . They are told by them that the highest right is might. . . ."[22] Whether this sort of ethical positivism was actually taught by the original Thrasymachus is a matter of conjecture.

Callicles of Acharnae (late fifth century B.C.) is reported by Plato[23] as teaching another version of the "might is right" theory. Callicles' argument is that laws are made by the many weak men in order to control and restrain the few who are strong. The right and the just thus become mere conventions imposed by the popular majority. The early Greek poet Pindar is quoted as saying that according to "natural justice," unimpeded by the devices of popular legislation, might would be right, for the stronger would have their way without challenge. Hippias of Elis (fifth century B.C.) was still another Sophist who emphasized the conventional and artificial character of moral law and advocated self-satisfaction as the ethical ideal.[24]

Despite the fact that he left no written works and gave no formal teaching, Socrates can well be regarded as the founder of ethical studies. In Athens (470–399 B.C.) he engaged in informal discussions in public places and private homes. Sometimes he talked with Sophists and older scholars but his audience usually consisted of young men who were curious about Socrates' views and amused by his professed ignorance and his ability to reveal the pretensions of their teachers. His thought is now partly known through various reports in Xenophon, Aristophanes, and Plato. Later classic explanations of Socratic wisdom (from Aristotle down to writers in the early Christian period) are abundant and divergent. He was and is, however, the one man generally admitted to have best personified the life of the philosopher. Aristophanes presented him (in *The Clouds*) as a semiludicrous figure. Xenophon (in *Memorabilia*) recorded several Socratic discussions, admired his rugged personality, but possibly simplified his profound thoughts. Plato was the one witness who had the understanding and literary power to transmit Socrates' wisdom to us. The problem with the Platonic account is that it is too rich: Socrates is the chief speaker in most of Plato's dialogues. It is difficult to know where the real Socrates ends and the literary Plato begins to offer his own thoughts through the mouth of his spokesman, "Socrates." Plato's *Apology, Crito,* and *Phaedo* tell the touching story of Socrates' final days, of his trial on trumped-up charges and his death in prison.

There are books that present Socrates as an ethician with teachings on most of the key issues of traditional ethics. One of the best of these, by Miles Dawson, offers nineteen chapters on a broad variety of topics.[25] Its selections deal with the rational character of virtue, the scientific basis of ethics, the soul, man's highest good, happiness as the goal of life, rewards and punishments, immortality, the future life, human character, theory of education, the value of the fine arts, duties to the gods and to other men, duties within one's city and within one's family, the rights and duties of women, and duties to friends and to self. There is even a closing chapter on death. One has the feeling, however, that much of this is post-Socratic and that an account of Socrates' ethical position should be somewhat simpler.

The method of philosophic discussion used by Socrates was characterized by three features: the asking of questions, the profession of ignorance, and the search for definitions. He may have thought that definitive knowledge of man or of courage and the other virtues implied the independent existence of "forms," such as manhood and courage. If so, then he actually was the originator of the theory of ideal forms and Plato merely took it and developed it. Socrates clearly did think that all the moral virtues are rooted in practical wisdom. "It is evident," he said, "that justice and every other virtue is wisdom."[26] Most of his reported discussions emphasize the importance of self-examination, observation of other worthy men, reflection on the meaning of our moral convictions, and moderation in feeling and action. Indeed, as Plato testified,[27] Socrates personified the two moral imperatives attributed to the Delphic oracle: "know thyself" (*gnōthi seauton*) and "avoid excess" (*mēden agan*).

At times Socrates seems to be saying that if one knows what is right and good one will do it. This sort of moral intellectualism is probably overoptimistic in its view of human conduct. Certainly that is what Aristotle thought of it: "Socrates in one respect was on the right track, while in another he went astray; in thinking that all the virtues were forms of practical wisdom he was wrong, but in saying they implied practical wisdom he was right."[28]

Socratic well-being (*eudaimonia*) consists in the actual doing of what is good. This is a dynamic theory of happiness and moral success. To do good (*eu—prattein*) is to fare well.[29] Socrates avoided offering a formal standard for the determination of what is good but insisted that earnest discussion and reflection could discover the ideals of temperate, just, and courageous living. Kierkegaard was not wrong when he said: "Socrates was thus a man whose energies were devoted to thinking; but he reduced all other knowledge to indifference in that he infinitely accentuated ethical knowledge."[30]

More than his formal teaching in ethics, the story of Socrates' life has had a tremendous ethical influence. People have admired and wondered at his reported self-control, his reasonableness, his superiority to passing fancies and discomforts, his interest in the views and pleasures of others, his reputation of being warned against evildoing by his familiar spirit (*daimon*). He is the personification of the pagan "sage." Little wonder that even Christians hailed him as "saint" Socrates.[31]

Three minor schools of Greek philosophy took over and developed diverse aspects of Socrates' teaching and character. The Megarics, founded by Euclid of Megara (fl. 420 B.C.), were primarily interested in dialectic. They came to stress the importance of a clear knowledge of the good. Euclid identified the Good with the One, which he also recognized under the names of reason, understanding, and the divine.[32] A century later, another Megarian named Stilpo was teaching in Athens that indifference to feeling (*apatheia*) is the special virtue of the good men. Stilpo taught Zeno the Stoic who in turn exploited this idea of apathy. In another such school, the Elean—Eretrian group, Menedemus of Eretria taught that virtue is one with knowledge.

More important in the history of ethics was the Cynic school, named perhaps from the Greek word for dog, because of the Cynics' disdain for conventional behavior. The founder, Antisthenes (fifth century B.C.) studied under Gorgias the Sophist and knew Socrates. He admired the independence and self-sufficiency of Socrates' personal character. The Cynic ideal of virtue thus became *simplicity* of living, a renunciation of wealth, pleasure, adornment, and ambition. The Cynic paragon was a sort of pagan ascetic represented in popular legend by the fourth-century Diogenes of Sinope, who was said to have lived in a tub. Diogenes was an Athenian beatnik, imitating a dog in disdain for the amenities of life and the rules and customs of polite society. Cynicism became another name for vulgarity and at its lowest ebb was a moral skepticism as extreme as any to be found in the ancient world. As late as the fifth century A.D., Augustine testified that there were still Cynics wandering about imitating the behavior of Diogenes.[33] He even tells the old story that the ancient Cynics went so far in imitating the "naturalness" of dogs as to copulate openly in public places. Crates of Thebes (fourth century B.C.) was a more cultivated Cynic who influenced the development of Stoic ethics. Cynicism was a negative kind of ethics that stressed a lack of interest in personal and social satisfactions.

Aristippus of Cyrene (*ca.* 435–355 B.C.) founded the third Socratic school. After studying under Protagoras, he attended some of the discussions conducted by Socrates in Athens, and on his return to Cyrene, taught there in the Cyrenaic school. Aristotle considered Aristippus a Sophist.[34] He thought that personal pleasure was the thing to aim at in life: any act that tends to secure such satisfaction on the sense level would be good. This is the first known occurrence of egoistic hedonism in the history of ethics. Aristippus seems to have started from the Socratic ideal of well-being (*eudaimonia*) and independence of the person (*autarkia*), eventually concluding that personal pleasure is the highest good.[35] Later, this theory was to be developed by the Epicureans but there is no known connection between Aristippus and Epicurus. Little more than the names of later Cyrenaics remains: Theodorus the Atheist (who is said to have identified pleasure with mental satisfaction), Hegesias, and Anniceris.[36]

If these three Socratic schools offer only partial appreciations of the ethical thought of Socrates, there is no question that his moral views were given ample development in the next school of ethics, the Platonic. Plato (427–347 B.C.) was the first Greek philosopher to write on nearly all the problems of philosophy and to leave us almost his entire literary product. With various interruptions for travel and political activity in Sicily, he taught in his school in Athens (the Academy) for about fifty years. Around twenty-five authentic dialogues are extant plus a number of letters. There is a strong tradition that Plato delivered a famous lecture *On the Good* (*Peri tagathou*) which was recorded by Aristotle when he was Plato's pupil.[37] This lecture is not now extant, of course, but the final lines of the *Eudemian Ethics* imply that it identified the one and the Good. This would mean that Plato was already attempting to identify fullness of being (unity) with moral perfection (good) and was thus inaugurating a type of self-perfection ethics. It is probable that the sixth book of Plato's *Republic* offers a closely related doctrine.

As already noted, one group of Platonic dialogues (*Apology, Crito, Phaedo*) deals with the last days of Socrates and his thoughts before death. Socrates was not afraid to die: he looked forward to some sort of life after death. One of the chief arguments for personal immortality of the human soul (*psychē*) is found in the *Phaedo*: the soul is the principle of life within each man, death is the opposite to life, the process of change from one opposite to another always entails a return from one extreme to the other, thus the soul always reverts from the extreme of death to that of life, hence "the souls of the dead are in existence and the good souls have a better portion than the evil" (*Phaedo*, 72D). There are several such arguments for immortality offered in this dialogue.

It is likely that they represent something of the actual thought of Socrates, as revised by his pupil, Plato.

Another set of Platonic dialogues present Socrates as the dominant speaker and are probably closely related to some of the actual discussions that Socrates held in Athens and its vicinity. Nearly all of these Socratic dialogues deal briefly with the nature of certain virtues, or with definite moral problems. In the *Euthyphro*, for instance, Socrates talks about the virtue of piety (respect for one's parents and country, and the gods), hears a standard definition from Euthyphro ("piety is that part of justice which gives the gods their due") and then criticizes this definition as a trivial account of man's dealings with the gods. As in most of the dialogues, no positive conclusion is reached, no dogmatic teaching is offered, but the discussion raises many moral and ethical problems and stimulates the serious reader to do some personal thinking. Similar debates are found in other early Platonic dialogues: *Laches* deals with courage, *Charmides* with temperance or the moderating of sensual desire, *Lysis* treats friendship, *Euthydemus* covers prudence or practical wisdom. Some scholars think that the early books of the *Republic* (in which several definitions of justice are reviewed and criticized) date from this first Socratic period and were incorporated into the longer dialogue during Plato's maturity.

More general ethical questions are discussed in later dialogues where Socrates is still the main character. We have seen that the *Protagoras* presents the problem of the teachability of moral virtue. Socrates argues that, if virtue is knowledge and can be taught, then all successful and wise men would certainly teach their sons to live as they do (*Protagoras*, 319–326). The discussion turns to the problems of whether wisdom, temperance, courage, justice, and piety are reducible to one key virtue that could be acquired by education. There is some suggestion that a theory of the good life would have to pay some attention to pleasure and pain and that knowledge is not the only factor in moral character. "Socrates" in this dialogue ends by arguing that no man voluntarily chooses evil: "to prefer evil to good is not in human nature" (*Protagoras*, 358). The implication is that one will always do what one thinks good— and that education helps one to make reliable judgments on what is good. In other dialogues this discussion is related to the exploration of the "good life" (in the *Gorgias*) and to the problem of voluntary and involuntary error (in *Hippias Minor*).

A group of dialogues extending from the middle of Plato's writing career to his old age provide outlines of his personal thinking on the nature and problems of ethics. He does not reject the moral intellectualism of Socrates but expands it and places it in the context of a developed view of reality and of man's psychic functions. These dialogues include the *Symposium* (on the good and the beautiful), the *Republic* (on

justice, both individual and social, and on many other matters), the
Phaedrus (on love and the relation of man's appetites to reason), the
Philebus (on pleasures and the good for man), and the *Statesman* (on
the division of sciences into practical and theoretical, the problems of
political rule, the doctrine of the mean, the origin of state laws, and the
importance of reason in all areas of virtue). Finally, the longest and
apparently the last of Plato's dialogues is the *Laws*, which offers a less
idealistic and more practical consideration of most of the questions that
had been raised in the *Republic*. Politics is there (*Laws*, I, 650B)
identified with the art of managing the natures and habits of men's
souls—a notion that is easily transformed into totalitarianism. Many readers think that the *Laws* reproduce the thought of an aging, or even
senile, Plato.

Very distinctive in the background of Plato's ethics is his theory of the
"parts" of man's soul. These are not precisely faculties, nor are they mere
functions: they are divisions of psychic reality and activity but certainly
not physical parts. In the *Phaedrus* (246, 253) he compares the soul
to a pair of winged horses plus a charioteer. One horse is ill-bred and
ignoble, inclined to pursue brutish pleasures: this one symbolizes the
appetitive or concupiscent part of the soul (*to epithumētikon*). The other
horse is well-bred and noble, inclined to soar upward toward honor and
glory: this is the spirited part (*thumos*) of man's soul. Obviously, they
represent two appetites in man, the desire for sensual satisfaction and the
aspiration for success and fame. The driver of these two horses must know
where he is going, love the better things, and assert his orderly control
over his unruly steeds: reason (*logos, to logistikon*) is this highest part of
man's soul. Philosophy is designed to train man's soul so that all three
parts work together for happiness (*Phaedrus*, 254–256).

The same theory of the tripartite soul is found in the *Republic* (Bk. IV,
431–439). Two levels of psychic activity are there distinguished: the
rational and the irrational. The rational (*to logistikon*) is that part which
reflects and acquires knowledge. In the irrational are two parts: one feels
anger, indignation, and the ambition to excel—it is the spirited element
(*thumos*); the other part desires the pleasures of food, sex, and so on—
it is the element of desire or appetite (*to epithumētikon*). Each part of
the soul has its special perfection or virtue. The rational part is perfected by
practical wisdom (*phronēsis, sophia*). Courage or manliness (*andreia*)
develops the spirited part. Temperance (*sophrosune*) is the virtue that
moderates desire, especially in the concupiscent part, but it perfects all
parts of man's soul. Finally, justice (*dikaiosune*) as a virtue of the
individual man is that general condition of soul in which each part
performs its proper function. The just man only does what is right in
his external actions as a citizen of a state—he does the right because his
soul is internally well-ordered.[38]

Plato thought that the wise and just man requires some sort of standard, some ideal, on which to pattern his judgments and his conduct. The theory of intelligible "forms" supplies such a criterion. One approach to the ideal forms is through the four levels of cognition described in the sixth book of the *Republic*. Two lower ways of knowing deal with the world of appearances: the lowest is perception of things through images (*eikasia*), it "takes sensible appearances and current moral notions at their face value[39]; the second level is belief (*pistis*) in the reality of the things perceived by the senses, and also it is belief in the right moral opinions *without understanding why they are right*. Two higher modes of cognition have as their objects certain intelligible realities that are unchanging in character. The objects of understanding (the ideal forms) include mathematical items, such as unity and equality; and moral standards, such as perfect justice, goodness, and so on. These Platonic forms may be known directly and intuitively in themselves; this is the highest level of cognition, called intelligence (*noēsis*) or knowledge (*epistēmē*). Or they may be known indirectly, through other things or acts of knowing, by discursive reasoning, by the process of thinking (*dianoia*).[40] It may be observed that the *Republic* definitely illustrates this analysis by reference to moral or ethical judgments: some people have moral opinions without seeing the grounds or reasons for these views; other people clearly understand the basis for their moral convictions. Ethics, for Plato, would consist in the second (and highest) kind of cognition.

The allegory of the cave (*Republic*, Bk. VII, 514–521), is another device used by Plato to suggest what the ideal forms are. Men are described as chained in an underground cavern where they can see only the shadows of physical objects cast on one wall. In this condition, they would think that these shadows are all that can be known and all that can be. If one of these cave dwellers were released, he might look at the physical things themselves which cause the shadows and think that reality consists in such bodies. Further, if he is allowed to come out of the cave into the higher world of sunlight, he might be dazzled by the brightness and think that the reflections of visible things are the best objects to look at. Eventually, he might adapt to the upper world so that he could steal brief glances at the sun itself. This higher world symbolizes the realm of intelligibility, the sun is the "essential Form of Goodness." To live well, with clear understanding, one must rise to a vision of the idea of the Good.[41] Many readers see Plato's form of the good as identical with what God would be in a more obviously monotheistic philosophy.[42]

This is not an easy ethics to grasp; it is far from a crude intuitionism. Plato's ideally educated man would be the product of long years of study, particularly of mathematics (here Pythagoreanism is an obvious influence), and years of training in good habits. The Platonic sage would be an elderly, well-balanced character, free from ordinary mundane concerns, enamored of beauty and good order, perfected in intellect so that he might easily and accurately see the principles of good living. This may well be an idealization of the personality of Plato's teacher, Socrates.

But Platonic ethics is not simply an intellectualism. The notion of well-being (*eudaimonia*) is retained and explored in the last books of the *Republic*. There had been some suggestion at the beginning of the treatise that injustice, if not detected, might be approvable. This possibility is explored in the story of Gyges, which is told in the second book of the *Republic*. A Lydian shepherd named Gyges happened to find a gold ring and he put it on his finger. At the monthly meeting of the royal shepherds Gyges discovered that whenever he turned the setting of the ring inside his hand he became invisible to his companions. With this magic device Gyges went to the royal court, seduced the queen, murdered the king, and took over the throne. Plato asks whether even a just man, equipped with such a ring that would enable him to escape all discovery and punishment for his acts, could be expected to resist all wrongdoing. He even suggests that "people would think him a miserable fool if they found him refusing to wrong his neighbours." This introduces a very important consideration into the history of ethics: whether the moral quality of human conduct is to be determined solely by the consequences of the action. Returning to this theme in the ninth book, Plato there argues that justice pays, that to live justly is to live profitably. He even examines the nature of pleasures and attempts a classification of them. His scale of personal satisfactions depends on the tripartite analysis of the soul: there are pleasures of sensual satisfaction, of competitive achievement, and of rational accomplishment. None is essentially bad or immoral; yet the pleasure associated with the perfect use of reason is obviously held to be best.[43]

Plato's ethics is fundamentally eudaimonistic. He saw the good life for man in terms of the personal attainment of well-being; in this condition man's reason would regulate and order all the functions of the irrational appetites. The movement within each man toward the ideal personality is an original version of self-perfection ethics. The development of the basic virtues is a personal process, of course, and varies from one man to the next. Yet Plato, like most of the Greeks, was well aware of the social dimensions of human life and well-being. A good life requires association with other persons. Ethics is but a part of politics—which deals with how to live well in the state (*polis*). In the fourth book of the *Republic* the descriptions of personal kinds of virtue are paralleled by the accounts of the functions of the three classes of citizens. The lowest class is productive and acquisitive: its social virtue is temperance. A second class is spirited, competitive, and warlike: its distinctive virtue is courage. The highest class (the rulers or guardians) is distinguished by its rationality: its special virtue is practical wisdom. When all three classes work well together, the state is marked by the virtue of justice. In the *Laws* Plato offers a very detailed and less idealistic description of the good society. There are to be precisely 5040 households in this state. A council of 360 members is to be in charge. The guardians of the law are to number thirty-seven. Such precisions are based on a sort of numerology: the number 5040 is chosen, for instance, because it has fifty-nine divisors! This dialogue, written in Plato's last years, maintains the parallelism between personal moral goodness and political good order but it stresses throughout the superiority of political virtue over the attainments of the individual. Since state "morality" is identified with the divine good, the *Laws* offer a suggestion of totalitarianism. Even in the *Republic* Plato had taught that the rulers may lie, if it is for the good of the state as a whole. This is one of the least attractive features of Plato's social ethics.

Another dimension in Plato's ethics involves the afterlife. There is little question that he taught that man's soul is immortal. We have already noticed how the *Phaedo* offers dialectical arguments to show that the *psyche* cannot end with physical death. Several other dialogues (*Gorgias, Symposium, Phaedrus*, and *Republic*) contain myths suggesting something of the nature of the afterlife of the soul.[44] The most impressive is the Tale of Er, which is told in the last book of the *Republic*. This man, Er, is pictured as going after death to a place of judgment, from which he eventually returned to earth to tell his story. Er saw many souls of the dead being offered the choice of various sorts of lives: they were free to choose what they thought best. This choice depended on what each man felt the good life should be. Obviously, Plato considered it most important to be ready to make this choice: "Each of us should lay aside all other learning, to study only how he may discover one who can give him the knowledge enabling him to distinguish the good life from the evil."[45]

CHAPTER II

Teleological Eudaimonism: Aristotle

PLATO'S EMPHASIS on the good life for the individual man is continued and expanded in the ethical thinking of his pupil Aristotle. The eudaimonism of Aristotelian ethics, however, is teleological: it stresses the purposiveness of human nature. For Aristotle the goal of moral activity is achieved when man develops his understanding and appetitive powers so that he can habitually act in accord with the moral virtues. His early studies in biology doubtless influenced Aristotle's conception of maturity as an ideal stage in the development of any living being. His father was a physician named Nicomachus who served as court physician to a Macedonian king in the town of Stagira in northern Greece, where Aristotle was born in 384 B.C. After studying with his father, he went to Athens at the age of eighteen and worked in Plato's school for about twenty years. Aristotle eventually established his own school in Athens and taught there from 335 B.C. until shortly before his death in 322.

The philosophic writings of Aristotle are numerous and extensive, covering almost all the divisions known to classic philosophy: logic, philosophy of nature, psychology, metaphysics, ethics, politics, rhetoric, and poetics. Indeed, these names and many others that have become traditional to philosophy are due in great part to Aristotle. He is likewise the originator of much of the terminology that is still used in ethical discussions. Several ethical writings are attributed to Aristotle and accounts of his moral philosophy differ, depending on which treatise is emphasized. Three popular treatises stem from his youthful period (ca. 355 B.C.) and they were ethical in character. The Protrepticus was an essay in praise of philosophy as a way of life, stressing the view that eudaimonia consists in intellectual contemplation.[1] In the dialogue Eudemus Aristotle discussed the nature, origin, and destiny of the human soul in Platonic terms. The contents of another early dialogue, On Justice, are not now known. In fact, we have only fragments and indirect reports on these early works.

Aristotle's two main works in ethics are the *Eudemian Ethics* and the *Nicomachean Ethics*. Books IV, V, and VI of the *Eudemian* are identical with V, VI, and VII of the *Nicomachean Ethics*. Although there is still some dispute on the matter, most Aristotelian scholars now think that Aristotle wrote the *Eudemian Ethics* in his early period and used some of the same material when he compiled the *Nicomachean Ethics* later.[2] It is possible that the former work was a compilation made for or by a person named Eudemus and that the latter was dedicated to Aristotle's father or son, both of whom were named Nicomachus. The *Nicomachean Ethics* is the most complete, and apparently the most mature, ethical treatise. Most of our discussion of Aristotle's ethics will be based on it.

A third version of Aristotle's ethical teaching is printed among his works, under the title *Magna Moralia*. This has but two books (both quite long) and they duplicate material from the *Eudemian Ethics* and *Nicomachean Ethics*. It is generally agreed that the *Magna Moralia* is a compilation made after the death of Aristotle and that it adds nothing to his thought. The same thing may be said of the short treatise *On Virtues and Vices*, found in the collected works of Aristotle. Some of the other authentic works of Aristotle (such as the *Rhetoric, Politics, De Anima,* and *Metaphysics*) contain passages which throw light on his ethical position.

Before turning to Aristotle's main ethical teachings, a few preliminary observations on his theory of human nature are in order. As a long-time pupil and assistant teacher under Plato, Aristotle was much influenced by Platonism. The key role assigned to *eudaimonia* and the concept of the regulation of the irrational movements of the soul by the rational are two important examples of this debt. There are other similarities: the description of the moral virtues, the picture of the ideal moral person as an Athenian aristocrat, and of course the basically intellectual approach to moral life.

However, Aristotle is also very critical of certain aspects of Plato's thought. Generally speaking, he is less otherworldly and more naturalistic than Plato. This is very evident in the critique of the theory of ideal forms: Aristotle thinks that the world of sensible things is the real world and that there is no realm of intelligible entities. Instead of "forms" as constituents of another and higher world Aristotle speaks of forms as co-principles with matter of all physical substances. Dogs are not such by virtue of a Platonic participation in an idea of dogness; rather, each dog has the formal and specific nature of dogness within him. Such natures are the sources of various activities characteristic of their species. Trees grow and reproduce but do not see; dogs include sense perception and locomotion among their activities; men have all of these plus the ability to reason. The natures of things are dynamic, that is, they are equipped with various powers (*dynameis*) to act and to be acted upon. Such activities are the operations or workings of these powers, movements from potency to act. Appropriate activities tend to perfect their powers by bringing them to the condition of habituation (*hexis*) and, in turn, this process perfects the beings to which the powers belong. A dog's use of his sense and motor powers is generally self-perfective and the same may be said about human activity. It is clear that the ethics stemming from such a view of dynamic natures is going to be a type of naturalistic self-perfectionism.

The psychology of Aristotle's *De Anima* is an application of the foregoing to specifically human functioning. The soul (*psychē*) in man is the principle or source of his vital activities: growth, assimilation of food, sexual reproduction, self-movement, appetition, sensory and intellectual cognition. Man's soul is never very clearly described by Aristotle; some of his immediate followers thought that he understood the *psychē* as simply the orderly arrangement (*harmonia*) of the living body—which would disappear at death. Other interpreters (especially medieval Christians) noted how the third book of *De Anima* spoke of human intelligence as separable, impassible, and unmixed—and when "set free from its present conditions it appears as just what it is and nothing more: this alone is immortal and eternal" (III, 5, 430a17-24). Whatever Aristotle personally thought about the possibility of immortality, he made no use of this notion in his ethics: the good life that he tried to describe is the life of men on earth. Unlike Socrates and Plato, he did not teach anything about rewards or punishments in a future life.

One other feature of Aristotle's theoretical view of human nature is important here. All natures are thought to be tendential, inclined toward a certain optimism of activity, end-directed. This is Aristotelian teleology. As a biologist, Aristotle thought chiefly in terms of living things and he was convinced that they are always tending toward a goal or end (*telos*). Each living thing is born with a set of unused and undeveloped potencies: as it moves through its life cycle, it inclines toward mature perfection and reproduction within its kind. This ongoing process includes the notion of internal finality: the final cause (purpose) of each man's activities is the continued perfect use of his potencies. This end is not some goal outside the man's own nature: it is the condition of "entelechy," of having reached the full perfection of the *telos* within the individual person. Such self-perfection is, of course, not incompatible with the welfare and perfection of the human species and of society.

It is with the foregoing in mind that we should head the famous opening sentence of the *Nicomachean Ethics*: "Every art and every inquiry, and similarly every action and pursuit, is thought to aim at some good; and for this reason the good has rightly been declared to be that at which all things aim." Aristotle proceeds to argue that some such ends or goods are external products and others are immanent activities. It is generally agreed that what men aim at above all else is *eudaimonia*; this includes the notions of living well and doing well. As noted in the terminology of Socrates and Plato, the Greek word *eudaimonia* is often translated as "happiness." Literally, it does mean being in good spirits but Aristotle gives it a much more dynamic signification. For him, *eudaimonia* is not a state or possibility of enjoyment or even of well-being: it is perfect *activity* (*energeia*) performed for its own sake.[3] One misses the point of Aristotle's ethics if he does not grasp this claim that immanent action is an end in itself. What all men desire, as Aristotle sees it, is not some product or consequence of action, nor some conformity of activity with a law or sense of duty, nor even some highly rewarding pleasures. Aristotelian *eudaimonia* is (1) that to which all men aspire as a fulfillment, (2) a continued and perfect activity, and (3) a whole human life embodying this activity in a favorable context of possessions and friends.[4]

Of course the activity that crowns the successful human life must be of a special kind. Many expositions of Aristotelian ethics simply identify it with intellectual contemplation. There is little doubt that Aristotle did have a very high regard for speculative understanding but it is hardly *eudaimonia* in his special sense. Much of the tenth book of the *Nicomachean Ethics* is devoted to the description of the really good and successful person. Aristotle again emphasizes that human happiness or well-being is an activity and not a habitual state (*hexis*). Then he argues that it is an activity of intellectual understanding (*nous*), continuous, pleasant, and sufficient unto itself. Suddenly he remarks: "But such a life would be too high for man; for it is not insofar as he is man that he will live so, but insofar as something divine is present in him."[5] We should strive, of course, to cultivate this "divine" factor and to make ourselves immortal. Regretfully, it would seem, Aristotle then proceeds to describe a second-best type of good life: this includes various activities in accord with virtue. Always central to these virtuous activities, of course, is the use of intelligence.

Aristotle's insistence on virtue, in the last book of the *Nicomachean Ethics*, is but the climax of his whole argument in the treatise. His ethics is not a deontology, although he recognized the importance of duty (*to deon*).[6] Nor is his ethics a legalism, although he stressed both natural and legal justice. The truth is that the theory of the virtues is the key to Aristotle's ethics. He distinguishes three factors within the human soul—emotions (*pathē*), powers (*dunameis*), and habitual states (*hexeis*)—and concludes that virtues are good habits.[7] Vices, of course, are bad habits.

This requires Aristotle to explain how one distinguishes between good and bad habits. At times (*Nicomachean Ethics*, 1113a25–30) he suggests that we have to depend on observing what the "good man," the pillar of society (*to spoudaios*) approves and tends to, in order to discover what is morally good. This theory of the wise or prudent man as the measure of morality is reminiscent of later theories of ethical intuitionism but Aristotle is far from intuitionism in his developed theory. Certainly it is not a deductive system, which starts from a certain definition of man and reasons to definite rules governing human activity.[8] Nor does Aristotle agree with Plato that the good is a unity of which there is one great science or wisdom.[9]

The doctrine of the mean (*mesotēs*) plays an important role in Aristotle's study of the moral virtues. As we saw in the Pythagorean view, most human affective attitudes admit of states or feelings which may be excessive on the one hand or defective on the other. The desire for food, for instance, may become habitually too great or too little. The habitual state of such desire in excess would be the vice of gluttony; similarly, habitual disinterest in eating would be a vice of defect. The middle state, or mean, is not one precise point midway between extremes; the moral mean varies for different persons, in different circumstances. What is moderate for an athlete may be immoderate for a sedentary person. In determining the mean of virtue, in the concrete, one uses a capacity for perceptive appraisal rather than formal reasoning.

Aristotle describes in great detail the application of his theory of the mean to many states of moral character. Many later lists of virtues and vices, in classical, medieval, and early modern ethical treatises stem from the Aristotelian descriptions in the second books of both the *Nicomachean Ethics* and the *Eudemian Ethics*.[10] The following table lists the chief moral means with their respective extremes of vice:

EXCESS	MEAN	DEFECT
foolhardiness	courage	cowardice
licentiousness	temperance	insensibility
prodigality	liberality	illiberality
vulgarity	magnificence	meanness
vanity	highmindedness	littlemindedness
ambition	[moderate aspiration]	lack of ambition
irascibility	gentleness	impassivity
boastfulness	truthfulness	mock modesty
buffoonery	wittiness	boorishness
obsequiousness	friendliness	surliness
bashfulness	modesty	shamelessness
envy	righteous indignation	spite

It will be observed that the "means" listed above name virtues which have to do with affective states of consciousness. This is the area of the "passions" in medieval moral treatises. It is the field in which the doctrine of the mean has its most effective application. Moderation, after all, is an obvious ideal in human feelings. Aristotle also uses the notion of the mean in treating intellectual virtues and especially in discussing the moral virtue of justice. Since it deals with transactions between men, justice is the habit of voluntarily doing what is good for other people and of avoiding acts that are harmful to others (*Nicomachean Ethics*, 1129a1–1138b12). There are different kinds of justice, in Aristotle's view, and the mean differs in each. First of all, there is that ordinary kind of justice with is a habitual inclination to act in accord with the recognized laws: this is legal justice. It aims at the good of men in groups—what will in later Aristotelianism be called the "common good" and the public welfare. Legal justice pertains to what is right in most cases and in the ordinary run of things. However, there are extraordinary occasions when to follow the law slavishly is to be unfair. A special virtue is needed enabling one to judge and do what is right in exceptional circumstances. It is called equity (*epieikeia*) and is the best kind of justice (*Nicomachean Ethics*, 1137b9). The mean in these types of justice consists in voluntary action that preserves a reasonable balance in dealing with others.

Aristotle also considers justice as it relates to the good of the individual person (particular justice), and he here describes two kinds. One type is a habit of fairness in distributions of public advantages (or disadvantages) to various individuals. This sort of justice (distributive) recognizes pertinent inequalities among persons and endeavors to adjust honors and monies that are apportioned from the common fund, in such a way that a sort of geometric proportion is achieved. The mean in such transactions is a complicated ratio between the value to the community of the person who receives and the value of the thing allotted to him. A second type of particular justice deals with simple transactions between individual persons (sales, loans, promises, deposits, etc.). In such dealings the private persons are regarded as equals and the appropriate type of justice (commutative) looks to an arithmetic equality in exchanges.[11]

The term "voluntary" has been used in the foregoing discussion of the mean. Aristotle made an important contribution to the history of ethics in his analysis of what voluntariness implies. Although the usual English terminology suggests a close connection with the notion of will (*voluntas*), Aristotle's language does not. He talks about some of man's actions as being *hekousia*, that is, with the knowledge and approval of the agent. It is such actions that are called voluntary in English. Other activities of man are performed consciously but with a certain amount of repugnance: these Aristotle calls *akousia* (not coming from within the agent, not spontaneous) and we speak of them as involuntary. Obviously, involuntary actions may be partly voluntary. Still other human activities are quite outside his personal control (one type would be those performed as a result of complete ignorance); these Aristotle calls not-voluntary.[12] Obviously, moral actions must be voluntary to some extent. Aristotle's definition of the voluntary as "what is done not under compulsion and not through ignorance" is recognized in contemporary ethics as a still-valid approach to the determination of moral responsibility.

There is no tendency toward legalism in Aristotle's ethics: he does not teach that there is some sort of set of moral precepts which all men are bound to obey. Later Aristotelians, under influences other than the thought of Aristotle, will develop various theories of natural moral law. The *Nicomachean Ethics* has nothing to say about natural law, beyond the basic suggestion that there is a naturally right way of acting; this is the *dikaion* of the fifth book. Rather, it is the theory of the virtues that is characteristic of Aristotelian ethics. Books III, IV, and V of *Nicomachean Ethics* treat the moral virtues, as we have seen. Books VI and VII discuss the intellectual virtues and the concept of right reason.

Five intellectual virtues are studied by Aristotle: all are habits of the intellect described in *De Anima* (430a15) as capable of becoming all things that are intelligible. Three of these habits are theoretical and speculative in character: there is a more or less innate habit of intuiting first principles; there is an acquired habit of reasoning to demonstratively established judgments; and there is philosophic wisdom, the habit of considering the highest objects of knowledge by a sort of fusion of intuitive understanding with demonstrative reasoning.[13] Wisdom in the speculative order (as directed simply to pure knowing) is treated in Aristotle's *Metaphysics*. The sixth book of *Nicomachean Ethics* turns to the other aspect of wisdom: when it is a habit of considering how to act well and rightly, it becomes practical wisdom, prudence (*phronēsis*). If we speak of *phronēsis* as prudence, it must be remembered that it does not mean a self-seeking astuteness (as in much contemporary usage) but the habit of deliberating and judging well about one's own problems of moral action. Unlike moral science, Aristotle's prudence is not teachable; it is a skill which must be acquired, if at all, by personal effort. In part, Aristotelian prudence is concerned with *knowing* how to act as a human being—but it is also involved in the direction, the rectification, of one's own voluntary activities. In this second sense, prudence governs actions and is a moral virtue.

As a habit of practical understanding, prudence makes it possible to reason to judgments that some actions are good and others are evil. Aristotle takes it that children are born with certain natural tendencies toward virtuous activity: acquired prudence merely develops these inclinations so that they become conscious elements in the living of a good life.[14]

Pleasure is regarded by Aristotle as a sort of satisfaction attendant upon the perfect use of one's powers. There is a pleasure that accompanies sensory perception and one that is associated with the understanding of the most excellent objects. These pleasures are not identical with their concomitant activities but they are, along with perfection of action, constitutive of ideal well-being (*eudaimonia*). It has been argued that Aristotle's ethics started as a hedonism (pleasure being the ultimate good for man) and moved toward eudaimonism in its later formulations.[15] There is, indeed, greater stress in the seventh book of the *Nicomachean Ethics* on the ultimate desirability of pleasure than there is in the tenth book. However, we do not know enough about the chronology of these books to found any theory of the evolution of Aristotle's thought on such evidence. At best, we can say that he always regarded some degree of pleasure as a proper accompaniment for that perfection of human activity in which *eudaimonia* consists.

The tenth and last book of the *Nicomachean Ethics* tries to restate Aristotle's notion of the good life. Continued intellectual contemplation is the highest activity of man—and the most rewarding. Such activity is the use of "the most divine element in us." Yet Aristotle has some hesitation in concluding that intellectual speculation is by itself the good life for man; "such a life would be too high for man; for it is not insofar as he is man that he will live so, but insofar as something divine is present in him."[16] He then argues that, perhaps, *eudaimonia* consists in activity in accord with moral virtue, requiring also a certain amount of material prosperity, freedom from worries, and the consolations of having some good friends. Such a "good life" is obviously limited to some favored people and is restricted to life on earth.

In the final lines of the *Eudemian Ethics* a somewhat different emphasis is found. Here we are told that all other goods that we may seek are merely means to enable us to advance to the highest good for men. Man's final felicity consists in "serving and contemplating God."[17] Some interpreters think that this terminating passage is an addition by some later scribe, with Christian views on the destiny of man.

The successor of Aristotle as head of the Peripatetic school was Theophrastus (*ca.* 375–288 B.C.), a man who did some work in ethics. In addition to his *Ethical Characters*, he wrote a treatise *On Eudaimonia*. Cicero (*De finibus*, V, V, 12) is our source for the report that Theophrastus emphasized the need for good fortune and material possessions as constituents of the good life. Some historians think that Theophrastus criticized the theological orientation of the ethics of Aristotle.[18] Also, a certain Andronicus (whether this is Andronicus of Rhodes, first century B.C., is not known) produced a short treatise *On the Passions* which is Aristotelian in spirit. He may also have written a treatise on the various "parts" or subdivisions of the four chief Aristotelian virtues: prudence, temperance, courage, and justice. The Greek medical doctor Claudius Galen (*ca.* 130–200 A.D.) produced a treatise, *On Moral Customs*, known through an Arabic summary of the twelfth century. This treatise was one of the first sources of information among Moslem scholars concerning certain elements in Aristotle's ethics.[19] During the Middle Ages a Latin treatise entitled *Liber de Bona Fortuna* was widely circulated as a source of information on Aristotelian morality. It was a compilation from the *Eudemian Ethics* and the *Magna Moralia*.

Greek paraphrases and commentaries on Aristotle's ethical writings were produced at intervals during the first fifteen hundred years of the Christian era. Aspasius (fl. 125 A.D.), the Pseudo-Alexander of Aphrodisias (unknown dates), an anonymous commentator (first centuries, A.D.), Bishop Eustratios of Nicaea (fl. 1052–1120 A.D.), Michael Ephesius (fl. 1070 A.D.), and the Pseudo-Heliodorus (fourteenth to sixteenth century, precise dates unknown) constitute this group. These men are little read and seem to have had but small influence on the history of ethics.

Latin commentaries on portions of the *Nicomachean Ethics* begin to appear in the twelfth century. In the 1240s, Robert Grosseteste made a complete Latin version of the *Nicomachean Ethics* and wrote *Notulae* to explain it.[20] In the ensuing decades of the thirteenth and fourteenth centuries many Christian writers (Albert the Great, Thomas Aquinas, Siger de Brabant, Giles of Rome, Anthony of Parma) produced formal commentaries or series of questions dealing with the *Nicomachean Ethics*. To the extent that they modify Aristotelianism, they belong in the history of medieval ethics. The influence of Aristotle on present-day ethics is evident in some Thomistic works and particularly in the thought of W. D. Ross and Henry B. Veatch.

CHAPTER III

Hellenistic Ethics:
Stoic, Epicurean, and Neoplatonic

THE LAST THREE CENTURIES before Christ witnessed the development of
three different schools of ethics: Stoicism, Epicureanism, and Neoplatonism. This Hellenistic period actually extended well beyond the time of
Christ. The last great figure in pagan Greek philosophy, Proclus, lived in
the fifth century of the Christian era. We have, then, eight centuries in
which there were many students and teachers of ethics. Many scholars
wrote commentaries on the thought of the earlier Greek philosophers but
some original thinking was done in ethics. With the growth of Roman
culture, Greek philosophy was translated into Latin and adapted to the
problems and interests of the new Roman empire. Christianity was born
in the middle of this period and it introduced a new outlook on the good
life for man. However, we shall postpone our treatment of Christian
ethics until the next chapter. In the present one we shall concentrate on
the ethical views of the thinkers who represent the last stages of Greek
philosophy.

In general, later Greek philosophy was less speculative and more practical in its interests than the thought of the early Greeks. While problems
of knowledge and reality continued to be investigated, the main thrust of
Hellenistic philosophy was toward the discovery of how men might live
well. Religious teachings became part of these philosophies. Man's ultimate
destiny and his possible relations with the divinity now came to the
forefront of attention. Some philosophers, particularly in the Stoic and
Neoplatonic schools, became the equivalent of religious leaders. In the
first centuries after Christ, an intellectual brand of neopaganism appeared,
for a time, to rival Christianity. All these developments left their effects on
ethics.

Stoic Ethics

Stoicism began early in the fourth century B.C., when Zeno of Citium (336–264) came to Athens to teach at a place that had a porch (*stoa*), whence came its name. Zeno wrote a number of treatises—*On Human Nature, On Living in Accord with Nature,* and *On Duty*—but except for fragments in later writings these works have been lost.[1] Zeno's successors, Cleanthes (331–232) and Chrysippus (282–204), also were important in the history of the ethics of the first Stoics. Roman Stoicism falls in a much later era, the first and second centuries A.D.; its leading ethicians were Seneca, Epictetus, and Marcus Aurelius.

The Stoic view of reality was thoroughly materialistic: all that exists is matter. Stoicism taught the usual ancient theory of four elements (earth, air, fire, and water) but regarded fire as the ultimate substance. Souls and God are subtler kinds of fire than that of crass bodies. Growth and change are due to certain seedlike rational forms (*logoi spermatikoi*) which are present in matter. There is a pattern, an understandable plan (*logos*), for everything that exists and happens in the nature of things. Knowledge is fundamentally sense perception: Stoicism is usually classified as a sensism. However, the Stoics obviously thought that men are able to understand the orderly character of mundane events, so they recognized the function of reason. Stoic logic was a highly sophisticated theory of reasoning that differered radically from the Aristotelian syllogistic. In particular, the Stoics maintained that certain general notions are given to men prior to sense experience, so their theory of knowledge bordered on innatism.[2] Although the Stoics were generally deterministic in regard to causality, this did not prevent them from granting a certain personal freedom to human agents. A man is not able to control the general course of events in the world but he is able to control his own inner acts of assent, his own desires, and his affective responses to internal experience.

Ethically, the Stoics still thought in terms of Greek eudaimonism. Their concept of *eudaimonia*, however, was more static than that of Aristotle. The end, or ultimate goal, to which they looked was a condition of undisturbed happiness, "a calmly flowing life." The Stoic sage would be a person who had acquired such a degree of rational control of his feelings that he would rarely, if ever, be inclined to any excess of emotion. Affective movements of consciousness, pleasure (*hēdonē*), sorrow (*lupē*), desire (*epithumia*), and fear (*phōbos*) are irrational and incompatible with human nature. The ideal of virtue is *apatheia*, a condition in which passionate feelings are not merely controlled but virtually eradicated. It is good to live in accord with nature; nature is fundamentally rational in character; hence, the second Stoic maxim, that the good life is in accord with reason. The highest instance of reason is God (Zeus) and divine law orders and governs all events universally. This respect for the universal and natural law of reason was evident in one of the earliest writings, Cleanthes' famous *Hymn to Zeus*. It is worth reading in its entirety.[3]

Most glorious of the Immortals, many named, Almighty for ever.
Zeus, ruler of Nature, that governest all things with law,
Hail! for lawful it is that all mortals should address Thee.
For we are Thy offspring, taking the image only of Thy voice,
    as many mortal things as live and move upon the earth.
Therefore will I hymn Thee, and sing thy might forever.
For Thee doth all this universe that circles round the earth obey, moving
    whithersoever Thou leadest, and is gladly swayed by Thee,
Such a minister hast Thou in Thine invincible hands;—the two-edged,
    blazing, imperishable thunderbolt.
For under its stroke all Nature shuddereth, and by it thou guidest aright the
    Universal Reason, that roams through all things, mingling itself with the
    greater and the lesser lights, till it have grown so great, and become
    supreme king over all.
Nor is aught done on the earth without Thee, O God, nor in the divine
    sphere of the heavens, nor in the sea,
Save the works that evil men do in their folly—
Yea, but Thou knowest even to find a place for superfluous things, and to
    order that which is disorderly, and things not dear to men are dear to
    Thee.
Thus dost Thou harmonize into One all good and evil things,
    that there should be one everlasting Reason of them all.
And this the evil among mortal men avoid and heed not; wretched, ever
    desiring to possess the good, yet they nor see nor hear the universal Law
    of God, which obeying with all their heart, their life would be well.
But they rush graceless each to his own aim,
Some cherishing lust for fame, the nurse of evil strife,
Some bent on monstrous gain,
Some turned to folly and the sweet works of the flesh,
Hastening, indeed, to bring the very contrary of these things to pass.
But Thou, O Zeus, the All-giver, Dweller in the darkness of cloud, Lord of
    thunder, save Thou men from their unhappy folly,
Which do Thou, O Father, scatter from their souls; and give them to dis-
    cover the wisdom, in whose assurance Thou governest all things with
    justice;
So that being honoured, they may pay Thee honour,
Hymning Thy works continually, as it beseems a mortal man.
Since there can be no greater glory for men or Gods than this,
Duly to praise for ever the Universal Law.

In this compendium of early Stoic ethics several points may be noticed. For the first time in Greek ethical teaching, the notion of an all-pervading "law" is introduced. Some of the pre-Socratics, it is true, spoke of *nomos* as a principle of regularity and harmony in change; but the view that a divine Ruler governs all events, including human activities, under universal law is an important innovation in Greek thought. This is the nearest approach to a theory of divine providence that we will find outside the Judaeo-Christian teaching. Cleanthes is saying that all things are ordered according to a rational plan (*logos*) which is implanted in the material universe and which is, at the same time, implicit in the Reason of God. Christian moral writers for many centuries were impressed by this Stoic doctrine of the law of nature. It is one of the chief sources of natural-law ethics.

The third head of the Greek Stoic school was Chrysippus of Soli (*ca.* 280–204), who is sometimes credited with turning the attention of Stoicism to the nature of man as opposed to its original interest in the nature of the universe.[4] However, because we have practically no source materials, it is impossible to assess the personal contributions to ethics of the earliest Stoics; beside those mentioned there were: Persaeus, Aretus, Sphaerus, Aristo, Zeno the fourth scholarch, Diogenes of Seleucia, Antipater, and Crates. They bring the school down to the second century B.C.

The name "middle Stoicism" is given to the teaching of a group of Greek thinkers who combined the original views of the school with parts of the philosophies of Plato and Aristotle and who transmitted this eclectic but practically oriented philosophy to Roman students and writers. Panaetius of Rhodes (*ca.* 189–109) taught for a time in Rome but became scholarch (head of the Stoic school) in Athens in 129 B.C. Due to the influence of Panaetius, the Stoic ethics that the Romans learned in the second century before Christ was less insistent on the ideal life of the sage, less interested in the restrictive virtue of *apatheia*—and more favorable to the view that the good life consists in a reasonable moderation in all things. One of Panaetius' pupils, Poseidonius (*ca.* 135–51 B.C.), taught Cicero at Rhodes and so made a profound impression on Roman culture.

Two important ethical ideas came to the Romans from middle Stoicism. The first was a development of the original Stoic teaching that all nature is rationally ordered under the supreme Reason of the Deity, and that man is morally obliged to conform his conscious life to the force of universal reason.[5] Second, Stoicism provided Roman and early Christian moralists with a practical psychology that emphasized the distinct functions of various cognitive, appetitive, and motor faculties (*dynameis*) of the soul.[6] In this theory there is a growing emphasis on the function of willing (*boulēsis*), viewed as rational wishing. Moreover, middle Stoicism introduced the concept of the *hēgemonikon,* a faculty that rules and governs the other powers of the soul. In various versions of Christian ethics, the role of the *hēgemonikon* will sometimes be played by the will, sometimes by the intellect.

Roman Stoicism begins to develop in first-century (B.C.) reports found in Latin writers who do not fully share the ethical positions of the Stoics. This is probably true of M. Terentius Varro (116–27 B.C.), whose encyclopedic writings are mostly nonextant. Through references and quotations in Augustine of Hippo (*City of God*, XIX, 1–3), we know that Varro transmitted 288 Greek views on the end of man and the nature of happiness. We also have the works of M. Tullius Cicero (106–43 B.C.), in which there is a great deal of information about Stoic ethics. Books III and IV of *De finibus* contain a lengthy exposition of the ethics of Stoicism, in the words of a Roman spokesman, Cato Uticensis. He was a real person and a contemporary of Cicero in Rome. One feature of this version of Stoic ethics in Rome was its social-mindedness. Even the Greek Stoics were noteworthy for their concern about the common good of humanity: if they had lived in the twentieth century, the Stoics would have been strong supporters of the United Nations. Cicero further emphasized the importance of human brotherhood in his personal revision of Stoicism.[7]

Of all the moralists of ancient Rome, L. Annaeus Seneca (*ca.* 4 B.C.–65 A.D.) was one of the most voluminous and widely read. His *Letters* and *Moral Essays* show no great interest in ethical *theory* but develop a practical doctrine of human virtues. Long lists of these good qualities of the human person are found in his works. Self-control, moderation of desire, rational reflection, and self-sufficiency (*per se sufficientia*) are typical Senecan virtues. He wrote with great respect for the higher mental aspects of man's nature, as well as for the influence of the Deity on human life, with the result that later Christian moral writers make abundant use of his descriptions of virtue and the good life.[8]

The greatest ethician among the later Stoics was Epictetus of Hierapolis (*ca.* 50–138 A.D.). A Greek slave in Emperor Nero's service, Epictetus was freed and taught philosophy in Rome and in Nicopolis. One of his pupils, Flavius Arrianus, made records of Epictetus' lectures and these reports constitute the four extant books of *Discourses* (*Diatribai*) and the little manual called the *Enchiridion*. As a pupil of the lesser Stoic, Musonius Rufus, Epictetus returned to the epistemological and physical views of early Stoicism: a sensistic explanation of knowledge (with a special insight into first principles, *syneidesis*), plus a generally materialistic notion of reality which did not exclude freedom of choice and assent within the consciousness of each man. Extramental things and the activities of the body are not under the control of one's will and it is the mark of the wise man to recognize this. As the opening lines of the *Enchiridion* put it:

Of things some are in our power, and others are not. In our power are opinion, movement towards a thing, desire, aversion, turning from a thing; and in a word, whatever are our acts. Not in our power are the body, property, reputation, offices (magisterial power), and in a word, whatever are not our own acts. And the things in our power are by nature free, not subject to restraint or hindrance; but the things not in our power are weak, slavish, subject to restraint, in the power of others.[9]

Yet Epictetus thought that all men have enough natural ability and information to govern their internal dispositions according to right reason (*orthos logos*). The original notions (*prolēpseis*) of good and evil are innate but the study of philosophy and ethics is necessary to assure a reasonable development of moral judgment and a fair application of principles to various concrete problems of life. Epictetus retained the earlier teaching of a ruling power (*hēgemonikon*) in man whereby one knows the difference between good and evil, makes choices, and controls the activities of the lower psychic powers. This governing power is almost identical with will. All human evil reduces to a perversion of will. Personal contentment (*ataraxia*) comes from learning to accept the course of external events and the divine regulation of men and the universe. Epictetus succinctly states this in his *Discourses*:

And will you be angry and peevish at the ordinances of Zeus, which he defined and ordained together with the Fates who spun in his presence the thread of your begetting? Do you not know how small a part you are compared with the whole? That is, as to the body; for as to the reason you are not inferior to the gods, nor less than they; for the greatness of the reason is not determined by length nor by height, but by the decisions of its will.[10]

Much the same point of view is found in the *Meditations* of Emperor Marcus Aurelius (121–180 A.D.). He is, perhaps, less materialistic in his teaching on man's nature. He divides the human person into three parts: body (*sōma*), soul (*psychē*), and intelligence (*nous*). The last is the ruling power (*hēgemonikon*) for Marcus Aurelius. Each man's personal intelligence is his guiding spirit (*daimon*) or conscience: in turn, this guiding power is subject to the will of God.[11]

The practical ethics of Marcus Aurelius may be summed up in the following nine rules of conduct: (1) be ready to forgive your neighbor when he offends you, since we all exist to serve each other; (2) reflect on the unfortunate effects which the bad actions of others have upon these others; (3) avoid making moral judgments on other persons; (4) remember your own moral defects; (5) remember that you do not know the internal attitudes of your fellow men; (6) when the occasion for anger arises, remember that you will soon be dead; (7) it is not the sins of others that really bother us but only our own opinions about others; (8) remember that anger and grief can be worse for a person than the external consequences of another man's actions; (9) remember that kindness and friendliness to others are best for all concerned.[12]

In popularized versions such as the foregoing, Stoic ethics was the dominant school of thought in pagan Rome and continued to be so during the first two centuries of Christianity. Platonism was too lofty and difficult; Aristotelianism was not well known and was felt to have little literary appeal. Besides Stoic ethics the only important contemporary moral philosophy was Epicureanism, and it was never anything more than a minority view, as we shall see.[13]

Epicurean Ethics

Among the post-Socratic schools, the Cyrenaics had taught that personal satisfaction is the test of the morally good act. This is hedonism in its simplest form. The line of connection between Epicurus (341–270 B.C.) and the Cyrenaics is not clear but it is evident that Epicurean ethics is also a hedonism. Where the Stoic located the focal point of moral good and evil in the conscious attitude of the moral agent (and so, remotely, anticipated certain deontological or intuitionistic types of modern ethics), the Epicurean ethician looked to the consequences of man's actions for his criterion of morality (and so, equally remotely, presaged modern utilitarianism in its individualistic versions). For some unknown reason, most of the writings by Epicurus have been lost: we now have three letters and some fragments, mostly from a work *On Nature*.

Like the Stoics, Epicurus divided philosophy into three parts: theory of knowledge, physics, and ethics. He was, however, comparatively uninterested in the logic of discursive reasoning and had no teaching that compares with Stoic logic. Epicurus' theory of knowledge is sensistic. He concentrates on sense perception (*aisthesis*) and the judgments consequent upon it. There are no innate notions: all knowledge comes through sense experience. The test of true knowledge is clarity. Concepts are memory images, usually following many sense perceptions.[14] Epicurus' theory of the nature of things was a version of the earlier materialistic atomism found in Democritus. Only bodies exist and all bodies are constituted out of innumerable little particles. It is possible that Epicurus originated the notion of the "swerve" in the falling of the atoms, to account for the various configurations of collections of atoms and possibly to allow room for some sort of freedom in an otherwise rigidly mechanistic explanation of the universe.

It was ethics that interested Epicurus most and he may simply have adopted from his predecessors those epistemological, psychological, and metaphysical views which were calculated to form a basis for his moral theory. He thought that most of the evil and suffering in man's world is due to the ignorant and superstitious acceptance of polytheism. He may not have been an atheist, in any fundamental sense, but he was very critical of the popular paganism of his day. Epicurus believed that most men live in terror of death and in fear of the gods. Hence he taught that there is no personal survival after death and that the gods are not concerned with human affairs. Epicurean ethics is naturalistic, then, in a special sense: it endeavors to deal with moral good and evil without any recourse to the divine will of Zeus, or to any supernatural laws or ideals of duty.[15]

Just as clearness of perception is the test of truth in the acquisition of knowledge, so the feeling of pleasure or pain is the criterion of right choice and action. Pleasure is the "first good innate in us," but this does not mean that all pleasures are equal in value, or that every pleasure is to be chosen. Sometimes the wise man will choose a present pain to secure a future pleasure. In any case, pleasure does not mean to Epicurus "drinkings and revellings, nor the satisfaction of lusts . . . but sober reasoning, searching out the motives for all choice and avoidance, and banishing mere opinions, to which are due the greatest disturbance of the spirit." The goal of morally good activity, then, is peace of mind (*ataraxia*), freedom from mental perturbation.[16] Epicurus held that study and personal effort will enable a man to acquire the virtues that lead to the equanimity of the sage. Primary among these are prudence (*phronēsis*) and friendship (*philia*): the former is more precious even than philosophy and is the root of all other virtues; the latter is the crown of the perfected life.[17] Evidently, Epicurus was far from teaching libertinism or the selfish pursuit of sensual satisfactions. Indeed, in the long run, the Epicurean and the Stoic ideally good men were not too different. Both were supposed to be men controlled by reason, interested in their own true good and that of other persons, pursuing a high-minded ideal of natural human perfection.

The most complete treatise, still extant, from Roman Epicureanism is Lucretius' poem *On the Nature of Things*. T. Lucretius Carus (*ca.* 96–55 B.C.) introduced Latin readers to the teachings of Epicurus. At the beginning of several of the six books *On the Nature of Things*, Epicurus is addressed in glowing terms as the wisest and best of men.[18] Epicurean atomism and sensism are explained at great length by Lucretius—who does not seem to have added anything to the basic theory. Epicurus' "atheism" and critique of popular religion are much stressed by Lucretius; it is possible that the Roman poet was more antireligious than the Greek philosopher. Lucretius shows himself to be a great admirer of the philosophy of nature. The more we know about physical realities, the more we realize that we should not crave any special satisfactions in life. "Nec nova vivendo procuditur ulla voluptas" (by living we cannot forge for ourselves any new pleasure).[19] The key attitude of the morally good man, according to Lucretius, is resignation, based on an understanding of the way things are. Like Epicurus, Lucretius insisted that friendship (*amicitia*) is the bond of the good human society.[20]

Neoplatonic Ethics

In the first five centuries of the Christian era, several types of ethics were developed by Greek writers who were more or less under the influence of Platonism. The common denominator in this Neoplatonic ethics is the view that the good life consists in a flight from the world of sense experience to a closer relationship with a supreme principle. These Neo-platonists use a variety of ways to explain the culmination of this other-worldly ethics. Chief among these were Philo Judaeus, Plutarch of Chaeronea, and Plotinus.

Philo Judaeus (*ca.* 25 B.C.–40 A.D.) was a Jewish scholar who lived in Alexandria and wrote about forty works in Greek.[21] Most of these writings are allegorical commentaries on the Old Testament. He was convinced that the same basic truths are found in Scripture and in Greek philosophy. The higher forms (or ideas, as in Plato) are created by God in the divine Reason (*logos*). In turn, the material things of the universe are fashioned from the four elements after the pattern of the forms.[22] Man is a creature with a mind ruling his body in somewhat the way that God rules the universe. Man's soul is made in the image of God and, while on earth, is on a journey away from God. It is the destiny of the soul to free itself from the burden of matter and to rise to a union with the divine wisdom. This "flight from the body" is what should be the aim of the perfected and good man.

> Depart out of the earthly matter that encompasses thee: escape, man, from the foul prison-house thy body, with all thy might and main, and from the pleasures and lusts that are its jailers. . . . if thou desire to recover the self thou hast lent and to have thine own posses-sion about thee, letting no portion of them be alienated and fall into other hands, thou shalt claim instead a happy life, enjoying in per-petuity the benefit and pleasure derived from good things not foreign to thee but thine own.[23]

Clearly, this poetical description of a mystical journey of the soul to rejoin its God is not a philosophical ethics. Yet there are adaptations of the Platonic vision in Philo's thinking and he exercised a good deal of influence on Plotinus and many Christian moralists.[24] His ethics would seem to stand at the opposite pole to the this-worldly naturalism of both Stoics and Epicureans.

Plutarch of Chaeronea (*ca.* 46–120 A.D.) was another ancient moralist who built a sort of practical ethics on a modified Platonic view of man. He combined an acceptance of much of the popular Greek religion with a desire to know God in a purely intellectual manner. His God is transcendent and in no way the cause of evil: the World-Soul is the source of mundane evil, even though it emanates from God. The intelligence (*nous*) in man is superior to the soul (*psychē*). It is the intelligent mind that may, by living virtuously and possibly by the practice of certain religious rites, achieve happiness in a future life after separation from the body. Unlike most of his contemporaries, Plutarch showed some acquaintance with Aristotelian ethics. He embraced the theory of virtue as a mean between excess and defect. Like the Stoics, he advocated the brotherhood of man as an ideal for the organization of human society.[25]

There is a sort of ethics in the group of Greek writings emanating from Alexandria, Egypt, and purporting to be the teachings of Hermes Tresmegistos. One discourse speaks of a rebirth of the soul and a mounting to some sort of culminating vision in the afterlife.[26] This teaching is expressed in very obscure myths and cannot be called a formal ethics but it serves to illustrate a point of view in paganism during the first Christian centuries. It placed the good for man in a nonterrestrial happiness.

Plotinus (205–270 A.D.) was the greatest philosopher in these centuries—yet he is rarely mentioned in histories of ethics. He studied at Alexandria and began to teach in Rome when he was about forty. Partially blind, Plotinus devoted much of his time to solitary meditation. He knew the philosophies of Plato, Aristotle, and the Stoics and used all of them in his personal thinking. His lectures were edited by his pupil, Porphyry, in six books with nine chapters in each and so were called the *Enneads* (the "Nines").

The whole of things is viewed by Plotinus as originating from a supreme principle, the One. This unitary beginning is beyond all predicates: one cannot even say that It *is*, for it is beyond being. Some interpreters identify the One with a personal God: Plotinus uses both personal and impersonal pronouns in speaking of It and he does suggest that It is divine. From the One there issues a first hypostasis, Intelligence (*nous*). This first emanation contains the Ideas (like Plato's ideal forms). In turn, the Intelligence gives rise to a second emanation, Soul (*psychē*). This is a cosmic soul: in itself it is not associated with the corporeal, it is the nous thinking itself. On a lower level the world soul animates the whole physical universe. Matter is the limit of the process of emanation: as such, matter is relative nonbeing. Each human being is a composite of a portion, as it were, of Soul plus some bodily matter. Man is poised, then, in a precarious position of existence, capable of going up or down in the scale of reality. If he goes down, by becoming more material, his life becomes evil. If he goes up toward his origin in the One, he is perfected and becomes a better man. The whole of reality is in process: what is real is not static substance but dynamic energy of an incorporeal sort.[27]

The process of emanation from the One is a necessary movement from goodness to evil, a descent into the imperfection of matter. Much of the first *Ennead* is dedicated to the proposition that the good life for man consists in a voluntary ascent of the individual soul toward the One: this is why these chapters are called the "ethical treatises."[28] The fourth chapter, for instance, is a discussion of *eudaimonia*: Greek ethics is eudaimonistic even in its last stages. Plotinus offers a review of his predecessors' notions on well-being; he covers the views of Plato, Aristotle, the Stoics, and the Epicureans. Like Aristotle, Plotinus insists on the active character of *eudaimonia* and is quite critical of the Stoic restriction of final happiness to the rational soul alone. All life is capable of *eudaimonia* and, just as there are different levels of life, there are different degrees of happiness. Similarly, the sixth chapter in *Ennead* I shows how the beautiful (*to kalon*) provides a starting point from which the soul may rise to the contemplation of its own beauty and eventually of the ideal Beauty. This description of the ascent of man's soul toward a peak of perfection is a moral reworking of the thought of several of Plato's dialogues, notably the *Phaedrus*, *Symposium*, and *Theaetetus*.[29] In another place, Plotinus suggests that this ascent of the soul toward the highest Beauty is a mystical phenomenon which he has experienced himself.

> Often I awaken to myself by escaping from my body: thus cut off from other things, in the intimacy of my self, I see a beauty that is as marvelous as can be. Above all, then, I am convinced that I have a higher destiny; my activity is the highest degree of life; I am in union with the divine and, once I have reached this peak of activity, I fasten to It above the other intelligible beings.[30]

In the immediately preceding chapter (7), Plotinus is very insistent on the incorruptibility of man's soul (he offers several arguments from Plato's *Phaedo*) and on the generic similarity between the life of the soul and the divine life. What makes it possible for the spirit of man to ascend to union with the divine is a purification (*catharsis*) from material concerns, an advance in the knowledge of the soul itself and intelligible things, and a process of self-perfection through virtues such as temperance and justice. The second chapter of *Ennead* I is an exposition of a highly developed theory of moral virtue (*aretē*). There are four levels: (1) the virtues required to live well among men in society (*aretai politikai*): these are temperance, courage, justice, and prudence; (2) the virtues needed to cleanse the soul from interest in the body and sense objects (*kathartikai*); (3) the virtues of the already purged soul (*virtutes purgati animi* in the fifth-century summary made by Macrobius, *In Somnium Scipionis*, I, 8); and (4) the exemplary virtues (*aretai paradeigmatikai*), which qualify the soul for the intelligible vision of the One.[31] The following passage from the sixth *Ennead* shows how this fits into the ethics of the soul's ascent:

For the soul by its nature refuses to go down to absolute nothingness; when it descends it goes as far as evil, which is a non-being, but not as far as absolute non-being. In going upward, it does not ascend to a being different from itself; rather, it returns into itself and dwells in nothing other than itself. As soon as it lives within itself alone and not in lower being, it is by that fact present in It. For It is a reality which is not an entity (*ousia*) but beyond entities; to this the soul is united. If a person is aware of his self becoming It, he sees his self as an image of It. If he goes beyond this stage, moving from the image to the reality Itself, he thus reaches the end of the journey. When a person falls back from such contemplation, it is possible for him to revive the virtue (*aretē*) that is within. Then he understands his internal orderliness and rediscovers the upward tendency of his mind: thus, through virtue one moves up to the Intelligence (*nous*), and through wisdom (*sophia*) ascends to the Highest. Such is the life of the gods and of godlike and morally successful men (*anthropōn theiōn kai eudaimonōn bios*): to free oneself from things here below, in a life finding no value in lower things, in a solitary flight toward the One.[32]

From the foregoing it will be evident that Plotinus' ethics is a remarkable version of self-perfectionism. It is a teleological theory, for the quality of good action depends on its being rationally directed toward the attainment of a contemplative and loving union with a supreme End. However, since the perfection achieved in this final union is the highest degree of incorporeal life, and since man's soul is life itself, this ultimate *eudaimonia* is but the final stage in the perfection (*aretē*) of the soul itself. Plotinus' ethical vision fascinated many spiritual-minded thinkers in the ensuing centuries: Greeks, like Dionysius the Areopagite and Maximus the Confessor; Latins, like Marius Victorinus, Augustine of Hippo, Scotus Erigena, Meister Eckhart, and Nicholas of Cusa; Moslems, like Avicenna and Al-Ghazzali; Jews, such as Avicebrón; and a host of Renaissance "Platonists."

Plotinus' immediate followers among the pagan Greek philosophers did not improve the ethics of Neoplatonism. Porphyry of Tyre (233–*ca.*

305 A.D.) edited his master's *Enneads* and wrote his life and also produced personal treatises which attempt a combination of Plotinus' ethical mysticism with a rather crude version of polytheism. Porphyry came to see himself as the prophet of a revived neopagan religion, in which the intelligible universe of Plotinus was filled with demons and spirits who required to be propitiated and managed by magic and esoteric rites. He was a forceful critic of Christianity. One of Porphyry's pupils was a Syrian, Iamblichus of Chalkis (d. *ca.* 330 A.D.). He adopted the four-level theory of virtue and even added a higher type: the priestly virtues, through which the soul is united in ecstasy to the divine One. Iamblichus pushed Neoplatonic ethics further toward a cult in which were practiced divination, theurgy, and magic.

The Greek Neoplatonic school ends with Proclus Diadochus (410–485 A.D.). He was a serious philosopher: his *Elements of Theology* is a highly systematized version of the metaphysics of Plotinus. His more personal writings on *Providence and Fate, Problems concerning Providence,* and the *Subsistence of Evils* are now preserved in Latin versions made in the thirteenth century by the Christian translator William of Moerbeke. Proclus was interested in the theory of the soul's ascent; he distinguished in this process these three stages: the initial *love* of the beautiful, *true knowledge* of reality, and *faith* in the union with the One.[33]

As we shall see in our next chapter, Neoplatonic psychology and ethics were adapted to Christian use by both Greek and Latin writers. The first thousand years of philosophical teaching in Christian centers were characterized by a dominant preference for Neoplatonism.

PART TWO

PATRISTIC AND MEDIEVAL THEORIES

CHAPTER IV

Patristic and Early Medieval Ethics

IN THIS CHAPTER we propose to treat the ethical position taken by key figures in the Christian tradition during the period from the first to the twelfth century A.D. This is actually about a thousand years, for the first Christian writings (apart from the New Testament) that could be called ethical in any philosophical sense, were produced toward the end of the second century. The first part of this millennium is termed the patristic period from the fact that the Fathers (*Patres*) of the Church lived and taught then. While the term is used with some vagueness, it is agreed by most authorities that a "Father" is marked by three special characteristics: he must be orthodox in his religious doctrine, he must be of considerable influence in his teaching and writing, and he must be noted for the personal holiness of his life. Men like St. John Damascene in the Greek Church and SS. Ambrose and Augustine among the Latin writers are universally recognized as Fathers.[1] Boethius, on the other hand, although a Christian and an outstanding writer, was never called a Father; he was not a member of the clergy. We shall examine, then, the views of these patristic and medieval Christian teachers to see what they contributed to the history of ethics. It is significant that none of these teachers knew Aristotle's *Nicomachean Ethics* (which became very influential from the thirteenth century onward). Their contemporaries in the Islamic and Jewish schools knew Aristotelian ethics long before the Christians did. We shall reserve for the next chapter our examination of these non-Christian schools of medieval ethics.

The relation between the sort of moral teaching found in the Bible and philosophical ethics is not understood in the same way by all present-day writers on the subject. To some scholars, morality that is based on belief in God's commands is not ethical theory at all.[2] To others, no ethics presuming to offer guidance for real living is possible without some reference to right and wrong as determined by God's Law or Will. As the outstanding contemporary Protestant theologian Emil Brunner puts it: "The Good consists in always doing what God wills at any particular moment."³ Without attempting to settle this metaethical problem, we will take it that a moral teaching based on a well-promulgated set of precepts backed by divine authority does involve an ethical position, provided it makes some effort to relate its views to recognized positions in moral philosophy. We do find such "theological approbative theories"⁴ in the writings of Christians before the thirteenth century and feel that they have a place in a historical survey of ethics.

The earliest Christian moral writers made no complete break with ancient Jewish traditions in which it was claimed that God had conveyed directly to Moses ten general commandments to regulate human conduct. This "Decalogue" was known and accepted by Christians from the beginning. For them, as for the Jews, the reason why a man was obliged to honor his elders, or to avoid killing and stealing, was simply that God had so commanded. New Testament morality did not negate the precepts of the old Jewish law but rather suggested a greater emphasis on love as the inner motivation of the believer who wished to live righteously. The two Christian precepts of charity (Matthew 22:37–40, "Thou shalt love the Lord thy God" and "Thou shalt love thy neighbor as thyself") are usually understood as fulfillments of divine law (Romans 13:8) and not as cancellations of the traditional rules of the Old Testament. In the Sermon on the Mount it is clearly stated: "Do not think that I [Christ] have come to destroy the Law or the Prophets: I have not come to destroy, but to fulfill."⁵

It can hardly be denied that there was a certain tension in early Christian writings between a strictly *juridical* approach to moral problems and a contrary tendency to emphasize mercy, love, and good will. Although the latter is what is typical of the spirit of Christian morality, the Fathers and medieval writers on ethics all accepted a code of moral precepts as imposed by divine command. This sort of legal view of moral obligation is unlike anything in Greek or Roman philosophy. The closest approach to it is in the universal "law" of the Stoics, but that was not a set of precepts promulgated by a transcendental Deity.

Actually, the first speculation about ethical obligations and their relation to laws may have taken place among Christians who were neither Greeks nor Latins. We sometimes have a tendency to forget that the "Oriental" Church, in the Near East and in North Africa, had many learned men during the first Christian centuries. Quite recent studies have thrown light on the work of an early Syrian Christian, Bardaisan of Edessa (154–222), who faced the problem of reconciling classical philosophy with Christian doctrine.⁶ His *Book of the Laws of Countries* admits that man's bodily activities are subject to external controls, and even to fate, but Bardaisan argues that man is internally free to choose right or wrong actions. Unlike some later Christian writers who tended to stress similarities in the laws of great nations (as evidence of their dependence on one natural law), Bardaisan found a certain support for moral freedom in the fact that laws in various countries differ and are easily changed. The full ethical significance of this early Christian thought in the Near East has not been properly studied as yet.

Greek Christian Writers on Moral Theory

Much the same admission would have to be made concerning our lack of knowledge of the beginnings of philosophy in the Greek Christian schools. We lack not only technical studies of the ethical thought of these people but also critical editions and good translations of their writings. There was, for instance, a Greek writer named Hippolytus whose precise dates are unknown but who was "probably a pupil of Irenaeus." This would place Hippolytus in the last half of the second century. He is thought to be the author of a treatise entitled *Philosophumena* in which much of classical Greek philosophy is appraised from the viewpoint of Christianity.[7] It contains an approving survey of Plato's ethics: the immortality and tripartite character of the human soul, the notion of rewards and punishments in a future life, the four virtues described in the *Republic*, and the notion (as suggested in the tale of Er) that our lives are only partly in the hands of fate and that we have some choice as to our destiny. This early Christian treatise also treats evil as a privation of goodness in a being where such goodness would be expected. The impressive feature of Hippolytus' thought is his unquestioning acceptance of the practical philosophy of Plato.

In the same period, a very active and productive school of Greek Christian thought was developing at Alexandria. This was a very cosmopolitan city: it had a famous library and outstanding Greek schools from the third century B.C. The first Alexandrian Christian writer to turn his attention to philosophy was Clement of Alexandria (ca. 150–215 A.D.). One of his writings, the *Miscellanies* (*Stromata*), offers many comparisons between pagan philosophy and Christian teachings. Clement was a noted classical scholar before his conversion to Christianity but he generally took the position that many of the same truths are found in philosophy and in religious revelation. He criticizes the Epicureans, however, as atheists and materialists. Such unfavorable appraisals of the school of Epicurus are common in early Christian writers. In the sixth book of the *Miscellanies* Clement develops a theory of practical wisdom (*phronēsis*) as a universal principle of beings and of the functions of the human soul. This appears to be an adaptation from the rationalism of Platonic ethics and the right reason theory of the Stoics. We should strive to live in such a way that we will become more and more like God (a rule also found in Hippolytus), even though, as Clement frankly admitted, we can know with certainty little or nothing about God's nature.[8] He does discuss certain moral problems concerning moderation in eating, drinking, and clothing but is little inclined to speculate about the philosophical basis for making ethical judgments. Perhaps Clement's greatest contribution was to have given a certain respectability to philosophy by virtue of his incorporation of some of its teachings in a widely read Christian work.

Another Alexandrian who produced Greek works with ethical content was Origen (185–254). His treatises *Against Celsus* and *On First Principles* contain some teachings similar to those of Plotinus; this is probably due to the fact that they studied under the same teacher, although Origen was at least twenty years older than Plotinus. Origen is less optimistic than Clement about the value of philosophy: it is alien to Christianity. In his psychology, Origen has some views that are generally considered unorthodox for a Christian and these teachings affect his moral theory. He is certain that each human soul is immortal but he speculates on the possibility that the soul may exist before union with its body, that it may sin in this pre-existence, and that it may be punished by being bound to a body in earthly existence.[9] This is a Christian version of something like the Plotinian descent and eventual ascent of the human soul. Man is free to go up or down: the soul "may either descend from the highest good to the lowest evil or be restored from the lowest evil to the highest good." Reason and free will are present in each soul and make it possible to control base tendencies and to live a good life. The test of what is good or bad action is found in the divine precepts (the Decalogue and certain New Testament injunctions to avoid anger, swearing, and to encourage the fainthearted and support the weak), which are to be literally understood and obeyed.[10] In the final outcome, all things will be restored to their source in God and there will no longer be any evil.

In less radical form, this theory of the ascent of the soul to its God is found in Gregory of Nyssa (335–*ca.* 394). He rejects the pre-existence of souls but admits the ultimate return of all things to God. Gregory's version of this psychic ascent entails one of the earliest accounts of Christian mysticism. He emphasizes the need for special divine assistance (grace) to enable man to rise to union with God.[11]

The most influential Christian exposition of this flight-of-the-soul ethic is also the most mysterious and historically baffling. At some time during the fifth century a group of five works in Greek come to be known in Christian learning; they were called the *Corpus Dionysiacum* (or *Areopagiticum*). Their writer is unknown but he is called Dionysius the Pseudo-Areopagite. He professed to have lived in apostolic times and to have witnessed certain New Testament events; in reality, these writings are obviously under the strong influence of Neoplatonic philosophy and contain literal passages from Proclus (fifth century). So, they could not have been written in the time of the apostles. These treatises are: *On the Celestial Hierarchy, On the Ecclesiastical Hierarchy, On the Divine Names, Mystical Theology,* and ten *Letters.* They were highly regarded in the Middle Ages—even though their message is obscure and their orthodoxy as Christian teachings is open to suspicion.

The fourth chapter of *On the Divine Names* is devoted to the meaning of "good" as applied to God, and it is in connection with this "name" that Dionysius reveals his predilection for Neoplatonic ethics. Here the problem of evil is raised and treated in terms of the Plotinian claim that evil is merely a privation of goodness.[12] This text is one of the two media (the other, of course, is Augustine) through which the privation theory of evil comes to thinkers of the thirteenth century. Angelic spirits and human souls are called evil, in this view, because of their "deficiency of good qualities and activities and in the failure and fall therefrom due to their own weakness."[13] The positive explanation of good human activity, according to the Pseudo-Dionysius, is given in terms of the soul rising to a personal union with God. In its yearning for the Beauty and Good of its Source, the soul goes through three typical motions: (1) a *circular* turning from the multiplicity of external things inward to itself; (2) a *spiral* movement of discursive and dialectical reasoning; and (3) a *straight forward* movement toward the simple unity of contemplative acts.[14] This theory is tersely and obscurely developed in the short treatise on *Mystical Theology.* Very influential on later moral theologians was a formula used by Pseudo-Dionysius to summarize his views on the good (*to agathon*): "The good stems from a cause that is one and entire; but the evil comes from defects that are manifold and pertaining to various parts."[15] This is taken to apply to both physical and moral evil, and to mean that a good action must be approvable in every one of its circumstances, while an action becomes immoral if any one of its required circumstances is missing.[16]

Maximus of Scythopolis (580–662) expanded and helped to popularize these views of Pseudo-Dionysius. His treatise on *Ambiguities* (*Patrologia Graeca* 91, 1072–1085) teaches that man rejoins God through knowing the good and feeling an ecstatic love of the divine Beauty. This terminates in a phase of divinization (*theōsis*) of all things. Man and the universe return to the unity of their divine Ideas. At the end, God will be All in All.[17]

The last Greek writer whom we will consider in this period is John Damascene (*ca.* 675–749). His large work, *The Source of Knowledge,* has as its third part a section on the basic truths of Christianity that was put into Latin in the twelfth century by Burgundio of Pisa under the title *De fide orthodoxa* (*On the True Faith*). In this Latin form, it was very influential in the thirteenth century and much quoted in the various *Summas* of theology. John Damascene introduces us to a teaching that is different from the Neoplatonic-Christian flight-of-the-soul theories. There is an analysis of the powers and functions of man which Damascene takes from a treatise by the Greek Bishop Nemesius, *On the Nature of Man* (written *ca.* 400 A.D.), who in turn adapted his theory from the pre-Christian teaching of Poseidonius of Apameia. The following passage shows how John Damascene understood the moral powers of man; it is translated directly from Burgundio's Latin version.

We should note that our soul has twofold powers (*virtutes, dynameis*), some cognitive, others vital (*zoticas*). Now the cognitive ones are: understanding, mind, opinion, imagination and sense. The vital or appetitive powers are counsel [*consilium*, a mistranslation of *boulēsis*, which means volition] and choice (*electio, proairesis*). It should also be noted that there is naturally present in the soul an appetitive power which is according to nature, and it is directed to all objects which are associated with nature; it is called will (*voluntas, thelesis*). For substance inclines (*appetit*) to be, to live, and to be moved, in accord with sense perception and understanding, craving its own natural or complete being. Therefore they describe this natural willing (*thelēma*) in this way: willing, that is the *voluntas*, is a rational, vital appetite, based on natural tendencies only. The power of will (*thelēsis*), that is *voluntas*, is itself natural, vital and subject to reason, an appetite for all the components of nature, a simple power (*virtus*). There is another appetite for other things and it is not rational, nor is it called will (*voluntas, thelēsis*). Now volition (*boulēsis*) is in every way natural; thelēsis is the will, the natural and rational appetite for any sort of thing. There is present in the soul of man a power of rational appetition. Since it is naturally moved, this rational appetite for any object is called *boulēsis* [spelled in Burgundio's Latin, *bulisis*], that is will. Now boulesis, that is will, is a rational appetite and desire for any object. It is called *boulēsis*, that is will (*voluntas*), both in regard to objects that are in our power and objects that are not; that is, in regard to possible and impossible objectives.[18]

In this halting and none too clear analysis we have the beginnings of a special moral psychology in which the notion of natural (and so, physically necessary) volition of the good is distinguished from a deliberated, rationally governed (and so, free) movement of the human will. Under the influence of this text, Thomas Aquinas and some other thirteenth-century thinkers taught that there are two kinds of human volition: *voluntas ut ratio*, which is free; and *voluntas ut natura*, which is not free.[19] Moreover, this text from John Damascene introduces the claim that there is more to appetition in man than rational willing.

Sensory appetition includes two powers: concupiscible appetite (whose movements are simple desires or aversions in regard to individual things perceived in sensation) and irascible appetite (whose movements are efforts to evade or attack dangerous or difficult aspects of sense objects). This teaching influenced the moral psychology of Aquinas and other writers in the Scholastic tradition so that they adopted a three-appetite view of human activity: will, and irascible and concupiscible appetites.[20]

Latin Writers on Moral Theory

In the period before the thirteenth century, the Western or Latin section of the Christian Church produced a good many writers who touched on fundamental questions of ethics. Of the Latin Fathers, Ambrose and Augustine are the most prominent in this field. Some of their ethical views are still under discussion in the twentieth century. Boethius, as we shall see, had a good deal to say about the moral life in his *Consolation of Philosophy*. Erigena and Anselm developed quite different versions of Christian Platonic ethics in the ninth and eleventh centuries respectively. Peter Abelard, however, best typifies the tensions between the subjective demands of personal conscience and the objective requirements of a moral law that transcends human nature. We shall take a look at the more significant ethical theories of key figures in this Latin tradition.

One of the earliest Christian moralists was a North African, Tertullian, who lived from about 160 to 240. Frequently associated with his name is the phrase "credo quia absurdum" ("I believe because it is absurd"), but it is difficult to decide just what he meant. Quite possibly he was simply saying that faith has its mysteries which lie beyond the scope of reason.[21] In his treatise *On the Soul* (chapter 19), Tertullian suggested that the human soul is of a bodily nature and that the souls of children come from the father's semen. In spite of this apparently materialistic view of man's spirit (few Christian writers have shared it), Tertullian was a strong advocate of personal freedom and did much to make precise the meaning of person.[22] In his moral teaching, Tertullian advocated a very rigid and strict regulation of all aspects of Christian living. Christianity provides a detailed code of conduct: the reward for complete obedience is eternal happiness with God, the punishment for disobedience is eternal suffering. As one patristic scholar sums up Tertullian's legalism: "The God whom he cherished is the inflexible and jealous Judge Who has established *timor* (fear) as the basis for man's salvation."[23]

Less extreme is the position of another African Christian, Lactantius (*ca.* 250–330), who also wrote in Latin. In his *Divine Institutes,* Lactantius took the position that pagan philosophy has no truth in it (Book III is entitled *De falsa sapientia*). The sixth book in this treatise presents the basic principles of Christian morality and treats these directives as the immediate commands of God. This is a good example of a moderate type of theological approbative ethics in the early Church. While he is little inclined to theorize about ethical problems, Lactantius recognizes the importance of education in practical wisdom.[24]

It is usual to mention Ambrose, Bishop of Milan (340–397), as a practical-minded moralist. His treatise *On the Functions of the Clergy* is indeed a practical application of Cicero's *De officiis* to the Christian setting. In this sense, Ambrose has influenced Christian moral theology.[25] Quite another aspect of his work in philosophy has been discovered recently in connection with research into the background of Augustine's thought. Briefly, Ambrose appears to have had more than a passing interest in Neoplatonic philosophy. The group of sermons gathered under the title *De Isaac et anima* show that he adopted the Plotinian view that evil is nothing positive, but a privation of good, and that he was under the same influence in his treatment of virtues and vices. Furthermore, Ambrose pictured the good life as a flight of the soul from the world to God.[26] He was, then, a medium for the transmission of Greek philosophical ideas to the early Latin Church.

The Latin Father of the Church who has the most completely developed moral theory is Augustine of Hippo (354–430). He had something to say on most of the problems that later ethicians have studied. Augustine's ethical views are still under discussion in twentieth-century ethics.[27] No one work contains his moral teaching. We will use several of the early dialogues, the *Confessions, City of God, On the Trinity, Enchiridion,* and other writings for our exposition.[28]

That all men desire and strive for happiness (*beatitudo*), Augustine did not doubt. His ethical position is as eudaimonistic as any in classical Greek thought. He did not know Aristotle's *Nicomachean Ethics* (except through reports in Latin writers such as Cicero) and his acquaintance with the dialogues of Plato was very limited. He seems to have read parts of the *Enneads* and some of the short moral works of Porphyry. Platonism (under which he included the thought of Plotinus) appeared to Augustine to be the best of the pagan philosophies (*City of God,* VII, chapters 4–7). In his day, however, the popular philosophies were Epicureanism and Stoicism. They were quite wrong in their ethics, Augustine felt. Interestingly enough, Augustine sums up the Epicurean ultimate object of desire as "pleasure of the body," and the Stoic ideal as "steadfastness of spirit."[29] His own view is that man's final felicity cannot consist in some mere perfection of the human person (such as virtue or knowledge) but rather in a special sort of union, after the death of the body, with God.[30]

The really important part of man, as Augustine sees it, is the soul (*anima, animus, spiritus*). Man is a soul using a body as instrument ("*anima utens corpore*," *De moribus ecclesiae*, I, 27, 52). As knowing, this soul is called mind (*mens*); as keeping all objects within it, the same soul is memory (*memoria*); and as the source of any psychic action through the body or apart from it, the soul is called will (*voluntas*). This trinitarian psychology is expounded in Books IX to XIV of the treatise *On the Trinity*.[31] Man's soul is able to direct its attention to various objectives by an act of volitional turning (*versio*). One may turn to concentrate on bodies (all of which are inferior to soul) and this is a perversion. It is not that Augustine considered bodily things evil; they were made by God and are good things (*De natura boni*, 1); rather, he was convinced that the soul as the seat of life, consciousness, and all human effort is obviously better than any inanimate thing.[32] So, the soul only degrades itself by concentrating on corporeal values. When the soul turns in upon itself, it finds a better nature but still something imperfect and subject to temporal changes. Introspection reveals the grandeur of the human spirit, of course (see the famous description of memory, *Confessions*, X, 8–26), but further consideration indicates the inferiority of the soul to God. In looking to God, man's soul finds the source of all reality and goodness.

God will enlighten the minds of men who turn to Him and seek His help. Divine illumination is available to all men, to show them the initial truths of knowing, existing, and acting. God's "Light" is not merely a cognitive principle but also a source of moral information and guidance. Our first notions of equality, order, right thinking (*prudentia*), moderation (*temperantia*), strength of character (*fortitudo*), justice (*recititudo, justitia*), and other such ethical ideals, come to us through a personal intuition which is made possible by the divine light.[33] The following passage shows how Augustine presented this intuition of the eternal standards (*rationes aeternae*) of ethical judgment:

So also among the objects of the understanding, there are some that are seen in the soul itself: for example, the virtues (to which the vices are opposed), either virtues which will endure, such as piety, or virtues that are useful for this life and not destined to remain in the next, as faith, by which we believe what we do not see, and hope, by which we await with patience the life that shall be, and patience itself, by which we bear every adversity until we arrive at the goal of our desires. These virtues, of course, and other similar ones, which are quite necessary for us now in living out our exile, will have no place in the blessed life [in Heaven], for the attainment of which they are necessary. And yet even they are seen with the understanding . . . distinct from these objects is the light by which the soul is illumined, in order that it may see and truly understand everything, either in itself or in the light. For the light is God himself. . . .[34]

Another way that Augustine has of describing the object of moral illumination puts it in terms of eternal law. As he says in his early dialogue On Order (II, 8, 25): "This teaching (disciplina) is the very law of God, which ever abiding fixed and unshaken with Him, is transcribed, so to speak, on the souls of the wise, so that they know that they live a better and more sublime life in proportion as they contemplate it more perfectly with their understanding and observe it more perfectly in their manner of living." This eternal law is both the reason and the will of God: lex est ratio divina et voluntas Dei (Contra Faustum, XII, 27). It is immutable and universal. In pre-Mosaic times, the eternal law was naturally known through man's reason (and so is occasionally called lex naturalis by Augustine) and it was delivered in part, in written form, to Moses: it is said to be "impressed on our minds" or "written in our hearts." Man's conscience (conscientia) thus becomes immediately aware of rules such as: Do not do to others what you would not have them do to you (Enarrationes in Psalmos, Ps. 57, 1). Many other rules of this kind are naturally known.[35]

Thus far, the ethics of Augustine appears to be a legalistic version of Christian morality. His thought has, however, another important ethical dimension. Despite his insistence on obedience to God's law, Augustine takes second place to no ethical writer in his insistence on personal freedom, the importance of good will, and the need of proper internal motivation. In mature life he wrote a famous treatise On the Spirit and the Letter (De spiritu et littera, 412 A.D.) to explain that a person must be moved by the love of God before he can get any credit for acting in conformity with moral law. As he now expresses his view: "If this commandment is kept from fear of punishment and not from love of righteousness, it is servilely kept, not freely, and therefore is not kept at all. For no fruit is good which does not grow from the root of charity" (De spiritu et littera, 14, 26). Fear of punishment is not an adequate motive, even for the negative avoidance of immorality (Epistola 145, 3, 4). In another letter (Epistola 155, 4, 13) Augustine makes the love of God the principle of good living:

> In this life, although there is no virtue save that of loving what ought to be loved, prudence lies in choosing it; fortitude in not being turned from it by any troubles; to be allured from it by no seductions is temperance, and by no pride is justice. But what ought we to choose as the object of our principal love but that which

we find to be better than anything else? This object is God; and
to set anything above or even equal to Him is to show that we do
not know how to love ourselves. For our good becomes the greater
the more we approach Him than whom there is nothing better.

It is in terms of the foregoing that one should understand the much-
quoted Augustinian text: "Love, and do what you will" (*dilige, et quod
vis fac*).[36] Augustine did not mean that a good person could break
all the laws of God, provided such a person felt a great love for something or other! What he did mean was that a man who truly loves God
is of such good will, so well motivated, that he will almost automatically
act in full accord with all the precepts of divine and moral law. Such
perfection of will and character comes to a man through the gift of
divine grace only. The love that motivates all good moral actions is
the theological virtue of charity.[37]

In spite of the intensely religious coloring of this teaching, Augustine
did think of his wisdom as an ethics. As he formally outlined the matter,
in the eighth book of the *City of God*, the third and last part of
philosophy is moral, what the Greeks call *ethica* ("quam Graeco vo-
cabulo dicunt *ethiken*"). He proceeds to explain how he understands
the field of ethics:[38]

It deals with the supreme good, by reference to which all our
actions are directed. It is the good we seek for itself and not because
of something else and, once it is attained, we seek nothing further
to make us happy. This, in fact, is why we call it our end, because
other things are desired on account of this *summum bonum*, while
it is desired purely for itself.

Augustine's ethics is a theocentric eudaimonism: man's ultimate well-
being consists in the possession of God (*De moribus ecclesiae*, I, 6, 10).
Many people consider it the greatest example of Christian ethics.[39]

Another version of early Christian ethics is found in the next century
in the writings of the Roman senator Anicius Manlius Torquatus Sev-
erinus Boethius (*ca.* 470–525). His best-known work is the *Consolation
of Philosophy*. Some shorter theological treatises are also sources for his
views in ethics. Boethius' psychology is similar to Augustine's but he
knew more about Greek philosophy than did Augustine. In particular,
Boethius would seem to be the first Latin scholar in the Christian Church
who was well acquainted with the *Nicomachean Ethics*. Despite his
knowledge of Aristotle, Boethius preferred the teaching of Plato on
many problems and was also favorably impressed by many features in
the practical philosophy of the Stoics. At the end of the nineteenth
century, it was fashionable among historians of philosophy to question
the Christianity of this author: today, no serious scholar doubts that he
was a Christian.

There are, for Boethius, four levels of cognition: the lowest is sense, which perceives the shapes and qualities of things clothed in matter; the next level is imagination, which views bodily forms without their matter; the third is reason (*ratio*), which penetrates to the universal nature that may be present in many individuals (this is the cognitive power that is distinctive of men living on earth); and the highest power is intelligence, which intuits perfect "forms" existing apart from matter (*intellectibilia*): this is a divine capacity, men share in it only occasionally, when they get flashes of understanding. Theology is a divine science that cultivates the highest knowledge of God and divine properties.[40] At the beginning of a short treatise on metaphysics which came to be called *De Hedomadibus* in the Middle Ages, Boethius listed nine propositions which he took as axiomatic to the rest of his argument.[41] The first described a "common conception" as a statement which one would approve as soon as it is heard. These are of two types: some, such as the geometric axiom of equality, are understandable to all men; other propositions, such as "incorporeals cannot occupy space," are grasped only by the learned. A second type, such as "equals added to equals result in equals," is knowable to all men. This theory of initial axioms and definitions in philosophy, plus the theory of intuitive intelligence, combine to influence the later Scholastic teaching on first principles of speculative and practical knowledge (including ethics). Taken together with a deductivist emphasis on discursive reasoning (which stems from Boethius' textbooks on syllogistic logic), this Boethian tradition of demonstrative science is the source of much of the system-building that characterized Christian moral philosophy and theology in the later Middle Ages.[42]

Quite a different approach to ethics is suggested in the actual metaphysics of the treatise *De Hebdomadibus*. This is a thoroughly Platonic discussion of how the many inferior instances of good are good by participation in One, Highest Good. Such metaphysical goodness is not identical with the ethical meaning of good. At the end of this treatise we are told that "all things are good but all things are not just." Justice is a species of activity and there are acts that are not just.[43]

Books III and IV of the *Consolation of Philosophy* give further evidence of how Boethius attempted to build a practical philosophy of life by using elements of Platonism, Aristotelianism, and Stoicism within the context of a Christian morality. Like the Greeks, Boethius saw men as striving for the attainment of ultimate well-being (*beatitudo*). Different men have thought that happiness is dependent on obtaining bodily goods (strength, health, beauty), or goods of the spirit (knowledge, virtue), or even goods of social intercourse (fame, political power, good reputation). Boethius argues that all these ends are imperfect and not lasting: there must be some Perfect Good which is the objective terminus of these human aspirations for happiness. Such reasoning requires one to see that God exists as the perfect and fullest good.[44] This way of arguing to the conclusion that God is the objective goal of all moral striving becomes an important element in the teleological ethics of later Scholasticism.

There are, of course, numerous writings on detailed questions of practical morality in the centuries immediately following Boethius. Many of these are unedited and unstudied. Comparatively unknown, for instance, is the Bishop of Braga, Martin of Dumio (ca. 515–580). His works are under titles such as *Formula for an Honest Life*, *The Four Virtues*, *How to Put Down Pride*, and so on. In general, Martin adopted Seneca's teaching on the leading moral virtues and applied it to Christian living. Much the same could be said of the moral content of encyclopedic writers such as Gregory the Great (540–604) and Isidore of Seville (ca. 570–630). They were not as dependent on pagan sources as Martin, but their ethical views result from a combination of classical humanism with a fundamentally Christian view of life. Gregory's *Moral Exposition of the Book of Job* is much quoted later but it is an exaggeration to call it the classical *Grundwerk* from which medieval ethics sprang.[45]

In the ninth century, John Scottus Erigena (ca. 810–877) put into a Latin work the whole Neoplatonic ethics of the flight of the soul to its Source. His *De divisione naturae* is a vast metaphysical structure purporting to explain how all things, including men, come forth from the one cause and eventually return to this divine Principle. Plotinian emanationism is thus combined in a startling way with Christian creationism. All reality is called "nature" (*natura*): God as Source is *natura creans sed increata*; the divine Ideas constitute *natura creans et creata*; the universe and men make up *natura increans sed creata*; and finally God as End is *Natura increans et increata*.[46] A human being is initially "a certain intellectual idea formed eternally in the divine mind."[47] At the end of his life on earth each man undergoes another "division" of his nature: the soul divides from the body, and the body disintegrates into its material components. However, in a third step man's body is reunited with his soul and is progressively spiritualized; in a fourth step the spiritualized man rejoins his archetypal Idea in God; and in a final stage of the return all the world will go back to its Source.[48] Man is free to adapt his will to this return, and indeed it is his duty as a Christian to develop his higher capacities so that his whole being is transmuted into pure thought. Divine grace is needed to enable man to rise to this higher state of existence. As Erigena explains in the fifth book *On the Division of Nature*, the man who lives a morally good life not only reunites with God, as all men eventually do, his ultimate condition is a becoming like God (*deifactio*). This deification is granted only to the good.

After Erigena there is no Latin writer on morality of comparable stature until we come to St. Anselm in the eleventh century. Anselm of Canterbury (1033–1109) was an Italian who was trained in a Benedictine monastery in France and became one of the most renowned bishops of the English see of Canterbury. His importance in the history of ethics lies in his emphasis on the personal attitude of the moral agent as the determinant of moral good or evil. One historian goes so far as to say that, with Anselm, "morality is defined independently of any consideration of utility and, generally speaking, of any consideration of ultimate end."[49] This is the first known instance of a medieval ethician who broke away from the eudaimonism of Plato, Aristotle, and the Stoics.

Of course, St. Anselm is very much indebted to Augustine, particularly in his moral psychology. The will is the most important aspect of the soul. Man's will is subject to two possible dispositions (*affectiones*) prior to any moral activity. By one of these predispositions, the *affectio ad commodum*, every man is subjectively inclined to seek various goods that are appropriate to his ordinary state of existence. This inclines him to desire to build a home and cultivate his fields, for instance. The second of these dispositions, the *affectio justitiae*, enables some men to incline volitionally toward a better than natural good. This is the justification of the will by divine grace.[50] To see what this "higher justice" means to Anselm we must look briefly at his theory of truth. In the *Dialogue on Truth* he described many instances of the true (*verum*): true statements, true opinions, true volitions, true actions, true sense perceptions, true things. Like a good Platonist, Anselm argued that these many instances are true because there is one supreme Truth in which they all share. To be true, then, is to be right (*rectus*) in relation to some immutable standard of rightness (*rectitudo*). The general definition of truth (*veritas*) is: "rightness perceptible to the mind alone."[51]

Applying this to the problem of morality, Anselm decided that justice is rightness of will that is preserved for its own sake.[52] In other words, a person is just, not so much because of *what* he wills as because of the *reason why* (*propter quod*) he wills it. Anselm is here broaching the important theme of ethical motivation: he is suggesting that a moral agent is *right*, not because his action achieves a certain result but because of a certain quality of the initial attitude, or volitional inclination, of the person. Since he insists that rectitude must be willed for its own sake alone (true freedom is defined as "the power of preserving rectitude of will, for the sake of rectitude itself"), Anselm is here anticipating something of Kant's theory of the pure and good will.[53] Of course, Anselmian moral rectitude is far from mere subjective rightness; he is not an ethical formalist; one's will is right by conforming with an objective Rightness—which is God.

One of the few writers in the early Middle Ages to use the term "ethics" was Peter Abelard (1079–1142). His treatise *Ethica seu liber dictus scito teipsum* is a landmark in ethical discussions in the Middle Ages. As an opponent of the usual (in his time) realistic approach to universals, Abelard could not maintain that a concrete instance of good (*bonum*) is such by virtue of participation in an existing essence of universal goodness (*bonitas*). Somewhat under the influence of Anselm, he maintains that sin consists in consent (*consensus*) to what is improper. Since the improper is what is opposed to the laws of God, the consent to sin is equivalent to contempt for God. He proceeds to argue forcefully that what is morally good or bad is not the execution of a given action but the prior disposition of the agent's will. Using an example much favored in present-day situationism, Abelard says: "The sin, then, consists not in desiring a woman, but in consent to the desire."[54]

Abelard had no direct knowledge of the *Nicomachean Ethics* and was thus unable to use Aristotle's analysis of voluntariness. In the key third chapter of his *Ethics* Abelard hesitated to say whether sin necessarily involves an act of willing or not. He discussed several examples of things done "against one's will" and yet seeming to involve responsibility, guilt, and sin. He did much to highlight the important difference between fault (*culpa*) and guilt (*poena*) but his terminology and thought on such points fluctuated. In some chapters the *Ethics* speaks of intention (*intentio*) as the focal point of moral good and evil: in this usage "intention" means the same as consent. Throughout the work he insists that the doing or omitting of an action adds nothing to the moral value of the consent or intention.

Abelard's ethics is not a pure subjectivism: a man's intention must be right, and this means in objective conformity with God's laws. He knows that some people have suggested that an intention is right "when anyone believes that he acts well."[55] He firmly insists that the only good intention is one that actually pleases God. However, he did not indicate how ordinary people can know what does please God, objectively.[56]

The view that morality is a matter of some quality of rightness within the soul of each person (what modern writers would call "intrinsic morality") was rather general in the twelfth century. Even a great critic of the orthodoxy of Abelard's theology, like Bernard of Clairvaux (1090–1153), was in full agreement with the idea that consent to the good is what enables a person to merit an eternal reward in Heaven.[57] St. Bernard was not an ethical theorist: more than any other medieval moralist he simply insisted on the importance of loving God with as pure and exalted motives as are possible. This is the theme of his treatise *On the Necessity of Loving God* (*De diligendo Deo*). Of course, this is not moral subjectivism: there is a suprahuman standard to which right willing must conform; this norm is eternal law. Bernard is not juridical-minded, but he is far from saying that goodness is simply having a good feeling. He condemns the man who values merely self-will: "each one made a universal and eternal law."[58] This is a perversion of the desire to imitate God.

During the twelfth century, ethics or moral philosophy came to take an accepted place among the disciplines taught in many Christian schools. Many anthologies (florilegia) and eclectic treatises were produced to serve as texts in the training of boys in the monastery schools and in other scholastic centers. Most of these works are anonymous. There is, for instance, the Teachings of the Moral Philosophers (Moralium dogma philosophorum), which has been attributed to William of Conches, Gauthier of Chatillon, and others. There is the Moral Philosophy of the Good-in-itself and the Useful Good (Moralis Philosophia de honesto et utili) printed among the works of Hildebert of Tours but of uncertain authorship. And there is the Oxford Collection of Moral Writings (Florilegium Morale Oxoniense), only recently edited. What these and other works of this kind have in common is a desire to cull what is best from the classic Greek and Roman moral writers and to adapt these exemplary readings to the requirements of Christian life. This movement is sometimes called "Christian Socratism." The ancient authors who are especially prized are Plato, Cicero, Seneca, and certain minor writers, such as Macrobius and Andronicus. Ethically, these twelfth-century collections represent a spiritually oriented version of self-realization. Instead of emphasizing moral obligation by law, they advise the improvement of moral character by the cultivation of the theological (faith, hope, charity) and the cardinal (prudence, temperance, fortitude, and justice) virtues. These virtues are subdivided into many "parts" and the result is a lengthy listing and description of many good habits (virtues), often accompanied by criticisms of the opposed bad habits (vices).[59]

Certain groups with heterodox religious views appeared on the scene in the twelfth century and may have had some negative influence on the central current of medieval Christian ethics. One such movement was that of the Cathari. In southern France, they had a center in a town called Albi and came to be known as Albigensians. In Italy, two groups of Cathari were found in this century: the Albanenses in the Bergamo-Verona area, and the Concorenses (Garatenses) in the region of Concorezzo. Basically, Catharism was a revival of Manichaeism, a religious teaching that there are two ultimate Principles: one is the source of all good things and events, the other is the source of all evil. Usually these were regarded as coeternal, and equally powerful, gods. In twelfth-century Catharism the basic dualism of Mani was adapted to several different views of the Christian life. Two effects of this movement may be observed in the ethics of the period. First of all, most of the

Cathari embraced a very rigorous and puritanical attitude toward moral behavior. They regarded all sexual activity as morally evil, for instance, and required their perfect believers to abstain from procreation, even in marriage. Extreme asceticism was professed. On the other hand, since the original Manichaeism (of Persian origin, Mani lived in the third century A.D.) held that evil was as real and positive as good, and that there are two wills in every man (one evil and one good), many later followers took it that immorality was inevitable. One could disclaim responsibility for an evil action by saying that it stemmed from his bad will and not from the good will, with which latter he would identify.[60]

Another religious movement with ethical overtones originated in the views of Joachim of Flora (1145–1202), a Cistercian abbot in northern Italy. He advocated a return to the simplicity and rigor of the early years of Christianity. It is probable that he felt that all academic or theoretical ethics is pagan nonsense, so Joachim would represent an odd type of ethical skeptic, critical of such philosophical activity as not pertinent to the salvation of one's soul.[61] His theological and scriptural writings suggest an apocalyptic view of history, which was pushed to an extreme in a treatise entitled the *Eternal Gospel*, written in 1254 by Gerardus de Borgo San Domino. Among many other things, this Joachimist treatise advocated a complete reform of the moral conduct of Christians and stressed a code of behavior so ascetic that it outdid the Stoic ideal of apathy. The results of this work were felt in the lives of religious communities (particularly the Franciscans) in the thirteenth century. It did not produce a formal ethics, but Joachimism was partly responsible for an extreme otherworldly attitude in some varieties of late medieval ethics.

It is obvious that much of the ethical speculation in these Christian writings before the thirteenth century is derivative from the seminal notions to be found in the Bible and in the Platonic and Stoic schools of Greek ethics. However, two important new emphases were brought into the subject during this period. First of all, the view that God's will, or the eternal law, is the ultimate and absolute norm of all ethical judgments now comes to the fore in these patristic and medieval moralists. This norm is equally stressed, as we shall see in the next chapter, by the theistic ethicians in the medieval Jewish and Moslem traditions. Until well after the time of Kant, in the eighteenth century, this conviction that there is a divine source of absolute ethical obligation remained almost unchallenged in the history of ethics.

In the second place, the ethical concept of motivation, of personal attitude toward external events in which one is involved, became a focal point for moral discussions during this period of medieval ethics. As we have seen, men like Augustine, Anselm, and Abelard are quite modern in their ethical claims that what is morally significant is not so much the material character of one's action but rather the inner motivation of the person involved. Perhaps more than we usually realize, this new emphasis is due to the great importance that the medieval Christian attached to the human person as a creature of God. The Augustinian theme of the supreme moral significance of the love of God is but another way of saying this. It typifies Christian ethics up to the thirteenth century—and well beyond it, of course.

CHAPTER V

Medieval Jewish and Moslem Ethics

THE FIRST FIFTEEN CENTURIES after Christ produced other types of ethics than those taught in the Christian schools. We will examine in this chapter some of the ethical views of scholars associated with two other religions that flourished during the Middle Ages: Judaism and Mohammedanism. Both cultures have been somewhat neglected in general histories of ethics and, indeed, in the usual histories of medieval philosophy. Both, at times, gave a prominent place to ethical thinking and exerted a strong influence on the ethics of Western civilization.

Jewish Ethics in the Middle Ages

Judaism is more a way of life than a special theology or religious creed. There have not been as many philosophers in the Jewish tradition as one might expect. We have already seen the role played by Philo Judaeus in the development of Hellenistic ethics. He felt that he could find many parallels between the wisdom of the Old Testament and the thought of the Greek philosophers. But Philo is the only prominent Jewish philosopher before the medieval period.

While is it quite true that the Bible is not a technical philosophical work it does contain seeds of practical wisdom that continued to grow during the centuries which we are considering. Yahweh orders all things "in measure, number, and weight." Yet the God of the ancient Jews was also a loving deity: "But thou sparest all, because they are thine, O Lord, who lovest souls."[1] He is above all a stern dispenser of justice. His commands are absolute and inescapable. The most famous listing of these divine obligations is found in the Ten Commandments, which are found in the books of Exodus and Deuteronomy. Since these precepts are discussed and used as illustrations by many later writers on ethics, we give the Decalogue in full, here:

You shall have no gods except me.

You shall not make yourself a carved image or any likeness of anything in heaven or on earth beneath or in the waters under the earth; you shall not bow down to them or serve them. For I, Yahweh your God, am a jealous God and I punish the father's fault in the sons, the grandsons, and the great-grandsons of those who hate me; but I show kindness to thousands of those who love me and keep my commandments.

You shall not utter the name of Yahweh your God to misuse it, for Yahweh will not leave unpunished the man who utters his name to misuse it.

Remember the sabbath day and keep it holy. For six days you shall labour and do all your work, but the seventh day is a sabbath for Yahweh your God. You shall do no work that day, neither you nor your son nor your daughter nor your servants, men or women, nor your animals nor the stranger who lives with you. For in six days Yahweh made the heavens and the earth and the sea and all that these hold, but on the seventh day he rested; that is why Yahweh has blessed the sabbath day and made it sacred.

Honour your father and your mother so that you may have a long life in the land that Yahweh your God has given to you.

You shall not kill.

You shall not commit adultery.

You shall not steal.

You shall not bear false witness against your neighbour.

You shall not covet your neighbour's house. You shall not covet your neighbour's wife, or his servant, man or woman, or his ox, or his donkey, or anything that is his.[2]

In the second and third of these precepts, Yahweh speaks of himself as a strict Judge who will punish all disobediences. From this attitude arises another aspect of Old Testament morality, the so-called *lex talionis*, which required that the punishment of an injury to another be equal and of like character. It is still quoted in discussions of the morality of capital and other forms of legal punishment: "And he that killeth any man shall surely be put to death . . . as he hath done, so shall it be done to him; breach for breach, eye for eye, tooth for tooth."[3] Balancing this rigid view are Biblical approximations of the golden rule. Thus, Proverbs 24:29 reads, "Say not, I will do to him as he hath done to me"; and Tobit 4:15(16) states, "Do that to no man which thou hatest."[4]

Judaism has often been accused of excessive legalism. Early rabbinical works distinguished 613 commandments in the law.[5] Yet this juridical tendency was tempered by the spirit of love and forbearance. The "Great Commandment" enjoining love of God and neighbor is in the Old Testament. Deuteronomy 6:5 says, "Thou shalt love the Lord thy God with all thy heart, and with all thy soul, and with all thy might." Leviticus 19:18 adds, "Thou shalt love thy neighbor as thyself." It has recently been argued that Judaism stresses the love of man for God (and is more interested in ethics and human conduct) while Christianity emphasizes the love of God for man (and thus tends to be more theological).[6] According to this view, the two great themes in ancient Jewish ethics are "holiness" (*kadosh*), expressing both ontological and moral transcendence, and "glory" (*kavod*), expressing the contrary immanence of God in the lives of men, the manifestation of the divine in history.

One of the first medieval Jews to touch on formal problems of ethics was Saadia ben Joseph al-Fayyumi (882–942)[7] who wrote a *Book of Doctrines and Beliefs* at Baghdad in the year 933. His work has much the same purpose as Maimonides' later and better-known *Guide for the Perplexed*. Saadia offers an explanation of the relation between reason and faith, for the enlightenment of educated Jews who may be puzzled by alleged contradictions between what scientists and philosophers say and the teachings of the religious Law.[8] Some men have doubts because of defects in their sense observation of the facts of a problem; others suffer deficiencies in reasoning from sense data, either because they do not understand the method of reasoning or because they are hasty or neglectful in demonstrating their conclusions. Saadia's theory of knowledge and moral psychology are worked out in terms of the attempt to remove such sources of doubt.

He distinguishes two kinds of laws governing human conduct: laws of reason and laws of revelation.[9] He was convinced that mankind *could* have reasoned to a workable code of moral precepts, if divine revelation had not conveyed such a guide to men. However, Saadia thinks that revelation made it possible for men to know their obligations more immediately and more accurately than if they had been left to use unaided reason. Reason "dictates" four points that summarize the moral law: (1) one must return the kindness of every benefactor in some fitting manner; (2) the wise man will refuse to be treated with contempt and, with greater reason, a wise God will expect to be treated with respect; (3) no one should trespass on the rights of another by any sort of aggression; and (4) it is reasonable to employ a workman and to pay him, simply so that he may earn something. In retrospect, these rules of reason rather obviously apply to man's relations to God as well as to his fellow men. Saadia proceeds to list various precepts imposed by God on men (to be just, truthful, equitable, and impartial; to avoid homicide, adultery, theft, tale-bearing, and trickery in dealing with others). Moreover, "the Believer should love his neighbor as he loves himself." These are revealed rules, but "in regard to all the things which He commands us to do, He has implanted approval of them in our Reason."[10] He would appear to say that, given enough experience of life and adequate education of the rational powers, every man may "see" his duty. It is a version of deontologistic ethical intuitionism, with God's law to guarantee it from on high.

Saadia knows about hedonism, that some people argue that the good is that which causes pleasure. Such a view, he claims, ends in manifest contradiction: acts, such as rape, which bring pleasure to one person may be quite painful to another. "But every theory which involves a self-contradiction is invalid." The revelation and moral guidance which come through the prophets are needed, however, to ensure a certain perfection in moral behavior. Though man is the "center of the universe," he must recognize that the Biblical law is eternal and can never be abrogated.[11] Saadia says that reason confirms his Jewish beliefs but does not replace them.

One of the most important ethical treatises in the eleventh-century Jewish tradition was the *Fountain of Life*. Until about the mid-nineteenth century, the author of this *Fons Vitae*, ibn-Gabirol, whom Latin scholars of the Middle Ages called Avicebrón, was not known to be a Jew. Ibn-Gabirol (*ca.* 1021–1058) wrote in Arabic (as did most medieval Jewish philosophers) and was evidently a theist, so many readers felt that he might be a Christian, possibly Syrian. However, through the research of Solomon Munk we now know that the famous and long treatise called *Fons Vitae* (*Fountain of Life*) in Latin was written by an eleventh-century Jew. It is under the strong influence of Neoplatonic emanationism. All things in the universe, including men and angels, are compounds of matter and forms. God is the Creator but works through Universal Will which efficiently produces lower things by a progressive descent of forms. Man is a microcosm in which all features of the subhuman world are formally contained.[12] As in any version of Neoplatonism, the good life consists in a process of self-perfecting within each man, whereby he renders himself less corporeal and more fitted for union with the higher forms. This is not treated at any length by ibn-Gabirol but it is clear that education, intellectual improvement, and good will are requisite to the movement back to the source of all. Eventually, the good man returns not to God (who is so transcendent that He is inaccessible) but to the Universal Will which appears to be God's Power (*Virtus*). The nature of this Will is not clear in the *Fons Vitae*.[13]

Each medieval religious tradition has one thinker who bluntly rejects philosophy as a study that is not helpful for salvation: Islam has its al-Ghazzali, Christianity its St. Bernard, and Judaism is represented by Judah Halevi (b. *ca.* 1080). His *Sefer ha-Kuzari* is a dialogue in which the chief speakers are the King of the Khazars (a convert to Judaism) and a learned Rabbi. In the course of their discussion two things are brought out that have some bearing on the history of ethics. First of all, Judah

Halevi insists that there is no other source of obligation or moral guidance for men than the will of God as conveyed through divine law in the Bible.[14] This, then, is a purely religious type of morality. Judah Halevi does say that there are "rational laws" that are present and needed in every society, but that these general principles, as well as the more detailed rules of legal and ceremonial behavior found in the Old Testament, are all issued by the absolute divine will.[15] In the second place, Judah Halevi taught that "intention" is not enough to merit a moral reward: wherever action is possible, "actions must be perfected to claim reward."[16]

A more detailed system of morality is found in the *Duties of the Heart* by Bahya ibn Pakuda (eleventh to twelfth century). The treatise has ten "gates" (chapters), each discussing a distinct duty. Thus, the first duty is to recognize God as existent, one, and uncreated; the second duty is to meditate on the evidences in creatures of the divine wisdom. The third chapter deals with the duty to serve God in physical actions, thus stressing with his contemporary, Judah Halevi, that good intentions must be completed by good deeds. The remaining nine duties are not novel but it soon becomes clear that Bahya sets philosophy in a much higher place than does Judah Halevi. Besides faith in divine revelation, chapter 4 presents three other sources of information: sensory observation, intellectual intuition, and logical inference. In this theory of knowledge (which owes something to Saadia), insight into the requirements of moral duty falls on the second level, that of intellectual intuition. The tenth chapter treats the duty to love God and argues that awareness of this obligation arises from an innate urge in the mind. Divine grace is needed for the perfection of this love but there is a natural and philosophical preparation for it. The love of God grows in man's soul "when the believer's heart has been emptied of love of this world and freed from its lusts, as a result of perception and understanding."[17]

The greatest Jewish ethician in the Middle Ages was, of course, Maimonides. Born in Córdoba, Rabbi Moses ben Maimon (1135–1204) had a distinguished career in Spain before moving to Cairo, where he spent his mature years. Maimonides was a rabbi, legal expert, and physician. His best-known writing is the *Guide for the Perplexed* but his *Mishneh Torah* and a *Letter on Astrology* are also important sources for his ethics. He was convinced that the rational investigation of morality is incumbent on the educated person.

Much of Maimonides' thinking and writing was devoted to the problem of the relation between religious belief and philosophical rationalism. His best-known work, the *Guide for the Perplexed*, was written to inform Jewish believers who were disturbed and in doubt concerning this point. Although he was quite ready to criticize the "philosophers" (Aristotle's facts are useful, his theories are not), Maimonides had great respect for the life of understanding.[18] The opening pages of the first and second parts of the *Guide* offer an elaborate explanation of the role of divine revelation (the law) in contrast with the use of natural reason. In sum, he argues that but few men are equipped intellectually to probe the depths of metaphysics and, even among those who can be philosophers, the road to philosophical truth is long and paved with errors.[19] Maimonides' acquaintance with the philosophers was broad: he knew the teachings of all the major schools of Greek philosophy but particularly valued Plato and Aristotle. Much of his detailed information came through the encyclopedic writings of the Moslem scholars, such as al-Farabi and Avicenna.

The moral psychology used by Maimonides is an adaptation of Aristotelianism. Man is equipped with cognitive and appetitive powers. External sense experience is retained in imagination. The power of understanding with which man is born is minimal: the "hylic" (material) intellect is little more than the passive capacity of the imagination to receive actual understanding from above the soul. Study, sense experience, and a righteous moral attitude prepare some men for "acquired intellect."[20] Personal freedom is much prized by Maimonides: "Free will is bestowed on every human being. If one desires to turn towards the good way and be righteous, he has the power to do so. If one wishes to turn towards the evil way and be wicked, he is at liberty to do so."[21]

The ethical views in the third part of the *Guide* are almost identical with the teaching of the *Mishneh Torah*, usually called the *Code*. There is so much discussion of the law and its many precepts (as mentioned above, 613 commandments are enumerated in the rabbinical tradition) that one gets the initial impression of a strict legalistic ethics. However, this juridical emphasis is tempered in Maimonides by the idea that joy and love are the proper dispositions for the morally developed person. Righteousness (*sedaqah*) and loving-kindness (*hesed*) are more important than formal compliance with rules.[22] This is evident in a frequently quoted passage from the *Fundamental Principles of the Torah, Repentance*, X:

> Whoever serves God out of love occupies himself with the study of the Law and the fulfillment of the commandments and walks in the paths of wisdom, impelled by no external motive whatsoever, moved neither by fear of calamity nor by the desire to obtain material benefits; such a man does what is truly right because it is truly right, and ultimately, happiness comes to him as a result of his conduct.[23]

This text shows clearly that we are still dealing with a type of ethics which is eudaimonistic. The ultimate end of man is happiness or well-being. Both the welfare of the body (orderly social intercourse) and the well being of the soul (correct opinions in the multitude concerning their capacities) are aimed at in the divine law.

Moral virtues are, of course, important aids to a good life. The doctrin of the mean between extremes of excess and defect establishes the right way of feeling and acting. Saints may be more scrupulous and incline toward extreme dispositions but the ordinary person should strive to follow a middle path.[24] Moral rules are not made to cover exceptional people or cases; they are directed to "things that occur in the majority of cases." Maimonides seems to admit that natural moral law is knowable to people who have not received divine law but revelation is necessary for those who wish to attain to complete personal perfection.[25] It is in the acquisition of the "rational" virtues, however, that this highest human perfection lies. There are passages in Maimonides that suggest that intellectual development is all-important, at least for those favored few who are highly intelligent and able to secure a good education. The following text is but one among many such.

> His ultimate perfection is to become rational in actuality, I mean to have an intellect in actuality; and that is to know everything concerning all the beings that it is within the capacity of man to know in accordance with his ultimate perfection. It is clear that this ultimate perfection does not comprise either actions or moral habits and that it consists only of opinions arrived at through speculation and made necessary by investigation.[26]

Such a development of theoretical understanding requires a prior acquisition of moral virtue, and even a moderate freedom from bodily discomforts, but it remains speculative and theoretical in character. This intellectualist tendency was due in part, at least, to Maimonides' explanation of prophecy. Some men can prepare themselves by study, experience, and good moral conduct, to receive an infusion of special information into their perfected imaginations.

> Know that the truth and essence of prophecy consist in its being an emanation from God, the Mighty and Majestic, through the mediation of the Active Intellect to the rational faculty in the first place and thereafter to the imaginative faculty. This is the highest degree of man and the ultimate perfection that can exist for his species; and this state is the ultimate perfection of the imaginative faculty. This is something that can in no way exist in every man.[27]

Certain judgments of Maimonides on more specific moral questions have had an important influence on the history of ethics. He made an influential contribution to the theory of mental reservation in his *Letter on Apostasy* (written *ca.* 1160). In connection with persecutions of the Jews by the Moslem community at Fez, he was asked whether a Jew might repeat the formula expressing praise for Allah as the only God and Mohammed as his Prophet, provided the Jew thought in his heart that this prayer was not true. With some qualification, Maimonides replied that one might do so, under coercion.[28] This judgment that it is not immoral, under certain circumstances, to express something different from what one thinks to be true, was taken over by various Christian Scholastic ethicians and developed into the theory of mental reservation.

Concerning the view of the astrologers that a man's life is determined by the position of the stars at the time of his birth, Maimonides vigorously rejects such fatalism and argues that both religion and Greek philosophy support the personal freedom of every man to work out his own destiny.[29] He was well aware of the difference between scientific astronomy and the pseudoscience of astrology. Similar reasonableness is indicated in Maimonides' views on ascetic practices. For the average man, he advised moderation in this area, as in all others.

> The Sages accordingly enjoined us that we should only refrain from that which the Torah has expressly withdrawn from our use. No one should, by vows and oaths, inhibit to himself the use of things permitted. 'Do not the prohibitions of the Torah suffice thee,' say our Sages, 'that thou addest others for thyself?' Our wise men prohibited self-mortification by fasting.[30]

There is no question that Maimonides' ethics is a version of theological approbatism. Man's moral obligations stem ultimately from divine law. Such law is not the arbitrary expression of God's will: it springs from divine wisdom, as well as divine will, and is the essence of fairness and reasonableness.[31]

After Maimonides there were other medieval Jewish ethicians of secondary importance. Hillel ben Samuel (1220–1295) commented on and defended the views of Maimonides. His chief treatise was The Rewards of the Soul (Tagmule ha-Nefesh). He does not diverge from the teaching of his master. At the beginning of the fourteenth century, Levi ben Gerson (Gersonides, 1288–1344) produced a treatise in Hebrew, Milhamot Adonai (Wars of the Lord), which touches on ethical questions in its early, psychological section. Hasdai ben Abraham Crescas (1340–1410) showed some interest in ethics in Or Adonai (Light of the Lord). Crescas opposed the use of Aristotelian philosophy in Jewish schools, while Gersonides favored it.[32]

A very interesting treatise was written in fifteenth-century Spain by Joseph Albo (ca. 1380–1444). This was the Sefer ha-ikkarim (Book of Principles). Its fifth chapter accords more importance to natural law than Maimonides had wanted. This natural law is required to preserve justice in all human societies and to eliminate wrongdoing. As Albo saw it:

> This order [in society] would comprise protection against murder, theft, robbery, and the like, and in general, whatever would preserve the political association and arrange it so that people might live in a

proper manner. This order the wise men called by the name of natural law—that is to say, that it is something that man needs in respect of his nature—whether it is ordered by a wise man or by a prophet.[33]

He further argues (chapter 6) that divine law is also necessary to lead people to the attainment of happiness. His very systematic treatment of various types of laws (divine, natural, and conventional) suggests that Albo may have borrowed some things from the Latin writers of his period. With his work, the story of Jewish ethics in the Middle Ages comes to a close.

Islamic Ethics in the Middle Ages

Before the Prophet Mohammed (*ca.* 571–632 A.D.) founded the religion of Islam there were some learned Christians writing in Persian, Arabic, or related languages, who helped to preserve and translate Greek ethical writings. This Syrian Christian activity continued throughout the Middle Ages. In the ninth century, for instance, Hunaïn ibn-Ishaq translated Porphyry's *Commentary on the Nicomachean Ethics* into Arabic. Both the Greek and Arabic versions of this *Commentary* are now lost but something of its content is preserved in Moslem ethical treatises.[34] The Jacobite Christian, Yahya ibn-Adi (d. 974 A.D.), wrote an ethical treatise entitled *The Correction of the Dispositions* (*Tahdhib al-Akhlaq*) that was an epitome of Greek moral thought; it served as a source for later Moslem writers, such as Miskawaihi.[35] As late as the thirteenth century we find a Syrian Christian, Gregorius Abu al-Faraj (known to the Latins as Abulfaragius and Bar-Hebraeus), producing a moral treatise (*Book of the Dove*) and a work entitled *Ethikon* (written in 1278) which incorporated much of the ethical teaching from al-Ghazzahi's *Ihya al-Ulum*.[36] Little historical work has been done on this school of Syrian ethical scholars but it is suspected that they knew classical writings no longer extant today in the original.[37]

Early in the seventh century the Koran (Qur'ān) appeared as the writing of the Moslem religion. According to Moslem belief, it was divinely revealed to Mohammed through the angel Gabriel. Mohammed was regarded as the last and greatest of the prophets: his chief predecessors were Adam, Noah, Abraham, Moses, and Jesus. As a prophetic religion, Islam occasioned many studies—religious, psychological, and philosophical —of the act of prophecy. From the ninth century onward, an important school of philosophers associated with Islam developed. There were many more Moslem "scholastic" philosophers than there were Jewish philosophers in this period. And long before Latin Christians had translations of the key works of the major Greek ethicians the Mohammedan teachers were familiar with these classics. The moral code of duties imposed in the

Koran included five basic obligations: (1) to profess the faith daily; (2) to pray five times in every twenty-four hours, facing Mecca; (3) to give alms to the poor; (4) to fast from dawn to dusk in the holy month of Ramadan; and (5) to make a pilgrimage to Mecca once in one's life. Teaching and discussion of these and other religious duties induced Moslem teachers to investigate the grounds and nature of moral judgment and obligation. Their study of prophecy contributed to the growth of remarkable analyses of the psychic functions of man.[38]

In the ninth century a theological movement called the *kalam* ("word" or "speech") developed within Islamic thought: this is the school of thinkers called *Loquentes* in later Latin treatises. These Moslem theologians gave a place to both reason and faith, and they differed from the stricter interpreters of the Koran in affirming the freedom of man, the justice of Allah, and in denying rigid predestination. A certain appreciation of the possibilities of philosophy stemmed from this school. We find al-Kindi (*ca.* 796–866), for instance, writing treatises in the ninth century on nearly all the problems of classical philosophy. Within a few decades, Mohammed ibn-Zakariya al-Razi (865–925) wrote two ethical treatises which gave a very important role to natural reasoning. Using the Platonic psychology of the tripartite soul, al-Razi argued that reason should control the passions and the virtue of justice should balance the interests of all three parts. Moderation is stressed as the keynote to a good moral character. The problem of telling a lie is already taken as an example of the influence of intention on moral activity. Al-Razi decided that a lie is bad, if directed to a bad purpose.[39]

Though these thinkers made important contributions to Islamic philosophy, the first really great Islamic philosopher was al-Farabi (d. 950). He studied in Baghdad under the Christian teacher Yuhanna ibn-Haylan (a Syrian), who was a link with the traditions of the earlier school at Alexandria. The writings of al-Farabi are encyclopedic in scope and character and they were used for the next four centuries, not only by Moslems but also by Jews and Christians, as sources of information concerning the philosophies of Aristotle, Plato, and other Greek schools.[40]

Plato's *Republic* and *Laws* are of primary importance in the practical philosophy of al-Farabi. He tries, however, to effect a harmony between Platonism and Aristotelianism. One view which he finds in both is the notion that ethics is but a part of the architectonic science of politics. In the fifth chapter of the *Enumeration of the Sciences*, al-Farabi lists three practical sciences: politics, jurisprudence, and theology (*kalam*). This does not mean a downgrading of ethics. He simply sees the moral life of man as but one aspect of political and religious life. Good and bad actions are distinguished to the extent that they promote or hamper the attainment of happiness. It is in a future life, after the death of the body, that true happiness may be achieved. As al-Farabi expresses it: "Distinguishing the actions and ways of life, it [political science] explains that the ones through which true hapiness is attained are the goods, the noble things, and the virtues, while the rest are the evils, the base things, and the imperfections."[41]

From Aristotle and al-Kindi comes a complicated theory of the stages of human understanding which, with modifications in Avicenna and Averroës, continues to ground the moral psychology of medieval Aristotelianism up to the thirteenth century. As Aristotle did in his De Anima, al-Farabi distinguished sense perception from intellection. Sensation receives impressions from individual aspects of bodies; these "phantasies" are retained in sensory memory; eventually sense experience provides a preparation for personal understanding of the universal meanings of the objects experienced through the senses. The power of understanding with which man is born is, for al-Farabi, 'aql hayulani (intellectus materialis), the passive potency to receive understanding. Above all men there exists a higher Intelligence which is always knowing; this is the 'aql fa'al, the Dispenser of Forms (Dator Formarum, in the Latin versions). We have here an interpretation of the two intellects (potential and agent) that are obscurely described in Aristotle's De Anima (III, 4–5). When the passive power of understanding is informed from above by the Dispenser of Forms, man's soul achieves actual understanding, 'aql bi'l-fi'l (intellectus in actu). One is in this actuated condition when actually thinking of the conclusion to a theorem in geometry, for instance. Actual understanding of any given universal notion is but temporary: even Einstein could not always think about one universal truth. So, the basic power of understanding, after being actuated, reverts to an intermediate state from which it may more easily and promptly be actuated the next time; this state of habitual understanding is called 'aql bi'l-malaka (intellectus in habitu). It is the way in which all higher learning, skills in arts and sciences, remain in man's soul; habitual understanding is intellectual memory, science, wisdom. Other stages of the basic power of understanding are distinguished by al-Farabi and his followers in psychology. There is, for instance, that special skill that enables some people to teach others; and there is an even higher intellectual perfection, which enables a few men to receive and transmit special information from above, concerning future events, the higher meaning of the sacred writings, and so on: this is the understanding of the prophet. From the point of view of ethics, al-Farabi's theory of the stages of human understanding is of primary importance. Since it implies that even rather ordinary men are informed from above, from a higher Intelligence, concerning the meaning of items such as happiness, virtue, goodness, and so on, this teaching suggests that the standards of ethical judgment have a suprahuman origin which is, nevertheless, not outside the realm of nature. The suprahuman Dispenser of Forms is not Allah but simply a higher kind of spirit, an angel. In some versions of the theory, this Intelligence is identified with the Mind of the Prophet, Mohammed.[42]

It is in the light of the foregoing that we must interpret al-Farabi's account of the attainment of happiness. His view of the personal perfection of man is thoroughly intellectualistic. There are five generic faculties in man: theoretical reason, practical reason, appetitive power, imagination, sensory power. "Happiness, which only man can know and perceive, is known by the theoretical-rational faculty and by none of the remaining faculties."[43] Education is for the few who can profit from it; they are people with the capacity to become happy.

A similar ethical teaching is found in the work of al-Ameri (d. 992). His book *On Seeking and Causing Happiness* has not been translated but the editor of the original text reports in his introduction that it combines the moral positions of Plato and Aristotle.[44]

The outstanding Moslem ethician before the thirteenth century was Ahmad ibn-Muhammad-ibn Yaqub Miskawaihi (932–1030). His *Tahdhib al-Akhlaq* (*Correction of the Dispositions*) has been printed many times and is still influential in the Islamic schools. He is not well known outside his own culture. Like the other early Mohammedan thinkers that have been mentioned, Miskawaihi was from the east; he served as a librarian at Shiraz and Ray, in what is now Iran.

In his psychology, Miskawaihi distinguished three faculties of the human soul: (1) the power to exercise thought (*al-fikr*), discrimination (*al-tamyiz*), and observation (*nazar*); (2) the power which gives rise to anger (*al-ghadab*), firmness (*al-najda*), and initiative (*al-iqdam*); and (3) the power of sensual desire (*al-shahwa*) for food, sexual pleasure, and similar goods.[45] Obviously, these powers are the equivalents of reason, and irascible and concupiscible appetites, in the terminology of contemporary Latin thinkers in the Aristotelian tradition. Chapter 3 of Miskawaihi's *Tahdhib* offers an almost verbatim passage from a work of Aristotelian origin called *Fada'il al-Nafs*. This would seem to be the *De Virtutibus et vitiis* composed by some follower in the later Greek school of Aristotle. A pupil of the Syrian translator, Hunaïn ibn-Ishaq, named abu-Uthman al-Dimishqi (809–877), had translated the Aristotelian treatise into Arabic.

Miskawaihi uses his theory of three powers or parts of the soul to expound a teaching on the four virtues—wisdom (*hikma*), purity ('*iffa*), courage (*al-shaja'a*), righteousness ('*adala*)—that is close to that in Plato's *Republic*, Book IV.[46] He then distinguishes seven "species" of practical wisdom: acuteness of intelligence, quickness of intellect, clearness of understanding, facility of acquisition, precise discrimination, retention, and recollection. This is followed by a description of eleven species of courage, twelve species of temperance, and nineteen species of justice. We are obviously in the midst of a typical Aristotelian exposition of the "parts" of each of the cardinal virtues. There are dozens of virtues (*fada'il*) and vices (*radha'il*). Virtue is a mean between extremes of vice. The fifth chapter of Miskawaihi's *Tahdhib* offers an analysis of different types of love. Man's ultimate end is happiness. This complete good is that to which all men aspire: health, wealth, fame, honor, success, and right thinking. Some degree of this happiness is attainable in this life; Miskawaihi is not as completely otherworldly as some of his colleagues.[47] However, he insists that divine justice is supreme in the realm of morals. It is a religious ethics that has incorporated a good deal of Greek naturalism.

Avicenna, abu-'Ali al-Husayn ibn-Abdallah ibn-Sīna (980–1037), was the greatest of the Eastern school of Moslem philosophers. An almost universal genius, poet, medical doctor, theologian, lawyer, this man would be ranked by many historians with the ten greatest philosophers of all time. The year 1952 marked the millennium of his birth, according to Moslem chronology, and witnessed the publication of many studies of the life and thought of Avicenna. His *Shifa* (*Book of Healing*) is an encyclopedic work treating all the branches of speculative knowledge available in the eleventh century. Its four parts cover respectively logic, physics, mathematics, and metaphysics. Ethics receives only occasional mention. The *Najat* (*Salvation*) is a shorter version of the *Shifa*. It was the *Shifa* that was translated into medieval Latin and which gave Christian scholars some idea of the riches of Moslem learning, particularly in the fields of psychology, physiology, and physics.

The psychology of Avicenna was a development of the same basic Aristotelianism that we encountered in al-Farabi. His analysis of the human soul and its functions is found in the sixth book of the Physics section of the *Shifa*; it became known in Latin as *Liber Sextus Naturalium*, or simply *De Anima*.[48] Five internal senses are distinguished by Avicenna: common sense, phantasy, cogitative (imaginative), estimative, and memorative (*De Anima*, I, cap. 5). In the functions of cogitation and estimation man knows and makes judgments of a particularized sort concerning individual bodies and their concrete meanings. Thus, if a man were attacked by a snarling dog and came up with the decision "This animal is dangerous to me," he would make this judgment in his estimative power, not in his intellect. Understanding for Avicenna, as for most Aristotelians, looks to universal objects only. He did not put much emphasis on the ethical significance of this teaching but it had a profound influence on Latin Scholasticism. In the thirteenth century, ethics as a science of universal judgments concerning human conduct was kept quite distinct from the habit of prudent reasoning about one's own concrete problems of morality. The latter involves judgments made in "particular reason" (an internal sense power to cogitate under the general direction of the rules of intellectual reasoning). Avicenna is, in good part, the source of this position.[49]

Part of Avicenna's ethical position is discernible from his writings on the mystical life. One such work is the *Story of Hajj Son of Yaqzan*.[50] This enigmatic description of Moslem mysticism has recently been shown to involve most of the philosophical teachings of Avicenna.[51] Briefly, man's soul starts on a journey and encounters a guide named Hayy (living) son of Yaqzan (awake). This guide seems to be the Universal Agent Intelligence. Man's soul is conducted to various places in the West (the realm of matter) and in the East (the realm of form). Various temptations are encountered by the soul in its quest for knowledge and peace; it struggles with external and internal impediments; a variety of helps are provided it. Finally, it reaches the King, is enraptured with admiration and love, and achieves an ineffable peace.[52] The meaning of the work is veiled in symbolism and romantic imagery.

Perhaps this is the "ethics" of Avicenna. He obviously thinks that there are two classes of people: the many unlearned and material-minded, the few who are educated and spiritual-minded. The souls of the many face downward to the world of sensory images: for such people it is good to follow the guidance of an imam, a spiritual and religious leader. In the case of the intellectual elite, their souls face in a different direction and are ordered to a higher perfection. What is good for them is the acquisition and development of personal understanding, a process which begins with the study of science, philosophy, and religious teachings, in this life—and which continues to develop in a future life, in the company of the angels and the divine presence. As he says, "Through this science [ethics] one knows how man ought to be in his moral habits and his actions so as to lead a happy life here and in the hereafter. This part is contained in Aristotle's book on ethics."[53]

In the Eastern school, the last great personality in medieval Islam was al-Ghazzali, abu-Hāmid Muhammad (1059–1111). He came to be known in Latin as Algazel. This man was generally critical and suspicious of pagan philosophy. His *Tahafut al-Falasifa* was a vigorous refutation of twenty philosophical conclusions, mostly taken from Avicenna. Al-Ghazzali's autobiographical *Deliverance from Error*[54] tells how he studied the philosophers and decided that their views were not in accord with Moslem teachings. This negative aspect of his doctrine is usually emphasized in histories of philosophy. Other works of al-Ghazzali show him as one of the greatest of Mohammedan theologians, by no means an obscurantist but much concerned to preserve the original spirit of the Koran. The *Ihya al-Ulum al-Din (Revivification of the Religious Sciences)* and the *Risalat al-Laduniyya (Inspired Treatise)* show that he was in the early twelfth century the "best known writer on ethical subjects."[55]

The *Risalat* offered ten rules of personal conduct: (1) maintain a good intention; (2) aim to serve Allah only; (3) conform to truth; (4) oppose procrastination; (5) avoid innovation and follow established practice; (6) cultivate humility toward others; (7) seek salvation through faith, fear, and hope; (8) pray devoutly; (9) banish all but Allah from your heart; (10) seek the knowledge that leads to the vision of Allah.⁵⁶ This is a purely religious ethic in which values such as gratitude, repentance, trust, and fear of God are stressed in a manner quite foreign to the moral philosophy of the Greeks.⁵⁷ For al-Ghazzali all ethical problems can be answered by consulting the will of Allah as revealed in the Koran and as interpreted by orthodox theologians. This is theological approbative ethics at its purest.

In his discussion of lying,⁵⁸ al-Ghazzali used an example that appears in many later treatments of the same problem, notably that of Immanuel Kant.

Understand that falsehood in speech (al-kidhb) is not forbidden (haram) in itself, but because of such injury as may be in it to the speaker, or to others. . . . Maimun ibn al-Mohr said that falsehood is at some times better than truth (al-sidq). For example, if you see that a man is trying to fall upon another man with a sword in order to kill him, that he has entered the gate and has come to you and has said, 'Have you seen such a person?' You will not say, 'I have seen him,' but you will say, 'I have not seen him.' This type of falsehood is required, for we say that speech is but a means to an end.

In addition to the interest of the illustration, this passage shows the forthright position of a Moslem theologian who thinks that, in this problem, the end does justify the means.

Al-Ghazzali's influence in ethics extended beyond his century and outside his religious culture. In the thirteenth-century Ethikon by Bar-Hebraeus there is a series of chapters (on the soul, its training, wantonness, the tongue, anger and envy, worldly desires, avarice, hypocrisy, pride and boasting) that parallel ten chapters in al-Ghazzali's Ihya.⁵⁹

Another Persian moralist contemporary with al-Ghazzali but with a different notion of the happy life was Omar Khayyam (d. ca. 1123). His poems, gathered under the title Rubáiyát, have provided in the English paraphrase by Edward FitzGerald (1859) one of the most quoted expressions of ethical hedonism.

> A book of Verses underneath the Bough,
> A jug of Wine, a Loaf of Bread—and Thou
> Beside me singing in the Wilderness—
> Oh, Wilderness were Paradise enow!

> Some for the Glories of This World; and some
> Sigh for the Prophet's Paradise to come;
> Ah, take the Cash, and let the Credit go,
> Nor heed the rumble of a distant Drum!

A member of the Sufi sect, Omar was not an epicurean ethician but used lyrical imagery to convey his mystical and somewhat pessimistic views.[60]

Western Islamic philosophy centered in southern Spain. One of the first ethical treatises was written there by ibn-Hazm, abu-Muhammad Ali ibn-Ahmad iba-Sa'id (994–1064). This was the *Kitab al-Akhlaq Wa-l-Siyar* (*Book of Dispositions*). Just as "ethics" comes from a Greek word (*ethos*) meaning custom or habitual disposition, and "morals" from a Latin word (*moris*) with the same meaning, so does the Arabic *akhlaq* have the same meaning, and it has come to be used for the discipline of ethics. Ibn-Hazm's work is a moral essay advising zealous study in order to develop a spirit of repose, good manners and conduct, friendliness, and practical honesty in dealing with others.[61] It contains information on how to heal broken characters and how to profit from study sessions.

More influential was ibn-Bajjah, abu-Bakr Muhammad ibn-Yahya (*ca.* 1087–1138), known in Latin as Avempace. He was learned on many subjects (music, medicine, astronomy, mathematics, as well as all divisions of philosophy) but most interested in moral philosophy. He knew the major works of Aristotle quite well, including the *Nicomachean Ethics*. For the unlearned, ibn-Bajjah had no concern; their interests are base. His treatise *Governance of the Solitary* is directed to the cultured Moslem who had time and ability to study philosophy.

> The man of wisdom is therefore necessarily a man who is virtuous and divine. Of every kind of activity, he takes up the best only. . . . When he achieves the final end—that is, when he understands simple essential intellects, which are mentioned in the *Metaphysics, On the Soul,* and *On Sense and the Sensible*—he then becomes one of these intellects. It would be right to call him simply divine.[62]

With ibn-Bajjah, we are obviously in an ethics that is Aristotelian and intellectualistic. Human actions are clearly distinguished from nonvoluntary, animal functions. Appetition is quite different from cognition. Right opinion based on the study of speculative philosophy (note the metaphysical and psychological works of Aristotle mentioned in the quotation) is the norm of ethical judgment.[63]

In the short work *Fi ittisal al-'aql bi-l-insan* (*On the Union between the Intellect and Man*), ibn-Bajjah used the term *ittisal* to name that conjunction (which is cognitive, moral, and ontological) between the internal sense power of a man (prepared by the acquisition of phantasms and by study) and that separate Agent Intelligence which dwells in the sphere of the moon and is available to all humans as a source of actual understanding. This is fundamentally an intellectual perfection. It is necessary for any real advance on the road to happiness.[64]

Less Aristotelian but open to the value of practical philosophy is the Spanish Moslem, ibn-Tufail, abu-Bakr Muhammad ibn-'Abd-al-Malik (*ca.*

1100–1185), known to the West as Abubacer. His only known work is a sort of philosophical novel bearing the same title as Avicenna's mystical treatise, Hayy ibn Yaqzan. Ibn-Tufail starts his much longer story with the solitary birth of a boy on a deserted island. Unaided by other humans, this child learns to care for himself and to deal with his material environment. From the death of a gazelle that had helped to mother him, Hayy grasps the notion that a life spirit has departed from this dead animal. Observing the upward movement of flame suggests that this hot vapor may have some kinship with the principle of life and that it strives to rise into the celestial regions. He meditates on his own body-spirit constitution and rises to the thought of a Perfect Being. Eventually he meets two humans from a neighboring island and gets some experience of social life. He comes to realize that most men "are like irrational animals" but that "all wisdom, guidance to the right path, and good fortune reside in the utterances of the apostles of God and what is set forth by religious Law."[65] There is also the implication at the end of this romance that there is a secret meaning to the story and that men of intelligence will know what it is.

The story has fascinated people through the ensuing centuries and has been read in many languages. Apart from its obvious literary influences the story of Hayy was an important source of inspiration for the greatest Moslem thinker of the West, Averroës, and probably affected the thought of radical Aristotelians in the Latin schools of the thirteenth century, such as Arnold of Brescia and Siger of Brabant. When the Bishop of Paris, Etienne Tempier, condemned as religious errors (in 1277) two propositions saying that happiness is attainable in this life through the intellectual and moral virtues, he was objecting to a position originally taken by ibn-Tufail. The implication of the story of Hayy is that "the philosopher, left to his inner light, is capable of attaining to supreme bliss."[66] More amazing is the claim that ibn-Tufail was an inspiration to George Fox (1624–1691), the founder of the Quakers.[67]

The greatest Aristotelian scholar in the history of Islam was Averroës: he was named the Commentator (on Aristotle), even in the Christian writings of the later Middle Ages. Ibn-Rushd, abu-al-Walīd Muhammad ibn-Ahmad (1126–1198), wrote commentaries of three types (epitome, middle, and long) on most of the major writings of Aristotle. Averroës was not as interested in ethics as in speculative philosophy and produced only a middle commentary on the Nicomachean Ethics. This is extant in Hebrew and Latin versions but not in the original Arabic. His explanation of Aristotelian ethics follows the original closely and need not be detailed here.

Averroës' more personal treatises have some bearing on ethics. The Fasl al-maqal (Decisive Treatise) deals with the problem of the role of philosophy in the studies and life of a learned Moslem. He was accused, from the thirteenth century onward, of teaching the doctrine of the "double truth": that a conclusion may be true according to reason but false according to religious belief, or vice versa. Modern historians point out that he actually rejected such a view.[68] Throughout the *Decisive Treatise*, Averroës insists that al-Ghazzali did not understand the peripatetic philosophers and was mistaken in his condemnation of them.[69] He argues that the study of philosophy is quite useful for those intelligent enough to profit from it and that it is, indeed, obligatory in the religious law.

> Since all this is now established, and since we, the Muslim community, hold that this divine Law of ours is true, and that it is this Law that incites and summons us to the happiness that consists in the knowledge of God, Mighty and Majestic, and of His creation, that [end] is appointed for every Muslim by the method of assent that his temperament and nature require.[70]

Some men, he proceeds to explain, base their assent on demonstrative reasoning: philosophy is useful to them, of course. A second kind of men are convinced by dialectical arguments, and a third type reach assent through rhetorical arguments. For each the appropriate arguments may be used by religious teachers; without question Averroës places the first kind of men in the highest place. He is simply saying that, where it can, faith should seek understanding.

There has been a great deal of controversy as to whether Averroës denied or supported personal immortality for man. He interpreted Aristotle's *De Anima* much as al-Farabi and Avicenna had. However, where Avicenna seemed to grant a potential power of understanding to each human soul at birth, Averroës is rather definite in saying that the highest cognitive potency that man has at birth is the cogitative power (*fikr*), which is not the same as Avicenna's estimative. Whether the Averroistic cogitative is originally an intellect or merely sensory is a disputed point.[71] Those who read Averroës as saying that, at birth, man is little more than a beast, conclude that he denied personal immortality for all except those few who merit everlasting life by study and good behavior. Actually, the *Decisive Treatise* states that the knowledge "of happiness and misery in the next life" is available to each of the three classes of men named above.[72] He did think, then, that philosophic demonstration of the future life for the individual person is possible. For Averroës, as for most Mohammedan ethicians in the Middle Ages, the good life culminates in a personal union in actual understanding with the Agent Intelligence, which is always knowing and offering information to men.[73]

The most representative treatise on ethics by a medieval Moslem philosopher was the *Akhlaq-i Nasiri* (*The Nasirean Ethics*), written in Persia about the year 1235 A.D. The author, Nasir ad-Din Tusi (1201-

1274), was a scholar and man of affairs in thirteenth-century Persia. It must be admitted that Nasir was not a great speculative mind but he did write a work which gives "a conspectus of most of the significant moral and intellectual preoccupations of the medieval Islamic world."[74] His book is actually an exposition of the three traditional divisions of Aristotelian practical philosophy: ethics (morality of individual conduct), economics (right and wrong in family life), and politics (moral direction of the state). Most of the following analysis will be confined to the ethical theory in Nasir's first *Discourse*.

In the first division of Discourse One, Nasir describes the three souls present in man: vegetative, animal, and human. The vegetative soul has three basic faculties, the nutritive, augmentative, and generative powers. The animal soul has two generic faculties: organic perception and voluntary motion. The first is divided into two sets of subfaculties: (1) external senses—sight, hearing, smell, taste, touch; (b) internal senses, which are common sense, fantasy, reflection, estimation, and recollection. Voluntary motion is assigned two sub-faculties: concupiscible and irascible powers. The human soul has one generic faculty, rationality, which apprehends without an organ and discriminates among the objects thus known. Rationality is subdivided into speculative intelligence, through which one knows existent beings and various types of intelligible objects; and practical intelligence, through which one directs the control of objects, distinguishes good from evil actions, and exercises discovery in the sphere of the arts. There is no special faculty called will; volition on the level of desire and emotional reaction to irritants and dangers are the functions of the concupiscible and irascible powers of the animal soul; volition, which is expressive of rational motivation and choice, is the function of practical intelligence.

Nasir next describes: (1) faculties whose operations come under control of will and reason and that lead to meritorious effort; (2) faculties whose functions work by nature and receive no added perfection from their use. The first kind are obviously the sort of actions that would be called voluntary by Nasir's Latin contemporaries; these are the operations that are ethically interesting. Three of the previously listed faculties initiate acts of this ethical kind: rationality, concupiscible power, and irascible power. Through the concupiscible one experiences attraction for benefits, or pleasures (food, drinks, women); through the irascible a person reacts to injuries, faces perils, yearns for authority and fame.

In the fourth section of the first discourse, Nasir introduces the basis for the discrimination between good and evil. Even the vegetative soul has the ability, he explains, to be attracted to the wholesome and to shake off the unwholesome. One date palm may show affection for another tree! It is in brute animals, however, that one finds a certain voluntariness and the power to sense. Similarly, the distinguishing features of human acts are their ranks of perfection determined according to volition (*irada*) and reason (*ru'yat*). It is possible that the latter term simply means cogitation or mental perception.[75]

Next, Nasir describes three levels of human perfection: (1) that of people skilled in the mechanical arts and the use of instruments; (2) that of people skilled in knowledge, the sciences, and virtues; and (3) that of persons skilled in receiving knowledge of truths and laws from above. Man is originally stationed in a middle position, able to go up or down. To know what to do, most people need guidance from prophets, philosophers, and other wise teachers. The wise man is called rational, which signifies:

> the faculty of perceiving intelligibles and the power of distinction and reason, by which one discriminates between fair and foul, reprehensible and praiseworthy, and disposes of them according to the will. It is on account of this faculty that Man's actions are divided into good and bad, and fair and foul, and that he is characterized by felicity or affliction, as against the other animals and the plants. Thus, whoever applies this faculty properly, and by will and endeavour reaches that virtue towards which he was directed at creation, such a one is good and blissful; but one who neglects to tend that property, either by striving in an opposite direction or by sloth and aversion, is evil and afflicted.[76]

At this point, Nasir approximates a "right reason" theory of ethics, not far removed from the contemporary views of Christian moralists in the Latin tradition.

The difference between the theoretical faculty and its speculative perfection and the practical faculty with its perfection in activity is further dicussed in the sixth section. Both speculative and practical perfection are needed for felicity: "Theory without practice is abortive, and practice without theory is absurd." The most sublime happiness is found in the divine Presence. Nasir is very critical of hedonism, whether directed to sensual pleasure in this world or the next: people who cherish such a goal "are the companions of the dog and the pig." Two moral feelings promote good moral judgment, shame occasioned by the unfitting and love of a fair action.

At times, Nasir is concerned to show that his ethics is in accord with the teachings of the Koran. Thus he cites passages in the sacred writings to show that his threefold division of souls is supported by the religious doctrine of the Imperative, Reproachful, and Peaceful souls. He is well aware that Plato's *Republic* has much the same division of psychic parts. In other places Nasir echoes some teaching of Aristotle: "Every action is in order to attain a purpose," for instance. Or, the "Absolute Good" is that to which all men must aim. The attainment of future felicity "is vested in reason and the intelligence." Long passages are quoted almost verbatim from the *Tahdhib al-Akhlaq* of Miskawaihi.[77]

The second division of Discourse One is devoted to Ends. The three moral faculties are again described, with the enumeration of many species of virtue perfecting each. These virtues are habitual dispositions that serve as means to the achievement of good ends. He has the doctrine of the mean: "Every virtue is, so to speak, a middle-point." As a science, ethics is "to give fundamental principles and rules, not to calculate particulars."[78] Rather specific moral questions are treated in connection with the virtues of temperance and courage. Suicides, for instance, are judged to be cowards.

In the seventh section of the second division, Nasir discusses justice and stresses the idea that its central notion is equivalence (the Aristotelian "equity," *epieikeia*). Other types of justice are distributive, commutative, and legal. Nasir even claims that the *Nicomachean Ethics* teaches that the greatest law may be from God.

Intellectual union of the soul with Truth (*ittisal*) is the end of the cultured and perfected man, viewed subjectively. Various sorts of felicity are discussed, bodily, psychic, and civic. This portion of the treatise parallels the discussion of goods of the body, soul, and society, in the tenth book of the *Nicomachean Ethics*.

Moral vices are described as "sicknesses of the soul." There are many more of them than there are virtues, for there is an indefinite number of ways of going wrong. Nasir cites Master Miskawaihi to show that it is not reasonable to grieve at the death of relatives. Suppose a certain prince and all his descendants were to remain alive for four hundred years. They would number more than ten million people in this one family! The surface of the habitable earth would not permit them space to stand. Eventually, they would have to stand on each other's heads. Thinking on something like this shows how ignorant and absurd it is to wish that people would live forever.[79] Obviously, the possibility of overpopulation of the earth did occur to medieval thinkers.

There is a sort of humorous and even earthy quality to Nasir's examples and conclusions that served to make his work popular. He cites al-Ghazzali to the effect that the concupiscible faculty is like a revenue agent, inclined to take everything. To men whose attention is wont to stray from their wives to other women, Nasir points out that all women are basically rather similar: why not be satisfied with what you have at home? On the same subject, in the second discourse (which deals with problems of family life), Nasir says that the main thing that a husband should instill in his wife is awe. He offers four "stratagems" which may be used to rid oneself of a bad wife. Here, and in many of the later sections of the treatise, the discussion descends to mere details of etiquette. Ethical notions that occur in the third discourse (on Politics) are not novel: the influence of Aristotle's *Politics* is evident.

In the fifteenth century another popular treatise on ethics was written in Persia by Jalal al-Din Muhammad ibn-Asad Dawani (d. 1502). His *Aklaq-i Jalali* (*Jalal's Ethics*) is merely an abbreviated and somewhat corrupted version of Miskawaihi and Nasir ad-Din Tusi.[80] The work is still read; numerous editions in modern India attest to its popularity in that country.[81]

Despite the difficulties of communication and translation in the Middle Ages, particularly from various Middle Eastern and Semitic languages into Latin, it is clear that the ethical learning of the Jews and Moslems did reach their Christian contemporaries. The twelfth century saw many versions from Jewish and Mohammedan writings made at two busy translating centers: Toledo in Spain and Naples in the Sicilian Empire. It was from these translations that Latin scholars of the thirteenth century got their first taste of Aristotelian ethics. Before long, the Christian scholars were clamoring for complete translations from the Greek text of Aristotle. The continuing influence of Avicebrón, Maimonides, Avicenna, and Averroës is everywhere evident in the Christian schools of philosophy in the last part of the Middle Ages. Greek rationalism and eudaimonism became part of medieval culture through these intermediaries.

CHAPTER VI

Right Reason Theories

FROM THE EARLY thirteenth century to the fifteenth century a very large number of men were interested in ethics. This was the period when the first universities of Europe came into being; their courses in liberal arts usually included some study of ethics. It was a time in which two religious orders (Dominicans and Franciscans) were founded and gave opportunities to their members for study and writing in this field. Aristotle's *Nicomachean Ethics* became generally available in Latin at this time and stimulated much discussion of ethical problems. Christian theology was highly organized in the thirteenth century and this doctrinal study always included sections on moral theology that paralleled the contemporary work in ethics. There were even certain popular fads (such as the vernacular poetry of courtly love) that challenged established academic and ecclesiastical moral teachings. In the present chapter we will examine some of the main contributions made to ethics by Latin writers between 1200 and 1500. The dominant ethics of the period centered around the theory of right reason but there were other interesting positions.

The *Nicomachean Ethics* of Aristotle was not known to the Latin scholars of the early Middle Ages. Its second and third books were put into Latin during the twelfth century and became known as the *Ethica vetus* (*Old Ethics*). Book I was translated early in the thirteenth century and was called *Ethica nova* (*New Ethics*). Together, these three books were used as texts in *scientia moralis* in the Arts Faculty of the University of Paris between 1230 and 1250. By March 19, 1255, the statutes of the Arts Faculty at Paris required the reading of four books of the *Nicomachean Ethics*. About the year 1240, Robert Grosseteste produced a complete Latin version directly from the Greek. At about the same time, at Toledo, Hermannus Alemannus translated an Arabic paraphrase of the *Nicomachean Ethics* into Latin. It was Grosseteste's version which became the base for commentaries by Albert the Great (1245–1252), Thomas Aquinas (1265–1272), Giles of Rome, and many others in the thirteenth century. The next century saw similar commentaries by Walter Burleigh, Gerardus Odonis, Jean Buridan, John Baconthorpe, and others. Leonardo Bruni d'Arezzo (1369–1444) made a new translation of the Nicomachean Ethics in the fifteenth century. The Magna Moralia was translated by Bartholomew of Messina at Naples (1258–1266) but the only book of the Eudemian Ethics that was in Latin in the thirteenth century was the seventh, through the compilation called De bona fortuna. We shall see later in this chapter how extensively the thought content of Aristotle's ethics affected the writers of the later Middle Ages.

Apart from academic writings in Latin there was in the vernacular poetry of the troubadours a romantic view toward life and love that exerted a certain influence on medieval ethics. It is probably too much to say that "courtly love is an ethics, a religion, an obsession."[1] Many people in the thirteenth (as in any other) century were fascinated with the ideal of unrequited love. This was the publicly professed admiration of a knight for his unattainable lady love. What made courtly love different was the claim that the lover was ennobled, morally improved, by his unfulfilled love. In spite of efforts to fuse it with spiritual love of God, courtly love was essentially an idealized form of sensual love. It may have some background in Moslem philosophy (Avicenna's mystical love) but this romantic movement in popular European literature indicates one important fact in the thirteenth and following centuries; many medieval people sought happiness in this life and in the pleasures of the flesh. In 1277 the Bishop of Paris condemned a long list of erroneous teachings. Among the errors noted by Bishop Etienne Tempier were the following: "that happiness is possessed in this life and not in another; that there are fables and falsehoods in the Christian law just as in others; and that simple fornication, namely, that of an unmarried man with an unmarried woman, is not a sin."[2] That the bishop had in mind the courtly love ideals is evident from his prologue to the list of errors; in it he expressly mentions the treatise On Love with its opening and closing lines. This is the De amore written about the year 1185 by Andreas Capellanus; it was probably the most influential treatise produced by this movement.

The theme of human love found different emphasis in Franciscan spirituality. Many people consider St. Francis of Assisi (1182–1226) the typical medieval man: otherworldly, impractical perhaps, guided by feelings. He was typical of but one tendency in a complex period. No scholar himself, Francis founded a religious community (the Order of Friars Minor, started about 1208) which, within a few decades, included professors at Paris, Oxford, and other university centers. St. Francis produced no technical writings on ethics and, indeed, the Flowers of St. Francis is a fourteenth-century compilation incorporating materials from the early days of the Franciscans. He is mentioned here only because of his influence on the moral attitudes of many late medieval Christians. Brand Blanshard calls his exaltation of feeling over reason "an immensely important experiment in morality."[3] Francis did feel that love is all-important and his spiritual disciples in their later and more learned works always retained something of his respect for the affective and volitional approach to moral and religious values.

More distinctive of the ethical thinking of these centuries was the contrary tendency. From the thirteenth to the sixteenth century most writers on the theoretical basis of moral judgment espoused some version of right reason (*recta ratio*) as the ethical standard. To avoid repetition, we will first state the general character of this theory and then indicate the individual attitudes of key thinkers in this period toward the common teaching. The background of right reason ethics is complex. Patristic and medieval Biblical scholars produced many commentaries on the Book of Genesis (the usual name for such a work was Hexaëmeron, "On the Work of the First Six Days"). In these there developed the teaching that God as Creator had a divine Plan (*Ratio*) in mind for all things that He created. Each creature was known eternally to God and thus the eternal Idea (*ratio aeterna*) of every distinct thing served as an exemplar or archetype for the existence and functioning of that thing. In this sense there is a "reason" for each human person and this reason is present eternally in the creative mind of God (*in arte Dei*). The first chapter of Genesis describes how God finished making all things on the sixth day: "And God saw everything that he had made, and behold, it was very good." This was understood to mean that God compared the products of His creative activity with their exemplars in the divine mind and judged that these creatures were well made and pleasing. This is divine exemplarism; it is accepted by all medieval Christian thinkers. According to this view a man performs good actions when he functions in accord with the requirements of his "eternal reason" in God's mind. This is the religious element in the doctrine of right reason.

Most medieval philosophers also knew about the theory of ideal forms, as found in Platonic dialogues such as the *Symposium, Republic,* and *Theaetetus.* In this tradition, there was a perfect archetype for each and every *species* of things in this world. In some sense, all men were thought to share in the ideal form of man. This is Platonic participation of the many in the One. As a theory, it also carried the implication that a good horse will act in conformity with the archetypal "horseness"—and the good man will act in accord with the ideal "humanity." In Latin versions or paraphrases of Plato, these ideas are often called "reasons" (*rationes*). Thirteenth-century Latin writers came to know the way in which Aristotle modified Plato's teaching without entirely rejecting it. Aristotelian metaphysics and philosophy of nature rejected the supposition of a separate world of ideal forms but retained the view that all members of a real class (or species) of things have the same specific form. These "forms," whether substantial or accidental, are not things in themselves but they are constitutive factors in the existing being of each individual thing. Thus, for Aristotle, there is in each horse the substantial form of "horseness"—not existing as a universal essence but individuated and proper to each horse. Each man is similarly constituted of substantial form and prime matter. The substantial form of a man specifies the way in which this individual person exists and operates. Reason, the ability to understand and make inferences (*logos* in Greek, *ratio* in Latin), is the *specific difference* that distinguishes man from brute animal. Man acts in a good way, according to Aristotle, when he realizes as fully as possible in his operations the potentialities of his formal nature as a *rational* animal. This clearly includes the suggestion that the good man must think rightly about his proposed activities. Such practical reasoning is right reason (*orthos logos*), when carried out in a manner befitting a human nature. This Platonic-Aristotelian teaching is the second element in the constitution of medieval right reason ethics.

From the Stoics came the third and last influence. As much as Hegel, these Greeks thought that the world is completely rational in character. There is a reason (*logos*) for everything that occurs. If men were completely wise, they would be able to grasp all these "reasons" and would not hesitate to adjust their interior, conscious attitudes and judgments to the requirements of reason. This is another way of saying that law (*nomos*) is simply what reason, as universalized, dictates. What characterizes the lawmaker is not a will to bind his subjects to the performance of certain actions. Such a voluntaristic account of universal law never occurred to the pre-Christian Greeks. "To order is the function of reason," Thomas Aquinas wrote,[4] and he was echoing both Stoicism and Aristotelianism. Now, the Stoics saw all things as interrelated in a comprehensible manner: some things are useful or suitable for other things, some are not. Such suitability is a relation, an order, a "ratio" in the mathematical sense. In Greek it is a *logos*. The order of nature is a vast complexus of such intelligible relations. As part of that natural order, each man is able to discern those things and actions that are really fitting for him. It is reasonable enough for a stone to stay in one place for all its existence: this behavior is not fitting or suitable for a man. Such a judgment ultimately rests on an intelligent appraisal of what a man is and how he stands in relation to other things. There is a rational order in which man finds himself. Moral law is nothing but the expression of what is fitting for human agents in view of their significant relations with other beings. Right reason is simply another name for a correct or justifiable understanding of the natural order. Universalized, right reason is expressed in general rules; applied to particular actions right reason is a personal decision as to the suitability or unsuitability of this individual action in its present conditions.

We have noted how a certain amount of Stoic ethics entered th

Christian tradition through writers such as Ambrose and Augustine. St. Jerome (340–420) was probably the first to introduce into Latin the term *synderesis*, which may be a corruption of the Stoic word for insight (*syneidesis*). In a Biblical commentary[5] Jerome spoke of synderesis as the spark of conscience (*scintilla conscientiae*). At the start of the thirteenth century this terminology was picked up by theological writers and developed into a special teaching.[6] Generally speaking, synderesis came to mean the human ability (variously interpreted) to distinguish in a general way between moral good and evil, while conscience was reserved for the personal discrimination between good or evil in individual action. In other words, the deliverances of synderesis are universal, the decisions of conscience are particular. Moral reasoning is considered by most medieval thinkers as starting with the general rules or laws grasped through synderesis and as proceeding step by step through various other judgments derived from religious faith or rational experience, or both, to conclude in: (1) more specific but still general judgments concerning right and wrong types of actions (these would be conclusions of "moral science," *scientia moralis*, either ethics or moral theology, depending on whether one used natural reason and information only, or along with supernatural revelation and divine law); and (2) completely particularized moral judgments about the goodness or badness of an individual human action in its context of actual circumstances (such a decision or judgment is called conscience, *conscientia*). The process of practical reasoning to individual (nonuniversal) decisions concerning moral problems is not part of ethics; but when well done it is called right reason (*recta ratio*). The virtue of prudence, or practical wisdom (*prudentia*), is the good habit of reasoning rightly to good practical judgments about individual actions. It reaches its term in good actions. Thus, right reason in its most concrete form is translated from the sphere of mental experience (which may be both cognitive and affective) into the order of action or *praxis*. There are many variations in the explanations of how such a transition is effected but the general pattern is suggested in the foregoing.

Of course the theory of prudential reasoning owes a great deal to the *Nicomachean Ethics*. The versions used in the thirteenth century were, as we have seen, a twelfth-century translation of the first three or four books and the complete translation made by Robert Grosseteste (ca. 1168–1253). Grosseteste also produced a fragmentary commentary (*Notulae*) on the *Nicomachean Ethics* and its Greek commentators. These "Notes" are partly printed with a commentary made by Walter Burleigh in the fourteenth century.[7] In addition to his pioneer work as translator and commentator, three things may be remembered in connection with Grosseteste's contribution to ethics. First, he was one of the first lecturers on the liberal arts in the schools at Oxford. The university was granted a charter there in 1248 but long before that time Grosseteste was teaching at the Franciscan house of studies, although not himself a member of that order. From 1229 to 1235, he was the first lecturer in theology for the Oxford Franciscans.[8] In 1235, he became Bishop of Lincoln (and thus is often cited as *Lincolniensis*). So, Grosseteste was doubtless one of the first to lecture on ethics in England. The second thing for which Grosseteste is important in this field was his general emphasis on natural science, mathematics, and the observation of nature. He is thus partly responsible not only for the continuing British interest in the philosophy of science but also for an emphasis on empirical information as an important source of ethical judgment. He was convinced that natural experience is a necessary element in all learning and that mathematics supplies the key to the interpretation and understanding of the speculative and practical significance of such experience. Grosseteste's third contribution was a blunt explanation of right reason as a direct conformity between a thing or an act and its exemplar in the divine mind. His version of *recta ratio* is a simple theological approbative theory, as the following text shows.

This rule [of rightness, *rectitudo*] is nothing other than the eternal reason (*ratio aeterna*) of the thing in the divine mind. . . . But if it be said that this is the right reason according to which the thing should be thus, it is asked again: where is this reason seen to be the right reason of this thing and such as it should be, except, in turn, in its reason? And so there will always be a regress until the thing is seen to be as it should be in its first reason which is right according to itself. And, therefore, the thing is as it should be because it conforms to that. All created truth, then, is evident in so far as the light of its eternal reason is present to the person observing, as Augustine testifies.[9]

Grosseteste's most famous pupil and admirer was Roger Bacon (*ca.* 1214-1292), who entered the Franciscan Order in 1257 after teaching liberal arts at Oxford and Paris for many years. Bacon was highly critical of most of his contemporaries and advocated a complete reform in Christian learning. (Both Grosseteste and Bacon anticipated by several centuries the more famous "idols" and "new method" of Francis Bacon.) While in Paris, Roger Bacon had met a canon lawyer named Guido Fulcodi and told him of his plans for reform. Roughly, what Bacon wanted was more emphasis on natural science, mathematics, and the study of ancient languages as aids for the interpretation of Scripture. In 1265 Guido became Pope Clement IV. He wrote to Bacon requesting a copy of his writings and ordering that this be sent regardless of any Franciscan regulation to prevent the publishing of Bacon's views. This is the first intimation that Bacon was in some difficulty with his superiors.[10] He had written various short treatises but he now began the *Communia Naturalium* (a *Summa* of all types of knowledge). Soon he saw that this grandiose work could not be finished in time to satisfy the pope's interest in a plan for the reform of Christian education, so Roger started the *Opus Majus* (*Greater Work*) to cover much the same ground but more briefly. With a few other writings, the *Opus Majus* was dispatched by messenger to Rome in the year 1268. The treatise is of some importance in the history of ethics, since the seventh and last part of the *Opus Majus* is an essay on moral philosophy.[11] Somewhat in the manner of Auguste Comte in the nineteenth century, Roger Bacon argued that ethics should be placed at the peak of the sciences and that all other disciplines should be propaedeutic to it. Indeed, Roger also shared with Comte a sort of positivistic attitude toward ethics: he was quite frank in saying that canon law is an important source of moral judgment, along with the Scriptures.

However, Roger Bacon had little else in common with Comte. One has only to read a few pages of the *Opus Majus* to realize that, like Augustine, Bacon takes "philosophy" as Christian wisdom and makes little distinction between philosophy and theology. The Bible, canon law, and the "philosophers" are all sources of moral instruction. Among his favorite authors were Augustine, Seneca, and Avicenna. Many parts of the essay on moral philosophy are verbatim extracts from one or the other of these writers. In the third section of this treatise (*Opus Majus*, VII, 3) Bacon argues that the views of the ancient philosophers are frequently superior to the practices of Christians—yet he frequently asserts that Christian revelation is needed for a really good life. He is very close to Grosseteste's position that moral goodness consists in direct conformity with the law of God as manifested in the Scriptures. God's will is the standard of moral judgment. Most people learn what their moral obligations are through the dictates of canon law. There is also a moral illumination that comes in the inner mental experience of at least some men, but it is difficult to ascertain the extent and content of this sort of special communication. Some texts suggest that it is a theory of innate ideas.

In connection with his discussion of politics (civil science, which he takes as a part of moral philosophy) Roger Bacon introduces a threefold division of man's moral relations which is retained by some later Scholastic ethicians (notably Francis Suárez). First of all, man is considered in relation to God; then in relation to his neighbor; and thirdly in relation to himself.[12] On each of these levels, Bacon feels man has certain rights and responsibilities. He does not seem to see that the third relationship (of man to himself) is not interpersonal, as are the other two, and can hardly involve "duties" in the same sense as the two external relations. In spite of his protestations concerning the high role of moral philosophy in Christian education, Bacon did not actually contribute much to the development of the theory.

The Franciscan school at Paris was also active in the realm of practical philosophy. From about 1236 onward they had one or two of their members teaching continually as theology professors at the University of Paris. Alexander of Hales (ca. 1186–1245) was an elderly Parisian professor (though born in England) before entering the Order of Friars Minor in 1236–1237. His admirers in the order compiled in his honor a large encyclopedic work of theology which came to be known as the Summa Fratris Alexandri. It contains the first treatise on law in the Summa literature and exerted some influence on Aquinas' better-known discussion of various types of law.[13] One of Alexander's successors as a Franciscan professor at Paris was the French scholar John of La Rochelle (died in 1245). His treatise On the Soul became the standard exposition of Franciscan psychology in the thirteenth century.[14] Many of the teachings of this type of psychology (no real distinction between the soul and its powers, a different mode of cognition for corporeal things and for immaterial beings, and much stress on the affective-volitional functions of the human soul) become influential in the work of later Franciscan moral writers, such as Bonaventure, Duns Scotus, and even William of Ockham.

The great figure in Franciscan thought at Paris in the thirteenth century was Bonaventure (ca. 1217–1274). Born Giovanni di Fidanza in Italy, he joined the Franciscans at an early age, studied theology and liberal arts in Paris, received his doctorate in the same year as Thomas Aquinas (1256–1257,) and was made general minister of his order at that time. As an administrator for the rest of his life, Bonaventure wrote mostly short treatises and sermons. However, he had definite views on the role of philosophy in Christian life and represented a very distinctive approach to the ethical theory of right reason.

Psychology is most important in Franciscan thinking. In the thirteenth century their analysis of the human soul and its functions embodied elements from Augustine, Damascene, and Aristotle.[15] Starting with Alexander of Hales and John of La Rochelle, continuing with Bonaventure and Matthew of Aquasparta (ca. 1240–1302), Franciscan psychology insisted on the unity and simplicity of man's soul (and so refused to make radical distinctions between powers such as intellect and will), and this psychology further maintained that volitional activity and affective experience are more distinctive of man than is any cognitive activity. Bonaventure would say, for instance, that man is a "rational" animal but he would understand rationality as expressed in volitional decision and activity. The test of this view is found in Bonaventure's notion of ultimate beatitude: the good man's final union with God is essentially an act of love, and not an act of intellectual knowledge as Aquinas was teaching in the same years at Paris. This is what is meant when Bonaventure is called a voluntarist. He is not extreme in his views but he is opposed to the idea that the intellect is man's highest power.

It was as a consequence of this psychological position that Bonaventure decided to place synderesis in the function of volition. As he explained in his lectures on Peter Lombard's *Sentences:*

> Just as from the very creation of the soul the intellect possesses a light which is for it a natural seat of judgment (*naturale judicatorium*), directing the intellect in its acts of knowing, so also does the affective capacity (*affectus*) have a sort of natural weight (*naturale quoddam pondus*), directing it in its acts of appetition . . . and in this way, synderesis only denotes this weight of the will (or the will plus this weight) in the sense that it has the function of inclining toward that which is good in itself (*ad bonum honestum*).[16]

He goes on to say that conscience (*conscientia*) is different from synderesis. As a habit in the order of cognition, conscience belongs to practical understanding and even has a certain moving character (*rationem motivi*), inasmuch as it prompts and inclines the soul to action.[17] So, for Bonaventure conscience is a habit of the practical intellect which inclines a person to know both general principles of moral rectitude and the particular character of good or bad actions. The source of this "rightness" is a moral illumination which involves the light of sacred Scripture. In one of his shorter treatises, the point is expressed as follows:

> Accordingly, in the consideration of rectitude there is seen the rule of life. For he indeed lives rightly who is guided by the regulations of the divine law, as is the case when the will of man accepts necessary precepts, salutary warnings, and counsels of perfection that he may thereby prove the good and acceptable and perfect will of God. And then is the rule of life right when no obliquity can be found therein.[18]

Obviously, then, the moral philosophy (*philosophia moralis*) of St. Bonaventure employs the data of religious faith and is a moral theology.

At the same time that the Franciscans were developing their affective approach to moral theory the Dominicans were beginning to emphasize the role of practical reason in the moral life. The first teacher in the Order of St. Dominic to develop an ethics was Albert the Great (1206–1280). He was accused by Roger Bacon of teaching philosophy without having had any teacher in the subject. This was probably correct: Albert taught liberal arts courses based on his own voracious reading of all the ancient, patristic, and early medieval treatises that he found available in Latin. At the beginning of several of his commentaries on works of Aristotle, he stated his intention to make Aristotelian philosophy

known to the "Latins." However, Albert's views in speculative philosophy
are not simply Aristotelian: he combined Neoplatonism, Christian Platonism, Avicennism, and Augustinism with his own meditations. His metaphysics is not identical with that of his pupil Thomas Aquinas: Albert-
inism is a complicated theory that has not yet been fully investigated.

On moral questions, Albert's writings are very extensive and their
chronology is not yet completely established. However, the following
works are important: *Tractatus de natura boni* (written before 1240),
as yet unedited, treats detailed moral questions; *Summa de creaturis*
(1244–1249), one part: *De homine*, has information on the moral psychology and theory of knowledge, another part, *De bono*, contains data on
moral science; *Commentaria in libros Sententiarum* (1244–1249), Albert's theology lectures on Peter Lombard's *Sentences*: books two and
three are important for ethics; *Lectura in libros Ethicorum Aristotelis*
(1248), a course of lectures on the *Nicomachean Ethics*, recorded in the
handwriting of Thomas Aquinas; *Commentaria in libros Ethicorum Aristotelis* (1256–1270), a much later paraphrase of the *Nicomachean Ethics*;
and the *Summa Theologiae* (1270–1280), a very late work with much
material on moral science but frequently incompatible with the earlier
views of Albert.[19]

It is evident that Albert was one of the first thinkers in the thirteenth
century to develop a moral philosophy based in good part on man's
natural experience and reasoning. He believed that there is an eternal
law in the mind of God, of course, but was quite anxious to investigate
what the Greek and Arabian philosophers had to say about ethics.
The theory of right reason (*recta ratio*), as outlined earlier in this
chapter, is central to Albert's thinking. Synderesis is the intellectual
capacity to understand the first principles of moral reasoning—which are
general rules of natural law (*jus naturale*). In his *Lectures on the
Ethics* (1248) he explained:

> Just as there are in speculative thinking certain general principles
> from which one reasons to particular conclusions, so in moral con-
> siderations there are some general principles by which one discovers
> rules for actions, such as "theft is forbidden" and similar rules;
> every man is expected to know these and he can, because he has
> the process of reason for this purpose, and these rules are called
> the natural law.[20]

The process of practical reasoning starts with such a general rule and
moves through more particular judgments (factually grounded in experience) to individual conclusions. Conscience (*conscientia*) is the name
that Albert uses for these concluding judgments of practical reasoning.[2]

The expression *jus naturale* (in both Albert and Thomas Aquinas
is usually translated as "natural law." This may cause misunderstanding

in English. Other modern vernaculars have a special word for *jus* (*Recht*, *droit*) as opposed to *lex* (*Gesetz*, *loi*). In authors such as Albert and Aquinas, *jus* means what is objectively right (adjusted) in the concrete. So, it is *just* for a male and female of the same biological species to reproduce and care for their offspring. This is not because some lawmaker has so willed but because there is in the real relation between male and female a certain suitability (*convenientia*) which is not present between male and male, or between members of two different species. Provided other circumstances are reasonable, it is thus good for male and female to engage in reproduction. Man apprehends this good quality of his actions by observing what is in accord with his nature and what flows from his nature as a reasoning being.[22]

According to Albert, the most general rule known through synderesis is: "Good should be done; evil should be avoided" (*bonum faciendum*; *malum vitandum*).[23] However, Albert thought that other broad rules of conduct (such as: honor your parents, help those in need, do no injury to any man, avoid fornication, commit no theft or murder, love God, etc.) are known to all men by natural insight. These are *jura*, i.e. right things. His whole approach to law, moral or otherwise, is intellectual and realistic. Command is the work of reason.[24] The expression of such an intellectual order is a law (called either *jus* or *lex*), and the will of the lawmaker is no more active in declaring a moral law than it would be in a mathematician who states that equals added to equals must result in equals. After hundreds of years of emphasis on the notion that a law must be enacted by the will of the legislator, it is difficult for a twentieth-century man to appreciate this intellectual view of law which characterizes one line of late medieval ethics, starting with Albert and running through Thomas Aquinas, Soto, Medina, and Robert Bellarmine.

Thomas Aquinas (1224–1274) remains the outstanding ethician of the thirteenth century and perhaps of the whole Middle Ages. A colleague of Albert in the Order of Preachers, Thomas had studied liberal arts at the royal University of Naples before becoming a Dominican. After further studies in philosophy and theology, under Albert at Cologne and in the University of Paris, Thomas taught philosophy and theology at Paris, in several study centers of his order in the vicinity of Rome, and finally as a professor at the University of Naples. His writings with important ethical content are: *Commentary on the Sentences* (1252–1256), *On the Truth of the Catholic Faith* (*Summa Contra Gentiles*, 1259–1264, Book III is on moral science), *Commentary on the Nicomachean Ethics* (at any time from 1263 to 1272), *Disputed Questions on Evil and on the Virtues* (1268–1272), and the first and second sections of Part II of the *Summa Theologiae* (1268–1272).

Broadly speaking, the ethical theory of Thomas is similar to what we have seen in Albert; the Thomistic position is much more thoroughly developed, however, and is more internally consistent than the Albertinian ethics.[25] Thomistic ethics is often classified as a "natural law" theory,[2] but this is unfortunate for two reasons. In recent terminology, law implies a command with an origin in the will of a legislator: this is not Thomas' view. He defined law as "an ordinance of reason promulgated by someone in charge of the community for the common good."[2] Second, the meaning of "natural law" has been so diversified in late medieval and modern discussions that the term is no longer accurately descriptive. Thomas' ethics is eudaimonistic and teleological; it stresses internal motivation as well as the consequences of moral action; it is moreover, a self-realization theory.[28]

Man as a moral agent is analyzed in great detail by Aquinas. Human functions range from vegetative acts of assimilating food, growing, and reproducing, through the range of animal activities of sense perception, appetition (concupiscible and irascible emotions), and kinesthesis, to the typically human actions of understanding simple meanings, reasoning discursively to logical conclusions, and intellectual appetition (also called volition). Important in this complicated moral psychology is the distinction between man's sensory experience (cognitive and affective), which is concerned with the *individual* aspects of bodies; and man's rational experience (cognitive and appetitive), which deals with the *universal* meanings of reality. Moral actions must be voluntary, that is they must come under the control of human understanding, must be done (or omitted) with some end in view, with some knowledge of the nature of the act under consideration, and with some approval on the part of the agent himself. This excludes from the domain of voluntary action purely accidental actions, merely physical or biological functions, and acts resulting wholly from external violence. It should be emphasized that, in Thomism, voluntary does not mean volitional. There are four powers in man which are the centers of moral activity: concupiscible appetite (feelings of sensual desire and the contrary), irascible appetite (emergency feelings in response to threats from sense objects), intellectual appetite (personal inclinations toward or away from the universal objects of intellection), and potential intellect (the functions of understanding, judging, and reasoning about universal objects). Each of these moral powers is open to being perfected by an appropriate moral habit: temperance (*temperantia*) may be acquired in the concupiscible appetite and is the moral virtue of reasonable *moderation* in sense desires; courage (*fortitudo*) is the chief habit of the irascible appetite, and brings *firmness* to one's emotional responses to emergencies presented in sense experience; justice (*justitia*) may habituate the intellectual appetite (*voluntas*) so that it customarily wills what is good for other persons, and *equality*, either simple or proportional, is the keynote of justice; and fourthly, prudence (*prudentia*) or practical wisdom is the chief practical habit of man's intellect, and is the moral virtue of reasoning well about, and commanding, good moral actions. Only one of these cardinal virtues is a habit of the will. This is a fundamental difference between the ethical theory of Thomas Aquinas and that of the other scholastics: most others think that will (*voluntas*) is the only essentially moral power in man.[29]

As to Thomas' particular approach to right reason and the distinction of morally good from evil action, he did, of course, think that God knows all the rules of morality and has perfect judgment of individual human actions. But Aquinas did not teach that we humans know all that God knows.[30] Some part of God's moral wisdom is conveyed to men by way of revelation (as in the case of Moses and the Decalogue); other partial knowledge of eternal Justice is acquired by ordinary natural experience and rational reflection on it (as in the case of thoughtful pagans like Aristotle and Cicero but also in philosophers of every era). Aquinas was convinced that "God is not offended by us except by what we do against our own good."[31] In other words, actions are not morally right or wrong because of some arbitrary fiat of divine will: what is good for man is what may be understood as fitting (*conveniens*) to this kind of agent, under certain concrete circumstances, in relation to the purpose that this agent intends to accomplish, in the real environment of the actions including other persons individually and collectively. This complicated set of relations is what Thomas Aquinas means by right reason. As expressed in universal judgments about the kinds of actions that are morally appropriate or inappropriate for a human agent, the conclusions of right reasoning are identical with the rules of natural moral law. As applied by the prudent person to practical decisions about individual moral problems, right reasoning terminates in moral conscience, a practical judgment of choice, and right action.

Thomistic ethics, in its original form, is a eudaimonism but it differs from the theory of Aristotle in that Thomas regards the ultimate end of a good human life as not merely internal well-being (*eudaimonia*) in the moral person but also as a positive approach to an external and real objective: the Perfect Good which is God. Thomism is not simply a self-realization ethics, then; it has certain resemblances to "good will" ethics (as found in Anselm, or later in Kant) by virtue of the emphasis on right intention. On the other hand, Thomas' stress on a prudent consideration of the purpose and predictable results of each voluntary action has something in common with utilitarianism and naturalistic pragmatism.

Some of Thomas' contemporaries were even more naturalistic, however. At some time during the 1260s a movement began at the University of Paris that has been variously called Latin Averroism, and heterodox or radical Aristotelianism. It was basically an attempt by certain teachers in the Arts Faculty (all of them Catholic priests) to give a great deal of autonomy to naturalistic philosophy. Leaders in this school of thought were Siger of Brabant (ca. 1240–1284) and Boethius of Dacia (fl. ca. 1270). As far as their ethical teaching is concerned, these professors were Aristotelians who attempted to philosophize without using the data of their Christian faith. Our information on their views is defective, because we have very few of their writings today and because our reports on them are mostly derived from their thirteenth-century critics and opponents. Siger wrote a *Book on Felicity*, now nonextant. Boethius produced a short treatise on the highest good.[32] It appears that they taught that the good life for man consists in the cultivation of speculative understanding. In his famous *Condemnation of 219 Propositions* (1277 A.D.) Bishop Etienne Tempier was concerned about the teachings of these Aristotelian professors. Among the "errors" to which he objected were these:

> That there is no more excellent state than to study philosophy; that all the good that is possible to man consists in the intellectual virtues; that happiness is found in this life and not in another; that a man who is ordered as to his intellect and his affections, in the manner in which this can be sufficiently accomplished by means of the intellectual and moral virtues of which the Philosopher [Aristotle] speaks in the *Ethics*, is sufficiently disposed for eternal happiness.[33]

At least three anonymous *Commentaries on the Nicomachean Ethic* from the late thirteenth century have been discovered as evidences of the spread of this naturalistic ethical trend in the period.[34]

Giles of Rome (ca. 1247–1316) shows the continuing influence of Aristotelian ethics in the latter part of the thirteenth century. His letter on the *Distinction of Rhetoric, Ethics and Politics* simply repeats peripatetic doctrine.[35] One distinctive view in Giles's work is the subordination of politics to moral philosophy, on the theory that the latter is the complete science of human action. This same view carries over into Giles's famous treatise *On Ecclesiastical Power*, where he argues for the subordination of civil authority to that of the Church: "The duty of earthly power is to prepare the materials in order that the ecclesiastical ruler may not be hampered in spiritual matters."[36]

It is in this second half of the thirteenth century that we find the beginnings of ethical voluntarism. We have already noted how Franciscan psychology emphasized the affective and volitional side of man's nature. Peter John Olivi (d. 1298) was one of the first Franciscans to teach that "either the will is free, or it is not a will."[37] Prior to this in patristic and medieval thought there is no discussion of free will (*liber voluntas*) but only of free choice (*liberum arbitrium*). From the time of Olivi onward, more and more people insist that the human will is an essentially free power.[38]

This emphasis on volition is not confined to the Franciscan thinkers. Henry of Ghent (*ca.* 1217–1293) was a prominent professor in arts and theology at the University of Paris who taught that the will of man is in every way the most distinctive human power. Will directs the intellect in its functioning but the will "by its own power of knowing can direct itself."[39] As a result of this view, Henry thought that moral law and obligation issue directly from the will of the legislator. While he may still speak of right reason, Henry of Ghent stands at the beginning of a different theory of moral and legal obligation. To command now becomes a function of a will that is autonomous and undetermined by external judgments of intellect. What the lawmaker wills to be done is what is right and no other justification is required.

Associated with this "Neo-Augustinian" trend in thirteenth-century thought is the remarkable Catalan writer Ramón Lull (*ca.* 1232–1315). A layman and married, Lull devoted the last part of his life to the project of converting the Moors to Christianity. On the island of Mallorca he founded a university which continues to this day as a center of Catalan culture and Lullism. His psychology is that of St. Augustine: the human soul has no separate powers, it is utterly simple but has three main functions—memory, understanding, and willing. Of these the last is most distinctive, and volition reaches its peak in love. Lull's famous "Great Art" was simply the teaching that man intuits (by means of divine illumination, as in Augustine) a number of self-evident notions. These principles are: goodness, greatness, eternity, power, wisdom, will, virtue, truth, and glory. The foregoing may be used as predicates with various basic concepts and relations to form true and useful judgments in the practical order.[40] Although Ramón Lull was not a theoretical ethician, he has some importance in ethics as an advocate of a rather simple version of intuitionism. One might even suggest that his semi-autobiographical novel, *Blanquerna*, has many of the attitudes that characterize recent phenomenological ethics. The following passage illustrates Lull's emphasis on concrete emotions:

> "Justice," said Blanquerna, "what thing desirest thou in my will?" Memory answered for Justice: "I desire therein contrition and fear; I desire tears in thine eyes, in thy heart sighs, and in thy body afflictions." "And thou, Liberality, what desirest thou in my will?" Understanding answered for Liberality: "I desire to possess it wholly, for love, for repentance and for the despising of the vanities of this world." "And thou, Mercy, what desirest thou of my memory and understanding?" Will answered for Mercy: "I desire thy memory

wholly, for remembrance of the gifts of Mercy and her pardon, and thine understanding wholly for comprehension of the same, and these yet more for the contemplation of Mercy herself." So Blanquerna gave himself wholly to that which the virtues of his Beloved desired of him.[41]

From these lines it will be obvious that existential commitment is not without its medieval antecedents and that "irrational man" found a place in the century of right reason.

Another very unusual thinker at the end of the thirteenth century was Meister Johannes Eckhart (ca. 1260–1327). He was a Dominican, as were Albert and Thomas Aquinas, but Eckhart's philosophy was a complicated blending of Neoplatonic speculation with Christian mysticism. The peak or spark of the soul (scintilla animae) is the highest part of man, above both reason and will. It is in this "citadel" that God contacts man in mystical union. As one historian describes Eckhart's theory: "The gradual purification of the soul from contact with matter by its turning toward God, its final liberation by union with him in a region beyond knowledge and being—all this reminds us of Plotinus' flight of the soul to the One and its absorption in it."[42] It is in his Sermons that we see Eckhart developing a "good will" doctrine of human conduct that owes something to the right intention theories of Abelard and Anselm and that anticipates the famous teaching of Immanuel Kant.

> If you have good will, you shall lack for nothing, neither love, humility, nor any other virtue; what you will with all your strength you shall have, and neither God nor any creature can deprive you—if, again, your will is sound, divine and wrapt in God. . . . Good will is not less powerful for good than bad will is for evil. . . . With a will that is purely bad, I commit as great sins as if I were to murder all the people in the world, even though I did not lift a finger toward the crime. Why should not the same power reside in good will?[43]

Still another nonacademic personality who should be mentioned briefly is the poet Dante. Dante Alighieri (1265–1321) was widely read in philosophy and introduced much of his learning into his literary works. He was not, of course, a professional in the field of ethics but deserves mention here for two reasons. He agreed with Thomas Aquinas and the Aristotelians that reason in man "is especially his life and the actuality of his noblest part."[44] Moreover, Dante offers in the Divine Comedy and De monarchia an instructive picture of the moral attitudes of the Christian noncleric in the thirteenth century.

Comparatively little historical work has been done on the ethics of the fourteenth century—yet it was rich in its thought and exerted no little influence on the Renaissance and early modern period. Most of the ethical writers who treated the subject in the sixteenth and seventeenth centuries studied some type of fourteenth-century philosophy. The outstanding schools were either Scotistic, terminist, or Thomistic in orientation.

John Duns Scotus (ca. 1265–1308) was a Franciscan who taught for only a few years at Oxford and Paris. He died before he could say his best word on the problems of ethics. Until recently his writings have been badly edited and they are not yet wholly available in critical texts. The Ordinatio is Scotus' own edition of his several series of lectures on Peter Lombard's Sentences. In the Prologue to the first book of the Ordinatio we find a great deal of his philosophy expounded, including his ethics. There is some information on ethics in the Quodlibetal Questions, which were conducted in Paris and contain his most mature thought. Duns Scotus is known as the "Subtle Doctor." Very intelligent and learned, he was one of the most brilliant intellects produced in the British Isles. He differed on fundamental points of philosophy from Thomas Aquinas. Perhaps the most important items in the speculative thought of Scotus are his doctrine on the object of the human intellect (ens in quantum ens, being without any qualification) and his teaching that the will is free and rational by nature and is superior to the intellect.[45]

In spite of his general opposition to the philosophy of Thomas Aquinas, Duns Scotus supports the view that right reason is the basis on which to judge good human action. He offers, in fact, one of the clearest explanations of the meaning of recta ratio, in these lines from the first book of the Ordinatio:

> Just as beauty (pulchritudo) is not some absolute quality in a beautiful body but is the aggregation of all items that are suitable to such a body (that is, matters of size, shape and color) and also the aggregation of all the relations (which pertain to these suitable aspects) in regard to the body and among themselves—so also the goodness (bonitas) of the moral act is something like the decorous character (decor) of the act, including the aggregation of due proportion to all items to which it is to be proportioned (for instance, to the power, to the object, to the end, to the time, to the place, and to the manner of acting) and this especially according as they are dictated by right reason (ratione recta) to be suitable to the act. Consequently, we may say in all cases that the suitability (convenientia) of the act to right reason is that which, once it is present, renders the act good. For since every act is concerned with a definite kind of object, if the act is not in accord with right

reason in the agent (that is, if he does not have right reason in acting), then the act is not good. Primarily then, the conformity of the act to right reason—fully dictating concerning all the proper circumstances of this act—is the goodness of the moral act.[46]

There is no question that Duns Scotus upheld the standard of right reason in ethics. "The moral goodness of the act," he explains elsewhere, "is the entirety (*integritas*) of all those items which right reason judges to be required to fit the act itself, or to be suitable to the agent involved in his action."[47] However, unlike Aquinas, Scotus teaches that every moral action is an act of willing, either completed within the will (*actus elicitus voluntatis*) or performed by some other power under command of the will (*actus imperatus voluntatis*). Every deed (*praxis*) for which man is morally responsible is a will act.[48]

The notion that will, either in God or man, is the source of moral law is rejected by Scotus. He carefully reviews the teaching of Henry of Ghent to the effect that conscience (*conscientia*) resides in the affective part of man's soul and is like a universal mover prompting man to action ("universalis motor stimulans ad opus"). But this view is subjected to severe criticism by Scotus.[49] Then he proceeds to explain that synderesis is the habit whereby practical principles are known—and it is in the intellect, not the will. Furthermore, Scotus treats conscience as the habit of the practical intellect which elicits judgment as to the conformity or nonconformity of concrete actions with the principles of right reason.[50] In the next distinction he repeats his explanation of what right reason means: a reasonable agreement (*convenientia*) of a proposed action with the end the agent has in view, with the free character of the agent (*efficiens*), with the generic character of this kind of action, with the manner in which the action is executed, and finally, with various extrinsic circumstances of time, place, and other such conditions.

If Scotistic ethics is a right reason theory that insists on the intrinsic character of the good or evil moral action, the next great thinker in the Franciscan school does not agree. William Ockham (*ca.* 1280-1349) marks the beginning of ethical extrinsicism: the theory that moral good and evil have nothing to do with the internal character of man or his action but rest on the external attribution of a moral quality. Moreover Ockham is the first prominent ethician to reject eudaimonism. He did not think that man is naturally ordered to the pursuit of personal well-being or happiness. The only objective which can satisfy the human will is God; but ethics cannot show that there is such an ultimate end for man. Hence, Ockham also rejected the medieval theory of the finality of man's nature. He *believed* that God is the ultimate goal of human aspiration but he stoutly maintained that he did not *know* this philosophically. This is the start of the "modern way" (*via moderna*) in ethics. William Ockham's works with ethical content are the *Ordinatio* (a commentary on the first book of Lombard's *Sentences,* written by Ockham himself); the *Reportatio* (a written record by listeners at Ockham's lectures on the last three books of the *Sentences;* the *Seven Quodlibets;* and the *Treatise on Predestination and Divine Foreknowledge.*[51] His political writings deal chiefly with the Church-state problem and the internal frictions in the Franciscan Order arising from the efforts of a group desiring to return to the pioneer poverty and spirituality of St. Francis.

The speculative philosophy of Ockham sets the stage for his moral views. He has a logic and a philosophy of nature but no metaphysics. The only realities are existing individuals, material or immaterial things. Universals (humanity, goodness, justice) are general words and, in a special sense, generalized concepts. Sometimes Ockham explains the universal concept as a *fictum,* that is, a mental construct produced by intellectual abstraction to represent several similar individuals. In his later period he gave more reality to the universal concept by identifying it with the abstractive *act* of understanding.[52] In any case, the real objects of human understanding are individual things. It becomes difficult for Ockham to assign a difference between sense perception and understanding, since both types of cognition are concerned with individuals.

Ockham's logic includes his epistemology. He has a very strict notion of the requirements of demonstrative science, being convinced that the philosopher could not prove all the things that Thomas Aquinas, or even Duns Scotus, had tried to demonstrate. For instance, Ockham flatly denied that a person could have evident knowledge "by reason or experience" that the intellective soul is the form of the human body.[53] As to the effort to demonstrate the existence of God, Ockham felt that our success depends on how God is initially defined. If God means "some thing more noble and more perfect than anything else besides Him, then it is impossible to demonstrate by natural reason that there is only one God, or even that God, in this sense, exists. On the other hand, if God be understood as "that than which nothing is more noble and more perfect," it may be possible to show that He exists but it is impossible to prove philosophically that He is unique.[54]

While he limited the power of human reason to prove philosophical conclusions, Ockham believed in the usual articles of Christian faith. He was particularly impressed by the omnipotence and freedom of God— and frequently appealed to these attributes in his reasoning about man's capacities and actions. Like Duns Scotus, Ockham identified moral action with volitional activity: "No act is virtuous or vicious unless it is voluntary and in the power of the will."[55] In discussing this, Ockham shows how he considers the will of God to be the ultimate source of morality. God may will that any action be good or bad, provided He does not become involved in contradiction. For instance, God could command a man not to love God for a certain time—and this would become a good action for that period.[56] Of course William still speaks of the need to be guided by right reason ("every right will is in conformity with right reason"), but this does not mean that reason rectifies the volitional act; rather, reason is right *because God has willed it* to be so.[57]

Thus begins in Christian thinking about morality the authoritarian teaching that God could rightly order man to do almost anything and, in view of the absolute omnipotence of God, the consequent actions would be good. Evidently, Ockham did not mean that, having established one set of moral rules, God is going to change them arbitrarily. But he did think that it is within the absolute power of God to alter most of the accepted precepts of morality. The consequences of this Ockhamistic doctrine are tremendous: moral law is reduced to positive divine law, obligation is contingent, and it is doubtful that a valid ethics can be constructed apart from theology.

Ockhamist ethics, then, is truly authoritarian. It is the clearest example in medieval Christian thought of a theological approbative theory. God is the boss and whatever He wills to be right is what is morally good. This became the standard teaching of this type of nominalistic Scholasticism. Gabriel Biel (1425–1495) continued this doctrine in the next century. His writings were studied by many of the early modern ethicians and influenced some of the prominent figures in the Reformation.

Natural law ethics contrasts with the positivist character of Ockhamism. There were some medieval writers who developed the notion of the "law of nature" within the context of jurisprudence. Henry de Bracton (d. 1268) exemplified this lawyer's approach to the right and the good in his book *On the Laws and Customs of England*.[58] Two centuries later, Sir John Fortescue (ca. 1385–1476) continued the same natural law tradition in his work *On the Merits of the Laws of England*. Fortescue's views are close to the teaching of Aristotle. He quotes with approval the *Nicomachean Ethics*: "Natural law is that which has the same force among all men."[59] In fact, Fortescue's version of the right reason theory is very similar to what we saw in Thomas Aquinas.

At the end of the Middle Ages there were frequently three chairs of philosophy (and theology) in the great European universities. A student had a choice of Scotism, Ockhamism, or Thomism. To some extent the same divisiveness carried over into moral science and ethical theory. There were many commentators in each of the three schools but they showed little originality. Among the Thomist writers, Antoninus of Florence (1389–1459) was a bishop who expanded and updated Thomas' teaching on the moral problems of social life. He is considered a pioneer thinker on the moral aspects of economics. Antoninus' basic ethical position is Thomistic.

An oddity in the same period is the vernacular moralizing of the German priest Albrecht von Eyb (1420–1475). He was not interested in ethical theory: his two treatises contain long lists of virtues and pious maxims addressed to the common people rather than the world of scholarship. Von Eyb's forthright but simple teaching was not unlike that of Martin Luther in the next generation.

Two English writers bring to a close the history of right reason ethics in the Middle Ages. Reginald Pecock (ca. 1393–1460) was a Catholic bishop who became concerned about the effects of the Lollard movement within Christianity. In opposition to the view that simple faith and Bible reading offer adequate moral guidance for the good life, Pecock wrote a series of English treatises that stressed the primacy of reason. The natural function of reason, he argued, is to decide what ought to be done.[60] God accepts no good deed unless it be in accord with the judgment of reason ("the doom of resoun"). It is the natural function of man's will to do what right reason dictates. Bishop Pecock distinguished two branches of practical knowledge: moral philosophy and theology. At times he implied that ethics is the more important for salvation. As can be expected, he encountered much criticism both from his Catholic colleagues and from the Lollards. Toward the end of his life he wrote:

> I . . . confess and acknowledge that I here before time [was] presuming of mine own naturall witt, and preferring the judgment of naturall reason before the New and Old Testaments, and the authority and determination of our modern Holy Church.[61]

In point of fact, Pecock's ethical position was very close to that of Thomas Aquinas, although the bishop's optimism about the salvific role of moral philosophy in the life of the Christian no doubt exceeded that of St. Thomas.

Our last representative of this type of ethics, Richard Hooker (1553–1600), takes us well beyond the Middle Ages, but his version of right reason is well developed and very much in the tradition of the Middle Ages. He has been called the Anglican Aquinas. The first book of his *Laws of Ecclesiastical Polity* is an excellent summary of basic Thomistic ethics. Hooker taught that besides the supreme eternal law, which rests in "God's bosom," there is a second eternal law, which consists in the order of things in this universe. Man comes to understand this real order and its requirements from his natural experience and by the use of ordinary reasoning. He did not think that this view demands that one be a Platonist: "We are not of the opinion therefore, as some are, that nature in working hath before her certain exemplary draughts or patterns. . . ."[62] It is erroneous, he argues, to think that we need no reason besides God's will in order to do the good. His opposition to ethical voluntarism is evident in the following typical explanation:

Where understanding therefore needeth, in those things reason is the director of man's Will by discovering in action what is good. For the Laws of well-doing are the dictates of right reason. . . . In the rest there is that light of Reason, whereby good may be known from evil, and which discovering the same rightly is termed right.[63]

Hooker's description of the law of reason in relation to other laws makes a fitting conclusion to this chapter on the ethics of right reason:

Now that law which, as it is laid up in the bosom of God, they call Eternal, receiveth according unto the different kinds of things which are subject unto it different and sundry kinds of names. That part of it which ordereth natural agents we call usually Nature's law; that which Angels do clearly behold and without any swerving observe is a law Celestial and heavenly; the law of Reason, that which bindeth creatures reasonable in this world, and with which by reason they may most plainly perceive themselves bound; that which bindeth them and is not known but by special revelation from God, Divine law; Human law, that which out of the law either of reason or of God men probably gathering to be expedient, they make it a law. All things therefore, which are as they ought to be, are conformed unto this second law eternal; and even those things which to this eternal law are not conformable are notwithstanding in some sort ordered by the first eternal law.[64]

PART THREE

EARLY MODERN ETHICS: 1450–1750

CHAPTER VII

Humanist Ethics in the Renaissance

THE PRIMARY CHARACTERISTIC of ethical thinking in the Renaissance was its humanism. Man became the focal point of attention in the arts, in education, in philosophy, and eventually in religion. The view that man the microcosm epitomizes the whole of things was not unknown to the Middle Ages[1] but the fact remains that man was not the most fascinating object of investigation for the medieval scholar: God was, for both Christian and non-Christian. If we insist that Renaissance ethics was homocentric, that does not mean that the period was irreligious or atheistic. The good and right for man were still ultimately determined by reference to the law or will of God. The point is that even the more religious-minded ethicians at the dawn of modern philosophy focused their interest on the individual human person, his unlimited capacities, his freedom, his opportunities not only for future salvation but for terrestrial accomplishment.

In his *Oration on the Dignity of Man*, Giovanni Pico della Mirandola puts the following speech in the mouth of God. It is typical of this humanistic attitude.

> We have given you, O Adam . . . according to your desire and judgment, whatever place, whatever form, and whatever functions you shall desire. The nature of other creatures, which has been determined, is confined within the bounds prescribed by Us. You, who are confined by no limits, shall determine for yourself your own nature, in accordance with your own free will, in whose hand I have placed you. . . . You may fashion yourself in whatever form you shall prefer.[2]

No twentieth-century existentialist would criticize the thrust of this declaration of man's freedom to make of himself whatever he willed. However, the *Notebooks* of Leonardo da Vinci (1452–1519) show that all is not optimism in the Renaissance outlook on man. At one point Leonardo warns prophetically:

Creatures shall be seen upon the earth who will always be fighting one with another, with very great losses and frequent deaths on either side. These shall set no bounds to their malice; by their fierce limbs a great number of the trees in the immense forests of the world shall be laid level with the ground; and when they have crammed themselves with food it shall gratify their desire to deal out death, affliction, labours, terrors and banishment to every living thing. And by reason of their boundless pride they shall wish to rise towards heaven. . . .[3]

Tied in with this humanism was Renaissance classicism. Most of the Greek and Roman ethicians were edited, printed for the first time, and avidly studied in the fifteenth and sixteenth centuries. Plato, Aristotle, the Stoics and Epicureans, Seneca, Cicero, and Plotinus were now re-examined. Nor were the classics of Christian wisdom neglected: there was a renewed interest in the Greek and Latin Fathers of the Church and even in the teaching of Scholastics such as Thomas Aquinas and Duns Scotus. Mankind became newly conscious of the worth of its heritage from the past at the same time that it looked forward to a greater future on earth.

Platonic Ethics in Italy

One branch of this neoclassicism involved the revival of Platonism. The Church Council of Florence (1438–1445) was concerned with the project of reuniting the Greek and Latin branches of Christendom. Greek scholars (Gemistus Pletho, Georgios Scholarios, Teodoro Gaza, and Cardinal Bessarion) wrote on philosophical as well as religious topics. There was a tendency to downgrade Aristotle and to stress the thought of Plato and his school. Under Cosimo de' Medici a Florentine school of Platonic studies developed, partly as a courtly fad but also as a serious center of renewal in Christian education. Scarcely any formal writing or academic teaching of ethics was carried on in this school but its influence on other types of Renaissance ethics was profound. In this group we shall consider the thought of men like Nicholas of Cusa, Laurentius Valla, Marsilio Ficino, Giovanni Pico della Mirandola, Giordano Bruno, and Tommaso Campanella. All of them made some contribution to the growth of new philosophical attitudes in Italy.

Nicholas of Cusa was neither an Italian nor a simple Platonist but we will consider him here because he did much of his work in Italy and he incorporated a good deal of Platonism into his highly personal approach to ethics. His name was Nicholas Kryfts (Krebs) and he was born at Kues (Cusa) on the Moselle River, in 1401. His education at Deventer, Heidelberg, and Padua led to a doctorate in canon law and various services as an ecclesiastical diplomat. Raised to the cardinalate in 1448, Nicholas died at Todi (Italy) in 1464. In spite of his involvement in the external affairs of his Church, he managed to write a good number of philosophical works. Of these, the treatise *On Learned Ignorance* (1440) and the work *On the Vision of God* (1453) deserve special mention. They combine several strains of Greek philosophy (Plato, Pythagoras, Plotinus) with various types of Christian thought (Augustine, Albert, Meister Eckhart) and even include a certain amount of dabbling in writers on magic and the mystery religions of the East. Some commentators see Nicholas as a continuator of the nominalism of William of Ockham.

Nicholas is critical of Aristotelian philosophy and its effects on theology and moral teaching. He sees the principle of contradiction as the keynote to the method of Aristotle. In his *On Learned Ignorance* (with a further development in the contemporary *De conjecturis*) he argues that contradiction may be overcome in infinity. In the absolute maximum of reality there is a *coincidentia oppositorum*, a fusion of contraries, which transcends the ordinary oppositions of syllogistic logic. This maximum is at once Creator and creature.[4] Human nature exists in the individual only but in the case of the human nature of Christ we find the absolute maximum, the unique instance of the microcosm which combines perfections of the lowest and highest order. The notion of "learned ignorance" goes back to Socrates, of course, but Nicholas sees this ignorance as the essence of wisdom. When he faces the infinite, man most requires the humility that consists in realizing his intellectual limitations.

Ethically, Nicholas is a teleological eudaimonist. Man's "intellect has a natural movement towards the most abstract truth as being the end of all its desires and its final and most delectable object."[5] This ultimate end of moral activity is God. To understand how to achieve final union with God one must start with faith. "In every science certain things must be accepted as first principles if the subject matter is to be understood; and these first postulates rest only upon faith."[6] There is, however, a natural desire in man's mind for the eternal. Thus the study of the good life for man (ethics) involves a combination of faith and natural understanding.

Very much interested in the eventual union of all men in one religion, Nicholas argued that there are a small number of initial moral rules known intuitively by all nations. These he takes to be roughly equivalent to the precepts of the Decalogue and the two Christian precepts of charity. All moral laws can be traced back to love as their source. His treatise *On the Peace of Faith* (1453) is a dialogue that develops this idea that men of all religions and all nationalities are in basic moral agreement on how to live well. Optimistically, Nicholas concludes this treatise: "Therefore, it was concluded from reason that in heaven a harmony is somehow permitted."[7] The influence of this remarkable thinker is found not only in his immediate successors of the Italian Renaissance but in much German mystical and moral speculation and even in the metaphysical edifices of Spinoza, Schelling, and Hegel.

One of the first Italian humanists to treat of ethical problems was Laurentius Valla (1406–1457). He was a blunt critic of Aristotelian philosophy and his *De voluptate* offers a defense of Epicurean ethics. Valla argued in the treatise *On Free Choice* that the relation of human freedom to divine omnipotence is such a great problem that philosophy cannot solve it. Like his contemporary, Nicholas of Cusa, Valla felt that faith was a necessary starting point for philosophy and that some problems can only be handled with the resources of Christian belief.

The two outstanding Platonists of this period in Italy were Marsilio Ficino and John Pico della Mirandola. Ficino (1433–1499) was the central figure in the Florentine academy and he made the first Latin translation of Plotinus' *Enneads*. He also translated and commented on several Platonic dialogues. The work in which his own somewhat eclectic ethical view is best seen is the *Platonic Theology* but he also developed his teaching in the *Book on Pleasure* and the treatise *On Divine Love*. Like Nicholas, Ficino exalted love as the ideal standard of moral living: the love that binds all men in one species as children of God is called *humanitas*.[8] This ideal "humanity" is the source not only of the goodness and beauty in the life of the individual man; it is the standard of perfection in the arts and all human endeavors. Ficino is a pioneer in the introduction of humanism into modern philosophy. Like all followers of Plotinus, he taught that true happiness requires a turning from the earthly to the transcendent: "Our soul by means of the intellect and will, as by those twin Platonic wings, flies toward God."[9]

The same theme of "flight from the world" is evident throughout the writing of Giovanni Pico della Mirandola (1463–1494). Echoing passages from the Old and New Testaments in a text that is basically Platonic, Pico says:

> Let us therefore fly from the world, which is confirmed in evil [cf. I John 5:19]; let us soar to the Father in whom are the peace that unifies, the true light, and the greatest happiness. But what will give us wings to soar [cf. Ps. 44:7]? The love of the things that are above [cf. Col. 3:1–3]. What will take them from us? The lust for the things below, to follow which is to lose unity, truth, and goodness.[10]

As we saw at the beginning of this chapter, Pico epitomized the Renaissance optimism in regard to the future of mankind in his *Oration on the Dignity of Man* (1486). While he was eclectic in his ethics and openly expressed his aspiration to combine the philosophies of Plato and Aritotle, Pico was actually the funnel through which Platonic ideals poured into sixteenth-century ethical writings. British Platonism is particularly indebted to him, as can be seen from Thomas Elyot's translation of Pico's *Rules of a Christian Lyfe* (1534), and from Thomas More's translation of the *Life of Pico della Mirandola* (1510), which was written by John Pico's nephew Gianfrancesco.

Even more influential was Giordano Bruno (1548–1600), who produced three ethical treatises: *The Expulsion of the Triumphant Beast* (1584), *The Cabal of the Horse Pegasus* (1585), and *The Heroic Frenzies* (1585). His speculative philosophy was much influenced by Neoplatonism and the theory of the *coincidentia oppositorum* of Nicholas of Cusa. The result in Bruno is something very close to a pantheism. Man as an individual is merely a modification of infinite substance. Yet man does live some sort of moral life by taking a personal stand in relation to the ongoing process of cosmic nature under the direction of divine necessity. It is clear that Stoicism lies in the background of Bruno's ethical theory and Spinozism in its foreground. One interpreter sums up Bruno's view of the ethical life as follows:

> When man, through wisdom, knows the eternal law and accepts it in his will, and he tends toward the goal assigned to the universe by God and in a social life regulated by the Law he represents the perfection of the world—he then becomes God's instrument in the accomplishment of the ends of the Cosmos.[11]

The "heroic frenzy" in Bruno's poetic language means the agony that the human individual undergoes in trying to assert some degree of freedom and personality in a universe which is ruled by necessity and in which a man is but a bubble in the infinite.

Fragments of ethical theories of quite diverse origin appear disconcertingly in Bruno's writings. Thus in the work *On the Infinite, Universe and Worlds* he suggests that "there is in the spirit of everyone a certain natural holiness, which sits in the inmost shrine of the intellect, and distinguishes between good and evil."[12] This may simply be an echo of the Scholastic theory of synderesis. On the other hand, his notion that the heart is the center, or monad, from which radiate all the forces of human life and feeling, is frankly attributed by Bruno himself to Pythagoreanism.[13] So conceived, the "heart" becomes (with reason, concupiscence, and will) one of the four powers in which virtue may grow. Prudence in practical reason, fortitude in the heart, temperance in the concupiscible power—all three are subsumed under justice as a general virtue. This is, of course, very much like the teaching in the fourth book of Plato's *Republic*. Bruno's rather chaotic ethics may have influenced Leibniz and Spinoza; there is no question that he was popular with some of the German idealistic ethicians from Hegel onward.

With Tommaso Campanella (1568–1639) we are much removed from the simple Platonism of the early Florentine school. Yet his *City of the Sun* is a utopian work which owes something to Plato's *Republic*. Although his theory of knowledge seems to reduce all human knowing to sense perception, Campanella speaks of the soul introspecting and finding that its three inner attributes are power (*posse*), cognition (*nosse*), and will (*velle*). These are paralleled by the divine attributes: omnipotence, omniscience, and goodness. He even suggests that the ideal state will have three rulers corresponding to the foregoing: Power (in charge of war and peace), Wisdom (in charge of arts, sciences, and education), and Love (in charge of the procreation and upbringing of children). What is good for the individual citizen depends on the promotion of the welfare of society. In this teaching he may have anticipated in a vague way the later theory of social utilitarianism.

Platonic Ethics in England

A similar trend toward the philosophy of Plato is also found in England. Underlying all versions of Platonic ethics is the conviction that there are certain universal standards of goodness, rectitude, temperance, courage, equality, and so on. In Christian Platonism (which is what is found in the Renaissance) these ideals of virtue are considered to exist as exemplars in the mind of God. Such a view was very widespread in European centers of learning at the beginning of the modern era. Even thinkers like Bruno and Campanella who came to be regarded as heretics by ecclesiastical authorities did not challenge this teaching. Nor did the Protestant Reformation necessarily require the abandoning of the Platonic position in ethics, even though it became more and more difficult to maintain such a universalism in company with a nominalistic theory of knowledge and reality. The fact is that many personalities in the early Reformation movement did combine Platonism with their moral and religious views. Nowhere was this more evident than in early British humanism.

We have seen in the preceding chapter how Richard Hooker, in the last half of the sixteenth century, taught a kind of ethics that is in direct continuity with the *recta ratio* doctrine of Thomas Aquinas in the thirteenth century. To many readers at the end of the Renaissance (and to many today), Hooker would look like an ethical Platonist.[14] Much the same judgment could be made on that little-understood school of British philosophers called the "Cambridge Platonists." They, too, are Platonist in only a very special sense; we shall examine their ethical position in the next chapter. At present we are concerned with the rather direct influence of some of Plato's philosophy on English ethicians of the Renaissance. It would be possible to discuss many writers under this category, since nearly all English classical scholars of the period have some interest in Plato's moral dialogues, but our survey will be limited to three leading figures.

One of the most unusual humanists in Renaissance England was Thomas More (1478–1535). A Catholic layman, he became lord chancellor of England and was executed for refusing to acknowledge that Henry VIII was head of the Church in England. More's *Utopia* was written in Latin and published on the Continent forty-five years before its posthumous appearance in English from a London printer. The work is obviously influenced by Plato's *Republic*. It also appears to be a reaction to Machiavelli's *The Prince* (1513), but the fact is that More did not know the Italian treatise.[15]

The ethical position taken by More in his *Utopia* is deliberately marked off from Biblical and early Christian moralizing. After arguing that reason may develop certain principles of natural religion, More proceeds to a theory of psychological hedonism limited only by a reasonable concern for the welfare of society. Few secondary works seem to note this important statement of ethical egoism a whole century before Hobbes, and of the theory of natural religion a hundred years in anticipation of Herbert of Cherbury. Speaking of the Utopians, Thomas More writes:

> They define virtue thus, that it is a living according to Nature, and think that we are made by God for that end; they believe that a man follows the dictates of Nature when he pursues or avoids things according to the direction of reason; they say that the first dictate of reason is the kindling in us a love and reverence for the Divine Majesty, to whom we owe both all that we have and all that we can hope for. In the next place, reason directs us to keep our minds as free from passion and as cheerful as we can, and that we should consider ourselves as bound by the ties of good-nature and humanity to use our utmost endeavors to help forward the happiness of all other persons. . . .[16]

Thus far, More's view does not differ from that of many open-minded and socially conscious Christians. However, he next draws his own inferences about the value of seeking personal pleasure, in the immediately following lines:

> And from thence they infer, that if a man ought to advance the welfare and comfort of the rest of mankind, there being no virtue more proper and peculiar to our nature than to ease the miseries of others, to free from trouble and anxiety in furnishing them with the comforts of life, in which pleasure consists, Nature much more vigorously leads him to do all this for himself. A life of pleasure is either a real evil, and in that case we ought not to assist others in their pursuit of it . . . or if it is a good thing, so that we not only

may, but ought to help others to it, why then ought not a man to begin with himself? Since no man can be more bound to look after the good of another than after his own; for Nature cannot direct us to be good and kind to others, and yet at the same time to be unmerciful and cruel to ourselves. Thus, as they define virtue to be living according to Nature, so they imagine that Nature prompts all people on to seek after pleasure, as the end of all they do.[17]

Later More defines pleasure as "every motion or state, either of body or mind, in which Nature teaches us to delight." Within the next few pages he lists and examines in some detail what these mental and physical satisfactions are considered to be. Hobbes no doubt read all this and liked it.

If Thomas More's ethics is Platonic in a broad sense (as inspired by the *Republic* and a view that man's universal nature indicates the way of virtue to each person), then the outlook of Sir Thomas Elyot (*ca.* 1490-1546) is more strictly in the classic tradition of Plato. We have already noted that Elyot was associated with Italian Platonism by virtue of his translation of *The Rules of a Christian Life* written by Giovanni Picc della Mirandola (1534). Several years earlier Elyot had composed *The Boke Named the Governour*, in continuation of the medieval literary tradition of the "Book for Princes." Elyot's ethical foundation for the education of a political ruler follows close upon the Greek doctrine of the great virtues. Prudence, justice, fortitude, and temperance are discussed with all their "parts" or associated virtues. The one nonclassical virtue inserted by Elyot is that of faith.[18] Aristotle is much quoted throughout but Plato is "the most noble Philosopher." Perhaps the greatest contribution from Thomas Elyot to English ethical writing is his coining of many new vernacular terms to express the nuances of practical discourse. He, more than any other, may be regarded as the father of ethics written in English.[19]

Although a poet and not a moral philosopher, Edmund Spenser (c. 1552-1599) probably did more than any philosophical writer of the period to transmit the Platonic outlook on the good and the beautiful to England. Compare him with a contemporary named William Baldwin who published in 1597 A *Treatise of Morall Philosophy, Wherein Is Contained the Worthy Sayings of Philosophers, Emperors, Kings, and Orators.* The contribution of Baldwin's work is minimal.[20] On the other hand, Spenser Foure Hymnes publicized the doctrine that there are ideal standards of aesthetic and moral judgment which immutably and eternally regulate the proper expressions of human taste. Thus the *Hymne in Honour of Beaut* speaks of the "goodly Paterne" from which the Creator ("the grea Workmaister") has formed all things on earth. It further suggests that the human soul is similarly informed from above with the "seede of vertue Spenser's stress on the moral influence of high-minded love indicates the source of this poem: the treatise *De amore divino* of Marsilio Ficino. In point of fact, most British writing on Platonic ethics is tributary to Italian humanism.

Aristotelian Ethics in the Renaissance

The works of Aristotle that have survived are not elegant and attractive literary pieces. In the estimation of a period which valued aesthetic appeal, the *Nicomachean Ethics* ranked quite low. Yet one of the earliest of the Italian classicists, Leonardo Bruni, or Aretino (1369-1444), translated it along with the *Politics*. Even in his own *Introduction to Moral Instruction* (*Isagogicon Moralis Disciplinae*) Leonardo Bruni gives preference to the ethics of Aristotle, although he offers brief glimpses of the moral philosophies of the other Greek schools.[21]

In Renaissance Italy the great center of Aristotelian studies was Padua and many of the books written in this school were published by the printers of nearby Venice. The Paduan Aristotelians, unlike the majority of Renaissance scholars, were nonclerics. Medical doctors in north Italy took up the study of the scientific works of Aristotle and expanded their interests in the direction of the Averroistic interpretation of the peripatetic psychology and philosophy.[22] Their commentaries stressed the empirical and materialistic tendencies of the original works. In the area of practical philosophy, their Aristotelianism was somewhat deterministic and materialistic in orientation. The annotations of men like Alexander Achillini (1463-1512), Agostino Nifo (1473-1546), Marcantonio Zimara (d. 1532), and Giacomo Zabarella (1533-1589) were printed with the early Latin editions of Aristotle's works. They influenced even Scholastic writers of the period (such as Cardinal Tommaso de Vio, known as Cajetan, 1469-1534) so that they hesitated to offer philosophical arguments for the spirituality and immortality of the human soul and for the freedom of man and the noneternity of the world.

Pietro Pomponazzi (1462-1525) actually criticized the Averroist interpretation of Aristotle, in his treatise on the *Immortality of the Soul*. Yet he also argued that Aquinas had been too optimistic in thinking that he could establish the spirituality and immortality of the soul by using Aristotle's philosophy. Pomponazzi insisted that he *believed* these things but did not *know* them philosophically.[23] The thirteenth and fourteenth chapters of the *Immortality of the Soul* show that Pomponazzi viewed *eudaimonia* in terms of man's natural life on earth. The moral goal that is attainable by all men is a life in accord with the usual moral virtues. Man's oft-mentioned desire for immortality is not really different from the brute animal's natural desire to avoid death. Thus we have a version of Renaissance Aristotelian ethics which is completely naturalistic.

Pomponazzi always professed to believe in Christianity but one of his followers, Lucilio Vanini (1585–1619), pushed this position to its extreme in openly attacking the established religion in England. Vanini was eventually convicted as a libertine and atheist, at Toulouse. In contemporary Soviet scholarship, Vanini is regarded as an important predecessor of Diderot, Helvétius, and d'Holbach, as well as of dialectical materialism.[24]

A quite different school of Aristotelian ethics is found in Catholic Scholasticism. Its activities were centered in Spain and Portugal but extended somewhat into other countries of Europe. Typical of this movement was Francisco de Vitoria (1480–1546), a Dominican professor at the University of Salamanca. His *Commentary on the Second Part of the Summa Theologiae* is a well-informed study of the moral teaching of Thomas Aquinas. In his treatise *On the Law of War* (1532), however, Vitoria shows more of his personal ability as a practical thinker on problems of international relations. In the thirteenth century, Thomas had stated three conditions that would have to be satisfied before a country could be justified in waging war: (1) that it be waged by the authority of a sovereign state; (2) that it be waged for a just cause; and (3) that it be waged to promote some good or to avoid some evil.[25] Vitoria discusses each of these conditions very thoroughly. As to what is a good reason for going to war, he denies that difference of religion, extension of empire, or the glory of a prince are just causes for making war. He concludes: "There is a single and only just cause for commencing a war, namely, a wrong received. . . ."[26] The other two conditions are similarly clarified by Vitoria. More significant today, he adds a fourth condition of his own: the just war must be conducted in a reasonable and moderate manner. Thus he raises the important ethical question of the use of proper means. In particular, Vitoria emphasizes the point that the good results of a war should exceed the evil consequences: "If any war should be advantageous to one province or nation but injurious to the world or to Christendom, it is my belief that, for this very reason, that war is unjust."[27]

As a consequence of views such as the foregoing, Vitoria is regarded by many as the founder of the theory of international law. He lived at a time when national spirit and the theory of sovereignty reached their peak yet he strongly supported the project of one world state and of a law that would be truly international. This Vitoria viewed as not merely a matter of political expediency; his moral disapproval of refusal to cooperate with world regulation is frankly expressed. "It is clear," Vitoria wrote, "that they who violate these international rules, whether in peace or in war, commit a mortal sin." No Scholastic philosopher could be more forthright.

Besides the Dominican writers in the Iberian Peninsula the outstanding group of Aristotelian Scholastics was found in the Society of Jesus. Almost from the beginning the textbook for philosophical studies in the Jesuit course of studies was the *Opera Omnia* of Aristotle. A Renaissance Jesuit, Sylvester Maurus (1619-1687), provided the standard printing, with commentary, of Aristotle in Latin. In the textbook series published by the Jesuits of Coimbra (the famous *Cursus Conimbricensis*) the commentary on the *Nicomachean Ethics* went through many printings.[28] The Jesuit, Juan de Mariana (1536-1624), was very much in the tradition of Aristotle in his treatise on *The King and the Education of the King* (1599). In opposing the idea that whatever the ruler decreed was morally binding, Mariana was one of the originators of the theory of limited monarchy and of the origin of political power in the people.

The founder of the Jesuits, Ignatius of Loyola (*ca.* 1491-1556), had studied philosophy and theology at the University of Paris. He came away with a tremendous respect for Aristotle. The Jesuit concept of the education of the whole man owes a good deal to the ideals of classical humanism.[29] One of the early scholars who developed this ideal was Robert Bellarmine (1542-1621). It is possible that he was the Renaissance Jesuit who best understood the practical philosophy of Thomas Aquinas, but his *Lectures on the Summa of Theology* have never been edited although they are preserved in the archives of the Gregorian University in Rome. We do know that on the thorny question of freedom of choice Bellarmine maintained that the act of human election is a joint function of intellect and will. Thus freedom is a function of the whole man and not merely of his will. In fact, the will "is free in electing, not because it is not necessarily determined by the last and practical judgment of reason, but because this ultimate and practical judgment is in the power of the will."[30]

Francisco Suárez (1548-1617) was the most important and influential ethician in the Renaissance. This Spanish Jesuit exerted a strong influence on many textbooks in ethics, in both the Catholic and Protestant traditions, well into the nineteenth century. Even today Suárez is important in the moral writings of Catholic thinkers in Spain and the Latin-American countries. Until a generation ago most ethics textbooks produced by British and United States scholastic ethicians were Suarezian in inspiration.

The works of Suárez that are of significance in the history of ethics are four. He taught a course *On the Soul* when he was a young man (possibly at Segovia, 1571), which he partly revised before his death; this is the *De Anima* published in 1621. It gives a good exposition of his early psychological views. Second, Suárez gave a series of lectures in moral theology (remotely based on Aquinas, *Summa Theologiae*, I-II) at the Roman College of the Jesuits, probably in 1580-1582. This course was posthumously published as a series of disputations entitled *On the Ultimate End, the Voluntary, and the Goodness of Human Acts* (*Opera Omnia,* Tome IV). Third, in his early twenties Suárez made a plan for a huge treatise in metaphysics; it was eventually finished and published in 1597 under the title *Metaphysical Disputations*. The tenth of the twenty "disputations" in this work treats of goodness in all its aspects, including the moral goodness of human acts. Fourth, his treatise *On Laws* was published in 1612; it is very important for his theory of obligation and of the relation of natural law to positive laws.[31]

Suárez continually cited almost two hundred authors from among his predecessors. He developed his own ethical position as a combination and rethinking of the views of Thomas Aquinas, Henry of Ghent, Duns Scotus, William of Ockham, and many others. He regarded himself as a Thomist but his philosophy, in the field of ethics especially, is not identical with that of Thomas Aquinas. Suarezian metaphysics deals with being as conceived almost univocally; the analogy of intrinsic attribution admitted in this theory is far removed from the Thomistic notion of analogy. Essence and *esse* are not radically distinguished by Suárez and his theory of matter and form grants a certain entity to matter that would not be admitted in Thomism. But the two points in Suárez's speculative philosophy which have a most important bearing on his ethics are his diminution of the reality of the universal as a nature, and his depreciation of the role of final causality. He has been accused of nominalism (that is, the view that universal natures, such as humanity, are merely terms or signs) but his actual position seems somewhere between the terminism of Ockham and the moderate realism of Thomas. Suárez thought that a universal is a concept produced by the discursive action of the possible intellect moving from its initial conception of individual beings to a generalized meaning.[ ] As a result of this diminished reality in the universality of human nature, Suárez is forced to adopt a teaching on ethical obligation that stresses the basing of this oughtness on God's will.

Of equal importance is the growth of the doctrine that the only important kind of causality is efficiency. In Aristotle, and in his commentators up to the fourteenth century, the final cause or end of an event was thought to be at least as important in the explanation of operations as was the efficient cause or agent. All the different kinds of things, trees and dogs and men, were thought to have natures with a finality (end-directedness) peculiar to each type of being. In such a metaphysics, the good actions of each species of being were those that promoted the development of this being as tending naturally toward its end. Ockham was one of the first thinkers to challenge this teaching on the finality of human nature. By the time that Francisco Suárez began to teach, it caused little or no stir when he bluntly called the causality of the end a metaphor.[33] This takes much of the force out of a teleological approach to ethical judgment. It is usually said that Francis Bacon threw final causes out of scientific explanation: they had already been thrown out in the fourteenth century.

The language of Suárez's ethics, then, is reminiscent of that of Thomas but the actual thinking is different. When the Spanish Jesuit says the human nature is the proximate standard of ethical judgment, he means what has come to be called in Suarezian textbooks *"natura humana adequate considerata,"* that is, man viewed in all his essential relations. Internally, each man (the individual, not the universal) is composed of certain vegetal, sensory, and rational capacities; externally, each man is related to God, other men, and to subhuman things, in an order of rights and duties. This contextual view of the individual person is what a Suarezian means by human nature adequately considered.[34]

Suárez is a natural law ethician. He was a law student before becoming a Jesuit and he retained something of the mentality of the legal thinker. Natural law, for Suárez, is that part of the eternal law in which God freely decrees with His will the order to be observed in the free actions of intellectual creatures.[35] Moral law may be viewed in two ways: actively, as issuing from the divine will; passively, as received and accepted by men. Man's reason is the power in which natural law is known. We still have the language of "right reason" in Suárez's moral writings. This *recta ratio* is now "the capacity (*vis*) of distinguishing between actions that are suitable and those that are unsuitable to human nature."[36]

A contemporary Jesuit, Gabriel Vásquez (*ca.* 1551–1604), was teaching that natural moral law is identical with man's rational nature. Suárez disagreed, arguing that law (*lex*) has a more definite and limited meaning than nature. Natural law is equivalent, he thought, to the judgments of right reason.[37]

Suárez situates his own position between two extremes that he finds in earlier Scholasticism. Gregory of Rimini (d. 1358) is understood by Suárez as saying that natural law merely "indicates" to man what should or should not be done. As he reads Gregory, this natural law does not really command man but simply shows him the way to live well. In other words, Gregory recognized very little obligation in the constitution of natural law. On the other hand, Suárez takes William of Ockham as a rather thorough divine voluntarist: God's will is the sole source of all distinctions between moral good and evil. So understood, Ockhamism would be a pure extrinsicism: nothing in the nature of man or his actions would ground ethical judgments. Suárez tries to find a middle way: as he sees it, natural law has an obligatory force from the will of God but the fact that some actions are good for man is not the result of an arbitrary divine fiat; it is implied in a man's relations to his environment. Interpreters of the ethics of Suárez differ as to whether this is a moral voluntarism or an intellectualism.

In any event, three kinds of precepts make up the content of natural law, in Suárez. Primary precepts are rules known immediately and intuitively by all normal human beings: the standard example is, "Do good and avoid evil." Secondary precepts are more specific and limited; they require a certain amount of experience and thought so that their terms may be understood, but these are also self-evident principles. Examples are: "Do no injury to anyone" and "Live temperately." Suárez thought that these primary and secondary principles of ethical judgment do not change, except in the sense that new conditions or new knowledge may broaden the meaning of their component terms.[38] Lastly, there are tertiary precepts of moral law which require study and discursive reasoning to ground them. They are not self-evident but are derived from more basic rules. Precepts of this character are exemplified by: "Lying is always immoral" and "Usury is unjust."[39]

In his De Anima (4, 10, 9) the youthful Suárez had taught that moral conscience is not merely an act of practical judgment but that it is a habit of practical reason. In his later works, however, he described conscience as that judgment of practical understanding by which a man distinguishes between concrete good and evil (bonum et malum) and between what is commanded or prohibited (praeceptum vel prohibitum). In this development he tended to agree with Thomas Aquinas.[40] So defined, conscience may be certain or doubtful. If certain, one must act in accord with conscience in order to do good. If doubtful, moral conscience is not an adequate guide; something should be done to remove the doubt, either by getting more information about facts or law, or by using "reflex principles." One such principle is the rule of tutiorism when in doubt always do what is morally "safe." Another reflex principle is that of probabilism: when in doubt one may follow the guidance of any respected authority or expert, even if his judgment is not a majority opinion.[41] The application of these rules for the solution of problems of conscience is worked out in great detail. With other such reflex principles they have become part of the standard procedure used in that kind of applied moralizing which is called casuistry.

It would be difficult to overstate the scope of Suárez's influence in ethics. Many of the leading modern philosophers from Hobbes to Schopenhauer studied ethics in textbooks written from a partly Suarezian viewpoint. The seventeenth century saw the publication of dozens of manuals of moral philosophy written by both Catholic and Protestant ethicians. In most of these academic books the ethics of Suárez had some influence. Two examples of this sort of thing may be taken as typical. In Holland, Francis Burgersdijck (1590–1635) published a much used textbook, Idea philosophiae moralis (Leiden, 1644). This book is a Protestant version of Suárez. It was the work that introduced John Stuart Mill to ethics.[42] Another Dutch Protestant ethician, Adriaan Heereboord (1614–1661), studied under Burgersdijck at the University of Leiden and eventually wrote his own textbook, Philosophia rationalis, moralis et naturalis (Leiden, 1654). Heereboord is often treated as a follower of Descartes; he was also an admirer of the ethics of Suárez.

Protestant Reform Ethics

This introduces the problem of the status of moral philosophy in the scholarship of the Reformed Churches. Philosophy, whether theoretical or practical, did not occupy a high place in the esteem of some of the initiators of the Protestant Reformation. As one historian puts it: "Luther and the early reformers were bitter in their attacks upon Scholasticism and the influence of Aristotle, 'the damned heathen,' although later Protestants were not averse to explaining their theology by scholastic methods." Indeed, Martin Luther (1483-1546) had little use for philosophical ethics; he has been called "that most unphilosophical of characters."[43] Yet he did exert a great influence on later ethics and provided an excellent example of theological approbative ethics in a very pure form. A recent history sums up Luther's view: "The only true moral rules are the divine commandments; and the divine commandments are understood in an Occamist perspective—that is to say, they have no further rationale or justification than that they are the injunctions of God."[44] In *The Bondage of the Will*, Luther wrote:

> But a man cannot be thoroughly humbled until he comes to know that his salvation is utterly beyond his own powers, counsel, endeavours, will, and works, and absolutely depending on the will, counsel, pleasure, and word of another, that is, of God only.[45]

The positive influence of Luther on modern ethics would seem to lie chiefly in his view of personal freedom. In spite of the fact that Luther wrote his *Bondage of the Will* to refute Erasmus' *Treatise on Free Choice* (*De libero arbitrio diatribe sive collatio*, 1524), it is clear that Luther placed the act of faith, or individual submission to the Will of God, in the "heart" or will. His denial of "free will" in man, at the conclusion of *The Bondage of the Will*, is simply a statement of the limitations under which human volition operates. Luther did a great deal to bring this problem of man's freedom under God to the forefront of attention in modern ethics. This emphasis on the individual man continued in the writings of Martin Bucer or Butzer (1491-1551), who was originally a Dominican friar and who preached on the importance of personal love of God as the keynote of the moral life, during his period at Strasbourg (1523-1549) and eventually at Cambridge University in England (1549-1551).

One of the most learned men among the early reformers was Philip Melanchthon (1497-1560). He did not share the general antipathy to Aristotle but lectured on the *Nicomachean Ethics* at Wittenberg and published his *Scholia* in 1542. Melanchthon also wrote a textbook in ethics (*Elementa philosophiae moralis*). His personal teaching in ethics was distinguished by a theory of innate ideas (which may have influenced Leibniz). He thought that every man is endowed with a natural light (*lumen naturale*) that enlightens him with the idea of God and with certain inborn ethical principles from which his moral conduct may be directed.

John Calvin (1509–1564) was another reformer who, though not a formal ethician, left his mark on practical philosophy. His teaching on original sin made men subject not only to the punishment for the sin of Adam but also with a nature vitiated by "the pollution to which the punishment is justly due."[46] Convinced of the utter depravity of all men, Calvin drew up a strict and harsh code of human conduct and then showed his opinion of academic ethics by saying: "Now let those who are of the opinion that the philosophers have the only just and orderly systems of moral philosophy show me, in any of their works, a more excellent economy than that which I have stated."[47] There is in Calvin's teaching on the absolute control of men by the divine will a view of moral law which is antithetic to the whole idea of natural law.[48]

Of course, there were some early Protestant scholars who wrote and taught ethics of a more conventional and academic sort. We have already noted how people like Burgersdijck and Heereboord carried on much of the Scholastic tradition. Erhard Weigel (1625–1699) produced in Germany a version of Aristotelian ethics in geometric style: *Analysis Aristotelica ex Euclide restituta* (1658). Leibniz was probably referring to this work when he mentioned an *Ethica Euclidea* that was a source for Pufendorf.[49] Another German textbook writer who was much in vogue on the Continent and in England was Bartholomaeus Keckermann (1571–1608). His *System of Ethics* (1607) is very critical of Aristotelian Scholasticism. Keckermann was associated with the attempt to supplant philosophy with rhetoric, in the movement founded by Pierre la Ramée (1515–1572) in French Calvinism.

Entirely apart from the academic tradition in ethics was the thought of the Silesian shoemaker Jakob Böhme or Behmen (1575–1624). He was a very unusual thinker, something of a mystic and something of a Protestant heretic. He saw God as a combination of good and evil (probably under the influence of some preacher who had read Nicholas of Cusa). At times Böhme seems to have adopted a dualistic theory of evil in which man's falling away from moral goodness is attributed to Satan, as a primordial cause of evil. An eschatological thinker, Böhme believed that all men would probably be brought back to goodness in the final days of creation. He took some of his teachings from another Protestant moralist, Valentine Weigel (1533–1588, not to be confused with Erhard Weigel in the seventeenth century). Valentine Weigel wrote both in Latin (*Libellus de beata vita,* Halle, 1609) and in German

(*Erkenne dich selbst,* Neustadt, 1615). He was a devotee of the thought of Nicholas of Cusa. These men, especially Böhme, exerted a great influence on the ethical and religious thinking of the later German romantics.[50]

Neoclassical Ethics in the Renaissance

Platonism and Aristotelianism were by no means the only kinds of classical philosophy to be revived in this period. The three other schools that gave rise to some ethical speculation were skepticism, Epicureanism, and Stoicism. We shall examine each briefly.

Ethical skepticism might be defined as any point of view that denies that the moral philosopher has anything of value to teach. In this broad sense, Luther, Calvin, and many other religious teachers who are suspicious of ethics, would be skeptics. A Catholic layman, Franz von Baader (1765–1841), expressed this attitude pungently: should the devil ever appear on earth, said von Baader, it would be in the garb of a professor of moral philosophy!

Besides this sort of thing there are several Renaissance examples of men who took the position that it is nonsense to try to distinguish moral good from evil. Niccolò Machiavelli (1469–1527) is one of the first names to come to mind. His treatise *The Prince* (1513) and his *Discourses on Livy* (1517) are now classic examples of the view that if you want something badly enough you may do almost anything to get it. He was fascinated by the problem of political power: his solution to this problem is frankly amoral, as these lines indicate:

> It is necessary for a prince, who wishes to maintain himself, to learn how not to be good, and to use this knowledge and not use it, according to the necessities of the case. . . . Some things which seem virtues would, if followed, lead to one's ruin, and some others which appear vices result in one's great security and wellbeing.[51]

This political cynicism seems to be based on a thoroughgoing ethical skepticism. Human actions are good or bad solely in terms of their technical competence as means to achieve a given end, in this case the preservation of political power. This may be viewed as an anticipation of utilitarianism of a peculiar sort: the standard is the advantage of the individual who happens to exercise civil power. This is not a formal species of ethics, perhaps, but it is an ethical position which has had many adherents.

More in the tradition of the Greek skeptics were some of the philosophers of sixteenth-century France. Michel de Montaigne (1533–1592) has had a minor role in the history of ethics. His *Essays* (first published in 1580, revised several times by Montaigne) show a mind which is very pessimistic about the value of any kind of natural science or wisdom. He felt that the teachings of Christianity are at least as believable as any of the deliverances of the philosophers. Montaigne adds, however:

> Should I examine, finally, whether it be in the power of man to find out that which he seeks, and if that quest wherein he has busied himself so many ages has enriched him with any new force or any solid truth: I believe he will confess, if he speaks from his conscience, that all he has got by so long an inquiry is only to have learned to know his own weakness. We have only by long study confirmed and verified the natural ignorance we were in before.[52]

As one historian has expressed it very well, Montaigne's best advice as a moralist reduces to this rule: "Be content with your own human reality and learn to enjoy it moderately under its temporal, composite, and habit-forming conditions."[53] There is some resemblance between this "situationism" of Montaigne and the existential stance adopted by a thinker like Albert Camus. The great difference is that Montaigne felt that he could live a decent human life, whereas Camus was never quite sure of that.

Other examples of Gallic skepticism in Renaissance ethics are not hard to find. Pierre Charron (1541–1603) was a French priest who also based his moral philosophy on a special kind of skepticism. His work on *The Three Truths* (1593) was actually a defense of theistic belief and of Christian teachings. But his treatise *On Wisdom* (1601) criticized what he saw as the pretensions of philosophical wisdom. Theoretical philosophy had little appeal for Charron but he thought that there was a place for the practical wisdom of the ordinary man. Stoic ethics, with emphasis on a reasonable following of nature, is combined with a simple acceptance of God's providence.

A Portuguese physician, Franciscus Sanchez (ca. 1552–1632), became an instructor in medicine at Montpellier and Toulouse. He was impressed by the classic doubt of Pyrrho and also by an argument from Nicholas of Cusa. To know any one thing well a person would have to know all things, and this is impossible. Sanchez's treatise *That Nothing Is Known* (1580) not only presents this negative conclusion; it suggests that empirical knowledge (as contrasted with syllogistically deduced systems) is possible. Because Sanchez stressed introspective experience of man's psychic functions, he was a contributing factor in turning the attention of philosophers and ethicians in the next generation, or so, to the study of personal consciousness.

Epicureanism, in the sense of an ethic of personal pleasure, had some devotees in Renaissance Italy. We have seen that Laurentius Valla wrote an essay on pleasure (*De Voluptate*) that combined Plato with

Epicurus. The fifth dialogue in Giordano Bruno's *Concerning the Infinite* quotes at length from Lucretius' Epicurean poem *On the Nature of Things*. However, the primary example of ethical hedonism in the Renaissance is the French priest Pierre Gassendi (1592–1655). Chronologically, Gassendi is quite late to be considered as in this period (he is a contemporary of Descartes) but the ethical content of his writings is similar to that of many Renaissance writings, being merely a revival of the material on Epicurus and his teaching, as found in the tenth book of Diogenes Laërtius. Two points, however, are distinctive in Gassendi's version of the ethics of pleasure. First, unlike the original Epicureans, Gassendi believed that personal happiness is not attainable in this life but may be secured in the future life. His treatises *On the Life and Moral Teachings of Epicurus* (1647) and *Outlines of the Philosophy of Epicurus* (1658) offer a fusion of diluted Christian ethics with hedonism. Second, just as the Greek hedonists questioned the Stoic acceptance of the law of reason in nature, so Gassendi preceded Hobbes in attacking ethics based on the immutable and universal laws of nature. It is noteworthy that Ralph Cudworth treats Gassendi, along with Hobbes, as the prime opponent of the theory of natural justice.[54] On the Continent, then, Pierre Gassendi represents a transitional stage of ethical egoism.

Stoicism was much more popular than Epicureanism among ethical theorists of the Renaissance. In the Low Countries, Justus Lipsius, or Joest Lips (1547–1606), translated Seneca into the vernacular and wrote an *Introduction to Stoic Philosophy* which attempted to combine the practical wisdom of St. Augustine with the ethics of the Stoics.[55] Unlike the skeptics who were his contemporaries and who were all influenced by the ethics of Stoicism, Lipsius had a high regard for the theoretical part of Stoicism. He thought that their view of nature and reason does provide a sound basis for a system of ethics.[56]

Equally prominent as a Neo-Stoic ethician was Guillaume Du Vair (1556–1621). He, too, started as a translator, making one of the first vernacular versions of Epictetus' *Enchiridion*. His *Moral Philosophy of the Stoics* (1585) was soon translated into English, as was Lipsius' *Two Books of Constancy*, and these works helped to spread the doctrine of Stoicism in the formative period of British ethics. Besides the usual emphasis on practical wisdom that is characteristic of the Stoic, Du Vair developed his ethics in terms of other virtues held up as ideals: clemency, justice, charity, and constancy. He was one of the first to write on these ethical ideals in French.

Neo-Stoicism was never as influential in British ethics as it was on the Continent. Some of the English humanists were interested in classical Stoicism, of course, but they did not produce an ethics. It has been suggested that the famous translator of Homer, George Chapman (1559–

1634), offered a "flamboyant" morality based on Stoicism in his plays.[57] It is hardly a theoretic ethics. One could argue that Herbert of Cherbury (1583–1648) was a British Stoic ethician. His treatises *On Truth* (1624) and *The Religion of the Gentiles* (1645) expound a theory of innate ideas (*notitiae communes*) that provides a foundation for both natural religion and ethics. The terminology is certainly Stoic, and so, possibly, is the inspiration. Lord Herbert's five innately known truths (as listed in his *De veritate*) are: (1) that God exists; (2) that God should be worshiped; (3) that a life of virtue is the best form of worship; (4) that sins are to be repented; and (5) that there are moral sanctions in the future life.[58] This is much more than Stoicism; it is a type of ethical a priori, long before Immanuel Kant.

In concluding this chapter on the ethics of the Renaissance, one should point out that few, if any, distinctive ethical theories originated at this time. That is the reason why the period is usually omitted from histories of ethics. Yet it should also be evident that the Renaissance marked an important transitional stage from the ethics of the classical and medieval thinkers to the better-known theories of the modern ethicians. In particular, it was in the Renaissance that a new and secular spirit came into ethical thinking. From this time onward, moral philosophy or ethics was no longer the exclusive domain of the cleric. It soon was recognized as a standard discipline in the liberal arts programs of the great university centers. In many, the teaching of philosophy bifurcated into the dual professorate of mental and moral philosophy. This was the real beginning of ethics in the academic institutions of the modern world.

CHAPTER VIII

British Egoism and Its Reactions

IN THIS CHAPTER we shall examine British ethics running through the seventeenth and into the first part of the next century. Most of our thinkers are clergymen in the Anglican or Presbyterian Church; a few are laymen. Many ethical treatises are still written in Latin but English is more and more the language of publication and controversy as the seventeenth century progresses. The central problem in ethics is seen as the explanation of the origin of man's notions of moral good and evil. Practically all these British thinkers assert that the divine will is the ultimate source of moral distinctions, but much diversity is found in their various explanations of how the individual man comes to know what God wills. Much of the ethics in this period consists of indignant rebuttal to Thomas Hobbes's assertion that the moral good is simply whatever pleasure may satisfy a man's desires. Few ethicians in his century accepted that answer, which has come to be called egoistic naturalism.

Something of a transition to the new ethics of the seventeenth century is found in the thought of Francis Bacon (1561–1626), who was actually a Renaissance man. His works still show the influence of medieval Scholasticism, neoclassicism, and empiricism. He wrote no treatise on formal ethics but there is a section in his famous *Advancement of Learning* (1605) where he gives a brief outline of his ethical thinking. The *Essays* (1597) contain much practical moralizing but little ethical theory. Bacon's *New Atlantis* is a utopian fragment that illustrates his interest in the use of knowledge to improve the material conditions of human life.

In the *Advancement of Learning* moral philosophy is described as "that knowledge which considereth of the Appetite and Will of Man."[1] It has two parts: one studies the exemplars of good, virtue, duty, and felicity; the other (the "Georgics of the mind") has to do with cultivating these seeds in the practical life of the individual man. Bacon feels that his predecessors have done rather well with the theory of the good life but earlier moralists have failed to show how these "exemplars" may be applied in practice. He criticizes Seneca, Virgil, Zeno the Stoic, Epictetus, but especially Aristotle, on this score. Aristotle was wrong in taking the life of speculative contemplation as morally the best: the active life is better. Francis Bacon always treats Christian theology (Divinity) with great respect; he professes to approve its teaching that the highest felicity can only be attained in the future world. However, after making his bow to religion he proceeds to ignore it almost entirely. One gets the impression that what is important for Bacon is a good life on earth.[2]

Bacon distinguishes, in the same section of the *Advancement of Learning*, between the private good of the individual man and the common good of human society. The latter is the more important and it is most plainly treated in "Christian law." (This, of course, is but an echo of Scholastic moral teaching.) He gives very little information as to what the requirements of this law may be. There is throughout these chapters the suggestion that moral good and duty somehow are related to the welfare of human society. Bacon's utilitarianism is not obvious but it is there. It is in strong contrast with the egoistic attitude of his one-time secretary, Thomas Hobbes, which we will now consider in some detail.

Hobbes's Ethical Egoism

The moral theory that found somewhat random development in the various writings of Thomas Hobbes (1588–1679) has been one of the most noted and most criticized in the history of the subject. Actually, Hobbes has three systems of ethics: one is a theological approbative theory in which the will of God is the immediate ground of good and evil; the second is a social utilitarianism in which right and wrong are determined by the sovereign power of the state; and the third is the view that has come to be called egoism, in which moral good and evil are equivalent to pleasure and pain for the individual man. It is the third position that is most important historically, for it elicited a great variety of critical responses in the readers of Hobbes.

Hobbes wrote both in Latin and in English. The first work of ethical significance was *The Elements of Law, Natural and Politic*, written in Paris about 1640, partly published in 1650, completely edited and published in 1889. Two parts of this were entitled *Human Nature* and *De corpore politico* (*On the Body Politic*). His *De cive* (*On the Citizen*) was written and first published in Paris (1642). Hobbes's most controversial work was published in 1651: *Leviathan, or the Matter, Form and Power of a Commonwealth, Ecclesiastical and Civil*. This was the book that most disturbed his contemporaries: its general message was that might is right. Some fifteen years later Hobbes finished and published *De corpore* (*On Body*) and *De homine* (*On Man*); these were published in London in 1655 and 1657.

The general philosophical position adopted by Hobbes may be summed up in two words: corporealism and sensism. All reality, he thought, was bodily; all events are of the nature of motion in place. As he describes it: "Motion is a continual relinquishing of one place, and acquiring of another." In men, motions are either *vital* (physiological functions) or *animal* (desire, aversion, and all functions of will). These two kinds of motion include all human activities. This is a thoroughgoing mechanism and it entails the teaching that the function of knowing is merely the motion of certain parts of the human body. "Sense, therefore, in the sentient, can be nothing else but motion in some of the internal parts of the sentient; and the parts so moved are parts of the organs of sense."[3] Understanding becomes simply a motion in the human brain; reasoning is the "addition and substraction" (sic) of sensory images. Will is merely the last act of desire or aversion in any process of deliberation.

Pleasure is that which "helps" vital or animal motion; pain hinders it. Good means whatever is the object of any man's appetite or desire; evil is the object of his aversion.[4] Thus, Hobbes's rule of egoism may be stated: "It is natural, and so reasonable, for each individual to aim solely at his own preservation or pleasure."[5] The distinction of good and evil, then, depends on the relation of the objects of appetite to the person who desires or hates them. In the context of civil society (the commonwealth), actions are good or evil depending on their relations to the laws of a given state. "For it was shown that the civil laws were the rules of *good* and *evil*, *just* and *unjust*, *honest* and *dishonest*; that therefore what the legislator commands, must be held for *good*, and what he forbids for *evil*."[6] And within the framework of the Kingdom of God, what God commands is good and what He forbids is evil.

Hobbes writes, of course, that the law of nature is the "dictate of right reason."[7] This should be understood in reference to his previously mentioned views on intellectual knowledge and its objects. There is no suggestion in Hobbes of a universal human nature that grounds such a law; humanity is merely a name that is conventionally given to some generalization that philosophers find useful in conversation.[8] Hence Hobbes bluntly states: "This *right reason*, which is the law, is no otherwise certainly right than by our making it so by our approbation of it and voluntary subjection to it."[9]

It is well known that Hobbes taught that man, in a state of nature before agreeing to form an organized society, is entirely selfish. This is the condition in which there is *bellum omnium contra omnes* (war of everyone against everyone) and it gives rise, Hobbes says, to the first "law of nature": "that every man ought to endeavour peace, as far as he has hope of obtaining it; and when he cannot obtain it, that he may seek, and use, all helps, and advantages of war."[10] The reason for asserting his first precept is that Hobbes was convinced that every man "has a right to every thing." Of course, men may agree to limit this egoistic claim to all things. This gives rise not only to Hobbes's theory of the conventional contract by which civil society is established but also to his second precept of the law of nature:

> that a man be willing, when others are so too, as far forth, as for peace, and defence of himself he shall think it necessary, to lay down this right to all things; and be contented with so much liberty against other men, as he would allow other men against himself.[11]

Hobbes has such a high opinion of this second precept that he calls it the "law of the Gospel" and the golden rule. Logically it is an odd law of nature, for it enjoins men to get away from the state of nature. If asked why men should obey this second precept, Hobbes would have to say because it promotes the pleasure or preserves the life of each individual who submits to such a limitation of his "natural" appetites. It will be clear to any reader that Hobbes's notion of natural law is quite different from the traditional theory of Richard Hooker or of Thomas Aquinas.

To these two initial precepts of the law of nature Hobbes adds twelve more detailed rules: (1) "that men perform their covenants made"; (2) "that a man who receives benefit from another of grace, endeavour that he which gives it, have not reasonable cause to repent of his good will" (3) "that every man strive to accommodate himself to the rest"; (4) "that upon caution of future time, a man ought to pardon the offences past of them that repenting, desire it"; (5) "that in revenges . . . men look not at the greatness of the evil past, but the greatness of the good to follow" (6) "that no man by deed, word, countenance, gesture, declare hatred or contempt of another"; (7) "that every man acknowledge another for his equal by nature"; (8) "that at the entrance into conditions of peace, no man require to reserve to himself any right, which he is not content should be reserved to every one of the rest"; (9) "that such things as cannot be divided, be enjoyed in common, if it can be; and if the quantity of the thing permit, without stint; otherwise proportionably to the number of them that have right"; (10) "that the entire right; or else, making the use alternate, the first possession, be determined by lot"; (11) "that all men that mediate peace, be allowed safe conduct"; and (12) "that they that are at controversy, submit their right to the judgment of an arbitrator."[12] In case it is not possible for all men to remember all these excellent rules (from Scripture, Roman law, canon law, and classical an-

Scholastic ethics), Hobbes contracts them "into one easy sum," which is a negative formula of the golden rule: "Do not that to another, which thou wouldst not have done to thyself." These laws are immutable and eternal, according to Hobbes, "and the science of them is the true and only moral philosophy."

Often classified as an ethical naturalist, Hobbes would admit that there is a sense in which this is correct: at the lowest level he reduces the ground of ethical judgment to individual approval or disapproval. Yet Hobbes's ethics is also a crude version of the theological approbative theory: God's will or power (they are identical) is the source of the right of nature (*jus naturae*). This does not mean that God has created men in a universe whose ontological structure requires certain types of human behavior (this would be the natural law theory of the thirteenth century); rather, Hobbes explains, these laws stem from His "irresistible power."[13] Or, as he puts it in the *Philosophical Rudiments*:

> The same law which is *natural* and *moral*, is also wont to be called *divine*, not undeservedly; as well because reason, which is the law of nature, is given by God to every man for the rule of his actions; as because the precepts of living which are thence derived, are the same with those which have been delivered from the divine Majesty for the *laws* of his heavenly kingdom, by our Lord Jesus Christ, and and his holy prophets and apostles.[14]

Very few writers in his century were able to accept this pious declaration as genuine. Many wrote in rebuttal.

One of the first of these critics was John Bramhall, Anglican Archbishop of Armagh (*ca.* 1594-1663). He called the *Leviathan* a "horrendous monster." Bramhall's original objections to Hobbes had to do with the denial of free will in Hobbesian psychology.[15] In later essays Bramhall accused Hobbes of overturning all law with his teaching on the "irresistible power" of God.[16]

There are exceptions, of course, to the contemporary resentment of Hobbesian egoism. Sir Thomas Browne (1605-1682)), the author of *Religio Medici* and *Christian Morals*, was quite undisturbed by Hobbes. Browne granted a certain autonomy to moral philosophy but felt that religion was a higher and surer guide. His advice was to "look beyond Antoninus, and terminate not thy morals in Seneca or Epictetus. . . . Be a moralist of the Mount, an Epictetus in the faith, and Christianize thy notions."[17]

One of the first extended criticisms of Hobbes was the treatise *Leviathan Drawn Out with a Hook* (1653) by Alexander Ross, which objected especially to the religious aspects of Hobbes's teaching. Sir James Tyrrell's *A Brief Disquisition of the Law of Nature* (1692) was another typical attack on the moral philosophy of Hobbes. In the second half of the seventeenth century, more than fifty such works appeared in opposition to the religious, political, and ethical views of Thomas Hobbes.[18]

Ethics in Cambridge Platonism

Among the reactions to Hobbes's moral philosophy some of the more important positive developments are found in the writers called the Cambridge Platonists. They were mostly scholars from Emmanuel College, Cambridge (a Puritan center), but their interest lay in the practical applications of Christianity to life. They were not "Platonists" in the sense of devotees of Plato's *Dialogues* but in the broader sense of being epistemological realists, of stressing the universality, immutability, and reality of the objects of human reason. Both natural and supernatural knowledges were understood by these men as manifestations of divine Reason. As Nathanael Culverwel (*ca.* 1615–1651) wrote: "God is the Spring and Head of reason."[19] The Cambridge Platonists were rationalists, not in the continental sense of logical system-builders but in the classic Greek sense of cultivators of the *logos* in all reality. We shall concentrate on the two men in this school who made significant contributions to ethics: Ralph Cudworth and Henry More.

It is not easy to decide where Ralph Cudworth (1617–1688) learned his philosophy: the tradition of Emmanuel College would hardly explain his grasp of the ethics of "right reason," which we examined in Chapter VI. The influence of Hooker is evident but hardly sufficient to explain the metaphysical and ethical philosophy of Cudworth. His *The True Intellectual System of the Universe* first appeared in 1678 and his *Treatise concerning Eternal and Immutable Morality* was finished within the next ten years but not published until fifty years later (London, 1731).

The chief object of Cudworth's contempt is the theory that "arbitrary will" is the source of all distinction between good and evil. Plato, Aristotle, Protagoras, Polus, and Callicles are accused of this sort of voluntarism; so are Ockham, Pierre d'Ailly (1350–1420), and Andreas de Novo Castro. But his greatest scorn is reserved for the modern supporters of this view, Gassendi and Hobbes. Cudworth quotes from the *Leviathan* and points out that Hobbes makes "the Arbitrary Will and Pleasure of God" the first rule and measure of good and evil.[20] In his second chapter, Cudworth states his own understanding on the basis of ethical judgment:

> For though the will and power of God have an absolute, infinite, and unlimited command upon the existences of all created things to make them to be, or not to be at pleasure; yet when things

exist, they are what they are, this or that, absolutely or relatively, not by will or arbitrary command, but by the necessity of their own nature. There is no such thing as an arbitrarious essence . . . the natures of justice and injustice cannot be arbitrarious things, that may be applicable by will indifferently to any actions or dispositions whatsoever. . . . We must needs say that nothing is morally good or evil, just or unjust by mere will without nature, because every thing is what it is by nature, and not by will.[21]

Later in the *Treatise*[22] Cudworth suggests that man has two kinds of knowledge, that which originates in sense perceptions and that which the activity of the mind produces within itself. From this second source come innate ideas of wisdom, prudence, vice, honesty, justice, injustice, plus notions of many relations (cause and effect, means and end, etc.). This is the origin of man's knowledge of the immutable principles of morality. These *noeta* are the proper objects of all sciences, the intelligible essences of things, and as necessary verities they "exist no where but in the Mind it self." Whether this is an anticipation of the a priori of Kant[23] is not clear; historically it is evident that Cudworth's view was never popular in British philosophy.

If he failed to convince Englishmen that morality and law do not depend on the will of the legislator, Cudworth did exert a strong influence with his qualified explanation of free will.[24] Cudworth's huge essay on this subject, A *Discourse of Liberty and Necessity*, is now partly edited and partly lost. In it Cudworth disagreed with both Hobbes and Bramhall concerning free will. It is obvious that he would object to Hobbes's physical determinism but he is just as much opposed to Bramhall's "Scholastic" notion that will is a separate faculty. Cudworth takes will as the "whole soul redoubled upon itself,"[25] in much the same way that St. Augustine had understood *voluntas*. As will, the soul of man is not indifferent to good and evil; it is naturally inclined toward the good. Freedom of choice remains in those cases where the distinction of good from evil in action is not clearly evident. Free action is not rare. We know that we have free will because we experience it within us, we praise and blame free activity in other persons, we need freedom as the basis for moral life.

Cudworth rarely attempted to develop specific rules of ethical behavior, preferring to treat the theoretical ground of such judgments. His follower, Henry More (1614–1687), showed no such hesitation. More's *Enchiridion Ethicum* (1667) is an almost geometric exposition of the intellectual principles (*noemata*) that constitute "right reason." Speaking of the intellectual part of the soul, More says:

I will take from this storehouse, therefore, certain principles which are immediately true and needing no proof, but into which almost all moral doctrine is plainly and easily resolved, even as mathematical demonstrations are resolved into their common axioms. Since these are the fruit of that faculty which is properly called *Nous*, I thought it not inappropriate to call them *Noemata*.[26]

Astonishingly, More's first *Noema* states that a good is that which is pleasant, agreeable, and suited to the preservation of the recipient. This, of course, is Hobbes's definition of good! However, More proceeds to argue that one good may be superior to another in nature, duration, or both (*Noema* IV), that the superior good should be sought (*Noema* V), and that the cardinal virtues may be acquired by following these and similar *noemata*. Right reason, then, "is that which by certain and necessary consequences may be ultimately resolved into some Intellectual Principle that is immediately true" (*Noema* XXIII). This listing of many principles of moral reasoning by More anticipates the procedure of several later theorists: of the Deists and moral-sense ethicians, and of the Scotch common-sense thinkers. Richard Cumberland (1631–1718), for instance, represents a transitional stage between Platonist ethics and utilitarianism. His Latin treatise on the *Laws of Nature* (1672) insisted that "the nature of things in the universe ought first to be considered" before reasoning to an explanation of human faculties and human happiness.[27] This is combined with the further claim that "the common good of all is the supreme law." This leads into a utilitarian ethic, and we shall return to Cumberland in Chapter X, where British utility theories will be treated together.

Although he has a distinctive ethical position, John Locke (1632–1704) is not the great figure in the history of ethics that he is in epistemology. His thought has some relation to the kind of ethics that is found in Cambridge Platonism. Locke's early *Essays on the Law of Nature* (1660-1664) have only recently been published (1954). Presenting a theory of moral law, known naturally, these *Essays* are obviously much indebted to fourteenth-century Scholasticism. Here we find a completely voluntaristic explanation of moral law. The definition of natural law is "an ordinance of the divine will knowable by the light of nature, showing what is in agreement or disagreement with rational nature and in the same act commanding or prohibiting it."[28] Like the Cambridge Platonists Locke indicates that there are but three ways in which natural law could be known by man: by innate inscription, by hearsay, or by reasoning from sense perception. However, he is already much opposed to any suggestion of innate ideas and he criticizes this theory throughout on whole *Essay*.[29] In regard to the second manner of learning about the principles of morality, Locke admits that we acquire a good deal from our parents and other such sources but this mode of knowing is from the dictates of men and not the *dictatum rationis*. It is by the third method, then, that we obtain our basic knowledge of natural law, that is, by reasoning from the data of sense experience.[30]

Longer and better-known than these recently discovered *Essays on the Law of Nature* are the sections of the famous *Essay concerning Understanding* (1690), which constitute Locke's most extended treatment of moral philosophy. Although his *Two Treatises of Civil Government* (1690) throw some light on his concept of the state of nature (in which men are less belligerent than in Hobbes's account), they have little to say about ethics. Locke has left other essays and fragmentary writings that deal with ethics; for instance, there are short essays entitled "Of Ethics in General" and "Thus I Think."

Another distinctive feature of the ethical position of John Locke stems from his epistemology. This is Locke's empiricism. The main message of the *Essay concerning Human Understanding* is the contention that all knowledge arises from experience, either sensation or reflection. Book I of the *Essay* is a thoroughly developed refutation of innatism. Whether it be the theory of Herbert of Cherbury, René Descartes, or the Cambridge Platonists, Locke cannot accept any suggestion that man is endowed with inborn notions. Neither speculative nor moral principles can be explained in this way. Reflection on the relations that we find among our acquired ideas (all objects of understanding are called "ideas") is our only way to reach primary rules of ethical judgment. Ethically, Locke is an empiricist.

The second point in the general philosophy of Locke that influences his ethics is his depreciation of the problem of free will. This is a pseudo-problem, Locke thinks, because "will" means a power to prefer or choose, whereas "liberty" is a different power, "to begin or forbear, continue or end several actions of our minds, and motions of our bodies."[31] It is the mind that exerts both these powers but they should not be confused by asking whether there is liberty of will: "Voluntary, then, is not opposed to necessary, but to involuntary." Desire is explained by Locke as a certain "uneasiness" at the absence of anything.

Good and evil are equated, then, with that which is apt to cause pleasure or pain; and happiness is desired by all men, for it is "the utmost pleasure we are capable of."[32] Not all pleasures necessarily move man's desire, only those which seem to be required for happiness. This is a remnant of classical eudaimonism but it is also not far removed, in its expression, from Hobbes's egoism.

Among the relations of ideas that become evident through inner reflection are those of moral relations: cases of "conformity or disagreement men's voluntary actions have to a rule. . . ."[33] There are three sorts of these moral rules or laws: divine, civil, and philosophical. God promulgates His laws "by the light of nature, or the voice of revelation." This is the only true touchstone of moral rectitude; so, Locke is fundamentally a theological approbative ethician. In the second place, there is civil law. It is enacted "by the commonwealth" to distinguish criminal from inno-

cent actions. Thirdly, there is philosophical law, which distinguishes virtue
from vice. It is alo called the law of "opinion or reputation." Concerning
this law, Locke adds:

> Thus the measure of what is every where called and esteemed
> "virtue" and "vice," is this approbation or dislike, praise or blame,
> which by a secret and tacit consent establishes itself in the several
> societies, tribes, and clubs of men in the world, whereby several
> actions come to find credit or disgrace amongst them, according
> to the judgment, maxims, or fashions of that place. . . . By this
> approbation and dislike, they establish amongst themselves what they
> will call "virtue" and "vice."[34]

This form of the social approbative approach to ethics is Locke's most
notable contribution to the subject.

In Book IV of the *Essay*, Locke returns to the description of the
science of ethics, relating it to divinity in the following lines:

> The idea of a Supreme Being, infinite in power, goodness, and
> wisdom, whose workmanship we are, and on whom we depend; and
> the idea of ourselves, as understanding rational beings, being such as
> are clear in us, would, I suppose, if duly considered and pursued,
> afford such foundations of our duty and rules of action, as might place
> morality among the sciences capable of demonstration: wherein I
> doubt not but from self-evident propositions, by necessary conse-
> quences, as incontestable as those in mathematics, the measures of
> right and wrong might be made out to any one, as he does to the other
> of these sciences.[35]

Later Locke repeats that "moral knowledge is as capable of real certaint
as mathematics." There is a certain quality of idealistic intuitionism ir
volved in this claim. Our moral ideas are "archetypes" like our mathe
matical ones; and our scientific certainty in ethics or mathematics is bu
"the perception of the agreement or disagreement of our ideas." So, i
the end, Locke's empirical ethics is transmuted into an ethical intuitionism

The influence of Locke is most obvious on Lord Shaftesbury (Anthon
Ashley Cooper, 1671–1713). Most important are his *Inquiry concernin
Virtue* (1699) and *The Moralists, A Rhapsody* (1709); both are reprinte
with other pieces in the *Characteristics* (1711). The contemporary po
ularity of this three-volume work is amazing: it went through eleve
editions in England before 1790; Diderot adapted it to French under th
title *Essai sur le Mérite et la Vertu* (1745); and a complete German ve
sion was published at Leipzig in 1776–1779.

Shaftesbury was one of the first British thinkers to treat ethics i
dependently of religion. In this he anticipated one of the features
Deism; indeed, he has been called the most important and plausib

member of that amorphous school. At the beginning of the *Inquiry* he made it clear that Cudworth's ethics seemed to Shaftesbury to confuse theology with ethics. It was not that Shaftesbury denied the existence of a divine law which applies to human actions; rather, he insisted that men must first understand goodness, obligation, and virtue *in a natural way* before they can recognize and interpret the supreme requirements of God's law.

As the first prominent writer to speak of a moral sense, Lord Shaftesbury claimed that just as men have an aesthetic sense of the beautiful and the ugly, so do they have a moral sense of right and wrong.[36] Two things should be noted in his account of this moral sense. First, it is a function of man's understanding or reason; and second, it involves a feeling for what is decent and virtuous. Shaftesbury made a rather lengthy survey of the "affections" of man and came up with three conclusions about them. First, natural and kindly affections directed toward the public good are the source of our greatest personal joy. Second, too strong personal affections are the source of personal misery. Third, unnatural affections are neither in the public nor the private interest and they lead to misery in the highest degree.[37] In his discussion of the public good or interest, Shaftesbury several times uses the notion of the good of the species and speaks of the "common nature" of man. This is a Scotistic term, a way of looking at human nature as neutral in regard to both individuality and universality. It is impossible to establish the precise significance of Shaftesbury's usage of the term. He appears to have a somewhat more realistic notion of what constitutes the human species than either Hobbes or Locke. We shall see how his optimistic confidence in man's ability to reach a natural basis for moral judgment influences people like Bolingbroke and Alexander Pope in the Deist movement.

Shaftesbury's theory of the natural affections is an obvious reaction to Hobbes's view of man as naturally selfish. There were many more anti-Hobbes treatises at this time. Archbishop William King of Dublin (Established Church of Ireland, 1650-1729) published in 1702-1704 a Latin treatise *On the Origin of Evil*; it was put into English by Edmund Law and published in 1731, with dissertations by John Gay (1699-1745) *Concerning the Fundamental Principle of Virtue or Morality*. Gay surveyed the various attempts that have been made to find a criterion of virtue: "Some have placed it in acting agreeably to nature, or reason; others in the fitness of things; others in a conformity with truth; others in promoting the common good; others in the will of God, &c." He eventually argued that the will of God is the sole standard of virtue.[38]

A more fundamental attack on Hobbes is found in the work of Samuel Clarke (1675-1729), an Anglican clergyman. His *Discourse on Natural Religion* is actually a series of eight sermons or lectures, delivered in 1705 and printed in 1706. In rather forceful language, Clarke suggested that

Hobbes had no basis for denying that the difference between good and evil is rooted in "the Nature of Things." He particularly objected to the idea "that all Obligation of Duty to God, arises merely from his absolute irresistible [sic] Power, and all Duty towards Men, merely from positive Compact."[39] Clarke's own position is that right reason discovers good and evil, and this is the law of nature.[40] Acknowledging his debt to Plato, Cicero, and especially to Cumberland, Clarke mentioned the Deists as "ranting" opponents of his theory. Oddly, a reply to the *Discourse on Natural Religion* was published in 1730 by a schoolmaster of Hull named John Clarke (not related, John lived from 1687 to 1734), under the title, *The Foundation of Morality in Theory and Practice* This work claims that Dr. Samuel Clarke relies on the principle of benevolence and a universal moral sense to ground his ethics. John objected that even benevolence is reducible to private pleasure: "The main Use of the Moral Sense, and the Principal Intention of Nature therein, seems to be to put the Mind of Man upon the Hunt, to see if such actions as appear at first sight Beautiful, may not be attended with greater Pleasures . . ."[41] It is evident that John Clarke came under the influence of Hobbe and that he thought that the impetus for moral sensism ("a very pretty ingenious Speculation") came from the teaching that all human actions spring from self-love.

Somewhat similar to the view of John Clarke is that of Bernard Mandeville (1670–1733), a Dutch physician who made his home in England He first wrote *The Grumbling Hive: or, Knaves turned Honest* (1705) this was later revised into *The Fable of the Bees: or, Private Vices, Publi Benefits* (1714). In the second edition of the *Fable* (1723) there appeared his *Enquiry into the Origin of Moral Virtue*. Mandeville directed his argument against Shaftesbury's notion that morally good actions are thos directed to the public good. Instead, said Mandeville, it is obvious tha "private vices" contribute most to the public welfare. By "vices" in th *Fable of the Bees* he means selfish tendencies; so, his point is that peopl who seek their own personal pleasures do more to advance the good c society than do the superficial altruists. A society of moral rigoris would be static in all ways, whereas a group of rugged individualists i search of material satisfactions would be a dynamic union. The publ toleration of organized prostitution in Amsterdam was given as an e ample of vice contributing to the general good of a city. In his *Enqui* Mandeville showed that he was more than a literary cynic. At one point remarked: "It is impossible to judge of a man's performance, unless v are thoroughly acquainted with the principle and motive from which I acts."[42] He proceeded to discuss pity as a motivating passion and to arg that this altruistic feeling is the source of much immorality. In one se tence he anticipated much of Nietzsche. A few lines later, Mandevi mentioned the "love of goodness" as a motive and admitted that people so moved "have acquired more refined notions of virtue than those I have hitherto spoke of." This could have been said by Kant. In point of fact, much of Berkeley's *Alciphron* is a refutation of Mandeville. Since the *Fable* maintains that "vicious" people are big spenders, it is even possible that laissez-faire economics owes something to Mandeville.

Deistic Ethics

Our survey of this period in English thought requires a brief notice of the ethical views of those writers who have become known as Deists. Deism has been given a variety of meanings but we will use it here to name a point of view that developed in the seventeenth and early eighteenth centuries in England and France and that maintained that man can reason from his natural experience to the existence and some of the attributes of God, that revelation and the mysteries of faith may be unnecessary, and that the good life for man finds adequate guidance in philosophical ethics. It is the last feature that justifies mention of the movement in this history. Virtually all of the leading philosophers in these centuries (Hobbes, Locke, Descartes, Leibniz, Spinoza) have been called Deists. We shall briefly examine a group of less noted men who are nearer to the core of the movement.

We have noted at the end of Chapter VII how Herbert of Cherbury proposed a modified Stoic ethics that suggested to English readers that revealed religion might not be the sole source of moral guidance. Herbert was probably the founder of Deism in England. A hundred years later, William Wollaston (1659–1724) wrote the treatise which is, however, the best exposition of Deistic ethics: *The Religion of Nature Delineated* (1722). Its first section deals with religion. Truth is defined as "the conformity of those words or signs, by which are exprest, to the things themselves."[43] Wollaston never tires of saying that "every thing is what it is." Moreover, "if there is a supreme being," then this Deity is the author of nature, is truth itself, and his will is "revealed in the books of nature." Truth distinguishes right from wrong, and "moral good and evil are coincident with right and wrong."[44] The following passage shows that we have here a right reason theory:

> They who make right reason to be the law, by which our acts are to be judged, and according to their conformity to this or deflexion from it call them lawful or unlawful, good or bad, say something more particular and precise. And indeed it is true, that whatever will bear to be tried by right reason, is right; and that which is condemned by it, wrong. And moreover, if by right reason is

meant that which is found by the right use of our rational faculties, this is the same with truth: and what is said by them, will be comprehended in what I have said.[45]

Wollaston's use of the hypothetical form in speaking of God does not mean that he doubted the divine existence: he thought that reason established the fact that God exists. It should be remembered that the first centuries of reformed Christianity generally distrusted philosophy and exalted personal belief, so Wollaston (whose views are not far removed from thirteenth-century Scholasticism) was given the reputation of an atheist, rationalist, and opponent of institutional religion. Actually, he insisted that the obvious distinction between moral good and evil necessarily implies the truth of religion, and that every intelligent being should act in accord with truth.[46] The second section of Wollaston's Religion of Nature treats of happiness. Like Hobbes, he starts with the claim that pain is a real evil and pleasure a real good. From this he proceeds to a detailed examination of pains and pleasures in the light of "truth." This is a sort of moral arithmetic that anticipates Bentham's moral calculus.

A similar argument that natural ethics justifies Christianity is found in the writings of a medical doctor, Thomas Morgan (1680–1743). His Physico-Theology was published in 1741, and his treatise The Moral Philosopher in 1738. We are now getting into an era in which this view of religion is more popular, at least among literary figures. It is well known that the Essay on Man (1734) by Alexander Pope (1688–1744) is a poetic summary of Deist psychology and ethics. Its famous last line ("One truth is clear, Whatever is, is right") is but an echo of Wollaston. Must of the poem repeats Shaftesbury almost verbatim. Pope was a friend of Henry St. John Bolingbroke (1678–1751), who is said to have supplied the philosophical base for Pope's Essay. A notorious rake, Bolingbroke did the cause of Deism no good in his personal mode of life. However, his writings (Letters on the Study of History and On Authority in Matters of Religion, both published shortly after Bolingbroke's death) had wide literary appeal for his contemporaries and influenced many serious writers. He was critical of organized Christianity and argued that moral obligations cannot be deduced from the revealed attributes of God.

Although this is a chapter on ethics in the British Isles, it should be noted that Deistic ethics extended to other countries. Shaftesbury is considered by some historians as instrumental in this transmission: we have seen how his writings were quickly translated into French and German. Voltaire (François Marie Arouet, 1694–1778) included entries on Deism in his Philosophical Dictionary (1765). Denis Diderot (1713–1784) moved from an early adherence to Deism to a later naturalistic pantheism. His Philosophical Thoughts on the Sciences (1746) presented a moral view partly inspired by Deism. The Abbé Étienne Bonnot de Condillac (1715–1780) pushed Locke's theory of knowledge to its extremity; in the *Traité des sensations* (1754) all knowing is reduced to the working of the sense of smell. Good means "whatever pleases our smell or our taste."[47] What there is of ethics in these French thinkers is closely associated with Deism.[48]

It is a commonplace to say that many of the founders of the United States of America were Deists. Of course they did not write treatises on ethics. However, the *Autobiography* of Benjamin Franklin shows his general acquaintance with Deistic ethics. He tells of compiling a little treatise on the virtues, for his own edification, and then he comments on it as follows: "Though my scheme was not wholly without religion, there was in it no mark of any of the distinguishing tenets of any particular sect."[49] It is probable that Franklin's Deism was closer to the French than the British variety.[50]

America also played a role in the career of another British thinker, Bishop George Berkeley (1685–1753) of Cloyne, Ireland. In 1729 he traveled to America in the interest of establishing an Anglican college in Bermuda but spent three years in residence at Newport, Rhode Island, and there wrote his *Alciphron, or the Minute Philosopher* (1732) in which he criticized freethinkers such as Shaftesbury and Bernard Mandeville. As a young man (before 1720) Berkeley had started write a treatise on psychology and ethics but it was lost in an accident; he never took the trouble to rewrite it. The critique of Shaftesbury's moral sensism in the third dialogue of *Alciphron* is based on Berkeley's conviction that ethics requires Christian theology to ground it. There is a passage in his *Principles of Human Knowledge* (1710) where he says that there is little advantage in making abstract considerations of happiness or goodness and that such abstractions render morality difficult.[51] In the original edition of 1710 he had added this:

> One may make a great progress in *school ethics*, without ever being the wiser or better man for it, or knowing how to behave himself, in the affairs of life, more to the advantage of himself, or his neighbours, than he did before. This hint may suffice to let any one see that.[52]

This would suggest that Berkeley was a skeptic as far as the value of academic ethics is concerned. His own position in the early notes that constitute his *Philosophical Commentaries* (1707–1708) is surprisingly eclectic. At one point he says that sensual pleasure is the *summum bonum*.[53] But on the same page he argues that such pleasure is good only when desired by a wise man, and he implies that those who are not motivated by a desire of heaven cannot perform good actions.

An essay by Berkeley on *Passive Obedience* (1712) has some sec
tions (4–15, 28–34, 41, 42, 53) that outline a type of theological
utilitarian ethics. As some people grow more mature, Berkeley tells
us, they learn to look to the remote consequences of their actions
to see "what good may be hoped, or what evil feared . . . accord
ing to the wonted course of things."[54] At this same place he makes
it plain that the real measure of good and bad actions is the will of
God. To the extent that he has an ethics, Berkeley always thinks in
terms of such a theory as a derivative from divine law.

Much more important in the history of ethics was the teaching
of another bishop in the Anglican Church, Joseph Butler (1692–
1752). He presented his ethics in fifteen *Sermons* (1726) and in *A
Dissertation upon the Nature of Virtue*, printed as an appendix to
his *Analogy of Religion* (1736). Sermon I shows that Butler is con
cerned about the possible effects of Hobbes's egoism but that he is
not convinced that men like Shaftesbury and Wollaston have all
the truth on their side. There are three motivating principles in man's
moral life, Butler suggests: a principle of benevolence, which inclines
him to act for the good of other persons; a principle of self-love,
which makes him tend toward his private good; and a principle of re
flection (conscience), which enables man coolly to approve or dis
approve of the motivations of the first two.[55]

The second and third sermons expand the meaning of conscience
and relate it to human nature. It is a mistake to think that Butler
takes human nature as something universal and common to all men.
Like nearly all philosophers of this period, Butler is a nominalist.
The nature of man is merely a set of tendencies that each man may
discover within himself: thus self-love is natural, in the sense that I
find myself instinctively disposed toward it. The compulsion of "duty"
is similarly natural. Conscience is a sort of cool, disinterested, passion
less viewing of the claims of these natural inclinations. As Butler
explains:

> The whole argument . . . may thus be summed up. . . . The
> nature of man is adapted to some course of action or other. Upon
> comparing some actions with this nature, they appear suitable and
> correspondent to it: from comparison of other actions with the same
> nature, there arises to our view some unsuitableness or dispropor-
> tion. The correspondence of actions of the nature of the agent
> renders them natural: their disproportion to it, unnatural. . . . Rea-
> sonable self-love and conscience are the chief or superior principles
> in the nature of man: because an action may be suitable to this
> nature, though all other principles be violated; but becomes un-
> suitable, if either of those are.[56]

In the *Dissertation* conscience is described as the "approving and disapproving faculty" that each person experiences within himself. It reflects upon actions; it discerns that some require reward and others punishment; it "compares" these actions with the capacities of the agent; it involves a calm appraisal of one's own interest; and it recognizes the appeal of benevolence but does not regard it as the only mark of virtue.[57]

We must be cautious in classifying the ethical theory of Butler. It is an ethical intuitionism; one historian calls it "autonomic intuitionism."[58] Of course it is a deontological theory, for the awareness of duty is central to Butler's thought. It has been called a "sophisticated formalist theory" but it is not close to the sort of formalism that attempts to establish general rules of moral obligation. Rather, Butler's view resembled "act-utilitarianism" without the utilitarianism! That is to say, his conscience "compares" each proposed action or tendency to act, within the individual person, and comes up with a verdict of natural and suitable, or the opposite. This is the way that moral good and evil are distinguished in the concrete, by a personal intuition of certain inclinations within the agent.

Contemporary with Butler are two men with similar but less well-developed theories of ethics. Archibald Campbell (1691-1756) was a Scottish professor of church history at St. Andrews University who wrote *An Enquiry into the Original of Moral Virtue* (1728). Lord Kames (Henry Home, 1696-1782) published his *Essays on the Principles of Morality and Natural Religion* in 1751. The latter stresses the requirement that good action must conform to "the common nature of the species" and the power to perceive this suitability is moral sense.[59] Eventually, Kames identifies moral sense with "the voice of God within us."

The fullest treatment of the theory of moral sensism is given in the ten works produced by Francis Hutcheson (1694-1746). We shall examine but three of them: the *Inquiry into the Original of Our Ideas of Beauty and Virtue* (1725), the *Essay on the Nature and Conduct of the Passions* (1728), and *A System of Moral Philosophy* (1755). The first sentence of the *Inquiry* states: "The Word Moral Goodness . . . denotes our Idea of some Quality apprehended in Actions, which procures Approbation, and Love toward the Actor, from those who receive no advantage by the Action."[60] Notice the use of "Quality" and also an intimation of the disinterested or impersonal spectator theory. Objects that excite personal or selfish pleasure seem to Hutcheson *naturally* good but those that are advantageous to other persons are *morally* good. The principle of benevolence is already foremost. God has given us an internal sense of the beautiful and harmonious; similarly "he has given us a MORAL SENSE, to direct our Actions, and

to give us still nobler Pleasures; so that while we are only intending
the Good of others, we 'undesignedly promote our own greatest private
Good.' "[61] In the next section, Hutcheson dwells on this contention
that moral good must be directed to the good of others (God or fellow
men) by a love of benevolence.

Explaining the working of the moral sense, Hutcheson introduces into
British ethical writing the notion of the good of the greatest number
He suggests:

> In comparing the moral Qualitys of Actions, in order to regulate
> our Election among various Actions propos'd, or to find out which
> of them has the greatest moral Excellency, we are led by our moral
> Sense of Virtue to judge thus; that in equal Degrees of Happiness,
> expected to proceed from the Action, the Virtue is in proportion
> to the Number of Persons to whom the Happiness shall extend; . . .
> so that, that Action is best, which procures the greatest Happi-
> ness for the greatest Numbers; and that, worst, which, in like man-
> ner, occasions Misery.[62]

This anticipation of utilitarianism is modified, in this same passage
by the suggestion that happiness or pleasure varies in quality as well
as in quantity.[63] Possibly under the influence of Wollaston, Hutcheson
proceeds to a sort of moral arithmetic to be used by the moral sense
on "computing" the morality of actions. Six axioms are proposed a
guides in this computation: (1) "The moral Importance of any Agent
or the Quantity of publick Good produc'd by him, is in a compoun
Ratio of his Benevolence and Ability"; (2) "the Moment of privat
Good, or Interest produc'd by any Person to himself, is in a compoun
Ratio of his Self-Love, and Abilitys"; (3) "when in comparing th
Virtue of two Actions, the Abilitys of the Agents are equal; the momer
of publick Good produc'd by them in like Circumstances, is as th
Benevolence"; (4) "when Benevolence in two Agents is equal, an
the other Circumstances alike; the Moment of publick Good is :
the Abilitys"; (5) "the Virtue then of Agents, or their Benevolenc
is always directly as the Moment of Good produc'd in like Circur
stances, and inversely as their Abilitys"; and (6) "the entire Motiv
to good Actions is not always Benevolence alone; . . . we must lo
upon Self-Love as another Force, sometimes conspiring with Benev
lence, . . . sometimes opposing Benevolence."[64] Hutcheson later su
gests that the ideas of obligation and moral right may be "deduce
from the deliverances of moral sense.[65]

The *Essay on the Passions* appeared just before Hutcheson w
appointed to the chair of moral philosophy at Glasgow, thus beginni
a long line of distinguished ethicians in Scotland. (Hutcheson, hir
self, was born in Ireland.) This work, of course, develops a psycholo

of human feeling, but its contribution of an analysis of internal sensation is more important to ethical theory. He now has four internal senses: the aesthetic, public ("to be pleased with the Happiness of others, and to be uneasy at their Misery"), moral (to "perceive Virtue or Vice, in themselves, or others, as an Object"), and the sense of honor and shame.[66] The other noteworthy feature of this shorter work on the passions is a general tendency to criticize any use of final causality, such as Aristotle's notion that moral good depends on the directing of an action to an ultimate end. Hutcheson will have none of this; each affection is its own complete motive.

Hutcheson's *System of Moral Philosophy* is a very large work (two volumes) edited from his lectures at Glasgow and posthumously published.[67] The basic components of his teaching remain the same. In later life, Hutcheson read more of the classic Greek and Latin moralists and this interest shows in the *System*. The moral sense becomes something like the *hēgemonikon* of Hellenistic ethics: "This moral sense from its very nature appears to be designed for regulating and controlling all our powers."[68] The principle of benevolence is still dominant in the operation of the moral sense, "it makes the generous determination to public happiness the supreme one in the soul, with that commanding power which it is naturally destined to exercise." In the second book of the *System*, an effort is made to "deduce" various key concepts of morality (righteousness, obligation, moral right) from the moral sense. The theory is also extended into the discussion of special problems of morality and economics.

Hutcheson's writings in ethics influenced the whole later course of British moral philosophy. From this point onward, any attempt to discuss moral good in terms of an abstract relation, an ideal of goodness, will be unpopular in England. "Good" now means a certain perceived *quality* in a personal action or attitude. As we shall see in Chapter X, Richard Price will eventually try to reinstate the theory of an ideal human nature, but without great success.

In his *Foundation of Moral Goodness* (1728) John Balguy (1686–748) claims that "Mr. Hutchinson" can demonstrate nothing about morality with his theory.[69] Balguy himself has a variant of the right reason teaching: "The Dictates and Directions of Right Reason are the very Rule which the Deity Himself inviolably observes, and which therefore must needs affect all intelligent Creatures."[70]

Another type of criticism directed against the moral sense theory of Hutcheson derived from the associationist psychology in the writings of David Hartley (1705–1757). Under the influence of John Locke, Hartley's *Enquiry into the Origin of the Human Appetites and Affections* (1747) suggested that all the "affections" of self-love, benevolence, and piety toward God originate in sense impressions. Certain elementary feelings of pleasure and pain are associated with other ideas to form more complex emotions of the aesthetic, moral, and religious types. Of itself the human mind is a *tabula rasa*, without any predispositions toward the beautiful or the good. If true, this associationist psychology kills the whole idea of a moral sense. However, Hartley proceeded in his *Observations on Man* (1749) to refurbish the principle of benevolence by explaining how psychological analysis explains the development of acquired dispositions to benevolence, piety, and moral sense.[71]

It was Abraham Tucker (1705–1774) who (in *The Light of Nature Pursued*, 1768) pointed out that Locke and Hartley had demolished innatism and that Hutcheson's moral sense involved some claim to innate moral dispositions. Tucker advocated a "translation" theory that relied on associationist psychology to explain how man's initially selfish and low-grade feelings may be transmuted into altruistic, moral, and high-grade attitudes. Comfortingly, Tucker assures us that there is a sort of bank or storehouse of happiness which is ever increasing under divine guidance; in the end, God will see to it that every man gets an equal share of happiness![72] His ethics is utilitarian, of course. In our tenth chapter, we shall take up the growth of the ethics of utility, in eighteenth-century and nineteenth-century England.

CHAPTER IX

Rationalistic Ethics on the Continent

EUROPEAN ETHICIANS in the seventeenth and eighteenth centuries made moral philosophy an important and distinctive study. At this point ethics became a subject for university study but it was also cultivated by nonacademic writers in order to complete the practical dimensions of their philosophies, to provide a foundation for their theories of society and law, to explore the moral bearings of the new directions of religion. In general, these continental writers on ethics, from Grotius to Kant, are somewhat deductive in their approaches to the subject; they are inclined to fit ethics into the vaster framework of their entire philosophies. Moreover, these European ethicians are theists who retain a certain confidence in the ultimate character of the law of God, even as they investigate the principles of goodness and justice in the "light of natural reason." In the case of those continental ethicians who are interested in jurisprudence (and many are), their way of proceeding is to start with some very general principles of law and right, then to move by reasoning to more specific rules, eventually to apply these broad regulations to individual cases. This contrasts with the tendency in British legal thinking to work from individual court cases, taken as precedents, toward a growing body of laws which accumulate as a living tradition. Continental thinking in moral philosophy is not usually inductive, during this period of the Enlightenment, even though there is a general move toward empiricism in the field of the sciences.

The Dutch Protestant jurisprudent Hugo Grotius (1583–1645) is a good example of an ethician exhibiting the foregoing characteristics. His treatise *On the Rights of War and Peace* (1625), written in Latin, continues much of the Scholastic tradition of right reason and natural law. It is still recognized as a classic contribution to the theory of international law. He wrote other things. The treatise *De imperio Summarum Potestatum circa sacra* (1661) has not been translated but it is his most philosophical treatment of natural law morality. Grotius' *Inleiding tot de Hollandsche Rechts-Geleerdheid* (1631; *Introduction to*

the Jurisprudence of Holland) is not only a source of legislation in the
Netherlands; it is still used today in countries that have come under
Dutch cultural influence, for instance, in the Union of South Africa.[1]

Reference works often suggest that Grotius abandoned the Scholastic
and Catholic approach to natural law and adopted the lawyer's attitude
that man's "social nature" and not metaphysics or theology constitutes
the ground for legal judgment.[2] Nothing could be farther from the truth.
This caricature of Grotius' teaching was drawn by his follower, Samuel
von Pufendorf, for reasons of his own. The fact of the matter is that
Grotius was very close to the right reason type of moral philosophy that
we found in Thomas Aquinas.[3] Grotius did write that there would be
a valid natural law, "even if it were granted that God does not exist,"
but this does not mean that he denied the ultimate foundation of natural
law in the eternal law.[4] It was the recognized teaching of the Thomistic
school of jurisprudence, particularly in Renaissance Spain, that once
God had established certain laws for men and the universe He would not
change them. Some eccentric Scholastics, such as Gregory of Valencia
(1551–1603) and Rodrigo de Arriaga (whose *Cursus philosophiae* was
published in Antwerp in 1632), taught that the dictate of right reason
(*dictamen recta rationis*) would provide a basis for natural law, even if
God did not exist.[5] It is in the light of this background, with which
Grotius was very familiar, that we should read the following explanation of natural law.

> *Natural right* (*jus naturale*) is the dictate of right reason, showing
> the moral turpitude or moral necessity of any act from its agreement
> or disagreement with a rational nature, and consequently that such
> an act is either forbidden or commanded by God, the author of
> nature. The actions, upon which such a dictate is given, are either
> binding or unlawful in themselves, and therefore necessarily under-
> stood to be commanded or forbidden by God. This mark distin-
> guishes natural right, not only for human law, but from the law,
> which God himself has been pleased to reveal, called by some the
> voluntary divine right.[6]

Grotius is not a nominalist nor a voluntarist in his practical philosophy
The above quotation obviously continues the realistic theory of a rationa
moral order, as it is described by the Spanish Thomist, Gabriel Vasque
(*ca.* 1551–1604), in his *Commentary* on Thomas' *Summa Theologiae*
Even Grotius' emphasis on "*socialitas*" (the inclination of all men to com
bine in society) is not a break with the Scholastic teaching. Al
Scholastics had agreed with Aristotle that man is by nature a socia
animal. Grotius simply continued this emphasis on the "common good,
or the welfare of the people (*salus populi*), in his *De imperio* (cha
4, sect. 6) with his theory of right reason as the ground of ethical jud;

ment. No less an authority than Leibniz says as much in one of his letters: "In my judgment, Grotius rightly combined the Scholastic teaching on eternal law with the principle of sociality."[7]

The ethical views of Samuel von Pufendorf (1632-1694) tell quite a different story. He is the second noted Protestant advocate of natural law ethics, on the Continent. Pufendorf is in the tradition of William of Ockham, however, holding that all moral distinctions are imposed directly by God's will. Moral law is no longer "natural" in the sense of proclaiming what actions are suitable or unsuitable to the specific nature of a human being acting in the world of nature. For Pufendorf, an act is good because God willed it to be so: there is nothing else to it. As manifested through supernatural revelation, God's will is the divine law; as shown through the "light of natural reason," the same prescription of divine will is the natural law. In other words, we have here a theological approbative theory of natural law.

Pufendorf served as professor of natural and moral philosophy at Heidelberg from 1660 to 1668 and later taught jurisprudence at Lund, Sweden. Hence, he was probably the first occupant of a university chair of ethics in Germany. His huge work on *The Law of Nature and of Nations* (1672) had a tremendous influence. It was translated from the original Latin into most of the European vernaculars. He also wrote in Latin an *Elements of Jurisprudence* (1660), a study of the *Duties of Man and of the Citizen* (1673), and a reply to critics of his treatise on *The Law of Nature* under the title *Eris Scandica* (1686).

The first thing to notice about Pufendorf as an ethician is his almost pathological prejudice against the Scholastics. In one of the treatises in the *Eris Scandica*[8] he names "Thomas, Papa Suaretz, Molina, Vasquetz, Valentia, the Conimbricenses and Sanchietz" and then intemperately castigates their teachings as nonsensical, empty, ornamented with frivolous subtleties, and so on. He frequently asserts that Scholastic philosophy was nothing but bad Aristotelianism. In reviving the moral teaching of the Stoics, plus the true message of Christian Moral Theology (*Theologia Moralis Christiana*), Pufendorf's professed aim was to exterminate the "jejune ethics of Aristotle from the Protestant schools."[9]

From his teacher, Erhard Weigel, Pufendorf took the notion that ethics could be developed as a demonstrative science using the method of mathematics. He much resented Grotius' admission that there cannot be as much accuracy and certitude in moral reasoning as there is in mathematics.[10] Actually, Pufendorf's main contribution to the development of such an ethics was to pick up the notion of "sociality" from Grotius and suggest that it is the basis of natural ethics.[11] His own position is a combination of Grotius and Hobbes, resulting in a doctrine that uses the language of natural law to promote a voluntaristic and positivistic theory. As we shall see, Christian Thomasius, his most noted follower in Germany, became critical of Pufendorf as he grew more mature. Pufendorf's *Law of Nature* was highly regarded by John Locke, however, and was much read at Oxford in this period.[12]

In France, this sort of rationalistic ethics made its appearance in the early seventeenth century. René Descartes (1596–1650) is not as important in the history of ethics as he is in other parts of philosophy. However, he has said a few things that have influenced other ethicians. These are to be found chiefly in his *Discourse on Method* (1637), *Principles of Philosophy* (1644), *Passions of the Soul* (written about 1649), and in a few *Letters* to the exiled Princess Elizabeth of Bohemia. It is, of course, helpful to read his *Rules for the Direction of the Mind* (1628) and *Meditations* (1641) in order to understand his conception of the work of the philosopher. There is no treatise by Descartes that is devoted mainly to moral philosophy.

Dissatisfaction with the kind of philosophy that he had been taught at the Jesuit Collège Henri IV (it was a modified Suarezianism), plus a great admiration for the method and certitude of mathematics, led Descartes to attempt to begin philosophy all over again. He decided to doubt almost all the things that he had accepted as a youth, so that he might eventually see clearly what views would pass the test of rational examination. His criterion of truth was the clarity and distinctness of his ideas. He found that he could not doubt that he existed himself as a thinking thing (*res cogitans*) and he reasoned from his mental experience to the fact of the existence of God, and by considering that a good God would not permit him to be so continually persuaded of the reality of bodies he eventually concluded to the existence of the extramental world. He thought that his philosophy would logically culminate in a new moral philosophy but he never succeeded in reaching this goal.

The Preface to the *Principles of Philosophy* speaks of four degrees of pre-philosophical "wisdom" and suggests that there is the possibility of a fifth wisdom (philosophical) which would be a definitive moral philosophy growing out of the use of Descartes's method.[13] Descartes compares philosophy to a tree whose highest branches would be medicine, mechanics and ethics. He had not reached these branches by 1644, and he never did. However, he says that this exalted ethics would be based on the principles presented in the *Principia Philosophiae*, because they are very clear and all other truths can be deduced from them.[14] He leaves no doubt then, that his ethics would be the product of deduction. The character of his principles has been suggested in the preceding paragraph.

In the same Preface, we are reminded that there is "an imperfect ethic" sketched in the *Discourse on Method*, written some seven years earlier. This is the famous provisional code of morality found in Part III of the *Discourse*. There, after throwing many of his convictions into the hopper of methodic doubt, Descartes listed the practical maxims for living in this period of trial. They were: (1) to obey the laws of his country and to adhere to his Catholic faith; (2) to act firmly and decisively once a course of action has been adopted; and (3) to conquer self rather than externals or fortune. Concluding this "code of morals" was the resolution to study different ways of living, using the light of reason to distinguish truth from error, keeping in mind "that all that is necessary to right action is right judgment."[15] The impression that one gets is that the higher ethics which would be "perfect" in relation to the provisional morality is a demonstrative science in the practical order.

Descartes's *Passions of the Soul* was written in the late 1640s, in part as a response to questions about ethical matters asked in a series of letters exchanged with the exiled Princess Elizabeth of Bohemia. He submitted a version of the treatise to her before it was published. The work describes psychic "passions" as perceptions, feelings, or emotions in the soul caused by movement of the "spirits."[16] These animal spirits are something like physiological vapors coursing through the body and making contact with, and moving, the soul through the pineal gland. The appearance of a ferocious animal excites various changes in the bodily senses, stimulates the imagination to think of similar previous experiences that have been painful to the body, results in movements of the animal spirits and eventually terminates in certain disturbances in the soul. These emotions are classified by Descartes into major types of feelings. Such passions are all basically good by nature but they have a tendency to go to excess and to disturb the higher functions of willing and reasoning. So, they require to be controlled by the will.[17] This is effected by rational effort and also by cultivating certain helpful passions, of which the main example is generosity. It helps a person to feel his true relationship to things based on a wise estimate of himself. This reduces to the realization that one's will is the main thing that one can control. The ethical problem remains one of knowledge, however, for good desire results from true knowledge and bad desire springs from error.[18] This is not as intellectualistic as it first appears, since Descartes always thought that error is caused by a defective act of assent in the will.

In one letter to Princess Elizabeth, Descartes starts from Seneca's *De vita beata* to describe the happiness that is attainable on earth.[19] It is constituted of virtue and wisdom (which we can control) and of honors, wealth, and good health (not entirely under our control). To this modified Stoicism are now added three basic maxims of moral living which are very similar to the rules in the provisional code of morality. Another letter to the Princess[20] gives two requirements for sound moral judgment: to know the truth, and to form the habit of assenting to this knowledge. Included in the knowledge of the truth are four objects of practical cognition: (1) God, (2) the nature of the human soul, (3) the vastness of the universe, and (4) the larger societal group of which man is part.

The strong intellectualist bent of Descartes's incomplete ethical view is obvious. This is somewhat balanced by the important role assigned to will in the governance of the passions. Like Socrates, Descartes felt that if you see the truth clearly you will do good actions.

A long line of thinkers in Europe attempted to follow in Descartes's footsteps and work out the higher wisdom of his ethics. One of these was a Belgian, Arnold Geulincx (1625–1669), who started as a Catholic professor of philosophy at Louvain but eventually became a Protestant and taught moral philosophy at Lyons and Leiden. He is chiefly known in histories of philosophy for his occasionalistic interpretation of Cartesian dualism. An example of the concomitance of human will and bodily motions as illustrated by two synchronized clocks was used by Geulincx long before Leibniz picked it up.[21] Actually, Geulincx wrote more in the field of ethics than in theory of knowledge or metaphysics. He produced an *Ethics,* in six treatises (1665–1709), which has only survived in part. He also wrote *Disputations on the Highest Good* and a series of *Ethical Disputations* (1664–1668).

His approach to ethics stresses the need for a metaphysical foundation for practical wisdom. In a set of *Notes,* he lays down the rule that "moral and ethical matters are based on natural and physical things."[22] Influenced by Jansenism, Geulincx contrasts the radical imperfection of the *brutum* (which seems to mean the material universe) and the weakness and servitude of the natural man with the glorious power and liberty of man under the influence of God's grace. Like Descartes, he needed God in his philosophy and was fascinated by the concept of the omnipotence of God. Interestingly, he repudiated the "moral medicine" of the *Passions of the Soul* and would not accept it as part of the Cartesian ethics. Geulincx's *Ethica* is really a theory of virtue. Its six parts treat: I. Virtue in General; II. the Particular Virtues; III. The End of Virtue: the Good; IV. Passions; V. Reward for Virtue; VI. Prudence (unfinished). This position is restated in the *Ethical Disputations:*

> Ethics is concerned with virtue. Virtue is the unique love of right reason. In this I do not understand by "love" just any sort of passion, or a weak and mild affection . . . but a firm resolve (*firmum propositum*), an efficacious act of willing.[28]

As he works out the details of this ethics of virtue, it becomes evident that Guelincx stresses the voluntarism that is implicit in Cartesianism, falling back on God's will as the explanation of moral right and wrong.[24]

In 1692 some anonymous compiler put together a French summary of *Cartesian Ethics.* This was put into Latin, as the *Ethica Cartesiana,* and published in Germany in 1719. Its subtitle tells its story: "The art of living well and happily developed according to the clearest reasons and the ideas of a sound mind and the most solid principles of René Descartes."[25]

The Cartesian influence is also obvious in the thought of Benedict de Spinoza (1632–1677). He published a résumé of the first two parts of Descartes's *Principles of Philosophy* (in 1663) but he was much more than a Cartesian. In spite of a certain vague and unfinished quality in his moral philosophy, Spinoza stands out as a key figure in modern ethics. There are many excellent studies of his treatise, named *Ethics*, but it is hard to find a coherent account of his moral philosophy, because most interpreters stress his metaphysics.

In 1658–1660 Spinoza wrote a *Tractatus brevis de Deo et homine ejusque felicitate*; this has been lost but two Dutch versions of it were discovered in the middle of the nineteenth century and have been printed. This *Short Treatise* is an advance sketch of the *Ethics*. He insists in it that there can be but one substance and that it will have various attributes and accidents.[26] Even at this early date, he is vague in discussing personal immortality but quite certain about the "eternity of mind."[27]

Spinoza's great work, of course, is the *Ethics Demonstrated Geometrically*. The first draft dates from 1665; he revised it several times; it was published posthumously in 1677. As a Jew residing in Amsterdam, with unorthodox religious views, Spinoza was regarded with distrust by most people and he hesitated to publish his writings, even in that bastion of freedom which was seventeenth-century Holland. Two later treatises (*Tractatus Theologico-Politicus*, 1670, and *Tractatus Politicus*, about 1675) throw some light on the relation between Spinoza's moral and religious thought.

The *Ethics*, as we now have it, is in five books: I. On God; II. Nature and Origin of Mind; III. Origin and Nature of the Emotions; IV. Strength of the Emotions; and V. Power of Understanding, or On Freedom. Each part begins with a set of definitions or with certain axioms and the argument progresses through numbered propositions, with corollaries and explanatory notes. Spinoza was quite serious about using the style of geometric demonstration. Much of the work is taken to present his monistic metaphysics but this is necessary to the exposition of his moral philosophy.

Substance exists in itself and is conceived through itself; it is consequently one, infinite, and identical with God.[28] Of substance there are infinite attributes (ways in which intellect may conceive the essence of substance) of which but two are known to us: thought and extension. The influence of Descartes's dualism of mind and matter is at work here. Nothing that exists or occurs in the universe is contingent; nor is there free will in the domain of mind.[29] Men are mistaken in attributing final causality to the universe; there is no final end for all things. The only kind of teleology that is admissible is the conscious direction of human effort toward proximate goals. Modes are modifications of substance. They may be either infinite or finite. Like "accident" in Scholastic terminology, a Spinozistic mode exists in another and is conceived through another.

Body is God (or substance) existing determinately as an extended thing. Idea is the conception that is actively formed by mind. Will (*voluntas*) and understanding (*intellectus*) are identical and they are simply individual volitions and ideas. Each human mind is a limited aspect of the divine intellect—and is the idea of some thought-object (*ideatum*) that is actually existing.[30] The idea which is the human mind has as its object a certain mode of extension, which is the body. Man, for Spinoza, is constituted of a number of modes, some in the attribute of thought and others in the attribute of extension. Elsewhere, Spinoza calls man an "atom" in the eternal order of universal nature.[31] In another place, we are asked to imagine a worm existing in the blood stream and viewing the various particles about it as if they were individuals, and to compare this worm with a man living in the universe and thinking that he is surrounded by many individual things.[32] Each one of us is but a speck in the vast infinity of substance.

The second book of the *Ethics* also introduces us to Spinoza's three levels of knowledge (Proposition XL). The lowest kind is called opinion or imaginative perception: it is the ordinary (one might even say "common sense") way of looking at man and nature. The second level of perception of knowing is that in which "we have notions common to all men, and adequate ideas of the properties of things." Spinoza calls this "reason" and sees it as operative in science. The highest kind of knowledge is "intuitive"; it "proceeds from an adequate idea of the absolute essence of certain attributes of God to the adequate knowledge of the essences of things."[33] What is important here is that Spinoza thinks that a true moral philosophy must be worked out on the third level, i.e. ethics must view human actions in terms of principles originating in mind and having a reference to the divine attributes. At the end of Book II of the *Ethics* there is a note that criticizes Descartes's *Passions de l'âme* as an inadequate theory of human feelings. The physiology of the pineal gland does not appeal to Spinoza.

At the start of the next book (III, prologue), Spinoza says: "I shall consider human actions and appetites just as if I were considering lines, planes, or bodies." His approach to the emotions is reminiscent of the naturalism of Hobbes but it is also very rationalistic. Spinoza defines "affects" as "modifications of body by which the power of acting of the body itself is increased, diminished, helped, or hindered, together with the ideas of these modifications."[34] Such affects involve both the attribute of extension and that of thought. Man is the inadequate cause of some of his affects, these are *passions*; he is the adequate cause of other affects and they are *actions*. This is important to grasp, because his whole program in the remainder of his ethics consists in showing how man may, and should, convert his passions into actions. This is a gradual process of gaining self-control, or better mental initiative.

There is in each man what Spinoza calls the *conatus*: that basic and ongoing effort whereby everything tries to persist in its own being.[35] As "will" the *conatus* is mental; as "appetite" it belongs to both body and mind. The longer Cartesian list of passions of the soul, or emotions, are reduced by Spinoza to three primitive expressions of human feeling: desire (*cupiditas*), joy (*laetitia*), and sorrow (*tristitia*). The last two carry some connotation of bodily pleasure and pain, as well as the mental feelings corresponding thereto. Now, Spinoza does not think that the Stoics and Descartes were correct in simply saying that these feelings need to be curbed by reason or will, in the ethically developed person. At the beginning of the fourth part of the *Ethics*, the notion of "human bondage" to the emotions is introduced. Man must learn to be alert to the tendency of his passive feelings to take over his life; he must try to transmute his passive affects into dynamic actions. (One may see some similarity here between Spinozism and existentialism.)

Good and evil name nothing positive in things; they are simply comparative notions that we form. Good suggests an approach toward some idea of perfection, as described in these words:

> By "good," therefore, I understand in the following pages everything which we are certain is a means by which we may approach nearer and nearer to the model of human nature we set before us. By "evil," on the contrary, I understand everything which we are certain hinders us from reaching that model.[36]

The aim of Spinoza's ethics is to enable us to move toward a more intuitive, and philosophical, understanding of this process of self-perfection in man. This process is further described in a series of points (there are thirty-three) which constitute the Appendix to Book IV. In the main, they restate in orderly fashion most of the steps that we have followed above.

The last book of the *Ethics* shows how a man may develop himself by striving to detach disturbing affects from the thought of an external cause in order to connect it with inner thoughts. Further, man must come to realize that an affect loses its passivity as soon as he can form a clear and distinct idea of it; and this can be done for all affects that appear to arise from some modification of the body.[37] The import of this is that one becomes more perfect as a man in this effort to advance toward a personally developed understanding of initial mental disturbances. ("Peace of mind" books in present-day applied psychology owe something to Spinoza.) Moreover, the mind may come to know that all things are necessary, and so connected with God, and so they should be consciously related to the idea of God. To know God is to love Him, and this is what man should do above all.[38] All of this is summed up in Proposition XXV, where he says that the highest mental endeavor and virtue is to understand things through the third level of knowledge. And his proof is as follows:

> The third kind of knowledge proceeds from an adequate idea of certain attributes of God to an adequate knowledge of the essences of things . . . in proportion as we understand things more in this way, we better understand God; therefore the highest virtue of the mind, that is, the power, or nature, or highest endeavor of the mind, is to understand things by the third kind of knowledge.[39]

Some years later, in the *Theological-Political Treatise*,[40] Spinoza set forth his views concerning man's duties to recognize and to obey God. These are not remarkable in their content but they are grounded entirely on natural reasoning and they have thus had a considerable influence on the later Deists. Spinoza's debt to Hobbes becomes more obvious in this treatise. There is no such thing as "natural" law or justice, since all events and tendencies in nature are equally natural. Before civil laws there is no difference between pious and impious: "wrong is conceivable only in an organized community."[41] The same rationalized naturalism is discernible in the *Political Treatise*. Natural right means the very laws or rules of nature. "Man, whether guided by reason or mere desire, does nothing save in accord with the laws and rules of nature." And later Spinoza adds: "I am altogether for calling a man so far free, as he is led by reason."[42] In the state of nature, wrongdoing is impossible, everything that you do is natural. In organized society, state law determines what is right and wrong. Frequently now, Spinoza mentions "utility" but this simply refers to the general human welfare and does not have the hedonistic connotation that is sometimes given the term in British writing.

It is impossible to fit Spinoza's ethics into the ordinary classifications of ethical theory. He is a naturalist only in the broadest sense: he did not think that the data or methods of the empirical sciences (his second-level knowledge) are directly applicable in moral philosophy. Yet he committed the "naturalistic fallacy" with complete abandon, by defining good in terms of several other features in his metaphysics, and so his ethics might be called a rationalistic naturalism.[43]

Descartes was a Catholic, Spinoza was originally of the Jewish faith, and our next rationalistic philosopher was an outstanding Protestant: Gottfried Wilhelm von Leibniz (1646–1716). A brilliant and learned scholar, Leibniz wrote in Latin, French, and even in his native German. He did not produce a treatise on ethics, as such. Most of his views on the subject are found in his works on jurisprudence and on miscellaneous subjects.[44] In the case of Leibniz, it is not essential to have a thorough knowledge of his theoretical philosophy in order to understand his ethical views. We might simply note that he was convinced that there is a reasonable explanation for everything that exists and happens, although he did not claim to know all these reasons. All reality is constituted of "monads," which are simple substances, indivisible and nonextended. These monads are like atomic force-centers which give rise to two kinds of activities: perceptions and desires. There is a very large number of created monads constituting the physical and mental universe. Monads do not interact (they have no windows) but each monad mirrors all the external universe in its internal perceptions. Monads with only *petites* (unconscious) *perceptions* cluster to form bodies. Monads with *grandes* (conscious) *perceptions* are souls which function as the entelechies (directive principles) of living bodies, including humans. God is the supreme Monad and does not have a body. Human soul monads have intelligence and free choice. The soul monads are destined for personal immortality.[45]

In 1693 Leibniz prepared and published an edition of documents dealing with the law of peoples (*Codex Juris Gentium Diplomaticus*) with a special Preface. Here, right (*jus*) is defined as "a kind of moral power, and obligation is a moral necessity." Moral means "something equivalent to natural for a good man." And a good man is "one who loves all men, so far as reason permits."[46] In the same place, wisdom is described as "nothing but the science of happiness itself." In a later commentary on this *Code of the Law of Peoples* (*Mantissa codicis juris gentium*, 1700) Leibniz singled out and stressed a definition of justice which he had given in the Preface. "Justice," he said, "is nothing but the charity of the wise man."[47] This leads to an explanation of the importance of the love of God but it does not mean that Leibniz is a voluntarist: the ultimate basis of ethical distinctions is not the will of God but divine wisdom or reason. He mentions an objection to his view: "It is more perfect so to submit to God that you are moved by his will alone and not by your own delight." To this anticipation of Kant's good-will theory, Leibniz replies that this objection "conflicts with the nature of things, for the impulse to action arises from a striving toward perfection, the sense of which is pleasure, and there is no action or will on any other basis." He adds that "even our evil purposes are moved by a certain perceived appearance of good or perfection."[48]

It is clear that Leibniz's ethics equates the good with an advance toward perfection. In a paper *On Wisdom*, written in German during the decade 1690-1700, he explained: "I call any elevation of being a perfection," and he adds that "perfection shows itself in great freedom and power of action."[49] As in Spinoza, the approach to personal perfection is a progress in understanding. Leibniz may be even more of an intellectualist than Spinoza, however. As he puts it in the same place, "Nothing serves our happiness better than the illumination of our under-

standing, and the exercise of our will to act always according to our understanding."

The view that moral obligation rests on the requirements of natural
law as known through human reason, is strongly supported by Leibniz.
About the year 1702 he wrote a French essay, *Reflections on the Common
Concept of Justice*. It is very critical of the notion that law is simply a
volitional command. Quoting the Latin dictum "*Stat pro ratione voluntas*" (Let my will stand for a reason), he insists that this is the motto of
a tyrant:

> All our theologians, therefore, and most of those of the Roman
> Church, as well as the ancient Church Fathers and the wisest and
> most esteemed philosophers have favored the second view, which
> holds that goodness and justice have grounds independent of will and
> of force.[50]

As Leibniz sees it, Hobbes wrongly adopted the position of Thrasymachus
that might is right, for he "fails to distinguish between right and fact.
For what *can* be is one thing; what *ought* to be is another." The "formal
reason" of justice, or what is right, must be common to God and man.
To show this Leibniz uses the example of arithmetical numbers and
relations: they must be the same in meaning for all intellects, even God's.
So also, "the term or word *justice* will have some definition or intelligible
meaning. And, by using the incontestable rules of logic, one can draw
definite consequences from every definition."[51] Precisely as one can develop logic, metaphysics, and arithmetic by deductive demonstration from
initial definitions, so can one produce the *science de droit* by reasoning.

This same point of view is evident in the *Nouveaux essais sur l'entendement humain* (written in 1704, not published until 1765). There,
after reviewing Locke's theory that moral rules are established by human
custom and convention, he mentions the suggestion that morality depends
on the will of the divine lawgiver. Leibniz's spokesman in this dialogue
(Theophilus) disagrees with this: "I prefer for myself to take as the
measure of moral good and of virtue the invariable rule of reason which
God is charged with maintaining."[52] Throughout this important twenty-
eighth chapter Leibniz offers a theory of morality that reasons from an
initial definition of goodness and the view that right action must conform
to nature, to general rules of moral conduct.[53] This point of view is in
complete accord with the *Reflections on Justice*, which we have been
considering: in this work of the same period we read, "We may ask what
is the true good. I reply that it is merely whatever serves the perfection
of intelligent substances."[54]

About the year 1675, Leibniz visited Spinoza in Amsterdam and was
shown a manuscript draft of the *Ethics* from which he made some notes.
It is difficult to determine the extent of the impression which Spinoza's

made upon him. Leibniz is very much like Spinoza in his esteem for the "serenity of the spirit, finding pleasure in virtue."[55] Such high-minded Stoicism was very much in the air at this time. In a summary appended by Leibniz to his *Essais de Théodicée* (1710) he began an explanation of moral obligation by quoting Seneca, "*semel jussit, semper paret*," which Leibniz took to mean that God commanded but once and then He obeys His own laws always. God's law imposes a type of necessity that is not physical but analogical.

This necessity is called moral, because, to the sage, *necessity* and *what ought to be* are equivalent things; and when it always has its effect, as it really has in the perfect sage, that is, in God, it may be said that it is a happy necessity. The nearer creatures approach to it, the nearer they approach to perfect happiness.[56]

It is in this passage that Leibniz enunciates his "principle of the best"—that God, or a perfect will, always chooses what is best. This is the source of his tremendous moral optimism and his confidence that God has made the best possible world.

The theme of the "love of God" runs through all of Leibniz's practical thinking. At the end of *Principes de la nature et de la Grâce* (1714) there is a beautiful and oft-quoted passage in which he speaks of this highest love which "makes us enjoy a foretaste of future felicity." Such love is disinterested, yet it gives us complete confidence in God as the guarantor of all our hopes and the assurer of happiness in a future life for those who live well.[57] He sees all men united under God as ruler of the "City of God" which is "a moral world within the natural world."[58] Supreme goodness is especially manifested in this most perfect state. In keeping with these views, Leibniz was a most tolerant man religiously and worked assiduously for the reunion of Christendom.

While Leibniz wrote no treatise on ethics, a Leibnizian manual of moral philosophy was produced by one of his followers, Christian von Wolff (1679-1754). He was the original "Herr Professor" of German philosophy and, indeed, has been called the schoolmaster of Europe. Wolff wrote very systematic, and very rationalistic, textbooks for all the traditional divisions of philosophy. In fact, though Aristotle had done a rather exact job of naming the parts of philosophy, Wolff added more divisions and names and we are still using them.[59] In 1738-1739 he published his two-volume textbook *Universal Practical Philosophy*, in an academic Latin that has been blamed on the Scholastics. A good deal is told about Wolff's character by the dedications: the first volume is addressed to Cardinal Melchior de Polignac, the second to Frederick Wilhelm, king of Prussia! This "practical philosophy" is intended to provide the principles for ethical, domestic, and political philosophy. These principles are the precepts of natural law (*lex naturalis*) which "makes known the sufficient reason (rationem sufficientem) within the essence and nature of man and of things."[60] His expansion of this teaching is based on Grotius and Leibniz. Everything is simple for Wolff; he solves the problem of a ground for moral obligation in a few words. "Granted, then, the essence and nature of man and things, obligation is granted, and it comes from the law of nature."[61] At times, Wolff's simplistic rationalism is but a caricature of Leibniz.

The great textbook is, of course, Wolff's Moral Philosophy, or Ethics Treated by the Scientific Method (1750–1753). Its five volumes are also well dedicated; one is to Charles, the Duke of Brunswick, another is to Andrzej Zaluski, Bishop of Cracow! Their subjects are: I. On the Intellect and Its Faculties and on the Intellectual Virtues; II. On Willing and Not-Willing (De voluntate et noluntate); III. On the Virtues and Moral Duties in regard to God; IV. On the Virtues and Moral Duties in regard to Ourselves; V. On the Virtues and Moral Duties in regard to Other People. This takes care of almost everything. The opening sentence of Volume I, page 1, reads: "Moral philosophy or ethics is a practical science, teaching the way in which man may perform his free actions in accord with the law of nature." All the rest of his ethics follows from this with Leibnizian rigor.

Christian Wolff's textbooks have had a tremendous influence. Their teaching is in the background of Kant and much of German idealistic ethics. In another tradition, Wolffian teaching has been accommodated to Catholic Scholastic ethics and was thought, until recently, to be the authentic doctrine of Thomas Aquinas. Not a few textbooks in "Christian Ethics," written for use in modern Protestant schools, owe a great debt to Wolff.

Another version of natural law ethics was developed by the German Protestant philosopher of law, Christian Thomasius (1655–1728). As a young writer he followed the views of Pufendorf and produced a number of books on jurisprudence and on the life of virtue, written in Latin or German. Thomasius helped to adapt the German vernacular to the use of practical philosophers. His emphasis was on the general utilitarian aspects of Pufendorf's theory of morality.

At the beginning of the eighteenth century in France, the leading practical philosopher was Charles Louis de Secondat, baron de Montesquieu (1689–1755). His Spirit of the Laws (1748) carried on the tradition of Cartesian rationalism but with good sense and moderation. Laws, according to Montesquieu, "are the necessary relations arising from the nature of things."[62] All law is an expression of an original reason in God that establishes relations between it and other beings and among all other beings. In itself, this rational order is natural law. Human laws are "positive" in the sense that they are established on particular occasions by men or societies in order to regulate human intercourse and to curb excessive force. The relations among all things under God all together constitute the "Spirit of Law." The main thing that Montesquieu brings to ethics in France is a growing awareness of the possibility of an empirical study of right and justice as realized in human customs and society.

Another French writer of this period was Jean Jacques Rousseau (1712–1778), who was born in Switzerland but lived in Paris for many years. His *Discourse on the Arts and Sciences* (1749–1750) introduces one of the basic themes in his practical philosophy: that man existed originally in an innocent state of nature, unregulated by laws but naturally good and unspoiled by "civilization." Right at the beginning of Part II of this *Discourse*, Rousseau shows that he even regarded the usual learned disciplines, including ethics, with suspicion: "Astronomy was born of superstition, eloquence of ambition, hatred, falsehood, and flattery; geometry of avarice; physics of an idle curiosity; and even moral philosophy of human pride."[63] In another work, the *Discourse on the Inequality of Men* (1754–1755), Rousseau further treats man in the state of nature and his passage into the artificial conditions of societal life. Unlike Hobbes, Rousseau does not see the "natural" man as warlike and quarrelsome. His happy savage only gets into difficulties with his fellows when he thinks of claiming exclusive title to a piece of land: from this point onward, laws must be devised and they are artificial and not natural. In a sense the possibility of evil, in the way of illegal activity, is attendant upon man's fabrication of positive laws. Rousseau also wrote novels that helped to popularize the importance of "naturalness" in moral and social living, and in education.

The famous *Social Contract* (1762) is Rousseau's most serious effort to explain how human society and its laws come into being. In it he describes two principles in man's nature that are prior to reason and that incline him toward his personal good and toward the good of others. These a priori factors were taken over later by Kant. Here is what Rousseau says of them:

> Meditating on the first and simplest operations of the human soul, I think that I perceive two principles prior to reason, one of which makes us intensely concerned about our well-being and personal self-preservation, and the other inspires us with a natural repugnance to seeing any other being that is capable of feeling, and especially those of our own species, die or suffer.[64]

It is the suggestion that man has some innate endowments in the moral order and prior to experience that will interest Kant, but there is still another teaching in the *Social Contract* which influenced later ethicians and especially Kant. This is the theory of the "general will" (*la volonté générale*). In a well-organized society, as Rousseau understands it, the judgment of the people on moral and social questions is the general or

popular will. It is usually expressed by the vote of the majority but it is, fo
Rousseau, no ordinary counting of opinions. There is something mystica
and almost divine about the general will. It is infallibly right and pure
it requires obedience from all citizens. It is the social expression of what i
right and moral.[65] Rousseau did not develop this "general will" into
theory of ethics but it is an important antecedent to Kant's doctrine of th
autonomous will.[66]

Critical of Rousseau's "moral naturalism" and of John Locke's em
piricism was Cardinal Sigismond Gerdil (1718–1802), an Italian by birt
and long residence in Rome but French in culture. His fundamentall
Augustinian philosophy is now little known (partly because he taught
theory condemned later by the Catholic Church, his ontologism, whic
held that all things are known by men on earth through seeing them i
the divine essence). His dependence on the Christian spiritualism o
Malebranche (whom we shall treat in Chapter XII) is generally recognizec
Gerdil's main writing in ethics is the Metaphysical Principles of Christia
Morality (published posthumously in 1806). In this work, Gerdil presents
"natural law" ethics which asserts that man knows the principles c
morality and justice by seeing them in the wisdom of God.[67] His teachin
is a simple and forthright theological approbatism. In effect, he denies a
difference between revealed and ordinary knowledge, and between supe
natural and natural wisdom. Despite official ecclesiastical disapproval c
his views, Cardinal Gerdil was read by many Catholics who saw his bran
of Christian spiritualism as a bulwark against the novelties of Locke an
the French "philosophes."

Germany in the early eighteenth century witnessed the growth of a
academic ethics that was under the influence of the Leibniz-Wolffian a
proach to the subject; that is, it started with a very general theory
practical reasoning, plus certain initial definitions, and then reasone
deductively to various derivative ethical judgments and to an applic
ethics that treated typical moral problems. Martin Knutzen (1713–1751
who was Immanuel Kant's teacher at Königsberg, belonged to this scho
of thought. He wrote a Philosophical Proof of the Truth of the Christi
Religion (1740). More important as a writer in the field of ethics was
contemporary professor at Frankfurt, Alexander Gottlieb Baumgart
(1714–1762), who usually appears in histories of philosophy as the found
of German aesthetics. Actually, Baumgarten produced the textbooks
metaphysics and ethics that were used by Kant as a young teacher. Spec
ically, Kant taught his first courses in ethics from two Latin books
Baumgarten, Philosophical Ethics (1740) and the Elements of First Pr
tical Philosophy (1760). These texts were followed closely in Kan
teaching between 1775 and 1781.[68]

Wolff's philosophy was not unopposed, of course. Professors like J
chim Lange (1670–1744) at Halle and Johann Andreas Rüdiger (167

1731) at Leipzig criticized his rationalism and mathematicism. Particularly in the area of ethics, one of Wolff's outstanding German critics was Christian A. Crusius (1715-1775). He is mentioned by Kant as teaching that the will of God is the objective ground of morality and was called a "theological moralist."[69] In another work, Kant reports that Crusius rejected the Leibniz-Wolffian principle of sufficient reason but substituted his own, equally fundamental, principle: "That which I cannot think except as true is true."[70] This does not meet with Kant's approval but, in general, Kant had a high regard for Crusius.

The most important ethician in this whole rationalist school was Immanuel Kant (1724-1804) and many experts think that he was the greatest moral philosopher in modern times. In his teaching and writing at Königsberg, Kant began a revolution in ethics which is still important in the twentieth century. It is usual to divide his thought into the precritical and critical periods. His first Critique (of Pure Reason) was printed in its first edition in 1781. During the decade preceding this publication he had been turning away from Wolffian philosophy toward a more personal way of thinking. His Inquiry into the Distinctness of the Principles of Natural Theology and of Morals (1764) is the main ethical work of the precritical period. It deals with the question of whether strict geometrical demonstration is possible in ethics and philosophical theology.[71] The Lectures on Ethics were edited from students' notes taken in his classes at Königsberg during the years 1775 to 1781. As we have seen, they show a professor dealing wittily and often eloquently with the systematic outlines of Baumgarten's ethics. At this point, Kant is in transition toward his own critical ethics. The Foundations of the Metaphysic of Morals (1785) is one of his important contributions to ethics. The other is the Critique of Practical Reason, published in 1788 after the appearance of the second edition (B) of the Critique of Pure Reason. Much of the same subject matter is treated in the Foundations and in the Critique of Practical Reason but the order of the arguments is different and the style of the former is more popular in comparison with the rigorous and systematic procedure of the second Critique. In 1797 Kant published his Metaphysics of Morals which carried his ethics into the philosophy of law (Part I) and the theory of special duties and virtues (Part II). In the last decade or so of his life Kant produced a good many notes and miscellaneous essays which contain some material on his later ethical views.[72] Among other things, the Opus Postumum shows that the elderly Kant is ready to grant a more immediate and real role to God as a moral legislator.[73]

Just how much of Kant's speculative philosophy one needs to know in order to understand his ethics is problematical. Certainly one would have to study the Critique of Pure Reason before attempting any thorough study of the practical philosophy.[74] Kant distinguished three cognitive faculties in man. Sensibility is man's receptivity to sensory data under the subjective forms of space and time. Understanding (*Verstand*) is the faculty of synthesizing sense data so that they may be thought in terms of the categories of human knowledge. Reason (*Vernunft*) is the faculty that transcends the conditions of experience and spontaneously gives rise to certain ways of relating the objects of understanding among themselves and to some higher principle. It is by reason that our knowledge of objects is ordered into systems. What reason contributes apart from the data of experience is a priori, from within the very constitution of man's consciousness. The phenomenal objects which are constructed in the imagination out of the presentations of sense experience as formed by the categories of sensibility and understanding are not things-in-themselves. These latter are by definition unknown, for, if they were known they would be in consciousness and not in themselves. When Kant investigates "pure" reason, he is endeavoring to discover what is characteristic of the mind and its functioning, quite apart from the empirical or received elements of thought.

The part of the *Critique of Pure Reason* devoted to the "Transcendental Dialectic" has a section that deals with the antinomy of natural causality and human freedom.[75] One may argue that another sort of causality, that of freedom, is necessary; and one may also argue that freedom has no place in the explanation of the phenomenal world. In attempting to resolve this conflict of reasonings, Kant suggests, in the following passage, that morality is a domain to which pure reason may be extended:

> The legislation of human reason has two objects, nature and freedom, and therefore contains not only the law of nature, but also the moral law, presenting them at first in two distinct systems, but ultimately in one single philosophical system. The philosophy of nature deals with all that *is*, the philosophy of morals with that which *ought to be*.[76]

This provides an important transition to Kantian ethics: in effect, complete theory of pure reason would have to extend into the sphere of practical reason.

The *Foundations of the Metaphysic of Morals* is easier than the *Critique of Practical Reason* to digest; so, we will use its argument as the main part of our consideration of Kant's ethics. What he is attempting in this work is a general account of what is needed to reason out theory of ethics. Kant proposes to explain the formal basis of moral judgment. A complete ethics would include material received from experience (practical anthropology) interpreted in the light of certain laws or principles provided prior to experience from the resources of reason itself. More particularly, in discussing these "foundations" or fundamental principles, Kant is dealing with the preconditions to a general philosophy (metaphysics) of ethical judgment. (He wrote the "metaphysics" of ethics in the treatise published in 1797, *Metaphysik der Sitten*.) The first section of the *Foundations* shows how we move from common rational knowledge of morals to a philosophical knowledge. It is here at the start that Kant introduces one of his most famous ethical doctrines: the only unqualified good is a good will. Moreover, he insists that it is the function of practical reason to give rise to such a volition.[77] This leads to the enunciation of three propositions of morality: (1) to have moral worth an action must be done from duty; (2) the action does not derive its moral worth from its results but from the maxim which produces it; and (3) duty is the necessity in an action performed out of respect for law. Already at this point there is also the suggestion that the rule, or maxim, from which moral activity springs must be capable of becoming a universal law.

Section two of the *Foundations* considers the process from popular moral philosophy to a metaphysics of morals. All moral concepts have their seat in reason prior to all data of experience. Natural (or physical) events always occur according to laws; only rational beings, however, act according to *conceptions* of laws. This implies a peculiar and distinctive ability in men. "This capacity is will. Since reason is required for the derivation of actions from laws, will is nothing else than practical reason."[78] The formula of any command of reason is an imperative, of which there are two kinds: hypothetical (if you wish this, then do that) and categorical (commanding an action that is of itself objectively necessary). Thus we are introduced to the name and notion of a "categorical imperative." In the ensuing few pages,[79] three formulations of this absolute kind of command are given by Kant. The first is: "Act only according to that maxim by which you can at the same time will that it should become a universal law." A few paragraphs later is the second: "Act as though the maxim of your action were by your will to become a universal law of nature." The third formula is given later: "Act so that you treat humanity, whether in your own person or in that of another, always as an end and never as a means only." What we have here is an attempt by Kant to show the most basic formal pattern that would regulate the expression of more specific ethical or moral judgments.

The categorical imperative is "formal" in the sense of containing no definite subject matter but providing a principle of all moral commands. It has given rise to various other formulations of the principle of universalization or generalization, in more recent ethics.) Implied in Kant's discussion of these formulas is the notion of the "autonomy of will"— suggesting that practical reason (which is "will" as legislative) has here something of the force of Rousseau's general will.[80] Furthermore, the idea of a "realm of ends" is brought out here. In fact, the principle of autonomy is stated in such a way as to be equivalent to another formula for the categorical imperative: "Never choose except in such a way tha the maxims of the choice are comprehended in the same volitions a universal law."[81] As opposed to autonomy of will, Kant speaks of he eronomy of will (choosing for motives apart from the maxim implied i the categorical imperative) as the source of all spurious principles c morality. Explicitly, the concept of perfection and the notion of a mo: perfect divine will are regarded as heteronomous principles.

The third section of the *Foundations* is devoted to the process fro: the metaphysics of morals to pure practical reason. Here, freedom become the most important presupposition of the autonomy of will. A ration: being may consider himself as belonging to the world of sense and natur or as part of the intelligible world under laws that derive from reason. . is the idea of freedom that makes one a member of the intelligib world. Freedom makes the categorical imperative possible.[82] At the en of the *Foundations*, Kant admits that we do not fully understand tl unconditional necessity of the categorical imperative but argues that v do grasp its incomprehensibility.

In the *Critique of Practical Reason*, Kant covers much the same grou: but more thoroughly and in reverse order. We saw that the *Foundatio:* begins with moral law and freedom and analyzes them to find the grounds. The second *Critique* is synthetic in its method, starting wi experience and moving toward a more general organization of the da of morality. Perhaps the chief conclusion which the practical *Critiq* adds to the *Foundations* is the demonstration of the great unity betwe practical and theoretical reason. Still another formulation of the ca: gorical imperative is offered in the *Critique of Practical Reason:* "So a that the maxim of your will could always hold at the same time as principle establishing universal law."[83] This is probably the best-knov statement of the categorical imperative. It is again intimately related the autonomy of will as practical reason.

In the *Critique of Practical Reason* the famous postulates of ethics : clearly presented.[84] Kant had shown in the first *Critique* that it is i possible, in the context of his principles, to demonstrate the exister of God, the freedom of the human agent, and the immortality of t human soul. Now, in the light of the demands of practical reason, argues that freedom must be granted in order that moral action possible, that God is needed to guarantee man's independence from t world of sense, and that immortality is required to provide a durati adequate to the fulfillment of moral law.

Kant's ethics is a deontology. In the last resort the basis for do: good and avoiding evil is one's personal awareness of duty. There i: much quoted passage in the *Critique of Practical Reason* where he h: duty as that which requires obedience without threatening, which mo without enticing, and which provides a law that is unconditionally bi:

ing.[85] Obedience to moral duty cannot be motivated by fear of punishment or the desire for happiness, although practical reason suggests that happiness will follow upon action that is motivated by good will. This is an idealistic and high-minded ethics. It demands a degree of intellectual integrity and sophistication which is rare even among men of learning.

Much German ethics in the nineteenth century consists of controversies between the followers and the critics of Immanuel Kant. Many thinkers accept part of his teaching but attempt to modify other elements. Typical is Salomon Maimon (1753-1800), who agreed that the supreme law in ethics is an a priori datum of consciousness.[86] Yet Maimon could not agree that the desire for happiness should be excluded from the motivation for good action. He also felt that Kant had neglected the impact of moral feelings on the human agent: high-minded pleasure seemed to Maimon to be a most valuable incentive to good behavior.[87] We shall see in Chapter XI how Kantian ethics continued to play a central role in later German thinking.

PART FOUR

MODERN THEORIES

CHAPTER X

Utilitarian and Subjectivist Ethics in Britain

IT WAS in the eighteenth and nineteenth centuries that the contrast between the utilitarian and the intuitionist approaches to ethics came to the fore. This division is not restricted to British thinkers but it is most evident in their attempts to do practical philosophy. The utilitarian thinks that judgments about human actions to the effect that they are good, right, and ought to be done (or contrariwise, that they are bad, wrong, and ought to be omitted) are justified by considering the knowable consequences of such actions to the agent or to other persons, or to both. These consequences or results may be viewed either in terms of the advantage of the individual agent (egoistic utilitarianism), or in the light of the advantage of a plurality of persons other than the agent (universal utilitarianism). Sometimes the first type is called hedonism and the second simply "utilitarianism."[1] In its broadest sense utilitarianism maintains "that the right or wrong of an action is to be judged by its utility in the production of happiness."[2] J. S. Mill thought that he had picked up the term "utilitarianism" from John Galt's novel *Annals of the Parish* (1821), but it had been used as early as 1781 by Jeremy Bentham.[3]

Ethical intuitionism, on the other hand, is the view that a person directly knows or feels the good (or "oughtness") of an action or moral judgment, without any need to consider other items, such as consequences, in justification. As Henry Sidgwick understood the term: "Writers who maintain that we have 'intuitive knowledge' of the rightness of actions usually mean that this rightness is ascertained by simply 'looking at' the actions themselves, without considering their ulterior consequences."[4] Broadly understood, intuitional ethics would include some right reason theories, some types of deontology, moral sensism, and psychological approbative types of ethics. For the present chapter, we will simply understand intuitionism as the ethics that concentrates on the subjective attitude of the moral agent, rather than on the results of his action, in discussing what is morally good or bad. In the eighteenth century, what is under discussion is not always the individual action but may be the premises of moral reasoning. This is why the term "subjectivist" is used in the title of this chapter: it simply means an ethical approach that starts from something experienced within the moral person or subject. We shall see that many ethicians manage to combine intuitionism with utilitarianism; it is only as pure positions that they are mutually incompatible.

At the end of the seventeenth century, Richard Cumberland had introduced the theory, but not the name, of universal utilitarianism into English ethics. In his Latin *Treatise of the Laws of Nature* (1672), he had argued that it is not "possible to determine what is the best thing a man can do in each instance, unless the effects, remote as well as near, which may result in every variety of circumstances, be foreseen and compared among themselves."[5] This statement of the method of utilitarianism is followed by a remarkable enunciation of the principle of the greatest happiness to the greatest number. Cumberland calls this proposition the "fountain of all natural laws."

> The greatest benevolence of every rational agent towards all, constitutes the happiest state of all in general and of each in particular, as far as is in their power to procure it; and it is necessarily requisite in order to attain the happiest state, to which they can aspire; and therefore the common good of all is the supreme law.[6]

This brand of utilitarianism (combined in Cumberland with a right reason view of moral law) was not acceptable to David Hume (1711–1776). He tended to distrust deductive reasoning in ethics and he could not see why the common good should take precedence over private interests. The complicated ethical position which Hume eventually reached is still a most important factor in the thinking of twentieth-century British ethicians. He rejected the notion that reason can command or move the human will and insisted that ethics should concentrate on certain impressions or feelings of approval or disapproval within the agent. In Hume's thinking, "an action, or sentiment, or character, is virtuous or vicious, because its view causes a pleasure or uneasiness of a particular kind."[7] He adopted, then, an ethical position which is subjectivist in the sense that we have just seen.

The problem of interpreting Hume's ethics is made more difficult by his own later dissatisfaction with the doctrine of his famous *Treatise of Human Nature* (1739–1740). Its third book is frequently made the basis for expositions of Hume's ethical position but Henry Sidgwick[8] claims that the *Treatise* was "expressly repudiated" (apparently referring to Hume's admitted disappointment with the reception of the *Treatise* as noted in the *Autobiography*), and Sidgwick confines his analysis to the *Inquiry concerning the Principles of Morals* (1751). We will take a look at the doctrine of both works. There is also some material of ethical significance in the popularly written *Essays, Moral and Political* (1741–1742).

To understand Hume's argument in his practical philosophy we should think briefly of his view of man. Both the *Treatise* and the *Enquiry concerning Human Understanding* (1748) give a phenomenalistic account of the human agent. Hume tried to use Newton's method of empirical science in the whole field of philosophy. What is given in initial human experience is a series of "perceptions." These are both cognitive and emotional presentations. They combine in various patterns of association and thus form more complicated events in experience. Psychology (not yet developed as a distinct discipline in Hume's day) would be the study of these atoms of experience and their various modes of association. There is no mind, in the sense of an immaterial substance or power that thinks or feels these data; there is no person, in the sense of an individual being endowed with intelligence and volitional freedom. Hume continues to speak of persons and selves but in a very special way. A mind or person is a series of separately existing and discrete perceptions, occurring in such a way that one perception seems to give rise to the next.[9] When perceptions occur forcefully they are called impressions; when they are weak they are termed ideas. Perceptions are related according to three modes of association: resemblance, contiguity in time or place, and cause-effect.

In Book III of the *Treatise* (sec. 1) we are told that "reason or science is nothing but the comparing of ideas, and the discovery of their relations." So viewed, reason is wholly inactive and cannot be a source of moral experience. As Hume now says:

> Those who affirm that virtue is nothing but a conformity to reason; that there are eternal fitnesses and unfitnesses of things which are the same to every rational being that considers them; that the immutable measures of right and wrong impose an obligation, not only on human creatures, but also on the Deity himself: All these systems concur in the opinion, that morality, like truth, is discerned merely by ideas, and by their juxta-position and comparison. . . . Since morals, therefore, have an influence on the actions and affections, it follows, that they cannot be derived from reason; and that because reason alone, as we have already proved, can never have any such influence.[10]

This neatly disposes of Cudworth and all such rationalists. From this point onward, in British ethics, it will be generally agreed that Hume has shown the folly of speaking about natural laws, right reason, and all such nonsense.

In this same section of the *Treatise*, Hume introduces the approbative portion of his theory. To say that an act or character is vicious simply means that one has a feeling or sentiment of blame in viewing it. Vice and virtue are perceptions in the mind, just as sensible qualities (sounds, colors, heat) are perceptions and not present in objects. So, in the second section of Book III, he offers his version of a moral sense theory. This is the function of feeling pain at the perception of an action which is then called vicious, and of feeling pleasure in viewing another action which is virtuous. Some such moral feelings are original instincts and are "natural"; other virtuous feelings arise by means of artifice from the needs of mankind and are called "artificial." Justice is an example of such an artificially contrived virtue.[11]

Book II of the Treatise is devoted to the passions as moral principles. If reason cannot be a source of action, then feelings can. Some passions are primary and simple feelings and others are derivative and follow upon ideas. There are also self-regarding and other-regarding feelings. Of the latter, sympathy is important in Hume's ethics. As he sees it, sympathy arises when there occur ideas of the effects in others of something such as a painful surgical operation: these ideas may give rise to stronger impressions which, in turn, precede feelings of pain in the observer who is not under surgery.[12] As a vicarious emotion and other-directed, sympathy is an important principle for moral feelings and actions. Along with self-interest and custom, sympathy is used to explain the working of moral sense.[13]

One final contribution of the Treatise to the history of ethics may be noted. In a famous passage he states the "is-ought" problem very clearly:

> In every system of morality, which I have hitherto met with, I have always remarked, that the author proceeds for some time in the ordinary way of reasoning, and establishes the being of a God, or makes observations concerning human affairs; when of a sudden I am surprized to find, that instead of the usual copulations of propositions, is, and is not, I meet with no proposition that is not connected with an ought, or an ought not. . . . As this ought or ought not expresses some new relation or affirmation, it is necessary that it should be explained; and at the same time that a reason should be given for what seems altogether inconceivable, how this new relation can be a deduction from others which are entirely different from it.[14]

Many ethicians, particularly in the twentieth century, have attempted t solve this problem of the relation of ought to is. In alternative te: minology it may be stated as the problem of how to get values fror facts.

The Enquiry concerning the Principles of Morals is Hume's ow revision of the third book of the Treatise, done after ten years in whic few readers paid any attention to this new start in British ethics. There are important differences between the two works. Instead of "sympathy" the *Enquiry* dwells upon "humanity" as a sentiment which all men have in common and which gives a sort of open and public character to moral attitudes. The distinction between "natural" and "artificial" is excluded as a verbalism in the *Enquiry*. More important, the handling of justice shifts from a Hobbesian emphasis on self-interest modified by sympathy as a basis for the virtue of justice to the concept of utility to society.[15] Utility has the meaning of "tendency to *ulterior* good"; it is the basis for several moral virtues but it is not the sole source of virtue; other qualities—courtesy, modesty, cheerfulness—contribute to virtue.

The following summary passage shows how Hume tried to combine a sentimental approbative theory of ethics with a measure of public agreement that is closely related to utility.

> The notion of morals implies some sentiment common to all mankind, which recommends the same object to general approbation, and makes every man, or most men, agree in the same opinion or decision concerning it. It also implies some sentiment, so universal and comprehensive as to extend to all mankind, and render the actions and conduct, even of the persons the most remote, an object of applause or censure, according as they agree or disagree with that rule of right which is established.[16]

Hume's influence in ethics has been extensive and profound. His stress on social utility leads into British utilitarianism in its several varieties. His emphasis on feelings of approval or disapproval is eventually taken up by psychological approbative ethics and, especially, by the school of emotive ethicians. In the *Essays, Moral and Political* ("Of the Original Contract") these two aspects of his thought are clearly brought out. Of two kinds of moral duties, one proceeds from natural instinct and is quite independent of ideas of obligation or public utility: love of children, gratitude to benefactors, and pity for the unfortunate are given as examples. A second type of moral duty is performed solely from a sense of obligation, an awareness of the necessities of human society. This is Hume's ethics in brief.

An almost immediate reaction to Hume's ethics is found in the *Review of the Principal Questions in Morals* (1758) by a Unitarian minister named Richard Price (1723–1791). Price disagrees with the epistemology and psychology which he finds in Hobbes, Locke, and Hume. Bluntly, Price says that Hume's assertion that all our ideas are either impressions or copies of impressions is "destitute of all proof."[17] Combining in a surprisingly consistent way the views of Cudworth, Samuel Clarke, and Butler, Price proposes a theory of "eternal and immutable" morality. He tries to reinstate "understanding" as the human power to grasp the unchanging natures of actions and realities. What Price contributes to the discussion is something which may have been implicit in earlier writers but is only now made explicit. The "understanding" is not the same as the "power of reasoning." By the latter we investigate certain relations between objects—but that is not what understanding does. As he explains it, to understand is to see something:

> As bodily sight discovers to us visible objects; so does understanding (the eye of the mind, and infinitely more penetrating) discover to us intelligible objects; and thus, in a like sense with bodily vision, becomes the inlet of new ideas.[18]

In effect, Price teaches that men enjoy an intellectual intuition of certain principles of moral judgment. This, plus his insistence that "rectitude" must be the motive for virtuous activity, may be the reason why some historians treat Price as a precursor to Kant.[19]

More impressed by Hume's position was Adam Smith (1723–1790), who is well known as a pioneer political economist but not so well recognized as an ethician. Smith was professor of moral philosophy at Glasgow and wrote his *Theory of Moral Sentiments* (1759) long before his famous *Wealth of Nations* (1776). Taking the principle of "sympathy" from Hume's *Treatise,* Smith investigated this altruistic feeling at great length and made it the sole foundation of ethical judgment.[20] He did not accept a special "moral sense," as such, but spoke of a sense of propriety quite distinct from the perception of utility. In fact, Adam Smith disliked the idea that usefulness to society might be taken as a criterion of morality. We make certain judgments of approbation or disapprobation of the conduct of other persons and these other-directed views and feelings are fundamental to ethics. When we attempt to judge our own conduct, we reverse the process, as it were, and try to see our selves as others see us. Here Smith made considerable use of the "impartial spectator"—a disinterested observer whose attitudes provide a foun dation for the sense of obligation and for ethics.[21] David Hume had used the idea of the impartial spectator throughout the third book of the *Treatise.* Adam Smith was the last important exponent of the mora sense theory, even though he substituted other terms (such as the sense of propriety) for it.[22] Smith's "impartial spectator" was not far removed from an active Presbyterian conscience, and that is close to a sense o morality.

Much of the activity in British ethics at this time centered in Scotland Adam Smith's successor as professor of moral philosophy at Glasgow wa Thomas Reid (1710–1796), founder of the school of "common-sense" philosophy. (Actually, a French Jesuit named Claude Buffier had firs proposed the appeal to common sense against Cartesianism. Buffier's ideas are found in the *Traité des premières vérités* published in 171₋ Both Reid and Dugald Stewart read Buffier.) The platform of th₋

"common-sense" philosophy was very much like one part of the teaching of Boethius. In reaction to what seemed the excessive subtlety and complication of British epistemology from Locke to Hume, Reid asserted (in his *Inquiry into the Human Mind on the Principles of Common Sense*, 1764) that it is wrong to make "ideas" the objects of human knowledge. As far as Reid was concerned, when I see a tree I know an existing thing and not an idea.[23] In the moral area, there are certain universally accepted principles which need no philosophic proof. An example is: "No man ought to be blamed for what it was not in his power to hinder."[24] Man's moral faculty is his conscience which, on the basis of the common principles of right and wrong, dictates man's duty. Moral instruction and guidance are needed to develop good ability in moral reasoning but the whole business is not as tricky and sophisticated as Hume would suggest.[25]

At Edinburgh, Adam Ferguson (1723–1816) taught moral philosophy from 1764 to 1785 and was much influenced by his friend David Hume. Dugald Stewart (1753–1828) became professor in 1785 and introduced a modified version of Reid's common-sense ethics. His *Philosophy of the Active and Moral Powers of Man* (1828) was one of the first English textbooks in ethics used in the United States. Stewart taught that ethical propositions are just as true as mathematical ones: "In both cases we have a perception of *truth*, and are impressed with an irresistible conviction that the truth is immutable and independent of the will of any being whatever."[26] Stewart's pupil Thomas Brown (1778–1820) carried on the common-sense tradition at Edinburgh and exerted some influence on French ethicians of the nineteenth century, such as Victor Cousin. At Aberdeen, James Beattie (1735–1803) was a critic of Hume and taught ethics in the common-sense tradition.

In 1768 John Witherspoon (1723–1794) came to America from Scotland to serve as president (and *ex officio* to teach philosophy) at the College of New Jersey, later to be known as Princeton University. A century later, James McCosh (1811–1894) brought the common-sensism of the Scottish school to the same American institution.[27] In this manner, the realistic, Biblically oriented, middle-of-the-road ethics from Scotland became a pioneer influence on higher education in the United States.

The great conservative thinker in British politics, Edmund Burke (1729–1797), was not a great ethician but he deserves to be mentioned here. He was not—contrary to what one recent study has tried to show—an exponent of the ethics of Thomas Aquinas.[28] There are superficial resemblances among all supporters of tradition and of natural law—but the differences can be more remarkable. Burke's *Philosophical Inquiry into the Origin of Our Ideas on the Sublime and Beautiful* (1756) and his *Appeal from the New to the Old Whigs* (1790) reveal a man who is eager to reinstate the classical function of "understanding" into English practical philosophy.[29] The idea that "utility" is the criterion of moral judgment is clearly under widespread discussion at this time, for Burke takes a whole section to reject it. He shares, however, his era's general distrust of any attempt to found ethics on metaphysical abstractions, as this text from the *Appeal* indicates:

Nothing universal can be rationally affirmed on any moral, or any political subject. Pure metaphysical abstraction does not belong to these matters. The lines of morality are not like the ideal lines of mathematics. They are broad and deep as well as long. They admit of exceptions; they demand modifications. These exceptions are not made by the process of logic, but by the rules of prudence.[30]

Much more confident of his knowledge of ethics was the Anglican cleric and Cambridge tutor William Paley (1743–1805). He is usually remembered for his version of the argument for the existence of God from mechanical design in the universe; however, Paley's *Principles of Moral and Political Philosophy* (1785) was used as a textbook at Cambridge for more than fifty years.[31] Rejecting the notion of a moral sense, Paley made "utility" (in regard to both the particular and the general consequences of actions) the test of moral goodness.[32] The will of God determines the difference between moral right and wrong. It is conveyed to men in two ways: as revealed in Scripture and as known through the "light of nature." Virtue consists in "doing good to mankind, in obedience to the will of God, and for the sake of everlasting happiness." The ethics of William Paley is a neat combination of Christian morality with the principle of social utility.

A major figure in the history of British ethics, even though he did not pretend to be an ethician, was Jeremy Bentham (1748–1832). His primary interest was in the philosophy of law and politics but this required him to develop certain notions as to the relationship between morality and social organization. Estimates of the value of his suggestions in ethics vary widely. John Stuart Mill has called Bentham "the great subversive," yet Mill learned a great deal from Bentham.[33] It has been asserted that Bentham deliberately reduced all moral problems to technical ones.[34] In any case, the treatise that is ethically significant is Bentham's *Introduction to the Principles of Morals and Legislation* (1789). John Bowring's compilation, entitled *Deontology* (1834), is of doubtful value as a source.

In an anonymous publication in the year 1776 (*Fragment on Government*), Bentham revealed his early distrust of "natural law" thinking. The *Fragment* is an open attack on Sir William Blackstone (1723–1780) for his advocacy of natural law in his famous *Commentaries on the Law of England* (1765–1769). Blackstone had maintained that

the law of nature being coeval with mankind, and dictated by God himself, is of course superior in obligation to any other. It is binding over all the globe, in all countries, and at all times: no human laws are of any validity if contrary to this; and such of them as are valid derive all their force and all their authority, mediately or immediately, from this original.[35]

At one point in the *Fragment* Bentham characterized a view such as Blackstone's as "a sink that with equal facility will swallow any garbage that is thrown into it."[36]

Bentham helped to introduce the teaching that all laws governing human conduct are commands of a sovereign, backed by sanctions, and retained by a habit of obedience. The test of a good law is its "utility," which means "that property in any object, whereby it tends to produce benefit, advantage, pleasure, good, or happiness . . . to the party whose interest is considered."[37] The interest involved may be that of the individual person or that of the community but Bentham is inclined to take the interest of the individual as more basic, since the community is nothing more than a collection of individuals. He admits that he took the notion of "utility" from the French thinker Claude Adrien Helvétius (1715–1771), who had defined probity as that which has some usefulness (*utilité*) for the individual or his country.[38] In his treatise *De l'Homme* (1772), Helvétius described virtue in terms of "the confused idea of some quality useful to society."[39] In point of fact, the notion of utility as an ethical principle was becoming a commonplace in the late eighteenth century.

Perhaps Bentham is best known in ethics for his description of pleasure and pain in terms of quantity, and for his consequent theory of a "calculus of pleasures." As Mill noted,[40] Bentham could see no qualitative distinctions in pleasures: "quantity of pleasure being equal, push-pin is as good as poetry." So Bentham developed a method of calculating the amount of pleasure to the individual by using the four determinants: (1) intensity, (2) duration, (3) certainty or uncertainty, and (4) propinquity or remoteness. In relation to the interest of a group of persons, Bentham added two more circumstances of pleasure to be included: (5) fecundity and (6) purity. To decide morally between two proposed actions, then, one has only to add up and compare their respective quantities of pleasure and select the greatest!

Motivation is not ignored by Bentham; the tenth chapter of his *Principles of Morals* is devoted to this subject. He thinks that "motive" has two senses: literally it means an incident that tends to arouse pleasure or pain, and so move the will; figuratively motive designates any fictitious entity within the mind (such as avarice, indolence, benevolence) considered as prompting the mind to take a certain course. Bentham makes an extended list of such motives at the end of his *Principles of Morals*.

Perhaps the most competent follower of Bentham was James Mill (1773–1836), the father of John Stuart. The elder Mill published an *Analysis of the Phenomena of the Human Mind* (1829) which simplified associationistic psychology by concentrating on the relation of contiguity. Personal pleasure and pain clearly function as the internal motives of moral action. Education is the chief means for the development of a better awareness of how to employ the utilitarian principle.

Not all British practical thinkers at this time agreed with Bentham. William Godwin (1756–1836) was also a utilitarian in his ethics, and, like Bentham, he was not primarily interested in ethical theory. Godwin's *Inquiry concerning Political Justice and Its Influence on Morals and Happiness* first appeared in 1793. It was intended as a rebuttal to Burke's *Reflections on the Revolution in France* (1790). Godwin was an ardent advocate of political and social freedom. However, he disagreed with Bentham's espousal of individual pleasure and pain as the key factors in moral judgment. Godwin's utilitarianism used the principle of the greatest happiness for the greatest number of people, long before John Stuart Mill formulated it. Of course, it should be remembered that this formula occurs in Bentham. The first note (written by Bentham) to the *Principles of Morals* speaks of "the greatest happiness or greatest felicity principle" and explains it.[41] However, Bentham had put little stress on the social dimension of utility, whereas Godwin insisted that personal pleasure and pain are not morally good motives for action. The latter thought that "reason" was the best moral motivation and in this he approached the better-known position of Immanuel Kant.[42]

One of the first British scholars who really knew something about Kant's ethics was the poet Samuel Taylor Coleridge (1772–1834). As his *Philosophical Lectures* (1818) reveal, Coleridge was reading Kant as early as 1804. He was much taken by Kant's arguments and tried to make them known in England. However, it was not until late in the nineteenth century that Kant's ethics made much impression on the British universities. Professors of ethics (John Grote, 1813–1866, at Cambridge; and James Ferrier, 1808–1864, at St. Andrews) distrusted the apparent agnosticism in the sage of Königsberg. Another well-known philosopher, Sir William Hamilton (1788–1856), was somewhat influenced by Kant but chiefly in the area of epistemology and in the direction of phenomenalism. Hamilton's views were brought to a wider audience by means of J. S. Mill's *Examination of Sir William Hamilton's Philosophy* (1865). As far as ethics is concerned, Hamilton combined Kant's teaching on the absolute and necessary character of primary moral principles with the down-to-earth moderation of Reid.

The "positivistic" quality of Bentham's theory of law was found also in the writing of John Austin (1790–1859). His *Province of Jurisprudence Determined* (1832) is not only the initiation of analytic jurisprudence; it is a forthright essay in utilitarianism. More clearly than Bentham, Austin taught that whatever the sovereign commands and can enforce is the law. This is what "positivism" means in the philosophy of law: there can be no appeal to a law of nature, a "higher law," or to the will of God.

Even in morals, what the state law enjoins is what is right. Austin obviously influenced John Stuart Mill. One commentator writes that "Mill learned more of moral philosophy [from John Austin] than he could have learned from Bentham."[43]

A British Catholic thinker who had some impact on the ethics of this period was John Henry Newman (1801–1890). At Oxford he had been a pupil of Richard Whately (1787–1863), who was an outstanding logician and an authority on the ethics of Paley.[44] So, the ethics that Newman originally learned was doubtless a Christian approbative theory. However, in his *Grammar of Assent* (1870) Newman showed a highly personal approach to some of the problems of ethics. First of all, he distinguished notional from real assent: the former is abstract and unrelated to life, the latter is directed toward things and is concrete and unconditional.[45] There is a certain impatience with conceptual knowledge and system building, in Newman, that resembles the attitude of the twentieth-century existentialist. Reason is able to create a world of ideas for itself; it is also able "to investigate its reasonings."[46] It is the second function that interests Newman. He thinks that informal inference is more important (especially in practical matters) than the syllogistic of Aristotle. So, we are offered the theory of the "illative sense"—the mind's power of concluding to a concrete and certain judgment. As Newman sees the matter:

> An ethical system may supply laws, general rules, guiding principles, a number of examples, suggestions, landmarks, limitations, cautions, distinctions, solutions of critical or anxious difficulties; but who is to apply them to a particular case? Whither can we go, except to the living intellect, our own, or another's? . . . It is a capacity sufficient for the occasion, deciding what ought to be done here and now, by this given person, under these given circumstances.[47]

Newman adds that this illative sense (which is a function of reason) is very much like Aristotle's *phronēsis*, the habit of reasoning well about practical matters. It is not really ethical theory, then, but the problem of applying any theory to life, that concerns Newman. In this he much resembles St. Augustine. His influence on the moral thinking of recent Catholic philosophers, such as Maurice Blondel (1861–1949) and Erich Przywara (1889–   ), is widely recognized.

Another British ethician, James Martineau (1805–1900), produced a much read survey of the subject in his *Types of Ethical Theory* (1885). Besides its obvious historical value, his work brings the whole problem of psychological motivation to the forefront in British ethics. To Martineau, morality is not an affair of the consequences, or even of the human action in itself. "That in which we discern the moral quality is, we have found, the *inner spring of action.* . . ."[48] The motive is known as good or evil by an immediate intuition. In addition to this view, Martineau is

also recognized for his advocacy of indeterminism in the perennial problem of free will.[49]

The outstanding personality in nineteenth-century British ethics, however, was John Stuart Mill (1806–1873). A precocious child educated
under the direction of his father, James, but without any training in
revealed religion, John Stuart Mill made ethics the focal point of his
personal interests. His contributions to theory of knowledge, psychology
and logic are well known. Against the realism of Hamilton, he argued
that what we know consists of mental states, and his notion of man
and his mind is basically that of David Hume. In logic Mill's theory of
induction is a landmark.

We will confine our examination of Mill's ethical theory to the two
key works. On the Logic of the Moral Sciences is actually the last part
of his System of Logic, first published in 1843. At this time he was in
close touch with the French social positivist Auguste Comte, and Mill's
treatment of the methods of social science shows this influence. The
other work is from twenty years later: it is the essay entitled Utilitarianism
(1863).

The Logic of the Moral Sciences is prefaced by a lengthy quotation
in French from Antoine Nicholas de Condorcet (1743–1794), who, in
his Historical Sketch of the Progress of the Human Mind (1794), had
insisted that the philosopher should form his opinions on the basis of
experience. With this empirical note established, Mill argues that a general
science of human nature is possible, and that within this science the
subject of psychology would be "the uniformities of succession, the law
whether ultimate or derivative, according to which one mental state
succeeds another—is caused by, or at least is caused to follow, another."
Next, Mill proposes a new science, "Ethology," which is to study the
formation of character, national and collective, as well as individual
character. This ethology is to be deductive in its method, contrasting
with psychology, which is inductive, as Mill sees it.[51] Character study,
however, is not ethics. Mill proceeds to discuss the methodology of the
various social sciences: economics, sociology, political science, and also
history. He does not think that they should, or can, use purely experimental methods; nor need these social sciences pretend to the sort of
accuracy that is characteristic of chemistry.

The twelfth chapter brings Mill to moral knowledge and he immediately makes it clear that he regards ethics as an "art" and not
science. Ethics employs the imperative mood and this is typical of an
art. Where there is an established law or rule (e.g. in a court of law)
the process of reaching a judgment is ratiocination or syllogism. This
contrasts with the procedure of the legislator whose function of establishing laws employs the opposite method. The legislator must look for the
reasons or grounds for his rule. Matters of fact (expressed in terms of
"is") are quite different from ought-propositions. Even in injunction

and recommendations (where "ought" is employed) some matter of fact is asserted, of course, namely "that the conduct recommended excites in the speaker's mind the feeling of approbation."[52] This is not enough; ethics must find general premises and deduce certain principal conclusions from them, in order to form a body of doctrine which will be the "Art of Life." It will have three divisions: morality, policy, and aesthetics —corresponding to the Right, the Expedient, and the Beautiful. This ethics as the art of life remains to be developed. Intuition of moral principles, if possible, would only take care of the start of the division of morality. Practical policy (prudential judgment) and aesthetics would require a different sort of principle. So, John Stuart Mill admits:

> I merely declare my conviction, that the general principle to which
> all rules of practice ought to conform, and the test by which they
> should be tried, is that of conduciveness to the happiness of mankind,
> or rather, of all sentient beings: in other words, that the promotion
> of happiness is the ultimate principle of Teleology.[53]

This is as far as the principle of universal utilitarianism is developed in Mill's *Logic*.

We have noticed how John Austin influenced John Stuart Mill. In Bentham there was always some ambiguity as to whether resultant utility was a test of the morality of a proposed individual action, or of a general type of activity. Speaking of human action, Austin said:

> Trying to collect its tendency . . . we must not consider the
> action as if it were *single* and *insulated*, but must look at the *class*
> of actions to which it belongs. The probable *specific* consequences
> of doing that single act, or forbearing from that single act, or of
> omitting that single act, are not the objects of the inquiry. The
> question to be solved is this:—If acts of the *class* were *generally*
> done, or *generally* forborne or omitted, what would be the probable
> effect on the general happiness or good?[54]

This helps us to understand the approach to the subject which Mill used in his *Utilitarianism* (1863).

First, Mill rejects the moral-sense theory: the existence of such a sense is not proved and even if we take it to be a function of our reason the deliverances of such a moral faculty would only be "the general principles of moral judgments."[55] The question of the morality of an individual action is not to be solved by direct perception but by applying a law to his case. Mill thinks that both ethical intuitionists and inductivists agree on this point. So he puts forth the utilitarian "creed" as his solution to the problem, after warning that it has nothing to do with the popular notion of "utility" as opposed to pleasure. Here is Mill's best statement of what it does mean:

The creed which accepts as the foundation of morals, Utility, or the Greatest Happiness Principle, holds that actions are right in proportion as they tend to promote happiness, wrong as they tend to produce the reverse of happiness. By happiness is intended pleasure, and the absence of pain; by unhappiness, pain, and the privation of pleasure.[56]

To this Mill adds two clarificatory points. What is involved is not the greatest happiness of the individual agent but "the greatest amount of happiness altogether." Moreover, there are different kinds of pleasure; variations in quality must be noted, as well as in quantity. On this point Mill is departing from Bentham.

The main way of justifying the principle of utility seems to Mill to consist in an examination of its ultimate sanction. He frankly asks: "What is the source of its obligation?"[57] The only answer that he can give is that his test is "the same as of all other moral standards—the conscientious feelings of mankind." Mill is convinced that it is generally agreed that men do desire happiness—and he concludes that virtue is what is truly conducive to happiness.

The fifth chapter of *Utilitarianism* associates utility with the notion of justice. Mill is well aware that many people have thought that men have a natural instinct or feeling for the just. He offers a very thoughtful account of the historical origin of men's acceptance of justice. Stressed in this is the idea that intelligent beings tend to grasp a "community of interest" and to develop the capacity to sympathize with human beings generally.[58] He even suggests that Kant's formula "So act, that thy rule of conduct might be adopted as a law by all rational beings" is an acknowledgement of the interest of mankind collectively. At the end, Mill decides that the duties of justice are simply the highest kind of social utilities; there are other things to do that are of utility, besides the obligations of justice. Justice has more definite commands and its sanctions are sterner.

Probably the outstanding British follower of John Stuart Mill was Alexander Bain (1818–1903). His *Mental and Moral Science* (1868) combined two works that developed the psychological and ethical implications of Mill's thought. Bain's *John Stuart Mill, A Criticism: With Personal Recollections* (1882) is a still-useful introduction to utilitarianism. It was Bain who introduced this way of thinking into the universities of Glasgow and Aberdeen.

Some people think that Henry Sidgwick (1838–1900) was the greatest of British ethicians. Certainly he was one of the best informed historically and the most learned. His *Methods of Ethics* (1874) and *Outlines of the History of Ethics* (1886) are evidences of the scholarship that he brought to his teaching at Cambridge. Sidgwick felt that, in the long run, there were really only three distinct approaches to the central problem of ethics, which is the justification of ethical or moral judgment. These are egoistic hedonism, universalistic hedonism (or utilitarianism), and intuitionism.[59] Of these, Sidgwick bluntly rejected Hobbes's egoism. This seemed to Sidgwick to be no ethics at all. Like a good academician, he tried to combine the best features of the other two theories, intuitional and utilitarian ethics. Yet he differed from John Stuart Mill on the matter of the ground of the greatest happiness principle. Mill, he thought, had confused the issue by attempting to show what men *ought* to desire from what they *do* desire. In other words, Sidgwick was concerned about something like the naturalistic fallacy well before G. E. Moore invented that striking name.

It was to avoid what seemed a circle in Mill's argument (happiness is desirable because we all desire it) that Sidgwick claimed an intuition of the principle of utility.[60] Of course, there are places in Mill's *Utilitarianism* where some recognition is given to the suggestion that we instinctively intuit the ground of moral obligation. But of all his predecessors, Samuel Clarke was the moral philosopher who seemed to Sidgwick to have had the most to offer. In this judgment, Sidgwick was also passing sentence on British ethics of the nineteenth century.

In his poem entitled *The Latest Decalogue*, Arthur Hugh Clough (1819–1861) expressed his cynical verdict on the utilitarian ethics of his century:

> Thou shalt have one God only; who
> Would be at the expense of two?
> No graven images may be
> Worshipped, except the currency:
> Swear not at all; for, for thy curse
> Thine enemy is none the worse:
> At Church on Sunday to attend
> Will serve to keep the world thy friend:
> Honour thy parents; that is, all
> From whom advancement may befall:
> Thou shalt not kill; but need'st not strive
> Officiously to keep alive:
> Do not adultery commit,
> Advantage rarely comes of it:
> Thou shalt not steal; an empty feat,
> When it's so lucrative to cheat:
> Bear not false witness; let the lie
> Have time on its own wings to fly:
> Thou shalt not covet, but tradition
> Approves all forms of competition.

CHAPTER XI

German Idealistic Ethics

IN THE nineteenth-century German tradition ethics remained very muc under the influence of Kant. The theoretical philosophy is generall idealistic, i.e. most thinkers in this period take it as granted that th objects of understanding and reasoning are ideas of some sort. Philos phy was considered to begin with an investigation of the inner present tions of human consciousness. These "ideas" were not merely cognitiv of course; they revealed feelings, volitions, human attitudes, laws, an obligations. A good deal of the German philosophy of this century w: subjectivistic but there were attempts to reach an objective ground f both speculative and practical knowledge. Much of it was also dialectic in the sense that some sort of step-by-step pattern of development w. attributed to the ongoing process of reality. Finally, German ethics this century becomes more and more divorced from the religious co mitments of the Judaeo-Christian tradition. This is not universal but t general trend is toward a secular ethics.

Hundreds of German scholars were occupied with ethics at this tin it had become a popular subject in the university curriculum. We sh; concentrate on four key figures: Fichte, Hegel, Schelling, and Schope hauer. Less influential ethicians will be noted in passing.

Johann Gottlieb Fichte (1762–1814) initiates and personifies the ma tendencies of idealistic ethics. All his writings are of ethical significan but three of them will be sufficient for a brief treatment of his ethi Almost from the start of his writing career he showed his conviction tl the domain of practical reason is most important. We see this in t *Basis of Natural Right* (1796) and the *System of Ethics* (*Das Syst der Sittenlehre*, 1798). Written in more popular style is the *Vocation Man* (1800) which, however, presents most of the basic themes Fichtean ethics. There is, finally, the *Addresses to the German Nat.* (1807–1808), in which Fichte tried to rally his fellow countrymen telling them that the Germans have as their destiny the duty of becom "culture bearers" to the rest of humanity.

The aim of Fichte's methodology was to develop philosophy into a general theory of scientific knowledge (*Wissenschaftslehre*). This requires one organizing principle to explain all the presentations (*Vorstellungen*) of consciousness. Such data might be explained dogmatically and deterministically by attributing their origin to the "natural" world of matter. Such a move is repugnant to Fichte. The events of consciousness may also be explained mentally and freely by relating them to the mental character of the self or ego. This is what Fichte decides to do. From the very beginning, he takes the self as free, active, and moral.

One may think of the ego as contrasted with the nonego (or of the subject positing itself as object) within consciousness. One may experience the ego as a mental energy (will) which in acting meets with opposition—which is eventually revealed as but another aspect of will. As object or obstacle the nonego remains a function of the "Ich," the ever-present ego. So, Fichte's philosophy becomes an ethics as soon as it leaves the level of methodology. What is real for him is not some nonmental world of physical matter: the real is the resultant of the expression of volitional energy. He thinks that this is immediately evident within individual consciousness. "My will is mine, and it is the only thing that is wholly mine and entirely dependent on myself; and through it I have already become a citizen of the realm of freedom and of pure spiritual activity."[1]

Ethics deals with the realization of the ideal activity, both in the individual consciousness and in the moral order of the universe, which is a field for the development of infinite will. The ego first "posits" itself and thereby exists (thesis). It next sets up the nonego in opposition to itself, thereby becoming conscious of an otherness within itself (antithesis). Third, there comes an awareness that the ego without limitation (as absolute) must posit a certain limitation (or finitude) in both the ego and the nonego (synthesis). These are the stages of Fichte's dialectic: progress in knowledge and in morality will follow this triadic pattern.

There is an ordinary knowledge of morality common to all men because the "voice of conscience" speaks clearly and unequivocally within each of us.[2] In the second place, there is a philosophical science of what is right (ethics) that entails the understanding of the ground of morality in terms of Fichte's theory of knowledge. The main purpose of ethics is to show the development and realization of will, or moral consciousness, toward independence (*Selbständigkeit*). The resolve to become independent and free, in this sense, is called "Faith."[3] Thus, Fichte's ethical imperative is: "Act according to thine own conviction of duty." To act from motives arising from nature or authority is to abandon what is distinctively moral.

Fichte's moral conception of the state is in direct continuity with the foregoing. Will is not simply your mental energy or mine: there is the greater "will" (obviously reminiscent of Rousseau's general will), which posits itself in the life of the national state. Politics is but an extension of ethics. In the social community, the individual will must learn to limit itself in relation to the interests of other individual wills. Society, then, is "the relation of reasonable beings to each other . . . a free reciprocal activity founded on ideas."[4]

This ethics of Fichte is an important example of the self-realization theory. The process takes place in the ego, viewed both individually and cosmically. It is also a voluntarism but not an irrationalism, for Fichte's "will" remains within the limits of practical reason. In its social and political implications the doctrine of Fichte influenced some of the theoreticians of Hitler's national socialism. Fichte took a high-minded approach to the idea of a "national will"; it is easy enough to prostitute it. We shall see how the more personal facets of Fichte's voluntaristic ethics appear again in some existentialists of the twentieth century.

If Fichte neglected the Kantian realm of "things-in-themselves" and stressed the basic character of practical reason, one of his contemporaries Friedrich Schleiermacher (1768–1834), took the contrary path. His main treatise in ethics is entitled: Outlines of a Critique of the Doctrine of Morals up to the Present (1803). Schleiermacher felt that we do know Kant's noumena, and so he was very much opposed to what he saw as a Fichte's extreme subjectivism. That philosophy is concerned with a dialectic and that God is the transcendent identity of thought and being Schleiermacher agreed. It is not through practical reason that we reach God but by way of religious feeling and intuition. Schleiermacher's natural theology has been called a "fusion of Spinozism and idealism."[5] Although human egos are parts of the universal substance, for Schleiermacher, they remain free, self-determining, and quite individual. Reason is present in lower sense in nature, and on a higher level in man. All reality is rational; hence, the laws of nature and moral law are entirely compatible The fundamental imperative in Schleiermacher's ethics is: "Be a unique person and act in accord with your own distinctive nature."[6]

The place of G. W. F. Hegel (1770–1831) in the history of ethics is not easy to determine. Some histories of the subject simply omit him It could be argued that he has a philosophy of law, of history, of society and so on, but no ethics as such. However, he has influenced, positively and negatively, so many later writers in ethics that it is necessary to pay some attention to his views. We cannot attempt a complete exposition but will try to single out some of the more important teachings.

A group of early writings by Hegel dates from the last decade of the eighteenth century and contrasts Christian morality with Kant's philosophical ethics. These are the works translated as the Early Theological Writings. One of these studies (Life of Jesus, 1795) treats Christ as teacher of ethics. The *Phenomenology of Mind* (1807) marks the beginning of Hegel's personal approach to philosophy. This work has a good deal to say about the relation of ethics to the rest of philosophy. In 1821 Hegel published his *Outlines of the Philosophy of Right;* it is a major source for the study of his ethics. Various other volumes have been edited from Hegel's courses of lectures. The *Philosophy of History* is of this type. The posthumously published *System of Ethics* was outlined in 1802 by Hegel but it is a very imperfect formulation of Hegelian ethics and is only mentioned here for the sake of completeness.[7]

In the early works Hegel seems to have thought of ethics in terms of Kant's system. *The Spirit of Christianity*, for instance, teaches that Jesus advanced from the legalism (a morality of externally imposed commands) of the Judaic tradition to a new morality concerned with the satisfaction of human needs. This new morality of Jesus is grounded in the autonomy of the human will. In spite of the Kantian cast of this interpretation, Hegel accuses Kant himself of mistakenly speaking of a command requiring respect for a law which commands love." It is wrong, Hegel thinks, to base love on an imperative: "In love all thought of duties vanishes."[8]

During the first decade of the nineteenth century, Hegel worked out his own general notion of what philosophy is and does. His views now represent a reaction to those of Kant, Fichte, and Schelling (who, though contemporary, published several works that were read by Hegel). Hegel remained an idealist but pushed the theory beyond the original meaning of "idea" as a presentation of individual consciousness toward a doctrine in which all things and events occur in Mind objectified. Reality is completely rational: there is an intelligible explanation for everything and the method of philosophical explanation is dialectical. Hegel's dialectic is a three-step process moving from an original positive affirmation of some event or thing (thesis), through a second stage of negation or denial of the first (antithesis), to a final stage which cancels and transmutes the two preceding stages into a higher combination (synthesis). What is canceled but then rises to a higher meaning is said to be *aufgehoben.* The blooming of a rose is used as an example of the dialectic. First, there must be a rosebud (thesis); then the bud must stop being a bud (antithesis); and third, the canceled bud must give rise to a new item, the flower, which comes from the first two steps (this culmination is the synthesis). This is the patterned triadic process of all developments in mind and reality: all philosophical interpretation should make use of this new logic. The dialectical theory is described at great length in the *Phenomenology of Mind.*[9] Nature, consciousness, history, culture, art, and religion develop dialectically. So also does ethics, for it is but a distinctive way of tracing the evolution of Mind.[10]

God is the Idea, the universe considered potentially; Mind or Spirit

(*Geist*) is the realization of the Idea in concrete evolution. Mind expresses itself in many lines of development. The *Phenomenology of Mind* traces the dialectical process through methodology, various phases of consciousness and self-consciousness, reason in itself, in nature and in self-consciousness, through objectified spirit, morality, religion, art, to the ultimate stage of general philosophical science. Considering the phenomena of morality, Hegel says this:

> When we look at the moral view of the world . . . The first stage, which forms the starting-point, is the actual moral self-consciousness. . . . And, since what is moral only is at all so far as it is complete,—for duty is the pure unadulterated ultimate element (*Ansich*), and morality consists merely in conforming to this pure principle—the second proposition runs: "there is no actual existence which is moral." Since, however, in the third place, it is a self, it is inherently the unity of duty and actual reality. . . . In this final goal or aim of the synthetic unity of the two first propositions, the self-conscious actuality, as well as duty, is only affirmed as a transcended or superseded moment.[11]

In other words, ethics advances from some low-grade common concept of morality, through a stage which recognizes that this sort of morality is unrealistic, to a synthesis in which a philosophy of morality is proposed.

Hegel's *Philosophie des Rechts* offers such a higher ethics, expressed in terms of right and wrong. As objectified, Mind gives rise to "abstract right." The term *Recht* (like *jus* in Latin) has no precise English equivalent. In a broad way, it names the moral, the lawful, the approved good. Concretely, for Hegel, the institution of property (one's actual right to possess a thing) provides a thesis from which to begin the development of ethics.[12] A property right is one sort of objectification of the universal or rational will.[13] Will is that aspect of consciousness in which freedom becomes actual: there is both individual and universal will. Voluntary actions running contrary to rational will are wrong and antithetic to the original rightness.[14] For such wrongs there is a logical demand for punishment and retribution. Morality itself is the abstract harmony between the individual volition and the rational will or notion of what ought to be.

At one point in the *Phenomenology of Mind*[15] Hegel speaks of ethical life as substantially realized in a set of customs (*Sittlichkeit*) as something lower than morality (*Moralität*). However, the *Philosophie of Right* (some fifteen years later) sees morality as an abstract concept that is concretely objectified in the substance of the ethical life (*Sittlichkeit*). The latter is social, objective, and more profound than morality.[16] In the ethical dialectic a key series moves from (1) *purpose*, the subjective inclination of the individual person, through (2) *intention* and *well-being*, as the essential character of the act that is proposed, to (3) the final synthesis of *goodness* or *wickedness*. Fundamental to this is the concept of the "ethical system." This is described as follows:

The ethical system is the idea of freedom. It is the living good, which has in self-consciousness its knowing and willing, and through the action of self-consciousness its actuality. Self-consciousness, on the other hand, finds in the ethical system its absolute basis and motive. The ethical system is thus the conception of freedom developed into a present world, and also into the nature of self-consciousness.[17]

Duty, for Hegel, is the moral law issuing from the rational nature of will; while moral conscience is simply duty made effective.[18] The notion of "subjectivity" is important here to Hegel. Whether recent phenomenology is in lineal descent from the thought of Hegel is a matter of dispute today.[19] However, the phenomenological term "subjectivity" is used in a distinctively ethical manner by Hegel. This is evident in lines such as these:

Substantive ethical reality attains its right, and this right receives its due, when the individual in his private will and conscience drops his self-assertion and antagonism to the ethical. . . . Subjectivity is the absolute form and the existing actuality of the substance. The difference between the subject and substance, as the object, end, and power of the subject, forthwith vanishes, like the difference between form and matter.[20]

Hegel goes on to say that subjectivity is the foundation for the real existence of the conception of freedom, and in ethics subjectivity is the existence of personal self-determination and moral freedom.

Another very important Hegelian approach to the notion of "ethical system" lies in the development of social life. This may be one of Hegel's greatest contributions to ethics; it implies a special theory of history and of politics. As morality concretizes and becomes "substantial" in the family, civil society, and eventually the state, there is an evolution of the ethical life (*Sittlichkeit*). The family is the union of at least two persons in love.[21] Civil society is a condition in which there is a mutual dependence of all persons on all, yet as a collection of independent individuals. It is founded on a system of wants. The state is a concrete institution that unifies and gives a higher reality to the ethical lives of its individual members. At times, there is a sort of mystique about Hegel's state. In his *Philosophy of History* we are told that the state is "the embodiment of rational freedom," and that it is the "Idea of Spirit in the external manifestation of human Will and its Freedom."[22] Since God is also the Idea of the Spirit (Geist), this amounts to a rather extravagant divinization of the national state. It is but one step away from totalitarianism or étatisme.[23]

The later influence of Hegel's ethical writings has been extensive. At times (see the Preface to the Philosophy of Right) Hegel presented himself as the philosopher of Protestantism and the successor to Luther in the reformation of the religious life of Europe. A group of German theologians (including Karl Daub, 1763–1836, at Heidelberg; and P. K Marheineke, 1780–1846, at Berlin) applied his dialectic and ethical system to the study of Christian religion. They became known as right-wing Hegelians. Another school picked up Hegel's notion that religion is but a stage in the movement toward the synthesis which is his ethical philosophy and decided that Christianity had outlived its usefulness. These left-wing Hegelians (David F. Strauss, 1808–1874; and Ludwig Feuerbach, 1804–1872) stressed the materialistic and atheistic implications of Hegel's thought and influenced the thinking of Karl Marx. Practically all recent historians of philosophy have come under the influence of Hegel methodology. One of the first histories of ethics was written by a pupil of Hegel, Leopold von Henning (1791–1866), under the title Principie der Ethik im historischer Entwicklung (Berlin, 1824). Finally, we might note that existentialists from Kierkegaard to the present agree on little other than a shared suspicion and dislike for the conceptualizing system building of Hegel.

A follower of Kant who turned Kantian ethics into a spiritualist eclecticism was Jakob Friedrich Fries (1773–1843). Fries's main writings in ethics were his Doctrine of Right (1804) and his Ethics (1818). The role of ethics in these works is to analyze and verify the moral deliverances of common experience. In his psychology Fries made much use of the method of introspection and his ethics also stresses inner experience. There is in Fries's understanding of Kant's practical reason a notion of moral faith viewed as an expression of religious feeling Leonard Nelson (1882–1927) brought Fries's teachings to the United States, where the "Nelson Foundation" is still devoted to this school thought.

Reaction to the prevailing idealism of nineteenth-century Germany represented by Johann Friedrich Herbart (1776–1841). His pluralist metaphysics is reminiscent of the philosophy of Leibniz but Herbart's work in psychology helped to bring attention to the importance of empiric data in ethics. Apart from his Textbook in Psychology (1816), the Practical Philosophy (1808) is Herbart's chief contribution to the literature of ethics. His theory of knowledge is realistic: we know the material world as an aggregate of simple essences, in which real events occur. On the other hand, the human soul is not known in itself, as this text indicates:

The soul has no innate natural talents nor faculties whatever, either for the purpose of receiving or for the purpose of producing. . . . It has originally neither concepts, nor feelings, nor desires. It knows nothing of itself, and nothing of other things; also in it lie no forms of perception and thought, no laws of willing and action, and not even a remote predisposition to any of these.[25]

This vigorous rejection of the a priori leads to Herbart's claim that feelings and desires include acts of preference and rejection, plus "something objective." He is a pioneer in attempting an experiential approach to a science of objective and real values.

Herbart investigates the functions of feeling and willing from the point of view of aesthetics, of which one branch for him is ethics. Five kinds of will relations give rise to ethical judgments. We approve of (1) the relation of a person's will that is in keeping with his basic convictions (the idea of freedom); (2) the relation of an act of will in one person that is in accord with other efforts of the same will (idea of harmony); (3) the relation of one person's will to the satisfaction of the will of another person (idea of benevolence). We disapprove of (4) the relation in which several wills impede each other (idea of justice); and (5) the relation in which the intended good or evil is not compensated (idea of retribution). This is an interesting attempt to discover certain basic ethical notions in immediate experience.[26]

A somewhat similar use of psychology to establish a value theory and an ethics is found in the work of Friedrich E. Beneke (1798–1854). His Outlines of a Natural System of Practical Philosophy (1837) rejects the ethics of Kant and suggests a detailed theory of the process of valuing in terms of good and evil. He is more inclined than others to attribute to human nature a certain predisposition toward some types of valuation. Beneke describes five relations or bases for grading perceptions of good and evil: (1) the nature of the elementary faculties; (2) the development of the elementary faculties through impressions; (3) the degree of complexity in the products of these faculties; (4) the duration of these products; and (5) the purity of these products.[27] This is obviously an effort to provide an empirical scale for rating ethical values.

Another direction taken by German idealistic ethics is illustrated by the views of Friedrich W. J. von Schelling (1775–1854). Historians usually treat him before Hegel because he influenced Hegelianism, especially in the area of methodology and the notion of the Absolute in the development of nature. Like Fichte and Hegel, Schelling also uses the logic of dialectic (action, reaction, synthesis) to interpret various processes. However, we are interested here in the later ethical position of Schelling, when he turned away from rationalistic logic to the romanticism of religious feeling. The beginning of this romantic period can be set at the publication of his treatise On University Studies (1803), in which his whole early philosophy is summarized for popular reading. Key works in the later period are the *Philosophical Investigations on the Essence of Human Freedom* (1809 and *The Ages of the World* (1811).

Lecture XIV is the end of the series *On University Studies* and already in it we find the suggestion that the philosophy of art may be a source of religious and ethical information. As Schelling grew older and came under the influence of the two Schlegel families at Jena, and of the Catholic fideist Franz von Baader (1765–1841), he put more and more emphasis on the irrational, dark, obscure depths of human and divine consciousness. God and the world are one, in a sense, but Schelling defended himself against the charge of pantheism by explaining that God is the antecedent and the world the consequent. This comes out in the treatise *On Human Freedom*. He is sure that man is free, because he has the power of good and evil.[28] In the dark depths of man's spirit Schelling finds urges and impulses toward unreasonable and evil feelings and actions. As a person matures, these lower instincts are brought to light and somewhat controlled by increasing rationality. They remain something of the basis for human freedom, however. Perhaps this is the main point in his later ethical thought (which is much neglected in secondary studies of Schelling): there is a dimension of feeling and imagination in the ethical life that exceeds the limits of reason. If most German ethicians up to Schelling thought of ethics as a reasoned account of voluntary activities, he now insisted that there is more to ethical personality than that. Doubtless he influenced, directly or indirectly, the growing interest in the unconscious (Eduard von Hartmann, 1842–1906) and in the subconscious drives, which were stressed by Sigmund Freud (1856–1939).

The last major figure in the German ethics of the nineteenth century was Arthur Schopenhauer (1788–1860). Yet he was never fully accepted as a serious philosopher by the academic thinkers of the day. Schopenhauer's first great work was *The World as Will and Idea* (1819), in which a portion (secs. 55–71) of the fourth book is devoted to ethical topics. Years later, in 1839–1840, Schopenhauer wrote two lengthy *Prize Essays*, one on the freedom of the will, the other on the basis of morality. These were published (1841) together as *The Two Basic Problems of Ethics*. Finally, he has a miscellaneous collection of essays and notes, gathered under the title *Parerga und Paralipomena* (1851). It is from cheap editions and translations of selections from these popular essays that Schopenhauer has come to be known as the "philosopher of nursemaids."

The World as Will and Idea is a huge metaphysical treatise that explains that the fundamental energy which evolves in all things and produces all events is "will."[29] As Schopenhauer expresses this metaphysics: "The world as idea is the complete mirror of the will, in which it knows itself in ascending grades of distinctness and completeness, the highest of which man."[30] What we have here is another version of German idealism: instead of all things being variations of mind, they are now bubbles in an infinite will.

As individuals, men are part of the world of appearances, *phenomena*; as things-in-themselves (Kant's *noumena*), human beings are united in the eternal will. Freedom belongs to noumenal will but not to the order of individual phenomena; hence, individual men are not free.[31] Will is an ongoing process, ever striving, but with no ultimate objective. The whole series of volitional events which makes up the universe is nonpurposive. Here, Schopenhauer is running against the Hegelian, and generally idealistic, tradition that there is a reason why for everything. He thinks not. Satisfaction or happiness is quite negative. It consists in release from pain.[32]

Good and bad are the basic ethical conceptions for Schopenhauer but they are essentially relative. Good means "the conformity of an object to any definite effort of the will." What is good for one man may be bad for the next person. There can be no highest or absolute good (*summum bonum*); for that would be a final satisfaction of willing and, by the initial assumption of Schopenhauer, the will never ceases to desire and to strive. Intensity of volition is a source of inevitable suffering: the bad man must endure the sting of moral conscience and the good man must face the frustration of unending desire. To be just or right means to avoid denying the will that appears in another person. There is no moral imperative, or "ought," to prescribe to the eternally free will.[33]

A "principle of asceticism" (to see that individual differences and strivings are merely phenomenal, and thus to renounce the effort of individual volition), which amounts to a denial of the will to live, is offered in this passage:

> After our investigation has brought us to the point at which we have before our eyes perfect holiness, the denial and surrender of all volition, and thus the deliverance from a world whose whole existence we have found to be suffering, this appears to us as a passing away into empty nothingness. Before us there is certainly only nothingness.[34]

This is a blunt statement of Schopenhauer's ethics of pessimism: not even suicide will remove one from the pointless flow of will power; the suicide is merely another negative event in an eternal process.

The essay on *Freedom of the Will* won the prize offered by the Norwegian Scientific Society in 1839. It was regarded as a brilliant *tour de force*. In it Schopenhauer argues for about ninety pages that there can be no freedom in human willing. "The result of our preceding exposition was to recognize the complete annulment of all freedom of human action and its thoroughgoing subjection to the strictest necessity."[35]

However, Schopenhauer suddenly suggests at the end that, if we advert to the feeling of responsibility for our actions, we may take a new approach from this moral fact and conclude that human actions are "transcendentally" free, not as individual events but in the whole being and essence of man.[86] During the course of this essay, a very thorough and learned history of various theories of free will is provided by Schopenhauer.

In a second prize essay, *On the Basis of Morality* (which failed to win the prize offered by the Royal Danish Academy of Sciences in 1840), Schopenhauer offers a very severe and lengthy criticism of Kant's ethics.[87] He is briefer in subsequently rejecting Fichte's moral philosophy. Many of his remarks are unfair and intemperate and this is one reason why the Danes did not give him their prize. Yet in the latter part of this second essay Schopenhauer describes an ethical theory that is of some importance. His criterion, now, of an action of moral worth is that such action must be motivated by *compassion* for others.[88] This is Schopenhauer's famous ethics of pity or sympathy. "Only insofar as an action has sprung from compassion does it have moral value; and every action resulting from any other motives has none." His two great moral virtues, then, are altruistic. They are justice and loving-kindness; both have their roots in natural compassion. This feeling is the criterion of morality in ordinary knowledge. Metaphysically, Schopenhauer rests his ethics on the claim that the virtuous man "makes less of a distinction than do the rest between himself and others."[89] In other words, the real cause of evil is located in the phenomenal differences which separate people. To realize that we are all one will is ethically desirable. Schopenhauer was influenced by his reading in the religious writings of India to adopt a position which is similar to the Nirvana teaching.

Parerga and Paralipomena, the popular essays, include a wide variety of observations on life and people. Their style is terse and popular. In one he will explain why "there is a worm in every apple," and in another, why a beautiful woman always picks an ugly one as a companion. These illustrate his general pessimism in the moral order but are not of primary importance for the serious study of Schopenhauer's theoretical ethics. With important changes, Nietzsche carried on this voluntaristic movement in German ethics. We shall follow this line of influence in Chaper XVIII.

A very unusual development in German idealistic ethics is connected with the name of Max Stirner (1806–1856). He was a teacher in a Berlin school for girls and his real name was Johann Kaspar Schmidt. His book *The Individual and His Unique Quality* (1845) is a protest against the moral rules of society. Stirner seems to have been a nineteenth-century "beatnik" in his thinking but he is usually classified as an ethical anarchist. A left-wing Hegelian in his general philosophy, he felt that the individual person should be free to express himself without any social restraints. He ethical imperatives urged his contemporaries: "Be egoistic! Scorn the illusions of social morality! Don't be the slave of an idea!"[40] It is probable that Stirner pushed ethics as far as it would go in the direction of extreme egoism.

The medical doctor Rudolf Hermann Lotze (1817–1881) is noted in the history of philosophy for his revival of psychophysical parallelism in his large work entitled *Microcosmus* (1856–1864). His projected third volume on ethics, in his *System der Philosophie*, was never written but his *Metaphysics* (1841) shows something of what his approach would have been to moral philosophy. Student notes of his lectures (including those on ethics) were printed under the title *Kleine Schriften* (3 vols., 1885–1891). Lotze taught that the human will is powerless to cause anything to happen in the human body. If I have the impression that I can move my hand at will, this is due to the fact that "Nature" moves the body on the occasion of certain acts of will.[41] Ethically, this somewhat reduces the importance of the bodily aspects of moral activities.

In spite of an almost mechanistic view of human physiology and psychology, Lotze was much interested in Leibniz's metaphysics and in Fichte's ethical idealism. Rejecting the notion of a moral a priori predisposition in man, Lotze felt that there was some importance in Fichte's theory that a general moral consciousness expresses itself in the lives of individual persons. Thus, Lotze thought, our moral consciousness testifies to the purposiveness of the world and human life. The end to which man's moral efforts should be directed is the supreme value, God.[42] His efforts to deal empirically with valuation are important in the history of axiology.

The famous pioneer in empirical psychology, Wilhelm Wundt (1834–1920), also did considerable work in ethics. His textbook on *Ethics* (1886) was widely used in late nineteenth-century classes in ethics and had quite a success in English. Besides the introduction of much empirical material from social psychology about the moral notions of various peoples, Wundt's use of the general will as the source of objective moral standards was reminiscent of Rousseau and, of course, Kant. The end of the century saw an increase in interest in Kant's ethics, not only in Germany but also in France, England, and the United States. The noted interpreter of Kantian ethics was Friedrich Paulsen (1846–1908). At Marburg, Hermann Cohen (1842–1918) went back to the original ethics of Kant.

A series of books that developed the theory of an ethics of spiritual life were written at Jena by Rudolf Eucken (1846–1926). As the teacher of Max Scheler, Eucken influenced the early directions of German phenomenological ethics. His *The Value and Meaning of Life* (1907) and *The Life of the Spirit* (1908) were translated into English. A theory of "types of life" (the naturalist, the aesthete, the spiritual man) was developed by Eucken to demonstrate the superiority of the life of spiritual freedom.

This brings us to the end of our account of nineteenth-century German ethics. Its contributions to the subject are not always fully appreciated today, particularly in English-speaking countries. But there was a period, early in the twentieth century, when American and even many British ethicians looked to graduate work at the great German universities as the crowning feature in their preparation as teachers of the subject. Even today, as we shall see in subsequent chapters, the idealism of German ethics remains significant in the axiological, existential, and spiritistic types of moral philosophy.

CHAPTER XII

Franco-Latin Spiritistic Ethics

THE KIND OF ETHICS to be examined in this chapter is not well known to English readers. It is a moral philosophy that has grown out of the movement which is called *"la philosophie de l'esprit"* in France but it is also very important in Italy and Spain and is the dominant ethical view in most parts of Latin America. The notion of *esprit* is not conveyed by one English term. It means spirit and mind, of course, but it also suggests that reality which is discovered in the higher functions of human consciousness and which is quite immaterial. This "spiritism" sometimes stresses the intuitional and cognitive aspects of mind; in other cases it emphasizes the volitional or affective functions. In all cases it rejects materialism.

Many of the thinkers to be considered here are known as "Christian personalists." This term is much favored in Italy and the Spanish-speaking countries. There is a certain amount of idealism implied: what is real is best investigated through personal consciousness. The existence of a physical universe is not usually denied but bodies are regarded as less important and less real than minds. Most people who hold this kind of personalistic or spiritistic ethics have strong Christian religious commitments; many are Catholics. This does not mean that they are Thomists. Few of them have more than a nodding acquaintance with the thought of Aquinas. It is St. Augustine who is the important early source of inspiration. Descartes's emphasis on the *cogito* is also an influence, as are some of the teachings of the German idealists and romantics. On the whole, British and North American ethicians have had little interest in this sort of thing. Personalism means something rather different in the context of philosophy in the United States. The closest approach in this country would be the "Christian philosophy" of Orestes Brownson (1803–1876) who, in fact, was indebted to the philosophy of two of our spiritistic ethicians, Victor Cousin and Gioberti.[1]

The first spiritistic ethician was Father Nicolas Malebranche (1638–1715), something of a Cartesian but also a great student of Augustine. Histories usually treat his striking theory of knowledge and reality and neglect his ethics. Malebranche speculated that all things exist in their Ideas in God's creative mind and we know them (bodies and finite spirits) by seeing the "ideas" which God (as universal Reason) furnishes to our thought. It would not be necessary for trees and the ocean, and so on, to exist physically: God could provide us with these objective ideas, even if these created things did not exist. However, we believe on the basis of divine revelation that the world of finite creatures is in existence—but we do not know it, except through the divinely implanted ideas. This is what we are told in Malebranche's Search for Truth (1674) and Dialogues on Metaphysics (1688). It is a theory that adapts the Augustinian doctrine of divine illumination to the problems of Cartesian metaphysics and psychology.

However, Malebranche wrote extensively in the field of moral philosophy. An early treatise is the Christian Discussions in which One Justifies the Truth of Religion and Morality (1675). His Treatise on Morality was first published in 1683. In a revised edition of the Treatise (Lyons, 1697), he printed his Treatise on the Love of God. In these works, as in the speculative writings, we are continually told that my individual mind (esprit) is not universal but it is impressed or enlightened by divine Reason in such a manner that the objects of my understanding are common to all minds (esprits). Knowledge is "objective" in the sense of having a "validity for spirits everywhere and at all times."[2] This is the beginning of French spiritism, as neatly summarized by Malebranche:

> The reason of man is the word, or the wisdom of God himself; for every creature is a particular being, but the reason of man is universal. If my own particular mind were my reason and my light, my mind would also be the reason of all intelligent beings. . . . The pain which I feel is a modification of my own proper substance, but truth is a possession common to all spiritual beings. . . . Thus, by means of reason, I have or may have some society with God, and all other intelligent beings; because they all possess something in common with me, to wit, reason.[3]

Any suggestion that pleasure could be the criterion of virtuous activity is strongly opposed by Malebranche. As he explains it: "Pleasure i the reward of merit, and therefore cannot be the foundation of it." Nor can the order of nature (in the Stoic sense) be the ground fo moral law. The only basis that Malebranche can see for moral or ethica judgment is the "love of order," the will to live in harmony with God' general will. Two dispositions are required for the virtuous acceptanc of God's law in the love of order: "force of spirit" and "liberty of spirit." The habit of looking to universal Truth (another name for God) in order to acquire adequate ideas as to human behavior is the force of the spirit. On the other hand, the habit of rejecting all confused ideas, all notions which seem to come from the body (such as movements of concupiscence) is the liberty of the spirit. It is not easy to cultivate these two major virtues: the special assistance of divine grace is needed to advance in that love of God which culminates in eternal happiness.[5]

The ethics of Malebranche is a theological approbative theory: human actions are good because God immediately makes them so. Unlike William of Ockham, Malebranche does not suggest that God might, on occasion, "change His mind or will." The universality and objectivity of universal Reason are the bases for his confidence in the immutability of ethical principles. Implicit in this view of "spirit"—as transcending all individual limitations yet retaining the distinctive volitional and intellectual characteristics of personality—is the whole of later Christian personalism.

Another very unusual French Catholic thinker who belongs in this tradition is Maine de Biran (1766–1824). He was not a teacher or writer but a government official and the works that he has left are fragmentary and posthumously published. His essay on *The Relations between the Physical and the Moral in Man* was written in 1820 but only printed about ten years after his death. Also significant are the *Essay on the Foundations of Psychology* (1812) and the *New Essays in Anthropology* (1823). Henri Gouhier's selected texts (in French) is the most convenient for reference.

It is difficult to discover what Maine de Biran read; obviously Descartes and Malebranche lie in his background. He knew something of Kant and was influenced by him. The eighteenth-century philosophes were, of course, well known to him, in particular, Condillac. It is the soul, or spirit, that is of primary interest to Maine de Biran but, unlike Malebranche, he traces its basic energy to will. He looked not so much to God (although he was a pious man) for the explanation of the life of the spirit, as he did to the initial presentations of consciousness. "We feel our phenomenal individuality, or existence, but we do not feel the very substance of our soul."[6] What is important is to find the source, or primitive origin, of the activity that is the distinctive feature of the self. Maine de Biran introduces the "inner sense" (*sens intime*) as a function in which one intuits, or feels, his soul as a dynamic force. We have "an immediate feeling of force and that feeling is no other than that of our very existence, from which that of activity is inseparable."[7] This basic force, life, and existence in every person is what he calls will (*volonté*); it is efficient and free energy.[8] The starting point for his ethics is this psychological voluntarism, as he explains:

I will, I act (*cogito*), therefore I am (*ergo sum*). I am not in some indeterminate way a thinking being, but very precisely a willing force which passes from the virtual to the actual by its own energy, by determining itself or bringing itself to action.[9]

The good path for man's moral development is the way of self-determina tion, the improvement of the soul by the exercise of volitional freedom

At one time, Maine de Biran tried to locate the original awarenes: of willing in the consciousness of muscular effort; this was offered a: an alternative to Condillac's primitive fact of sensing. Maine de Birar always retained the notion that "effort" (*effort voulu*) is a most importan· feature of conscious moral life. Like Augustine, he thought that man' soul lives on an intermediate level between the life of the body, below and the life of God, above. But he felt that it was best for man's spiri to stay on its own level.

> This is the proper and natural condition of man, that in which he exercizes all the faculties of his nature, develops all his moral power in fighting the unruly appetites of his animal nature, . . . Above and beneath that state, there remains no struggle, no effort, no resistance, consequently no *I*; the soul is in that state of alienation, sometimes in deifying, sometimes in animalizing itself.[10]

What Maine de Biran has to offer, then, is not a theory of the bas: of ethical judgment or obligation (he would simply point to God, : asked about that sort of thing) but rather an expansion of the meanin of the "spirit" of man. It is dynamic force, free activity, self-determinin energy. It is a special mode of existence. This is important to late philosophers of the spirit and also to existentialists.

Not all French philosophers of the spirit are religiously inspired. I some, German idealism or Scotch common sense may substitute fe the love of God. Victor Cousin (1792–1867) called his own brand « thought eclecticism. He was an able historian of philosophy and fe that the way to build a teachable and useful philosophy is to use tl bricks gathered from the great philosophers of the past. He was or of the first French scholars to make a serious study of the thinking « men who lived in the Middle Ages. (His editions of the Latin wor of Peter Abelard are still used.) After teaching for a few years (1815–181€ Cousin went into administration, eventually becoming the director public education in France. His lecture notes were edited in sever series. *The True, the Beautiful, and the Good* (published in 1837) ai *History of Moral Philosophy in the Eighteenth Century* (publish« 1839–1840) are outstanding in the field of eclectic ethics. The latt contains much information on Scottish ethics and on moral sensis· He was well aware of developments in German idealistic ethics, als

Apart from the methodological suggestion that the study of the history of philosophy, done in a scientific manner, may be essential to a professional approach to working in modern ethics, Cousin has little to say that is novel or startling. One should try to derive his notions of the "good" from a prior study of the "true." Obligation, in ethics, is the will to achieve what is true and reasonable. Moral duties depend on societal existence; they are concerned with man's relations to his fellows. He is somewhat indebted to the German idealists for the important moral function that he assigns to the state and to public education.[11]

Not a formal Christian, Cousin saw much value in the cultural tradition of Christendom. As to the philosophy of the spirit, in the mind of Cousin, it meant the cultivation of one's intellect and will, by study, and by efforts at self-improvement particularly in the area of the fine arts. For the French, at this point, "un homme d'esprit" was a person with some natural gifts, trained to think and write logically, educated to the appreciation of music and painting. His follower Théodore Jouffroy (1796–1842) shared and propagated this aesthetic ideal. As the translator of Thomas Reid, Jouffroy helped to popularize the commonsense philosophy in France. His *Nouveaux mélanges philosophiques* (1842) contains an essay on moral eclecticism that simply extends the views of Cousin.

In Switzerland, the philosophy of the spirit was given a religious setting by the Protestant thinker Charles Sécrétan (1815–1895). He published an exposition of the philosophy of Victor Cousin (1868) but his personal thought is found in the *Philosophy of Freedom* (1849) and *The Principle of Morality* (1884). Like Maine de Biran, Sécrétan was a metaphysical voluntarist: will is the fundamental reality. God is the Christian divinity and is the source of all ethical distinctions. Hoewever, God is essentially freedom and is not bound by the logic of nineteenth-century rationalism. His Christian personalism is fundamentally a Protestant moral theology.

Two Italian thinkers of this period are part of the Christian spiritist movement: Rosmini and Gioberti. Although both were Catholics, their views were not typical of their religious tradition. Antonio Rosmini-Serbati (1797–1855) was a priest who tried to adapt Hegelianism to the Italian intellectual scene. Every man, according to Rosmini, has an inborn intuition of the idea of being which grounds and illuminates all other ideas, and which establishes the soul of man as a "spiritual" reality.[12] This is not merely an effort to account for the origin of human thoughts; it is a metaphysics of the human person. In a sense, the idea of being is also divine. This teaching brought Rosmini under official censure from Catholic authorities. There is much debate as to what

Rosmini actually meant by the intuition of an immutable object which is independent of all finite minds.

The fundamental ethical imperative for Rosmini is: "Follow the light of reason." There is a special science, *eudaemonology*, which treats of the human good, or happiness. Limited to the natural goods which may satisfy man's bodily and intellectual needs and aspirations, it is from the point of view of the *subjective* good (man's attainment of happiness) that eudaemonology is developed. Ethics, on the other hand, is the science of the *objective* good. Moral good is defined as objective good (identical with the idea of being) known by the intellect and willed by the will. As in Malebranche, the notion of "order" is a key one to Rosmini. Order is the relation between various grades of perfection and being. The good will loves the order of being. His position has been described as "an ethics in which 'obligation' and 'duty' find their foundation in the apprehension of ordered being by the light of natural reason . . . the free love of good acknowledged by intelligence and determined by reason."[13] There are many followers of Rosmini among the Christian spiritists of present-day Italy; the outstanding figure is M. F. Sciacca, whom we shall consider later in this chapter.

Contemporary with Rosmini was Vincenzo Gioberti (1801–1852), who also was a priest. He left Italy for political reasons and taught in Brussels for almost ten years. On his return to Italy, he became prime minister of Sardinia (1849) and then served as Italian ambassador to France. Eventually Gioberti died in poverty. At Brussels he had published a treatise *On the Good* (1848) and his *Primary Science (Protologia)* appeared in 1857. The *Course in Philosophy* (Brussels, 1841–1842) was published in 1947. Although he and Rosmini criticized each other severely, there is much resemblance between their teachings.

Gioberti reacted against Cousin's effort to base metaphysics on psychological evidence. For the same reason, he always opposed Rosmini for providing a theory of knowledge rather than an ontology. Gioberti tried hard to show the difference between starting with an intuition or an idea of being and a seeing of being. What is ontologically first (*primum ontologicum*) is different from what is psychologically first (*primum psychologicum*). He called his own position "ontologismo" and was criticized for practically teaching pantheism. But he tried to distinguish God in himself from God in us. The mature work *Della protologia* still maintains, however, that nature, providence, and revelation express variant views of the same reality.[14] Creation is simply the passage from being to concretely existing things.

The ethical theory offered in the treatise *Del buono* offers as a primary axiom "being creates existences," and insists that no thought or judgment is possible without this rule.[15] God is the prime cause of good, as He of being. He not only puts forth existents by the first moment of creation, God also recalls these existents to being by a second phase of creation. Thus the notion of moral good as a return to God (which we saw as early as Plotinus) makes a new appearance in the history of ethics. Being creates the good through the mediation of human choice. In turn, choice produces virtue by submitting feelings to law, and virtue gives rise to beatitude by reconciling affections with law. Ethics is necessarily purposive and teleological, because the good is the ultimate end of human actions. Like Fichte and Hegel, Gioberti thinks that man achieves a special moral perfection in society. In his case, of course, Italy is the state that has a special religious and ethical role in the eventual redemption of the nations.[16]

This is another version of the ethics of the spirit. Gioberti is still read in Italy and the Spanish language areas, as witness the recent printing of his philosophy course. There is something pious but amorphous in this personalistic ethics. Much of it is rhetoric. However, it is seriously regarded by many people in the Latin tradition as a high-minded moral philosophy. It would appear to resemble an idealistic version of self-realization ethics.

France continued in the nineteenth and early twentieth centuries as the main center of the *philosophie de l'esprit*. Charles Renouvier (1815–1903) called his theory personalism and used Leibniz's theory of monads as a model for his doctrine of plural realities, each of which is living and personal. His *Moral Science* (1869) retains God as guarantor of good moral order but regards Him as a finite divinity, since evil is not always prevented by Providence. Ernest Renan (1823–1892) was a notorious critic of institutional religion but strongly supported the transcending importance of the spirit. "Everything appertaining to the soul is sacred," he claimed.[17] Renan was very critical of Auguste Comte (whom we shall consider in Chapter XIII) because positivism has no place for "morality, poetry, religion or mythology."[18] To free the spirits of men from obedience to law is the higher morality.

Not a philosopher of the spirit but a critic of the whole movement was the French thinker Hippolyte Taine (1828–1893). His works *On Intelligence* contrasted the literary explanations of psychic events in terms of spiritual "forces" with his own scientific analysis of the mind into its basic facts.[19] A novel by Paul Bourget (*The Disciple*) accused Taine of debasing the spirit of man. Yet Taine developed an important theory of aesthetics and was obviously under the impression that the human mind is capable of high-minded endeavors in the field of art.

In the case of Marie Jean Guyau (1854–1888) we have a nineteenth-century French ethics that is completely divorced from the Judaeo-Christian religious morality. His doctoral thesis was on *The Moral Teaching of Epicurus and Its Relations to Contemporary Teachings* (1886). Later he wrote a survey of British ethics, stressing utilitarianism. Two books present his personal thinking in the field of ethics (he also made note worthy contributions to art theory): *Sketch of Morality Independent of Obligation or Sanction* (1885) and *The Non-Religion of the Future* (1887). His writings were translated into most modern languages and widely read.

The purpose of philosophy, as Guyau saw it, is to lead people to a better life. Scientific information should be used to find solutions to man's practical problems. He was particularly impressed with the possibilities of sociology but saw no reason to divorce it from metaphysics as in the work of Auguste Comte. The older notions of moral "obligation" and "sanctions" seemed to Guyau to depend on outmoded religious teachings. In their place he offered an awareness of life and its potentialities for development.

> Moral sensibility (*le sentiment moral*) is blended, as we see it, with the most intensive and extensive life that is possible, in the condition of awareness of its *practical fecundity*. The main form of this fecundity consists in action for others and sociability with other men.[20]

Life, so conceived, requires society for its full development. Morality is easier to treat in the social context, as a living part of a living whole. Life derives its "obligation" not from some mystical imperative but from the feeling of its own ability to act. Guyau's substitute for the famous Cartesian formula is: "I can, therefore I should" (*Je puis, donc je dois*).

In the *Sketch of Morality Independent of Obligation* we are presented with an "*anomie morale*," which is a condition of human existence without any fixed or categorical commands. This does not mean that Guyau would leave mankind without moral guidance. He felt that the virtues of pity and charity live on after the disappearance of religious dogmas. There is a sort of moral enthusiasm that he would require for the propagation of ethical idealism, but without myths and without threats of punishment or promises of rewards.[21] He even agreed with the basic eclecticism of Cousin:

> We think, on the contrary, that from all the varied theories on the principles of morality we can now draw a certain common fund of ideas, and make of it an object of instruction and of popular dissemination.[22]

This point of view is typical of the ethics that was taught in France in the last half of the nineteenth century. It is likely that Guyau influenced the thinking of Nietzsche more than most historians realize.

One more feature in the background of the twentieth-century *philosophie de l'esprit* was added by Émile Boutroux (1845–1921). Since

always doubted the deterministic rigidity of the physical laws of nature,
Boutroux came to think that there are many levels of reality, each
distinguished from that immediately below it by a greater degree of
freedom.[23] At the top is the most free being, which is God. On the
level of human spirits, all men are bound together in a union of ideal
love, described in the following quotation:

> This teaching of an original community of souls, of a principle
> of life, one, infinite and perfect, in which we are able to come
> back together with our fellows, each of us recovering and attaining
> our most complete development, not at the expense of others but
> by virtue of their own fulfillment, of a principle which humanity
> calls God—this teaching seems to us the end and the climax of all
> the experiences and reflections of the mystics.[24]

Thus does Émile Boutroux set the stage for a return to a more religious
meaning of "spirit" in contemporary French ethics.

Oddly, it was a thinker who started out as a biologist that restored
French spiritistic ethics to the realm of theistic morality. Little in the
early writings of Henri Bergson (1859–1941) pointed to the ethical
position that he eventually took in his now famous Two Sources of
Morality and Religion (1932). At first Bergson showed a great distrust
of the work of conceptualizing reason and of the determinism of physical
science. In good part he shared with many of his contemporaries an
antipathy to the system-building of Hegel. In the vital force (élan vital),
which his early works pictured as progressively evolving into higher and
higher levels of life and spirit, the basic characteristics were creativity
and freedom. As he said in Creative Evolution: "God, thus defined,
has nothing of the already made; He is unceasing life, action, liberty.
Creation, thus conceived, is not a mystery: we experience it within
us as soon as we act freely."[25] All of this is reminiscent of both
Guyau and Boutroux.

After many years Bergson wrote the treatise that contains his mature
ethics, the Two Sources. Its opening chapter treats moral obligation by
contrasting two kinds of societies, the closed and the open ones. A
society where almost every kind of activity is rigidly regulated by social
and moral laws and by strict religious codes of conduct must be static
or closed. For the majority of men, according to Bergson, "physical law,
social or moral law, all law is in their eyes a commandment."[26] This
legalism is a source of morality but Bergson leaves no doubt that it is
second-rate, in his estimation. The man who lives well under such
regulation is possessed of the closed soul (l'âme close) and he is not
the human spirit at its best. On the other hand, there is a society
which is dynamic, which gives full vent to the free development of
the individual person. In a sense, this open society is humanity in its

entirety.[27] It is the home of the open soul (*l'âme ouverte*), which is the spirit concerned with all mankind, whose love extends even to animals, plants, and all of nature.

To these two societies and types of men, Bergson applies their respective moralities. For the closed soul there is the ethics of law, strict codes of conduct, rigid moral obligation. For the open soul there is the ethics of freedom, of self-directed activity, of love rather than intelligence. It is not that obligation disappears in the life of the open soul: rather it is transformed. Of such obligation, Bergson writes:

> A constant vector force which is to the soul what weight is to the body assures the coherence of the group [in the open society] by inclining individual wills in the same direction. Such is moral obligation. We have shown that it may take on a new dimension in the society that is opened but obligation was made for a closed society.[28]

That there are two kinds of religion paralleling the two kinds of societies and souls, Bergson felt sure.

The third chapter of the *Two Sources* illustrates this theory of the two moralities by a discussion of certain human heroes. These are the people whom Bergson considers great souls, outstanding examples of the human spirit at its best. In turn, he reviews the characteristics of the Greek and Oriental mystics and the prophets of Israel. Though his own background was Jewish, he concludes that the finest example of moral "heroes" are to be found among the Christian mystics. He names various saints—Paul, Teresa, Catherine of Sienna, Francis, and Joan of Arc.[29] Bergson is quite aware that his ethics culminates in mystical union with God. Indeed, he is convinced that this sort of experience is an experimental demonstration of the existence of God. As one of his most able pupils has written: "the doctrine is the last word of the school of thought initiated by Maine de Biran."[30]

Another clear example of a philosopher of the spirit who developed an ethical position not only independent of, but opposed to, institutionalized religion was Léon Brunschvicg (1869–1944). His is a thoroughly rationalized version of the *philosophie de l'esprit*. Brunschvicg was, during the late twenties and early thirties, the chief opponent of the "Christian philosophy" movement led by Jacques Maritain and Étienne Gilson (both pupils of Bergson). Descartes's theory of mind merges with Kant's critique of reason (pure and practical) to form the background for Brunschvicg's ethical thought. *On the Knowledge of Self* (1931) is not primarily a psychology but a study of the past of the person with the intent to discover rules of development and growth in the realm of spirit. His *Philosophie de l'esprit* (1949) suggests that personal consciousness creates the values of truth and justice but not in an egocentric manner.[31] As men grow in rationality they find more ground for communion with each other; they are thus enabled to transcend selfish interests. This evolution of reasonable minds is the core theme of Brunschvicg's ethics.

Such moral thinking culminates in a religious teaching which is a sort of un-Christian Science. Brunschvicg's divinity is an impersonal but transcendent principle of value and goodness. As he explains it in *Reason and Religion* (1939), his God is not a being who reciprocates the love of men.

> He is not that higher Power to whom a being turns who lives in duration yet prays to be removed from the laws of his duration. He is the eternal truth in whom a thinking soul gains the sense and intimate experience of the eternity of thought.[32]

Both Catholic and Protestant philosophers in France have objected to this theory of a rationalized God as the object of higher human love.[33] It has been said with complete accuracy that Brunschvicg's thought combines "almost all the purely rationalist elements in the thought of our century."[34]

Vladimir Jankélévitch (1903–   ) continues in the footsteps of Bergson but uses phenomenological technique to study the human spirit and its duties. He attempts to describe human consciousness in terms of fleeting moments of irony, boredom, remorse, and inner struggle. Two ways are available to explain the world and the spirit: the way of "quiddity" and that of "quoddity." The quidditive approach stresses *what* reality and events are, and expresses itself in terms of rational concepts, laws, and causes. The quodditive view adverts to the fact that events are radically contingent, irrational, and sometimes open only to feeling experience. To attempt to conceptualize such experience is banal. It is from the quodditive approach that Jankélévitch does his ethics.

Although the book entitled *Bad Conscience* (1933) already shows the character of his ethics, Jankélévitch's *Treatise on the Virtues* (1949) is generally regarded as his main contribution in this field. Certain virtues are more basic expressions of the quodditive impulse within the spirit: this is the contentless feeling that "one must do something." It is a sort of formal categorical imperative that cannot be justified by reasoning. Courage, love, and humility are high in the scale of moral values, because they are dispositions to act in accord with this initial impulsion. On the other hand, friendship, justice, and modesty are more sophisticated and rationalized virtues; they are quidditive and fall lower on the scale of values. It is not easy to see where the quidditive ends and the quodditive begins for Vladimir Jankélévitch. He is a man with religious commitments, a Christian personalist who takes us into the related school of existential ethics. We shall look at this type of ethics in Chapter XVIII.

Two Catholic philosophers of the spirit in twentieth-century France have shown that Thomism is not the only type of philosophy cultivated by adherents of this traditional religion. (Of course, Gabriel Marcel is still another example, but he will be treated with existentialist ethics. René Le Senne (1882–1954) was a distinguished professor of moral philosophy at the Sorbonne. His contributions to metaphysics are at least as important as his work in ethics. We have made use, in this and earlier chapters, of his *Treatise on General Morality* (1942), which is a textbook with much material on the history of ethics. His other important book in the field of ethics are: *Duty* (1930) and *Obstacle and Value* (1934). Le Senne is an example of a first-rate French philosopher who is practically unknown to English readers.[35]

Like Bergson, Le Senne is opposed to "scientific" ethics. Science offers an account of what is and what cannot be; morality deals with what must be or cannot be. The moral is contingently subject to human decision. "Science is about the realized, morality about the realizable," is Le Senne's way of stating it.[36] He sees duty as something concrete and personal, as we may gather from this explanation:

> At the same time as it is the same for everybody, in the sense that no concrete duty can be a duty without applying the imperative universally, it is true, because of the inexhaustible fecundity of duty, that this duty, which imposes itself upon me, at such and such an instant, is a historical duty, that no other person is called upon to face, and which is incumbent upon me only by reason of what I am and what I want.[37]

The ethics of the *Traité de morale générale* is Bergsonian with overtones of Christian personalism and value theory. Le Senne makes a very thorough survey of various theories of moral conscience. After this, he asks whether, in the light of the history of ethics, one may still claim that metaphysics provides a basis from which morality may be deduced. Le Senne is as much opposed to deductive rationalism as Bergson was. However, he is convinced that values do provide a ground for moral judgment and decision. Value is a deliverance of the human spirit. Le Senne describes it as whatever is worthy of being sought. The unity and infinity of value are manifested within our mental experience by a multitude of presentations of humanized values. Items like truth, good, beauty, and love are cardinal values. The Absolute Value is God. Moral value is but one among many kinds of value: it is the value of the "I" (*le moi*) insofar as it is will.

Moral value, then, may be defined as the ought-to-be-done (*le devoir-faire*), where "done" means the doing of something. It is the value of action; and since action, in the sense in which it goes on according to a determination which serves as its end-directed or ideal rule, proceeds from the "I" that is made definite in the act of willing, moral value should be conceived as *the value of the will*, as truth is that of knowledge, beauty that of imagination, and love that of the heart.[39]

Part of what Le Senne means by "willing" is explained in the book entitled *Obstacle et valeur*. Man's spiritual energy is surging onward all the time; however, it sometimes meets obstacles or impediments which may be met with a special effort. Thus does will put forth volition and give rise to moral value.[40]

The other leading figure in the recent spiritistic school is Louis Lavelle (1883–1951). He was also a Catholic who worked through value theory toward a moral philosophy. Many of his insights are similar to what we have seen in Le Senne. Of Lavelle's extensive writings, we should mention *The Consciousness of Self* (1933), *The Error of Narcissus* (1939), *Four Saints* (1951), and *Conduct in Regard to Others* (1957). His basic moral theme is the notion of "participation." Some actions are creations but our potentially ethical actions are participations in a whole; they are "contained in the totality of things so that they are instrumental rather than creative."[41] To Lavelle, personal consciousness consists in freedom to initiate action. The same action displays both subjective and objective facets. Man does not create *things* but by his action he may make *beings* out of things. By participation the person consents to be; he thereby asserts the self on the level of value. This fulfillment of the person is the entry into the realm of morality and value.

Of philosophers who write in Spanish and Italian on ethical subjects many are in the school of Christian personalism. The "spirit" is the focal point of their attention, also. Some such thinkers are more in the tradition of Kant and the German idealists than of Descartes and Maine de Biran. Alejandro Korn (1860–1936), one of the greatest personalities in South American philosophy, was a practicing psychiatrist who also taught ethics at the University in Buenos Aires from 1906 to 1930. This is typical of many Latin American philosophers: they are not primarily engaged in teaching the subject but are lawyers, physicians, or politicians who teach and write philosophy as an avocation. Korn's books *Creative Liberty* (1922) and *Axiology* (1930) show the influence of both Nietzsche and Bergson. He was critical of any attempt to apply the findings or methods of physical science to the study of the spirit. Freedom is primarily experienced within spiritual consciousness and from this experience there stems an act of evaluation. Like Bergson, Korn taught that ethics must rely on intuition rather than reason. Will is very important in the constitution of the person. Culture and moral ideals are the product of the will, which is always seeking creative liberty (*libertad creadora*). This is the peak of personality, for Korn. Personality is the ideal terminus of man's historical and cultural growth. Moral values (good-bad) are but one among many types of worth that are projected in man's spiritual consciousness.[42] As successor to Korn at Buenos Aires, Francisco Romero (1891–1962) has carried on the tradition of personalistic ethics in his *Philosophy of the Person* (1938).

In Mexico, the outstanding exponent of personalist ethics has been José Vasconcelos (1882–1959). He has written extensively on the social culture of Mexico and published the first edition of his *Ethics* in 1932 It was against the importation of philosophies from other countries into Mexico that Vasconcelos reacted. In particular he resented the "Anglo Saxon" theory of evolution.[43] His own personalism, he argued, was no intentionally nationalistic but it led him to a heightened sense of patriot ism. Art is one of the highest manifestations of the human spirit. For this reason, he argues that aesthetic rhythm is a key to the higher value of human life.[44] In place of the famous three stages of the cultural development of mankind enunciated by Auguste Comte (whom we shall treat in Chapter XIII), Vasconcelos proposed a broader triad. His first stage is the material or warlike condition; the second is the intellectual or political; and the third is the spiritual or aesthetic phase. As he sees th process: "These three stages represent a process which will gradually free us from the empire of necessity and will, little by little, submit the whole of life to the higher norms of feeling (*del sentimiento*) and of fan tasy."[45] Vasconcelos fuses psychology, ethics, and an idealistic approach to politics into a view of life which avoids the materialism and mechanism of foreign philosophy. His basic themes are "individuality, freedom, pur posive creativity, cosmic reality in process, personality and God."

In contemporary Spain, the outstanding representative of Christian per sonalism is Xavier Zubiri (1898–   ). He has studied at several European universities and wrote his doctoral dissertation at Madrid on the phenom enological theory of judgment. Both Husserl and Heidegger taught him He also worked under Juan Zaragüeta, a Spanish priest who taught a modified version of Suarezianism. *Nature, History and God* (1953) i Zubiri's outstanding book.[46] A man of insights rather than a systematic philosopher, Zubiri appears to some scholars to be an existentialist However, he would seem to be rather close on many points to the philosophers of the spirit. Thus, he is fond of saying, "Personality is the very being of man."[47] Philosophy, he thinks, has already run through its three stages. With Descartes it concentrated on the subject; in the spec ulative philosophy of Kant the ego was the center of attention; and now following the lead of Kant's practical philosophy, the focal point is the person.[48] The volume of essays written by several Spanish writers, *Ho menaje a Xavier Zubiri* (1953), testifies to the esteem in which this unusual philosopher is held by his compatriots. His most recent book, *Sobre esencia* (1962), develops a metaphysics of the individual person which is not far removed from the views of Suárez.[49]

An Italian philosopher whose ethics is similar to that of the tradition in this chapter is Michele Federico Sciacca (1908–   ). Undoubtedly he is the leading representative of Christian personalism in Italy. Sciacca has lectured in many countries and his books are widely translated. As editor of the *Giornale di Metafisica* (Turin), he has had a great influence on other Catholic philosophers. His study, *The Moral Philosophy of Antonio Rosmini* (1955), indicates his debt to this earlier Christian ethician. He has also made an intensive investigation of the thought of St. Augustine, but Sciacca has little interest in Thomas Aquinas. His book in Portuguese on *Ethics and Morality* (1952) and the Italian work *Ethical Reason and Moral Intelligence* (1953) are representative publications in our field.

In an address delivered in 1963, Sciacca summed up his personalist ethics and showed how close he is to several of the thinkers that we have considered above. His words exemplify both the high-minded idealism and the unfortunate vagueness of this kind of ethics:

The unconditioned character of the norm is not an obstacle to liberty but rather a "guarantee" of its more valid exercise. It is liberty itself that takes on its own order and the absolute end that is constitutive of the will, which can refuse to choose or, having chosen, reject its choice. The determination of ends falls in the moral order, not the physical . . . there is no liberty without law and no law without liberty. What is free in the normative order is the Idea. Morality consists in acting according to the essence of the ideal (*secondo l'idealità*) "without any necessity stemming from reality" (Rosmini), with a view to the actuation of its extent in all things. And to actuate the essence of existing is the absolute choice, coinciding with the initiative of Existence.[50]

There is a good deal of similarity between this spiritistic ethics and the ethics of existentialism, which we shall take up in our final chapter.

CHAPTER XIII

Societal Ethics in Europe

DURING THE PAST three centuries a good many people have thought that a basis for ethical judgment is to be found in human societies as they develop historically. Most of these people are convinced that there are stages in the evolution of groups of men and that there is some sort of meaningful pattern to the sequence of these various periods of history. Some think that mankind as a whole is an ongoing group that gives rise to moral values as it moves forward through time. Others feel that a certain class of people (say the nobility, or the proletariat) are the bearers of a special set of ideals that may give direction to the ethical considerations of all men, whether they belong to the favored class or not. Still others have the idea that a certain people or nation (their own, of course) has a sort of corporate "soul" that carries with it the seeds of all human perfections. Some have been quite sure that a certain "race" of men are born to lead mankind to higher and better things, because they have better bodies or purer blood. And finally, some men have thought that ethics must be grounded in history itself, in those special meanings that are to be found in a philosophy of history. This sort of theory of ethics should not be confused with any version of utilitarianism. Societal ethics does not attempt to explain moral good and evil in terms of the consequences of certain personal attitudes or actions to the social welfare. Rather, this kind of ethics springs from the conviction that *prior to* any given moral action or ethical finding there is in the human group a ground for the justification of "oughts." People who hold this societal ethics, in one of its many varieties, usually think that the common good of the group takes precedence over the private interest of individual members. Such an ethical attitude is important to understand, because extremists in this school of thought feel that they are ethically justified in sacrificing the individual person for the sake of the general welfare which they see so clearly.

Early in the eighteenth century a rhetoric teacher in Naples wrote the first version of a work that pioneered in this school of thought. The

New Science of Giambattista Vico (1668–1744) first appeared in 1725. His second and definitive edition was printed in 1744. What he tried to do was to find wisdom in the history of mankind. One of Vico's greatest admirers in the twentieth century, Benedetto Croce, has expressed the project in a way that helps us to understand it:

> For Vico, politics, force, the creative energy of States, becomes a phase of the human spirit and of the life of society, an eternal phase, the phase of certainty, which is followed eternally, through dialectic development, by the phase of truth, of reason fully explained, of justice and of morality, or ethics.[1]

The first book of the New Science attempts a chronological account of the early history of man and then proceeds to establish the axioms, principles, and method to be used in the interpretation of the historical evolution of humanity. The key to much of his theory is found in Axiom XII, where he explains that common sense (senso commune) is not the same for all men. Rather, every group of men, or nation, or people may have its own distinctive ideals and standards of right and wrong. However, there are some general notions about natural justice that are found in all peoples and these are the bases of the law of peoples (diritto delle genti). It is taught to all by divine Providence.[2] This natural law is concerned with the "human necessities or utilities of social life." Vico also shows a strong sense of the evolution of civilization (evoluzione della viltà).[3] History itself has its own reality and its own laws of development. This theory is historicism. The temporal movement of the human spirit, in its collectivity, from finite and infinite, from the sensible to the idea, from passion to wisdom, is the object of Vico's philosophical interest. Vico did not like Cartesianism but some of the things that he said about wisdom in Book II of the New Science are reminiscent of Descartes's ideas on practical wisdom. In general, wisdom is the power that commands the acquisition of all the arts and sciences constituting the humanities. The highest wisdom would be that of metaphysics but Vico is sure that men have not yet reached the metaphysical stage of development. At this point in history one must settle for the "poetic" wisdom of the great theological poets. Homer is central here; in effect, he has provided the ideals of beauty, goodness, and virtue on which Western civilization is still living. From the trunk of poetic wisdom there is one great branch that produces logic, ethics, politics, and economics (the societal disciplines); from the other side springs the branch of physics and the other studies of nature. As far as Vico is concerned, it is time for men to concentrate at least as much of their efforts on the study of the branch concerned with society, as on the branch of nature. When we look at Croce's ethics (later in this chapter), it will become evident how important this emphasis on the reality of history and society can be.

France, in the same period, provides us with some good examples of both opposition to, and espousal of, societal ethics. A Benedictine monk, Dom Léger-Marie Deschamps (1716-1774), gave one of the most peculiar presentations of this kind of thought. His views are found in two works written in the 1770s: *The Voice of Reason* (1770) and *The True System, the Metaphysical and Moral Enigma* (published in 1939). Briefly, he thought that our present ethical standards are simply the product of human society; but, in order to get back to the true principles of morality, we will have to abolish society.[4] Deschamps was, then, a social anarchist. He was not precisely a societal ethician, for he did not think that society has provided us with an adequate morality. We are now in the stage of positive laws (*état des lois*); we look forward to that future state when laws will be replaced by morality (*état des moeurs*). This he saw as a dialectical process with the development of a true ethics as the final stage. In the period in which he was writing men had no moral consciences, no natural sense of right and wrong, of what is just or unjust. All the conceptions of human behavior were, to Deschamps, mere aspects of positive legality, of the law of the state.[5] An associate of thinkers like Rousseau and Diderot, Deschamps must have seemed somewhat extreme even to them.[6]

This is the place to mention the position of the Marquis de Sade (1740-1814). He was not a theoretical ethician but a man who wrote a number of books in which he expressed his violent rejection of the moral code imposed by the society of his day, particularly in the area of sexual behavior. If we recall that Rousseau's theory of the origin of moral distinctions in the general will was really a type of societal ethics, we can see that it was this sort of assumption that the Marquis de Sade professed to oppose. He makes this evident in the *Histoire de Juliette,* where he complained:

> Almost always, moreover, the laws of government are our compass for distinguishing just and unjust. We say, the law forbids such an action, therefore it is unjust. Nothing is more deceptive than this way of judging, for the law is directed towards the general interest; now nothing is in greater contradiction with the general interest than individual interest, and at the same time, nothing is more just than individual interest. Therefore, nothing is less just than law, which sacrifices all individual interests in the general interest.[7]

A contemporary of the Marquis de Sade, with equally impeccable family background, was the Marquis de Condorcet (1743-1794). The book which is of interest here is his *Sketch of a Historical Table on the Progress of the Human Mind* (1794). In the Introduction to this work, he tells us that metaphysics studies the development of the faculties of the human mind (this is from Condillac) and that his historical philosophy "studie this development as it manifests itself in the inhabitants of a certain area at a certain period of time." Obviously, Condorcet is not far removed from the historicism of Vico. He is studying the history of the evolution of various societies through time, with a view to the discovery of the general laws of such progress and the steps which mankind may take toward happiness. As a mathematician, Condorcet divides the history of civilization into ten neat stages. The ninth period runs from Descartes to the foundation of the French Republic and it has shown how the rights of man may all be deduced from the axiom "that man is a sentient being, capable of reasoning and of acquiring moral ideas."[8] Convinced that all errors in politics and morals are due to mistakes in philosophy and science, Condorcet looked forward to an ultimate period in history. The tenth stage of mankind will take place in that indefinite future of society in which all men will rise to the level of civilization that is characteristic of the French and Anglo-Americans! In it the moral code will be free of selfishness and superstition.[9]

Another member of the French nobility, Count Claude Henri de Saint-Simon (1760–1825), insisted that ethics is the science which aims at producing the greatest good for the greatest number of men. Of the continental thinkers in this period he most closely approaches the social altruism of British utilitarianism. There is but one kind of progress that is common to the whole of humanity: this is the development of the sciences.[10] The purpose of the New Christianity is to promote the social welfare of the human race. The science of ethics is far more important for the social community than all the physical and mathematical disciplines. In his Dialogue between a Conservative and a Reformer, Saint-Simon equated this ethics with the teachings of Christ:

> It is more than eighteen centuries since its fundamental principle has been produced, and since then none of the researches of the men of the greatest genius has been able to discover a principle superior in universality or precision to that formulated by the Founder of Christianity.[11]

The morality of "enlightened self-interest" is always negative and limited in character; true morality must be social in scope. A perfect ethics will make more use of feeling and love than of reason.

Another French social reformer who believed that all that is required for the improvement of human morality is the development of societal organizations in which life may be lived most fully was François Marie Charles Fourier (1772–1837). His ethical views are found in a large treatise entitled The New World of Industry and Society (1829–1830). He planned and helped to establish small social groups (about eighteen hundred persons) in which men would live simply and idealistically on a communal basis. Only one of these "phalansteries" was founded in

France but many were started in the United States of America. A pupil and ardent follower named Victor Considérant (1808–1893) set up one such community in Texas (near Dallas). Another such establishment was the famous Brook Farm, in Massachusetts.[12] Albert Brisbane, Charles A. Dana, Nathaniel Hawthorne, Father Thomas Hecker, and Orestes Brownson were Americans who came under the influence of Fourier's societal ethics during the nineteenth century.

The man who erected this societal ethics into a religion was Auguste Comte (1798–1857). His early thought was expressed in the six volumes of his *Course of Positive Philosophy* (1830–1842). This was soon published in a condensed form, by Harriet Martineau, in English (1853). In 1848, Comte published his *Discourse on the General View of Positivism*, which was followed by the *Catechism of Positive Religion* (about 1852). These works of the later period (after 1848) show a thinker who has moved away from his original faith in "science" to a faith in a new religion of Humanity, of which Comte is the founder.[13]

That Comte was the father of sociology is well known. He adopted and developed the view that we have seen in the opening pages of this chapter: the way to understand man and the laws governing human behavior lies in the study of the development of society. As he says at the start of the *Cours de philosophie positive*, "No conception can be understood otherwise than through its history."[14] Like Condorcet and the other French societalists, Comte thought that there is a dialectical pattern of the evolution of civilization and culture. Knowledge starts with *theology* (where explanations are fictitious), moves through a *metaphysical* period (in which abstract concepts are used), and reaches its ultimate growth in the *scientific* stage (where the positive method is employed). This is the famous law of three stages.

A famous classification of the "sciences" in the order of their logical development is next developed by Comte: mathematics (the "source of positivity"), astronomy, physics, chemistry, physiology, and social physics.[1] Sociology becomes the peak science in the original course of positive philosophy. The second volume of this *Course* divides the work of sociology into two parts, corresponding to the "anatomical" study of the order of society (statical sociology), and the study of the progress of society (social dynamics). Morality is best understood, according to the writing of this early period, by considering how the notions of human duties have changed in passing from the indirect and contradictory sentiments of the theological period, through the stress on self-interest in the metaphysical period, to the altruism of the positive period. This is explained as follows:

> Human faculties, affective as well as intellectual, can be developed only by habitual exercise; and positive morality, which teaches the

habitual practice of goodness without any other certain recompense than internal satisfaction, must be much more favorable to the growth of the benevolent affections than any doctrine which attaches devotedness itself to personal considerations.[16]

With the General View of Positivism, in 1848, Comte begins to give a special status to ethics. At this point he is moving away from Fourier's idea that the answer to all human problems lies in scientific knowledge toward the late Comtian view that makes a religion out of the cult of Humanity. Now the talk is about a new moral power that is rising in France which willl lead to the complete reorganization of society. Its guiding idea is the service of Humanity.[17] Within a few years, Comte will have quite definitely differentiated between sociology and ethics, as the following lines suggest: "Sociology studies the structure and the evolution of the collective beings formed by man. Ethics, on the contrary, studies individual man as developed for and by the collective beings: family, Fatherland, Humanity."[18]

Humanity is now deified and its cult and liturgy are formed into a complex religious institution, with Auguste Comte as high priest. Social feeling is proposed as the first principle of the new religion of humanitarian ethics. This Comtian ethics has "love for principle, order for basis, and progress for end."[19] No theoretical or systematic exposition of the positive ethics can be given, for that would be to reduce it to a metaphysical abstraction.

Still another version of societal ethics has greater contemporary significance. In Europe as of mid-twentieth century an astute observer of the history of philosophy could identify three major schools: the Communist, the Catholic, and the existentialist.[20] This may occasion some surprise to people not directly acquainted with contemporary philosophy on the continent. Few in the English-speaking countries of the world would select Communism as a major type of philosophy. Yet it is that for many people today: and that fact is our justification for including a brief survey of the ethical thinking of Marx and his followers in this history. We shall see that Marxist ethics is but a variant of the societal movement which is now under examination.

Karl Marx (1818–1883) was twenty years younger than Comte and had many of the same historical-minded and socially-oriented writers as the founder of positivism. Marx knew more about the German idealists, and one of his first important writings was a study of the Hegelian Philosophy of Rights (1843). From the beginning Marx was suspicious of the idealist metaphysics and the abstract system-building of Hegel. Yet he was impressed by the concept of a dialectical pattern in the development of human history. Such a dialectic is found not only in Hegel but in many other German idealists; it is also characteristic of nearly all the societal ethicians treated in this chapter. The names and notions of the stages may vary somewhat but the triadic pattern remains throughout. Marx's noted writings (*The Communist Manifesto*, 1848; and *Capital*, 1867–1894) have a very simple message. Up to his time, social philosophers concentrated on ethics or politics to the neglect of economics. As Marx saw things in the middle of the nineteenth century, Europe had had its Reformation, and Enlightenment, and even the start of its industrial revolution, but the ordinary man was worse off than ever. Only a radical change in the economic condition of that vast class of workers who make up the "proletariat" could result in real progress for mankind. The development of a truly human ethics, according to Marx, must await the coming of that future condition of mankind in which it will be possible to live well.

It will be recalled that Hegel taught that all development and progress take place in the ideal order and follow the dialectical pattern of thesis, antithesis, and synthesis. When young Marx was a university student at Bonn, Berlin, and Jena, this notion of dialectical evolution in all things was very much in the air and Marx accepted it in part. He did not agree with Hegel that all reality is ideal but he did have a high regard for the triadic dialectic as a principle of change. Marx felt, however, that Hegel's claim that the dialectical movement is always from a lower and more simple *thesis* to a higher and more complicated *synthesis* was simply wrong. Hegel had put the dialectic "on its head," and Marx undertook to turn it "right side up again" by making it move from the complexity of a prior synthesis to the simplicity of an eventual thesis.[21] The most important application of this reversal of the Hegelian dialectic, for Marx, was in the economic order. Here he saw the bourgeois system of private ownership, which had reached its peak in the industrial revolution, as an overorganized and objectionable synthesis. It would have to break down and be negated in an inevitable moment of revolution—which is the antithesis. Then would come the new thesis in human life, the simpler condition which is Communism.

The ultimate reality in which Marx sees this dialectic taking place is man. Left-wing Hegelians in early nineteenth-century Germany had tried to turn the idealism of Hegel into a materialism. Ludwig Feuerbach (1804–1872) represented a less radical view within this school, for he maintained that what is real is the concrete man. This influenced Marx although he could not agree to the supposition that man's environment is exclusively physical and that man is subject to complete determination by the forces of material nature. There is always in Marx's picture of man a certain emphasis on the importance of *society*, as the milieu in which human progress may be made and there is even a stress on the ability of mankind to achieve certain ends that are not dictated by the rigid laws of physical nature. While Marx's view of man has been called "materialistic," it should be remembered that this label was originally applied by historian with idealistic prejudices, to whom any nonidealistic position concerning human nature would be a materialism.[22]

One of the most important notions in Marx's teaching, from the point of view of ethics, is that of "alienation." He is convinced that the proletariat, that vast class of productive workers being exploited by a smaller class of rich owners, is the class of people on whom the ultimate salvation of mankind depends. Now, in the present industrial and economic system the worker becomes more and more separated from the product of his labor: it has a distinct existence, it is not controlled by the worker, it is alienated from him. Moreover, the worker is even separated from his activity as a human being; his own work become a means whereby other men dominate and exploit him.[23] What is necessary for the good life, according to Marx, is that this economic system be overthrown so that the proletariat may become the only class (the "classless" society) and its members may be enabled to live full and perfect human lives.

The ethics of Karl Marx is not, and cannot be, a theoretical system of morality. Rather, Marxian ethics would be that future condition of concrete moral practices which would characterize the real life of the worker under Communism. Such Marxist ethics grows inevitably out of the dialectical progress of man in society. For Marx, as one astute biographer stated it, "the only sense in which it is possible to show that something is good or bad, right or wrong, is by demonstrating that it accords or disaccords with the historical process, assists it or thwarts it, will survive or inevitably perish."[24] This ethics is a "Naturalism" —both in the sense of describing the moral good in terms of a life of economic well-being, and also in the negative sense of being opposed to all supernatural notions of divine obligation or eternal rewards and punishments. Moreover, Marx's ethics is normative. At the same time that Marx would call the present standards of morality merely relative and without absolute imperatives, he would also claim that the (as yet undeveloped) morality of the classless society of the future will impose absolute standards of moral judgment and behavior.[25]

Friedrich Engels (1820–1895) was a businessman with socialist interests who helped Marx to write several of his key works. In the book called Anti-Dühring (1878), Engels added one important thing to the preceding sketch of Marxist ethics. This was the notion that no morality can have absolute validity. All the ethical systems of the past have been produced by the economic stage of the societies in which they appear.[26] The three classes of modern society (feudal aristocracy, bourgeoisie, and proletariat) have their own special and purely limited morality. Even proletarian ethics is not eternal. There are eternal truths in mathematics and physics but not in the sociohistorical area. A truly human morality must await the coming of the classless society. It will contain the "maximum of durable elements," Engels felt, but even the morality of the proletariat will not be eternal.[27]

Among the older followers of Karl Marx the man who made the greatest effort to write a formal ethics was Karl Kautsky (1854–1938). His *Ethics and the Materialist Conception of History* (1927) compared Marxist ethics with other types and stressed the claim that all morality grows out of societal impulses.[28] There is some argument as to whether the term "dialectical materialism" is typical of Marx's original position. In Kautsky, who regarded himself as a very orthodox Marxist, the theory of Communism and its ethics come very definitely under the head of dialectical materialism. He is violently opposed to "revisionists," those who would modify the original thinking of Marx by combining it with some other type of philosophy. Kautsky sees the growth of society in purely economic terms and regards ethics as the set of human ideals emerging from the laws of the process of production. It is on these techniques that the entire future of mankind depends.[29]

Most of Marx's teachings were taken over and adapted to the conditions of Russian life and society by Vladimir Ilyich Lenin (1870–1924). With Lenin, Marxism became not only an organized economic crusade but also a political program. The Communist party now became a factor in world history and politics. On many points with some bearing on ethics, Lenin takes a more definite and harder line than Marx. Religion must be rooted out of socialist society and atheism must be adopted.[30] Lenin stressed the claim that Marxist thinking in all areas is solidly founded on positive science. The crude materialism of people like Ernst Mach is but a perversion of the true meaning of physical science.[31] Beyond giving support to the general Marxist claim that the proletarian class produces its own moral values, neither Lenin nor Joseph Stalin (1879–1953) contributed anything more to the theory of ethics. Before 1950 there is little use of the term "ethics" in Soviet academic literature. Morality is discussed under the ideology of dialectical materialism.[32] In the period between 1950 and 1965, a few articles, mostly historical in character, have dealt with moral philosophy in the U.S.S.R.

A prominent exponent of Marxist thought in contemporary Germany is Ernst Bloch (1885–   ). He objects to the emphasis on economic and historical determinism of human life, as he finds it in Russian Marxism and stresses the "principle of hope" as a freer and more human factor in the personal effort to live a good life. Bloch is, of course, regarded as a revisionist by Soviet Marxists.[33] Another non-Russian Marxist who is considered very influential is Georg Lukacs (1885–   ), a Hungarian who writes in German. As far as ethics is concerned, Lukacs has brought out the importance of the concept of alienation. It is undoubtedly true that certain types and conditions of work tend to dehumanize the people engaged in them. He has, however, vigorously criticized the idealist-existentialist version of Marxist ethics recently proposed by Leszek Kolakowski (1927–   ) of Warsaw. Lukacs rejects any charge that he himself is a revisionist.[34]

The recent literature of Marxism in Soviet Russia shows some growing interest in morality as a special field of study. The fundamental attitudes are very similar to what we have seen in Marx: a good morality grows out of a rightly ordered society; all ethical systems are relativistic; all classes have their own moralities but the proletariat has the only progressive type; the value of a given moral or ethical position is determined by its political and social results; the Communist party as the spearhead of proletarian ideals is the ultimate norm of moral judgment.[35]

Quite opposed to Marxism is another school of Russian thought, which takes its origins in the Orthodox Christianity of the Eastern Church. There is also a strong societal thrust in this kind of ethics. To be a Russian and a non-Latin Christian is to participate in the "soul" of Mother Russia. The ethical position of such a school is not systematized; it is much opposed to the "legalism" of Roman Catholicism; and it is emphatic in promoting values such as spirituality, freedom, and the development of the person. Much attention is paid to moral evil as an almost inevitable feature of all human life. The Russian novelists of the nineteenth century are primary examples of this point of view. However, there are philosophical and theological writers who have made this into a rather definite kind of ethics. Vladimir Soloviev (1853–1900) is one of the most influential of these. The Justification of the Good (1897) presents an ethics based on the spirit of the universal Church, the unity of Christendom, and the fundamental unity of mankind. As Soloviev sees it: "The moral significance of life in the last resort consists in the struggle with evil and in the triumph of good over evil."[36] Vladimir Soloviev is generally considered to be the source of most of the ethical views characteristic of the later school of Russian Christian ethics.

During his long residence in France, Léon Shestov or Chestov (1866–1938) was a most influential representative of this kind of ethics. His studies of the relation between the thinking of writers like Tolstoy and Dostoyevsky and contemporary existentialism are widely respected in Europe but little known elsewhere. Shestov knew Kierkegaard and the German idealists very well. Critical of the whole program of Christian philosophy, he avoided putting his moral insights into systematic form. In fact, he taught that human life is absurd and irrational—long before Camus and the French existentialists picked up this view. Impressed by the omnipotence of God, Shestov tended to think that nothing can limit the divine power, not even apparent contradictions and the facts of history.[37]

If Shestov is little known, except in France, Nikolai Berdyaev (1874–

1948) was another Russian philosopher in exile who popularized the tenets of this school. Many of Berdyaev's books (originally in Russian, German, or French) have been put into English and they are well known. The work which best presents his ethical views is *The Destiny of Man* (1935), which insists that "abstract *a priori* systems of morality have little value."[38] Throughout this book Berdyaev insists that it is what happens to man after death that gives meaning and value to his life. This eschatological emphasis involves the important notion of the finality of man. His view is not that of ancient or medieval eudaimonism, however; Berdyaev does not agree with Thomas Aquinas that a morally good life is the way to achieve everlasting happiness. Instead, Berdyaev argues that the more highly developed persons may suffer the most.[39] Actually, he does not think that the focal point of ethics is the norm of the good. Evil is just as important as good, ethically. The moral philosopher is concerned with the continual struggle during the course of time between good and evil. Much of Berdyaev's later ethical writing stressed the supreme value of personal freedom. He is often classified as a personalist. Creativity is the key to moral freedom.[40]

However, Berdyaev was also a societal and historical thinker from the beginning of his career as a writer. One of his first publications (*Subyektivizm i individualizm v obshchestvennoi filsofi*, St. Petersburg, 1901) stressed the objective and social character of ethics, in the following passage:

> Morality, of course, cannot be class morality, any more than truth can be class truth, but historically it takes on a class form and is borne by the social class which is carrying the banner of universal human progress. Later we will try to show that historically the *avant garde* of society always works to elevate the value of man and leads him toward consciousness of absolute justice.[41]

Though opposed to Communist proletarian ethics, Berdyaev remained convinced that ethics cannot be derived from speculative philosophy. It is the product of social values and the spiritual progress of man through history toward eternity. For Berdyaev, spiritual progress is a religious concept; his whole teaching in ethics is Christological.[42] Although he was not a cleric, his ethics came closer to being a moral theology than that of the other Christian ethicians from Russia.

Distinctively French societal ethics took a new start with the work of Émile Durkheim (1858–1917). In 1897 he founded one of the pioneer journals in sociology (*L'Année Sociologique*) and helped to develop the methodology of the social sciences. Durkheim held that "every social group naturally produces, as a sort of secretion, collective representation beliefs, and rules of behavior. . . ."[43] Each society has its own collective *conscience,* from which arise a religion, a morality, a political point of view, and so on. Sociology studies these cultural emergents. Ethics is not a part of theoretical or systematic philosophy; it is a useful moral code that should be taught to enable young people to adapt harmoniously to the *mores* of their group.

Long associated with Durkheim and a contributor to his journal was Lucien Lévy-Bruhl (1857–1939). His early book, *The Notion of Responsibility* (1885), is an essay in Kantian ethics. It is in *Ethics and Moral Science* (1903) that Lévy-Bruhl launches the *science des moeurs.* All questions of morality are now reduced to social facts: the "science of morals or customs" deals with what *is* and not with what *ought to be.* This sociological approach can go through various stages, as he describes them:

> In a primary form . . . the morality of a society is purely and simply a function of the other series of social phenomena. It may be called spontaneous. The second stage is that in which reflection begins to be applied to moral reality to validate it in the eyes of reason. This is the society of systems of morality which are attached to the rich complexity of moral life as to a single principle. Finally, today we see the beginning of a third period, in which social reality will be objectively studied.[44]

Thus, a purely theoretical ethics is, for Lévy-Bruhl, impossible. What one must do is to study what is transmitted from the collective consciousness (*la conscience*) of a given society. In relation to this group, the product of philosophical and scientific reflection on the standards of behavior approved therein is a relatively valid ethics.[45] In a sense, Edward Westermarck (1862–1939) simply extended this view in *The Origin and Development of the Moral Ideas* (1906) and *Ethical Relativity* (1932).

In the empirically based method of Frédéric Rauh (1861–1909) we find still another version of French societal ethics. He was interested in the methodology of both psychology and ethics. His book on *Moral Experience* (1903) uses the device of the impartial observer ("l'honnête homme") to provide a certain objectivity for ethical judgment. Moral opinion must be tested by contact with the milieu in which the agent lives. The ultimate criterion of moral certitude is the social conscience, according to Rauh: "Morality appears at the point when collective aspirations are narrowed down and refracted in the conscience of an individual person, in a conscience which by living these aspirations personally remakes and recreates them."[46] Rauh, then, attempts a combination of the societal origin of moral views with a more personal elaboration of these views within the spirit of the moralist. In this teaching, he was more disposed to effect a compromise between the factual morality of the sociologists and the rationalized ethics of the metaphysicians.

Equally important is the recent growth of societal ethics in Italy. Italian ethics in the twentieth century is very largely identified with the practical philosophies of Croce and Gentile, but unfortunately their thought is not well known to English readers. Both fall within the category of ethicians who take a historical and societal approach to their subject. Vico's ideas are still important but Hegel and his dialectic are even more influential. Both Croce and Gentile lived through that unfortunate period in Italy's history when Benito Mussolini attempted to restore the glories of ancient Rome. Croce was more opposed to Fascism than was Gentile but both contributed to a certain exaltation of the civil society, without which the philosophy of the fascist state would have been lacking in academic support. In any event Croce and Gentile are prime examples of men who identified the source of moral values with the history and social culture of the Italian people.

It was through reading the *Scienza Nuova* of Vico that Benedetto Croce (1866–1952) became interested in philosophy. Croce's basic contribution to philosophy lies in the fields of aesthetics and the philosophy of history. Always antagonistic to metaphysics, Croce made this attitude very clear in his famous address to the Sixth International Congress of Philosophy (1926). In it he denounced the concept of metaphysics as the study of a reality above and beyond experience, and as the notion of a systematic or final philosophy.[47] Croce there defined philosophy as "the abstract moment of historiography." The work of the philosopher he saw set forth in Hegel's *Philosophy of History*: to understand the laws and development of reality one must go back in history and relive the process whereby the Idea has moved dialectically in any given era. This is historicism: the meaning and value of human life can only be discovered from a philosophic study of the passage of the spirit of mankind through time.

In 1909 Croce published his *Philosophy of the Practical*, and it is the chief statement of his ethical position. In the order of *praxis* what is important is willing (*volizione*). Willing the particular belongs to economics; willing the universal pertains to ethics. The act of willing is not distinct from the practical action, since intention is realized in action only. Action is free every time there is a real volition. Some actions are amoral, being merely economic or political.[48] What characterizes the moral action, and the good action, for Croce, is its liberty. In the early works, freedom is identified with the good.[49] The later writings even more definitely make "liberalism" more than a merely political factor: thus, freedom becomes the form of what is ethical.[50] Right in the general sense (*diritto*) is not basically ethical and law (*legge*) is simply a willing of certain classes of actions, an abstract and unreal volition.[51]

Students of the practical philosophy of Croce point out his opposition to racism, imperialism, and dictatorship. He was, indeed, a stout critic of the aberrations of Italian Fascism. Yet there was in Croce's ethical thinking a certain exaltation of the state which is hard to reconcile with his support of personal freedom. Chapter thirty-six of the work translated as *The Conduct of Life* (*Frammenti di Etica*, 1922) deals with "The State as an Ethical Institution." In it he is opposed to the idea that "the State knows no law except its own power."[52] Yet he insists that the state requires its own virtues, that these are different from the ideals of Christianity, and he points to Machiavelli as a man who saw this truth. This is the way that Croce expresses his view: "The State is an ethical institution," and it is "the true Church," for it has "souls and not only bodies in its keeping."[53] It is not difficult to turn such a view to the support of totalitarianism.

An idealism of the human spirit which was much more personal and individualistic than Croce's historical idealism was meanwhile developed by Giovanni Gentile (1875–1944). Much influenced by both Kant and Hegel in his general theory of reality, Gentile shows in his treatise *The Theory of the Mind as Pure Act* (1912) that he identified the real with the ego (*Io*) in process of becoming. Both the particular and the universal meet and are combined, for Gentile, in the concrete spirit that is the individual ego.[54] This is the *actual idealism* of Gentile. *Act* does not designate an event but the existence or development of something in thought.

One might expect that Gentile's ethics would be a simple theory of the self-perfecting of the individual mind but this is not the case. He was very much impressed by Hegel's reification, and deification, of the state (as was Croce). In a posthumously published work on the *Genesis and Structure of Society*, Gentile describes a dialectic that shows the connection between his political and ethical position. His thesis in this dialectic is the immediate individuality of particular being, which involves a natural spontaneity. The antithesis is the force of universal being of law. This conflict is resolved, according to Gentile, in the process of the real formation of the ego (*processo dell'autocoscienza*). As he expands on this dialectical theme, Gentile makes it clear that this development of the individual mind or spirit only reaches its completion in the "bosom of society." There is no ethics of the individual as such. "The State completes the morality of the individual."[55] Whether he was "the philosopher of Fascism" or not (and there is still much debate on this question), Gentile was an ethician who thought that the good of the individual person is a function of, and is subordinate to, the higher good of the state or political society. This, of course, is the conclusion of nearly all societal ethics.

Societal ethics has held little attraction for English writers on ethics. Nearly every British philosopher is, of course, a social utilitarian at heart and convinced of the practical superiority of the moral ideals of society in England. The point is that usually he does not erect this prejudice into a substitute for ethical theory. So the mystique of the ethical State is not found in English ethics. A philosopher like R. G. Collingwood (1889–1943) stressed the role of history as a starting point for both metaphysics and ethics, of course, and he stoutly criticized the tendency of most British philosophers, and ethical intuitionists in particular, to ignore the historical dimension of their work. Plato is read as if he lived but yesterday. Ethics should be understood, according to Collingwood, in relation to the historical development of men and societies. Thus, Collingwood's *Autobiography* (1939) is a brief but eloquent defense of historicism in philosophy. Similarly, Morris Ginsberg (1889–   ) is a British sociologist who has written extensively on the relation between his subject and morality of law. His *Essays in Sociology and Social Philosophy* (1957–1960) show how a reflective application of sociological methods to the history of philosophy may produce new results. Ginsberg argues, for instance, that the observable diversity of cultural and moral views in different places and times is not a basis for concluding to ethical relativity.[56] That variations in moral opinion, when carefully examined, show an underlying pattern, is Ginsberg's basic contention. He argues as follows: (1) There is universal agreement that conduct has to be guided by reference to principle. (2) Variations of moral opinion are far from arbitrary; there are discernible levels of insight and experience corresponding to different valuations. (3) There is an observable growth of moral insight which is associated with an increase in the experience of human needs and social cooperation. These conclusions challenge the long-accepted inference by Edward Westermarck from cultural to ethical relativity. Ginsberg has not, however, made much impression on British writers on ethics.

Our final example of societal ethics in Europe is found in a group of writers who have claimed that all moral and cultural ideals are carried in the blood of a given race of men, and that certain races are superior and others inferior in this as in other respects. The writers whom we shall consider, very briefly, have suggested that the Aryan race is the bearer of the highest seeds of human culture. Their teachings were made the basis of the philosophy of German national socialism under Adolf Hitler but they are by no means exclusively German in origin. Racism is an attitude with ethical implications and it is found in many parts of the world.

A Frenchman, Count Arthur de Gobineau (1816–1882), wrote a lon treatise on the *Inequality of Human Races*, in the middle of the nineteenth century. In it he claimed that there was much scientific evidence to support the finding that the white race is in all ways superior to the black and yellow races. In energetic intelligence, courage, perseverance, physical power, and love of liberty, white people are outstanding, according to Gobineau.[57] He stressed the observations of some forgotten German physiologist who studied the capacity of different people to strike a blow with their fist. The best at this sort of thing were the English and the worst were the Negro and Australasian peoples. From "scientific" evidence of this kind, Gobineau concluded that the white race is by bodily and mental endowment naturally intended to lead and control the others. "I have been able to distinguish on physiological grounds alone, three great and clearly marked types, the black, the yellow, and the white." The negroid race "stands at the foot of the ladder."[58] He also assumed that the offspring of interracial breeding are inferior to the original stock of both races. (It should be unnecessary to point out, here, the flimsy factual and pseudoscientific foundation of this whole argument.)

Meanwhile, in Germany, Paul Anton de Lagarde (1827-1891; his father's name was Bötticher) picked up these notions and combined them with a violent dislike of Jews. Originally a Scripture scholar, Lagarde thought that St. Paul was responsible for corrupting the Christian Church by the introduction of Old Testament teachings into the New Testament. He published a set of essays entitled *German Writings* (1878-1881) that was very popular in Germany in the early 1930's. As the theoretical father of Nazi anti-Semitism, Lagarde stressed the nobility and moral value of the "spirit" that is found in all people of pure German blood.[59]

Another German writer with better academic credentials but similar racist attitudes was the sociologist Ludwig Gumplowicz (1838-1909). His family was actually Jewish, from Poland. This man was an advocate of what is called "conflict sociology"—the theory that primitive races originally hated each other and fought for supremacy. Civilization was supposed to have emerged out of this struggle. Gumplowicz's most influential work was called *The Race-Struggle* (1883) and it, ironically, was reissued in Germany during the period of Hitler's rise to power. The implication of his teaching was that the superior race is the one that wins all the battles.

England made its contribution to this school of writing through Houston Stewart Chamberlain (1855-1927). Educated in Germany, he married Eva Wagner, the daughter of the composer, and settled at Bayreuth. Chamberlain idealized German culture and institutions. His *Foundations of the Nineteenth Century* was first published in German, 1899, and it preached the doctrine of the purity of the German blood. Unlike Gobineau (whom he much admired), Chamberlain felt that the Jews were a threat not because of inferiority but because of their aggressive ability. Afraid that they were taking over Europe, Chamberlain concluded:

Were this to go on in this way for a few centuries, there would not be a single racially pure nation in Europe, other than the Jews. All others would be a herd of pseudo-hebraic half-breeds; without the slightest doubt they would be a physically, spiritually and morally degenerated people.[60]

We should note how Chamberlain included morality as a special inheritance within a race. This provided a ground for a version of societal ethics, in which the "society" is any group of people related by blood.

Leaders of the national socialist movement adopted what they found useful from the foregoing pseudotheories. One man was given the job of official philosopher for the Nazi party and he was told to publicize the doctrine of the cultural supremacy of the Aryan race. This writer was Alfred Rosenberg (1893–1946), whose Myth of the Twentieth Century (1930) sold hundreds of thousands of copies. He fabricated a new national religion based on the Teutonic myths in combination with the racial views that we have examined. Exalting the communal soul of the German people, Rosenberg insisted that "nobility is blood" (das Edelste ist das Blut).[61] The German is a Kulturträger, the natural bearer of cultural and moral values, and it is his duty to lead other nations to higher levels of culture.

This peculiar variant of societal ethics was taught for a few years in some German schools. It never gained wide academic recognition but it is a reminder that racist ethics is one tangent which societal morality may take. In ending this chapter with this unfortunate school of morality, we have no intention of suggesting that the inevitable climax of societal thinking is illustrated by the experience of national socialism; yet there is something of a totalitarian quality in most versions of societal morality.

PART FIVE

CONTEMPORARY ETHICS

CHAPTER XIV

Axiological Ethics

ᴀXIOLOGY IS the study of values. Wilbur M. Urban thought that he was ᴛhe first to use the adjective "axiological," but it had been used earlier ᴉᴺ Europe.[1] Perhaps the most helpful general meaning of "value" is the ᴀᴍous definition by R. B. Perry: "Value is any object of any interest."[2] ᵀo be interested, in this usage, means to be for or against something. ᴉᴺ the past century value theories have run the gamut from very realistic ᴀᴺd objective views (which maintain that values are extraconscious realities ᴉᴺ themselves or in things) to quite subjective theories (which equate ᴠalues with affective or cognitive states or acts of consciousness). Reᴄᴇnt philosophers speak of many kinds of value, in different fields of ᴇxperience: aesthetic, economic, religious, logical, and moral values. In ᴀct, value language is used, at least occasionally, by most contemporary ᴘhilosophers and the usage is so broad that the meaning has grown very ᴛhin.

What we propose to examine in this chapter is not, then, the whole ᴀeld of value ethics. John Dewey would have to be treated under such a ᴀeading, for his *Theory of Valuation* (1939) is quite important. Nor will ᴡe discuss R. B. Perry in the present chapter. They will be found with ᴀᴇr ethical naturalists in Chapter XVI. Here, axiological ethics designates ᴛhe theories of a group of German-Austrian philosophers and other related ᴛhinkers who have come under their influence. These people tend to offer ᴀ idealistic and objectivist teaching on values. In the moral order, they ᴀᴇn claim to have some sort of rather direct experience of a realm of ᴇᴛhical values that serve as norms or standards for practical judgment. ᴀere is some direct relation between this ideal value school of axiology ᴀᴺd phenomenology. We will devote Chapter XVIII to phenomenological ᴇthics, however.

ᴛhe kind of axiological ethics that we are now to consider is closely ᴀᴇlated to two other approaches to the subject. Ideal value theorists are ᴀᴇrly always intuitionists. What they claim to "see" is not some concrete ᴀᴇlity of good or bad in an action or attitude (as do the British intuitionists) but something like an essence of the good. Second, these axiological ethicians make use of the notion of self-realization: they tend to think (as do many other schools of ethics) that morally good activity fulfills or perfects the person in some distinctive way.

An Austrian priest, trained in Aristotelian and Scholastic philosophy, who left the Catholic Church after the First Vatican Council, initiated this movement. He was Franz Clemens Brentano (1838–1917), who taught philosophy and psychology at Vienna and had many distinguished pupils, including Sigmund Freud. His *Psychology from the Empirical Standpoint* (1874) and *On the Origin of Ethical Knowledge* (1884) provide the seeds from which Austrian axiological ethics developed. Brentano's theory of psychic activity stresses intentionality (*Intentionalität*): this is the characteristic of all acts of knowing, feeling, or willing whereby they are directed toward objects. Such objects may consist in contents of consciousness, or, in other cases, they may stand for extramental realities. Brentano's explanation simply says:

> Every act of knowledge is chacterized by what the Scholastics call the intentional (or mental) existence of an object; we call it the relation to an object, the direction toward an object; we could also call it immanent objectivity.[3]

The object (*Gegenstand*) for Brentano is not necessarily identical with an extramental reality. Rather, his object may owe its existence (and he argues that every object does exist, for consciousness) to some activity of the mind. Thus, while some objects may stand for physical realities (such as the Eiffel Tower), others may be imaginative items (such as a golden island), and still others may be meanings (such as the square root of three) that cannot be pictured. If ethical judgments are to be meaningful they must refer to objective contents of psychic activity.[4]

One of Brentano's outstanding pupils, Alexius Meinong (1853–1920) organized the theory of objects (*Gegenstandstheorie*) into a definite type of philosophy and formally related it to value theory and ethics. In an essay on the *Theory of Objects*, Meinong suggested that, when we feel joy or pity, or other emotions, the objects are not "joy" or "pity" but some items to which these feelings are directed. He used the term "directedness" (*Gerichtetsein*) for this characteristic which Brentano had called intentionality.[5]

For Meinong, many objects do not exist in reality (*wirklich*) yet they subsist (*bestehen*). Such objects are neither merely subjective mental states or acts, nor are they actual existents in the world of realities. Hence philosophy needs a third realm of being in which objects are given. A special and new part of philosophy is now to be devoted to the study of objects. "What can be known about an Object in virtue of its nature, hence *a priori*, belongs to the theory of Objects."[6] That some such object

re moral values, types of objective worth or oughtness, is brought out
y Meinong in a study of *Emotional Presentation* (1917). Just as there is
n objective content to what is presented in sense perception, so there
re objects-with-properties that are given in emotional experience. These
ncluded items such a goals, desideratives, and dignitatives.[7] These are
absistent ethical values that are not just personal appearances (*phe-
omena*) but are valid over and above subjective experience (*metaphe-
omena*). Whether this is to be called a realistic theory of values
Chisholm) or an idealistic theory (Hill) depends not so much on the
neory as on how we use the terms "ideal" and "real." Another philosopher
ho came under Brentano's influence in Vienna during the early 1880s,
as Edmund Husserl (1859–1938), who developed his "phenomenology"
ut stressing the realistic side of the theory of objects. Husserl influenced
nany of the phenomenological ethicians treated in our last chapter but
ad little to say about ethics for himself.

Still another follower of Brentano, Christian von Ehrenfels (1859–
)32), took a more psychological approach to the study of values. His
rstem of Value Theory (1897–1918) offers in its first volume a general
count of the genesis of values and, in the second volume, an explanation
' how ethics may be based on value theory. He understood value as an
bjective property arising from a person's act of desiring. Where Meinong
garded value as "given" in affective experience, Ehrenfels thought of
lue as projected from the subject's psychic inclination.

One of the greatest figures in the school of axiological ethics was Max
heler (1874–1928). One of his earliest ethical works, after his disserta-
n *On Logical and Ethical Principles* (1899), was the study entitled
ssentiment (1912). He borrowed this word from the French to name
e continued feeling of emotional reaction (or hostility) against a person
thing. This establishes Scheler's interest in the domain of emotional
periences as a source of moral notions. His chief contribution to ethics
the book on *Formalism in Ethics and the Non-Formal Value Ethics*
·913–1916; printed in *Werke*, II, 1954). Of the later writings, *The Nature
Sympathy* (1921) is important. Much unprinted material left at the
ne of his death has since been edited.

Scheler was not an Austrian (he was born in Munich) but came under
e influence of the phenomenology of values through Edmund Husserl.
· course, Scheler was also indebted to Augustine, Nietzsche, Bergson,
d Eucken. Fundamental in his thought is the notion of the *Mitwelt*
terally, with-world), a realm of experience shared with other persons
Thou relation). Four such interpersonal feelings are described by
neler: (1) community of feeling (*Miteinanderfühlen*), (2) fellow-feel-
: (*Mitfühlen*), (3) psychic contagion (*psychische Ansteckung*), and
) emotional identification (*Einsfühlung*). All are aspects of the basic

feeling of sympathy.[8] The capacity to enter into such relations with other is part of what it means to be a person.

Such an interpersonal relation is viewed as a sort of entity: being-with another subsists in the "ontic" realm of being, though it does not exist in the world of physical nature. This theory of real relations gives rise to Scheler's theory of "community" which is important in both his meta physics and his ethics.[9] Ordinary feelings of bodily pain or hunger, and so on, are not thus shared; these are entirely within the individual. Primary physiological feeling (*Gefühl*) is nonintentional but the higher feeling awareness of a feeling (*Fühlen*) is the value experience.[10] Since the higher, psychic feelings can be shared with others—emotions like joy and sorrow, remorse, despair, and happiness—it is on this level that ethical values are intuited. As interpersonal experiences, these feelings provide certain objectivity, universality, and absolute character to their value objects. Love is the most perfect feeling of community and it has a special status in moral experience. It is most important for ethics.[11]

Ethics studies the a priori content of what is given in such interpersonal feeling experience. Scheler's ethics is "material" (or nonformal) in the Kantian sense of having to do with the *content* of moral life. He think that Kant was generally right in his formal ethics but overlooked the whole area of objective moral values. Thus, there is no material a priori for Kant but there is for Scheler, who grants that there are many diverse "moralities" among different peoples, and at different times in history. The further question that Scheler asks is whether there is an underlying structure and unity in these various moralities which may be discovered in ethics. Ethics is a philosophical study of morality: the terms ethics and morality are not identical for Scheler.

One of the chief discoveries that Scheler makes as an ethician is scale of nonformal values. Working from the lowest values to the highest, he finds four levels. His principle of ranking uses the following features: (1) duration (a lasting value is better than a fleeting one); (2) extension (the quality of a value that may be shared by many persons without distintegrating); (3) independence (the higher value is never the foundation for the lower value); (4) depth of satisfaction (the more profound the value experience the higher the value).[12] With these standards he proposes the following scale of values. First, there are sensible values (*sinnliche Werte*), which include objects of pleasure and pain, and various sorts of utility. Second, there are life values (*Lebenswerte*): the noble and the mean, strength and weakness, good quality and bad quality Third, there are cultural values (*geistige Werte*), such as the beautiful and ugly, the legal and illegal, the knowledge of what is true. Final and highest are religious values (*Werte des Heiligen und Unheiligen*) beatitude and despair, feelings of holiness and the opposite.[13] This is hierarchy of values which has had a great influence on recent European ethics.

For Scheler, oughtness (Sollen) is of two kinds (1) ought-to-be, and (2) ought-to-do. The second rests in the first and together they establish the ground of ethical duty. Moral values do not correspond to the four levels of general value that have just been described. Instead, moral value arises when a person acts in such a way as to realize, or prefer, a thing-value (Sachwerte) of a higher level to a similar value on a lower level. All moral values are thus personal (Personwerte). Good as a value "rides on the back" of an act, as Scheler puts it.[14] In the long run, moral obligation consists in a special response in the person to the values that have been described.[15]

Much the same approach to value ethics is found in the work of Nicolai Hartmann (1882–1950). His three-volume Ethics (1926) is a more thoroughly organized version of Scheler's axiology. The first volume treats of moral phenomena; the second deals with moral values; and the third is devoted to moral freedom. His thought is better known to English readers than that of Scheler, because this large work of Hartmann's has been available for many years in translation. Born in Latvia of German parents, Hartmann did his university studies at Marburg. He came to know Aristotle quite well and was probably influenced by the Stagirite to take a slightly more realistic position on values than did Scheler. His historical study Die Philosophie des deutschen Idealismus (2 vols., 1923–1929) shows his extensive knowledge of earlier German idealism, particularly the thought of Hegel. Many people consider Nicolai Hartmann the greatest European ethician of the twentieth century.[16]

In Hartmann's view, values are essences in the ontic realm, essences somewhat like Plato's ideal forms. The world of subsisting values can be intuited through cognitive and affective acts of consciousness.[17] Value-objects are neither subjective phases of consciousness nor physically existing entities. They constitute a third realm of ideal reality.[18] Different persons are more or less open to the experience of values. All men perform some acts of approval, preference, and affective feeling of items which reveal an objective content of value. In this initial openness to value, feeling is most important.[19]

In the second volume of the Ethics, Hartmann makes a long investigation of the problem of ranking values and finding a value scale. Here he is indebted to Scheler but also critical of his simplicity. One must note that difference between the initial feeling of value and a secondary moment of ideal intuition of the value as object. Unlike Scheler, Hartmann thinks that the higher values are based on the lower ones; they depend, in some sense, on the inferior values.[20] Hartmann is very much aware of the history of philosophy, from Plato and Aristotle onward, and seems at times to get his gamut of lower to higher values from the great tradition of the ancient philosophers. On the other hand, he insists that higher values are not "stronger" but are generally "weaker" than the lower ones. What he means is that it is usually more serious to "sin" against a lower value than against a higher one. Yet to fulfill a higher value is better than to realize a lower one.[21] This means that Hartmann's table of values is not a unidimensional scale but a more complicated arrangement of objective standards of worth. The following value table attempts a summary of his teaching on this matter.

(I) *Elementary values:* modal oppositions of necessity and freedom, being and non-being, relational opposites of harmony and conflict, simplicity and complexity, qualitative and quantitative oppositions of universality and singularity, humanity and nation.

(II) *Values conditioning contents within the subject:* life, consciousness, activity, suffering, strength, freedom of will, foresight, purposive activity; values in goods: existence, situation, power, happiness.

(III) *Moral values:* (A) fundamental moral values: the good, the noble, richness of experience (common to many types of behavior); (B) special moral values: 1) values of the ancient moral system: justice, wisdom, courage, self-control, and other Aristotelian virtues; 2) Christian values: brotherly love, truthfulness, trustworthiness and fidelity, modesty, humility and aloofness, being true to one's own being, humor; 3) modern moral values (influenced by Nietzsche's transvaluation of values): love of the remote (humanity), radiant virtue, ethical ideals, personality, and personal love.[22]

It will be clear to the reader that an adequate account of this remarkable theory would require more space than can be given it here.

The study of the moral "ought" is much more fully developed in Hartmann than in Scheler. Both distinguish, of course, the "ought-to-be" from the "ought-to-do"—which latter brings us into the area of moral obligation and responsibility. All initial values have a teleological tendency toward being realized: "The *ought-to-be* is in its nature an *ought-to-be real.*" Only some values are of moral significance and have an exigency for action: to them the *ought-to-do* corresponds. Since values are in themselves independent of moral consciousness, they confer or point to absolute obligations for the ethical person. Accountability and responsibility for one's free personal acts are the key features of the moral life.

In his discussion of freedom, Hartmann is very critical of previous philosophic treatments of the subject. He is particularly opposed to indeterminism, for he feels that free acts are caused, both physically and psychically. Freedom is positive and entails the entry of new causal factor into an ongoing causal series. There is a freedom of the *ought-to-be* toward further realization—and there is a different freedom of action in the rder of the *ought-to-do*. The nature of moral responsibility and obligation s restated in terms of personal freedom.[24] In brief, the fact that conflicts mong values are quite possible leaves an opening for the person to intrude nto the interobjective tension and play the role of a determiner of the nanner in which "oughts" are fulfilled. Hartmann's ethics is, of course, a elf-realization theory. What makes it distinctive is his claim that one an intuit a whole range of ideal possibilities that may, and in some ases should, be realized. The validity of the whole construction depends n his initial assumption that such a realm of objective values is reached 1 human experience.

Although there were British idealist ethicians at the end of the nine-:enth and beginning of the twentieth century, and most of them used he language of value philosophy, the school of ethics under consideration 1 this chapter is not part of the English tradition. In the well-known nthology *Contemporary British Philosophy* (1925) neither Scheler or Hartmann is mentioned. Hartmann's *Ethik* was published a year iter, of course, but several of his studies in epistemology and ontology ad appeared earlier.

The closest approach to an axiological ethics in England was made by Villiam Ritchie Sorley (1855–1935). *Moral Life and Moral Worth* 1911) and the Gifford Lectures, *Moral Values and the Idea of God* 1918), are Sorley's most significant books. Nearly all of Sorley's phi-·sophy is ethically oriented. In his metaphysical thinking, he distrusted oth materialism and naturalism. Persons, he viewed as the "bearers of ilue" but not the constructors of standards of worth. Hence, moral ws and values are just as objective as the "laws of nature."[25] However, orley repudiated any suggestion that such values are experienced and iscovered philosophically through acts of feeling. If this means an rational approach (he quotes, "The heart has its reasons which the ason knows not," from Pascal), then such a method leads to the bank-iptcy of philosophy. Sorley is an *intellectual* idealist, not an emotional 1e, and this is where he differs radically from the Austro-German school ˙ axiologists.

Objectivity of values means to Sorley that these standards are there, hether we know them and are guided by them or not. The point is at "they ought to be our guides."[26] These moral values are part of the tal system of reality and they are simply revealed through the person. second characteristic of moral values, for Sorley, is their purposiveness. hey indicate a need of the human person for fulfillment. This is one the rare instances of the recognition of finality or teleology in recent ·itish ethics. The other context in which it appears is in some versions evolutionary ethics.

In the United States, until comparatively recently, German-Austrian axiology has had few devotees. Howard O. Eaton's study, *The Austrian Philosophy of Values* (1930), introduced the thinking of Brentano, Ehrenfels, and Meinong to American readers but did not treat the work of Scheler or Hartmann. Almost the sole representative of axiological ethics on the American scene was Wilbur M. Urban (1873–1952). His major publications in this field are *Valuation. Its Nature and Laws* (1909) and *The Intelligible World—Metaphysics and Value* (1929). The textbook *Fundamentals of Ethics* (1930, reissued 1949) is also important. *Beyond Realism and Idealism* (1949) states his mature thought on values and reality. Urban studied in Germany from 1895 to 1897, hence his knowledge of continental value theory goes back to the first members of the school, Brentano and Meinong, and even more to pioneers in German axiology, such as Wilhelm Windelband (1848–1915) and Heinrich Rickert (1863–1936).

Urban's early thinking on values and their relation to moral obligation stressed a psychological study of all the discoverable kinds of value. *Valuation* (1909) sought to discover through cognitive and affective acts of consciousness the whole gamut of values and the underlying principles in this field. He then described the act of valuation as the feeling aspect of a conative process.[27] The object of the act of valuing is not the product of this act: the value is already there as an object. The realm of values is midway between being and nonbeing.

A more definitely ethical orientation is required in Urban's textbook. There value is very simply defined as "that which satisfies human desire," even though, in *The Intelligible World* he had suggested that value is indefinable.[28] Now, value becomes the "basal concept" of Urban's ethics. Since ethics tries to find a standard or norm of human conduct, it is a normative science. However, such a norm is simply a description of "the morally good or humanly valuable."[29] Moral responsibility is implied in the acceptance of moral freedom. Duty is grounded in the axiom that "the good ought to be chosen rather than the bad, the greater rather than the lesser good."[30]

In his last major work Urban returned to the whole problem of the ontological status of values. As the title, *Beyond Realism and Idealism* implied, these are not ultimate philosophical classifications. A completely worked-out metaphysics will have to give first place to the realm of values as Urban sees it:

> From our present standpoint the entire issue, it seems to me, is one of priority or primacy. This primacy belongs to value for the reason, as I have long maintained, that there is a synthetic relation between them, such that there is a judgment of an "ought-to-be" implicit in all acknowledgment of value . . . the "ought-to-do" of moral agents being secondary and derived from this acknowledgment.[31]

In his mature thought, then, Urban held that ethics depends on metaphysics and that it is a specialized section of the general philosophy of value. There are some affinities between this position and that of Ralph Barton Perry, but we shall consider Perry as a representative of naturalism (Chapter XVI). *Humanity and Duty* (1951) offers a very explicit version of self-realization ethics, as developed in Urban's last period. The moral good is the fulfillment of an "ought-to-be" that consists in a drive toward realization.[32]

Continental Europe, in the period between the two world wars, saw many changes in philosophical thinking. Austrian axiological ethics came full circle with the work of Moritz Schlick (1882–1936), for his *Problems of Ethics* (1930) rejected the whole notion that values are objective and that they constitute independent norms for ethical judgment. Ethics was treated by Schlick from the viewpoint of the scientific positivism of the Vienna Circle and he had no sympathy with the idealism, or phenomenological realism, of the Brentano to Hartmann school. Schlick firmly rejected the assumption that the purpose of ethics is to formulate a conception of the good.[33] For him, ethics is reduced to a psychological study of the various observable motives for human conduct. Nor is it a normative science, in the ordinary meaning of the term "normative," as Schlick bluntly explains:

> For if ethics furnishes a justification it does so only in the sense just explained, namely, in a relative-hypothetical way, not absolutely. It "justifies" a certain judgment only to the extent that it shows that the judgment corresponds to a certain norm; that this norm itself is "right," or justified, it can neither show nor, by itself, determine.[34]

In his fifth chapter, Schlick gives a very accurate summary of the theory of absolute moral values. So conceived, value would have to be something wholly independent of man's feelings, identified with certain objects that are quite distinct from the ways in which we react emotionally to them. This absolutistic ethics would have as its moral imperative: "Act so that the events or things produced by your actions are as valuable as possible." In response to this, Schlick simply asks why he should obey this rule. His criticism of the theory of objective values uses the standard positivistic approach to verifiability. Value judgments are clearly not tautologies. If they are to be empirically verified, one may ask: Under what empirical conditions is the proposition, "this object is valuable," true? To say that moral values are any objects of pleasure is nonsense. One cannot find an objective fact in sense perception that would indicate objective value. It is necessary to conclude, according to Schlick, that values are not objective but are merely subjective feelings of pleasure.

Hartmann's claim that values are objective in the same sense that a mathematical proposition (2 plus 2 equals 4) is, being valid for all who think it, is not for Schlick a proper analogy. The hypothesis of absolute value is empty. What happens if I don't choose to realize a value? If values were in independent objective existence, "they would constitute an independent realm which would enter the world of our volition and action at no point."[35] Instead, Schlick suggests that moral values (and ethical judgments) are purely relative. Both pleasure and sorrow may be morally valuable feelings: "They owe their value to the joy they promise, which is the only measure of their value." Responsibility is simply the feeling that one is subject to punishment or reward for a given act.[36] It is generally agreed that Schlick's ethics amounts to ethical skepticism and that it is "axiological" only in the sense that this ethics continually uses the language of value.

If his positivism induced Moritz Schlick to create a far from idealistic type of value ethics, much the same diversity in theory now becomes apparent among his contemporaries. One group of philosophers in the United States represents a value theory of ethics that is not dependent on the Austrian school yet falls within the category of axiological ethics. C. I. Lewis (1883–1964), for instance, located value experience in the area of affective feelings. For Lewis, however, a value is not an object but a special and not easily described quality of the conscious experience of valuing. His book *An Analysis of Knowledge and Valuation* (1946) is usually classified as a naturalistic study and it does resemble John Dewey's efforts to make "valuation" more primary than value. Some commentators even reduce his position to hedonism,[37] but his distinction between *intrinsic* value (valuable for its own sake) and *extrinsic* value (valuable for the sake of something else) is very much like the Thomistic distinction between the *bonum honestum* and *utile*. In fact, Lewis puts extrinsic value under the heading of utility.[38]

An outstanding American personalist who used value language in his approach to ethics, Edgar Sheffield Brightman (1884–1953) stoutly defended the normative character of ethics and maintained that the purpose of ethics is to enunciate a coherent system of moral laws. Eleven basic laws of ethics are grounded in the value of the person.[39] As theist, Brightman regarded God as a necessary factor in any moral theory but he also insisted that moral law is more fundamental than religion.[40]

In his *Human Values: An Interpretation of Ethics Based on Study of Values* (1931), DeWitt H. Parker (1885–1949) developed teaching which depends on Perry's definition of value as "any object of any interest." Parker is more idealistic, or even subjectivistic, than Perry, since he places less stress on value as an object and more on the character of the "interest" involved. Ought-as-a-feeling has no meaning for Parker, unless it is related to some desire.[41] The highest good s a condition of harmony in which all desires are satisfied. Parker's ethics, in fact, fluctuates between the notion that the harmonious satisaction of the individual is all-important and the view that universal atisfaction is the supreme goal.[42]

Among more recent teachers in the United States, William H. Werkneister (1901–   ) has done a great deal to make the point of view of xiological ethics known in America. Born in Germany, Werkmeister inished his philosophical studies in the United States and has taught ere for many years. His exposition of the ethics of Scheler and Hartnann has formed the starting point for most of the recent studies by American scholars in this field. Werkmeister's own view may be gathered rom the tenth chapter of his Theories of Ethics (1961). One of the entral problems of ethics, as he sees it, is to work out the relation etween the axiological and the moral ought, for they are not identical.[43] Verkmeister finds a second pivotal problem in the many cases where ne's obligations are in obvious conflict.

A surprising number of Catholic ethicians, with more or less backround in Thomism, have gone into the field of axiological ethics. 'or example, Rudolf Allers (1883–1963) studied medicine in Vienna, sychology and philosophy at Milan, and then taught philosophy for any years at Catholic University and Georgetown University. One of llers' most influential books was his study of the development of the thical personality, entitled The Psychology of Character (1929) in the nglish version. Allers' work lies on the periphery of ethics but he aught and influenced many younger scholars who are doing promising ork in the subject. It was in a paper entitled "Reflections on Cooperation nd Communication" (1960) that Allers first supported the notion of realm of "insistent being" which would seem to parallel the ontic alm of Hartmann. Participation in this ontological region (in which meanings" and presumably values insist) enables human persons to mmunicate with each other.[44] In another paper, "Ethics and Anthrobology," Allers suggested that the social sciences may make important ctual contributions to ethics without forcing it into the camp of ethical lativism.

A German priest who started his scholarly career as a student of the ought of St. Augustine later became an ardent exponent of the pernalistic ethics of Max Scheler. This is Johannes Hessen (1899–   ). oth his study of Max Scheler (1948) and his Ethics: Foundations for a ersonalist Ethics (1954) remain untranslated but Hessen is regarded Europe as an important figure in post-World War II German ethics. milarly, Fritz von Rintelen (1898–   ) is another example of a Cathic ethician who has carried on the axiological approach to ethics in rent German scholarship.

Of course, Dietrich von Hildebrand (1889–   ), who taught for many

years at Fordham University, is well known for his many books in the
field of Christian ethics. Much of his thought is quite like the axiological
personalism of Max Scheler. *Fundamental Moral Attitudes* (1950), *Christian Ethics* (1953), and *True Morality and Its Counterfeits* (1955)
have made his views generally known in the United States. A symposium,
The Human Person and the World of Values (1960), was issued as a
tribute to von Hildebrand on his seventieth birthday. Its title was well
chosen: his interests are personalistic and axiological. For him, love is
the distinctive feature of the human person.[45] Some critics feel that von
Hildebrand's general emphasis on Christian belief as a ground for ethics
makes his thought a version of Catholic theology, rather than a moral
philosophy.

A native of the United States, Leo R. Ward (1893–   ) of Notre
Dame has made numerous contributions to the study of values and ethics.
His *Philosophy of Value* (1930) is a pioneer Thomistic work in the
field. Ward's recent *Ethics* (1965) makes use of much material from
value theory and the social sciences to develop a modified version of
Thomistic ethics. He has put more emphasis on special problems in
ethics than the theoretical foundations of the subject. Leo Ward offers
an excellent example of what might be called an "open" Thomistic
ethics, developed under the influence of DeWitt H. Parker and R. B.
Perry.

Much of the recent interest in axiological ethics in France is found
in the work of the *philosophie de l'esprit* school, whose contributions
we have noted already (Chapter XII). Louis Lavelle and René Le
Senne are primary examples of such a spiritual value approach to
ethics. The outstanding recent authority on axiology in France is undoubtedly Raymond Polin (1910–   ), whose survey article on the "Philosophy of Values in France" (1950) is the best guide to French activity
in axiology. Although Polin rejects the objectivity of values, his theory is
existential: value is something given in concrete human experience.
It has nothing to do, however, with "norms" in the sense of standards
imposed on persons by the authorities. Norms are not as good as
values. With this kind of axiology we have moved very far afield from
the original school of Brentano.

In a sense value ethics has been too successful. Practically all ethicians
now talk about values and mean many different things when they use
the term. As a result, the notion of value has become so diluted that
it is almost a transcendental term in contemporary ethics. Value enables
people to discuss the possibility of a rather ill-defined realm of moral
standards without too clearly committing themselves on their status in
being. And so, except for its usefulness as a general term, value is no
longer a major item in strictly contemporary ethics.

CHAPTER XV

Self-Realization and Utilitarian Ethics

MANY ENGLISH-SPEAKING moral philosophers during the past century have felt that ethical judgment must include some appraisal of the consequences of moral activity. Theoretically this view is directly opposed to Kantian formalism: the teaching that a good motive prior to external action, or a pure will, is the only indicator of a morally good act or person. The broadest meaning of utilitarianism would include any kind of ethics that stresses the *results* of moral attitudes, volitions, and activities. If these results are chiefly viewed in relation to the total fulfillment of the powers and personality of the moral agent, then we have a self-realization version of consequence ethics. On the other hand, if the consequences mainly include the welfare and advantage of other persons, of the society in which the agent acts, we have social utilitarianism. We shall see that the contrast between formalism and utilitarianism has grown much less acute in recent Anglo-American ethics. Philosophers are beginning to think that a "good will" is hardly possible without some concern for the predictable results of moral decisions, and that factual consequences are of ethical importance to the extent that they do or can qualify the motivation and prior dispositions of the moral agent. Even more striking is the manner in which some recent versions of utilitarian ethics have turned to the idea of generalization as a method of determining the moral value of consequences.

Some of the most influential voices in British ethics at the end of the nineteenth century were idealists. Many of these thinkers combined Kantianism, or some later kind of German ethics, with a general acceptance of Christian morality. James Martineau (1805–1900) is a good example of a holder of this general position. His *Types of Ethical Theory* (2 vols., 1886–1891) classified the various schools as: Unpsychological Theories (Plato, Descartes, Malebranche, Spinoza—all basing their ethics on some prior metaphysics); Unpsychological Theories based on physical science (Auguste Comte): Idiopsychological Theories, which focus ethical attention on a man's own inner conscience (Bentham,

Paley, and Martineau himself); Hetero-Psychological Theories, which are hedonistic and may be evolutionary types of ethics (Hobbes, Mill, Bain, Darwin, and Spencer); and Dianoetic Ethics, which employs some system of intellectual ideas or a moral sense (Cudworth, Clarke, Price, Shaftesbury, and Hutcheson). In point of fact, Martineau agreed with Kant that a person's inner awareness of his duty is the sole criterion of morality. His position is quite in keeping with that of his contemporaries, Bradley and Green, whom he classifies as ethical intuitionists, in the following text:

> Mr. F. H. Bradley tells us: "Morality has not to do immediately with the outer results of the Will:" "acts, so far as they spring from the good will, are good:" "what issues from a good character must likewise be morally good." And with equal distinctness, Professor Green insists that "it is not by the outward form that we know what moral action is. We know it, so to speak, on the inner side. We know what it is in relation to us, the agents; what it is as our expression. Only thus indeed do we know it at all."[1]

Instead of Kant's very formal imperative, Martineau takes as the basic axiom of his ethics: "Every action is RIGHT, which in presence of a lower principle, follows a higher: every action is WRONG, which in presence of a higher principle, follows a lower."[2] To illustrate, he gives the example of a son who decides to pay his father's large debt. Motivated by a "sense of justice," his act is morally good; if he had been motivated by a love of wealth and had decided otherwise, he would have been moved by the lower motive and his act would be bad. To provide criteria for the judgment of motivation, Martineau developed a table of "Springs of Action" that ranked thirteen different levels of motives, from low-grade passions of vindictiveness and suspicion to high-grade feelings of compassion and reverence.[3] His principle of ranking is obviously British social opinion in the nineteenth century.

British self-realization ethics reached its peak development in the writings of Thomas Hill Green (1836–1882). His general philosophical view was Kantian, ahthough he never accepted Kant's teaching on the thing-in-itself. Green thought that there is an eternal consciousness in which the individual person shares. The awareness of moral duty is one aspect of this participation in the consciousness, which he sometimes calls divine. Essentially, then, Green's ethics is a working out of what is required for the development or realization within each self of the potentialities of this universal consciousness. This is how he expresses his position, in the Prolegomena to Ethics:

> It is clearly of the very essence of the doctrine above advanced that the divine principle, which we suppose to be realising itself in man, should be supposed to realise itself in persons, as such.

But for reflection on our personality, on our consciousness of ourselves as objects to ourselves, we could never dream of there being such a self-realising principle at all, whether as implied in the world or in ourselves.[4]

Earlier in the same work, Green had asked whether the working out of the destiny of eternal consciousness might simply be accomplished through some impersonal Humanity; in the passage just quoted, he made it clear that its realization is personal and individual. However, there is a social dimension to Green's ethics, because he insisted that many of the higher capacities of man depend on his status within his social group. The "common good" thus becomes a pivotal concept in Green's moral philosophy.[5]

Green's pupil Francis Herbert Bradley (1846–1924) was a quick realizer of his potentialities: he published his famous *Ethical Studies* in 1876, seven years before Green printed his *Prolegomena*. Bradley soon showed that he was a great metaphysician. His *Appearance and Reality* (1893) provided a theoretical background for his ethics. The opposition between good and evil is not absolute; it is overcome in the totality of the Absolute. Self-realization is the movement of the person from the condition of discrete and pluralized pleasures (hedonism) to a higher integration of the self in an infinite whole.

The best presentation of Bradley's ethics is in the famous Essay II, entitled "Why Should I Be Moral?"[6] Here, he is inclined to minimize the notion of "moral consciousness" and to stress the effort to make one's personal will merge with the infinite whole. Two sentences in the essay make this clear:

"Realize yourself as an infinite whole" means "Realize yourself as the self-conscious member of an infinite whole, by realizing that whole in yourself." When that whole is truly infinite, and when your personal will is wholly made one with it, then you also have reached the extreme of homogeneity and specification in one, and have attained a perfect self-realization.[7]

Another of Bradley's essays, "Duty for Duty's Sake," takes up the Kantian theme of the good will. This is not a departure from self-realization, as Bradley understands it, since a pure act of will is, to him, fulfillment of the reality of the person. In this process, I become an end unto myself. In an effort to say more definitely what good will means, Bradley lists four special characteristics. First, the good will is *universal*; it is not the volition of particular men but a common standard above you and me. Second, it is *free* will: it is not conditioned or determined by anything other than itself. Third, it is *autonomous*: in willing what is valid for itself, it legislates for all. Fourth, it is *formal*: the good will acts not for the sake of some given content but for itself as without content or matter.[8] Nothing indicates better than the foregoing how basically Kantian is the self-realization ethics of Bradley. Much the same sort of ethics is found in the many writings of Bernard Bosanquet (1848–1923). Two of his most influential works in this field are *The Principle of Individuality and Value* (1912) and *The Value and Destiny of the Individual* (1913). A series of fourteen articles by Bosanquet in the *International Journal of Ethics* made his teaching well known to American readers.[9] The "individual" is a very positive concept with Bosanquet, and its characteristics are integrity, completeness, and wholeness. Hence, the Absolute is an individual. Moreover, Bosanquet felt that the ethical theory of F. H. Bradley deserved to be better known. It interpreted Kantian ethics in a way that Kant "would have disowned" but, in Bosanquet's mind, Bradley's ethics really satisfies the theoretical demand which the *Critique of Practical Reason* had left unfulfilled.[10] This enthusiasm for Bradley's ethics was fully shared by J. H. Muirhead (1855–1940), who devoted much of his time to the job of making it better known.

The thinking of Hasting Rashdall (1858–1924) also falls within the scope of British self-realization ethics but with different emphases from the foregoing thinkers. Rashdall's *Theory of Good and Evil* (1907) is actually an example of ideal utilitarianism. Moral good is intuited through the faculty of reason. As a strong theist, Rashdall insists that God is needed in any theory of morality. His thinking is also much more dependent on teleology than are other versions of British idealist ethics. There is a sharp criticism of self-realization in the *Theory of Good and Evil*, where Rashdall points out that if to make the self real means to realize what is real, the view is nonsense.[11] If it means, on the other hand, to realize some potentiality of the self, then the theory is doubtless true but obscure. Certainly the point cannot be that one must realize all the capacities of human nature, for it is frequently necessary to choose between competing potentialities. Finally, if self-realization means developing one's whole nature—physical, intellectual, emotional—then this is simply impossible, as Rashdall sees it. To perfect one aspect of personality, say the intellectual, entails a certain depreciation of another side of one's nature, say the physical. Yet Rashdall thinks that self-realization is as good as any other approach to ethics; it is possible he finally admits, that all attempts to define morality must move in a circle.[12]

A famous Plato scholar, A. E. Taylor (1869–1945), was critical of the self-realization theory of ethics but sympathized with the theistic approach of Rashdall. Taylor's *Problem of Conduct* (1901) and *The Faith of a Moralist* (1930) combine an idealistic value theory with certain elements of natural law ethics. Equally well known for his work in the field of Greek philosophy and also very active in the field of ethics, W. D. Ross (1877-1940) shared something of Taylor's idealism. Ross's *The Right and the Good* (1930) acknowledges a debt to H. A. Prichard and G. E. Moore but it is also strongly influenced by Kant. To Ross, right does not mean the same as good. This is clear, he thinks, from the fact that the words are not convertible; that is, one cannot be substituted for the other. When we say this act is "right," we mean that it ought to be done, or is morally obligatory. Eventually he suggests that moral rightness is intuited and that duties are of two general kinds: prima facie duties are certain types of activity (fidelity, reparation, gratitude, justice, beneficence, self-improvement, and nonmalevolence) that are generally right and obligatory unless some higher duty intervenes. Proper moral duties, on the other hand, apply in concrete situations and are the only guide that we have to what is morally right.[13] However, good is a quality of a thing, or action, or a character, that is connected with virtue, pleasure, or knowledge. Thus understood, moral good is probably indefinable.[14] Consequently, some acts may be right and not good, and vice versa.

In the *Foundations of Ethics* (1939), Ross makes some of these points more explicit. Right is a legalistic term suggesting obedience to law, while good suggests that which satisfies desire or obtains an end.[15] Both notions are important to ethics but that of right is more basic. Motives seem to determine goodness, whereas the suitability of an action is central to the notion of rightness.[16] In the final analysis, although most agents strive to achieve objective rightness, the ultimate obligation is determined by subjective rightness. That is, what a person thinks, or feels, that he must do is all-important. One's personal decision in the moral order rests on a comparison of prima facie duties.[17] For example, a policeman who finds that his mother is a habitual shoplifter is confronted by two prima facie duties, his obligation to secure obedience to the laws of his country, and his obligation to respect and honor his mother. His final decision, as moral judgment, rests on the resolution of the conflict of these types of duty. That one should decide in terms of promoting the most, or greatest, good is not always obvious. Intuition of what is right is often a surer guide.

A similar theory is advocated by H. A. Prichard (1871-1947) in a series of miscellaneous studies dating back as early as 1912 but published together under the title *Moral Obligation* (1949). Suspicious of utilitarian procedures, Prichard stated his view in a much reprinted article, "Does Moral Philosophy Rest on a Mistake?" (1912). It was not that he doubted the value of ethical investigation but rather that he wondered whether ethics had been asking the right questions, for he felt that one cannot offer "proof" or reasons for a duty. It is there and one simply sees it. This is a radical example of ethical intuitionism.[18]

A popular version of self-realization ethics was made the theoretical basis for the ethical culture movement in nineteenth-century United States. It was a Cornell University professor, Felix Adler (1851–1933), who established the first Society for Ethical Culture, in 1876, at New York City. Other groups were founded elsewhere in the United States and an international organization came into being in 1887. W. M. Salter, Stanton Coit, and Percival Chubb took a prominent part in the spread of ethical culture. Aimed at improving the moral life of individual members and their communities, without regard for theological or philosophical opinions, this semireligious movement has not had a great impact on academic ethics but it is an example of a widespread effort to popularize the ideals of ethical self-realization.

The greatest name in idealistic ethics in the United States is that of Josiah Royce (1855–1916). With William James (whose views were very different) Royce attracted European interest to American thought, for the first time. His *Religious Aspect of Philosophy* (1885), *The World and the Individual* (1900–1901), *Studies of Good and Evil* (1902), *The Philosophy of Loyalty* (1908), and *The Hope of the Great Community* (1916) are all ethically oriented books. In general, Royce's philosophical position is an absolute idealism quite unlike the similarly named philosophy of his British contemporaries. Kant, Schelling, Lotze, and Schopenhauer are important in Royce's background, and Hegel, of course, is central in his great work, *The World and the Individual.*

In his study of knowledge and reality, Royce came to think that the real objects of thought cannot be outside consciousness; for, if they were completely so, they would never be known. Moreover, the possibility of intercommunication between persons, and the possibility of error within the thinking of one person, led him to conclude that there is an infinite Thought which contains all objects, all relations, and even all errors, that can be thought.[19] Thus, Royce's God is Absolute Experience, embracing all selves, all thoughts, and all volitions.[20] Ideas (viewed either within the consciousness of the individual man or in universal consciousness) have a sort of life of their own: they intend and will "objects," which are the external fulfillment of the internal idea. Such externality does not mean extraconsciousness but simply an independent reality within the realm of thought. As Royce states this idealistic theory: "To be, in the final sense, means to be just such a life, complete, present to experience, and conclusive of the search for perfection which every finite idea in its own measure undertakes when it seeks for any object."[21]

In the context of such a position, Royce's ethics is a type of self-realization, or better, self-perfectionism. A good moral life is to be guided neither by rules derived from the "facts of nature" (realism) nor from the codes of behavior current in actual societies (social relativism). Evolutionary ethics was coming into prominence in his day, and confronted with the suggestion that man should act so as to achieve a higher state of evolution, Royce asked how we know that the later stages in evolution are any better morally than the earlier ones.[22] Instead, Royce based his ethics on an ideal moral order which embodied something of the Greek notion of living in accord with "reason," a good deal of the love-ethic of early Christian teaching, and much of Kant's theory of a kingdom of ends. As a young man, Royce's basic ethical imperative was: "In so far as in thee lies, act as if thou wert at once thy neighbor and thyself."[23]

A more distinctive teaching is developed in *The Philosophy of Loyalty*. There Royce treats "loyalty" as the fundamental moral experience and standard, and adds that loyalty means the willing and thorough devotion of an individual to a cause. As such, loyalty is for the individual person a supreme good. Two special features distinguish loyalty: decisiveness and fidelity. However, conflicts of causes or interests do arise and with them come conflicts of loyalties. A man may find that in taking a certain job he is depriving another person of work; a representative of one profession, or one state, or one school of thought, may find that his interest is in opposition to that of others; a patriot may discover that the citizens of an enemy nation are just as loyal to their country as he is to his own. In a famous lecture Royce proposed that the way to overcome these conflicts is to be "loyal to loyalty." What makes for conflict among the ideals or causes that people espouse is the limited way in which these causes are conceived. It is morally superior for the individual interested in his own welfare to think of a whole lifetime rather than a moment of pleasure. It is better to think in terms of the good of a larger group than a smaller one. Ultimately, one should strive to be loyal to all mankind; and this, Royce thinks, is to be loyal to God, and to loyalty itself. All special moral duties and all virtues are to be interpreted, then, in terms of loyalty to the whole duty of man.[24]

It was almost inevitable that Royce would go on to apply this ethical view to some of man's practical problems. *The Hope of the Great Community* (1916) expressed something close to the heart of American idealism in the social, political, and religious orders, when it proposed that all men should try to overcome petty differences in the total interest of humanity. The "great community" could be an international organization to promote peace, on one level; or, again, it might mean the community of all the faithful, which Royce took to be the essence of Christianity.[25] These high-minded ethical views did much to show other peoples that Royce's country was not solely devoted to material values.[26]

Royce's younger colleague in the famous Harvard department of philosophy, George Santayana (1863–1952), was an entirely different kind of thinker. Sometimes he was quite skeptical about the value of ethics. "Any feeling," he wrote, "nursed and kept close in the dark, may fester into a categorical imperative."[27] At other times Santayana took a naturalistic and somewhat hedonistic view of ethics. One must consider the consequences of our decisions and actions, and so, utilitarianism has some truth in it. Pleasure is obviously good and pain is evil. This was his position in *The Life of Reason: or the Phases of Human Progress* (1905-1906). As he put it, "Conduct that should not justify itself somehow by the satisfactions secured and the pains avoided would not justify itself at all."[28]

Later, Santayana came to his theory of "essences"—possibly under the influence of Plato.[29] Items like nature, history, and self are notions of things, images whose being is purely internal to them. These essence "possess no substance or hidden parts, but are all surface, all appearance." More generally expressed, Santayana's essences are "the characters possessed by such things as happen to exist, together with the character which all different things would possess if they existed."[30] One might expect him to equate moral values with some of these essences but he does not; in themselves, essences are morally neutral. Value, both aesthetic and moral, is constituted by personal approval of some item in the realm of essences. "Values accrue to any part of the realm of essence by virtue of the interest which somebody takes in it."[31] So, from this point of view, Santayana's ethics (which he himself calls "naturalistic") is an example of psychological value theory.

In other places, Santayana's skepticism leads him to take a different attitude. Morality, he thinks, should mean actual allegiance to this or that ideal of life. Most of Royce's writing fell into this category and there is no doubt that Santayana respected Royce. On the other hand, ethics would be for Santayana a descriptive science recording the history of moral allegiances, the circumstances and effects involved in the historical shifts of moral perspective. In other words, Santayana sometimes treated ethics as the "science of manners," in the French sociological sense.[32] It might be just as well to admit that Santayana was not strongly committed to any ethic; he preserved an attitude of aristocratic disdain for ethical "enthusiasm" and was not especially loyal to anything.

The tradition of idealistic self-realization ethics was continued in the teaching of Hocking and Jordan. William Ernest Hocking (1873-1966) was Royce's most faithful follower at Harvard. *Human Nature and Its Remaking* (1918) shows that Hocking placed more emphasis on traditional theistic belief as a bulwark for ethical judgment. Moreover, Hocking was a very explicit defender of democracy and political freedom as ethical values. Elijah Jordan (1875-1953) never attracted the same amount of attention as Hocking, while he was alive, but Jordan's thought is now becoming better recognized as an important contribution to ethics and social theory in the United States. *The Good Life* (1949) offers a self-realization theory based on objective idealism. In it, Jordan opposed subjectivism in value theory and was particularly critical of the notion that moral value can be reduced to some sort of personal "interest."[33]

Academic philosophers have paid little attention to the writing of Albert Schweitzer (1875–1965), at least, in the field of ethics; yet to many people in the contemporary world he represented the personification of the ethical spirit. There are periods in the history of ethics when the key writers are anything but professors; at other times (and the twentieth century is one such), it is almost necessary to be affiliated with university work before one can get a hearing in ethics. In any case, Schweitzer's decision to abandon a promising medical career in Europe (the family was Alsatian) and to establish a hospital in Africa made him a universally esteemed figure. Not all of his admirers realized that he was an excellent scholar in philosophy and theology. Schweitzer's *Civilization and Ethics* (1922) was originally a series of lectures, delivered in French, at Mansfield College, Oxford, but published in German, as were the originals of his other books. Dr. Schweitzer did a great deal of reading as background for these talks and his book is the best short history of ethics that has appeared since Henry Sidgwick's *Outlines*.[34] Schweitzer's own ethical position is very simple: "Reverence for life affords me my fundamental principle of morality, namely that good consists in maintaining, assisting, and enhancing life, and that to destroy, to harm, or to hinder life is evil."[35] The term that he used in German is *Ehrfurcht*, which suggests both respect and awe for the living. Life was intended to include both its human and nonhuman examples. Other than this vitalistic principle, Schweitzer's ethics has little to distinguish it from any other simple theory of self-realization.[36]

The most straightforward presentation of self-realization ethics is to be found in the writing of Henry W. Wright (1878–1959). His main publication is entitled *Self-Realization* (1913); he expounds his theory there in terms of the development of the individual self, the social self, and the universal self. The ends of the individual are pleasure and culture, of the social self they are altruism and humanitarianism, and of the universal self the goal is "universal progress," which involves resignation to the divine will and trust in divine wisdom.[37]

An Englishman who taught for many years at Princeton, Walter T. Stace (1886–   ) is a good example of the advocate of a refined hedonism. His chief work in ethics is *The Concept of Morals* (1937). Ethical relativism based on a hasty interpretation of data from the social sciences is subjected to very severe criticism by Stace, for he regards such an ethics as defeatism in morals. Stace has also insisted that without free will ethics is nonsense but that such freedom must admit of a certain amount of causal determinism.[38] His own ethics takes pleasure as the test of what is morally good and suggests that mental pleasures must rank above those of the body.

Another American thinker, Brand Blanshard (1892–   ), has been an outstanding critic of the noncognitivism and subjectivism of recent British ethics. His *Reason and Goodness* (1961) represents a revision of the Gifford Lectures at St. Andrews and the Noble Lectures at Harvard. Blanshard has a broad knowledge of different types of ethics, and, in particular, is one of the few contemporary ethicians who knows anything about medieval ethics.[39] At times, Blanshard's own ethics comes very close to Kant, but he prefers to be known as a rationalist. Sometimes, Blanshard can sound positively classical in explaining the role of reason, as in the following sentence:

> Rationality, as we conceive it, does not lie merely in letting reason appoint one's beliefs, hard as that is; it means carrying a rational spirit into the ramifications of practice, making it permeate one's feelings and pervade all the decisions of one's will.[40]

Like Rousseau and Kant, Blanshard distinguishes between personal fluctations of desire and volition (the actual will) and the rational will "which is what on reflection would commend itself as the greatest good."[41] In working out the features that constitute rationality, he presents a theory of human nature that is not far removed from Aristotelian ethics. It is not as close to Aristotle, of course, as the work of Henry B. Veatch (1911–   ), whose *Rational Man: A Modern Interpretation of Aristotelian Ethics* (1962) was written as a formal answer to the phenomenological work *Irrational Man*, by William Barrett.

Kantian deontology is combined with self-realization ethics in the work of A. C. Garnett (1894–   ). His *Ethics: A Critical Introduction* (1960) surveys all the main types of ethical theory and has been helpful at many points in the present history. Specifically expert contemporary scholarship in the ethics of Kant is represented in England by H. J Paton (1887–   ) and in the United States by Lewis White Beck (1913–   ). Both have provided translations and interpretations of the practical works of Kant.

In the rest of the present chapter, it is proposed to offer a brief summary of two special trends in recent ethics which have some relation with consequence ethics. Oddly both provide a bridge between formalism and utilitarianism. The first is the theory of games as applied to ethic and the second is the development of "act" and "rule" utilitarianism

Games theory goes back to the efforts of mathematicians to investigate the rules of strategy that govern the winning of table games such a chess. It is generally known that only a certain number and pattern of moves are required for success in such games and probability theory can be applied to this sort of problem. A pioneer article in this field was the German study "On the Theory of Playing Games" (1928), by J. von Neumann. With O. Morgenstern, von Neumann later applied this technique to the making of decisions in the sphere of economics. It is not a matter of going through a complicated calculus of all the possibilities that may be available for achieving a certain end. Nor is games theory anything like a calculation of the relative weights of pleasures that may result from a given action. As applied to decision-making, the method becomes rapidly simpler the nearer the agent is to his goal, since the number of possible moves diminishes rapidly, after the opening moves. It should be noted from the beginning, however, that this theory has nothing to offer in regard to opting for an end or goal of action. It is only after a moral agent has established his objective, that games theory may help him with the selection of the best means to that end.

The most discussed book applying the theory of games to ethics was written by R. B. Braithwaite (1900–   ) of Cambridge University. His *Theory of Games as a Tool for the Moral Philosopher* (1955, reissued 1963) was the inaugural lecture, delivered when he became professor of moral philosophy at Cambridge. This version of the theory is explained by discussing a definite problem that is moral, in a sense, but also somewhat like a game. The problem is later used in another context of ethical discussion by R. M. Hare.[42] Two men live in the same building: one plays piano and the other plays trumpet and the building is so constructed that one man's playing interferes with the other man's enjoyment. With this background (plus a few more details that are here omitted), Braithwaite asks:

> Can any plausible principle be devised stating how they should divide the proportion of days on which both of them play, Luke alone plays, Matthew alone plays, neither play, so as to obtain maximum production of satisfaction compatible with fair distribution?[43]

While it is impossible to summarize the mathematical steps used to suggest a solution, it may be noted that Braithwaite eventually decides that out of 43 evenings the piano player should play on 17, while the trumpet player should play on 26. That other solutions are theoretically possible, Braithwaite admits.

Two observations may be made concerning games theory and ethics. First, if one uses a teleological approach to ethics, such as this method implies, the really difficult problem centers on the option for ends, rather than the choice of means to secure these ends. This is generally recognized by people who work from the point of view of value theory: is easy to set up proximate standards of worth but very hard to justify ultimate values. In other words, the theory of games may have some limited utility in helping people to make moral decisions, *if they already* *have an objective clearly in view.* Mathematical computation does no seem to help in determining such an ultimate objective for life. Second while some moral decisions may be reducible to the competition-be tween-two-persons pattern, it does not seem that this is generally the case. Some moral problems may not directly involve other person at all; and other questions may include so many affected persons an so many variations of detail that the simplicity of Braithwaite's case ma be deceptive. In any event, it is interesting to note how what looks lik a very formal suggestion in recent ethics actually entails a consideratio of ideal consequences, in the guise of what one means by "winning th game."

The other recent trend in utilitarian ethics has to do with the differenc between using an appraisal of consequences to make a judgment of a act and of a *rule.* Act-utilitarians included most of the now classi thinkers in this school, notably Bentham and J. S. Mill. However, the may not have been entirely conscious of the point now under discussior The act-utilitarian does not attempt to generalize; he asks, "Wha effect will *my* doing *this* act in *this* situation have on the gener balance of good over evil?" On the other hand, the rule-utilitaria thinks that moral action should always be governed by a general ru that has been established by asking whether this general kind of actio if done by everyone, would result in general good or evil.[44]

An important contemporary representative of act-utilitarianism is th Australian J. J. C. Smart (1920–   ). His *Outline of a System of Uti tarian Ethics* (1961) discusses both kinds of consequence ethics an opts for the utilitarianism that concentrates on the act. The basic o jection to rule-utilitarianism, according to Smart, is that it can lead judgments that one should abide by a rule even in situations where will not be beneficial to do so. Moreover, Smart insists that there is difference between the person who thinks that all pleasures are equal quality and the ethician who considers mental pleasures, for instanc superior to bodily ones. It is ideal utilitarianism that requires qualitati distinctions of pleasures.

Actually, Smart distinguishes two moments in the thinking of an ac utilitarian: he must first evaluate the consequences, and then he mu judge the various acts that might lead to these consequences.[45] Admittir that there are difficulties in estimating the value of the consequenc Smart takes the example of the recent physiological experiments on ra which can be electrically stimulated so that they appear to enjoy almc endless feelings of pleasure. Whether humans thus artificially stimulat to feel pleasures on the sensual level might represent the ideal go which the ethician envisions, now becomes Smart's main query. It indeed a question whether this sort of thing is true human happiness

As Smart sees the act-utilitarian teaching, the only reason for per-
forming act A rather than act B is that doing A will make mankind
happier than will doing act B. He feels that people who work in ethics
and value general happiness will tend to agree that his is a most acceptable view.[47] Smart does not ask for altruism but simply for benevolence: the view of the agent who wishes others as much good as he
gets himself. There is always the problem of deciding whether one
should promote the maximum of happiness for all men as a group, or
whether one should strive for an equitable distribution of possibly lesser
happiness to all men. Here Smart admits that one might need to use
mathematical probability theory in order to secure complete equity.
It is at this point that one realizes how thin the wall now is between
a sophisticated utilitarian ethics and a formalism that shows some concern for the facts of life. In point of fact, as Smart notes, if one begins
to think of possible rules in utilitarianism then one approaches the
position of Kant.[48]

Another major contribution to this problem of ethical method has
been made by Marcus G. Singer (1926–   ) in his *Generalization in
Ethics* (1961). He has no use for act-utilitarianism—which he calls "direct" utilitarianism. Utility as traditionally understood is an ambiguous
standard and leads to insurmountable ethical difficulties. However,
Singer is willing to take a second look at what he calls "indirect"
utilitarianism. This is the view that one may look to the consequences to
evaluate various *kinds* of actions. "One thus considers the consequences
that actions of that kind may generally be expected to have, and by
such means directly determines the morality of that *kind* of action."[49]
This indirect utilitarianism is, of course, but another version of rule-
utilitarianism. That it is an improvement over act-utilitarianism but still
subject to criticism is Singer's appraisal.

Singer's own ethical position is an attempt to refine the categorical
imperative of Kant. It will be recalled that Kant said that one should
act so that his very action could become a general rule of conduct.
There is much ambiguity in this rule. Hence, Singer expands the generalization *argument* in these words: "If everyone were to do that, the
consequences would be disastrous (or undesirable): therefore, no one
ought to do that."[50] On the other hand, he phrases the generalization
principle as follows: "what is right (or wrong) for one person must be
right (or wrong) for any similar person in similar circumstances."[51] To
Singer's mind, the categorical imperative can be interpreted so as to
form an adequate guide for ethical judgment.[52] It is admitted that the
consequences of an action—in the sense of the foreseeable results—
are quite relevant to moral consideration. In fact no serious ethician
would wish to exclude consequences from ethical discussions, and so
Singer concludes with the odd suggestion that the major problem in

"morals" is not one of theory but rather the difficulty of determining the facts in concrete cases. Surely no previous formal ethician has been this willing to grant a role to material morality.

This is something of what has happened, then, to recent thinking within the limits of classical ethical theories. What remains to be seen in our final chapters will be what is new in strictly contemporary ethics.

CHAPTER XVI

Naturalistic Ethics

ʜᴇɴ G. E. Moore said that moral philosophers who attempt to define
'ood" in terms of anything else are committing the "naturalistic fal-
cy," he not only coined a phrase but also gave a name to a school of
hics. Naturalistic ethics has since come to mean that kind of theory
nich attempts to define the moral good in terms of certain elements of
ır ordinary experience of life. In the next chapter we shall see that
ıoore himself considered that the predicate "good" names a property
at is not a natural quality or any grouping of such qualities. Good,
ıoore felt, is a nonnatural, specially intuited property. "Naturalism,"
ıoore said, "offers no reason at all, far less any valid reason, for any
ıical principle whatever."[1]
Since Moore wrote this, in 1903, many ethical philosophers have
ıagreed with him on this point and have taken considerable delight in
ımmitting the naturalistic fallacy. In the broad sense, then, any ethics
naturalistic that endeavors to define moral good by identifying it with
ıll-being, pleasure, obedience to God's law, conformity with human
ture, or with any principle other than good itself. Thus broadly un-
ɾstood, any ethics other than Moore's might be labeled "naturalism."[2]
There is, however, a more restricted meaning for naturalism in con-
ınporary philosophy: this stresses an empirical, scientific, non-super-
tural approach to the subject. To speak simply, the contemporary
turalist tries to couch his explanations in terms of what he experiences
the world about him. In this narrow sense, naturalistic ethics has
ır special features. First, all its explanations are expressed in terms of
s world and it is opposed to the use of any transcendental principles,
ɦ as God or an ideal Absolute. Second, the data of ethical philosophy
lude not only the presentations of ordinary experience but also the
dings of modern science, interpreted by the techniques of science,
ɾecially of the social sciences.[3] Third, naturalistic ethicians are dedi-
ɾd to the notion of ongoing progress, of the continual advance of
n and their institutions toward higher levels. This tends toward the

view that any new change is an improvement.[4] And fourth, in opposi
tion to analytical philosophers and positivists the naturalistic ethiciar
maintains that ethical statements may be true and capable of verification

Another way of stating the program of ethical naturalism is to say
that it is possible to derive an *ought* from an *is*, or a value from a fact
We shall see in the next chapter that most British ethicians of the
twentieth century are convinced that there is some sort of impassable
gap between factual descriptions and moral prescriptions. American
moral philosophers, until very recently, have tended to assume that there
is a rather close connection between knowing what a problem is, wha
conditions surround it, what scientific experts think about it, and being
able to discover what one should do about it. This is the naturalistic
approach: get the facts, consult the experts, interpret the data with the
help of scientific methods, if possible—then decide what ought to be
done, without too much talk about God's law, a future life, or any sort
of absolute standards or ideals.

In the present chapter we shall center our attention on American
naturalistic ethics but will include some other types of naturalism that
are either contributory to this kind of thought (such as evolutionary o
psychological approbative ethics) or are tangential to it (such as som
versions of natural law ethics).

When Charles Darwin (1809–1882) first published his famous *Origi
of Species by Means of Natural Selection* (London, 1859), it was im
mediately apparent that his theory was pregnant with implications tha
went well beyond science into the area of religion and ethics. Its mea
ing is still a matter of speculation in the twentieth century.[5] Ethicall
there was the initial tendency to identify moral improvement wit
biological change. Thus, Darwin spoke of "the rearing of the greate
number of individuals in full vigor and health under the conditions t
which they are subjected."[6]

The leading philosopher of evolutionary theory was Herbert Spenc
(1820–1903). His *Principles of Ethics* (2 vols., 1892–1893) assum
throughout that the more evolved man displays the better conduct. I
Spencer's view, life is taken as a fundamental value. Human condu
requires "an improving adjustment of acts to ends, such as furthers tl
prolongation of life." Hence, it is good to preserve and strengthen tl
life of the individual and that of the race. Right and wrong ha
meaning only in relation to creatures capable of pleasures and pain:
Although he speaks of the possibility of an absolute morality, Spenc
insists that the ethics that we now know is not absolutely right but on
relatively so. Moral science (like "mechanical" science) has evolved fro
a primitive teaching developed by the Greeks, through a theologic
period, to its present incipient scientific state. As a consequence, mo

perfection could not be attained by an individual man unless he existed
in the environment of the ideal state.[8]

Oddly, Thomas Henry Huxley (1825–1895) took the opposite view.
Admitting the importance of the evolutionary hypothesis in biological
and related sciences, Huxley (in his Romanes Lecture of 1893 entitled
Evolution and Ethics) argued that the law of the survival of the fit
was not an ethical principle. Man, he felt, must do his best to overcome
the law of the jungle and to establish his ethical ideals on a non-
evolutionary basis.

> The practice of that which is ethically best—what we call good-
> ness or virtue—involves a course of conduct which, in all respects,
> is opposed to that which leads to success in the cosmic struggle for
> existence. In place of ruthless self-assertion it demands self-re-
> straint. . . .[9]

Still another version of evolutionary ethics is found in the writings of
a Russian contemporary of Spencer and Huxley, Prince Pëtr Alekseevich
Kropotkin (1842–1921). In a book entitled *Mutual Aid, a Factor of
Evolution* (London: Heinemann, 1915) Kropotkin claimed that it is
not competition but mutual assistance which is the law of evolutionary
progress. He buttressed this idealistic version of evolutionary ethics in
his *Etika*, where he offered a rather extensive survey of classical and
modern ethical theories as support for his own ethics.[10] Kropotkin's
own position is a type of naturalistic ethics that offers moral science as
substitute for religion, stresses the development of "social conscience"
in mankind, but pays little attention to biological progress.[11] Thus,
Kropotkin's ethics culminates in an altruistic form of social utilitarianism.

Outstanding among more recent works in evolutionary ethics is *A
Modern Theory of Ethics* (1929) by Olaf Stapledon (1886–1950). In
general, Stapledon attempted to put the theory of teleological order
back into the interpretation of human conduct. Human activity is
teleological in the sense that it shows definite tendencies toward some
sort of completion in the future. Good designates such tendential activity, as free, fulfilling, or as instrumental in the ongoing perfection of
cosmic processes. He does not reduce man to the purely mechanical or
deterministic processes of physical nature, however, for Stapledon thinks
that man can rise in "ecstasy" to the level of moral experience which
is only a little lower than mysticism. However, "in the final ethical
analysis it turns out that in *all* value-judgments, an objective situation,
such as organic fulfilment or personal fulfilment, is simply judged good
in and for itself."[12]

Very influential on the ethical attitudes of practical psychologists,
psychiatrists, social scientists, and many writers of novels, has been the
psychoanalytic teaching of Sigmund Freud (1856–1939). This Viennese

medical doctor who spent the last part of his life in London was not really a theoretical ethician; yet the history of contemporary ethics would not be complete without some account of his teaching.[13] Freud admitted little debt to earlier philosophers but he did study under Franz Brentano and knew the general position of the Austrian value school.

Freudian psychoanalysis was initially a form of mental therapy developed to treat emotional disorders. It grew into a psychological view of man and his functions. Originally, moral attitudes played little part in Freud's work. His tendency was to ignore and even play down ethical considerations as factors in clinical practice. Thus Freud is frequently classified as an ethical skeptic.[14] However, as his theory of human endowments and functions grew broader, Freud took positions that have had profound ethical importance and influence. For instance, he opposed the "rationalism" of the Enlightenment and of nineteenth-century German idealism with the contention that men, in the concrete findings of the clinic, show themselves to be irrational and capricious.[15] This stress on the irrational has been picked up by contemporary existentialism. Moreover, as an ethic, Freud's later teaching adjures the supernatural, the otherworldly, the traditionally religious, the system-building of the idealists, and adheres to a rather simple naturalism. This is obvious throughout *Civilization and Its Discontents* (1939), Freud's key work in the field of ethics.

The basic analysis of the human psyche, on which Freudianism stands, is rather generally known. Freud distinguished the large and lower area of the unconscious from the smaller and upper field of consciousness.[16] Many instinctive impulses are thought to surge up from the unconscious and seek realization in conscious activities, and the main instinctual drives are sexual and aggressive.[17] To deal with these impulses, Freud postulated three functional levels within the human psyche: (1) the "id" is the unconscious considered as the seat of bodily appetites; (2) the "ego" is the middle level, the area of conscious and rational decision and activity; and (3) the "super-ego" is judgmental and critical, a sort of moral dictator, cruel and self-punishing.[18]

There is a partial similarity between the foregoing psychology and Plato's three parts of the human soul. Freud was well aware of this. He did not assign the highest role to reason, however, but put it in the middle as the field of mediation between lower instincts and higher tendencies toward inhibition. Unlike Plato, he denied that the lower impulses should be restrained at all costs; in fact, Freud felt that such restraint is the start of personality disorders. The dictates of the superego tend to be identified by Freud with the conventions of civilized society and the repressive teachings of traditional religion and ethics. What good for man is an ethic of honesty in which the individual will strive to be open, frank, and uninhibited in speaking of and acting out his

asic drives.[19] All secrecy, subterfuge, hypocrisy, and repression are bad.
t is good to express oneself but one must learn to respect the interests
f others in order to live peacefully in society.

During the same period, William James (1842–1910) was studying
medicine, teaching psychology, and finally turning his attention to phi-
osophy in the United States. He eventually became a member of the
istinguished philosophy department at Harvard which included G. H.
almer, Royce, and Santayana. There, James made numerous contri-
utions to empirical and educational psychology and was one of the
ioneers in the development of American pragmatism. There are natural-
tic moments in William James's thought (for instance, his account of
abit formation in humans as the "grooving of channels for nerve
essages") but he is not anti-metaphysical in his general philosophy,
or is he inclined to reject entirely the values of theistic belief and
aditional religion. Like Henri Bergson, James felt that the Christian
ints are models of moral perfection.[20] We have several short studies
f ethical significance from James's pen but the most important is his
cture "The Moral Philosopher and the Moral Life" (1891).

No great interest is shown by James in a ready-made ethical theory:
There can be no final truth in ethics any more than in physics, until
e last man has had his experience and said his say."[21] In true prag-
atic style, James views a realistic ethics in terms of three questions.
he first is psychological: What is the historical origin of our moral
tions? He reviews certain attempts to answer this but shows no fas-
nation for the history of the subject. The second great question in
mes's ethics is metaphysical: What do key words in ethics, terms like
od, evil, and obligation, mean? In considering this, James rejects
solutism and any suggestion that ethics might be grounded in meta-
ysics as a systematic construction. Since he sees good and obligation
the objects of feeling and desire, James concludes that they have no
othold in metaphysical being. His third question is "casuistic": What
the measure whereby good may be distinguished from evil? In answer-
g this, he suggests that the morally good is simply that which satisfies
mand, any demand. "That act must be the best act, accordingly,
ich makes for the best whole, in the sense of awakening the least
m of dissatisfactions."[22]

Among the people impressed by James's pragmatic ethics was the man
o became the most prolific and best-known American ethician, John
ewey (1859–1952). He began his philosophical career as an idealist,
ongly under the influence of German thought, and his early writings
ethics show this affiliation. However, Dewey soon adopted a more
turalistic and practical approach to moral philosophy. In the famous
tbook Ethics (1908), which he wrote in collaboration with J. H. Tufts,
e second part was written entirely by Dewey and has recently been

separately published as *Theory of the Moral Life* (1960). It was already evident in this work that Dewey had reached, before 1910, his instrumentalist version of pragmatic ethics. Moral theory is only called for when some problem arises involving a practical conflict of ends or standards of conduct.[23] Thus, instrumentalist ethics is an attempt to offer a reflective answer to such a human problem. To this end, Dewey reviewed various historical theories concerning the supreme goals of human aspiration and concluded that they all have some partial validity as practical ideals, but he refused to draw up a table of such moral values, suggesting instead the importance of forming the habit of making wise and reflective judgments in ethics.[24] Eventually he proposed a delicate balance between the claims of egoism and altruism, with the preference going slightly to the latter because the social interest is more inclusive.

The next major ethical work by John Dewey is the seventh chapter of *Reconstruction in Philosophy* (1920), where the idea that serious reflection is central to the work of the ethician is further developed. Here, Dewey contrasts the position of those who base ethics on duty as deriving from some supreme law, with the theory that ethics seeks the moral good in self-realization, happiness, or some other ideal end. He now asserts that every moral situation is unique and cannot be judged by any ready-made law or rule. Each moral problem must be faced pragmatically. An intelligent and serious inquiry is required to come up with a judgment and choice concerning a given situation. These are to be the best that can be made in view of the predictable consequences of the proposed action.[25]

In *Human Nature and Conduct* (1922) Dewey reacts against the Freudian theory of unconscious instinctual drives. There is, as far as Dewey is concerned, no evidence that we have a distinct "psychic realm" for our instincts. Nor will he accept the notion of an original individual consciousness such as one finds described in Freud.[26] This is one of the most effective criticisms of Freudian psychology and through it John Dewey has influenced the modifications of psychoanalytic theory that have developed in the United States.[27] Dewey was then quite definite in his exclusion of any search for fixed standards of ethical judgment. He turned rather to the study of "ends-in-view" and endeavored to describe how these proximate goals arise and function within the field of human action. They are not final goals but function as "turning points" in activity. All ethics must devote some attention to the consequences of human action; even deontologists do this under the guise of "meaning well" or being properly motivated for moral decisions.[28] All ends-in-view may become means for other ends.

The *Quest for Certainty* (1929) shows Dewey's growing interest in value theory. In it, he clearly distinguished valuation from value: all values may be liked or enjoyed (that is a question of psychology but not all acts of enjoyment are truly valuable. Since value judgments focus on the *objects* of our experiences, they constitute judgments about the *regulation* of "our desires, affections and enjoyments."[29] Psychological and scientific reports of human preferences have only "instrumental" utility in the discovery of value judgments. This is a revision of his earlier position and it distinguishes Dewey from the positivist who accepts socal science data as the last word on ethical questions. On his part, Dewey always insisted on the need for reflective interpretation of all empirical materials, whether from science or from ordinary experience.

Further explanation of the important difference between acts of "prizing" and the values that are the objects of such actions is offered by Dewey in *Theory of Valuation* (1939). Now he is very critical of the positivist assertion that value judgments are unverifiable and thus without philosophic meaning.[30] To support his contention that such verification is possible, Dewey turned to modern experience in medical practice, where various means are clearly evaluated in terms of their fitness to achieve desired ends. Rather convincingly, he argued that value judgments as to the fitness of certain things for given purposes are practical generalizations and that they are justified in terms of the means-end relation. They can be tested rigorously by observing their actual results in comparison with their intended consequences.[31]

This kind of naturalistic ethics is still quite important in American thought, although not as popular as it was in the twenties and thirties. The influence of John Dewey in the moral judgments of social scientists and experts on educational theory is still strong. Noteworthy, also, is the growing number of sympathetic studies of Dewey's ethics written by American Catholic philosophers in the past two decades.

The view that reality is ever in process underlies Dewey's general philosophic position, and this same theme was strongly reinforced in the thought of Alfred North Whitehead (1861–1947). Although he did not develop a detailed theory of ethics he deserves to be remembered here because of the indirect influence of his thought on certain tendencies in contemporary ethics. As the author (with Bertrand Russell) of *Principia Mathematica* (1910–1913), Whitehead brought about a revolution in philosophic notions about logic and methodology. While it did not deal with the logic of ethical discourse, this work, in the view of many scholars, "dealt a blow" to faith in any sort of philosophic absolutes.[32] Another indirect influence stems from Whitehead's theory of a finite God.[33] This has impressed contemporary thought about the role of God's will in the moral area, particularly in the thinking of some recent Protestant Christian ethicians. We shall see in our final chapter that Christian ethics, which was formerly quite idealistic and absolutistic, has now become aligned with existentialism. This is true of only one branch of Protestant ethics, of course, that which is now identified as situationism.

The expositions of Whitehead's philosophy of God by followers such as Charles Hartshorne (1897–) and Henry Nelson Wieman (1884–) have been especially influential in the thinking of recent Christian ethicians.

As we saw earlier, value ethics has frequently adopted a naturalistic stance. It was Ralph Barton Perry (1876–1957) who provided the generic definition of value from which later naturalistic ethicians took thei starting point. In his General Theory of Value (1926) Perry defined value as "any object of any interest."[34] Thus used, interest is any "organization that consistently acts for its own preservation," while mora good consists in the fulfillment of any organization of interests.[35] T Perry, duty consists in the enlightened recognition of the good. For th ranking of values, Perry proposed four criteria: correctness, intensity preference, and inclusiveness. Actually, the last three have to do wit degrees of value, whereas the first is the test of whether something i a value or not.[36] In the final analysis, Perry's basic moral imperativ becomes: "Cultivate that kind of will that is qualified to bring harmon through its universal adoption."[37]

Some moral philosophers have continued to base their views on variou versions of the general theory of evolution. The biologist Samuel Jackso Holmes (1868–) equated moral goodness with that which promote the preservation of the life of the individual or of the species. In his turr Julian Huxley (1887–), the grandson of Thomas Huxley, delivere the Romanes Lecture in 1943 and took the occasion to correct his granc father. Julian's Evolutionary Ethics insists that the development of mor. consciousness is a part of the general process of evolution, and he ti in the growth of awareness of moral values with the level of civilizatio in which a person lives.[38] It is well known that Julian Huxley h: had a considerable influence on the philosophic outlook of the UNESC program.

In Europe, naturalism was not lacking in twentieth-century supporte A remarkable Jesuit scientist, Pierre Teilhard de Chardin (1881–1955 shared many of Julian Huxley's naturalistic views but assimilated the to a theistic account of man and the universe. Teilhard's Phenomenon Man (posthumously published, in French in 1956, in English in 195 pictures the evolution of man from physical nature as a continuo process, springing from the presence of psychic energies in even t lower levels of bodily nature. As things evolve they become more co plex; we are now in the stage of the "noosphere," at which mind h appeared. Optimistically, Teilhard saw evolution as an upward proc toward ever higher and better things. The whole movement is tendi toward an ultimate stage, the omega point, which will be the clim of the development of the noosphere. Although infinite and transcende nevertheless the omega point will remain in immanent continuity with the ongoing process of nature.

There are ethical and religious implications in the *Phenomenon of Man* but the most interesting of Teilhard's published works, from the point of view of moral philosophy, is *The Divine Milieu* (1960). This work stands out as a highly spiritual account of the natural environment (the *milieu*) of man as transfused by charity (divine love) which becomes the stable principle of natures and powers.[39] Through Christ humanity is to be "divinized" in the love of God. This involves the concerted union of all human spirits in moving toward God as the "ultimate point" at which all realities converge.[40] There are similarities between the evolutionary thinking of Teilhard de Chardin and the ethics of Julian Huxley (they were quite friendly) but most commentators see Teilhard as close to the views of Bergson in the *Two Sources of Morality and Religion*.[41] It has even been suggested that Teilhard's ethic of divine love takes us one step beyond existentialism.[42]

In England, a noteworthy attempt to gather the resources of anthropology and ethnology in the service of ethics has been made by Alexander Macbeath (1888–1964). His *Experiments in Living* (1952) is a serious attempt to test the claim of ethical intuitionists, like G. E. Moore and Henry Sidgwick, that there are certain "deliverances of moral consciousness" that are self-evident to all men. Among other things which Macbeath notes in his first lecture, are the lack of precision and ambiguity of the propositions usually offered as ethically self-evident. He also points to the lack of agreement among people like Sidgwick, Moore, and Ross as to the precise nature of these initial judgments of intuitionist ethics. However, the major part of *Experiments in Living* is given over to the examination of published reports on the moral convictions of primitive peoples in many parts of the world. At the end Macbeath offers five conclusions: (1) He finds few, if any, primitives who consider that their moral rules apply to all men. (2) Although there are similarities among the general formulations of rules of life in various tribes, the concrete interpretations of these vary among different peoples. (3) Some of the prima facie duties known to British intuitionists are quite unknown to primitive peoples. (4) These various tribes think of their rules of living as limited to the conditions of their own life. (5) There are some rules recognized by primitive peoples that we would not approve on a moral basis at all.[43] It is only fair to note that Macbeath's rather negative findings are partly contradicted by other competent anthropologists with an interest in the moral significance of their work.[44]

The "social adjustment theory" of Stephen C. Pepper (1891–   ) is one of the most important recent American efforts to work out an axiological approach to naturalistic ethics. His *Sources of Value* (1958) is the best study since Perry's *General Theory*. In his *Ethics* (1960), Pepper devotes a dozen chapters to a thorough survey of all the great empirical theories of ethics. At the end, he suggests that each of these theories uses a "selective system" of evidences for its teachings on moral values. Each is limited by its particular point of view. Pepper lists the selective systems used in the important empirical types of ethics: *individual value* systems (hedonists use purposive structures and stress the work of prudence; self-realizationists use personality structure and the harmonious integration of the person); *social values* (pragmatists use the social situation and aim at the reduction of social tensions; cultural relativists concentrate on the cultural pattern and stress positive conformity to this structure); *biological values* (evolutionary ethicians emphasize progress in accord with natural selection). From this survey of naturalistic values Pepper concludes that natural ethical norms do exist.[45] His own social adjustment theory has two main conclusions. When no special problem of social adjustment arises, then the ordinarily recognized naturalistic norms work alone. However, in cases of conflict, one's decision may depend on the degree of social pressure in a given society. Ethics, according to Pepper, is the "study of the structure and operation of selective systems bearing on human activity and the lines of legislation running through them."[46]

In the broad meaning of "naturalism" most of the ethics that has been developed by Roman Catholic thinkers in recent times is naturalistic. That is to say, they do feel that one may derive an "ought" from an "is." It is usual in Catholic writings to distinguish moral theology (the study of most of the traditional problems of ethics from the point of view of divine revelation, Biblical teaching, Christian traditions, and ecclesiastical law) from moral philosophy or ethics (which is restricted to information gained from ordinary experience and interpreted philosophically). In practice, of course, the views and positions taken in ethics by some Catholic philosophers may be indirectly influenced by the religious commitment, as is doubtless the case with all thinkers having either pro or con attitudes toward traditional religion.

One of the best-known Catholic philosophers in the twentieth century is Jacques Maritain (1882–   ). His efforts to make Thomism known and respected in contemporary circles are widely recognized. One of his books, *Science and Wisdom* (1935), takes a somewhat different position concerning the relation of moral theology and ethics from the view just stated above. In it, Maritain argues that a Christian thinker may and can, borrow certain items of information from what he believes in order to produce a more adequate ethics. That is to say, if one believes in original sin and its debilitating effects on mankind, and if one believes that men have been raised by God's special grace so that they may aspire to a future vision of God in heaven provided they live well on earth, then one's ethics may be more completely and practically developed under the influence of these Christian teachings. Such a "Christian ethics," as Maritain sees it, would be better and more practical than an abstract version of purely philosophical ethics. Thus envisioned, Maritain's ethics would be "subalternated" to moral theology.[47] Such an approach to a Catholic Christian ethics is not the usual view of Catholic ethicians, as is indicated by the rather severe criticisms aimed at Maritain by J. M. Ramirez and others.

The *Nine Lectures on the First Notions of Moral Philosophy* (1951) have not been translated into English, although this book is Maritain's most noteworthy effort to treat some of the central problems in ethics. The relation of good and value, the final end of man, the concept of moral obligation, and the role of moral sanctions are discussed. Most distinctive in this and later writings of Maritain is his theory of "connatural knowledge." This implies that, in the area of practical philosophy, man's initial judgments are preconceptual and are guided by certain affective inclinations. Consequently, ethical propositions are not purely cognitive but involve certain natural tendencies stemming from human appetites. Maritain professes to find some basis for this teaching in Thomas Aquinas' doctrine on man's natural desire to see God. Many readers think that Gabriel Marcel, the Catholic existentialist, has influenced this tendency in Maritain to stress affectivity in the context of ethical judgment.

In 1960 Maritain published the first volume of his large work entitled *Moral Philosophy*. (The second volume, subtitled "Doctrinal Examination of the Great Problems," has not appeared.) This first volume surveys many of the great theories in the history of ethics, from Socrates to Bergson, but it exhibits two important lacunae: no effort is made to treat the ethics of the Middle Ages—and British ethics is completely ignored! Except for certain tangential remarks and the various criticisms which Maritain offers, this *Moral Philosophy* does not expound his own ethics.

Much more open to the use of scientific data (and so, more naturalistic in the narrow sense) is the ethics of the Austrian Catholic scholar Johannes Messner (1891–   ). His treatise *Ethics and Facts* (1952) discusses five basic problems or tendencies in human life: the impulse toward sexual satisfaction, toward general happiness, toward freedom in choice and action, toward society, and toward the satisfaction of intellectual curiosity. Messner's openness to empirical information and all types of contemporary ethics is striking. On the last page of this book, he restates his solution to the fact-value, or is-ought, problem. Briefly, Messner does not think that ethical judgments can be verified by a simple appeal to the facts of sense experience. What he does claim, however, is that "the consequences of moral principles" can be tested in the life of each man and of society. For people who would like to know what contemporary Thomistic ethics stands for, reading Johannes Messner can help to balance the more theology-oriented thought of Maritain. Interestingly enough, Messner is a priest and Maritain is not.

Natural law ethics still holds the attention of many modern Catholic thinkers, and of a good many who are not Catholics. Of course, there are many variations in the explanations of what natural law is and requires. One prominent Belgian Catholic writer, Jacques Leclercq, quite frankly admits that "natural law has never been systematically studied."[48] In his French study of natural law and sociology (1960), Leclercq adopts a surprisingly naturalistic and even relativistic view of morality. He admits, for instance, that poor children who grow up in an economically deprived area are almost inevitably driven by the force of circumstances into crime. To talk about what such children "ought to do" is next door to nonsense: their moral freedom is very much limited by the conditions of their lives.[49] There is still a good deal of talk among natural law ethicians about the obligations of human nature the need to work for an ultimate end, and the importance of somewhat abstract principles, but few advocates of this kind of ethics now claim that its rules are absolute and unchanging (except for very formal imperatives such as: "The good should be done and evil should be avoided") Nor are there many natural law thinkers today who would suggest that there is a ready-made code of natural moral laws.

Still other forms of naturalism look to studies related to psychology for guidance. Psychoanalysis, psychiatry, and clinical psychology continue to provide both data and problems for contemporary ethics. In France, the Swiss scholar H. Baruk (1897–   ) has made studies of the relation between delinquency and the level of moral judgment. He is the editor of a new Swiss journal devoted to the relation between science and ethics. The best-known name in the field of psychology and ethics is, of course, that of Erich Fromm (1900–   ), but his position is complicated by an interest in Marxism which introduces a third factor into an already difficult relationship. Fromm's *Escape from Freedom* (1941) illustrates very well his rather facile ability to make striking generalizations and popular summaries of the moral implications of science. For instance a negative way of looking at freedom sees it as a separation from mother a breaking of the ties to immediate community, church, and social caste. Later, he suggests that Protestantism and the growth of capitalism have favored the development of another and more positive freedom in the moral person. Commenting on selfishness, Fromm says: "To love other is a virtue, to love oneself is a sin."[51] It is not always clear how he grounds these insights in the data of psychology.

Man for Himself (1947) is Fromm's most serious attempt to give his ethical views. Chapter four is a famous criticism of the "authoritaria conscience" as the voice of external authority (parents, state, or other authorities) represented within the feelings of the moral agent. This version of moral conscience he identifies with Freud's superego. Although affectively internalized (that is, presented by moral feelings within the person), the authoritarian conscience actually rejects the possibility that the agent himself can *know* what is right or wrong for himself.[52] When it occurs as fear of the authorities such conscience is called bad; when it is the awareness of pleasing the authorities it is good. Psychoanalytic therapy will cure a person of these feelings of guilt and self-approval. In Fromm's ethics, man is a different sort of agent, however, from what he was in the original Freudian psychology. Perhaps the chief difference lies in Fromm's more extended role for human love.

Fromm calls his own position "humanistic" ethics, because he makes *man* the sole judge of his own ethical welfare and sets up man's personal development as the criterion of moral judgment. For Fromm self-interest does not exclude altruism and is not equivalent to selfishness.[53] Distinctive in this version of psychological ethics is Fromm's insistence on the "objectivity" of ethical principles: most psychological approbative ethicians adopt a relativistic and subjectivistic account of ethical judgment but Fromm always insists that the conclusions of his ethics are objective norms, open to public verification by the study of their consequences and by deductive reasoning.[54]

The *Sane Society* (1955) maintains the theme of "humanistic psychoanalysis." Fromm's naturalism is now evident in his discussion of man as an animal and as part of the evolutionary process. But man also rises above "nature" and, as thus separated, displays the functions of reasoning, self-consciousness, and moral conscience. Human needs and consequent rules of behavior become different from those of the brute animal.[55] This is the theme of the "human situation." Fromm now uses the concept of the "total needs of man" as his criterion of moral value: in facing a moral problem one finds that "one answer corresponds more to the total needs of man, and hence is more conducive to the unfolding of his powers and to his happiness than the other." At points, Fromm sounds like a natural law ethician, for he says that ethical judgment must be based on "our knowledge of man's nature and the laws which govern its growth."[56] In this book, also, Fromm points to growth in "creative love" as the positive ideal of higher human aspirations.

A similar approach is found in The Morality of Self-Interest (1965) by Robert G. Olson (1924–   ). Somewhat more insistent than Fromm on the welfare of society as a norm of judgment, Olson openly accuses "prevailing religious views" of undermining the practice of morality.[57] What Olson advocates is "religious naturalism"—a view that combines the left-wing naturalism of Bertrand Russell's "A Free Man's Worship"[58] with the right-wing religious optimism of John Dewey's A Common

Faith (1934). Religious naturalism, in this formulation, takes a middle path between Russell's pessimism and Dewey's optimism.[59]

One of the leaders of a similar "humanist" movement in ethics is Corliss Lamont (1902–   ). Much of his effort is given to criticism of traditional religious views (such as the belief in personal immortality) that have some bearing on ethics and the conduct of life. Thus, Lamont's *Humanism as a Philosophy* (1949) has a section devoted to the ethics of this form of thought.[60] As a sort of antidote to religion, humanist ethics is more a semipopular substitute for religion than a type of academic ethics.

American naturalistic ethics has received quite diverse presentations since the initial impact of John Dewey's instrumentalist ethics was felt in the United States. William R. Dennes (1898–   ), for instance, has directed attention to a certain basic similarity in the manifestations of human drives and needs in diverse cultures. *Some Dilemmas of Naturalism* (1960) is Dennes' eloquent plea for the reinstating of some sort of objective values as a basis for "oughtness" in the naturalistic enterprise. Sharing such a view is Eliseo Vivas (1901–   ), who began his career as a naturalist, changed his views, and then wrote a severely critical appraisal of this type of ethics, in *The Moral Life and the Ethical Life* (1950). Calling his own view "axiological realism" (under the influence of Nicolai Hartmann), Vivas complains of the naturalists' insensitivity to the tragic dimensions of twentieth-century existence. In particular, Vivas points to three errors of naturalism: (1) the belief that psychological data are logically prior to the definition of value; (2) the formation of a view of man that is a thin abstraction, paying lip service to scientific facts; and (3) "scientism," the notion that the method of the physicist is primary in philosophy.[61] Naturalistic ethics, according to Vivas, has thus neglected the "primacy of the person."[62] His criticism has been resented by some naturalists but it has elicited new clarifications of the naturalist position in ethics.

A thoughtful and important revision of naturalistic ethics has been propounded in the book *On the Knowledge of Good and Evil* (1955) by Philip Blair Rice (1904–   ). His first four chapters review the chief theories of ethics in twentieth-century British and American thought but the remainder of the book develops Rice's notions on how naturalism and emotivism (on which, see *infra*, Chapter XVII) may be related. Throughout, Rice maintains that value judgments have both descriptive and prescriptive parts. When one expresses a personal "ought," this indicates "the fact that a choice has been made, and serves as a signal to release the action."[63] Without some cognitive content, an ethical judgment is "empty and blind." So, certain "identifying properties" are required and they must be natural rather than nonnatural. Thus, Rice's basic imperative limits one's judgment to a definite state of affairs

"This is good means 'This has the Identifying Property of goodness; do or seek this under conditions C!' "[64] Such a justification of ethical principles appeals to "normativeness" in human nature and to man's goal-seeking tendencies. Rice admits that this is somewhat a priori. Empirically, Rice speaks of the observable development in man of a "second nature" that carries a sense of well-being and is somewhat like conscience. At another point it is called "an operative sense of rationality."[65] In a work such as this, we see a naturalistic approximation of a religiously neutral natural law ethics.

A valiant effort has been made by Abraham Edel (1908–   ) to work out some special methodology that would enable the naturalistic ethician to convert the data of social science to moral use. His *Ethical Judgment: The Use of Science in Ethics* (1955) and *Method in Ethical Theory* (1963) review the various techniques available in the field of sociology and statistical interpretation. Well aware of the difficulty of moving from *is* to *ought*, Edel has suggested, in a survey of the ethics of naturalism, that the ethician should take as his guidelines certain "fundamental global needs," things like peace, increased world productivity, and freedom for all men.[66] These, according to Edel, cannot be logically or scientifically justified, except in the sense that they are as obviously good as is the conclusion that health is better than sickness.

Taking a more critical approach, Patrick Romanell (1912–   ) has written an important reformulation of the naturalistic program in ethics, in his book *Toward a Critical Naturalism* (1958). He thinks that Dewey was wrong in requiring ethics to use the same *methods* as the empirical sciences; experimental verification works, according to Romanell, only for questions of fact. It is "not good for ethics proper, which deals with questions of norms or *what-ought-to-be-so*."[67] Admittedly, the justification of ethical norms is difficult. Traditional utilitarianism has some validity in its study of consequences but Romanell does not see it as a 'mature form of naturalistic ethics." Like Vivas, Romanell thinks we need to become more aware of the "tragic" dimensions of modern life, and to pay more attention to the meaning of the human person. These, of course, are ever-present themes in the personalistic and quasi-existential writings of Spanish and Italian philosophers, with which literature both Vivas and Romanell are well acquainted.

There has been some recent tendency to combine the position of British noncognitive ethics (emotivism) with a modified naturalism. Mrs. Philippa R. Foot has published a series of articles in British journals which maintain that there is more validity to naturalistic ethics than is usually granted in present-day England. One of her articles says some things that needed to be said about the rather dogmatic rejection of naturalism in British ethics, from G. E. Moore onward.[68] In reasoning from facts to values, according to this article, some things do "count in favor of a moral conclusion." She seriously questions the whole claim that an evaluative conclusion requires evaluative premises and bluntly asks how such a generalization can be proved. This is Humean heresy, of course, but Mrs. Foot suggests that present-day ethics should take a more careful look at the rules of evidence and should avoid the assumption that there is no possible proof for ethical conclusions.

A modified naturalism is combined with emotive ethics in Paul Edwards' (1923–   ) *The Logic of Moral Discourse* (1955). While Edwards agrees with the emotivists that moral judgments express attitudes of approval or disapproval, he does not limit them to what is merely subjective. There is an objective side to moral thinking, and moral disputes are capable of resolution, within certain limits, by an appeal to the facts of the case. He feels that it is wrong to exclude, arbitrarily, the observable facts of a moral situation from a reflective attempt to reach ethical conclusions.[69] Thus, moral disagreements are more than verbal disagreements. This is a great concession for an emotivist to make, as we shall see in the next chapter.

In spite of its indefiniteness concerning even pragmatic standards of ethical judgment, and its vulnerability to criticism (see the impressive work of E. M. Adams),[70] naturalistic ethics is a most promising approach to this subject. It is not limited to as narrow a method as British analytic ethics (which we shall examine next); nor is naturalism as antithetic to ethical *theory* as existential ethics seems to be. Doubtless the very narrow positive-science view of ethics which characterized the work of some naturalists early in this century is too restricted to produce useful results. Yet there is a present anticipation in many quarters that much of the future of this subject rests on the shoulders of those who will perfect the methodology of naturalism.

CHAPTER XVII

Analytic Ethics

BRITISH PHILOSOPHY in the twentieth century has emphasized the analysis of language. In part this approach has been a reaction against the idealism of T. H. Green and F. H. Bradley, which was couched in grandiloquent terminology and contained a good many obscure notions. Primarily, language analysis stemmed from a desire for clarity of meaning. A realistic and down-to-earth point of view was advocated early in the century by G. E. Moore and others who felt that philosophy should make its terminology understandable; many questions are hard to answer, because the questions are not clearly expressed. Eventually, many British philosophers came to think that this is the central activity of the philosopher: to examine critically the logic of linguistic discourse and to work out an explanation of how various meanings are best expressed in linguistic communication. This program was reinforced by the rapid growth of modern logics, in which the formal patterns of various types of rigorous thinking were examined. For a time after the publication of Russell and Whitehead's *Principia Mathematica* (1910–1913) hopes were high that an entirely new method of philosophizing would soon be discovered. Some thought that philosophy would eventually be carried on in a special symbolic language; others felt that the ordinary language of human intercourse was quite adequate and, indeed, that it was pregnant with the accumulated wisdom of the ages.

David Hume had set the stage for the application of this program of language analysis to ethics when he complained about the sudden way in which all moral philosophers shift from statements about what is so (God is a perfect being; or, man is rational, or immortal, or free) to *ought* statements (a man ought to keep his promises, he ought to avoid injuring others). This change from *is* to *ought*, as Hume saw it, requires justification or, at least, some explanation.[1] There is obviously a language problem here, for the difficulty may be expressed as the unexplained transition from the simple indicative mood to some oblique grammatical mood. How does the moral philosopher move from

the indicative (which states facts) to the subjunctive, the optative, th
hortatory, and the imperative (which express wishes, aspirations, er
couragement, choices, and commands)?

A great deal of British ethics in this century has been devoted t
Hume's problem. The consequent preoccupation with the analysis o
language, on the part of the British, has been a puzzlement to othe
Europeans (with the exception of the Scandinavians, who have bee
speculative grammarians since the Middle Ages and share this interes
in linguistic analysis) and it has set British ethicians apart from the mai
stream of continental thinking on the subject. The British do not "d
philosophy" the way that others do. The feeling of exclusion is mutua
Jacques Maritain once remarked concerning the ethics to be examine
in this chapter: "Je la tiens pour absurde!"[2]

In most versions of analytic ethics, it has become customary to spea
of three levels of practical discourse. This helps one to understand th
main thrust of British ethics. There is, first of all, the practical thinkin
of the agent trying to work out his own personal problems: this is th
level of *moral* discourse. Few analytic ethicians write about such problem
the level would be that of advice to the lovelorn. In the second plac
there is philosophic thinking about the principles, patterns, and methoc
of making decisions in regard to moral problems: this reflective examin
tion of practical thinking is the level of *ethical* discourse. Finally, ther
is the study of what might be called the logic and epistemology
ethics, the consideration of some very general problems which go beyor
the scope of ethical reasoning (such as the difference between ethic
and nonethical judgments, the nature and relation of freedom to ethic
the comparison of empirical science and ethics): this third level is th
of *meta-ethical* discourse.[3] Analytic ethics moves chiefly on the thi
level, that of meta-ethics. It does not attempt to tell you how to li
well, or even to provide the rules whereby you might decide for yourse
Analytic ethics attempts to find and explicate the logic of ethical d
course, but it sometimes goes into ethical (second-level) views ar
problems, in order to illustrate its points and show its applicabili
To work out a complete ethical theory, without first dealing with sor
of the problems of meta-ethics, would seem to the analyst to be foolis

At Cambridge University, George Edward Moore (1873–1958) ini
ated the new approach to philosophy with the publication (in 190
of his "Refutation of Idealism" and the book entitled *Principia Ethic
It is the first chapter of the latter that has occasioned a sort of C
pernican revolution in British ethics. Moore starts off with an ordina
definition of ethics as the study of what is good or bad in hum
conduct. In the first chapter, he asks what "good" means in such
usage. It cannot be defined, he thinks, because if you say that it
anything else other than good then you are shifting its meaning. '

explain this he takes the example of "yellow"—it is also a simple indefinable quality. You either know it or you do not know it. Hence, good may be taken to mean some quality that belongs to a thing (this sort of realism of sensory qualities is defended in Moore's "Refutation of Idealism") in much the same way that yellow is known to belong to a thing. Good cannot mean what is pleasurable, or that which promotes happiness, or any such natural property or complex of properties. To identify "good" with a natural property is to commit the 'naturalistic fallacy." Moore concludes that in the intrinsic ethical sense 'good" is a simple, indefinable quality, which is unique and non-natural, and which must be known directly in itself. There is a difference between this "good in itself" and "good as a means"; the first is the intrinsically good and that is what Moore finds most interesting.

In the Preface to *Principia Ethica* two questions asked by moral philosophers are stated: (1) What kind of things ought to exist for their own sakes? and (2) What kind of actions ought we to perform? The first is treated by Moore in his famous discussion of "good" and that is the part of his ethics that has had the most influence—positive and negative. Many people have failed to note that, in answering the second question, Moore argued that such queries can be treated empirically. To determine what kind of actions we should do, we may certainly consider which ones will produce the most good.[4] As far as he is concerned, all moral laws "are merely statements that certain kinds of actions will have good effects." Hence, in the concrete, each moral duty is the action that will cause more good to exist in the universe than any other alternative.[5]

Moore's shorter *Ethics* (1912) is an obvious attempt to make his views understandable to a larger audience. He devotes two chapters to utilitarianism, then argues that moral judgments are objective in the sense that "one and the same action cannot be both right and wrong," and finally he restates his views on duty and right and wrong actions.[6] Quite plainly, Moore now states that whether an action is right or wrong "*always* depends on its *actual* consequences."[7] While Moore admits that our awareness of duty has a certain element of feeling as well as of cognitive consciousness, he will not accept the claim that an action is right or wrong because "his society has some particular feeling towards actions of that class, nor yet that *some* man has."[8] Such a criterion (as social or subjectively personal attitudes) will not enable one to make an objective moral judgment. As far as Moore's teaching on the meaning of moral good is concerned, the *Ethics* of 1912 only modifies one major point in *Principia Ethica*. He is now ready to assert that pleasure is the only "ultimate good" but hastens to add that the ultimate good is different from the intrinsically good. The latter will involve a great deal more than pleasure.[9]

Two points are clarified in Moore's contribution to the volume entitled *The Philosophy of G. E. Moore* (1942). First of all, in his "Reply to My Critics," Moore discusses the pro and con arguments for Charles Stevenson's "emotive" meaning for good (which Moore knew through Stevenson's article in the 1937 issue of *Mind*). At first it seems that Moore is going to accept the emotive position but he finally rejects it as untenable.[10] This is in keeping with his earlier decision that feeling alone cannot lead to objectivity in judgment. The second thing that Moore tries to develop in this "Reply" is the meaning of natural and nonnatural, since neither is very clear in his earlier writing. Now he maintains that a natural property must be "descriptive" of the object to which it belongs.[11] However, Moore continues to insist that the nonnatural property ("good") is not perceptible to the senses and is not part of the description of the object.

There are obvious difficulties and lacunae in Moore's account of the meaning of good and right. He seems to need an intuition of the nonnatural quality which is good, yet he cannot accept Sidgwick's theory of intuitionalism. Of what the intrinsic good is a property is never entirely clear: most frequently, conscious states or attitudes are viewed by Moore as the bearers of the quality of being good, but the last chapter of *Principia Ethica* suggests that things like "Art or Nature" are also good in this intrinsic sense. In any event, after reading this epoch-making English treatise, moral philosophers divided into naturalists and non-naturalists.

In 1910 Bertrand Russell (1872–   ) wrote a series of articles for various journals, and they have been gathered under the title "The Elements of Ethics." If one has any doubt about the influence of G. E. Moore, he should read this little work of Russell's, for it is a very precise summary of *Principia Ethica*. At some later date, Russell wrote a note[12] in which he acknowledged his debt to his Cambridge colleague and added that he had changed his mind about the indefinability of good. Russell also came to think that the only objectivity that good possesses is "political," a notion which he claims to have found in Santayana. In this note Russell adds that he finds it difficult to work out any satisfactory view of ethics and, henceforth, he is refraining from further writing in the field.

Of course, it was not in Russell's temperament to remain silent on ethics for the rest of his life. Although he has not produced a major treatise on moral philosophy, Bertrand Russell has been a vocal member of the Cambridge school. In "A Free Man's Worship" (1903), he has looked upon morality as something imposed by traditional religious beliefs and suggested that "the world of fact, after all, is not good."[1] The free man's worship depends on emancipation from personal desire and a burning passion for eternal things.

By 1935, in the ninth chapter of his *Religion and Science*,[14] Russell is saying that questions of "good" and "values" are beyond the reach of science and, indeed, lie "outside the domain of knowledge." Hence, my statement that something has value is simply an expression of my own emotion. Ethics, in this period of Russell's thought, is an unsuccessful attempt to escape the subjectivity of emotional preferences.[15] It is this type of ethical skepticism that is usually associated with Russell's later views.[16]

The contribution of another Cambridge thinker, Ludwig Wittgenstein (1889–1951), to ethical theory is equally difficult to estimate. Yet he has had an impact in the field. A Viennese, Wittgenstein first (1908) studied engineering at Manchester University in England, read the first volume of *Principia Mathematica*, and went to study philosophy with Russell at Cambridge. The early twenties found him back in Vienna (living for a time on the grounds of a Benedictine monastery and considering entrance into this Catholic religious community) where he had some contacts with Moritz Schlick and other members of the Vienna Circle of positivists but never became a member of their famous group. At this time he published the first German version of the mediations which became known later (1922) as the *Tractatus Logico-Philosophicus*. Returning to Cambridge in 1929 as an advanced student in philosophy, Wittgenstein soon gathered about him a group of admirers and began to function as a master. Something very much like a personality cult developed about him, in which G. E. Moore oddly participated, and this mystique persists, even after Wittgenstein's death. It is necessary to understand this, that many people feel that he was a man of great wisdom, before one can grasp the impact that he had on British philosophy. In 1929 Wittgenstein succeeded Moore as professor of philosophy at Cambridge.

Wittgenstein's writings (along with the work of John Wisdom at Cambridge) are central to the whole movement of language analysis. Unlike many others (including Moore), Wittgenstein did not see words functioning primarily as symbols of things or of internal acts of consciousness. For him, words are more like dominoes with which people play different games. (He is not without responsibility for certain recent notions popularized by Marshall McLuhan to the effect that "communications theory" has to do with the manipulation of media.) As a result, Wittgenstein convinced many English philosophers that the main work of philosophy is simply to get things straight in regard to the use of language.[17] From logical positivism he brought the theory that propositions can be verified only if they are tautologous or if they accord with the direct evidence of sense perception. This makes nonsense of metaphysics, of religion as a creedal institution, and of theoretical ethics. In his *Tractatus* Wittgenstein had ruled out ethical propositions.[18]

At this time (1921), he admitted that one could speak of good and evil in concrete circumstances but he objected to ought-statements a meaningless.[19] So, the *Tractatus* teaches that we may express judgment of value in circumstances which make it sense to do so. For Wittgenstein this does not suggest that ethics should be equated with the social sciences; indeed, in 1942 he said that he did not consider the description of "the ways and customs of various tribes" to be ethics.[20]

We now have a published (1965) "Lecture on Ethics" which wa written and read in English (he was always more at home in German by Wittgenstein for some group at Cambridge, at some time betwee: September, 1929, and December, 1930. The talk begins with Moore' definition: "Ethics is the general enquiry into what is good."[21] T provide a sort of composite picture of the meaning of ethics, Wittgen stein next offers a series of "synonymous expressions." Thus, ethics the enquiry into what is valuable; into what is really important; into th meaning of life; into what makes life worth living; or into the righ way of living. "If you look at all these phrases you will get a rough ide as to what it is that ethics is concerned with," explains Wittgenstein.

Two ways in which "good" or any value word may be used are no distinguished: trivial or relative usage simply means that somethin comes up to a predetermined standard (this man is a *good* pianist; th is the *right* road); ethical or absolute usage is different and can l exemplified as follows. I tell a preposterous lie; a listener says to m "You're behaving like a beast"; I reply, "I know, but I don't want l behave any better"; he answers, "Well, you *ought* to want to beha better." Wittgenstein ends this bit of dialogue with the observatio "Here you have an absolute judgment of value."[23]

All relative judgments of value are mere statements of facts, t lecture adds, but there is no way in which an absolute judgment value can be grounded in statements of facts. Even an omniscie mind writing a complete factual account of the whole universe and all men and their states of mind, "would contain nothing that we wou call an *ethical* judgment or anything that would logically imply su a judgment." If this suggests that there is no ethics, for Wittgenstei that is not what he means. Characteristically, he now suggests that someone could write an ethics "which really was a book on Ethics this would explode and destroy all the other books in the world! Ethi is supernatural (sic) and our words will only express facts.[24] The mainder of Wittgenstein's talk is devoted to an expansion of the ther of the inexpressibility of ethical judgments. His final summary is th

> Ethics so far as it springs from the desire to say something about the ultimate meaning of life, the absolute good, the absolute valu able, can be no science. What it says does not add to our knowledge

in any sense. But it is a document of a tendency in the human mind which I personally cannot help respecting deeply and I would not for my life ridicule it.[25]

One additional point should be noted before we leave Wittgenstein. 1 his "Notes on Talks with Wittgenstein,"[26] Friedrich Waismann :corded some comments that Wittgenstein made concerning the ethics f Moritz Schlick. Among other things mentioned is Schlick's statement f two conceptions of ethics: (1) the good is good because God wills it; 1d (2) God wills the good because it is good. Wittgenstein then says 1at he prefers the first view: "Good is what God orders."[27] This in-icates that, in the ultimate analysis, Wittgenstein opted for divine)luntarism. His explanation for this preference is that it cuts off any tionalistic attempt to explain why something is ethically good. "A 1eory gives me nothing" either in ethics or in religion, adds Wittgen-:in, and this is probably his last word on the matter.

What Wittgenstein was saying was not some novel personal discovery 1at he had made; it was standard teaching in the Vienna Circle. One the main figures in this group, Rudolf Carnap (1891–   ), has writ-1 very little about ethics, but in *Philosophy and Logical Syntax* (1935) : included a passage which flatly states that the propositions of norma-'e ethics have no "theoretical meaning" and are not scientific (i.e. rifiable) propositions.[28] In another sense, Carnap explained, ethical 1tements may be taken as expressions of emotions or wishes within e speaker. Furthermore, these feelings may be investigated empirically psychology, or if you wish, in psychological ethics. Moritz Schlick was other member of the Vienna Circle who held these same views. is an early version of the emotive meaning of ethical statements.

Not all the philosophers at Cambridge fell victim to the spell of ittgenstein. Alfred Cyril Ewing (1899–   ) has staunchly defended uitional ethics against all opponents, and his *The Definition of Good*)47) is probably the outstanding book on intuitionism in recent 1ics. Ewing rejects (in this work) both naturalism and subjectivism 1 also dissociates himself from ideal utilitarians (who would otherwise m his closest allies). That Moore's "intrinsic good" is basic to all 1ical theory and that this good is known in itself, objectively, by 1ht-minded people, is assumed throughout by Ewing.[29] Concerning 3ht-judgments, Ewing is a deontologist with theistic commitments. To , "A ought to be done," is equivalent to saying, "A is commanded God."[30] However, Ewing does not agree with Wittgenstein that 3 is the end of the matter. What God commands is obligatory, ing thinks, because God is good. It is "goodness" in the objective 1 metaphysical sense that is the ground for ethical commands.[31] For ny years Ewing has stood almost alone in England in supporting such views. Vigorously attacked by A. J. Ayer (whose own position we shall examine shortly), he has been forced, since 1958 or so, to modify his ethical position. *Second Thoughts in Moral Philosophy* (1959) shows Ewing open to the sort of "reasoning" about duties and goods that is carried on by younger British thinkers in the "good reasons" school. Moreover, in a paper delivered in 1958,[32] Ewing listed naturalism, intuitive nonnaturalism, and subjectivism as the main divisions of contemporary ethics and then suggested that he could see the possibility of fusing the three into a single position. Willing now to abandon the indefinability of "good," Ewing still insists that "ought" is beyond definition. He agrees that ought-judgments express subjective feeling for or against something. However, what he now emphasizes is that ethical judgments must be "rationally justified and indeed imposed on us by the objective situation."[33] Ultimate justification can only be achieved by an appeal to empirical facts. But he still thinks that the main concepts of ethics are nonnatural. Ewing's ethics present many difficulties, even to those who are inclined to agree with his basic assumptions.[3]

Philosophers at Oxford University eventually took up language analysis and made it their own. Central to this movement was John Austin (1911–1960), who became professor of moral philosophy at Oxford in 1952. He published no books during his lifetime and the two issued posthumously (*Philosophical Papers*, 1961; and *How to Do Things with Words*, 1962) are only indirectly related to ethics. Being editions of two series of lectures, they show that Austin made the study of words and meanings central to his work at Oxford. One of his editors, James O. Urmson (1905–   ) has written *Philosophical Analysis* (1956) which is a valuable study of the whole movement. Urmson's most discussed contribution to ethics is a little paper "On Grading,"[35] where he talks about the experienced appraisal of the relative rank of various items (such as apples) in terms of "grading." In discussing various examples of grades, including the academic lists of "excellent, very good, good, fair, etc.," Urmson calls such classifications, into higher and lower, "grading labels." Naturalism, intuitionism, and emotivism (and also subjectivism and utilitarianism)—all have something to contribute, according to Urmson, to the understandng of ethical grading. At least we now know that to describe is one thing and to grade is quite another. Moral choice is much closer to a grading judgment than to a description but no one set of grading criteria for ethics imposes itself. Urmson ends with the suggestion that one might grade ethical criteria from the viewpoint of the ultimate grades, "enlightened and unenlightened. This is a good example of the sort of thing that Oxford analysts do from the "ordinary language" approach to ethics.

Eventually a philosopher from the United States joined the analysts. This was Charles L. Stevenson (1908–   ), who studied at both Harvard

nd Cambridge. In 1937 he published an article in *Mind* that was
ntitled "The Emotive Meaning of Ethical Terms."[37] This is a key
:atement of the emotive theory of ethics. In it, Stevenson listed three
:quirements for the meaning of "good" which is important in ethics:
1) it must be open to intelligent disagreement; (2) it must be "magnetic"
the quotation marks are Stevenson's); and (3) it must not be dis-
overable solely through scientific method. Two main uses of language
:e distinguished by Stevenson: first, to communicate beliefs and to
:press our feelings, or create moods (as in poetry); or second, to
:cite people to actions (as in oratory). The first usage is "descriptive"
id the second "dynamic." Emotive meaning (as employed by C. K.
•gden and I. A. Richards in a noted book on literary meaning)[38]
:emed to Stevenson to designate this second usage, as a tendency of
ords to produce affective responses in people. So his general contention
as been that ethical sentences are best understood in terms of such
notive meaning.

Stevenson's first book, *Ethics and Language* (1944), expands this same
isic theme, but he now insists that emotive meanings are not devices
r pushing aside ethics from the serious consideration of philosophers
it are precisely what the ethician must investigate.[39] For Stevenson
is very important to clarify two kinds of disagreement: a) in attitude,
• in belief. Since beliefs about facts may influence attitudes, there is
sense in which ethical statements may be true or false. If one will
ant one basic assumption to Stevenson (that "all disagreement in at-
ude is rooted in disagreement in belief"), then he feels that he may
vestigate the reasons that lie behind ethical judgments.[40] Discussion
this contention has led to the more recent versions of good reasons
hics, as we shall note later.

Facts and Values, Studies in Ethical Analysis (1963) does not rep-
:ent a rethinking of Stevenson's ethics but it is a useful collection
periodical articles and addresses (beginning with the *Mind* article of
37) on emotive ethics and other theories, such as John Dewey's. It
worth noting that the two American philosophers who most affected
:venson were R. B. Perry and Dewey. Perry's notion of value as any
ject of any interest is always a point of departure for the presentation
the emotive theory, as Stevenson understands it. From Dewey he
)k the important distinction between a psychological description of
: way in which ethical decisions are made and the authentically ethical
idy of "how we ought to proceed."[41] Stevenson's Preface (dated
52) states three questions: one asks for the kind of reasons that can
offered for normative conclusions; a second asks how the problems
normative ethics are different from those of the sciences; the third
:s how the key terms used in ethics differ meaningfully from scientific

terms. As he sees the situation, analytic ethics deals with these thre
questions.[42]

Contemporary with Stevenson is the British philosopher, Alfred Jule
Ayer (1910–   ), who is also a pioneer in emotive ethics. Ayer knew an
shared in the discussions of the men who constituted the Vienna Circle
Besides Schlick and Carnap, this group of logical positivists include
Herbert Feigl, Philipp Frank and Kurt Gödel. Interested in applyin
scientific method to philosophy, they tried to find some one versio
of this method that would be suitable for all parts of the philosophi
enterprise. Furthermore, they insisted on the verification principle: tha
all scientifically meaningful propositions must be either tautologies c
tested by empirical reference to sense data. Ayer shared these view
In the sixth chapter of *Language, Truth, and Logic* (1936), he explaine
that ethical philosophers put four kinds of propositions into their writing
(1) definitions of ethical terms, (2) descriptions of moral experienc
and their causes, (3) exhortations to live virtuously, and (4) son
actual ethical judgments. Ayer felt that only the first kind of propositio
really belong in ethical philosophy.[43] As he sees it, propositions of ty[
(2) belong in psychology or sociology, type (3) do not belong in ar
science, and type (4) defy classification but do not belong in ethic
Ayer's main conclusion is that ethics should "make no ethical pr
nouncements" but should give "an analysis of ethical terms."

At the end of this chapter, Ayer offered to "define the nature
all ethical enquiries." Eventually, it must be recognized that all concep
in ethics are pseudoconcepts and defy analysis, for ethical statemen
simply express the feelings of the speaker. They are completely subjecti
and it is nonsense to ask whether they are true.[44] This version
emotive ethics differs from Stevenson's in excluding ethics from t
category of philosophical sciences. It goes without saying, that Aye
subjectivism has been severely criticized—especially by C. E. M. Joa
who summarizes his objections in these words:

> If I consistently believe that the statement, "stealing is wrong,"
> does no more than express an emotion of horror at stealing, it
> will presently cease to express the emotion of horror. Not to put
> too fine a point on it, I shall cease to believe that stealing is wrong.[45]

On the other hand, Mary Warnock writes, in her survey of contempor:
ethics, that Ayer's formulation of the emotive theory "has great pla
bility and appeal for any empiricist."[46]

For the second edition of his book, Ayer wrote in 1946 a rat
lengthy new Introduction. Although he defends his earlier views
ethics, he now states that, when actions are called right or wrong
ethics, *types* of actions and not particular actions are the objects un
discussion.[47] This is an important point, for it opens Ayer's think:

to the possibility of universal ethical judgments. Also, in regard to Moore's argument that ethical subjectivism would make all disagreement about ethical statements impossible, Ayer now says that disputes about matters of fact are always possible (and he now admits that some ethical statements include factual elements) but no disagreements concerning questions of value are possible. While Ayer still denies theoretical meaning to ethical propositions, he admits that they may have some utility as means to influence the conduct of other persons. But Ayer continues to maintain that ethical expressions cannot be true or false: they simply express one's own feelings.

There has been some polite disagreement among British and American commentators as to who was first in the field of emotive ethics. Actually, neither Ayer nor Stevenson can claim this honor. In 1911 the Swedish philosopher Axel Hägerström (1868–1939) first suggested that ethical norms are not propositions but expressions of feelings, and that they cannot be verified empirically and so are neither true nor false.[48] We have a collection of Hägerström's studies, translated into English by C. D. Broad, under the title *Inquiries into the Nature of Law and Morals* (1953). The second essay, dated 1916, deals with "Law as an Expression of Will"; and the third essay, from 1917, treats "The Notion of Law." In both of these early studies, Hägerström takes an emotive position. Duty, he explains, involves a "feeling" of compulsion similar to that is found in a person who receives a command.[49] To Hägerström, the objectification of value or duty is associated with the "indicative form of expression for the simultaneous association which is present, while the expressions 'value' and 'duty' . . . refer primarily to a background of feelings." Moral imperatives stem from emotions usually expressed in the form: "that must (not) be done." Such commands are not self-explanatory.[50]

Hägerström was not the only Scandinavian to hold such views. Alf Ross was another Swedish philosopher of law who quite early took a positivistic approach to ethical norms.[51] In 1945 Ross was saying that the assertion that an ethical norm is "objectively valid" means that it can be verified (1) by immediate observation, or (2) by its coincidence with a wide experience not possessed by the immediate observer. Statements of value cannot pass these tests, according to Ross, so he concludes that propositions of value and oughtness are unverifiable and without logical meaning. In his book *On Law and Justice* (the original was published in 1953), Ross says: "To invoke justice is the same thing as banging on the table: an emotional expression which turns one's demand into an absolute postulate."[52] On questions of value, goodness, and duty, Alf Ross is a thorough positivist.

A widely esteemed book written from a modified analytic viewpoint the *Ethics* (1954) by P. H. Nowell-Smith (1914–   ), who studied at Oxford. Here, he takes the position that intuitionists have distorted the ethical situation by treating moral discourse as if it were descriptive.[53] Their constant talk about ethical "qualities" is, to say the least, misleading. If they were correct (W. D. Ross is the intuitionist that he has particularly in mind), then ethics would be a sort of implausible empirical psychology.[54]

After his critique of intuitionism, Nowell-Smith proceeds to examine the language in which ethical judgments are expressed. He insists on the major distinction between linguistic expression of *what is* and the expression of what *looks* or *feels* in a certain way.[55] In moral matters it is important to see that what is right may contrast with what seems right. We are asked to notice how adjectives have a variety of usages. A dress may be red, comfortable, and indecent. Red is a D-word, simply descriptive. Comfortable is an A-word, expressing aptness to arouse certain emotions pro or con. Indecent is a G-word, a gerundive usage, capable of inciting to action.[56] Not only single words but also sentences are used in these three ways. Often the usage is indicated by the context in which something is said. Hence, three rules of "contextual implication" are required. First, when a speaker states something in a sentence, it is contextually implied that he believes it to be true. Second, it is contextually implied that a speaker has good reasons for his statement. Third, what a speaker says is assumed to be relevant to the interest of his audience. The importance of these seemingly elementary rules lies in Nowell-Smith's contention that the work of the 'ethician is "to map the mutual relationships of moral words, sentences, and argu ments."[57]

A key chapter is devoted by Nowell-Smith to "Reasons for Choosing."[5] This section has helped to stimulate recent formulations of "good reasons" ethics. Nowell-Smith here agrees with the subjectivists that pro- and con-attitudes are basic motives for decision. An apparent exception is the choice of certain things as means to ends, rather than for their own sake (i.e. because we have a pro-attitude toward the means itself). Some times statements of fact function as motives: thus, if asked why I helped a man across a road, I could answer, "Because he is blind." Moreover aptness sentences may similarly function in lieu of motives. The whole problem of motivation is seen by Nowell-Smith as linguistically com plicated. This is not a mere problem of psychology, for he claims that "a motive is not an event or force inside you which functions as a antecedent cause; but is a disposition or tendency to behave in a certain way when certain events occur."[59] Here, too, Nowell-Smith stresses the relevance of the context of a problem, and because of this emphasis his ethics is sometimes called contextualism. Most of the latter part of his book is taken up with the practical problem of bridging the ga

etween the question, "What is the best thing to do?" and the even
1ore practical query, "What shall I do?"[60]

It is apparent that Nowell-Smith knows a good deal about the history
f ethics. Aristotle's theory of "voluntary" action figures prominently
1 his book, for instance. At one point, after talking about the ethics
f the great philosophers, Nowell-Smith takes an almost traditional stand
n the importance of human nature. These great philosophers, he says,

> do not seem to have been mistaken in their basic assumptions that
> the language of obligation is intelligible only in connexion with
> the language of purpose and choice, that men choose to do what
> they do because they are what they are, and that moral theories
> which attempt to exclude all considerations of human nature as it
> is do not even begin to be moral theories.[61]

A group of moral philosophers working from somewhat the same ap-
roach that we have seen in Nowell-Smith take what is now called the
;ood reasons" way of dealing with ethical questions. Admitting that
rmal verification of value judgments is not possible, they claim that
ch rigorous procedure is not necessary. It is enough, they think, to find
state some acceptable practical justification for one's choice or action.
mple intuitionalism is rejected by this group, mainly because they
1d no convincing evidence for the objectivity of moral properties such
goodness, or meekness, or rightness. Nor do the good reasons ethicians
ree with the emotive analysis of ethical propositions; for if moral
terances merely express emotion and encouragement to others, it is
ry difficult to explain why so much time and paper have been devoted
ethical discussion. In the positive sense, what the good reasons school
s done is to turn the attention of moral philosophers from the job
isolating and describing nonnatural properties to the more concrete
k of explaining how one thinks through to a morally good action.
ey are concerned with somewhat the same type of problem as that
ich Aristotle handled with his theory of the practical syllogism cul-
nating in a conclusion that is not a judgment but a right action.[62]

A leading exponent of the good reasons view is Stuart Hampshire
914–   ) who, like most of the thinkers in this group, represents the
ford type of ordinary language analysis. Hampshire's article "Fallacies
Moral Philosophy" is a good introduction to the position.[63] In this
icle, two quite different questions are stated. First, there is the meta-
ical query: "What are the distinguishing characteristics of sentences
ressing moral praise or blame?" (This is somewhat analogous to the
k of the art critic in passing judgment on an artist's work.) Second,
re is the moral question: "What are the distinguishing characteristics
moral problems as they present themselves to us as practical agents?"
his is somewhat like the problem of the artist facing a job that he

proposes to do.) Now, Stuart Hampshire argues that the work of ethics is more closely allied with the second question than with the first.[64] The main problem of ethics then becomes the determination of the procedure of practical deliberation. According to Hampshire, it is not necessary that such practical reasoning be logically conclusive in a strictly demonstrative sense. As he sees it, "All argument is not deduction, and giving reasons in support of a judgment or statement is not necessarily, or even generally, giving logically conclusive reasons."[65] Hampshire's book *Thought and Action* (1959) is thus an expansion of this program of good reasons ethics.

Another advocate of good reasons ethics who now teaches in the United States is Kurt Baier (1917–   ). In a significant address, "The Meaning of Life," delivered in 1957 at the Australian National University, Baier compared the views of traditional religion concerning the meaning and purpose of human life with the testimony of modern science on the same subject and suggested that the otherworldly attitude of much religious teaching is impractical today. To Baier, at this point, the Christian standard of perfection seemed unjustified.[66] So, what men need to do is to identify some "everyday" standard for making their moral decisions on earth. Baier's book *The Moral Point of View* (1958) is an effort to fill this need, and it has become much discussed and cited in recent ethical writing. In it he criticizes emotivism (which he calls the "impact theory"), because he feels that it implies that there are really no moral questions. Less interested than Hampshire in directing ethical attention to the purely practical problem of translating good thinking into action, Baier strongly supports the idea that moral "reasons" do not have to be proofs. Rather, these reasons involve the presentation of facts which will move a person to act in a certain way.[67]

As we have seen, one part of the good reasons program in ethics involves the rejection of objective, nonnatural moral qualities. This sort of criticism is exemplified in an article by Peter F. Strawson (1919–   ) entitled "Ethical Intuitionism" (1949), which simply denies that there are such objects. A rather different approach is taken by R. M. Hare (1919–   ) in his first book, *The Language of Morals* (1952), where he conducts a very general discussion of the difference between the "descriptive" and "prescriptive" use of language. For Hare, value judgments are prescriptive and, if they are calculated to influence action, they must contain some imperative. In turn, moral judgments are one type of value judgments.[68] In a rather abstract way, Hare then tries to show that various logical relations of implication, entailment, consistency, and so on, do hold among imperatives.

In a more recent book, *Freedom and Reason* (1963), Hare stresses three main points that he wished to make in *The Language of Morals.* The first claim is that moral judgments are one type of prescriptive

idgments. Second, moral judgments differ from other prescriptive judg-
ients in being universalizable. Third, as we have just seen, there are
gical relations between prescriptive judgments, including imperatives.[69]
1uch of the burden of Hare's second book goes to show that his
1eory is practical and applicable to problems of action. Thus, the first
entence of his Preface states that the work of ethics "is that of helping
5 to think better about moral questions by exposing the logical structure
f the language in which this thought is expressed." In spite of his
ew emphasis on the "practicality" of ethics, it is rather obvious that
Iare is not as interested in actual moral deliberation as Hampshire. Part
of *Freedom and Reason* is devoted to "Moral Reasoning" but the
:position remains rather abstract.[70]

Many students of contemporary ethics would regard *An Examination*
the Place of Reason in Ethics (1950) by Stephen E. Toulmin (1922–
) as the most important exposition of good reasons ethics. Perhaps
s most significant contribution is found in the eleventh chapter, where
oulmin describes two kinds of moral reasoning. One type simply takes
1 accepted moral code, asks whether an action that is in question comes
1der one of the provisions of this code, and then decides that the action
right or wrong. This gives a good reason for doing or avoiding many
tions. However, there is a second kind of practical reasoning that is
ed where the first is not applicable. In some cases one has to make an
timate of the social value of the consequences of a proposed action.
Iere Toulmin is not far removed from Dewey's instrumentalism.) This
rt of reasoning does not provide an absolutely certain solution but it is
e best thing that one can appeal to in cases of conflict of duties; and in
e final analysis, social harmony is the ideal on which such thinking is
sed.[71] Modestly, Toulmin makes no claim that he thereby discovers *the*
·ht way to act: he merely finds a good reason for so acting. As a conse-
ence it is not always clear whether the good reasons approach is an
1ical procedure or a method of moralizing.[72]

Analytic ethics has been chiefly a British phenomenon but it is spread-
5 rapidly in the United States, where many of the previously men-
ned moral philosophers are teaching or have taught on a temporary
sis. Few native Americans, other than Stevenson, have, as yet, become
ept in this kind of ethics. Perhaps John Rawls (1921–   ), who stud-
1 at Oxford, would be a leading exception. Paul Edwards shares many
the views of the analysts but he was originally an Austrian who did
;ood part of his philosophical studies in Australia, where the method
language analysis has been much cultivated. Canada has not shown
1ch interest in the theory. F. E. Sparshott (Toronto) has published
Enquiry into Goodness (1958), of course, but he is a native of
gland and a product of Oxford.

It is very difficult to offer any appraisal of the value and the future expectancy of analytic ethics, since, of late years, the efforts of the ordinary language school have branched off in many directions. Perhaps the most helpful thing that one can say is that analytic ethics is productive of more books and articles than any other kind of moral philosophy that is being cultivated in English. This means that its influence has been very extensive in many parts of the world, although it is not important in continental Europe, except for the Scandinavian countries. From the point of view of its content, analytic ethics has contributed most through its insistence on clarity. These twentieth-century British thinkers have continually stressed the supreme importance of understanding the meaning of, and the evidence for, ethical statements. Doubtless, this is a valuable lesson for any kind of ethician.

CHAPTER XVIII

Existential and Phenomenological Ethics

THE MORAL PHILOSOPHY to be examined in this final chapter is generically different from almost all the theories of ethics that we have considered in this *History*. It is not really a "theory" but an attitude (or set of attitudes) toward human life and its problems. What we are now to review cannot be called an ethics in the formal philosophical sense, yet it is ethically important to contemporary man. Some informed readers would claim that the existential point of view is the key to what is most significant in life today.[1]

We shall consider both existential and phenomenological ethics. Phenomenology is not identical with existentialism but most existentialists use some version of the phenomenological method. From the teaching of Franz Brentano in Vienna, one line of thinkers developed the Austian theory of values (whose ethics we saw in Chapter XIV) and another group of philosophers worked out the program of phenomenology. In the early phenomenological school, Edmund Husserl was the leading philosopher. For our present purposes we may state the method of phenomenology under two points. First, it starts with the facts of personal consciousness, with things as objects of knowledge and feeling, and it tries to make a very careful "description" of what is so given in consciousness. Whatever is thus given is a *phenomenon*, something that appears, hence the name phenomenology. Second, it seeks essential knowledge of what is, of the *essence* of the appearance and of the object which thus appears. As Husserl put it, phenomenology "will be nothing less than a theory of essence contained in pure intuition."[2] We have already looked two great German philosophers who made some use of phenomenological method in their ethics: Max Scheler and Nicolai Hartmann. Indeed, it is quite possible to interpret G. E. Moore's realistic theory of ethical qualities as but another version of phenomenology.[3]

Existentialism, on the other hand, names a reaction against the traditional philosophies which tended to stress *essences* as the most important aspects of reality. Hegel's absolute idealism, a system in which everything

is rational, everything has an understandable explanation, everything occurs according to a fixed pattern—this is the bête noire of all existentialists. One might think that existentialists would have no use for phenomenology, since it gives an important place to "essences"; but the
point is that phenomenology was also born out of resentment to Hegelianism and is quite opposed to his rationalistic account of immutable essences. Both phenomenology and existentialism also owe a good deal to
Descartes's *cogito;* his notion that the human mind is a "thinking thing"
(*res cogitans*) in which occur not only cognitions but doubts, affirmations,
denials, willings, refusals, imaginations, and perceptions (*Meditationes*,
II)—this constitutes a point of departure for both phenomenology and
existentialism.

The man who is generally regarded as the first modern existentialist,
Søren Kierkegaard (1813–1855), preceded the phenomenological movement. A Danish Protestant with deep religious convictions, Kierkegaard
protested against the established Church, the clergy, the professors, academic philosophy (Hegelianism), and all hypocrites. In his short lifetime
he wrote a large number of passionate and moving books, most of which
have now been put into English. The very titles—*Either/Or* (1843), *Fear
and Trembling* (1843), *The Concept of Dread* (1844), *The Sickness
unto Death* (1849), *Purity of Heart Is to Will One Thing* (n.d.)—suggest the nonacademic character of his writing.

In *Either/Or*, one of Kierkegaard's first works, we meet the characteristic
theme of *choice.* Unlike Hegel, whose dialectic was a both/and affair,
Kierkegaard insisted that the moral agent must take sides. "Both-and is
the way to hell," was his blunt warning.[4] This is the idea that will run
through most subsequent existentialism: to be a free and real person one
must commit oneself, make a choice at the major crossroads of life.

Kierkegaard felt that there are three levels at which a person may live,
the aesthetic, the ethical, and the religious. The aesthetic man is devoted
to cognitive perception, to the cultivation of the life of the senses, even
to sensual pleasure. He lives, as it were, on the surface of reality. The
ethical man fights and struggles with himself; his victory consists in putting
off the lust for pleasure for one hour.[5] In knowing himself he sees his
duty. Most of the second part of *Either/Or* is concerned with this ethical
level of existence, and Socrates becomes the personification of the ethical
person. This, however, is not the highest level of human life. The
Concluding Unscientific Postscript (1846) deals with how to become a
Christian. The truly religious man lives the highest form of existence.
Suffering is the keynote here; without some anguish no one can be a
religious person. The "leap" of faith brings one to an awareness of subjectivity, and of God's inward presence within the subject. Where Hegel
worshiped totality, Kierkegaard revered individuality. "Had I to crave a

inscription on my grave I would ask for none other than 'the individual,' " he wrote in his *Journals.*[6]

It is rather clear, then, that ethics cannot be an ultimate view of life, for Kierkegaard. Sin is more important that any ethical category and if ethics begins to pay attention to sin it goes beyond itself.[7] Like the Neoplatonists and Augustine, Kierkegaard thought that man is balanced on a precarious line between pleasure or suffering, between the lower and the higher; for the life decisions that he must make, academic ethics is of little avail.[8] Whatever the high religious significance of Kierkegaard's message, it must be recognized that he offers us not an ethics but an anti-ethics. Yet he continues to influence existential ethics.

Another personality in the early existentialist school was Friedrich Nietzsche (1844–1900), and he, too, was quite apart from the phenomenological movement. Like Kierkegaard (with whom he had, apparently, no contacts), Nietzsche was violently critical of Church and university. He also hated Hegelianism and other systematic kinds of German idealism, but it is doubtful whether Nietzsche shared the profound religious commitment of Kierkegaard. Some interpreters treat him as an immoralist," while others defend him as a supporter of a higher morality.[9] Something which makes it more difficult to reach the real Nietzsche is the fact that his sister, Elisabeth Förster-Nietzsche, edited the famous (or infamous) *Will to Power* (*Der Wille zur Macht*), from fragmentary materials and alleged private conversations, in such a way as to make Friedrich Nietzsche appear a Nazi before the fact.[10] The expression "will to power" does occur in the authentic writings of Nietzsche but it is not as much emphasized as many commentators think. His ethical views (which are far from orderly) are best seen in *The Birth of Tragedy* (1872), *Thus Spake Zarathustra* (1883), *Beyond Good and Evil* (1886), and *Toward a Genealogy of Morals* (1887).

Coming down from the mountains, Nietzsche's sage, Zarathustra, meets traditional saint who asks for gifts. Zarathustra hurries away from him, saying within himself: "Could it be possible! This old saint in the forest has not yet heard of it, that *God is dead!*"[11] This theme of the death of God runs through many of Nietzsche's works.[12] What it means is debatable. Possibly Nietzsche is saying that men have lost their contact with, and awareness of, the real God: in this sense, God has died within the awareness of mankind. (As we shall see, this is the way the "death of God" is understood in present-day "process theology.") On the other hand, Nietzsche may be taken as meaning precisely what he says, that there is no God, and this would be the core of his atheism. Following the second interpretation, it is usual to think of Kierkegaard as the pioneer theistic existentialism and Nietzsche as the originator of the atheistic school.

Another key theme in Nietzsche's ethical outlook is that of the devaluation of all values (*Umwertung aller Werte*). The traditional moralities stemmed from social and religious cultures that distorted man's ethical potential, according to Nietzsche. The Jews, for instance, are blamed for exalting the moral value of slaves and the poor, for saying that the noble virtues of power, courage, and joy are to be replaced with weakness, humility, and suffering as moral ideals.[13] Christianity, too, is an "old ladies' morality." What is needed Nietzsche says, is a reversal an overturning, of this perverted sense of traditional values. The ideal person is the "superman" (*Ubermensch*) who can rise above the petty limitations of ordinary morality. This aristocrat makes his own ethical values. Thus, "one has duties only toward one's equals; toward beings of a lower rank, toward everything foreign to one, one may act as one sees fit, 'as one's heart dictates'—in any event, 'beyond good and evil.' "[14]

To determine what Nietzsche really stands for, in ethics, is not easy In the *Genealogy of Morals* (which is the best source of information) he attacks and condemns the whole "ascetic" trend of Christian mo rality. But he also bitterly castigates those "freethinkers and scientists' who are "anti-idealists."[15] In any event, the antitraditionalism of Nietzsche has certainly had its influence on present-day existentialism. Positively perhaps the chief thing that he had to say was that the ethical person must assert himself, make his own choices, determine his own future

Feodor Dostoyevsky (1821–1881) is another figure in the prehistory o existentialist ethics. Popularly known as a novelist fascinated with th problem of evil, Dostoyevsky concentrated on this theme, with whic academic ethics has, perhaps, been too little concerned. *Crime and Punish ment, The Idiot, The Brothers Karamazov,* and Dostoyevsky's other storie have taken their place among the great works in world literature an they all deal with moral evil. For his anticipation of many of the theme of recent existentialism, Dostoyevsky's *Notes from the Undergroun* (originally published in 1864) is the important source.[16] Dostoyevsky "hero" is an unlikable, sick, unfortunate man. Fascinated with the "al surdity" of life, every sort of consciousness is for Dostoyevsky, "a disease. He feels some inner "gnawing" as a result of some hateful action an eventually finds a shameful sweetness in it. This anti-hero tends to thin of himself as a mouse rather than a man. Yet he prizes his "own fre unfettered choice" above all else.[17] Reason satisfies on man's ration side, but it is will that manifests life as a whole, in the view of Dostoye sky.

Dostoyevsky may not technically be an existentialist; but, if that is th case, then "Part One of *Notes from the Underground* is the best overtu for existentialism ever written."[18] The character Raskolnikov, in *Crim and Punishment,* is like Nietzsche's superman in determining his ov values, and he commits a completely absurd murder, like a person novel by Albert Camus. Thus, we find both the cult of unreason and f absurdity in Dostoyevsky.[19]

It is with Edmund Husserl (1859–1938) that we come to the beginning f the phenomenological school. We have seen that his *Ideas: General ntroduction to Pure Phenomenology* (1913) introduced the theory of escription of the presentations of consciousness and the notion that ese phenomena are essences. He did not work out an ethical theory imself. What he did offer, apart from the phenomenological method, as the suggestion that persons meet and intercommunicate *as subjects:* ot simply as one person viewing another as an object but in something f a sharing in the subjective experience of the other person.[20]

Of the followers of Husserl, Max Scheler was the most prominent in e history of ethics. We have looked at his work in Chapter XIV. Apart om Scheler, perhaps Alexander Pfänder (1870–1941) is the outstanding riter on the psychology of moral consciousness. His *Phänomenologie des ollens* (1930) is a valuable study of ethical motivation. Another member the Husserlian School, Herbert Spiegelberg (1904–   ), the well- own historian of the phenomenological movement, has published a set studies preliminary to a truly phenomenological ethics in his *Gesetz d Sittengesetz. Strukturanalytische und historische Vorstudien zu einer setzfreien Ethik* (1935).

Also falling within the broad category of phenomenological ethics was e greatest figure in contemporary Jewish thought, Martin Buber (1878–65). His main contribution was to have worked out in the setting of igious ethics the implications of intersubjectivity. In this field Buber's ost influential writings are *I and Thou* (1923) and *Good and Evil* nglish version, 1953). A long-time professor at the Hebrew University Jerusalem, Buber was respected throughout the world as an outstanding oponent of religious existentialism. Buber's basic contention is that we ould learn to know, and feel toward, and treat, the other person as "Thou" and not as an impersonal "It." As he expressed the point: Vithout *It* man cannot live. But he who lives with *It* alone is not a n."[21]

One of the comparable personalities in Christian ethics is Paul Tillich 886–1965), who is also frequently called an existentialist; but his ought is not that simple. Tillich's background combines Kantian ethics th Christian theology and moral relativism. Among his ethical writings : *The Courage to Be* (1952), *Love, Power, and Justice* (1960), and orality and Beyond* (1963). Of course, the *Systematic Theology* (3 vols., 51–1963) is necessary for the understanding of Tillich's thought, for he convinced that the attempt to separate theological ethics from philo- hical ethics is a bad thing; it smacks of a "double truth" approach.[22] lich calls his own position a "theonomous" ethics.

From the philosophical side (here Kant is very important), Tillich insists on an ontological basis for ethical judgment: "There is no answer in ethics without an explicit or implicit assertion about the nature of being."[23] On the religious side, he draws together the act of faith and obedience to the moral imperative: they are but one and the same act.[24] It is in this sense that his ethics is theonomous. Practical understanding is not enough; we must shift from reason to the *person* as the source of ethical decision.[25] Courage is a basic virtue and value. It is a universal self-affirmation, a positive assertion of one's being.

Tillich's existentialism stands out particularly in his rejection of eternal and immutable norms of moral behavior.[26] It is in this spirit that he criticizes rationalized laws and makes love (agape) the fundamental ethical principle. This affirmation of the primacy of "love" is the outstanding feature of theistic existential ethics. It is basic to the emphasis on the person-to-person encounter—which is almost as much stressed in Tillich as in Buber. The "other" can only be loved when he is recognized as an "I."[27] The claims of personal morality, religion, and social culture merge and even conflict within the human spirit, producing a situation of ambiguity and tension. With this ambiguous background, the ethical person makes his own resolution of each moral situation.[28] A man's decisions must be the best that he can make but they have only relative value.

Very important in Protestant Christian ethics on the American scene has been the thought of the two Niebuhr brothers. Reinhold Niebuhr (1892–   ) has the greater popular reputation; indeed, he is one of the few Americans chosen to deliver a series of Gifford Lectures, his *Nature and Destiny of Man* (2 vols., 1941–1943). Other key writings by Reinhold Niebuhr are *Moral Man and Immoral Society* (1932) and *An Independent Christian Ethics* (1935). Both books challenge the absolutism of traditional ethical standards. What the moral life requires, according to Reinhold Niebuhr, is "the nicely calculated less and more of the relatively good and the relatively evil."[29] This might suggest that rational calculation plays a part in this ethics: it does, but reason cannot be the sole base of virtue in man; "his social impulses are more deeply rooted than his rational life."[30] Reinhold Niebuhr is consequently very critical of natural law ethics, opposing it on three grounds: (1) human reason is too weak to sustain such a theory, (2) human nature is essentially mutable, and (3) love is ethically much more important than law or justice.[31] Here, again, the principle of love is given primary place in contemporary ethics. In fact, Reinhold Niebuhr says: "There is no possibility of giving any rational definition of a just relation between man and man and man and nation, or nation and nation, short of a complete love in which each life affirms the interests of the other."[32]

Less insistent than Reinhold on the social obligations of Christian ethics, was his brother, H. Richard Niebuhr (1894–1962). In "The Grace of Doing Nothing,"[33] Richard argued that the good Christian does not have to be a social activist. In his view, the concerns of Christian ethics rise above the constantly changing tensions of everyday life. Reinhold disagrees and insists that good faith requires action.[34] Richard Niebuhr's general ethical view is developed in *The Kingdom of God in America* (1937).

Of recent years, some writers on Protestant Christian ethics have emphasized what is called "situation ethics," or the "new morality." The name and basic concept goes back to a German book (*Gegenwart: eine kritische Ethik*) written in 1928 by Eberhard Grisebach (1880–1945). He simply claimed that there are no longer any universal rules or judgments in modern ethics, that each moral problem is unique and must be decided individually on its own conditions. This approach was called "Situationsethik."[35] During World War II, the Lutheran thinker Dietrich Bonhoeffer (1906–1945) became concerned about Hitlerism, eventually died in a Nazi prison as a result of his involvement in an attempt to overthrow Hitler. He left a quantity of fragmentary writings in which he protested against the older concepts of Christianity and its legalistic moral teaching. Bonhoeffer's *Ethics* has become the focal point of interest for a new generation of younger Christian ethicians.[36] The central notion in Bonhoeffer's ethics is that a person may do anything (such as killing a dictator), provided he is motivated by Christian love and concern for his fellow men. Each moral decision is unique and general rules are of little avail, as these lines suggest:

> The question of good is posed and is decided in the midst of each definite, yet unconcluded, unique and transient situation of our lives, in the midst of our living relationships with men, things, institutions and powers, in other words in the midst of our historical existence.[37]

Dietrich Bonhoeffer was not an existentialist philosopher, of course, but a religious-minded man trying to find a point of view from which to handle moral problems of immediate concern. He has become a leading figure in situational ethics.

Anglican Bishop John A. Robinson (1919–   ) has recently come to the fore as an exponent of situation ethics. His book *Honest to God* (1963) is a contribution to the "God is dead" literature which is closely associated with situationism. Robinson's *Christian Morals Today* (1964) insists that Christ's precepts were not legal rules and have no universal validity. Instead, they illustrate various applications of the principle of love in the period in which Christ lived. Hence, in a radical "ethic of the situation," nothing is required except love.[38] In the United States, a very similar approach to Christian ethics is taken in the work of Joseph Fletcher (1905–   ).

In continental Europe, the leading Catholic exponent of phenomenological existentialism is Gabriel Marcel (1889–   ). He has recently repudiated the name "existentialist" but his thought bears more resemblance to this school than to any other. Certainly, he is not a Thomist. Works like *Being and Having* (1935), *Homo Viator* (1944), *The Mystery of Being* (Gifford Lectures, 1949–1950), and *L'Homme problématique* (1955) show that Marcel has always been more interested in the ontology of man than in ethics. However, Marcel does have a good deal to say about the moral point of view; much of it is found in a newly translated work from his youth, *Philosophical Fragments 1904–1914*.[39]

Being opposed to systematic ethics and favoring a morality of love, Marcel directs his criticism against three kinds of ethics. First of all, the rationalistic ethics of the Enlightenment is no longer of any value, for it simply offered an artificial justification of the norms current in its time and milieu. Second, the theory (Hegelianism) that tried to ground an ethics on some concept of an abstract "Mind" is also useless, according to Marcel. Nor is an ethics based on "what science teaches" any better.[40] In the third place, Marcel attacks the sort of ethics that takes "life" as its supreme value. What life, Marcels asks, yours, mine, or life in general? Under this same heading, he condemns the whole program of American naturalistic ethics: it depersonalizes man, he thinks. Marcel has a tremendous capacity for disliking things. He does not care for Sartre's ethics, either. It is mistaken about the character of freedom (this is a foul blow, for Sartre thinks that he is an authority on freedom), and Sartrean existentialism is wrong about the self-creation of values. Moreover, as a strong-minded theist, Marcel resents Sartre's atheism.[41] Characteristically, he says: "I do not 'choose' my values at all, but I *recognize* them and posit my actions in accordance or in contradiction with these values. . . ."[42]

Marcel's view of human freedom is, first of all, based on a denial of other notions of it. Freedom is not "liberty of indifference," it is not a predicate belonging to the essence of man, and it is not an affair of causality. Freedom, as Marcel sees it, is "something that I decide," without any appeal.[43] The very existence of man is his freedom; and, like other philosophers of existence, Marcel stresses the personal encounter, the existential "We" and intersubjectivity.[44] A strong social emphasis adds a new dimension to Marcel's initially personalistic approach to morality. Obligation and moral responsibility are nothing without a being higher than oneself.[45] For Marcel, this being is God. Perhaps Georges Gusdorf (1912–   ) is the follower who has done most to write an ethics in the pattern of Marcellian thought. His *Traité de l'existence morale* (1949) stresses the immanence of moral values within the existing man, rather than the fact that they may come originally from a transcendent source.

Two great Spanish writers are sometimes called existentialists because they share some of the attitudes toward life and morality that distinguish that school. Miguel de Unamuno (1864–1936) studied German philosophy and came under the strong influence of Kierkegaard, whose thought he introduced into Spanish literature. Unamuno's great work in this field is the *Tragic Sense of Life* (1914). A giant protest against the pretensions of science and reason, it presents life, immortality, and faith as Unamuno's prime values. He thought that reason kills them. Long before other existentialists began their twentieth-century attack on rationalism, Unamuno was the apostle of irrationalism.

The second of these Spanish thinkers was José Ortega y Gasset (1883–1955), also a student of German philosophy, under the value philosopher Georg Simmel. Nietzsche appealed to Ortega and exerted a considerable influence on his writing. In Ortega's brand of personalistic idealism, "life" is all-important. In spite of his professed respect for traditional ethical values, Ortega held that the political hero (who has some of the attributes of the *Übermensch*) is not subject to the ordinary norms of ethical judgment. It is on this score that he is compared with existentialist moralists, but his chief impact has been on the philosophy of history and politics. In this area he has opposed totalitarianism.

The most formal contribution to phenomenological ethics that has been published in contemporary France is the *Eléments pour une éthique* (1962) by Jean Nabert (1881–1960). Unfortunately, he is little known outside France.[46] A very sincere Protestant, religious values were quite important to Nabert. His "ethics" is not, however, a moralizing treatise but a conscious account of man's effort to realize his will to exist on human level. Thus, Nabert offers a phenomenological "description" of a person's experience of moral failure ("*l'experience de la faute*"), the awareness of being blocked ("*l'échec*"), and the profound feeling of solitude.[47] This leads Nabert to a reflection on the meaning of moral consciousness and the development of an awareness of values. A long third section of Nabert's book deals with various aspects of personal existence, its teleological tendencies, its oughtness ("*le devoir de l'existence*"), its virtues viewed as spiritual forms, and its sources of religious veneration.[48]

Nabert's suggestive theory of values (in his fifth chapter) is close in many points to the position of Marcel. Both men regard freedom as the stuff of personal existence, and there is no immutability in ethical matters. As Nabert expresses the situation, toward the end of his book:

> The moral and religious categories by which we judge, the values whereby we appreciate, the rules themselves which we obey, in the most impersonal guise that they assume and with all their air of permanence—must be referred to highly contingent starting-points; they are contingent by virtue of the act which encompasses them, not by the principle which they produce.[49]

Much the best-known French existentialist, of course, is Jean Paul Sartre (1905–   ). A powerful writer who has used plays and novels, as well as philosophical writings, to put across his point, Sartre knows the technique of German phenomenology. Moreover, his *Outline of a Theory of the Emotions* (1939) shows his undoubted ability as a descriptive psychologist. *Being and Nothingness* (1943) is the basic work, however, both for the understanding of his ontology of man and for the foundations of his ethical views. *Saint Genet* (1952) is important for certain comments which it offers concerning the possibility of an ethics. Many people looked forward to his *Critique de la raison dialectique* (1960), in the expectation that it might be his long-awaited treatise on ethics. It is not that; at least in its first volume (the only one yet published), it is more concerned with Marxism than with ethics.

Two kinds of being are distinguished by Sartre: *être en-soi*, to be in-itself, is the reality of a static *thing*, the being of anything inanimate, with no openness to be anything else; and *être pour-soi*, which is to be consciously, to be human in the sense that the subject is able to be separated from himself, to be pregnant with dynamic potentiality.[50] It will be evident why "ambiguity" is a constant theme in Sartre: he feels that there are always internal and contrary tensions implicit in the human person.

Yet this radical contingency of human consciousness is its very existence, for Sartre. There is no human nature, or essence of man, to limit the openness of being *pour-soi*. This contingency is, of course, man's freedom.[51] To the extent that there is a Sartrean ethics, it consists in the exigency to actualize one's freedom. Hence, the ground of all moral values is in freedom.[52] The great virtue, according to Sartre, is "authenticity": a kind of honesty and courage. The authentic individual faces things which the inauthentic (and bad) person is afraid to face.[53] Not a mere attitude, Sartre's "authenticity" involves action and the making of free decisions. The worst vice, in Sartre's estimation, is "bad faith." It consists in the individual's negation of his own freedom, a failure to be a man.[54] The notion of intersubjectivity is also stressed by Sartre, as in all versions of phenomenological ethics. In his relations with other persons, a man comes to be a developed person; their awareness of him is a part of his own openness as a person. Some sort of intercommunion with others is implied in the very meaning of consciousness.

Ethics is described in *Saint Genet*[55] as a "synthesis of good and evil," a Hegelian *Aufhebung*. To have a wholly good person, Sartre feels would involve a separation of evil from the good, and this would result in an "alienation" of man. There is, then, something oddly impossible about a Sartrean ethics; for, an "ethic of praxis" would find the ego defined only by the "complex of its own decisions."[56] Clearly, such in ethics would be unteachable. Every value contains an inner contradiction: first, a tendency toward being incorporated into existence; and second, a need to stand beyond such realization. Here, again, we have an ineradicable ambiguity within value itself. "The moral agent can satisfy this twofold exigency only, so it seems, by giving his life to realize the ethical imperative and by dying as a result of not having achieved his goal." Obviously, it is not easy to be a Sartrean hero.

In *Critique de la raison dialectique* Sartre criticizes contemporary Marxists (notably the French theoretician, Pierre Naville) for their failure to develop the implications of Karl Marx's original teachings—and for their positive distortions of Marxism. Among other things, he accuses them of turning to an extreme materialism, because they have not understood how a dialectic can take place within the domain of consciousness or thought.[57] Sartre obviously thinks that his own view of consciousness is much better, but his accusation of crude materialism has been violently resented by more orthodox Marxists. Yet Sartre keeps on insisting that he is a true Marxist, in his social and political thought. But the French Marxists want nothing to do with him. A large part of the *Critique* is given over to an elaborate discussion of dialectic in history and he promises to finish off this question in a second volume.[58] What is quite evident is that this book does little to advance the ethical position of Sartre.

Some writers consider that Simone de Beauvoir (1908–   ) has produced the key work in existential ethics of the French school, in her *Ethics of Ambiguity* (1946). That judgment is somewhat exaggerated.[59] We find in her book much the same set of notions that have just been seen in Sartre. Ethics, she says, is "the triumph of freedom over facticity."[60] Here, as in Sartre, "facticity" means the contingency of being for-self.[61] Admittedly, Simone de Beauvoir makes it very clear how the Sartrean man is forced by this very odd notion of freedom to deny God. An existing God, as she explains, would set limits to man's radical freedom to create his own values. Consequently, she agrees with Sartre's reading of Kant, that any law that is not self-imposed is opposed to man's own dignity.[62]

There can be no definite judgments (and certainly no absolute ones) in Simone de Beauvoir's ethics. She discusses, for instance, the admitted violence practiced against many people under Stalinism in the Soviet Union. This was not necessarily evil, she argues, because what was done helped to alleviate the suffering of other people.[63] However, at other places she vehemently supports the value of respect for other people and their freedom. This has the status of an ethical imperative: "Such a law imposes limits upon action and at the same time immediately gives it a content."[64] For the ethics of ambiguity the great vice is seriousness. "*Le sérieux*" (the eager-beaver) is a man who prizes moral security, will take no chances, tries to do all the "right things." His attitude is the antithesis of conscious freedom.[65]

Two French phenomenologists with impeccable academic reputations have also made a peripheral contribution to ethics. One is Maurice Merleau-Ponty (1907–1961), who was most interested in the psychology and ontology of man. His *Sens et non-sens* contains material on the fringe of ethics and theology; and the book *Humanisme et Terreur* is a series of essays on the philosophy of history and Communism, in which Merleau-Ponty works out a theory of the *conscience engagée* (involved consciousness) that represents an advance beyond Sartre.[66] The other French thinker, Paul Ricoeur (1910–   ), used the phenomenological method in his *Philosophie de la volonté* (1950–1960) to develop a new approach to the affective side of man's nature. The second volume (*Finitude et culpabilité*) may be the prelude to a not yet developed phenomenological ethics.

Associated with Sartre and Simone de Beauvoir in the editing of a journal but eventually alienated as a result of a disagreement over Sartre's interests in Communism, Albert Camus (1913–1960) had a key role in the popularizing of existentialism. Camus's *Myth of Sisyphus* (1942) and *The Rebel: an Essay on Man in Revolt* (1951) are important parts of the literature of this movement. It is hardly possible to summarize what Camus represented in the field of ethical thinking, because his message is merely suggested in novels and plays. Quite opposed to systematic and rational thinking, Camus shows in his novels the complete absurdity of life. He certainly felt that academic ethics solves no practical problems. Yet Camus had a tremendous concern for people and a certain personal sincerity manifested in every line that he wrote.

In the United States, existentialism has had few adherents. One important book on phenomenological ethics (with no existentialist affiliations) has been published by Maurice Mandelbaum (1908–   ). His *Phenomenology of Moral Experience* (1955) is a scholarly effort which has a background in the thought of Max Scheler and some of the British ethicians, such as W. D. Ross and Prichard. Starting with description of four approaches to ethics—the metaphysical, psychological, sociological, and phenomenological—Mandelbaum explains that only the last employs "a direct examination of the data of men's moral consciousness."[67] Hence, his version of the phenomenological method is eductive rather than deductive: the answers to the problems of ethics are to be "educed from, and verified by, a careful and direct examination of individual moral judgments."[68]

Objecting forcefully to the separation of the normative and descriptive disciplines that has developed in much of recent ethics, Mandelbaum endeavors to bridge the gap by insisting on the generic character of moral judgments. In other words, he tried to restore the status of un-

ersal meanings in ethics.[69] From the fact that men do make moral
judgments Mandelbaum takes his start and distinguishes three levels of
uch conclusions. First, there are direct judgments of the moral rightness
or wrongness of the conduct of an individual person. Second, there
are judgments of rightness or wrongness, made at one remove from
he concrete. Third, come judgments of moral worth, concerned with
pecific traits of character or with the total character of a person.[70]
A whole later section of Mandelbaum's book treats virtues, vices, and
moral character in a fashion similar to what one would find in Max
Scheler or Nicolai Hartmann.

One of the more suggestive parts of Mandelbaum's ethics comes
with his explanation of what he regards as universally accepted principles
of moral judgment. It is here that he, quite obviously, tries to return
to the tradition of universal rules, calling his first principle that of the
primacy of the facts." Mandelbaum states it as follows: "To be valid,
the predication of a moral quality must arise as a direct response to
the apprehension of the non-moral properties which the object which
is praised or blamed actually possesses."[71] This is clearly a move in the
direction of naturalism. Mandelbaum's second rule is the "principle of
universality." Directed against relativism, it reads: "To be valid, a moral
judgment must make an assertion which is not restricted by a reference
to the conditions under which the judgment was made."[72] Finally,
Mandelbaum's principle of ultimacy states: "Any moral judgment which
is believed to be valid is incorrigible, and any incorrigible moral judgment
must be acknowledged to be binding upon thought and upon action."
In his final pages, Mandelbaum offers an impressive demonstration of
the use of these ethical principles in actual practice.[73] This effort of
Mandelbaum's represents something of a return to the rational procedures
of an earlier age but it is hardly typical of twentieth-century ethics in the
sixties.

At the end of this history of ethical theories, in which an attempt
has been made to let each type of ethics speak for itself without conscious
criticism from the writer, a word of final appraisal may be permitted.
Clearly, many of the older and more traditional kinds of ethics have
now lost their appeal for the philosophers of our time. Of course, many
people are still writing and teaching solid, but unremarkable, versions
of the various theories seen in the earlier pages of this survey. These,
however, do not represent the spirit of strictly contemporary ethics, in
which I see only three distinct approaches: naturalism, linguistic analysis,
and existentialism.

Of these three, existentialism really rejects theoretical ethics, and
language analysis offers no ethical content other than the moral attitudes
of the British gentleman who still remembers the period of Queen

Victoria. Neither a distinctive new method nor a new set of ethical judgments is forthcoming from these two schools. This leaves us with naturalism as a possible base for an ethics of the future. I do not mean that extreme position which entirely rejects the supernatural and relies on hard science only. There would seem to be some latent possibilities in a broad theory that ethical judgments might find their justification in the experienced facts of human life.

What is needed now is some spark of genius to provide a revised method of making such a reflective justification, perhaps not an entirely new method but one that will keep us open to empirical data and the dimensions of human personality, without shutting us off from the exercise of reason and the light of intuitive understanding. Some people think that "love" will take care of all of man's problems. I do not share this notion. Love is, indeed, a great virtue, but without intelligent reflection and clear factual information love easily degenerates into a dark morass of brute feeling. And I am not willing to accept that sort of thing as ethics.

Mark Twain once wrote: "To be good is noble, but to show others how to be good is nobler—and no trouble." To my mind, he was at least half right: it is an important undertaking to try to show others how to live well. Sometimes people who work at ethics forget that this is what they are really trying to do. Where Mark Twain was wrong, in my estimation, was in saying that such work is no trouble. On the contrary, ethics involves a great deal of trouble, and perhaps this survey will, at least, establish that point.

NOTES, BIBLIOGRAPHY, INDEX

Notes

CHAPTER I

1. The Greek fragments of these earliest philosophers are printed in H. els and W. Kranz, *Die Fragmente der Vorsokratiker* (Berlin: Weidmann, 56); there is a complete English translation in Kathleen Freeman, *Ancilla the Pre-Socratic Philosophers* (Oxford: Blackwell, 1948).

2. Freeman, *op. cit.* pp. 76–77 (Philolaus, frag. 14 and 22).

3. Aristotle, *Nicomachean Ethics*, II, 6; 1106a14–1107a25.

4. Freeman, *op. cit.*, p. 75 (Philolaus, frag. 11).

5. Freeman, *op. cit.*, p. 80 (frag. 3).

6. See fragments 1, 2, 45, 50, 72, and 115, in Freeman, *op. cit.*, pp. -32.

7. Joseph Owens, A *History of Ancient Western Philosophy* (New York: pleton-Century-Crofts, 1960), pp. 160–66, and C. Mazzantini, *Eraclito* orino: Vita e Pensiero, 1945), p. 24, speak of Heraclitus as the first ek moralist.

8. *Cf.* Frederick Copleston, *History of Philosophy* (Garden City, N.Y.: ubleday, 1962), Vol. 1, Pt. I, pp. 146–47.

9. Freeman, *op. cit.*, pp. 107–09 (frags. 170, 171, 187).

10. The translation of Democritus' fragment 31 is from Owens, *op. cit.*, 141.

11. Freeman, *op. cit.*, pp. 84–85 (frag. 12; *cf.* frags. 11, 13, and 14).

12. Aristotle, *Metaphysics*, I, 3–4; 984b18–985a20; compare Plato, *Phaedo*, ?–98D.

13. Aristotle, *Sophistic Elenchi*, 1; 165a21.

14. Plato, *Sophistes*, 231D.

15. Diogenes Laërtius, *Lives and Opinions of Eminent Philosophers*, trans. D. Hicks (Cambridge: Harvard University Press, 1950), IX, 51.

16. Plato, *Protagoras*, 361A–D.

17. Milton C. Nahm, *Selections from Early Greek Philosophy*, 3rd. ed. w York: Appleton-Century-Crofts, 1947, p. 239); *cf.* Plato, *Theaetetus*, A.

18. Plato, *Protagoras*, 318.

19. Nahm, *op. cit.*, citing *Pyrrhonenses Hypotyposes*, I, 216.

20. Aristotle, *Metaphysics*, IV, 5; 1008a35–1009a14.

21. Plato, *Republic*, 338C; the English is from F. M. Cornford, *Th Republic of Plato* (New York: Oxford University Press, 1956), p. 1

22. Plato, *Laws*, X, 889D–890A; trans. B. Jowett (New York: Rando House, 1937), II, 631.

23. Plato, *Gorgias*, 482E–484B.

24. *Cf.* Eduard Zeller, *Outlines of the History of Greek Philosoph* trans. L. R. Palmer (New York: Humanities Press, 1931), p. 103.

25. Miles Dawson, *The Ethics of Socrates* (New York: Putnam, 1924

26. Xenophon, *Memorabilia*, trans. E. C. Marchant (Cambridge: Harva: University Press, 1938), III, 7, 1–9, 1; *cf.* Hilda D. Oakeley, *Greek Ethic Thought from Homer to the Stoics* (New York: Dutton, 1925), p. 5

27. On the personality of Socrates, see the Platonic dialogues: *Charmid* 164D; *Phaedrus*, 230A; and *Philebus*, 45E.

28. *Nicomachean Ethics*, VI, 12; 1144b18–20.

29. Xenophon, *Memorabilia*, III, 9, 14; Plato, *Republic*, X, 621D.

30. Sören Kierkegaard, *Concluding Unscientific Postscript*, trans. D. Swenson and Walter Lowrie (Princeton, N.J.: Princeton University Pre 1944), p. 28.

31. *Cf.* R. Marcel, " 'Saint' Socrate," *Revue Internationale de Philosoph* V (1951), 135–43.

32. Diogenes Laërtius, *Lives*, II, 106; Seneca, *Epistulae*, IX, 1; on t teachings of the Megarics, see Copleston, *History*, 1, I, 138.

33. Augustine, *City of God*, XIV, 20; *cf.* Diogenes Laërtius, *Lives*, \ 69, and Cicero, *De Officiis*, I, 41.

34. Aristotle, *Metaphysics*, III, 2; 996a33.

35. Xenophon, *Memorabilia*, II, 1.

36. *Cf.* Zeller, *Outlines*, p. 132.

37. Alexander of Aphrodisias, *In Aristotelis Metaphysicam*, ed. M. H: duck (Berlin, 1891), 55, 20–57, 2.

38. *Cf.* R. N. Nettleship, *Lectures on the Republic of Plato* (Londc Macmillan, 1922; reprinted New York: St. Martin's Press, 1962), chap VII, especially p. 160.

39. Cornford, *The Republic*, p. 222.

40. The English terms for these four levels of cognition vary in differe translations. Cornford's terminology (p. 222) is used here.

41. *Cf.* Nettleship, *Lectures*, pp. 212–37; Paul Shorey, "The Idea Good in Plato's *Republic*," *Studies in Classical Philology* (Chicago, 189 Vol. I; Kevin Doherty, "God and the Good in Plato," *New Scholasticis* XXX (1956), 441–60.

42. See Basil Willey, *The English Moralists* (New York: Norton, 196 pp. 41–53.

43. For an interpretation of the intellectualism of Plato's ethics, couc in value terminology, see R. C. Lodge, *Plato's Theory of Ethics* (Lond Routledge, 1928, reprinted 1950).

44. On these stories see J. A. Stewart, *The Myths of Plato* (Lond Oxford University Press, 1905).

45. Cornford, *The Republic*, p. 356.

CHAPTER II

1. *Cf.* M. Moraux, "From the *Protrepticus* to the Dialogue *On Justice*," *Aristotle and Plato*, ed. I. Düring and G. E. L. Owen (Göteborg: Imqvist & Wiksell, 1960), pp. 113–29; see also A. H. Chroust, "Aristotle's On Justice' a Lost Dialogue," *The Modern Schoolman*, XLIII (1966) 249–3.

2. See W. D. Ross, *Aristotle* (London: Methuen, 1923), pp. 14–16; ore up-to-date information is found in the Introduction to *L'Ethique à icomaque*, ed. R. A. Gauthier (Paris: Nauwelaerts, 1958), I, 1*–90*.

3. *Nicomachean Ethics* (henceforth cited as *NE*), 1102a5; *Eudemian thics* (henceforth *EE*), 1219a32; *cf.* Jean Vanier, *Le Bonheur principe fin de la morale aristotélicienne* (Paris: Desclée de Brouwer, 1965).

4. *Rhetoric*, 1360b14–28; *cf.* Vanier, p. 186.

5. *NE*, 1177b25; the translation is from W. D. Ross's version, Oxford ranslation, Vol. VIII.

6. Gauthier, *op. cit.*, p. 569, notes that duty, in various verbal forms, curs 170 times in the Greek text of *NE*.

7. *NE*, 1105b20–1106a11; *EE*, 1220b11.

8. See Vanier, p. 53, with his criticism of J. D. Monan, *The Doctrine Moral Knowledge in Aristotle's Proptrepticus, Eudemian and Nicomachean thics* (Louvain: Nauwelaerts, 1959).

9. *NE*, 1096a20–1097b15; *cf.* Enrico Berti, *L'Unità del Sapere in Aristotele* 'adova: Cedam, 1965).

10. See *NE*, 1107b1–1108b10; *EE*, 1220b25–1222b15.

11. *NE*, 1130b30–1131a9.

12. For the discussion of voluntariness, see *NE*, 1109b30–1111b3; on e contemporary value of this theory, consult P. H. Nowell-Smith, *Ethics* altimore: Penguin, 1954), p. 292.

13. *NE*, 1139b15–1141a19; for the moral dimensions of practical wisdom *hronēsis*) see 1141a20–1144a35.

14. *NE*, 1144b9–10; see Pierre Aubenque, *La Prudence chez Aristote* aris: Presses Universitaires, 1963).

15. On pleasure, *NE*, 1174b15–1175a20; for a hedonistic interpretation Aristotle (which is not generally accepted) see J. Léonard, *Le Bonheur ez Aristote* (Bruxelles: Palais des Académies, 1948).

16. *NE*, 1177b26–28.

17. *EE*, 1249b15–24.

18. See Benjamin Farrington, *Greek Science* (Baltimore: Penguin, 1949), 17–27.

19. *Cf.* R. Walzer, *Greek into Arabic: Essays on Islamic Philosophy* ambridge: Harvard University Press, 1962), Essay 9: "New Light on len's Moral Philosophy."

20. See Odon Lottin, *Psychologie et Morale* (Gembloux: Duculot, 1942), 278–80; Daniel Callus, "The Date of Grosseteste's Translations," *Recher-s de Théologie Ancienne et Médiévale*, XIV (1947) 200–208; F. Van enberghen, *Aristotle in the West* (Louvain: Nauwelaerts, 1955).

CHAPTER III

1. Zeno is sometimes credited with introducing a technical term for duty (*to kathekon*) into Greek; it is found earlier in Plato's *Statesman*, 295B.

2. See Benson Mates, *Stoic Logic* (Berkeley: University of California Press, 1953); and H. Ritter et L. Preller, *Historia Philosophiae Graecae* (Gotha: Perthes, 1913), p. 411.

3. Trans. T. W. Rolleston, in *The Teaching of Epictetus* (London: Walter Scott, 1888), pp. 1–2.

4. See Copleston, *History of Philosophy*, 1, II, 139.

5. Cicero, *De natura deorum*, II, 11, 30–33, reports this teaching.

6. For this sophisticated Stoic psychology, see G. Verbeke, *L'Evolution de la doctrine du pneuma* (Louvain-Paris: Desclée, 1945), pp. 90–142.

7. *Cf.* A. P. Wagener, "Reflections of Personal Experience in Cicero's Ethical Doctrine," *Classical Journal*, XXXI (1935–36) 359–70; Milton Valente, *L'Ethique Stoicienne chez Cicéron* (Paris: Saint-Paul, 1956).

8. See W. C. Korfmacher, "Stoic *apatheia* and Seneca's *De clementia*," *Transactions American Philological Assoc.*, LXXVII (1946), 44–52; K. D. Nothdurft, *Studien zum Einfluss Senecas auf die Philosophie und Theologie des zwoelften Jahrhunderts* (Leiden: Brill, 1963).

9. Epictetus, *Enchiridion*, trans. George Long (Philadelphia: Altemus 1908), p. 56.

10. Epictetus, *Moral Discourses*, trans. W. A. Oldfather (Cambridge Harvard University Press, 1928), p. 97.

11. Marcus Aurelius, *Meditations*, ed. and trans. C. R. Haines (Cambridge Harvard University Press, 1930), V, 27, and XII, 1.

12. *Ibid.*, XI, 1.

13. *Cf.* W. W. Tarn, *Hellenistic Civilization* (New York: Longmans 1927), pp. 266–81.

14. Diogenes Laërtius, *Lives*, X, 30–34, is our chief source of information on this aspect of Epicurus' thought.

15. See the letter from Epicurus to Menoeceus in Epicurus, *The Extant Remains*, ed. Cyril Bailey (Oxford: Clarendon Press, 1926); *cf.* A. Festugière, *Epicurus and His Gods*, trans. W. Chilton (Cambridge: Harvard University Press, 1956).

16. *Cf.* John Ferguson, *Moral Values in the Ancient World* (London Methuen, 1958; New York: Barnes & Noble, 1959), p. 149; the quotation i from the Letter to Menoeceus.

17. Epicurus, *The Letters, Principal Doctrines, and Vatican Sayings*, tran R. M. Geer (Indianapolis: Library of the Liberal Arts, 1964), pp. 27–28.

18. Lucretius, *De rerum natura: On the Nature of Things*, trans. W. H. D Rouse (Cambridge: Harvard University Press, 1959); see the opening line of Bks. I, III, and V.

19. *Ibid.*, III, 1. 1081.

20. *Ibid.*, V, 1. 1019.

21. See Hans Lewy, *Three Jewish Philosophers* (New York: Harper, 1960), p. 109–10, for a detailed list of the writings of Philo Judaeus.

22. Philo Judaeus, *De opificio mundi*, I, 69–71, and IV, 16; in *Philo*, I. F. H. Colson and G. H. Whitaker (Cambridge: Harvard University ress, 1929), Vol. I; compare Lewy, *op. cit.*, pp. 54–55.

23. Philo Judaeus, *On the Migration of Abraham*, 9–11; in Lewy, p. 72.

24. H. A. Wolfson, in *Philo*, 2 vols. (Cambridge: Harvard University ress, 1948), possibly exaggerates Philo's influence on the Middle Ages.

25. Plutarch, *Moralia: Morals*, 14 vols., ed. and trans. F. C. Babbitt *et al.* Cambridge: Harvard University Press, 1927–58); in spite of the vast scope nd promising title of this work, it contains little evidence of original thinking ethics.

26. See G. H. Clark, *Selections from Hellenistic Philosophy* (New York: ppleton-Century-Crofts, 1940), pp. 211–16.

27. On this metaphysics consult A. H. Armstrong, *The Architecture of e Intelligible Universe in the Philosophy of Plotinus* (London: Cambridge niversity Press, 1940).

28. Cf. Plotinus, *The Ethical Treatises*, trans. Stephen MacKenna (Lon-n: Medici Society, 1926).

29. See Emile Bréhier's comment in *Ennéades* (Paris: Les Belles Lettres, 24–38), especially I, 94.

30. *Ennead*, IV, 8, 1; my English version is adapted from Bréhier's French, , 216.

31. See H. van Lieshout, *La Théorie plotinienne de la vertu* (Paderborn: höningh, 1926).

32. *Ennead*, VI, 9, 11; cf. Bréhier, *Ennéades*, VI, 188.

33. See Ferguson, *Moral Values in the Ancient World*, pp. 99–100; and pleston, *History of Philosophy*, 1, II, 221–24.

CHAPTER IV

1. For general information on the Fathers of the Church, see Johannes asten, *Patrology*, 4 vols. Westminster, Md.: Newman Press, 1950–66).

2. See R. B. Brandt, "The Use of Authority in Ethics," in *Ethical eory* (Englewood Cliffs, N.J.: Prentice-Hall, 1959), pp. 56–82; for the itrary view, that Christian ethics is the only adequate ethics, see Jacques iritain, *Science and Wisdom*, trans. Bernard Wall (New York: Scribner's, 40); and R. C. Mortimer, *Christian Ethics* (London: Hutchinson Uni-sity Library, 1950).

3. Emil Brunner, *The Divine Imperative* (Philadelphia: Westminster ss, 1947), p. 83.

. This terminology is used in T. E. Hill, *Contemporary Ethical Theories* ew York: Macmillan, 1950), pp. 97–113, to describe similar types of ntieth-century ethics.

. Matt. 5:17; Confraternity trans. (1941), p. 14.

. See Bardaisan of Edessa, *The Book of the Laws of Countries* (Syriac t plus English version), by H. J. W. Drijvers (Assen, Netherlands: Van

Gorcum, 1965); and the same scholar's biographical and doctrinal study, *Bardaisan of Edessa*, id., 1966.

7. On Hippolytus, see Étienne Gilson, *History of Christian Philosophy in the Middle Ages* (New York: Random House, 1954), pp. 24–26, 563–65.

8. See Gilson, *op. cit.*, pp. 33–35, 565–69.

9. *On First Principles*, III, 1, 13, and I, 8; see the trans. by G. W. Butterworth (London: Society for the Promotion of Christian Knowledge, 1936; reprinted, New York: Harper Torchbooks, 1966), pp. 181 and 67; cf. Jean Daniélou, *Origen*, trans. W. Mitchell (New York: Sheed & Ward, 1955), pp. 73–98.

10. *On First Principles*, III, 1–6; trans. Butterworth, pp. 161–249.

11. Gregory of Nyssa's *De hominis opificio* and *De vita Moysis* are now being critically edited under the direction of Werner Jaeger *et al.*; see Gilson, *op. cit.*, p. 583.

12. The immediate source for the Pseudo-Dionysius seems to be Proclus' *De subsistentia mali*.

13. *On the Divine Names*, chap. 4, sec. 24; trans. C. E. Rolt (London: Society for the Promotion of Christian Knowledge, 1920), p. 123.

14. *Ibid.*, sect. 9; trans. Rolt, pp. 98–99.

15. *Ibid.*, sect. 30; Rolt's trans. (p. 126) is modified here to conform to the Greek.

16. Thomas Aquinas (*In librum De divinis nominibus*, lectio 22, n. 572; ed. C. Pera, p. 213) will later make extensive use of this teaching.

17. See Gilson, *op. cit.*, p. 88.

18. My translation is made from *De fide orthodoxa*, MS Paris, Bibliothèque Nationale, 14557, fol. 204vb–205va, as transcribed by O. Lottin, *Revue Thomiste*, XXXVI (1931), 631.

19. For *bulesis* and *thelesis* in Thomas Aquinas, see *Summa Theologiae*, I, 83, 4, *ad primum*; and III, 18, 3c.

20. See O. Lottin, *Psychologie et Morale*, I, 393–424; and Vernon J Bourke, *Will in Western Thought* (New York: Sheed & Ward, 1964), pp 55–76.

21. For a discussion of the meaning of this notorious statement from *The Flesh of Christ* (chap. 5), see Gilson, *op. cit.*, p. 45.

22. *Adversus Praxean*, 12–18; trans. in *Writings of Tertullian* (Edinburgh Clark, 1870), XV, 357–72.

23. Pierre de Labriolle, *Histoire de la littérature latine chrétienne* (Paris Les Belles Lettres, 1947), I, 124.

24. *Cf.* de Labriolle, *op. cit.*, pp. 299–300.

25. Ambrose, *De officiis ministrorum*, is analyzed in N. E. Nelson, *Cicero' De officiis in Christian Thought* (Ann Arbor: University of Michigan Pres 1933); *cf.* R. Thamin, *Saint Ambroise et la morale chrétienne au IV siècle* (Paris: Masson, 1895).

26. For the evidences of Plotinian influence in Ambrose's *De Isaac e anima*, VII, 60–79, see Pierre Courcelle, *Recherches sur les Confessions d saint Augustin* (Paris: De Boccard, 1950), pp. 106–38.

27. See, for instance, Joseph Fletcher, *Situation Ethics* (Philadelphia: Westminster Press, 1966), p. 81.

28. Brief texts on ethical questions are found in *The Essential Augustine*, l. V. J. Bourke (New York: Mentor, 1964), chap. VII; for longer Latin lections, see G. Armas, *La Moral de San Agustin* (Madrid: Difusora del libro, 1954).

29. *Sermon* 150, in Quincy Howe, Jr., *Selected Sermons of St. Augustine* New York: Holt, Rinehart and Winston, 1966), pp. 89–110.

30. *De beata vita*, trans. as *The Happy Life*, by L. Schopp (New York: Fathers of the Church, Inc., 1948), I, 43–84.

31. *Cf.* Michael Schmaus, *Die psychologische Trinitätslehre des hl. Augustinus* (Münster: Aschendorff, 1927).

32. See *The Essential Augustine*, pp. 48–57.

33. *De libero arbitrio*, II, 19, 52; *Sermo* 341, 6, 8; *cf.* E. Gilson, *The Christian Philosophy of St. Augustine* (New York: Random House, 1960), t. I, chap. 5, for the theory of divine illumination.

34. *De Genesi ad litteram*, XII, 31, 59; trans. J. H. Taylor, in *The Essential Augustine*, p. 97.

35. For Augustine's views on law and morality, see *Confessions*, III, 7, 8; *Letter* 157, 15; *De libero arbitrio*, I, 6, 15; and Gustave Combès, *La doctrine politique de s. Augustin* (Paris: Plon, 1927); and Alois Schubert, *Augustins Lex-aeterna-Lehre nach Inhalt und Quellen* (Münster: Aschendorff, 1924).

36. *In Joannis Epistolam ad Parthos*, 4, 7, 8.

37. *Enarrationes in Psalmos*, 118, *Sermo*, X, 5.

38. *City of God*, VIII, 8; trans. G. Walsh *et al.* (New York: Doubleday Image Book, 1958), p. 155.

39. The best secondary work is Joseph Mausbach, *Die Ethik des hl. Augustinus* (Freiburg im Breisgau: Herder, 1909).

40. *In Isagogen Porphyrii*, ed. prima, I, 3 (Corpus Scriptorum Ecclesiasticorum Latinorum, XLVIII, 8–9); *De Trinitate*, ed. and trans. H. Stewart and E. K. Rand (Cambridge: Harvard University Press, 1918), pp. 8–12; Thomas Aquinas, *The Division and Methods of the Sciences*, trans. A. Maurer (Toronto: Pontifical Institute of Mediaeval Studies, 1953).

41. See Stewart and Rand, *op. cit.*, pp. 40–42.

42. *Cf.* J. Mariétan, *Le Problème de la classification des sciences d'Aristote à saint Thomas* (Paris: Alcan, 1901).

43. Stewart and Rand, *op. cit.*, p. 50; *cf.* Charles Fay, "Boethius' Theory of Goodness and Being," in *Readings in Ancient and Medieval Philosophy*, ed. James Collins (Westminster, Md.: Newman Press, 1960), pp. 164–72.

44. "Confitendum est summum deum summi perfectique boni esse plenissimum," Boethius, *De consolatione philosophiae*, III, 10, *prosa*; in Stewart and Rand, *op. cit.*, p. 268.

45. This is the view of Alois Dempf, *Ethik des Mittelalters* (München-Berlin: Oldenbourg, 1927), p. 56.

46. *On the Division of Nature*, I, 1, trans. in Herman Shapiro, *Medieval Philosophy* (New York: Random House, 1964), pp. 85–103.

47. *On the Division of Nature*, IV, 7; trans. in R. P. McKeon, *Selections from Medieval Philosophers* (New York: Scribner's, 1929), I, 117.

48. *Cf.* Gilson, *History of Christian Philosophy*, pp. 125–27.

49. Aimé Forest, *Le Mouvement doctrinal du IXe au XIVe siècle* (Paris: Bloud et Gay, 1951), p. 63.

50. *Liber de voluntate*, in *Patrologia Latina*, CLVIII, 487–90; *De concordia*, PL 158, 538–40; *cf.* J. Sheets, "Justice in the Moral Thought of St. Anselm," *The Modern Schoolman*, XXV (1948), 132–39.

51. *De veritate*, chap. 11; trans. McKeon, *op. cit.*, I, 172.

52. "Rectitudo voluntatis propter se servata," *ibid.*, chap. 12; in McKeon, I, 173–79.

53. "Potestas servandi rectitudinem voluntatis propter ipsam rectitudinem," *De libero arbitrio*, III; PL 158, 494.

54. *Ethica*, chap. 3; trans. by J. R. McCallum as *Abailard's Ethics* (Oxford: Blackwell, 1935); sixteen chapters are reprinted in Shapiro, *op. cit.*, see especially Shapiro, pp. 137, 141.

55. *Ibid.*, 12; in Shapiro, p. 162.

56. See Richard Thompson, "The Role of Dialectical Reason in the Ethics and Theology of Abelard," *Proceedings of the American Catholic Philosophical Association*, XII (1936), 141–48, who traces the theory of evil consent back to Augustine, *De continentia*, I, 23.

57. *De gratia et libero arbitrio*; see the English analysis in G. B. Burch, *Early Medieval Philosophy* (New York: King's Crown Press, 1951), pp. 90–93.

58. *On the Necessity of Loving God*, chap. 13; trans. in A. C. Pegis, *The Wisdom of Catholicism* (New York: Random House, 1949), p. 262.

59. Twelfth-century moral philosophy has not yet been fully studied; some idea of the possibilities may be gleaned from Philippe Delhaye research articles; see, for example, "L'Enseignement de la philosophie morale au XIIe siècle," *Mediaeval Studies*, XI (1949), 77–99.

60. *Cf.* Steven Runciman, *The Medieval Manichee* (Cambridge, Eng: University Press, 1947); and P. Alphandéry, *Les idées morales des hétérodoxes latins au debut du XIIIe siècle* (Paris: Leroux, 1903).

61. Joachim Abbatis, *Liber contra Lombardum*, ed. C. Ottaviano (Roma: Reale Accademia d'Italia, 1934); *cf.* H. Bett, *Joachim of Flora* (London: Cambridge Univ. Press, 1931); and M. W. Bloomfield and Marjorie E. Reeves, "The Penetration of Joachism into Northern Europe," *Speculum*, XXIX (1954), 772–93.

CHAPTER V

1. Wisdom 11:21 and 8:1.

2. Exodus 20:3–17; the translation is from *The Jerusalem Bible*, e Alexander Jones (Garden City, N.Y.: Doubleday, 1966), p. 102. Another listing of these precepts is found in Deut. 5:6–21.

3. Levit. 24:17–21.

4. For other formulations of the golden rule in various religious doc

ents, see Dagobert Runes, *Pictorial History of Philosophy* (New York: hilosophical Library, 1955), p. vii.

5. See Maimonides, *The Guide of the Perplexed*, trans. Shlomo Pines Chicago: University of Chicago Press, 1963), p. 509; also W. S. Sahakian, *stems of Ethics and Value Theory* (Paterson, N.J.: Littlefield, Adams,)64), p. 176.

6. *Cf.* Israel I. Efros, *Ancient Jewish Philosophy: A Study in Metaphysics d Ethics* (Detroit: Wayne State University Press, 1964), p. 179, note 22; a *kadosh* and *kavod*, see pp. 7–10.

7. For the sake of uniformity dates are given in the Christian Era.

8. Saadia ben Josef, *Kitab al-'Amanat wa'l-'I'tikadat* (Arabic original citten in 933), ed. S. Landauer (Leiden, 1880); trans. by Alexander ltmann as *Book of Doctrines and Beliefs*, in *Three Jewish Philosophers* 'hiladelphia: Jewish Publication Society, 1945; reprinted New York: arper Torchbooks, 1965); see Altmann, "Prolegomena," pp. 26–31.

9. *Ibid.*, chap. 3, sect. 2; Altmann, p. 94.

10. *Ibid.*, p. 97; Altmann adds that Saadia's use of the Arabic term akl) for "reason" indicates the influence of Mu'tazilite, and more re-otely, Stoic teachings here.

11. *Ibid.*, pp. 99–100, 111–15.

12. *Avencebrolis Fons Vitae*, ex arabico in latinum translatus ab Johanne ispano et Dominico Gundissalino, ed. C. Baeumker (BGPM I, 2–4) Münster: Aschendorff, 1892–95); see III, sects. 24–32, pp. 136–155.

13. *Cf.* Julius R. Weinberg, *A Short History of Medieval Philosophy* 'rinceton, N.J.: Princeton University Press, 1964), pp. 148–49.

14. Jehuda Halevi, *Book of Kuzari*, trans. Hartwig Hirschfeld (New rk: Pardes Publishers, 1946); abbreviated version by Isaak Heinemann, *Three Jewish Philosophers*, see pp. 86–90.

15. *Ibid.*, Bk. II, sects. 48–50, pp. 76–78.

16. *Ibid.*, Bk. V, sect. 27, p. 128.

17. Bahya ibn-Pakuda, *Hovot Halevavot*, trans. by Moses Hyamson as ties of the Heart, 5 vols. (New York: Bloch, 1925–47); the quotation is m V, 27.

18. *Cf.* Leon Roth, *The Guide for the Perplexed: Moses Maimonides* ondon: Hutchinson's Library, 1950), p. 58. (This is a doctrinal study, t a translation.) The best English version of the *Guide* is that by Shlomo es, cited above in note 5.

19. The influence of this view on Thomas Aquinas has often been noted; : Gilson, *History of Christian Philosophy*, p. 650.

20. *Guide for the Perplexed*, I, 72, and III, 27; see Pines, pp. 190 and 511.

21. J. S. Minkin, *The World of Moses Maimonides, with Selections m His Writings* (New York: Yoseloff, 1957), pp. 243–44, citing Mai-nides, *Repentance*, V.

22. *Guide*, III, 54; Pines, p. 630; *cf.* Roth, *op. cit.*, p. 119, citing Maimon-s, *Eight Chapters*, V.

23. *Cf.* Roth, *op. cit.*, p. 119; and Minkin, p. 188, where the passage m *Fundamental Principles* is quoted.

24. Maimonides, *Ethical Conduct*, Deot I, in Minkin, pp. 394–95.

25. *Guide*, II, 40; and III, 34.

26. *Guide*, III, 27; trans. from Pines, p. 511.

27. *Guide*, II, 36; this quotation is from the version in R. Lerner and M. Mahdi, *Medieval Political Philosophy: A Sourcebook* (New York: Free Press, 1963), p. 202.

28. See the text of this *Letter*, in Minkin, pp. 28–29.

29. Maimonides, *Eight Chapters*, VIII, in Minkin, p. 245; see also the *Letter on Astrology*, in Lerner and Mahdi, pp. 227–36.

30. *Deot* III, trans. in Roth, p. 107.

31. *Guide*, III, 26, in Pines, pp. 506–10.

32. On these three thinkers, see Isaac Husik, A *History of Medieval Jewish Philosophy* (Philadelphia: Jewish Publication Society, 1941), pp. 323–27, 329–61, and 388–405.

33. Joseph Albo, *Book of Principles*, V; the quotation is from Husik's version, reprinted in Lerner and Mahdi, p. 240.

34. In the *Tahdhib al-Akhlaq* of Miskawaihi, for instance; cf. M. M. Sharif, ed., A *History of Muslim Philosophy*, 2 vols. (Wiesbaden: Harrassowitz, 1963), see I, 475.

35. See D. M. Donaldson, *Studies in Muslim Ethics* (London: Society for the Promotion of Christian Knowledge, 1953), pp. 118–20.

36. Donaldson, *op. cit.*, pp. 136–37.

37. See Ezio Franceschini, *Il 'Liber philosophorum moralium antiquorum'* (Roma: Bardi, 1930).

38. Brief summaries of the moral teaching of the Koran are given in Donaldson, *op. cit.*, pp. 14–59, and in Sharif, *op. cit.*, pp. 136–55.

39. Cf. A. Badawi, "Muhammad ibn Zakariya Al-Razi, Moral Philosophy," in Sharif, I, 434–49.

40. For the extensive literature on al-Farabi, see Nicholas Rescher, *Al-Farabi: An Annotated Bibliography* (Pittsburgh: University of Pittsburgh Press, 1962); of original works of al-Farabi we have in English, *The Fusul al-Madani of al-Farabi* (*Aphorisms of the Statesman*), ed. and trans. by D. M. Dunlop (London: Cambridge University Press, 1961); and *The Philosophy of Plato and Aristotle*, trans. Muhsin Mahdi (New York: Free Press, 1962).

41. *Enumeration of the Sciences*, chap. 5; in Lerner and Mahdi, *op. cit.*, pp. 24–30.

42. Donaldson, *op. cit.*, studies this theory in detail, pp. 148–55.

43. *The Political Regime*, trans. F. M. Najjar, in Lerner and Mahdi, p. 34; cf. p. 61.

44. Al-Ameri, *As-Sa'adah Wa'l-Is'ad*, facsimile of copy by Mojtaba Minov (Teheran University) (Wiesbaden: Steiner Verlag, 1957–58).

45. Donaldson, *op. cit.*, p. 125.

46. Badawi, A., "Miskawaihi, Ahma ibn-Muhammad," in Sharif, *op. cit* I, 474, citing the Cairo, 1928, edition of *Tahdhib*, pp. 15–19.

47. Badawi, *op. cit.*, p. 476.

48. For a transcription of the Latin version, see *Avicenna De Anima* ed. G. P. Klubertanz (St. Louis, Mo.: The Modern Schoolman, 1949); the corresponding portion of the *Najat* is printed as *Avicenna's Psychology*

Arabic text and trans. F. Rahman (New York: Macmillan, 1952); chaps. 10–15.

49. *Cf.* G. P. Klubertanz, *The Discursive Power* (St. Louis, Mo.: The Modern Schoolman, 1952), pp. 89–105.

50. See H. Corbin, *Avicenna and the Visionary Recital,* trans. W. P. Trask (New York: Pantheon Books, 1960).

51. A. M. Goichon, *Le récit de Hayy ibn-Yaqzan,* commenté par textes d'Avicenne (Paris: Desclée, 1959).

52. The version by Corbin and Trask includes a *Commentary* by an unidentified Persian contemporary, indicating the popularity of the story of Hayy.

53. Avicenna, *On the Divisions of the Rational Sciences,* in Lerner and Mahdi, p. 97.

54. Al-Ghazzali, *Deliverance from Error,* trans. W. M. Watt, in *The Faith and Practice of al-Ghazzali* (London: Allen and Unwin, 1953), pp. 19–86.

55. *Cf.* Donaldson, *op. cit.,* p. 134.

56. *Ibid.,* p. 135.

57. *Cf.* Abdul Khaliq, "Al-Ghazzali, Ethics," in Sharif, *op. cit.,* I, 624–25.

58. Al-Ghazzali, *Ihya,* III, 48–50; trans. in Donaldson, *op. cit.,* pp. 142–43.

59. For detailed references, see Donaldson, *op. cit.,* p. 137.

60. *The Romance of the Rubaiyat,* ed. by A. J. Arberry, of Edward Fitzgerald's First Edition reprinted with Introd. and Notes (London: Macmillan: 1959).

61. Ibn Hazm, *Kitab al-Akhlaq Wa-l-Siyar, Epitre morale,* texte et traduction par Nada Tomiche (Beyrouth: Commission Internationale pour la Traduction des Chefs-d'Oeuvre, 1961).

62. Ibn Bajja, *Governance of the Solitary,* trans. L. Berman, in Lerner and Mahdi, pp. 131–32.

63. See M. S. H. Al-Ma'sumi, "Ibn Bajjah, Ethics," in Sharif, *op. cit.,* 523–24.

64. See also the Letter of Farewell, in Salomon Munk, *Mélanges de philosophie juive et arabe* (Paris: Franck, 1859), pp. 383–418.

65. Ibn Tufail, *Hayy the Son of Yaqzan,* trans. G. N. Atiyeh, in Lerner and Mahdi, *op. cit.,* p. 160.

66. B. H. Siddiqi, "Ibn Tufail," in Sharif, *op. cit.,* I, 537.

67. See *Encyclopaedia Britannica,* 14th ed., IX, 849.

68. Weinberg, *op. cit.,* p. 131; and Luis Alonso, *Teologia de Averroes* (Madrid: Instituto 'Miguel Asin,' 1947), p. 121.

69. Averroës, *Decisive Treatise,* trans. G. Hourani, in Lerner and Mahdi, p. 171, 172, and 178.

70. *Ibid.,* p. 169.

71. *Cf.* Klubertanz, *The Discursive Power,* pp. 110–22, with the references to Harry Wolfson's research studies.

72. *Decisive Treatise,* pp. 175–76; *cf.* Weinberg, *op. cit.,* p. 139.

73. Ahmed F. El-Ehwany, "Ibn Rushd," in Sharif, *op. cit.,* I, 364.

74. *The Nasirean Ethics,* trans. from the Persian by G. M. Wickens (London: Allen and Unwin, 1964); see the Introduction, p. 10.

75. *Ibid.*; in his note 141 Wickens gives these alternatives as suggested by George Hourani.
76. *Ibid.*, p. 49.
77. See the section on purity, *ibid.*, pp. 66–68.
78. *Ibid.*, p. 86.
79. *Ibid.*, pp. 140–41; *cf.* Donaldson, *op. cit.*, pp. 169–82.
80. See Wickens, "Introduction," p. 12.
81. On modern Islamic ethics, consult Donaldson, *op. cit.*, pp. 247–61.

CHAPTER VI

1. Crane Brinton, A *History of Western Morals* (New York: Harcourt, Brace, 1959), p. 185.
2. For Bishop Tempier's condemned propositions, see Lerner and Mahdi, *op. cit.*, pp. 335–56.
3. Brand Blanshard, *Reason and Goodness* (New York: Macmillan, 1961), p. 61.
4. *Commentary on the Nicomachean Ethics*, Bk. II, lectio 3; trans C. I. Litzinger (Chicago: Regnery, 1964), I, 126.
5. *In Ezekialem*, I, 1; PL 25, 22B.
6. *Cf.* O. Lottin, *Psychologie et Morale* (Gembloux: Duculot, 1948) Tome II, 103–350.
7. See Walter Burleigh, *Commentaria in Ethicam Aristotelis* (Venetiis 1521); *cf.* S. Harrison Thomson, "The 'Notule' of Grosseteste on the Nicomachean Ethics," *Proceedings of the British Academy*, XIX (1933)
8. *Cf.* A. C. Crombie, *Robert Grosseteste and the Origins of Experimenta Science* (Oxford: Clarendon Press, 1953).
9. Robert Grosseteste, *On Truth*, trans. in McKeon, *Selections from Medieval Philosophers*, I, 273.
10. See D. E. Sharp, *Franciscan Philosophy at Oxford in the Thirteenth Century* (London: Oxford University Press, 1930), p. 116.
11. This is translated as *Moral Philosophy*, by R. P. McKeon *et al.* in Lerner and Mahdi, *op. cit.*, pp. 355–90.
12. *Ibid.*, p. 359.
13. *Cf.* Ignatius Brady, "Law in the Summa Fratris Alexandri," *Proceedings of the American Catholic Philosophical Association*, XXIV (1950) 133–46.
14. Joanni de Rupella, *Summa de Anima*, ed. crit., Ignatius Brad (Quaracchi: Collegio San Bonaventura, 1967).
15. *Cf.* O. Lottin, *op. cit.*, Tome III, seconde partie (1949), pp. 393–42.
16. Bonaventure, *In II Sententiarum*, d. 39, 2, 1; *Opera Omnia*, II, 910
17. *Ibid.*, d. 30, 1, 1, concl.; II, 899.
18. Bonaventure, *Retracing the Arts to Theology*, trans. Sister E. Healy, reprinted in Shapiro, *Medieval Philosophy*, p. 382.
19. For more information on Albert's writings, see Gilson, *History of Christian Philosophy*, pp. 666–68.

20. Translated from a section of Albert's *Lectura* transcribed from the tuttgart MS by O. Lottin, *op. cit.*, III, seconde partie (1949), p. 544.

21. Albert, *Summa de creaturis*, II, De homine; ed. Borgnet, XXXV, 599.

22. *Summa de bono*, transcribed from MS Bruxelles Bibl. Royale 603, ol. 84 rb, in Lottin, *op. cit.*, p. 544.

23. *Cf.* Lottin, *Le droit naturel* (Bruges: Beyaert, 1931), p. 117.

24. Albert, *Commentaria in libros Ethicorum*, I, 5, 1; ed. Borgnet, VII, 7; *Summa de creaturis*, II, q. 65, 2, 3; ed. Borgnet, XXXV, 552.

25. On the relation of Thomas' ethics to the thought of his predecessors, ne of the most useful studies is Michael Wittmann, *Die Ethik des hl. 'homas von Aquin* (München: Hueber, 1933).

26. See, for instance, T. E. Hill, *Contemporary Ethical Theories*, p. 46; W. T. Jones *et al.*, *Approaches to Ethics* (New York: McGraw-Hill, 962), p. xviii.

27. *Summa Theologiae*, I–II, 90, 4, c.

28. Sahakian, *Systems of Ethics*, pp. 220–27, views Thomistic ethics in rms of self-realization.

29. Thomas Aquinas, *The Virtues*, trans. J. P. Reid (Providence, R.I.: rovidence College Press, 1951), pp. 22–51; see also *Summa Theologiae*, -II, qq. 49–56.

30. *Expositio in Job*, 11, lectio 1; see a partial translation in Vernon J. ourke, *Ethics in Crisis* (Milwaukee: Bruce, 1966), p. 125.

31. *Summa contra Gentiles*, III, 122; trans. in A. C. Pegis *et al.*, *On the ruth of the Catholic Faith* (Garden City, N.Y.: Doubleday, 1955–57), Bk. I, Pt. 2, p. 143, n. 2.

32. Boethius of Dacia, *De summo bono*, in M. Grabmann, *Mittelal-rliches Geistesleben* (München: Hueber, 1936), Bde. I, 200–204.

33. See Tempier's propositions numbered 1, 170, 171, and 172, in Lerner d Mahdi, *op. cit.*, pp. 338 and 351.

34. *Cf.* R. A. Gauthier, "Trois commentaires 'averroistes' sur l'Ethique Nicomaque," *Archives d'histoire doctrinale et littéraire*, XVI (1947–48), 7–336.

35. This letter is edited by G. Bruni in *New Scholasticism*, VI (1932), 12.

36. Giles of Rome, *De potestate ecclesiastica*, II, 6; see the English in rner and Mahdi, *op. cit.*, p. 399.

37. *Cf.* E. Bettoni, "La libertà come fondamento dei valori umani nel nsiero di Pier di Giovanni Olivi," *Atti del XII Congresso Internazionale Filosofia* (Venezia, 1958), XI, 45.

38. See A. San Cristobal-Sebastian, *Controversias acerca de la voluntad sde 1270–1300* (Madrid: Editorial y Libreria Co. Cul., 1958).

39. Henry of Ghent, *Quodlibeta*, I, q. 14; ed. Venetiis (1613), fol. 17D.

40. For details, see Gilson, *History of Christian Philosophy*, p. 352.

41. Ramón Lull, *Blanquerna*, trans. E. A. Peers (London: Jarrold, 1926), 478–79.

42. Armand Maurer, *Medieval Philosophy* (New York: Random House, 62), p. 301.

43. Eckhart, *Talks of Instruction*, trans. R. B. Blakney; reprinted in Jones, *Approaches to Ethics*, pp. 162–63.

44. Dante, *Convivio*, II, 1; and III, 15.

45. *Cf.* Efrem Bettoni, *Duns Scotus: The Basic Principles of His Philosophy*, trans. B. Bonansea (Washington: Catholic University Press, 1961), pp. 27–46, 81–86.

46. Duns Scotus, *Ordinatio*, I, d. 17, par. 1, qq. 1–2, n. 62; editio Vaticana, V (1959), 163–164; trans. Bourke.

47. Duns Scotus, *Quaestiones Quodlibetales*, q. 18, n. 3; ed. Wadding, XII, 475.

48. *Ordinatio*, prologo, pars. 5, qq. 1–2; ed. Vaticana, I, 156–58.

49. Duns Scotus, *Opus Oxoniense*, II, d. 39, qq. 1–2; this portion of the *Ordinatio* is not yet available in the Vatican edition.

50. *Ibid.*, II, d. 39, n. 926.

51. For data on William of Ockham's writings, see Philotheus Boehner Introduction, to *Philosophical Writings* (Edinburgh: Nelson, 1957).

52. See *ibid.*, pp. xxviii–xxix.

53. *Quodlibet*, I, q. 10; in Boehner, *Philosophical Writings*, p. 158.

54. *Ibid.*, q. 1; Boehner, pp. 139–40.

55. *Quodlibet*, III, q. 13; Boehner, p. 161.

56. *Ibid.*, pp. 162–63.

57. As Ockham puts it: "Eo ipso quod voluntas divina hoc vult, recta ratio dictat quod est volendum." *In I Sententiarum*, d. 41, q. 1, k; *cf In III Sent.*, d. 12, NN.

58. Henry de Bracton, *De legibus et consuetudinibus Angliae*, ed. G. E. Woodbine, 4 vols. (New Haven: Yale University Press, 1915–42).

59. Sir John Fortescue, *De laudibus legum Angliae*, chap. 16; see the trans. by S. B. Chrimes, in Lerner and Mahdi, *op. cit.*, p. 523.

60. Reginald Pecock, *The Reule of Crysten Religioun*, ed. W. C. Gree (London: Oxford University Press, 1927), pp. 24 and 227.

61. Reginald Pecock, *Book of Faith*, ed. J. L. Morison (Glasgow, 1909) p. 23.

62. Richard Hooker, *Of the Laws of Ecclesiastical Polity*, ed. J. Kebl (Oxford: Clarendon Press, 1839), I, 208.

63. *Ibid.*, I, 222.

64. *Ibid.*, I, 205.

CHAPTER VII

1. *Cf.* Rudolf Allers, "Microcosmus," in *The Philosophical Work c Rudolf Allers* (Washington, D.C.: Georgetown University Press, 1965) pp. 123–91.

2. *Oratio de dignitate hominis*, trans. M. McLaughlin, in *Portable Re aissance Reader* (New York: Viking Press, 1953), p. 478.

3. Leonardo da Vinci, *Notebooks*, trans. Edward MacCurdy (Londor Cape, 1928); reprinted in G. de Santillana, *The Age of Adventure* (Ne York: Mentor, 1956), p. 87.

4. *On Learned Ignorance*, III, 2.

5. *Ibid.*, chap. 10; trans. G. Heron, in *Unity and Reform*, ed. J. P. Dolan (Notre Dame, Ind.: Notre Dame University Press), 1962, p. 85.

6. *Ibid.*, p. 87.

7. *De pace fidei*, trans. J. P. Dolan, *op. cit.*, p. 236.

8. *Cf.* A. Maurer, *Medieval Philosophy*, p. 336.

9. Marsilio Ficino, *Platonic Theology*, trans. J. L. Burroughs, in *Portable Renaissance Reader*, p. 391.

10. Pico della Mirandola, *Of Being and Unity*, trans. V. M. Hamm (Milwaukee: Marquette University Press, 1943), pp. 33–34.

11. From J. R. Charbonnel, *L'Ethique de Giordano Bruno et le deuxième dialogue du Spaccio* (Paris: Champion, 1919), p. 210, trans. Bourke.

12. Bruno, *On the Infinite*, trans. Agapito Rey, in D. S. Robinson, *Anthology of Modern Philosophy* (New York: Crowell, 1931), p. 50.

13. Bruno, *De Monade numero et figura*, 2; trans. J. H. Pitman, in Robinson, pp. 56–57.

14. For a similar meaning of "Platonism" in contemporary philosophy, see the discussion in Morton White, *Toward Reunion in Philosophy* (Cambridge: Harvard University Press, 1956).

15. *Cf.* Copleston, *History of Philosophy*, 3, II, 134.

16. *Utopia*, trans. Ralph Robinson (New York: Lupton, 1890), p. 65.

17. *Ibid.*, pp. 65–66.

18. Elyot, *The Governour*, ed. F. Watson (New York: Dutton, 1907), p. 191.

19. *Ibid.*, pp. 298–308, for a lengthy Glossary.

20. *Cf.* Herschel Baker, *The Image of Man* (New York: Harper, 1961), p. 271.

21. See Felice Tocco, "L'Isagogicon Moralis Disciplinae di Leonardi Bruni Aretino," *Archiv für Geschichte der Philosophie*, VI (1892), 157–69.

22. The outstanding study is Bruno Nardi, *Studi sull'aristotelismo Padovano* (Firenze: Sansoni, 1958).

23. *Cf.* Maurer, *op. cit.*, p. 339.

24. See M. A. Dynnik, "Vanini et l'aristotélisme de Padoue," *Atti del XII Congresso di Filosofia* (Firenze: Sansoni, 1960), IX, 81–89.

25. Thomas Aquinas, *S.T.*, II–II, 40, 1, c.

26. Vitoria, *De jure belli*, see *Portable Renaissance Reader*, p. 367.

27. *Ibid.*, p. 371.

28. *Commentarii collegii conimbricensis, societatis Iesu . . . ethica Aristotelis* (Lugduni: Pillenotte, 1616), is but one example.

29. *Cf.* G. M. Ganss, *St. Ignatius: Idea of a Jesuit University* (Milwaukee: Marquette University Press, 1954).

30. Bellarmine, *De gratia et libero arbitrio*, 9; see Davitt, *The Nature of Law*, p. 200.

31. Selections are available in Suárez, *On the Laws*, trans. G. L. Williams et al., in *The Classics of International Law*, ed. J. B. Scott (Oxford: Clarendon Press, 1944), Vol. II.

32. Suárez, *Disputationes Metaphysicae*, VI, 2, 14; the best secondary study is J. M. Alejandro, *La gnoseologia del Doctor Eximio y la acusación nominalistica* (Comillas, Spain: Universidad Pontificia, 1948).

33. Suárez, *De Anima*, V, 3, 8.

34. For a typical explanation: Timothy Brosnahan, *Prolegomena to Ethics* (New York: Fordham University Press, 1941), p. 183; the teaching is based on Disputation X, in the *Disputationes Metaphysicae*.

35. Suárez, *De Legibus*, II, 5, 6–14.

36. *Ibid.*, sec. 9.

37. For an expanded report on this point, see Copleston, *History of Philosophy*, 3, II, 206.

38. Suárez, *De Legibus*, II, 13, 1–8.

39. *Ibid.*, II, 7, 5.

40. *De fine ultimo*, tract. III, d. XII, 1, 5, 6; in *Opera Omnia*, ed. Berton, Tome V, 438.

41. *Ibid.*, sects. 3–5; Tome V, 442–53.

42. *Cf.* Ueberweg *et al.*, *Die Philosophie der Neuzeit* (Berlin: Mittler, 1924), p. 275.

43. Giorgio de Santillana, *op. cit.*, p. 143.

44. Alasdair MacIntyre, *Short History of Ethics* (New York: Macmillan, 1966), p. 162.

45. Luther, *The Bondage of the Will*, trans. Henry Cole (Grand Rapids, Mich.: Zondervan, 1931); reprinted in Santillana, *op. cit.*, p. 148.

46. For a selection of ethical significance from Calvin's *Institutes*, see M. Mothersill, *Ethics* (New York: Macmillan, 1965), pp. 29–34.

47. *Ibid.*, p. 31.

48. *Cf.* L. G. Crocker, *Nature and Culture: Ethical Thought in the French Enlightenment* (Baltimore: Johns Hopkins Press, 1963), p. 148.

49. Leibniz, Letter to J. Thomasius, Sept. 2, 1663; in G. W. Leibniz, *Sämtliche Schriften und Briefe*, hrsg. von der Preussischen Academie der Wissenschaften, Darmstadt: Reichl, 1926, Zweite Reihe, Bde. I, p. 3.

50. On this influence, see James Collins, *Modern European Philosophy* (Milwaukee: Bruce, 1954), p. 572.

51. *The Prince*, trans. L. Ricci and C. E. Detmold (New York: Random House, 1940); reprinted in Jones, *Approaches to Ethics*, pp. 171–72.

52. Montaigne, *Essays*, 12, 2; in Santillana, *op. cit.*, pp. 177–78.

53. James Collins, *The Lure of Wisdom* (Milwaukee: Marquette University Press, 1962), pp. 25–26.

54. See Ralph Cudworth, *A Treatise concerning Eternal and Immutable Morality* (London, 1731), p. 6.

55. *Cf.* Collins, *Lure of Wisdom*, pp. 13–19.

56. Léontine Zanta, *La Renaissance du stoicisme au XVIe siècle*, (Paris: Champion 1914), pp. 225–36.

57. See R. W. Battenhouse, "Chapman on the Nature of Man," *English Literary History*, XII (1945), 89–92.

58. See the further analysis in Copleston, *History of Philosophy*, 5, I, 63.

CHAPTER VIII

1. *Advancement of Learning*, II, 20–21; see *Bacon Selections*, ed. M. T. McClure (New York: Scribner's, 1928), pp. 197–99.

2. This view of Francis Bacon is shared by Basil Willey, *The English Moralists* (New York: Norton, 1964), p. 125.

3. Hobbes, *De corpore*, 8, 10, and 25, 2; see *Hobbes Selections*, ed. F. J. E. Woodbridge (New York: Scribner's, 1930), pp. 83, 106.

4. *Leviathan*, I, 6; in Woodbridge, p. 188.

5. Henry Sidgwick, *Outlines of the History of Ethics* (London: Macmillan, 886; revised ed. of 1931, reprinted Boston: Beacon, 1964), p. 169.

6. *Philosophical Rudiments*, that is, the English version of *De Cive*; in *English Works*, ed. W. Molesworth (London: Bohn and Longmans, 839–45), II, 196.

7. *Ibid.*, cf. Woodbridge, p. 284.

8. *Elements of Philosophy, on Body*, 2, 4; *Human Nature*, 5; see Woodbridge, pp. 15–24.

9. *Questions concerning Liberty*, in *English Works*, V, 192.

10. *Leviathan*, chap. 16; in Woodbridge, p. 270.

11. *Ibid.*

12. *Leviathan*, chaps. 14–15; in Woodbridge, p. 309.

13. *Ibid.*, chap. 31; in Woodbridge, p. 384.

14. *Philosophical Rudiments*, in *English Works*, II, 50; cf. *De corpore politico*, in *Opera Philosophica*, ed. Molesworth, IV, 224.

15. John Bramhall, *A Defence of True Liberty . . . Answer to a Late Book of Mr. Thomas Hobbes* (London, 1655).

16. Cf. J. K. Ryan, "St. Thomas Aquinas and English Protestant Thinkers," *New Scholasticism*, XXII (1948), 146–58, for an account of Bramhall's argument.

17. Browne, *Christian Morals*, III, 21; cited in Willey, *The English Moralists*, p. 193.

18. For extensive discussion of these reactions to Hobbes, see John Bowle, *Hobbes and His Critics* (New York: Oxford University Press, 1952); and S. I. Mintz, *The Hunting of Leviathan* (Cambridge, Eng.: University Press, 962).

19. Culverwel, *An Elegant and Learned Discourse of the Light of Nature*, 652; in the ed. of Edinburgh, 1857, p. 162.

20. Cudworth, *Treatise concerning Eternal and Immutable Morality* (London, 1731), pp. 6–9.

21. *Treatise*, p. 17; or see B. Rand, *Classical Moralists* (Oxford: Clarendon Press, 1897), pp. 230–31.

22. *Treatise*, Bk. IV, 2, p. 148.

23. Willey, *The English Moralists*, p. 176, sees Cudworth as a preKantian.

24. See Mintz, *op. cit.*, chap. VI: "The Free-Will Controversy: Bramhall and Cudworth," pp. 126–33, especially.

25. Mintz, p. 131, gives MS citations from the unedited portions of Cudworth's A *Discourse of Liberty and Necessity*; the printed sections are in: A *Treatise of Free-Will*, ed. John Allen (London, 1838).

26. More, *Enchiridion Ethicum*, 3, 2; trans. E. K. Rand, in B. Rand, *Classical Moralists*, p. 242.

27. Richard Cumberland, A *Treatise of the Laws of Nature*, trans. J. Maxwell (London, 1727); in Rand, *Classical Moralists*, p. 248.

28. Locke, *Essays on the Law of Nature* (1660–1664), ed. Latina, W. von Leyden (New York: Oxford University Press, 1954), p. 110.

29. *Ibid.*, III, pp. 136–45.

30. *Ibid.*, pp. 146–59; *cf.* M. B. Crowe, "Intellect and Will in John Locke's Conception of Natural Law," *Atti del XII Congresso Internazionale di Filosofia* (Firenze, 1960), XII, 132–33.

31. *Essay concerning Human Understanding*, II, 21, 7; see L. A. Selby-Bigge, *British Moralists* (Oxford: Clarendon Press, 1897), II, 334.

32. *Ibid.*, 20, 2–21, 42.

33. *Ibid.*, 28, 4; in Selby-Bigge, p. 343.

34. *Ibid.*, 28, 10; in Selby-Bigge, p. 346.

35. *Ibid.*, IV, 3, 18.

36. Shaftesbury, *Inquiry concerning Virtue*, 1, 2, 3; and I, 3, 1; see the text in Selby-Bigge, I, 11–21.

37. *Ibid.*, II, 2, 3; in Selby-Bigge, I, 33.

38. John Gay, *Concerning the Fundamental Principle of Virtue or Morality*, sect. 3; in Selby-Bigge, II, 273.

39. Samuel Clarke, *Discourse on Natural Religion*, 1; in Selby-Bigge, II, 6.

40. *Ibid.*, 5; in Selby-Bigge, II, 29.

41. John Clarke, *The Foundation of Morality*; in Selby-Bigge, II, 242.

42. See Bernard Mandeville, *The Fable of the Bees*, ed. Douglas Garman (London: Wishart, 1934), pp. 82–85; the lines quoted are from Mandeville *Enquiry into the Origin of Moral Virtue*, in Selby-Bigge, II, 354–55.

43. William Wollaston, *The Religion of Nature Delineated*, 1; in Selby-Bigge, II, 362–65.

44. *Ibid.*, 8; in Selby-Bigge, II, 370.

45. *Ibid.*, 9; in Selby-Bigge, II, 372.

46. *Ibid.*, 10–11; in Selby-Bigge, II, 381–82.

47. Condillac, *Treatise on Sensations*, III, 1; the passage is translated in L. M. Marsak, *French Philosophers* (New York: Meridian, 1961), p. 196.

48. For well-chosen selections illustrating this point: L. W. Beck, *18th Century Philosophy* (New York: Free Press, 1966), pp. 164–91.

49. Franklin, *Autobiography*, ed. Herbert Schneider (New York: Liberal Arts Press, 1952), p. 90.

50. *Cf.* L. G. Crocker, *Nature and Culture: Ethical Thought in the French Enlightenment* (Baltimore: Johns Hopkins Press, 1963), p. 21.

51. Berkeley, *Principles of Human Knowledge*, 100; ed. A. C. Fraser (Oxford: Clarendon Press, 1901), II, 84.

52. This passage from the 1710 edition of Berkeley's *Principles* is r

rinted in G. Berkeley, A New Theory of Vision and Other Writings
New York: Dutton, 1925), p. 163, note 1.
53. Berkeley, Philosophical Commentaries, in Works, ed. A. A. Luce and
. E. Jessop (London: Nelson, 1948), I, 93.
54. Berkeley, Passive Obedience, in Works, VI, 19.
55. Butler, Sermons, I; in Selby-Bigge, I, 197–202.
56. Sermons, III: in Selby-Bigge, I, 224–25.
57. Butler, A Dissertation upon the Nature of Virtue, in Selby-Bigge,
246–53.
58. R. A. P. Rogers, Short History of Ethics (New York: Macmillan,
)11), p. 167.
59. Lord Kames, Essays on the Principles of Morality, II, 1–5; in Selby-
igge, II, 300–13.
60. Francis Hutcheson, Inquiry into the Original of Our Ideas of Beauty
xd Virtue, Introduction; in Selby-Bigge, I, 69.
61. Ibid., I, 8; in Selby-Bigge, I, 83.
62. Ibid., III, 8; in Selby-Bigge, I, 106–07.
63. Cf. James Bonar, The Moral Sense (Oxford: Clarendon Press, 1930),
77.
64. Hutcheson, Inquiry, III, 8; in Selby-Bigge, I, 110–11.
65. Ibid., VII; in Selby-Bigge, I, 153–54.
66. Hutcheson, Essay on the Nature and Conduct of the Passions, 1;
Selby-Bigge, I, 393–94.
67. An excellent analysis of the System of Moral Philosophy is provided
Bonar, The Moral Sense, pp. 95–99.
68. Hutcheson, System, I, 6; in Selby-Bigge, I, 420; cf. Bonar, p. 98.
69. Balguy, Foundation of Moral Goodness, art. 21; in Selby-Bigge,
195.
70. Ibid., II, art. 4; in Selby-Bigge, II, 188.
71. Cf. Henry Sidgwick, History of Ethics, pp. 218–22.
72. For the general philosophical position of Abraham Tucker, see Cople-
n, History of Philosophy, 5, I, 205.

CHAPTER IX

1. See Hans Thieme, Das Naturrecht und die Europäische Privatrechts-
chichte (Basel: Helbing, 1954).
2. See, for instance, An Encyclopedia of Religion, ed. Vergilius Ferm
few York: Philosophical Library, 1945), p. 316.
3. In a Letter to Benjamin Maurer (Epistola 154), Grotius formally
nmends Thomas' treatment of lex and jus.
4. Grotius, De jure belli et pacis, Proleg., 11.
5. For these writers, see the summary in F. Suárez, De Legibus, II, 6, 2.
5. Grotius, The Rights of War and Peace, I, 1, 10; trans. in B. Rand,
issical Moralists, pp. 208–09.
7. Leibniz, Epistolae ad Diversos, Leipzig, 1734–42, Vol. IV, n. 22.

8. Pufendorf, *Spicilegium Controversiarum*, printed in *Jus Naturae et Gentium* (Frankfurt, 1744), p. 174.

9. *Jus Naturae*, introd., p. 102.

10. *Ibid.*, I, 2, 9–10.

11. *Ibid.*, II, 3, 15.

12. See Sidgwick's severe comment on Pufendorf's lack of clarity on the golden rule, *History of Ethics*, p. 167; see also p. 270.

13. For an extended analysis, see Collins, *The Lure of Wisdom*, pp. 63–108.

14. Descartes, *Principles of Philosophy*, Preface; trans. J. Veitch (New York: Dutton, 1924), p. 153.

15. Descartes, *Discourse on Method*, in Veitch, p. 23.

16. Descartes, *Passions de l'âme*, I, 27; in Charles Adam et Paul Tannery, eds., *Descartes's Oeuvres*, XI, 349.

17. *Ibid.*, I, 45; XI, 363.

18. *Ibid.*, II, 144; XI, 436–37.

19. Descartes, *Lettre* 397, 4 août, 1645; in Adam et Tannery, IV, 263–68.

20. *Lettre* 403, 15 septembre, 1645; Adam et Tannery, IV, 290–96.

21. See Leibniz, *Monadology*, ed. R. Latta (London: Oxford University Press, 1925), p. 330, for an English version of the Geulincx text.

22. Geulincx, *Annotata ad Ethicam*, in *Opera* (The Hague: Nijhoff, 1891–93), III, 168.

23. Geulincx, *Disputationes Ethicae*, *id.*, III, 275.

24. *Cf.* Eugène Terraillon, *La morale de Geulincx dans ses rapports avec la philosophie de Descartes* (Paris: Alcan, 1912), pp. 173–74.

25. See F. Ueberweg *et al.*, *Die Philosophie der Neuzeit*, p. 247.

26. Spinoza, *Short Treatise*, I, 1, 9; see the text in H. Wolfson, *The Philosophy of Spinoza* (Cambridge: Harvard University Press, 1934), I, 71.

27. *Short Treatise*, II, 22, and App. 2; trans. in J. Wild, *Spinoza Selections* (New York: Scribner's, 1930), pp. 84–93.

28. Spinoza, *Ethics*, Pt. I, def. 3, and propositions 1–10.

29. *Ethics*, Pt. II, prop. 48.

30. *Ibid.*, prop. 11.

31. *Political Treatise*, 2, 8; trans. in *Chief Works*, by R. H. M. Elwes (London: Bell, 1883), I, 295.

32. Spinoza, *Letter to H. Oldenburg*, XXXII, 20 November 1665.

33. See Wolfson, *op. cit.*, II, 131–63, for a study of these three sorts of knowledge.

34. *Ethics*, Pt. III, def. 3.

35. *Ibid.*, props. 6–11.

36. *Ethics*, Pt. IV, preface; text cited from a modified trans. in Jones *Approaches to Ethics*, p. 203.

37. *Ethics*, Pt. V, props. 2–4.

38. *Ibid.*, props. 14–16.

39. *Ibid.*, prop. 25.

40. Spinoza, *Theological-Political Treatise*, p. 14; trans. Elwes, I, 182–87.

41. *Ibid.*, I, pp. 207–08, 246–47; *cf.* Crocker, *Nature and Culture*, pp 195–96.

42. *Theological-Political Treatise*, pp. 18–19.
43. It is so classified in Rogers, *Short History of Ethics*, pp. 143–46.
44. These works are conveniently excerpted in the *Philosophical Papers and Letters*, ed. L. E. Loemker (Chicago: University of Chicago Press, 1956).
45. This general theory is well outlined in N. Rescher, *The Philosophy of Leibniz* (New York: Prentice-Hall, 1967).
46. Leibniz, *Codex Juris Gentium*, praefatio, in Loemker, II, 690.
47. Loemker, II, 693.
48. *Ibid.*, II, 698.
49. *Ibid.*, II, 699–700.
50. *Ibid.*, II, 912–13.
51. *Ibid.*, II, 915–16.
52. Leibniz, *New Essays concerning Human Understanding*, trans. A. G. Langley (La Salle, Ill.: Open Court, 1916), II, 28, 5.
53. Rescher, *op. cit.*, pp. 137–39, attributes this "legalism" to the influence of mathematics and of Catholic theology on Leibniz.
54. See Loemker, II, 917.
55. *Ibid.*, II, 926–27.
56. Leibniz, *Philosophical Works*, trans. G. M. Duncan (New Haven: Yale University Press, 1890), pp. 231–32.
57. Leibniz, *Principles of Nature and of Grace*, 18; in Duncan, p. 217.
58. Leibniz, *Monadology*, nn. 85–86.
59. Wolff, *Preliminary Discourse on Philosophy in General*, trans. R. J. Blackwell (New York: Library of Liberal Arts, 1963), gives a good sampling of these terms.
60. Wolff, *Philosophia Practica*, I, 117.
61. *Ibid.*, I, 120.
62. Montesquieu, *Spirit of the Laws*, I, 1; trans. Thomas Nugent, reprinted in L. M. Marsak, *French Philosophers from Descartes to Sartre* (New York: Meridian, 1961), pp. 133–34.
63. Rousseau, *Discourse on the Arts and Sciences*, in *The Social Contract, and Other Works*, trans. G. D. H. Cole (New York: Dutton, 1926), p. 140.
64. Rousseau, *Contrat social*, in *Oeuvres*, ed. M. Raymond (Paris: La Pléiade, 1959), IV, 206.
65. See especially *Social Contract*, IV, 1, and the companion *Discourse on Political Economy*.
66. Cf. Bourke, *Will in Western Thought*, pp. 154–58.
67. Gerdil, *Principes métaphysiques de la morale chrétienne*, III, 2–7; in *Opere* (Rome: Poggioli, 1806–21), II, 48–70.
68. See Kant, *Lectures on Ethics*, trans. L. Infield (New York: Harper, 1963).
69. Kant, *Critique of Practical Reason*, trans. Beck (1949), p. 151.
70. Kant, *Natural Theology and Morals*, trans. Beck (1949), pp. 278–79.
71. See P. A. Schilpp, *Kant's Pre-Critical Ethics* (Evanston, Ill.: Northwestern University Press, 1938), on these early works.
72. These are in *Opus Postumum*, ed. Erich Adickes (Berlin: Reuter u. Reichard, 1920).

73. T. M. Greene, ed., *Kant Selections* (New York: Scribner's, 1929), pp. 371–74, gives some passages translated from Adickes' edition.

74. On the relation between the *Critique of Pure Reason* and Kant's ethics, see Graham Bird, *Kant's Theory of Knowledge* (New York: Humanities Press, 1962), especially pp. 189–204.

75. See this section of Bk. II, sect. 2, in Greene, pp. 195–97, 219–33.

76. Kant, *Critique of Pure Reason*, trans. N. Kemp Smith (London: Macmillan, 1933), A840–B868.

77. See *Critique of Practical Reason and Other Writings*, trans. L. W. Beck (Chicago: University of Chicago Press, 1949), pp. 53–64.

78. *Ibid.*, p. 72.

79. *Ibid.*, pp. 73–87.

80. For the important distinction between *Wille* and *Willkür* in Kant, see L. W. Beck, *Commentary on Kant's Critique of Practical Reason* (Chicago: University of Chicago Press, 1964), p. 91.

81. Beck, *Critique of Practical Reason and Other Writings*, p. 97.

82. *Ibid.*, pp. 107–15.

83. *Critique of Practical Reason*, I, 1, 7; trans. Beck (New York: Liberal Arts Press, 1956), p. 30.

84. *Ibid.*, II, 2, 3; Beck (1956), pp. 124–39.

85. *Ibid.*, I, 1, 3; Beck (1956), p. 89.

86. See Maimon, 'Ueber die ersten Gründe des Naturrechts," in *Fichte Niethammers Philosophisches Journal*, I (1795), 142.

87. *Cf.* David Baumgardt, "The Ethics of Salomon Maimon," *Journal of the History of Ideas*, I (1963), 199–210.

CHAPTER X

1. *Cf.* R. B. Brandt, *Ethical Theory* (Englewood Cliffs, N.J.: Prentice Hall, 1959), pp. 355–56, where various divisions of utilitarianism are discussed.

2. A. C. Garnett, *Ethics* (New York: Ronald Press, 1960), p. 159

3. *Cf.* Mary Warnock, "Introduction" to Mill, *Utilitarianism* (New York Meridian, 1962), p. 9.

4. *The Methods of Ethics* (New York: Dover, 1966), p. 96.

5. Cumberland, *Treatise of the Laws of Nature*, in Rand, *Classical Moralists*, p. 248.

6. *Ibid.*, I, 4; in Rand, p. 249.

7. Henry Aiken, *Hume's Moral and Political Philosophy*, p. 44.

8. *History of Ethics*, p. 205.

9. Hume, *Treatise on Human Nature*, I, 4, 6; ed. Selby-Bigge, p. 26

10. *Ibid.*, III, 1; ed. Selby-Bigge, p. 563.

11. For a more extended analysis of the argument of the *Treatise*, see Bonar, *Moral Sense*, p. 121.

12. *Treatise*, II, 1, 11; ed. Selby-Bigge, p. 320.

13. *Ibid.*, III, 3, 1; ed. Selby-Bigge, p. 576.

14. *Ibid.*, III, 1, 1; ed. Selby-Bigge, p. 541.

15. *Enquiry concerning the Principles of Morals*, III, 1; in *Hume Selections*, ed. C. W. Hendel (New York: Scribner's, 1927), p. 203.
16. *Enquiry*, III, 6, 1; in Hendel, p. 228.
17. Price, *Review*, 3; in Selby-Bigge, *British Moralists*, II, 123.
18. *Review*, 2; in Selby-Bigge, II, 120.
19. See, for instance, W. H. Werkmeister, *Theories of Ethics*, pp. 367–72.
20. Adam Smith, *Theory of Moral Sentiments*, Pt. I; in Selby-Bigge, I, 57–84.
21. *Theory*, III, 1–4; in Selby-Bigge, I, 297–306.
22. *Cf.* Bonar, *Moral Sense*, p. 175.
23. Reid, *Inquiry into the Human Mind*, 7, 4; ed. Edinburgh, 1819, 394.
24. *Essays on the Powers of the Human Mind*, ed. Edinburgh, 1819, 338.
25. See Reid's essay, "The Moral Faculty and the Principles of Morals," printed in Edwards and Pap, *A Modern Introduction to Philosophy* (New York: Free Press, 1965), pp. 288–96.
26. Ferguson, *Philosophy of the Active and Moral Powers*, 2, 5, 1; in *Collected Works* (Edinburgh, 1854), VI, 299.
27. *Cf.* R. B. Perry, *Philosophy of the Recent Past* (New York: Scribner's, 1926), p. 17.
28. P. J. Stanlis, *Edmund Burke and the Natural Law* (Ann Arbor: University of Michigan Press, 1965).
29. Burke, *Philosophical Inquiry*, 2nd. ed. (London, 1757), pp. 25–26.
30. Burke, *An Appeal from the New to the Old Whigs* (London, 1891), 19.
31. *Cf.* H. E. Cushman, *A Beginner's History of Philosophy* (Boston: Houghton Mifflin, 1920), II, 359.
32. Paley, *Principles*, II, 6.
33. See *Mill on Bentham*, in *Utilitarianism*, ed. Mary Warnock, p. 81.
34. Stuart Hampshire, "Fallacies in Moral Philosophy," *Mind*, LVIII (1949), 473–75.
35. For this text from Blackstone's *Commentaries*, see A. V. Dicey, *Introduction to the Study of the Law of the Constitution* (London: Macmillan, 1939), p. 62.
36. Bentham, *Fragment*, 54; in *Utilitarianism*, ed. Mary Warnock, p. 13.
37. Bentham, *Introduction to the Principles of Morals*, 1, 3; in Selby-Bigge, I, 340.
38. Helvétius, *De l'Esprit* (Paris, 1758); Essay II is on *Probity*; for a trans., see Rand, *Classical Moralists*, pp. 471–75.
39. Helvétius, *De l'Homme* (Paris, 1772); the trans. by William Hooper (1777) is reprinted in part in R. E. Dewey *et al.*, *Problems of Ethics* (New York: Macmillan, 1961), p. 8.
40. *Mill on Bentham*, in *Utilitarianism*, ed. Warnock, p. 123.
41. For this footnote, see *Utilitarianism*, ed. Warnock, p. 33.
42. This is the judgment of Sidgwick, *History of Ethics*, p. 272.
43. Mary Warnock, "Introduction" to *Utilitarianism*, pp. 22–23.
44. Richard Whateley, *Paley's Moral Philosophy* (London, 1859).

45. Newman, *Grammar of Assent*, 4, 2; in *The Essential Newman*, ed. V. F. Blehl (New York: Mentor, 1963), pp. 290–95.
46. Newman, *Fifteen Sermons*, in *The Essential Newman*, pp. 320–21.
47. *Grammar of Assent*, 9; in *The Essential Newman*, p. 327.
48. Martineau, *Types of Ethical Theory*, II, 29.
49. Martineau, *Study of Religion*, 2 vols. (Oxford: Clarendon Press, 1888).
50. Mill, *Logic of the Moral Sciences*, ed. H. M. Magid (New York: Bobbs-Merrill, 1965), p. 27.
51. *Ibid.*, pp. 37–53.
52. *Ibid.*, p. 145.
53. *Ibid.*, p. 147.
54. Austin, *The Province of Jurisprudence Determined*, lect. II; in *Utilitarianism*, ed. Warnock, p. 325; see also p. 23.
55. Mill, *Utilitarianism*, 1; ed. Warnock, p. 252.
56. *Ibid.*, p. 257.
57. *Ibid.*, p. 279.
58. *Ibid.*, pp. 307–08.
59. Sidgwick, *The Methods of Ethics* (London: Macmillan, 1874; reprinted, New York: Dover, 1966); see pp. 83–87.
60. *Ibid.*, pp. 381–82.

CHAPTER XI

1. Fichte, *Vocation of Man*, III; ed. R. M. Chisholm (New York: Liberal Arts Press, 1956), p. 106.
2. *Ibid.*, pp. 93–95.
3. Fichte, *System der Sittenlehre*, in the trans. of A. E. Kroeger, in Rand, *Classical Moralists*, p. 574.
4. Fichte, *The Nature of the Scholar*, lectures delivered in 1805, lect VII; see J. Collins, *Modern European Philosophy*, p. 563.
5. Frank Thilly and Ledger Wood, *A History of Philosophy*, 3rd ed (New York: Holt, 1957), p. 475.
6. Schleiermacher, *Monologues*, trans. H. L. Friess (Chicago: Open Court 1928); the second monologue is reprinted in Robinson, *Anthology of Modern Philosophy* (New York: Crowell, 1931), pp. 523–36.
7. *Cf.* H. A. Reyburn, *The Ethical Theory of Hegel* (Oxford: Clarendon Press, 1921), p. xiii.
8. See Hegel, *Early Theological Writings*, trans. T. M. Knox (Chicago University of Chicago Press, 1948), pp. 205–09.
9. Hegel, *Phenomenology of Mind*, trans. J. Baillie (London: Macmillan 1931), pp. 149–78: here, the dialectic is applied to sense certainty an perception.
10. *Cf.* Reyburn, *op. cit.*, p. 76.
11. *Phenomenology of Mind*, trans. Baillie, pp. 625–26.
12. Hegel, *Philosophy of Right*, sec. 44; these section nos. are retained i the Dyde and Knox versions, and also in Sterrett's digest.
13. *Ibid.*, sec. 75.

14. *Ibid.*, sec. 82.

15. See the Baillie trans., p. 381.

16. *Philosophy of Right*, secs. 142–57.

17. *Ibid.*, sec. 142; trans. S. W. Dyde, reprinted in Rand, *Classical* oralists, p. 605.

18. *Ibid.*, sec. 137; see Reyburn's comments, *op. cit.*, pp. 173–74.

19. Eugen Fink, *Sein, Wahrheit, Welt* (The Hague: Nijhoff, 1958), p. , denies such an influence; for the opposed view, see E. Gilson, T. Langan, d A. Maurer, *Recent Philosophy: Hegel to the Present* (New York: ndom House, 1966), p. 679.

20. *Philosophy of Right*, sec. 152; trans. Dyde, in Rand, pp. 608–09.

21. *Ibid.*, sec. 158.

22. Hegel, *Philosophy of History*, trans. J. Sibree (New York: Willey, 00), p. 47.

23. *Cf.* W. T. Stace, *The Philosophy of Hegel* (New York: Dover, 1955), 374–438; and the whole argument in Sidney Hook, *From Hegel to Marx* ew York: Reynal & Hitchcock, 1936; reprinted, New York: Humanities ss, 1950).

24. Herbart, *Textbook in Psychology*, trans. M. K. Smith (New York: pleton, 1891), III, 1; Robinson, *op. cit.*, p. 635.

25. *Ibid.*, trans. Smith; in Robinson, p. 634.

26. See the appraisal in Thilly and Wood, *History of Philosophy*, p. 495.

27. Beneke, *Grundlinien des natürlichen Systems der praktischen Philos-* ie (Berlin, 1837), I, 3; partly trans. in Rand, *Classical Moralists*, p. .

28. Schelling, *Philosophische Untersuchungen über das Wesen der mensch-* en Freiheit, in *Werke* (München: Hueber, 1928), IV, 244.

29. See Bourke, *Will in Western Thought*, pp. 205–08, for an extended lysis of this theory of volition.

30. Schopenhauer, *The World as Will and Idea*, IV, 54.

31. *Ibid.*, sec. 55.

32. *Ibid.*, sec. 58.

33. *Ibid.*, sec. 66.

34. *Ibid.*, sec. 71; trans. R. B. Haldane and J. Kemp (London: Kegan l, Trench, 1883–86).

35. Schopenhauer, *Essay on the Freedom of the Will*, trans. K. Kolenda w York: Liberal Arts Press, 1960), p. 93.

36. *Ibid.*, p. 97.

37. Schopenhauer, *On the Basis of Morality*, trans. E. F. J. Payne (New k: Library of Liberal Arts, 1965), pp. 49–115; his discussion of Fichte's cs is on pp. 115–19.

38. *Ibid.*, in Payne, p. 144.

39. *Ibid.*, p. 204.

40. Stirner's views are well outlined in Narcyz Lubnicki, "L'Homme et aleur," *Memorias del XIII Congreso de Filosofía* VII (Mexico, 1964), ff.

41. Lotze, *Microcosmus*, III, 1; trans. E. Hamilton and E. E. C. Jones w York: Scribner's, 1887), I, 286–87.

42. *Ibid.*, IX, 4, 2.

CHAPTER XII

1. See the outline of Brownson's views in Gilson-Langan-Maurer, *Recen Philosophy*, pp. 567–87.
2. For this objectivism in French idealism consult Gilson-Langan, *Moder. Philosophy* (New York: Random House, 1963), p. 99.
3. Malebranche, *A Treatise of Morality*, trans. James Shipton, in Ran(*Classical Moralists*, p. 286.
4. *Ibid.*, p. 293.
5. *Cf.* Gilson-Langan, *Modern Philosophy*, pp. 104–06.
6. These words of Henri Gouhier are quoted in Gilson-Langan-Maure *Recent Philosophy*, p. 182.
7. Maine de Biran, *Fondements de la psychologie*; see the text in H Gouhier, *Oeuvres choisies de Maine de Biran* (Paris: Aubier, 1942), p. 8
8. Maine de Biran, *Nouveaux essais d'anthropologie*, in *Oeuvres*, XIV 333.
9. *Ibid.*, p. 275; for more data on this voluntarism, see Bourke, *Will i Western Thought*, p. 94.
10. *Nouveaux essais*; English version from Gilson-Langan-Maurer, *Rece* *Philosophy*, pp. 189–90.
11. *Ibid.*, p. 236.
12. Rosmini, *The Origin of Ideas* (London: Kegan Paul, 1886), pars. 42ξ 33.
13. Gilson-Langan-Maurer, *Recent Philosophy*, p. 251.
14. Gioberti, *Della protologia*, ed. G. Balsamo-Crivelli (Torino: Paravi 1924), pp. 103–07.
15. Gioberti, *Del buono*, 8; in edition of Bruxelles: Méline, 1848, p 387–88.
16. For this nationalism, see Gilson-Langan-Maurer, *Recent Philosoph* pp. 255–61.
17. Renouvier, *Future of Science*, trans. by A. D. Vandam and C. Pitman (London: Chapman and Hall, 1891); this section is reprinted Marsak, *French Philosophers*, p. 362.
18. *Ibid.*, in Marsak, p. 369.
19. For a summary of Taine's critique of Cousin, see Gilson-Langa Maurer, *Recent Philosophy*, p. 758.
20. Guyau, *L'Irreligion de l'avenir* (Paris: Alcan, 1887), p. IX.
21. *Ibid.*, p. 346.
22. *Ibid.*, p. 350.
23. This theory is developed throughout Boutroux, *De la contingence c lois de la nature* (Paris: Germer-Baillière, 1874).
24. Boutroux, "La psychologie du Mysticisme," in Jean Baruzi, *Philosoph et savants français* (Paris: Alcan, 1926), I, 60–61.
25. Bergson, *L'Evolution Créatrice* (Paris: Alcan, 1907), p. 270.
26. Bergson, *Les deux sources de la morale et de la religion* (Par Alcan, 1932), p. 5.
27. *Ibid.*, p. 25.

28. *Ibid.*, pp. 287–88.

29. *Ibid.*, p. 243; in the English version by Audra and Brereton, pp. 27–28.

30. This is the judgment of E. Gilson, in *Recent Philosophy*, p. 316.

31. Brunschvicg, *Philosophie de l'esprit* (Paris: Presses Universitaires, 1949), Leçon 16.

32. Brunschvicg, *La raison et la religion* (Paris: Presses Universitaires, 1939), p. 74.

33. *Cf.* Roger Mehl, "Situation de la philosophie religieuse en France," *L'Activité philosophique*, ed. M. Farber, II, 273–76.

34. Colin Smith, *Contemporary French Philosophy* (London: Methuen, 1964), p. 107.

35. Le Senne's essay, "On the Philosophy of the Spirit," is available English in *Philosophic Thought in France and the U.S.*, ed. M. Farber, p. 103–20.

36. Le Senne, *Le devoir* (Paris: Presses Universitaires, 1930), p. 84.

37. *Ibid.*, p. 270.

38. Le Senne. *Traité de morale générale* (Paris: Presses Universitaires, 1942), pp. 685–711.

39. *Ibid.*, p. 702.

40. *Cf.* Colin Smith, *op. cit.*, p. 202.

41. *Ibid.*, p. 48.

42. See Francisco Romero, "Deustua, Korn, Molina y Vaz Ferreira, en ralelo," *Revista Mexicana de Filosofía*, I (1958), 19–21.

43. Vasconcelos, *Etica* (Madrid: Aguilar, 1932), pp. 20–26.

44. Vasconcelos, "The Aesthetic Development of Creation," *Philosophy d Phenomenological Research*, IX (1949), 463.

45. Vasconcelos, *Raza Cosmica* (Mexico: Espasa, 1948), p. 38.

46. A portion of Zubiri's *Naturaleza, Historia, Dios* (Madrid: Editorial acional, 1944), has been digested in English as "Socrates and Greek isdom," *Thomist*, VII (1944), 40–45.

47. *Naturaleza, Historia, Dios*, p. 369.

48. *Ibid.*, p. 370.

49. See Ferrater Mora, José, "The Philosophy of Xavier Zubiri," in *European Philosophy Today*, ed. George Kline (Chicago: Quadrangle Books, 1965), pp. 24–25.

50. Sciacca, "La Struttura della libertà nella 'costituzione' ontologica 'uomo," in *Memorias del XIII Congreso Internacional de Filosofía*, I Mexico, 1963), 26–27, trans. Bourke.

CHAPTER XIII

. Vico, *Politics and Morals*, trans. S. J. Castiglione (New York: Philohical Library, 1945), p. 65.

. *De universi juris uno principio*, I, 13.

. *Ibid.*, axioms 14–16.

. Deschamps, *Le vrai système* (Paris: Alcan, 1939), pp. 83–84.

5. Deschamps, *La voix de la raison* (Bruxelles, 1770), pp. 11–15.
6. Cf. Crocker, *Nature and Culture*, pp. 117–18.
7. *Histoire de Juliette*, IV, 178–79; the trans. is from Crocker, *ibid.* p. 198.
8. Condorcet, *The Progress of the Human Mind*, see the "Introduction," printed in L. M. Marsak, *French Philosophers*, pp. 266–69.
9. See Marsak, *ibid.*, pp. 279–81.
10. Condorcet's Letter I, in Marsak, p. 308.
11. *Ibid.*, p. 322.
12. On the American influence from Fourier, see Gilson *et al.*, *Recent Philosophy*, pp. 266, 751–52.
13. Jacques Maritain, *Moral Philosophy* (New York: Scribner's, 1964) pp. 261–350, provides a very detailed study of Comte's place in the history of ethics.
14. *The Positive Philosophy of Auguste Comte*, trans. H. Martineau (London, 1853), I, 1.
15. *Ibid.*, I, 20–24.
16. *Ibid.*, II, 312.
17. *General View of Positivism*, trans. J. H. Bridges (London: Routledge 1910), pp. 378–85.
18. This is from the Appendix by Pierre Laffitte to Comte's *Catéchisme positiviste*, p. 329; cited in English in Maritain, *Moral Philosophy*, p. 326.
19. *Ibid.*, Appendix, p. 59.
20. Cf. Jean Wahl, "The Present Situation of French Philosophy," in *Philosophic Thought in France and the United States*, ed. M. Farber (Buffalo, N.Y.: University of Buffalo, 1950), p. 38.
21. *Capital* (Moscow: Foreign Languages Publishers, 1954), I, 20.
22. See *The Economic and Philosophical Manuscripts*, trans. T. B. Bottomore, in E. Fromm, *Marx's Concept of Man* (New York: Ungar, 1961) Appendix.
23. *Ibid.*, for selected texts on Marxian "alienation," see Mann-Kreyche Approaches to Morality, pp. 253–60.
24. Isaiah Berlin, *Karl Marx—His Life and Environment* (New York: Oxford University Press, 1963), p. 140.
25. Cf. T. E. Hill, *Contemporary Ethical Theories*, pp. 141–45; and Jacques Maritain, *Moral Philosophy*, pp. 253–60.
26. Engels, *Anti-Dühring*, trans. E. Burns (New York: International Publishers, 1939), p. 110.
27. See the text in Mann-Kreyche, *Approaches to Morality*, pp. 274–7
28. Kautsky, *Ethics and the Materialist Conception of History*, trans. J. Askew (Chicago: Kerr, 1918).
29. Further analysis of Kautsky's ethics in Hill, *Contemporary Ethical Theories*, pp. 146–48.
30. See the selection "Socialism and Religion," from Lenin's *Selected Work* (New York: International Publishers, 1935–38), Vol. XI, Pt. III, in J. Hartmann, *Philosophy of Recent Times* (New York: McGraw-Hill, 1967 II, 123–26.
31. Lenin, *Materialism and Empirio-Criticism*, ed. C. Dutt, in *Collect*

'orks (Moscow: Foreign Languages Publishers, 1960), Vol. XIV; for selec-
·ns, see Edie, Russian Philosophy (Chicago: Quadrangle Books, 1965),
{, 410–36.
32. Cf. G. Wetter, Dialectical Materialism (New York: Praeger, 1958),
ap. 10.
33. See L. Labedz, Revisionism: Essays on the History of Marxist Ideas
Jew York: Praeger, 1962), pp. 166–78.
34. G. Kline, European Philosophy Today (Chicago: Quadrangle Books,
·65), pp. 136–37.
35. Cf. Viktor Antolin, "Communist Morality," Philosophy Today, I
·957), 107–08.
36. Soloviev, The Justification of the Good, trans. N. Duddington (London:
·nstable, 1918), p. 474.
37. This is the appraisal of Boris De Schloezer, "Un penseur russe:
·on Chestov," Mercure de France (Paris, 1922), pp. 82–115.
·8. Berdyaev, The Destiny of Man, trans. N. Duddington (New York:
·rper Torchbook, 1960), p. 15.
·9. Berdyaev, Dialectique existentielle (Paris: Janin, 1947), pp. 96–97.
·0. The Destiny of Man, pp. 40, 126–53.
·1. Berdyaev, Subjectivism and Individualism in Social Philosophy, trans.
Kline, in Edie, Russian Philosophy, III, 155.
·2. This point is well developed in R. Borzaga, Contemporary Philosophy
·lilwaukee: Bruce, 1966), pp. 245–48.
·3. Gilson et al., Recent Philosophy, p. 283.
·4. Lévy-Bruhl, La Morale et la science des moeurs (Paris: Alcan, 1903);
: English is adapted from S. Deploige, The Conflict between Ethics and
·iology (St. Louis: Herder, 1938), p. 187.
·5. Hill, Contemporary Ethical Theories, pp. 90–91, classifies Lévy-Bruhl's
·ught as a social approbative ethics.
·6. See for this summary of Rauh's view, E. Forti, "La Méthode scien-
·que en morale et en psychologie suivant l'oeuvre de Frédéric Rauh," Revue
métaphysique et de morale, XLI (1934), 22.
·7. Croce, "The Absolute Spirit," Proceedings of the Sixth International
·ngress of Philosophy (New York: Longmans, Green, 1926), pp. 551–54;
·1s. R. Piccoli, in Robinson, Anthology of Recent Philosophy (New York:
·well, 1929), pp. 162–65.
·8. Croce, Filosofia della pratica (Bari: Laterza, 1909), p. 133; cf. ibid.,
·245, and Elementi di politica (Bari: Laterza, 1925), where Croce speaks
·the "amoralità della politica."
·9. Filosofia della pratica, p. 139.
·o. Croce, Etica e Politica (Bari: Laterza, 1931), pp. 291, 324; and
Adriano Bausola, Etica e Politica nel pensiero di Benedetto Croce
·ilano: Vita e Pensiero, 1966), p. 133.
·1. Etica e Politica, pp. 327, 347.
·2. Croce, The Conduct of Life, trans. Arthur Livingston (New York:
·court, Brace, 1924), p. 270.
·3. Ibid., pp. 271–73.
·4. Gentile, Introduzione alla filosofia (Firenze: Sansoni, 1933), p. 49.

55. Gentile, *Genesi e struttura della società* (Firenze: Sansoni, 1946) pp. 46–67.

56. Ginsberg, "On the Diversity of Morals," in *Essays* (London: Heine mann, 1956), Vol. I; partly reprinted in Jones *et al., Approaches to Ethics* pp. 484–93.

57. Gobineau, *The Inequality of Human Races*, trans. A. Collins (New York: Holt, 1915), pp. 145–46, 207.

58. *Ibid.*, p. 205.

59. Lagarde, *Deutsche Schriften* (Göttingen, 1878), Bd. I, pp. 72–76 317.

60. Chamberlain, *The Foundations of the Nineteenth Century*, trans.] Lees (New York: Lane, 1912), p. 321.

61. Rosenberg, *Der Mythus des 20 Jahrhunderts* (München: Hoheneicher 1938), p. 268.

CHAPTER XIV

1. Urban, "Metaphysics and Value," *Contemporary American Philosophy* II (1930), 361, "The term 'axiological' was coined by me wholly inde pendently"; but on its earlier use, see E. S. Brightman, "Axiology," *Dictionar of Philosophy* (New York: Philosophical Library, 1942), pp. 32–33.

2. Perry, *General Theory of Value* (New York: Longmans, Green, 1926) pp. 115–20.

3. Brentano, *Psychologie vom empirischen Standpunkte* (Leipzig: Meine 1874), I, 111.

4. For English passages illustrating Brentano's theory of "objects," see] Chisholm, *Realism and the Background of Phenomenology* (Glencoe, Ill Free Press, 1960), pp. 39–75.

5. Meinong, "The Theory of Objects," trans. in Chisholm, pp. 76–11'

6. *Ibid.*, p. 109.

7. See Chisholm's *Introduction*, *ibid.*, p. 11.

8. Scheler, *The Nature of Sympathy*, trans. Peter Heath (New Haver Yale University Press, 1954), develops the theory of these feelings; s the analysis in Manfred Frings, *Max Scheler* (Pittsburgh: Duquesne Ur versity Press, 1965), p. 56.

9. *Cf.* James Collins, "The Moral Philosophy of Max Scheler," *Enc clopedia of Morals* (1956), pp. 517–24.

10. Scheler, *Der Formalismus in der Ethik* (Halle, 1913), I, 267–7

11. *Ibid.*, pp. 312–19; *cf.* Frings, *op. cit.*, pp. 67–80.

12. *Ibid.*, pp. 110–17; *cf.* W. H. Werkmeister, *Theories of Ethics*, p 259–60.

13. *Ibid.*, pp. 120–25.

14. *Ibid.*, p. 49.

15. *Ibid.*, pp. 200–25; *cf.* Frings, *op. cit.*, pp. 103–32; and Werkmeist *op. cit.*, pp. 261–67.

16. See, for instance, I. M. Bochenski, *Contemporary European Philosop* (Berkeley: University of California Press, 1956), p. 212; and Oliver Johnso *Ethics: Selections* (New York: Holt, Rinehart, 1965), p. 380.

17. Hartmann, *Ethics*, trans. Stanton Coit (London: Allen & Unwin, 932), I, 183–231.

18. On Hartmann's view of values as essences, see the texts in Jones *t al.*, *Approaches to Ethics*, pp. 453–55.

19. Hartmann, *Ethics*, I, 86, 100–02, 179; cf. Werkmeister, *op. cit.*, pp. 67–68.

20. Hartmann, *Ethics*, II, 25.

21. *Ibid.*, p. 52.

22. This table is condensed from *Ethics*, II, 170–380.

23. *Ethics*, I, 248 and 304; II, 247–50.

24. *Ethics*, III, 135–80.

25. Sorley, "Value and Reality," *Contemporary British Philosophy*, II 1925), 254–55.

26. Sorley, *Moral Values and the Idea of God* (Cambridge, Eng.: University Press, 1918), p. 238.

27. Urban, *Valuation. Its Nature and Laws* (New York: Macmillan, 1909), · 54.

28. Urban, *Fundamentals of Ethics* (New York: Holt, 1930), p. 16; cf. L. Blau, *Men and Movements in American Philosophy* (New York: rentice-Hall, 1952), p. 305.

29. *Fundamentals of Ethics*, pp. 353, 399.

30. *Ibid.*, p. 240.

31. Urban, *Beyond Realism and Idealism* (New York: Macmillan, 1949),). 207–08.

32. Urban, *Humanity and Duty* (New York: Macmillan, 1951), pp.)5–96; cf. Blau, *op. cit.*, pp. 302–12, for a good appraisal of Urban's hics.

33. Schlick, *Problems of Ethics*, trans. D. Rynin (New York: Prentice-all, 1939), pp. 8–28.

34. *Ibid.*, p. 17.

35. *Ibid.*, pp. 117–18.

36. *Ibid.*, pp. 142–56.

37. For this judgment, see R. B. Brandt, *Ethical Theory* (New York: entice-Hall, 1959), p. 314.

38. Lewis, *An Analysis of Knowledge and Valuation* (La Salle, Ill.: Open)urt, 1946), pp. 386–87.

39. Brightman, *Moral Laws* (New York: Abingdon Press, 1933), pp. 89–91, 5.

40. Cf. A. Reck, *Recent American Philosophy* (New York: Pantheon, 64), pp. 311–36.

41. Parker, *Human Values* (New York: Harper, 1931), p. 34.

42. For a further estimate, see Hill, *Contemporary Ethical Theories*, pp. 4–35.

43. Werkmeister, *Theories of Ethics* (Lincoln, Neb.: Johnsen, 1961), p. o.

44. See Jesse Mann, ed., *The Philosophical Work of Rudolf Allers: A ?ection* (Washington, D.C.: Georgetown University Press, 1965), p. 118.

45. Cf. J. V. Walsh, "Love and Philosophy," in *The Human Person and ? World of Values, A Tribute to Dietrich von Hildebrand*, ed. B. V. ıwarz (New York: Fordham University Press, 1960), pp. 36–48.

CHAPTER XV

1. Martineau, *Types of Ethical Theory* (Oxford: Clarendon Press, 1891 II, 25; the sub-quotations are from F. H. Bradley, *Ethical Studies*, p 207–08, and T. H. Green, *Prolegomena to Ethics*, p. 97.
2. *Ibid.*, II, 270.
3. *Ibid.*, II, 266; for the full table, see W. S. Sahakian, *Systems of Ethi* (Paterson, N.J.: Littlefield, Adams, 1964), pp. 93–94.
4. Green, *Prolegomena to Ethics* (Oxford, 1890), p. 191.
5. *Ibid.*, pp. 210–63.
6. Bradley's Essay II is reprinted in Melden, *Ethical Theories*, pp. 345–5
7. *Ibid.*, p. 357.
8. Bradley's *Essay* "Duty for Duty's Sake" is reprinted in Jones, A *proaches to Ethics*, pp. 369–70; for fuller analysis, consult A. J. M. Miln *The Social Philosophy of English Idealism* (London: Allen & Unwin, 1962 pp. 56–86.
9. These articles by Bosanquet run from Vol. 4 (1894) to Vol. (1910) in the journal now entitled *Ethics*.
10. Bosanquet, "Life and Philosophy," *Contemporary British Philosopf* I (1924), 58.
11. Rashdall, *The Theory of Good and Evil* (Oxford: Clarendon Pre 1907), Bk. II, chap. 3.
12. See the selection from Rashdall, *op. cit.*, in R. E. Dewey, *Proble* *of Ethics* (New York: Macmillan, 1961), pp. 257–60.
13. Ross, *The Right and the Good* (Oxford: Clarendon Press, 193(pp. 3–42.
14. *Ibid.*, p. 140.
15. Ross, *Foundations of Ethics* (Oxford: Clarendon Press, 1939), 10–11.
16. *Ibid.*, pp. 54–56.
17. *Ibid.*, pp. 148, 186.
18. Prichard, "Does Moral Philosophy Rest on a Mistake?" *Mind*, X (1912), 487–99; this article is frequently reprinted in books of readi in ethics.
19. Royce, *The Religious Aspect of Philosophy* (Boston, 1885), pp. 4 30.
20. Royce, *The Conception of God* (New York: Macmillan, 1898), 43.
21. Royce, *The World and the Individual* (New York: Macmillan, 190 I, 341–42.
22. *The Religious Aspect of Philosophy*, p. 27.
23. *Ibid.*, p. 149.
24. Royce, *The Philosophy of Loyalty* (New York: Macmillan, 190 lect. III, sect. 7, pp. 183–89.
25. Royce, *The Problem of Christianity* (New York: Macmillan, 191 II, 425.

26. This is the view of R. Le Senne, *Traité de morale générale*, (Paris: resses Universitaires, 1942), pp. 534–35.

27. Santayana, *Realms of Being* (New York: Scribner's, 1942), p. 474.

28. Santayana, *The Life of Reason, Reason in Common Sense* (New ork: Scribner's, 1906), p. 236.

29. Santayana, "Brief History of My Opinions," *Contemporary American hilosophy*, II (1930), 249.

30. Santayana, *Skepticism and Animal Faith* (New York: Scribner's, 1923), 77.

31. *Ibid.*, p. 129; cf. Hill, *Contemporary Ethical Theories*, p. 209.

32. Santayana, *Realms of Being*, p. 473.

33. See the excellent study of Jordan, in Reck, *Recent American Philos- hy*, (New York: Pantheon, 1964), pp. 276–310.

34. *Cf.* H. C. McElroy, *Modern Philosophers: Western Thought Since ant* (New York: Moore, 1950), p. 234.

35. Schweitzer, *Civilization and Ethics*, trans. John Naish (New York: acmillan, 1923), p. xvi.

36. See A. C. Garnett, *Ethics* (New York: Ronald Press, 1960), pp. 3–06, for two representative selections.

37. Wright, *Self-Realization. An Outline of Ethics* (New York: Holt, 24), chaps. 5 and 6.

38. Stace, *Religion and the Modern Mind* (New York: Lippincott, 1952), ap. 11.

39. Blanshard, *Reason and Goodness* (New York: Macmillan, 1961), pp. –69, for the ethics of feeling in St. Francis.

40. *Ibid.*, p. 409.

41. *Ibid.*, p. 397.

42. See Hare, *Freedom and Reason* (Oxford: Clarendon Press, 1963), p. 2.

43. Braithwaite, *Theory of Games as a Tool for the Moral Philosopher* ambridge: University Press, 1963), p. 9.

44. See W. E. Frankena, *Ethics* (New York: Prentice-Hall, 1963), pp. –35; and R. B. Brandt, *Ethical Theory* (New York: Prentice-Hall, 1959), . 396–400.

45. Smart, *An Outline of a System of Utilitarian Ethics* (Melbourne: elbourne University Press, 1961), pp. 6–7.

46. *Ibid.*, pp. 20–26.

47. *Ibid.*, pp. 29–32.

48. *Ibid.*, p. 14.

49. Singer, *Generalization in Ethics* (New York: Knopf, 1961), pp. 193– 4.

50. *Ibid.*, pp. 4, 67–68.

51. *Ibid.*, pp. 5, 17–20.

52. *Ibid.*, pp. 217–37.

CHAPTER XVI

1. Moore, *Principia Ethica*, chap. 1, secs. 10–14.
2. *Cf.* C. D. Broad, "Some of the Main Problems of Ethics," *Philosophy,* XXI (1946), 99; George Nakhnikian, "Contemporary Ethical Theories and Jurisprudence," *Natural Law Forum*, II (1957), 8.
3. See Vergilius Ferm, "Varieties of Naturalism," in *History of Philosophical Systems* (New York: Philosophical Library, 1950), pp. 429–40
4. This point is stressed in McGlynn-Toner, *Modern Ethical Theories* (Milwaukee: Bruce, 1962), pp. 63–64.
5. *Cf.* Nakhnikian, *art. cit.*, pp. 7–8.
6. Darwin, *Descent of Man* (New York: Appleton, 1876), p. 612.
7. Spencer, *Principles of Ethics*, Pt. I, chap. 2, n. 4; reprinted in Rand, *Classical Moralists*, pp. 682–88.
8. *Ibid.*, nn. 105–06; in Rand, pp. 698–702.
9. T. H. Huxley, *Evolution and Ethics* (London, 1893); cited in Blanshard, *Reason and Goodness* (London: Allen & Unwin, 1961), p. 381
10. Kropotkin, *Etika*, ed. N. K. Lebedev (Moskva, 1923); trans. as *Ethics Origin and Development*, by L. S. Friedland and J. R. Piroshnikoff (New York: Deal Press, 1924).
11. *Cf.* Hill, *Contemporary Ethical Theory*, pp. 126–27.
12. Stapledon, *A Modern Theory of Ethics* (London: Methuen, 1929) p. 251.
13. For Freud's ethical view, see McGlynn-Toner, *Modern Ethical Theories*, pp. 115–38; and Hill, *Contemporary Ethical Theories*, pp. 36–44.
14. He is so classified in Hill, *ibid.*, p. 37.
15. *Cf.* Philip Rieff, *Freud: The Mind of the Moralist* (Garden City N.Y.: Doubleday, 1961), p. 161.
16. Freud, *Beyond the Pleasure Principle*, trans. J. Strachey (New York Liveright, 1922), chap. 4.
17. Freud, *General Introduction to Psychoanalysis*, trans. Joan Riviere (New York: Garden City, 1943), p. 296.
18. Freud, *The Ego and the Id* (London: Hogarth, 1923), p. 30; for a fuller secondary account, consult Rieff, *op. cit.*, pp. 29–69.
19. This is Rieff's interpretation, *ibid.*, pp. 329–60.
20. *Cf.* J. P. Dougherty, "Introduction," in Mann-Kreyche, *Approaches t Morality*, p. 292.
21. James, *The Moral Philosopher and the Moral Life*, in *Essays o Faith and Morals* (New York: Meridian, 1962), p. 185.
22. *Ibid.*, pp. 185–205; the quotation is from p. 205.
23. Dewey, *Theory of the Moral Life* (New York: Holt, Rinehart Winston, 1960), p. 5; in the original *Ethics* (New York: Holt, 1908), p. 17
24. *Theory of the Moral Life*, pp. 59–60.
25. Dewey, *Reconstruction in Philosophy* (New York: Mentor, 1953), p 132–33.
26. Dewey, *Human Nature and Conduct* (New York: Holt, 1922), p 87–88.

27. On this point, see Rieff, *op. cit.*, p. 31.

28. *Human Nature and Conduct*, p. 227.

29. *The Quest for Certainty* (New York: Minton, Balch, 1929), pp. 260–75.

30. Dewey, *Theory of Valuation* (Chicago: University of Chicago Press, 1939), pp. 33–34.

31. *Ibid.*, pp. 28–35.

32. See L. Saxe Eby, *The Quest for Moral Law* (New York: Columbia University Press, 1944), p. 186.

33. Whitehead, *Science and the Modern World* (New York: Mentor, 1956), pp. 173–80.

34. Perry, *General Theory of Value* (Cambridge: Harvard University Press, 1926), pp. 115–24; see also Sahakian, *Systems of Ethics*, pp. 381–85.

35. Perry, *The Moral Economy* (New York: Scribner's, 1909), pp. 11–15.

36. *General Theory of Value*, pp. 630–36.

37. *Ibid.*, p. 682.

38. *Cf.* Hill, *Contemporary Ethical Theories*, pp. 129–31.

39. Teilhard de Chardin, *The Divine Milieu* (New York: Harper Torchbook, 1965), pp. 121–44.

40. *Ibid.*, p. 114.

41. *Cf.* James Collins, *Three Paths in Philosophy*, pp. 186–87.

42. Wilfrid Desan, "Introduction," in Mann-Kreyche, *Approaches to Morality*, pp. 579–80.

43. Macbeath, *Experiments in Living* (London: Macmillan, 1952), lecture 13; partly reprinted in R. E. Dewey, *Problems of Ethics*, pp. 375–80.

44. *Cf.* Margaret Mead, "Some Anthropological Considerations concerning Natural Law," *Natural Law Forum*, VI (1961), 51–64.

45. Pepper, *Ethics* (New York: Appleton-Century-Crofts, 1960), pp. 314–15.

46. *Ibid.*, pp. 326–35.

47. Maritain, *Science and Wisdom* (New York: Scribner's, 1940), p. 81.

48. Leclercq, "Natural Law the Unknown," *Natural Law Forum*, VII (1962), 15.

49. Leclercq, *Du droit naturel à la sociologie* (Paris: Spes, 1960), II, 02; three paragraphs from this passage are translated in my *Ethics in Crisis*, p. 113.

50. Fromm, *Escape from Freedom* (New York: Rinehart, 1941), pp. 4–26.

51. *Ibid.*, p. 105.

52. Fromm, *Man for Himself* (New York: Rinehart, 1947), pp. 8–12.

53. *Ibid.*, pp. 133–34.

54. *Ibid.*, pp. 16–20.

55. Fromm, *The Sane Society* (New York: Rinehart, 1955), pp. 7–69.

56. *Ibid.*, pp. 29–30.

57. Olson, *The Morality of Self-Interest* (New York: Harcourt, Brace, 1965), pp. v, 157–74.

58. Russell, *Mysticism and Logic*, pp. 46–57.

59. *Morality of Self-Interest*, pp. 176–77.

60. Lamont, *Humanism as a Philosophy* (New York: Philosophical Library 1949), pp. 273-97.

61. Vivas, *The Moral Life and the Ethical Life* (Chicago: University of Chicago Press, 1950), pp. 177-80.

62. *Ibid.*, pp. 326-46.

63. Rice, *On the Knowledge of Good and Evil* (New York: Random House, 1955), p. 109.

64. *Ibid.*, p. 122.

65. *Ibid.*, pp. 194, 255.

66. Edel, "Some Trends in American Naturalistic Ethics," in *Philosophi Thought in France and the U.S.* (Buffalo: Publications of the Universit of Buffalo, 1950), p. 610.

67. Romanell, *Toward a Critical Naturalism* (New York: Macmillar 1958), pp. 41-42, 44.

68. Foot, "Moral Arguments," *Mind*, LXVII (1958), 502-13; reprinte in Margolis, *Contemporary Ethical Theory* (New York: Random Hous 1966), pp. 176-90.

69. Edwards, *The Logic of Moral Discourse* (Glencoe, Ill.: Free Pres 1955), pp. 179-82.

70. E. M. Adams, *Ethical Naturalism and the Modern World-Vie* (Chapel Hill, N.C.: University of North Carolina Press, 1960), offers strongly critical view of the whole movement.

CHAPTER XVII

1. Hume, *Treatise of Human Nature*, ed. L. A. Selby-Bigge (1888), p 468-69.

2. Maritain, *Neuf Leçons sur les notions premières de la philosoph morale*, p. 42.

3. This division has become standard; cf. W. K. Frankena, *Ethics*, (Engl wood Cliffs, N.J.: Prentice-Hall, 1963), pp. 1-10.

4. Moore, *Principia Ethica* (Cambridge, Eng.: University Press, 1903 chap. 5, nn. 88-89.

5. Cf. Mary Warnock, *Ethics Since 1900* (London: Oxford Universi Press, 1960), pp. 48-51.

6. Moore, *Ethics* (London: Oxford University Press, 1965), p. 55.

7. *Ibid.*, p. 83; italics in the original.

8. *Ibid.*, p. 47.

9. *Ibid.*, p. 31.

10. Moore, "Reply to My Critics," in *The Philosophy of G. E. Moo* ed. P. A. Schilpp (Evanston, Ill.: Northwestern University Press, 194 p. 554.

11. *Ibid.*, p. 591.

12. Printed as a footnote to Bertrand Russell's "The Elements of Ethic in Sellars-Hospers, *Readings in Ethical Theory*, (New York: Appleton-Centu Crofts, 1952), p. 1.

13. Russell, *Mysticism and Logic* (New York: Norton, 1929), pp. 49–5.

14. See the section of *Religion and Science* reprinted in Edwards-Pap, *Modern Introduction to Philosophy*, pp. 297–302.

15. *Ibid.*, p. 298.

16. T. E. Hill, *Contemporary Ethical Theories*, pp. 13–15, notes that Russell has been associated with "three or four" different ethical positions.

17. See, for example, Wittgenstein's discussion of pain, in *Philosophical Investigations* (Oxford: Blackwell, 1953), pp. 88e–104e; reprinted in Weitz, *20th-Century Philosophy: The Analytic Tradition* (New York: Free Press, 1966), pp. 312–26.

18. Wittgenstein, *Tractatus Logico-Philosophicus* (London: Routledge, Kegan Paul, 1922), 6.42; see the digest by Rush Rhees, "Some Developments in Wittgenstein's Views of Ethics," *Philosophical Review*, LXXIV (1965), 17–26.

19. *Tractatus*, 6.422.

20. Rhees, *art. cit.*, pp. 23–24.

21. Wittgenstein, "Lecture on Ethics," *Philosophical Review*, LXXIV (1954), 4.

22. *Ibid.*, p. 5.

23. *Ibid.*, p. 6.

24. *Ibid.*, p. 7.

25. *Ibid.*, p. 12.

26. Waismann, "Notes on Talks with Wittgenstein," *Philosophical Review*, XXIV (1965), 12–16.

27. *Ibid.*, German, p. 13; English, p. 15.

28. Carnap, *Philosophy and Logical Syntax* (London: Routledge, Kegan Paul, 1936), chap. 1, sec. 4; reprinted in Morton White, *Age of Analysis* (New York: Mentor, 1955), pp. 216–18.

29. Ewing, *The Definition of Good* (New York: Macmillan, 1947), pp. 12–15, 166.

30. *Ibid.*, p. 106.

31. *Ibid.*, p. 109; cf. Hill, *Contemporary Ethical Theories*, pp. 312–14.

32. Ewing, "Ethical Judgments: Attempted Synthesis of Three Rival Views," *Atti del XII Congresso Internazionale di Filosofia* VII (Firenze, 1961), 155–60.

33. *Art. cit.*, p. 157.

34. See Blanshard, *Reason and Goodness*, pp. 288–89.

35. Urmson, "On Grading," *Mind*, LIX (1950), 145–69; reprinted in Paul Taylor, *The Moral Judgment* (New York: Free Press, 1966), pp. 211–37.

36. Taylor, p. 223.

37. Stevenson, "The Emotive Meaning of Ethical Terms," *Mind*, XLVI (1937), 10–31; in the reprint in R. E. Dewey, *Problems of Ethics* (1961), see p. 413.

38. This book is *The Meaning of Meaning* (London: Kegan Paul, 1938); for emotive meaning, see pp. 124–25.

39. Stevenson, *Ethics and Language* (New Haven: Yale University Press, 1944), p. 267.

40. *Ibid.*, p. 136.

41. Stevenson, *Facts and Values* (New Haven: Yale University Press, 1963), p. 97.

42. *Ibid.*, p. ix.

43. Ayer, *Language, Truth, and Logic* (London: Gollancz, 1936), p. 103.

44. *Ibid.*, pp. 112–13.

45. Joad, *Critique of Logical Positivism* (London: Gollancz, 1950), p. 146.

46. Mary Warnock, *Ethics Since 1900*, p. 91.

47. *Language, Truth, and Logic*, 2nd ed. (New York: Dover, 1952), p. 21.

48. See Harald Ofstad, "Objectivity of Norms and Value-Judgments according to Recent Scandinavian Philosophy," *Philosophy and Phenomenological Research*, XII (1951–52), 48.

49. Hägerström, *Inquiries into the Nature of Laws and Morals* (Stockholm: Almqvist & Wiksell, 1938), p. 138.

50. *Ibid.*, p. 154.

51. On Alf Ross, see Ofstad, *art. cit.*, pp. 53–54.

52. Ross, *On Law and Justice* (Berkeley–Los Angeles: University of California Press, 1959), p. 274.

53. Nowell-Smith, *Ethics* (Baltimore: Penguin, 1954), p. 25.

54. *Ibid.*, p. 30.

55. *Ibid.*, p. 52.

56. *Ibid.*, pp. 72–73.

57. *Ibid.*, pp. 81–83.

58. This section in chapter 8 is in *ibid.*, pp. 105–21.

59. *Ibid.*, p. 125.

60. *Ibid.*, p. 102.

61. *Ibid.*, p. 182.

62. Aristotle, *On the Motion of Animals*, 700b1–701b1; part of the ancient text on the practical syllogism is printed as an introduction to "good reasons" ethics, in R. E. Dewey, *Problems of Ethics*, pp. 434–35.

63. Hampshire, "Fallacies in Moral Philosophy," *Mind*, LVIII (1949), 466–82.

64. *Ibid.*; see the reprint in R. E. Dewey, *op. cit.*, p. 438.

65. *Ibid.*, in Dewey, p. 442.

66. See Weitz, *20th-Century Philosophy*, p. 379, for a portion of Baier's talk on "The Meaning of Life," (1957).

67. Baier, *The Moral Point of View* (Ithaca, N.Y.: Cornell University Press, 1958), chap. 1.

68. Hare, *The Language of Morals* (Oxford: Clarendon Press, 1952), 169.

69. Hare, *Freedom and Reason* (Oxford: Clarendon Press, 1963), p.

70. *Ibid.*, pp. 86–185; see G. C. Kerner's exposition of Hare's views in *The Revolution in Ethical Theory* (New York: Oxford University Press, 1966), pp. 138–96. Kerner is not sympathetic with this approach.

71. Toulmin, *An Examination of the Place of Reason in Ethics* (London: Cambridge University Press, 1950), pp. 148, 224.

72. *Cf.* Kerner, *op. cit.*, pp. 127–37, where again the criticism may be too severe.

CHAPTER XVIII

1. See William Barrett, *Irrational Man. A Study in Existential Philosophy* (Garden City, N.Y.: Doubleday, 1958), p. 21.

2. Husserl, *Ideen zu einer reinen Phänomenologie und phänomenologischen Philosophie*, ed. Willy Biemel (Ten Haag; Nijhoff, 1950), I, 154; *cf.* Quentin Lauer, *The Triumph of Subjectivity* (New York: Fordham University Press, 1958), pp. 1–19.

3. Thus Werkmeister, *Theories of Ethics* (1961), chap. 7, treats Moore together with Scheler and Hartmann.

4. Kierkegaard, *Either/Or*, trans. W. Lowrie (Princeton, N.J.: Princeton University Press, 1944), II, 163–64; on the same point, see Lowrie, *A Short Life of Kierkegaard* (Princeton, N.J.: Princeton University Press, 1942), p. 125.

5. *Either/Or*, II, 234–35.

6. Kierkegaard, *Journals*, 1847 entry, cited in Sahakian, *Systems of Ethics* (1964), p. 307.

7. *Cf.* Kurt Reinhardt, *The Existentialist Revolt* (Milwaukee: Bruce, 1952), p. 56.

8. This is the conclusion of Harald Höffding, *History of Modern Philosophy* (New York: Macmillan, 1924), II, 288.

9. For the "immoralist" interpretation, see A. W. Benn, "The Morals of an Immoralist—Friedrich Nietzsche," *Ethics*, XIX (1909), 1–13, 192–203; and for the contrary view, see A. C. Pigou, "The Ethics of Nietzsche," *Ethics*, XVIII (1908), 343–55.

10. See G. A. Morgan, *What Nietzsche Means* (Cambridge: Harvard University Press, 1941), for more information on the fabrication of *The Will to Power*.

11. Nietzsche, *Thus Spake Zarathustra*, in *The Philosophy of Nietzsche* New York: Random House, 1954), "Prologue," n. 2.

12. See, for instance, *The Gay Science*, in *The Portable Nietzsche*, ed. W. Kaufmann (New York: Viking Press, 1954), pp. 95–96.

13. Nietzsche, *Genealogy of Morals*, in *The Philosophy of Nietzsche*, . 7.

14. Nietzsche, *Beyond Good and Evil*, trans. M. Cowan (Chicago: Regnery, 955), p. 260.

15. See two illustrative passages from *The Genealogy of Morals*, in Mann-Kreyche, *Approaches to Morality*, pp. 616–26.

16. Part I of *Notes from the Underground* is printed in W. Kaufmann, *Existentialism from Dostoevsky to Sartre* (New York: Meridian, 1957), pp. 3–82.

17. *Ibid.*, in Kaufmann, p. 56.

18. This is Kaufmann's comment, *ibid.*, p. 14.

19. *Cf.* Borzaga, *Contemporary Philosophy*, pp. 238–39.

20. Cf. Lauer, op. cit., pp. 100–17.

21. Buber, I and Thou, trans. R. G. Smith (New York: Scribner's, 1958), p. 34.

22. Tillich, Systematic Theology (Chicago: University of Chicago Press, 1963), III, 266–67.

23. Tillich, Love, Power, and Justice (New York: Oxford University Press, 1960), p. 72.

24. Systematic Theology, III, 159.

25. Tillich, Courage to Be (New Haven: Yale University Press, 1952), p. 133.

26. Tillich, The Protestant Era (Chicago: Phoenix, 1957), pp. 151–54.

27. Systematic Theology, III, 45.

28. Ibid., pp. 95, 273–75.

29. Reinhold Niebuhr, Christian Ethics (New York: Meridian, 1960), p. 97.

30. Moral Man and Immoral Society (New York: Scribner's, 1949), p. 41.

31. See Love and Justice: Selections from the Shorter Writings of Reinhold Niebuhr, ed. D. B. Robertson (Philadelphia: Westminster Press, 1957), p 46.

32. Ibid., p. 53; see also Niebuhr, Christian Realism and Political Problems (New York: Scribner's, 1953), p. 173.

33. H. Richard Niebuhr, in The Christian Century, March 23, 1932 pp. 378–80; reprinted in Contemporary Moral Issues, ed. H. K. Girvetz (Belmont, Calif.: Wadsworth, 1963), pp. 321–25.

34. Reinhold Niebuhr, in The Christian Century, March 30, 1932, pp 415–17; see Girvetz, pp. 326–30.

35. For a full exposition in English of the ethics of Grisebach, see G. A Rauche, The Philosophy of Actuality (Fort Hare, Republic of South Africa Fort Hare University Press, 1964).

36. Bonhoeffer's Ethics was completed and edited by his friend, Pasto Eberhard Bethge, translated by Neville Smith (New York: Macmillan, 1965)

37. Ibid., p. 214.

38. Robinson, Christian Morals Today (Philadelphia: Westminster Press 1964), p. 39.

39. Marcel, Philosophical Fragments, 1904–1914 (Notre Dame, Ind.: Uni versity of Notre Dame Press, 1965).

40. Ibid., pp. 112, 181.

41. Marcel, The Philosophy of Existentialism (New York: Citadel Press 1965), pp. 69–87.

42. Ibid., pp. 88–89.

43. Marcel, The Mystery of Being (Chicago: Regnery, 1951), II, 113–17

44. Philosophical Fragments, 1904–1914, p. 10; and Homo Viator, tran E. Craufurd (Chicago: Regnery, 1951), p. 26.

45. Marcel, Being and Having, trans. K. Farrer (Boston: Beacon Press 1951), p. 15; Homo Viator, pp. 7–8.

46. The whole issue of Etudes Philosophiques, Vol. III, 1962, is devote to Nabert.

47. Nabert, *Eléments pour une éthique* (Paris: Presses Universitaires, 1943), pp. 19–58.
48. *Ibid.*, pp. 105–221.
49. *Ibid.*, pp. 218–19, trans. Bourke.
50. Sartre, *Being and Nothingness*, trans. Hazel Barnes (New York: Philosophical Library, 1956), pp. 74–90.
51. *Ibid.*, pp. 484–85.
52. Sartre, *Existentialism*, trans. B. Frechtman (New York: Philosophical Library, 1947), p. 21.
53. *Being and Nothingness*, p. 566.
54. *Ibid.*, pp. 34–35.
55. Sartre, *Saint Genet*, trans. B. Frechtman (London: Allen & Unwin, 1964), p. 186.
56. *Ibid.*, pp. 187, 190.
57. *Critique de la raison dialectique* (Paris: Gallimard, 1960), p. 123.
58. *Ibid.*, p. 755.
59. *Cf.* Ria Stavrides, "French Existentialism and Moral Philosophy," in *Encyclopedia of Morals*, by V. Ferm (New York: Philosophical Library, 1956), p. 167, places a high value on the ethics of Madame de Beauvoir.
60. Beauvoir, *Ethics of Ambiguity*, trans. B. Frechtman (New York: Philosophical Library, 1948), p. 44.
61. On "facticity" see Colin Smith, *Contemporary French Philosophy*, p. 28.
62. See James Collins, "Freedom as Atheistic Heroism," *Giornale di Metafisica*, IV (1949), 578.
63. *Ethics of Ambiguity*, p. 146.
64. *Ibid.*, p. 60.
65. *Cf.* Colin Smith, *op. cit.*, p. 212.
66. Merleau-Ponty, *Humanisme et Terreur* (Paris: Gallimard, 1947).
67. Mandelbaum, *The Phenomenology of Moral Experience* (Glencoe, Ill.: Free Press, 1955), pp. 16–30.
68. *Ibid.*, pp. 30–31.
69. *Ibid.*, pp. 32–39.
70. *Ibid.*, p. 45; for the theory of the virtues, see pp. 134–81.
71. *Ibid.*, p. 245.
72. *Ibid.*, p. 277.
73. *Ibid.*, pp. 291–309.

Bibliography

NOTE

THE LAST full-scale history of ethics in English is almost one hundred years
old. Henry Sidgwick's *Outlines of the History of Ethics* was written before
1886. In the sixth edition (1931), Alban G. Widgery added a chapter on
ethics in the first quarter of the twentieth century. Despite its obvious
lacunae, Sidgwick's work has remained a standard source of information
in this field. It is very weak on the ethics of the Middle Ages and on non-
British modern and contemporary ethics. Of course, a great deal has happened in twentieth-century ethics since the last revision of Sidgwick. The
Short History of Ethics written by R. A. P. Rogers in 1911 is briefer and
less informative than Sidgwick. After most of the research and writing on
the present book was completed, Alasdair MacIntyre's *A Short History of
Ethics* (1966) was published. He has chosen to concentrate on the ethical
views of about thirty main thinkers, from the Sophists to Sartre, and
to ignore lesser figures in the field. My effort has been to treat a much
larger number of ethicians.

Of histories of ethics in other languages, Ottmar Dittrich's four-volume
Geschichte der Ethik (1923–1932) is the most complete work. However, it
includes a great deal of material that is not central to ethics, and it does
not cover recent ethics, of course. The most helpful French history of the
subject is found in René Le Senne's *Traité de morale générale* (1942),
but it is not (and was not intended to be) a complete history of ethics.
Excellent surveys of the history of ethical thinking are now available for
most of the distinct periods of philosophy. The only era that is not well
covered by such special studies is the medieval; we are just beginning to
learn the history of medieval philosophy. Alois Dempf's work *Die Ethik des
Mittelalters* (1927) is extremely brief and its coverage is inadequate. There
is much more information on the ethics of the Middle Ages in a general
work such as F. C. Copleston's *History of Philosophy*. Most general histories
of philosophy, however, give little space to ethical theory.

The bibliographical lists offered herein are more complete than in most
other histories. Data on original writings in ethics, chief translations and
collections of texts, plus the most helpful secondary studies make up the
bibliographies appended to each chapter. In the case of Greek, Arabic, and

Russian works, the original titles and terms have been transliterated or given in translation. The difficulties of printing in non-Roman alphabets probably outweigh the value of having these data in the original. It is hoped that the information included on the literature of ethics will help to make up for the brevity and defects of the doctrinal expositions in this history.

GENERAL WORKS

Brinton, Crane. A History of Western Morals. New York: Harcourt, Brace, 1959.

Brunschivicq, Léon. Le progrès de la conscience dans la philosophie occidentale. 2 vols. Paris: Alcan, 1927.

Copleston, F. C. A History of Philosophy. 8 vols. Westminster, Md.: Newman Press, 1946–66; reprinted New York: Doubleday Image Books, 1962–65.

Dittrich, Ottmar. Geschichte der Ethik. 4 Bde. Leipzig: Meiner, 1923–32

Ferm, Vergilius (ed.). Encyclopedia of Morals. New York: Philosophical Library, 1956.

Hastings, James (ed.). Encyclopaedia of Religion and Ethics. 12 vols. Edinburgh: Clark, 1908–21. 7 vols. New York: Scribner's, 1924–27

Hobhouse, L. T. Morals in Evolution. A Study in Comparative Ethics London: Chapman & Hall, 1906; New York: Macmillan, 1951.

Janet, Paul. Histoire de la philosophie morale et politique dans l'antiquité et les temps modernes. 2 vols. Paris: Delagrave, 1852.

Jodl, Friedrich. Geschichte der Ethik als philosophischer Wissenschaft. 2 Bde Stuttgart: Cotta, 1906, 1912.

Kropotkin, P. A. Ethics, Origin and Development. Trans. L. S. Friedland and J. R. Piroshnikoff. New York: Dial Press, 1924; reprinted 1947

Lecky, W. E. H. History of European Morals from Augustus to Charlemagne 2 vols. New York: Appleton, 1869; reprinted in 1 vol., New York Braziller, 1955.

Leclercq, Jacques. Les grandes lignes de la philosophie morale. Louvain Paris: Vrin, 1946; 2me éd., 1964.

Le Senne, René. Traité de morale générale, Paris: Presses Universitaires 1942.

MacIntyre, Alasdair. A Short History of Ethics. New York: Macmillan 1966.

Maritain, Jacques. Moral Philosophy. Trans. Marshall Suther et al. New York: Scribner's, 1964.

Martineau, James. Types of Ethical Theory. 2 vols. Oxford: Clarendon 1866; New York: Macmillan, 1886.

Meyer, Hans. Abendländische Weltanschauung. 5 Bde. Paderborn: Schöning 1949–53.

Rogers, R. A. P. A Short History of Ethics, Greek and Modern. London Macmillan, 1911; reprinted 1964.

Schweitzer, Albert. Civilization and Ethics. New York: Macmillan, 192

Sidgwick, Henry. Outlines of the History of Ethics. London: Macmillan 1886; revised ed. of 1931, reprinted Boston: Beacon, 1964.

Wentscher, M. *Geschichte der Ethik.* Berlin: De Gruyter, 1931.
Werkmeister, W. H. *Theories of Ethics.* Lincoln, Neb.: Johnsen, 1961.
Westermarck, E. A. *The Origin and Development of Moral Ideas.* London: Macmillan, 1926.

CHAPTER I

Adkins, A. W. H. *Merit and Responsibility (Homer to Aristotle).* Oxford: Clarendon Press, 1960.
Aristophanes. *The Clouds,* ed. Cyril Bailey. London: Oxford University Press, 1921.
Boas, George. *Rationalism in Greek Philosophy.* Baltimore: Johns Hopkins Press, 1961.
Chroust, A. H. *Socrates, Man and Myth: The Two Socratic Apologies.* Notre Dame, Ind.: University of Notre Dame Press, 1958.
Dawson, M. M. *The Ethics of Socrates.* New York: Putnam, 1924.
Dickinson, G. L. *The Greek View of Life.* Garden City, N.Y.: Doubleday, Doran, 1925.
Diels, H., and Kranz, W. *Die Fragmente der Vorsokratiker.* Aufl. 8. Berlin: Weidmann, 1956.
Diogenes Laërtius. *Lives and Opinions of Eminent Philosophers.* Trans. R. D. Hicks. Cambridge: Harvard University Press, 1925, 1950.
Dittrich, Ottmar. *Geschichte der Ethik.* Bde. 1: *Vom Altertum bis zum Hellenismus.* Leipzig: Meiner, 1923.
Doherty, Kevin. "God and the Good in Plato," *New Scholasticism,* XXX (1956), 441–60.
Dudley, D. R. *A History of Cynicism, from Diogenes to the Sixth Century.* London: Methuen, 1937.
Ferguson, John. *Moral Values in the Ancient World.* London: Methuen, 1958; New York: Barnes & Noble, 1959.
Freeman, Kathleen. *Ancilla to the Pre-Socratic Philosophers.* Oxford: Blackwell; Cambridge: Harvard University Press, 1948.
Gould, John. *The Development of Plato's Ethics.* New York: Cambridge University Press, 1955.
Hackforth, R. *Plato's Examination of Pleasure (Philebus).* New York: Liberal Arts Press, 1957.
Helsel, P. R. "Early Greek Moralists," in *History of Philosophical Systems,* ed. V. Ferm. New York: Philosophical Library, 1950, pp. 82–92.
Jaeger, Werner. *Paideia. The Ideals of Greek Culture.* 3 vols. Trans. G. Highet. New York: Oxford University Press, 1939–45.
Kirk, G. S., and Raven, J. E. *The Presocratic Philosophers.* New York: Cambridge University Press, 1960.
Lachièze-Rey, P. *Les Idées morales, sociales et politiques de Platon.* Paris: Vrin, 1951.
Lodge, R. C. *Plato's Theory of Ethics.* London: Routledge, 1928, 1950.
Mazzantini, C. *Eraclito.* Torino: Vita e Pensiero, 1945.

Mondolfo, Rodolfo. *Moralisti Greci. La Coscienza morale da Omero Epicuro.* Napoli: Ricciardi, 1960.

Nahm, Milton C. *Selections from Early Greek Philosophy.* New York Appleton-Century-Crofts, 1947.

Nettleship, R. N. *Lectures on the Republic of Plato.* London: Macmillan 1922; reprinted New York: St. Martin's Press, 1962.

Oakeley, Hilda D. *Greek Ethical Thought from Homer to the Stoics* London: Dent; New York: Dutton, 1925; Boston: Beacon Press, 1950

Owens, Joseph. *A History of Ancient Western Philosophy.* New York Appleton-Century-Crofts, 1960.

Pearson, Lionel. *Popular Ethics in Ancient Greece.* Stanford, Calif.: Stat University Press, 1962.

Plato. *Opera,* ed. John Burnet. Oxford: Clarendon Press, 1910.

————. *The Dialogues.* Trans. R. G. Bury *et al.* 12 vols. Cambridge: Ha vard University Press, 1914–36.

————. *The Dialogues.* Trans. B. Jowett, 2 vols. London: Macmillan, 189: Revised in 4 vols., by D. J. Allan and H. E. Dale. London: Macmillan, 195

————. *The Republic of Plato.* Trans. with notes by F. M. Cornfor Oxford: Clarendon Press, 1941.

Robin, Léon. *La morale antique.* Paris: Alcan, 1939.

Sauvage, Micheline. *Socrates and the Human Conscience.* New York: Harp Torchbooks, 1960.

Schwartz, Eduard. *Ethik der Griechen,* hrsg. Will Richter. Stuttgart: Koehle 1951.

Shorey, Paul. "The Idea of Good in Plato's *Republic.*" (*Studies in Classic Philology,* Vol. I.) Chicago, 1895.

Snell, Bruno. *The Discovery of Mind. The Greek Origins of Europea Thought.* Cambridge: Harvard University Press, 1953; New York: Harp Torchbooks, 1964. (Chap. VIII: The Call to Virtue.)

Taylor, A. E. *Socrates.* New York: Nelson, 1939.

Tenkku, J. *The Evaluation of Pleasure in Plato's Ethics.* Helsinki: Societ Philosophica, 1956.

Untersteiner, M. *The Sophists.* Trans. K. Freeman. New York: Philosophic Library, 1953.

Versenyi, Lazlo. *Socratic Humanism.* New Haven: Yale University Pre 1963.

Vlastos, Gregory. "Ethics and Physics in Democritus," *Philosophical Revie* LIV (1945), 578–92; LV (1946), 53–64.

Wild, John. *Plato's Modern Enemies and the Theory of Natural La* Chicago: University of Chicago Press, 1953.

Xenophon. *Memorabilia Socratis dicta.* Trans. E. C. Marchant. Cambridg Harvard University Press, 1938.

Zubiri, Xavier. "Socrates and Greek Wisdom," *The Thomist,* VII (1944 40–45.

CHAPTER II

lexander of Aphrodisias. *De fato imperatoris*, ed. Pierre Thillet. Paris: Presses Universitaires, 1963.

ndo, Takatura. *Aristotle's Theory of Practical Cognition*. The Hague: Nijhoff, 1965.

ristotle. *Opera Omnia*, ed. I. Bekker. 4 vols. Berlin: Reimer, 1835–70.

———. *Works: The Oxford Translation*, ed. W. D. Ross and J. A. Smith. 12 vols. London: Oxford University Press, 1928–52.

———. *Ethica Nicomachea*, ed. I. Bywater. Oxford: Clarendon Press, 1890.

———. *Ethica Nicomachia*, ed. J. Burnet. London: Methuen, 1900. Trans. as *Nicomachean Ethics* by W. D. Ross (Vol. VIII of *Oxford Translation*). Also by J. A. K. Thomson. Baltimore: Penguin, 1955.

———. *Ethica Eudemia*, ed. F. Susemihl. Leipzig: Teubner, 1883. Trans. as *Eudemian Ethics* by J. Solomon (Vol. IX of *Oxford Translation*). Also by H. Rackham. Cambridge: Harvard University Press, 1952.

———. *Magna Moralia*. Greek text and trans., G. C. Armstrong. Cambridge: Harvard University Press, 1957.

ibenque, Pierre. *La Prudence chez Aristote*. Paris: Presses Universitaires, 1963.

ommentaria Graeca in Aristotelem. 23 vols. Berlin: Reimer, 1891–1909. (The ethical commentaries are in Vols. XIX, XXII.)

üring, I., and Owen, G. E. L. (eds.). *Aristotle and Plato*. Goteburg: Almqvist & Wiksell, 1960. (An important symposium.)

ilen. *On the Natural Faculties*. Ed. and trans., Arthur J. Brock. Cambridge: Harvard University Press, 1916.

iuthier, R. A. *L'Ethique à Nicomaque*. Introduction, traduction et commentaire (avec J. Y. Jolif). 3 vols. Louvain-Paris: Nauwelaerts, 1958–59.

———. *La Morale d'Aristote*. Paris: Presses Universitaires, 1958.

imburger, M. *Morals and Law: the Growth of Aristotle's Legal Theory*. New Haven: Yale University Press, 1951.

itch, W. M. *The Moral Philosophy of Aristotle*. London: Murray, 1879.

ger, Werner. "The Original Ethics," in *Aristotle: Fundamentals of the History of His Development*. Trans. Richard Robinson. Oxford: Clarendon Press, 1951; reprinted 1962.

ifa, H. V. *Thomism and Aristotelianism: a Study of the Commentary by Thomas Aquinas on the Nicomachean Ethics*. Chicago: University of Chicago Press, 1952.

ichim, H. H. *Aristotle, the Nicomachean Ethics*, ed. D. A. Rees. Oxford: Clarendon Press, 1951; reprinted 1962.

onard, Jean. *Le Bonheur chez Aristote*. Bruxelles: Palais des Académies, 948.

thardt, C. E. *Die Ethik des Aristoteles*. Leipzig: Meiner, 1876.

insion, Auguste. "Autour des Ethiques attribués à Aristote," *Revue Né-scolastique de Philosophie*, XXXIII (1931), 80–107, 216–36, 360–80.

Marshall, T. *Aristotle's Theory of Conduct*. London: Unwin, 1906.

May, W. E. "The Structure and Argument of the *Nicomachean Ethics*," *New Scholasticism*, XXXVI (1962), 1–28.

Monan, J. D. "Two Methodological Aspects of Moral Knowledge in the *Nicomachean Ethics*," in *Aristote et Problèmes de Méthode*. Louvain: Nauwelaerts, 1962.

Oates, W. J. *Aristotle and the Problem of Value*. Princeton, N.J.: Princeton University Press, 1963.

Prichard, H. A. "The Meaning of *agathon* in the Ethics of Aristotle," *Philosophy*, X, 37 (1935), 27–39.

Stewart, J. A. *Notes on the Nicomachean Ethics of Aristotle*. 2 vols. Oxford: Clarendon Press, 1892.

Theophrastus. *Characters*. Trans. J. M. Edmonds. Cambridge: Harvard University Press, 1929.

Vanier, Jean. *Le Bonheur principe et fin de la morale aristotélicienne* Paris: Desclée de Brouwer, 1965.

Veatch, H. B. *Rational Man; a Modern Interpretation of Aristoteliar Ethics*. Bloomington: Indiana University Press, 1962.

Wittmann, Michael. *Die Ethik des Aristoteles*. Regensburg-München: Hue ber, 1920.

CHAPTER III

Armstrong, A. H. (ed.). *The Cambridge History of Later Greek and Earl Medieval Philosophy*. Cambridge: Heffer, 1966.

Arnim, J. von (ed.). *Stoicorum Veterum Fragmenta*. 3 vols. Leipzig Teubner, 1914–21.

Arnold, E. V. *Roman Stoicism*. London: Cambridge University Press, 191١

Arnou, René. *Le désir de Dieu dans la philosophie de Plotin*. Paris: Alcar 1921.

Bevan, E. R. *Hellenistic Popular Philosophy*. London: Cambridge Universit Press, 1923.

Bonhoeffer, A. *Die Ethik der Stoiker Epiktet*. Stuttgart, 1894; reprinte Stuttgart: Fromman, 1965.

Bréhier, Emile. *The Hellenistic and Roman Age*. Trans. Wade Baskiı Chicago: University of Chicago Press, 1965.

Clark, Gordon H. *Selections from Hellenistic Philosophy*. New York: Aı pleton-Century-Crofts, 1940.

De Witt, Norman. *Epicurus and His Philosophy*. Minneapolis: Universi٭ of Minnesota Press, 1954.

Dittrich, O. *Geschichte der Ethik*. Bde. 2 u. 3. Leipzig: Meiner, 192

Dodds, E. R. *The Greeks and the Irrational*. Berkeley: University of Ca᷾ fornia Press, 1951.

Du Vair, Guillaume. *The Moral Philosophie of the Stoicks*, ed. R. Kiı New Brunswick, N.J.: Rutgers University Press, 1951.

Edelstein, Ludwig. *The Meaning of Stoicism*. Cambridge: Heffer, 1966.

ortin, E. L. *Christianisme et culture philosophique au cinquième siècle.* Paris: Etudes Augustiniennes, 1959.

arofalo, Gaetano. *La morale della Grecia nell'età dell'ellenismo.* Roma: Ciranna, 1961.

oodenough, E. R. *The Politics of Philo Judaeus.* New Haven: Yale University Press, 1938.

adas, Moses. *Essential Works of Stoicism.* New York: Bantam Books, 1961.

atz, Joseph. *Plotinus' Search for the Good.* New York: Columbia University Press, 1950.

risteller, P. O. *Der Begriff der Seele in der Ethik des Plotin.* Heidelberg: Abhandlungen z. Philosophie, 1929.

wy, Hans. *Chaldean Oracles and Theurgy: Mysticism, Magic and Platonism in the Later Roman Empire.* Cairo: Institut Français d'Archéologie Orientale, 1956.

eshout, H. van. *La Théorie plotinienne de la vertu.* Paderborn: Schöningh, 1926.

ancini, Guido. *L'Etica Stoica da Zenone a Crisippo.* Padova: Cedam, 1940.

ead, G. R. S. *Thrice Greatest Hermes.* New York: Holt, 1906.

erlan, Philip. *From Platonism to Neoplatonism.* The Hague: Nijhoff, 1953.

ore, Paul Elmer. *Hellenistic Philosophies.* Princeton, N.J.: Princeton University Press, 1923.

tes, W. J. *The Stoic and Epicurean Philosophers: Epicurus, Epictetus, Lucretius, Marcus Aurelius.* New York: Random House, 1940.

otinus. *Opera,* ed. Paul Henry et H. R. Schwyzer. Paris: Desclée de Brouwer, 1951 (crit. ed. in course of publication).

———. *Ennéades.* 6 vols. Texte établit et traduit par Emile Bréhier. Paris: Les Belles Lettres, 1924–38.

———. *The Ethical Treatises.* Trans. Stephen MacKenna. London: Medici Society, 1926.

———. *The Essential Plotinus.* Trans. Elmer O'Brien. New York: Mentor, 1964.

orphyry. *On Abstinence from Animal Food.* Trans. Thomas Taylor. Reprinted New York: Barnes & Noble, 1965.

oclus. *Elements of Theology.* Revised text with trans. by E. R. Dodds. London: Oxford University Press, 1933.

osdij, B. A. van. *Seneca als Moralist.* 2 vols. Leiden: Brill, 1961.

ter, H., et Preller, L. *Historia Philosophiae Graecae.* Gotha: Perthes, 1913.

san, L. J. *The Philosophy of Proclus: the Final Phase of Ancient Thought.* New York: Cosmas, 1949.

piro, H., and Curley, E. M. *Hellenistic Philosophy: Selected Readings.* New York: Scribner's, 1965.

n, W. W. *Hellenistic Civilization.* New York: Longmans, 1927.

uillard, Jean. *La purification Plotinienne.* Paris: Presses Universitaires, 1953.

ente, Milton. *L'Ethique Stoïcienne chez Cicéron.* Paris: Saint-Paul, 1956.

olfson, H. A. *Philo.* 2 vols. Cambridge: Harvard University Press, 1948.

CHAPTER IV

Alphandéry, P. *Les idées morales des hétérodoxes latins au debut du XII* *siècle*. Paris: Leroux, 1903.

Ambrose. *Some of the Principal Works*. Trans. H. de Romestin. Edinburgh Clark, 1896.

Ancient Christian Writers, The Works of the Fathers in Translation ed. J. Quasten and J. C. Plumpe. Westminster, Md.: Newman Pres 1946 ff.

Anselm. *Opera*, ed. F. S. Schmitt. 5 vols. Edinburgh: Nelson, 1938–5
———. *Proslogium and Other Works*. Trans. S. N. Deane. Chicago: Ope Court, 1903.

Augustine. *Opera Omnia*, in *Patrologia Latina*, Vols. 32–47. For mo recent editions consult:
———. *Essential Augustine*, ed. V. J. Bourke. New York: Mentor, 1964, p 249–56.
———. *La Moral de San Agustin*, ed. G. Armas. Madrid: Difusora del Libr 1954 (a complete selection of ethical texts in Latin).
———. *Basic Writings of St. Augustine*, 2 vols. ed. W. J. Oates. New Yor Random House, 1948.

Bardy, Gustave. *The Christian Latin Literature of the First Six Centurie* St. Louis: Herder, 1930.
———. *The Greek Literature of the Early Church*. St. Louis: Herder, 192

Bernard, St. *Select Treatises of St. Bernard*. Trans. W. W. Williams a B. R. V. Mills. Cambridge: Heffer, 1926.
———. *On the Love of God*. Trans. E. G. Gardner. London: Mowbra 1915. Also in A. C. Pegis. *The Wisdom of Catholicism*. New Yor Random House, 1949, pp. 230–68.

Bett, H. *Joachim of Flora*. London: Cambridge University Press, 192
———. *Johannes Scotus Erigena*. London: Cambridge University Press, 192 reprinted, New York: Russell & Russell, 1964.

Bigg, Charles. *The Christian Platonists of Alexandria*. Oxford: Clarend Press, 1886.

Boethius. *De consolatione philosophiae and Opuscula sacra*, ed. and tra H. F. Stewart and E. K. Rand. Cambridge: Harvard University Pre 1918; reprinted 1946.
———. *Consolation of Philosophy*. Trans. J. J. Buchanan. New York: Ung 1957. Also trans. Richard Green. New York: Liberal Arts Press, 1964.

Bourke, V. J. *Will in Western Thought*. New York: Sheed & Ward, 19(

Boyer, Charles. *Saint Augustin (Les Moralistes Chrétiens)*. Paris: Gabal 1932.

Brandt, T. *Tertullians Ethik*. Gütersloh: Universitäts Dissertation, 19:

Burch, G. B. *Early Medieval Philosophy*. New York: King's Crown Pre 1951.

Campbell, J. M. *The Greek Fathers*. New York: Longmans, Green, 19

Chadwick, Henry. *Early Christian Thought and the Classical Tradition.* New York: Oxford University Press, 1966.

Clement of Alexandria. *Writings.* 2 vols. Trans. W. Wilson. Edinburgh: Clark, 1868–69.

Cochrane, C. N. *Christianity and Classical Culture: A Study of Thought and Action from Augustus to Augustine.* London: Oxford University Press, 1944.

Corpus Christianorum. Series Graeca et Series Latina. The Hague: Nijhoff, 1953 ff.

Corpus Scriptorum Ecclesiasticorum Latinorum. Wien: Akademie der Wissenschaften, 1866 ff.

Delhaye, Philippe. "La place de l'éthique parmi les disciplines scientifiques au XIIᵐᵉ siècle," *Mélanges Arthur Janssen.* Louvain: Nauwelaerts, 1948, pp. 29–44.

———. "L'Enseignement de la philosophie morale au XIIᵐᵉ siècle," *Mediaeval Studies,* XI (1949), 77–99.

———. *Le problème de la conscience morale chez saint Bernard.* Namur: Editions Godenne, 1957.

Dempf, Alois. *Ethik des Mittelalters.* München-Berlin: Oldenbourg, 1927.

Dionysius, Pseudo-. *On the Divine Names, Mystical Theology.* Trans. C. E. Rolt. London: Society for the Promotion of Christian Knowledge, 1920.

———. *The Celestial Hierarchy.* Trans. by the Shrine of Wisdom Society. London: Shrine of Wisdom Manual, 1935.

Dittrich, O. *Geschichte der Ethik.* Bde. 2 u. 3. Leipzig: Meiner, 1926.

Dobler, E. *Nemesius von Emesa und die Psychologie des menschlichen Aktes.* Freiburg im Schweiz: Paulusdruckerei, 1950.

Enslin, M. S. *Ethics of Paul.* Nashville, Tenn.: Apex Books, 1963.

Fathers of the Church: a New Translation, ed. R. J. Deferrari. Washington, D.C.: Catholic University of America, 1947 ff.

Florilegium Morale Oxoniense, prima pars, ed. P. Delhaye. Lille: Giard, 1955. Secunda pars, ed. C. H. Talbot. *Id.,* 1956.

Forest, Aimé. *Le Mouvement doctrinal du IXᵉ au XIVᵉ siècle.* Paris: Bloud et Gay, 1951.

Gilson, Etienne. *History of Christian Philosophy in the Middle Ages.* New York: Random House, 1955.

Gregory, St. *Morals on the Book of Job.* 3 vols. Oxford, 1844–50.

Grou, S. J. *Morality Extracted from the Confessions,* Trans. P. Hudleston. London: Burns, Oates, 1934.

Harvey, J. F. *Moral Theology of the Confessions of St. Augustine.* Washington, D.C.: Catholic University Press, 1951.

Hausherr, I. *Philatie. De la tendresse pour soi à la charité selon saint Maxime le Confesseur.* Rome: Pontificium Institutum Orientalium Studiorum, 1952.

Heinig, H. *Die Ethik des Laktanz.* Leipzig, 1887.

Hunt, R. W. "English Learning in the Late Twelfth Century," *Transactions of the Royal Historical Society,* 4th series, XIX (1936), 19–41.

John Damascene. *De fide orthodoxa,* ed. E. M. Buytaert. St. Bonaventure, N.Y.: Franciscan Institute, 1955.

——. *Writings*. Trans. F. H. Chase, Jr. New York: Fathers of the Church, Inc. 1958.

Jolivet, Régis. *Le Problème du mal chez saint Augustin*. Paris: Beauchesne, 1936.

Koerner, Franz. *Vom Sein und Sollen des Menschen. Die existentialontologischen Grundlagen der Ethik in augustinischer Sicht*. Paris: Etudes Augustiniennes, 1963.

Labriolle, Pierre. *Histoire de la littérature latine chrétienne*. 2 vols. 3ᵐᵉ éd. Paris: Les Belles Lettres, 1947.

Lactantius. *Works*. Trans. William Fletcher. Edinburgh: Clark, 1871.

——. *Institutes*. Trans. E. H. Blakeney. London: Society for the Promotion of Christian Knowledge, 1950.

Library of the Nicene and Post-Nicene Fathers, ed. P. Schaff *et al.* 34 vols. New York, 1886–87; reprinted, Grand Rapids, Mich.: Eerdmans, 1952–56.

Lottin, Odon. "Le Problème de la moralité intrinsèque, d'Abelard à saint Thomas d'Aquin," *Revue Thomiste*, XXXIX (1934), 477–515. Reprinted in *Psychologie et Morale*. Gembloux: Duculot, 1948. II, 421–465.

McKeon, R. P. *Selections from Medieval Philosophers*. 2 vols. New York: Scribner's, 1929.

Martini Episcopi Bracarensis. *Opera Omnia*, ed. C. W. Barlow. New Haven Yale University Press, 1950.

Mausbach, Joseph. *Die Ethik des hl. Augustinus*. Freiburg im Breisgau Herder, 1909; reprinted, 1929.

Nelson, N. E. *Cicero's De officiis in Christian Thought*. Ann Arbor: University of Michigan Press, 1933.

Nothdurft, K. D. *Studien zum Einfluss Senecas auf die Philosophie und Theologie des zwoelften Jahrhunderts*. Leiden: Brill, 1963.

Origen. *On First Principles*. Trans. G. W. Butterworth. London: Society for the Promotion of Christian Knowledge, 1936. Reprinted, New York Harper Torchbooks, 1966.

——. *Contra Celsum*. Trans. H. Chadwick. London: Cambridge University Press, 1953.

Patch, H. R. *The Tradition of Boethius: A Study of His Importance in Medieval Culture*. New York: Oxford University Press, 1935.

Patrologia Latina. 221 vols. Paris: J. P. Migne éditeur, 1844–64. Series Graeca 162 vols. Paris, 1857–66.

Peter Abelard. *Ethica*, ed. L. M. De Rijk. Assen: Van Gorcum, 1966

——. *Abailard's Ethics*. Trans. J. R. McCallum. Oxford: Blackwell, 1935

Pra, Mario dal. *Scoto Eriugena ed il neoplatonismo medievale*. Milano Vita e Pensiero, 1941.

Puëch, Aimé. *Histoire de la littérature grecque chrétienne*. 3 vols. Paris: Les Belles Lettres, 1928–30.

Quasten, Johannes. *Patrology*. 4 vols. Westminster, Md.; Newman Press 1950–66.

Rashdall, Hastings. *Conscience and Christ*. London: Duckworth, 1933.

Rohmer, Jean. *La finalité morale de saint Augustin à Duns Scot*. Paris Vrin, 1939.

ousselot, Pierre. *Pour l'histoire du problème de l'amour au moyen-âge.* (BGPM VI, 6.) Münster: Aschendorff, 1908.

unciman, Steven. *The Medieval Manichee.* Cambridge, Eng.: University Press, 1947.

hnackenburg, Rudolf. *The Moral Teaching of the New Testament.* New York: Herder & Herder, 1965.

hiller, I. *Abelards Ethik im Vergleich zur Ethik seiner Zeit.* München: Universitäts Dissertation, 1906.

hubert, Alois. *Augustins Lex-aeterna-Lehre.* Münster: Aschendorff, 1924.

apiro, Herman. *Medieval Philosophy.* New York: Random House, 1964.

ortt, C. de L. *The Influence of Philosophy on the Mind of Tertullian.* London: Elliot Stock, 1933.

ebert, Otto von. *Die Metaphysik und Ethik des Pseudo-Dionysius Areopagita.* Jena: Pohle, 1894.

vitalski, Bruno. *Neoplatonism and the Ethics of St. Augustine.* New York: Polish Institute of Arts and Sciences, 1946.

ertullian. *De anima,* ed. J. H. Waszink. Amsterdam: Swets, 1933.

———. *The Apology.* Trans. A. Souter. London: Cambridge University Press, 1917.

———. *Apologetical Works.* Trans. R. Arbesmann *et al.* New York: Fathers of the Church, Inc., 1950.

amin, R. *Saint Ambroise et la morale chrétienne au IVe siècle.* Paris: Masson, 1895.

omas Aquinas. *In librum B. Dionysii de divinis nominibus Expositio.* Cura Fr. Ceslai Pera. Taurini: Marietti, 1950.

ouzellier, Christine (ed.). *Un traité cathare inédit du debut du XIIIe siècle, d'après le 'Liber contra Manichaeos' de Durand de Huesca.* Louvain: Publications Universitaires, 1964.

berweg-Geyer. *Die patristische und scholastische Philosophie.* Aufl. 11. Berlin: Mittler, 1928.

cant, A., Mangenot, E., et Amann, E. (eds.). *Dictionnaire de Théologie Catholique.* Paris: Letouzey et Ané, 1903 ff.

ndenbroucke, F. *La morale monastique du XIe au XVIe siècle.* Louvain: Nauwelaerts, 1966.

ulf, Maurice de. *History of Medieval Philosophy.* Vol. I. London: Longmans, 1935; reprinted, New York: Dover, 1952.

CHAPTER V

an, S. M. *Avicenna: His Life and Works.* London: Allen and Unwin, 1958.

Ghazzali. *The Alchemy of Happiness.* Trans. C. Field, London: Wisdom of the East Series, 1910.

———. *The Inspired Treatise.* Trans. Margaret Smith. London: Journal Royal Asiatic Society, 1936.

———. *Deliverance from Error.* Trans. W. Montgomery Watt, in *The Faith and Practice of al-Ghazzali.* London: Allen and Unwin, 1953.

———. *O Disciple!* Trans. G. H. Scherer. Beirut: Catholic Press, 1951
Arberry, A. J. *The Holy Koran, an Introduction with Selections.* London: Macmillan, 1953.
———. *The Koran Interpreted.* New York: Macmillan, 1964.
———. *The Romance of the Rubaiyat.* London: Macmillan, 1959.
Asin y Palacios, Miguel. *Algazel: Dogmatica, moral, ascetica.* Madrid-Saragossa, 1901.
Averroës (Ibn Rushd). *On the Harmony of Religion and Philosophy* Trans. G. F. Hourani. London: Luzac, 1961.
———. *Tahafut al-Tahafut: The Incoherence of the Incoherence.* Trans Simon Van den Bergh. 2 vols. London: Oxford University Press, 1954
———. *Commentary on Plato's Republic,* ed. and trans. E. I. J. Rosenthal London: Cambridge University Press, 1956.
Bahya Ibn Pakuda. *Duties of the Heart.* Trans. Moses Hyamson. 5 vols New York: Bloch, 1925–47.
Bar Hebraeus. *Book of the Dove,* with some chapters from his *Ethikon* Trans. A. J. Wensinck. Leiden: De Goeje Fund, 1919.
Bauer, Hans. *Islamische Ethik.* Halle, 1916, 1917, 1922.
Beiträge zur Geschichte der Philosophie des Mittelalters, hrsg. von Clemen Baeumker *et al.* Münster: Aschendorff, 1891 ff. (About 40 vols. now published; abbreviated as BGPM.)
Boer, T. J. de. *History of Philosophy in Islam.* Trans. E. R. Jones. London Luzac, 1903; reprinted, 1933.
Bokser, B. Z. *The Legacy of Maimonides.* New York: Philosophical Library 1950.
Cohon, Samuel S. *Judaism: A Way of Life. Introduction to the Basi Ideas of Judaism.* New York: Schocken Books, 1958.
Corbin, Henry. *Avicenna and the Visionary Recital.* Trans. W. P. Trask New York: Pantheon Books, 1960.
———. *Histoire de la philosophie islamique, I: Des origines jusqu'à la mo: d'Averroes* (1198). Paris: Gallimard, 1964.
Dawani, Jalal. *Practical Philosophy of the Muhammadan People: Akhlaq Jalali.* Trans. W. F. Thompson. London: Oriental Translation Fun 1839.
Donaldson, D. M. *Studies in Muslim Ethics.* London: Society for th Promotion of Christian Knowledge, 1953.
Duval, Rubens. *Anciennes littératures chrétiennes, II: La littérature syriaqu* 2me éd. Paris, 1900.
Efros, Israel I. *Ancient Jewish Philosophy: A Study in Metaphysics an Ethics.* Detroit: Wayne State University Press, 1964.
Gardet, Louis. *Mohammedanism.* Trans. William Burridge. New York: Ha thorn Books, 1961.
———. *Introduction à la théologie musulmane,* avec G. Anawati. Paris: Vri 1948.
Goldman, Solomon. *The Ten Commandments.* Chicago: University of Cl cago Press, 1962.
Guttmann, Julius. *Philosophies of Judaism.* Trans. D. W. Silverman. N York: Holt, Rinehart and Winston, 1964.

Iernandez, Cruz. *Historia de la Filosofia Española: Filosofia Hispano-Musulmana.* 2 vols. Madrid: Difusora del Libro, 1957.

Iourani, G. F. "Averroes on Good and Evil," *Studia Islamica,* XVI (1962), 13–40.

Iusik, Isaac. *A History of Medieval Jewish Philosophy.* Philadelphia: Jewish Publication Society, 1941.

bn Gabirol (Avicebron). *Fons Vitae,* ed. C. Baeumker. (BGPM I, 2–4.) Münster: Aschendorff, 1892–95.

——. *The Fountain of Life (Treatise Four).* Trans. H. E. Wedeck. New York: Philosophical Library, 1962.

bn Khaldun. *The Muqaddimah: An Introduction to History.* 3 vols. Trans. Franz Rosenthal. (Bollingen Series, 43.) New York: Pantheon Books, 1958.

on Tufail. *Hayy the Son of Yaqzan.* Trans. G. N. Atiyeh. In Lerner and Mahdi (see below), pp. 134–62.

oseph Albo. *Sefer ha-'ikkarim: Book of Principles,* ed. and trans. Isaac Husik. 5 vols. Philadelphia: Jewish Publication Society, 1946.

adushin, Max. *Worship and Ethics: A Study in Rabbinic Judaism.* Evanston, Ill.: Northwestern University Press, 1964.

azarus, M. *The Ethics of Judaism.* 2 vols. Philadelphia: Jewish Publication Society, 1900.

erner, Ralph, and Mahdi, Muhsin (eds.). *Medieval Political Philosophy: A Sourcebook.* New York: Free Press, 1963.

ewy, Hans, Altmann, A., and Heinemann, I. (eds.). *Three Jewish Philosophers.* Philadelphia: Jewish Publication Society, 1945; New York: Harper Torchbooks, 1965.

Iaimonides, Moses. *The Guide of the Perplexed.* Trans. Shlomo Pines. Chicago: University of Chicago Press, 1963.

——. *The High Ways to Perfection.* Trans. S. Rosenblatt. New York: Columbia University Press, 1927.

——. *The Main Principles of the Creed and Ethics of the Jews.* Trans. H. H. Bernard. Cambridge, England, 1832.

——. *The Eight Chapters on Ethics,* ed. and trans. J. I. Gorfinkle. (Columbia University Oriental Studies, VII.) New York: Columbia University Press, 1912.

inkin, J. S. *The World of Moses Maimonides, with Selections from His Writings.* New York: Yoseloff, 1957.

unk, Salomon. *Mélanges de philosophie juive et arabe.* Paris: Franck, 1859.

asir ad-Din. *The Nasirean Ethics.* Trans. G. M. Wickens. London: Allen and Unwin, 1964.

Leary, De Lacy. *Arabic Thought and Its Place in History.* London: Routledge, 1957.

trick, Mary Mills. "The Ethics of the Koran," *Ethics,* XI (1901), 321–29.

scher, Nicholas. *Al-Farabi: An Annotated Bibliography.* Pittsburgh: University of Pittsburgh Press, 1962.

oth, Leon. *The Guide for the Perplexed: Moses Maimonides.* London: Hutchinson's Library; New York: Longmans, 1950.

Saadia ben Josef. *The Book of Beliefs and Opinions.* Trans. S. Rosenblatt. New Haven: Yale University Press, 1948. Abbreviated version by A Altmann, in *Three Jewish Philosophers,* pp. 9–191.

Sharif, M. M. (ed.). *A History of Muslim Philosophy.* 2 vols. Wiesbaden Harrassowitz, 1963.

Snaith, N. H. *The Distinctive Ideas of the Old Testament.* New York Schocken Books, 1944.

Tresmontant, Claude. *A Study of Hebrew Thought.* New York: Desclée 1960.

Umaruddin, M. *The Ethical Philosophy of Al-Ghazzali.* Aligarh, India Muslim University Press, 1962.

Ventura, M. *La philosophie de Saadia Gaon.* Paris: Vrin, 1934.

Weinburg, Julius. *A Short History of Medieval Philosophy.* Princeton N.J.: Princeton University Press, 1964.

Wensinck, A. J. *The Muslim Creed.* London: Cambridge University Pres 1932.

Wickens, G. M. (ed.). *Avicenna: Scientist and Philosophers, a Millenar Symposium.* London: Luzac, 1952.

Wright, W. *A Short History of Syriac Literature.* London, 1894.

CHAPTER VI

Albert the Great. *Opera Omnia,* ed. A. Borgnet. 38 vols. Paris: Vivè 1890–99.

———. *Summa de Bono,* ed. B. Geyer. Vol. XXVIII of the new critical e Köln-Münster: Albertus-Magnus Institut, 1951.

———. *Commentaria in libros Ethicorum,* in *Opera Omnia,* ed. Borgne Vol. VII.

Alszeghy, Z. *Grundformen der Liebe. Die Theorie der Gottesliebe b dem hl. Bonaventura.* Rome: Gregorianum, 1946.

Andreas Capellanus. *The Art of Courtly Love.* Trans. J. J. Parry. Ne York: Columbia University Press, 1941.

Bettoni, Efrem. *Duns Scotus: The Basic Principles of His Philosoph* Trans. Bernardine Bonansea. Washington: Catholic University Press, 196

Binkowski, Johannes. *Die Wertlehre des Duns Scotus.* Berlin-Bonn: Dümmlc 1936.

Bizet, J. A. *Suso et le Minnesange, ou La Morale de l'amour courtois* Paris: Aubier, 1947.

Blakney, R. B. *Meister Eckhart: A Modern Translation.* New York: Harp 1957.

Boethius of Dacia. *De summo bono sive de vita philosophi,* ed. by Ι Grabmann. *In Mittelalterliches Geistesleben.* München: Hueber, 19: Bde. 1, 200–4.

Bonaventure, Saint. *Opera Omnia,* ed. crit. 10 vols. Quaracchi: Collegio San Bonaventura, 1882–1902.

———. *The Works of Bonaventure.* Trans. J. de Vinck. Paterson, N.J.: Anthony Guild Press, 1960 ff.

——. *Retracing the Arts to Theology*. Trans. Sister E. T. Healy. St. Bonaventure, N.Y.: Franciscan Institute, 1955.

onke, E. "Doctrina nominalistica de fundamento ordinis moralis apud G. de Ockham et Gabriel Biel," *Collectanea Franciscana*, CIV (1944), 57–83.

ourke, V. J. *St. Thomas and the Greek Moralists*. Milwaukee: Marquette University Press, 1947.

——. *Pocket Aquinas*. New York: Washington Square Press, 1960.

——. *Ethics in Crisis*. Milwaukee. Bruce, 1966.

andl, L. *Die Sexualethik des hl. Albertus Magnus*. Regensburg: Pustet, 1955.

avitt, Thomas. *The Nature of Law*. St. Louis: Herder, 1951.

ittrich, O. *Geschichte der Ethik*, Bde. 3: *Mittelalter bis zur Kirchenreformation*. Leipzig: Meiner, 1926.

merson, E. H. "Reginald Pecock: Christian Rationalist," *Speculum*, XXI (1956), 235–42.

tienne Tempier. "Condemnation of 219 Propositions." Trans. E. L. Fortin and P. D. O'Neill. In Lerner and Mahdi (see below), pp. 335–56.

airweather, E. R. *A Scholastic Miscellany: Anselm to Ockham*. (Library of Christian Classics, X.) Philadelphia: Westminster Press, 1956.

ickes, K. *Die Rechtfertigungslehre des Gabriel Biel*. Münster: Aschendorff, 1925.

eiler, W. *Die Moral des Albertus Magnus*. Leipzig: Universitäts Dissertation, 1891.

ancis of Assisi, Saint. *His Life and Writings*. Ed. by Leo Sherley-Price. Baltimore: Penguin, 1959.

arvens, Anita. "Die Grundlagen der Ethik Wilhelms von Occam," *Franziskanische Studien*, XXI (1934), 243–73, 360–408.

authier, R. A. "Trois commentaires 'averroistes' sur l'Ethique à Nicomaque." *Archives d'histoire doctrinale et littéraire*, XVI (1947–48), 187–336.

iles of Rome. *De differentia rhetoricae, ethicae et politicae*, ed. Gerardo Bruni, in *New Scholasticism*, VI (1932), 5–12.

——. *Errores Philosophorum*, ed. J. Koch, plus English trans. by J. O. Riedl. Milwaukee: Marquette University Press, 1944. Another version in Shapiro (see below), pp. 386–413.

ilson, Etienne. *Dante the Philosopher*. Trans. David Moore. New York: Sheed & Ward, 1949.

——. *Saint Thomas d'Aquin* (*Les moralistes chrétiens*). Paris: Gabalda, 1931.

enry of Ghent. *Summa Quaestionum ordinariorum*. 2 vols. Paris, 1520; reprinted St. Bonaventure, N.Y.: Franciscan Institute, 1953.

iller, Joseph A. *Albrecht von Eyb: Medieval Moralist*. Washington: Catholic University Press, 1939.

ooker, Richard. *The Works*, ed. John Keble. 3 vols. Oxford: Clarendon, 1839; 6th ed., 1874.

——. *Of the Laws of Ecclesiastical Polity*, ed. Ernest Rhys. 2 vols. London: Dent, 1960; New York: Dutton, 1963.

rett, Bede. *Saint Antonino and Medieval Economics*. St. Louis: Herder, 1914.

————. *Social Theories of the Middle Ages: 1200–1500*. London: Benn, 1926; reprinted, Westminster, Md.: Newman Press, 1942.

Johannes Eckhart, Meister. *Opera Latina*. Leipzig: Meiner, 1934 ff.

————. *Die deutschen und lateinischen Werke*. Stuttgart: Kohlhammer, 1936 ff.

John Duns Scotus. *Opera*, ed. Luke Wadding. 12 vols. Paris: Vivès 1891–95.

————. *Opera Omnia*. Ed. crit., Carolo Balić. Vatican City: Commissic Scotistica, 1950 ff.

————. *Reason and Revelation, A Question from Duns Scotus*. Trans. N Micklem. Edinburgh: Nelson, 1953.

————. *Philosophical Writings* (selections from the *Ordinatio*). Trans Allan Wolter. Edinburgh: Nelson, 1962.

John Fortescue, Sir. *De laudibus legum Angliae*, ed. S. B. Chrimes. London Cambridge University Press, 1942.

————. *The Works*, ed. Thomas Fortescue, Lord Clermont. London, 1869

Klubertanz, G. P. *Habits and Virtues*. New York: Appleton-Century-Crofts 1965.

Kluxen, Wolfgang. *Philosophische Ethik bei Thomas von Aquin*. Mainz Matthias-Grünewald, 1964.

Lacy, E. W. *Sir John Fortescue and the Law of Nature*. Urbana, Ill. University of Illinois Dissertation, 1939.

Lagarde, Georges de. *La naissance de l'esprit laïque au declin du moyen-âge* 5 vols. Paris: Droz, 1942–63.

Lauer, A. *Die Moraltheologie Alberts des Grossen*. Freiburg im Breisgau Herder, 1911.

Lehu, L. *La raison règle de la moralité d'après saint Thomas*. Paris: Gabalda 1930.

Lerner, R., and Mahdi, M. *Medieval Political Philosophy*. New York Free Press, 1963; see pp. 272–526.

L'Homme et son Destin, d'après les penseurs du moyen âge. Louvain Paris: Nauwelaerts, 1948.

Lottin, Odon. *Le droit naturel chez saint Thomas et ses prédécesseurs* Bruges: Beyaert, 1931.

————. *Psychologie et Morale aux XIIᵉ et XIIIᵉ siècles*. 7 vols. Gembloux Duculot, 1942–60.

————. *Etudes de morale*. Gembloux: Duculot, 1961.

McKeon, R. P. *Selections from Medieval Philosophers*. New York: Scribner' 1929, Vol. II.

Maurer, A. A. *Medieval Philosophy*. New York: Random House, 196

Meinertz, Max, und Donders, Adolf. *Aus Ethik und Leben. Festschri für Joseph Mausbach*. Münster: Aschendorff, 1931.

Miscellanea Moralia: In Honorem Eximii Domini Arthur Janssen. Louvain Nauwelaerts, 1948.

Nardi, Bruno. *Sigieri di Brabante*. Roma: Edizioni Italiani, 1945.

Noelkensmeyer, C. *Ethische Grundfragen bei Bonaventura*. Leipzig: Puste 1932.

Oakley, Francis. "Medieval Theories of Natural Law: William of Ockha and the Significance of the Voluntarist Tradition," *Natural Law Forum*, VI (1961), 65–83.

Oberman, H. A. *The Harvest of Medieval Theology: Gabriel Biel and Late Medieval Nominalism*. Cambridge: Harvard University Press, 1963.

Paré, G. *Le Roman de la Rose et la Scolastique Courtoise*. Paris: Vrin, 1941.

Pfister, A. *Die Wirtschaftsethik Antonins von Florenz*. Waldkirch: Universitäts Dissertation, 1949.

Pieper, Josef. *Die ontische Grundlage des Sittlichen nach Thomas von Aquin*. Münster: Aschendorff, 1929.

Powicke, F. M. *Robert Grosseteste and the Nicomachean Ethics*. London: Proceedings of the British Academy, 1930.

Prentice, Robert. *The Psychology of Love according to St. Bonaventure*. St. Bonaventure, N.Y.: Franciscan Institute, 1951.

Ramòn Lull. *Obres*. 17 vols. Palma de Mallorca, 1906–35.

———. *Blanquerna*. Trans. E. A. Peers. London: Jarrold, 1926.

Reade, W. H. V. *The Moral System of Dante's Inferno*. Oxford: Clarendon Press, 1909.

Reginald Pecock. *The Donet*, ed. E. V. Hitchcock. London: Oxford University Press, 1921.

———. *The Reule of Crysten Religioun*, ed. W. C. Greet. London: Oxford University Press, 1927.

Robert Grosseteste. *Summa in Ethica Nicomachea*. Lyons, 1542.

———. *Die philosophischen Werke*, ed. Ludwig Baur. (BGPM IX.) Münster: Aschendorff, 1912.

Roger Bacon. *Moralis Philosophiae*, ed. F. Delorme et E. Massa. Turino: In Aedibus Thesauri Mundi, 1953. Trans. as *Moral Philosophy* by R. P. McKeon, D. McCarthy, and E. L. Fortin, in Lerner and Mahdi (see above), pp. 355–90.

Rohmer, Jean. *La finalité morale chez les théologiens de saint Augustin à Duns Scot*. Paris: Vrin, 1939.

Sertillanges, A. D. *La philosophie morale de saint Thomas d'Aquin*, Paris: Aubier, 1946.

Siger de Brabant. *On the Necessity and Contingency of Causes*. Trans. J. P. Mullally. In Shapiro, *Medieval Philosophy*, pp. 415–38.

Stratenwerth, Günter. *Die Naturrechtslehre des J. D. Scotus*. Göttingen: Vandenhoeck und Ruprecht, 1951.

Suk, O. "The Connection of the Virtues according to Ockham," *Franciscan Studies*, X (1950), 9–32, 91–113.

Taylor, H. O. *Medieval Mind: A History of the Development of Thought and Emotion in the Middle Ages*. 5th ed. 2 vols. Cambridge: Harvard Univeristy Press, 1949.

Thomas Aquinas, Saint, *Opera Omnia*. 25 vols. Parma: Fiaccadori, 1852–73; editio Leonina, Rome: Commissio Leonina, 1882 ff. (17 vols. printed in 1966).

———. *Summa contra Gentiles*. Turin: Marietti, 1934. Trans. as *On the Truth of the Catholic Church*, by A. C. Pegis et al. New York: Doubleday, 1955–57.

————. *Commentary on the Nicomachean Ethics.* Trans. C. I. Litzinger. 2 vols. Chicago: Regnery, 1964.
————. *The Virtues.* Trans. J. P. Reid. Providence, R.I.: Providence College, 1951.
————. *Summa Theologiae.* 5 vols. Ottawa, Canada: Collège Dominicain, 1941–45. 60-volume Latin-English edition, ed. P. K. Meagher and Thomas Gilby. New York: McGraw-Hill, 1963 ff.
William Ockham. *Opera Plurima.* 4 vols. Lyons, 1494–96; reprinted, London, and Ridgewood, N.J.: Gregg Press, 1964.
————. *Opera Omnia.* Crit. ed., by E. M. Buytaert, E. A. Moody, et al. To be published from St. Bonaventure, N.Y.: Franciscan Institute.
————. *Philosophical Writings.* Trans. P. Boehner. Edinburgh: Nelson, 1957.
Wittmann, M. *Die Ethik des hl Thomas von Aquin.* München: Hueber, 1933.

CHAPTER VII

Artz, F. B. *Renaissance Humanism, 1300–1500.* Kent, Ohio: Kent State University Press, 1966.
Baker, Herschel. *The Dignity of Man.* Cambridge: Harvard University Press, 1947. Reissued as *The Image of Man.* New York: Harper Torchbooks, 1961.
Baldwin, William. *A Treatise of Morall Philosophy.* London, 1597.
Bellarmine, Robert. *Opera Omnia.* 12 vols. Paris: Vivès, 1870–74.
————. *Ascent of the Mind to God.* Trans. J. Brodrick. London: Burns Oates, 1928.
————. *De Laicis, or Treatise on Civil Government.* Trans. K. E. Murphy. New York: Fordham University Press, 1928.
Biéler, André. *L'Homme et la femme dans la morale calviniste,* Geneva: Editions Labor, 1963.
Boehme, Jakob. *Works,* ed. C. J. Barber. London: Watkins, 1909.
Boisset, Jean. *Sagesse et sainteté dans la pensée de Jean Calvin.* Paris: Ecole des Hautes Etudes, 1959.
Breen, Quirinus. *John Calvin: A Study in French Humanism.* Grand Rapids, Mich.: Zondervan, 1931.
Bruno, Giordano. *Dialoghi morali,* ed. G. Gentile. Bari: Laterza, 1908. Firenze: Sansoni, 1958.
————. *The Expulsion of the Triumphant Beast.* Trans. A. D. Imerti. New Brunswick, N.J.: Rutgers University Press, 1963.
————. *The Heroic Frenzies.* Trans. P. E. Memmo. Chapel Hill: University of North Carolina Press, 1963.
Bucer, Martin. *Opera Latina,* ed. F. Wendel. Paris: Presses Universitaires, 1954 ff.
————. *Deutsche Schriften,* ed. R. Stupperich. Gütersloh, 1960 ff.
Calvin, John. *Institutes of the Christian Religion.* Trans. F. L. Battles (Library of Christian Classics, 20–21.) Philadelphia: Westminster Press, 1960.

Campanella, Tommaso. *Civitas Solis*. Frankfurt, 1623. Trans. as *The City of the Sun* by T. W. Halliday, in Henry Morley, *Ideal Commonwealths*. London: Routledge, 1893.

Cassirer, Ernst. *The Individual and the Cosmos in Renaissance Philosophy*. Trans. Mario Domandi, New York: Harper, 1964.

Cassirer, Ernst, Kristeller, Paul, and Randall, J. H. *The Renaissance Philosophy of Man*. Chicago: University of Chicago Press, 1948; reprinted 1955.

Charron, Pierre. *De la sagesse*. Paris, 1601. Trans. as *Of Wisdom* by Samson Lennard. London, 1670.

Collins, James. *The Lure of Wisdom*. Milwaukee: Marquette University Press, 1962.

Du Vair, Guillaume. *La philosophie morale des stoïques*. Paris: 1585. Englished as *The Moral Philosophy of the Stoicks* by Thomas James, ed. by Russell Kirk. New Brunswick, N.J.: Rutgers University Press, 1951.

Elyot, Thomas. *The Boke Named the Governour*. London, 1531; ed. F. Watson. New York: Dutton, 1907.

Farrell, Walter. *Natural Moral Law according to St. Thomas and Suarez*. Ditchling, Eng.: St. Dominic's Press, 1930.

Garin, Eugenio. *Italian Humanism, Philosophy and Civic Life in the Renaissance*. Trans. Peter Munz. New York: Harper & Row, 1966.

Gassendi, Pierre. *Opera Omnia*. 6 vols. Lyon, 1658.

Giacon, Carlo. *La seconda scolastica*. 3 vols. Milano: Fratelli Bocca, 1944–50.

Gragg, F. A. (ed.). *Latin Writings of the Italian Humanists*. New York: Scribner's, 1927.

Grimm, H. J. *The Reformation Era, 1500–1650*, rev. ed. New York: Macmillan, 1965.

Harkness, Georgia. *John Calvin: the Man and His Ethics*. New York: Holt, 1931.

Harrison, J. S. *Platonism in English Poetry of the Sixteenth and Seventeenth Centuries*. New York: Macmillan, 1903.

Herbert of Cherbury, Lord. *De veritate*. London, 1633. Trans. by M. H. Carré. Bristol: University of Bristol, 1937.

———. *De religione laici*. Trans. H. R. Hutcheson. New Haven: Yale University Press, 1944.

Kahler, Erich. *Man the Measure*. New York: Pantheon Books, 1943.

Keckermann, Bartholomaeus. *Systema ethicae*. Hanoviae, 1607.

Koch, Karl. *Studium Pietatis: Martin Bucer als Ethiker*. Neukirchen: Neukirchener-Verlag, 1962.

Kristeller, Paul. *Renaissance Thought: the Classic, Scholastic and Humanist Strains*. New York: Harper & Row, 1961.

Lipse, Juste. *Tvvo Bookes of Constancie*. Trans. John Stradling, London, 1594. Ed. Russell Kirk. New Brunswick, N.J.: Rutgers University Press, 1939.

Litt, Theodore. *Ethik der Neuzeit*. München-Berlin: Oldenburg, 1926.

Luther, Martin. *Collected Works*, ed. Jaroslav Pelikan and H. T. Lehmann. St. Louis: Concordia, 1955 ff.

———. *Selections from His Writings*, ed. John Dillenberger. New York: Anchor Books, 1961.

Machiavelli, Niccolò. *The Prince and the Discourses.* Trans. L. Ricci and
C. E. Detmold. New York: Random House, 1940.
MacIntyre, Alasdair. *Short History of Ethics.* New York: Macmillan, 1966.
Chapter 10.
Mariana, Juan. *De rege et regis institutione.* Toledo, 1599. Trans. by G. A.
Moore as *The King and the Education of the King.* Washington: Country
Dollar Press, 1948.
Melanchthon, Philipp. *Scholia in Ethicam Aristotelis,* printed in *Aristotelis
Opera.* 4 parts in 2 vols. Basel: J. Oporinus, 1542.
————. *Selected Writings.* Trans. C. L. Hill. Minneapolis: Augsburg, 1962
Montaigne, Michel de. *Complete Works.* Trans. D. M. Frame. Palo Alto
Calif.: Stanford University Press, 1957.
More, Thomas. *Utopia.* Trans. Peter K. Marshall. New York: Washington
Square Press, 1955.
Mullaney, T. V. *Suarez on Human Freedom.* Baltimore: Carroll Press
1950.
Nardi, Bruno. *Studi sull'aristotelismo padovano dal secolo XIV al XVI*
Firenze: Sansoni, 1958.
Nicholas of Cusa, Cardinal. *Opera Omnia,* ed. E. Hoffmann and R. Klibansky
5 vols. Leipzig: Meiner, 1932–41.
————. *Of Learned Ignorance.* Trans. Germain Heron. London: Routledge
1954.
————. *The Vision of God.* Trans. by E. G. Salter. New York: Ungar
1960.
————. *Unity and Reform. Selected Writings of Nicholas de Cusa,* ed
J. P. Dolan. Notre Dame, Ind.: Notre Dame University Press, 1962
Pico della Mirandola, Giovanni. *Oration on the Dignity of Man.* Tran
by Robert Caponigri. Chicago: Regnery, 1956.
————. *The Rules of a Christian Lyfe.* Trans. Sir Thomas Elyot. London
1534.
Pomponazzi, Pietro. *Libri Quinque De Fato, De Libero Arbitrio et C
Praedestinatione,* ed. R. Lemay. Lucani: In Aedibus Thesauri Mund
1957.
————. *On the Immortality of the Soul.* Trans. W. Hay, in Cassirer et a
The Renaissance Philosophy of Man, pp. 280–381.
Popkin, R. H. *The History of Skepticism from Erasmus to Descarte*
Assen: Van Gorcum, 1960.
Rice, E. F. *The Renaissance Idea of Wisdom.* Cambridge: Harvard Un
versity Press, 1958.
Robinson, D. S. (ed.). *Anthology of Modern Philosophy.* New York: Crowe
1931.
Ross, J. B., and McLaughlin, Mary M. (eds.). *The Portable Renaissan*
Reader. New York: Viking, 1953.
Santillana, Giorgio de (ed.). *The Age of Adventure. The Renaissance Phil*
ophers. New York: Mentor, 1956.
Saunders, J. L. *Justus Lipsius: The Philosophy of Renaissance Stoicis*
New York: Liberal Arts Press, 1955.

Smith, Gerard (ed.). *Jesuit Thinkers of the Renaissance*. Milwaukee: Marquette University Press, 1939.
Suárez, Francisco. *Opera Omnia*, ed. C. Berton. 28 vols. Paris: Vivès, 1856–78.
————. *Disputationes Metaphysicae* in *Opera Omnia*, Vols. XXV–XXVI. Reprinted, 2 vols. Hildesheim: Georg Olms, 1965.
————. *De Legibus* in *Opera Omnia*, Vol. V.
————. Selections from *On the Laws*. Trans. by G. L. Williams *et al*. In *The Classics of International Law*, ed. J. B. Scott. Oxford: Clarendon Press, 1944. Vol. II.
Trinkhaus, C. E. *Adversity's Noblemen: The Italian Humanists on Happiness*. New York: Columbia University Press, 1940.
Ueberweg, F., Frischeisen-Koehler, M., and Moog, Willy. *Die Philosophie der Neuzeit*. Berlin: Mittler, 1924.
Vanini, Lucilio. *Amphitheatrum aeternae providentiae*. Lugduni, 1615.
Vitoria, Francisco de. *On the Law of War*. Trans. by Ernest Nys. Washington: Carnegie Institution, 1917. Also in J. B. Scott, *The Spanish Origin of International Law*, Part I. Oxford: Clarendon Press, 1934.
————. *Commentarios a la Secunda Secundae de Santo Tomás*, ed. Beltran de Heredia. 2 vols. Salamanca: Biblioteca de teologos españoles, 1934.
Weigel, Erhard. *Analysis Aristotelica ex Euclide restituta*. Wittenberg, 1658.
Wilenius, Reijo. *The Social and Political Theory of Francis Suarez*. Helsinki: Philosophical Society of Finland, 1963.
Zanta, Léontine. *La Renaissance du stoicisme au XVIe siècle*. Paris: Champion, 1914.

CHAPTER VIII

Bacon, Francis. *Works*, ed. J. Spedding, R. L. Ellis, and D. Heath. 14 vols. London: Longmans, 1858–72.
————. *Advancement of Learning, and New Atlantis*. New York: Oxford University Press, 1938.
————. *Complete Essays*, ed. H. L. Finch. New York: Mentor, 1963.
————. *Selections*, ed. M. T. McClure. New York: Scribner's, 1928.
Balguy, John. *Foundation of Moral Goodness, Or an Inquiry into the Original of Our Ideas of Virtue, in Answer to Hutcheson's Inquiry*. London, 1728.
Bandini Luigi. *Shaftesbury, etica e religione, la morale del sentimento*. Bari: Laterza, 1930.
Berkeley, Bishop George. *Works*, ed. A. A. Luce and T. E. Jessop. 9 vols. London: Nelson, 1948 ff.
————. *A Treatise concerning the Principles of Human Knowledge*, ed. A. C. Fraser. Oxford: Clarendon Press, 1901.
Blackstone, W. T. *Francis Hutcheson and Contemporary Ethical Theory*. Athens, Ga.: University of Georgia Press, 1965.
Bolingbroke, Henry St. John. *Philosophical Works*. 5 vols. London: Mallet, 1754.

Bonar, James. *The Moral Sense.* Oxford: Clarendon Press, 1930.
Bowle, John. *Hobbes and His Critics.* New York: Oxford University Press, 1952.
Broad, C. D. *Five Types of Ethical Theory.* New York: Harcourt, 1930.
Brogan, A. P. "John Locke and Utilitarianism," *Ethics,* LXIX (1959), 79–93.
Browne, Sir Thomas. *The Works,* ed. G. Keynes. 5 vols. London: Faber & Gwyer, 1928–31.
Butler, Joseph. *Works,* ed. S. Halifax. Oxford: Clarendon Press, 1874.
———. *Works,* ed. W. E. Gladstone. London: Oxford University Press, 1910.
———. *Fifteen Sermons,* ed. W. R. Matthews. London: Oxford University Press, 1949.
Campagnac, E. T. (ed.). *The Cambridge Platonists, Selections.* Oxford: Clarendon Press, 1901.
Carlsson, P. A. *Butler's Ethics.* The Hague: Mouton, 1964.
Cassirer, Ernst. *The Platonic Renaissance in England.* Trans. J. P. Pettegrove. Austin, Tex.: University of Texas Press, 1953.
Clarke, John. *Examination of the Notion of Moral Good and Evil.* London, 1725.
———. *The Foundation of Morality in Theory and Practice.* York, 1730.
Clarke, Samuel. *Discourse concerning the Unchangeable Obligations of Natural Religion.* London, 1706.
Crowe, M. B. "Intellect and Will in John Locke's Conception of the Natural Law," *Atti del XII Congresso Internazionale di Filosofia,* XII (Firenze, 1960), 129–35.
Cudworth, Ralph. *The True Intellectual System of the Universe.* London, 1678.
———. *Treatise concerning Eternal and Immutable Morality.* London, 1731. Ed. J. Harrison. London, 1845.
Cumberland, Richard. *De legibus naturae disquisitio philosophica.* London: 1672. Trans. J. Maxwell, as *A Treatise of the Laws of Nature.* London, 1727. Trans. J. Towers. Dublin, 1750.
De Pauley, W. C. *The Candle of the Lord: Studies in the Cambridge Platonists.* New York: Macmillan, 1937.
Duncan-Jones, A. *Butler's Moral Philosophy.* Baltimore: Penguin, 1952
Garin, Eugenio. *L'Illuminismo inglese: I Moralisti.* Milano: Vallardi, 1941
Gay, John. *Concerning the Fundamental Principle of Virtue or Morality* dissertations prefixed to Edmund Law's translation of Archbishop King's *Essay on the Origin of Evil.* London, 1731.
Harris, W. G. *Teleology in the Philosophy of J. Butler and A. Tucker* Philadelphia: University of Pennsylvania Press, 1942.
Hobbes, Thomas. *Opera Philosophica,* 5 vols. *English Works,* 11 vols. Ed W. Molesworth. London: Bohn and Longmans, 1839–45.
———. *Leviathan,* ed. M. Oakeshott. Oxford: Blackwell, 1946.
Hutcheson, Francis. *Works.* 5 vols. Glasgow, 1772.
———. *Inquiry into the Original of Our Ideas of Beauty and Virtue* London, 1725.

———. *Eassay on the Nature and Conduct of the Passions* and *Illustrations upon the Moral Sense*. London, 1728.

———. *A System of Moral Philosophy*, ed. William Leechman. Glasgow, 1755.

Kames, Henry Home, Lord. *Essays on the Principles of Morality and Natural Religion*. London, 1751.

King, Archbishop William. *De origine mali*. Dublin, 1702–04.

King, Lord. *The Life of John Locke*. 2 vols. London, Colburn & Bentley, 1830. (Contains *inedita*.)

Lamprecht, S. P. *The Moral and Political Philosophy of John Locke*. New York: Columbia University Press, 1918. Reprinted, New York: Russell & Russell, 1964.

Leland, J. *A View of the Principal Deistical Writers*. 2 vols. London, 1837.

Le Rossignol, J. E. *The Ethical Philosophy of Samuel Clarke*. Leipzig, 1892.

Locke, John. *An Essay concerning Human Understanding*, ed. A. C. Fraser. 2 vols. Oxford: Clarendon Press, 1894.

———. *Essays on the Law of Nature* (*1660–1664*), ed. W. von Leyden. New York: Oxford University Press, 1954.

———. *Locke Selections*, ed. S. P. Lamprecht. New York: Scribner's, 1928.

Mackintosh, James. *On the Progress of Ethical Philosophy during the XVII and XVIII Centuries*. Edinburgh: Clarke, 1830; Philadelphia: Carey & Lea, 1832.

Macmillan, Michael. "Bacon's Moral Teaching," *Ethics*, XVII (1907), 55–70.

McPherson, T. "The Development of Bishop Butler's Ethics," *Philosophy*, XXIII (1948), 317–31.

Mandeville, Bernard de. *The Fable of the Bees, or Private Vices Publick Benefits*. 2 vols. London, 1714. Ed. F. B. Kaye. Oxford: Clarendon Press, 1924.

———. *An Enquiry into the Origin of Moral Virtue*. London, 1723.

Mintz, S. I. *The Hunting of Leviathan*. Cambridge, Eng.: University Press, 1962.

More, Henry. *Enchiridion Ethicum*. London, 1667; London: Facsimile Text Society, 1930.

———. *The Philosophical Writings of Henry More*, ed. Flora Mackinnon. New York: Oxford University Press, 1925.

Morgan, Thomas. *The Moral Philosopher*. London, 1738. Reprinted, Stuttgart, Fromman, 1965.

Moskowitz, H. *Die moralische Beurteilungsvermögen in der Ethik von Hobbes bis J. S. Mill*. Erlangen: Junge u. Sohn, 1906.

Norton, W. J. *Bishop Butler, Moralist and Divine*. New Brunswick, N.J.: Rutgers University Press, 1940.

Petzäll, A. *Ethics and Epistemology in John Locke's Essay concerning Human Understanding*. Göteborg: Wettergren & Kerber, 1937.

Polin, Raymond. *La Philosophie morale de John Locke*. Paris: Presses Universitaires, 1961.

Pope, Alexander. *The Poems of Alexander Pope,* ed. John Butt. New Haven Yale University Press, 1966.
———. *An Essay on Man,* ed. Frank Brady. New York: Library of Libera Arts, 1965.
Rand, Benjamin (ed.). *Classical Moralists.* Oxford: Clarendon Press, 1897
Raphael, Daiches. "Bishop Butler's View of Conscience," *Philosophy,* XXIV (1949), 219–38.
Rogers, A. K. "The Ethics of Mandeville," *Ethics,* XXXVI (1926), 1–17
Selby-Bigge, L. A. *British Moralists, Being Selections from Writers Prin cipally of the Eighteenth Century.* Oxford: Clarendon Press, 1897. Re printed, New York: Bobbs-Merrill, 1964.
Shaftesbury, Lord. *An Inquiry concerning Virtue.* London, 1699.
———. *The Moralists, or Philosophical Rhapsody.* London, 1709.
———. *Characteristics.* 3 vols. London, 1711. Ed. Stanley Grean. New York Library of Liberal Arts, 1960.
Sidgwick, Henry. *The Methods of Ethics.* London: Macmillan, 1874; Chi cago: University of Chicago Press, 1962.
Taylor, A. E. "The Ethical Doctrine of Hobbes," *Philosophy,* XIII (1938) 406–24.
Tucker, Abraham. *The Light of Nature Pursued.* 3 vols. London, 1768. Ed H. P. St. John Mildmay. 7 vols. London, 1805.
Tyrrell, Sir James. *A Brief Disquisition of the Law of Nature (with Confutation of Hobbes).* London, 1692. 2nd ed., 1701.
Vigone, Lucia. *L'Etica del senso morale in Francis Hutcheson.* Milano Marzorati, 1954.
Whewell, William. *Lectures on the History of Moral Philosophy in England* London: Parker, 1852, 1868.
Willey, Basil. *The English Moralists.* New York: Norton, 1964.
Wollaston, William. *The Religion of Nature Delineated.* London, 172:
Zani, L. *L'Etica di Lord Shaftesbury.* Milano: Marzorati, 1954.

CHAPTER IX

Attisani, A. *L'Utilitarismo di G. G. Rousseau.* Roma: Foro Italiano, 193
Battaglia, Felice. *Cristiano Thomasio, filosofo e giurista.* Roma: Foro Italian 1935.
Barckhausen, Henri. *Montesquieu, ses idées, son oeuvre.* Paris: Alcan, 190
Baumgardt, David. "The Ethics of Salomon Maimon," *Journal of the Histo. of Ideas,* I (1963), 199–210.
Baumgarten, Alexander Gottlieb. *Initia philosophiae practicae primae.* Hall 1760.
———. *Ethica philosophica.* Halle, 1740.
Bayet, Albert. *La Morale des Gaulois.* Paris: Alcan, 1930.
Beck, L. W. *A Commentary on Kant's Critique of Practical Reason.* Chicag University of Chicago Press, 1960, 1964.
———. *Eighteenth-Century Philosophy.* New York: Free Press, 1966.

Becker, C. L. The Heavenly City of the Eighteenth-Century Philosophers. New Haven: Yale University Press, 1932.

Bidney, David. The Psychology and Ethics of Spinoza. New Haven: Yale University Press, 1940. 2nd ed., New York: Russell & Russell, 1962.

Cassirer, Ernst. The Philosophy of the Enlightenment. Trans. F. Koelln and J. Pettegrove. Princeton, N.J.: Princeton University Press, 1951.

Chroust, A. H. "Hugo Grotius and the Scholastic Natural Law Tradition," New Scholasticism, XVII (1943), 101–33.

Cohen, Hermann. Kants Begründung der Ethik. Berlin: De Gruyter, 1910.

Delbos, Victor. Le problème moral dans la philosophie de Spinoza. Paris: Alcan, 1893.

———. La philosophie pratique de Kant. Paris: Alcan, 1905.

Descartes, René. Oeuvres, ed. Charles Adam et Paul Tannery. 11 vols. Paris: Cerf et Vrin, 1897–1909, 1913.

———. Rules for the Direction of the Mind. Trans. L. J. Lafleur. Indianapolis: Bobbs-Merrill, 1961.

———. Discourse on Method. Trans. Lafleur, idem, 1960.

———. Principles of Philosophy. Trans. J. Veitch, in Descartes: Discourse on Method, etc. New York: Dutton, 1924.

———. Les passions de l'âme, in Oeuvres, Vol. XI.

———. Lettres sur la morale, ed. J. Chevalier. Paris: Vrin, 1935, 1955.

———. Philosophical Works. Trans. E. S. Haldane and G. R. T. Ross. 2 vols. New York: Cambridge University Press, 1911.

Duncan, A. R. C. Practical Rule and Morality. A Study of Kant's Foundations for the Metaphysics of Ethics. London-Edinburgh: Clarke, 1957.

Espinas, Alfred. Descartes et la morale. Paris: Bossard, 1925.

Ethica Cartesiana. Halle, 1719.

Frankel, Charles. The Faith of Reason: The Idea of Progress in the French Enlightenment. New York: Columbia University Press, 1948.

Gerdil, Sigismond Cardinal. Principes métaphysiques de la morale chrétienne, printed in Opere. Rome: Poggioli, 1806–21, I, 1–119.

Geulincx, Arnold. Opera Philosophica. 3 vols. The Hague: Nijhoff, 1891–93. Ethica, in Vol. III of Opera.

Gregor, Mary J. Laws of Freedom. A Study of Kant's Method of Applying the Categorical Imperative in the 'Metaphysik der Sitten.' New York: Barnes & Noble; Oxford: Blackwell, 1963.

Grotius, Hugo. De jure belli et pacis. Den Haag, 1625. Trans. by A. C. Campbell as The Rights of War and Peace. Pontefract, 1814. Also trans. F. W. Kelsey et al., in The Classics of International Law. Oxford: Clarendon Press, 1925.

———. Inleiding tot de Hollandsche Rechts-Geleerdheid. S'Gravenhage, 1631. Trans. by R. W. Lee as Introduction to Dutch Jurisprudence. Oxford: Clarendon Press, 1926.

Hallett, H. F. Benedict de Spinoza; the Elements of His Philosophy. New York: Oxford University Press, 1957.

Hazard, Paul. The European Mind: the Critical Years. Trans. J. L. May. New Haven: Yale University Press, 1953.

Hendel, C. W. *Jean-Jacques Rousseau: Moraliste*. 2 vols. New York: Oxford University Press, 1934. Reprinted, New York: Liberal Arts Press, 1963.

Hodges, D. C. "Grotius on the Law of War," *The Modern Schoolman*, XXIV (1956), 36–44.

Joachim, H. H. *A Study of the Ethics of Spinoza*. Oxford: Clarendon Press, 1901.

Joesten, Clara. *Christian Wolffs Grundlegung der praktischen Philosophie*. Leipzig: Meiner, 1931.

Kant, Immanuel. *Gesammelte Schriften*. 23 vols. Berlin: Reimer u. De Gruyter, 1902–56.

———. *Philosophia practica universalis*, hrsg. Paul Menzer. Berlin, 1924. Trans. by Louis Infield as *Kant's Lectures on Ethics*. London: Methuen, 1931.

———. *Grundlegung zur Metaphysik der Sitten*. Riga, 1785. Trans. by L. W. Beck as *Foundations of the Metaphysic of Morals*. New York: Library of Liberal Arts, 1963.

———. *Kritik der praktischen Vernunft*. Riga, 1788. Trans. by L. W. Beck as *Critique of Practical Reason*. Chicago: University of Chicago Press, 1949.

———. *Metaphysik der Sitten*. 1797. Trans. by J. W. Semple as *The Metaphysics of Ethics*. Edinburgh, 1886.
See also *The Metaphysical Principles of Virtue*. Trans. James Ellington. New York: Library of Liberal Arts, 1964. *Opus Postumum*, ed. Erich Adickes. Berlin: Reuter u. Reichard, 1920. *Kant Selections*, ed. T. M. Greene. New York: Scribner's, 1929.

Krieger, Leonard. *The Politics of Discretion. Pufendorf and the Acceptance of Natural Law*. Chicago: University of Chicago Press, 1965.

Kroner, Richard. *Kant's Weltanschauung*. Chicago: University of Chicago Press, 1956.

Le Chevalier, L. *La morale de Leibniz*. Paris: Vrin, 1933.

Leibniz, Gottfried Wilhelm. *Sämtliche Schriften und Briefe*. Darmstadt Reichl, 1926 ff.

———. *Leibniz: Textes inédits*, éd. par Gaston Grua. 2 vols. Paris: Presse Universitaires, 1948.

———. *Jurisprudence universelle*, éd. par G. Grua. Paris: Presses Uni versitaires, 1953.

———. *Philosophical Papers and Letters*, ed. L. E. Loemker. 2 vols. Chicago University of Chicago Press, 1956.

McKeon, R. P. *The Philosophy of Spinoza*. New York: Longmans, 1928

Maimon, Salomon. *Werke*, hrsg. Ernst Cassirer. 8 vols. Berlin: De Gruyter 1936.

Marsak, L. M. (ed.). *French Philosophers from Descartes to Sartre*. New York: Meridian, 1961.

Mesnard, Pierre. *Essai sur la morale de Descartes*. Paris: Boivin, 193(

Montesquieu, Charles Louis de Secondat. *Oeuvres complètes*, éd. par I Caillois. 2 vols. Paris: La Pléiade, 1958.

———. *The Spirit of the Laws*. 2 vols. Trans. Thomas Nugent. New York Hafner, 1949.

Paton, H. J. *The Categorical Imperative: A Study in Kant's Moral Philosophy.* Chicago: University of Chicago Press, 1948.

Popkin, R. H. (ed.). *Philosophy of the Sixteenth and Seventeenth Centuries.* New York: Free Press, 1965.

Pousa, Narciso. *Moral y Libertad en Descartes.* La Plata, Argentina: Instituto de Filosofía, 1960.

Pufendorf, Samuel. *Elementa Jurisprudentiae Universalis.* Leipzig, 1660. Trans. as *Elements of Universal Jurisprudence.* Oxford: Clarendon Press, 1931.

———. *De jure naturae et gentium.* 8 vols. Leipzig, 1672.

———. *Of the Law of Nature and of Nations.* Oxford, 1710. Also trans. C. H. and W. A. Oldfather. New York: Oxford University Press, 1934.

Reiche, Egon. *Rousseau und das Naturrecht.* Berlin: Junker, 1935.

Rodis-Lewis, G. *La morale de Descartes.* Paris: Presses Universitaires, 1957.

Ross, W. D. *Kant's Ethical Theory.* Oxford: Clarendon Press, 1954.

Rousseau, Jean Jacques. *Oeuvres complètes,* éd. par M. Raymond. 5 vols. Paris: La Pléiade, 1959.

———. *The Social Contract, etc.* Trans. G. D. H. Cole. New York: Dutton, 1926. Reprinted, New York: Hafner, 1947.

Schilpp, P. A. *Kant's Pre-Critical Ethics.* Evanston, Ill.: Northwestern University Press, 1938.

Spinoza, Baruch de. *Opera,* ed. J. van Vloten et J. P. N. Land. 4 vols. The Hague: Nijhoff, 1914.

———. *Short Treatise on God, Man and His Well-Being.* Trans. W. H. White. London: Black, 1910.

———. *Ethica ordine geometrico demonstrata.* Amsterdam, 1677. Trans. by W. H. White as *Ethics.* New York: Hafner, 1953.

———. *Chief Works.* Trans. R. H. M. Elwes. London: Bell, 1883.

Teale, A. E. *Kantian Ethics.* New York: Oxford University Press, 1951.

Terraillon, Eugène. *La morale de Geulincx dans ses rapports avec la philosophie de Descartes.* Paris: Alcan, 1912.

Thomasius, Christian. *Historia Juris Naturalis et Gentium.* Halle, 1719. Reprinted, Stuttgart: Frommann, 1965.

———. *Von der Kunst vernünfftig und Tugendhaft zu lieben: oder Einleitung zur Sittenlehre.* Halle, 1692. Reprinted, Hildesheim, Olms, 1965.

Welzel, Hans. *Die Naturrechtslehre Samuel Pufendorfs.* Berlin: De Gruyter, 1958.

Wolff, Christian L. B. *Vernünftige Gedanken von Gott, der Welt und der Seele.* Frankfurt-Leipzig, 1719. Excerpt from chap. 2 trans. as *Reasonable Thoughts on God, etc.,* in Beck, *Eighteenth-Century Philosophy,* pp. 215–22.

———. *Philosophia Practica Universalis.* 2 vols. Francofurti et Lipsiae, 1738–39.

———. *Philosophia Moralis, sive Ethica scientifica pertracta.* 5 vols. Magdeburg, 1750–53.

———. *A Preliminary Discourse on Philosophy in General.* Trans. R. J. Blackwell, New York: Library of Liberal Arts, 1963.

Wolfson, H. E. *The Philosophy of Spinoza*. 2 vols. Cambridge: Harvard University Press, 1934; Cleveland: World, 1958.
Zac, Sylvain. *La morale de Spinoza*. Paris: Presses Universitaires, 1959

CHAPTER X

Albee, Ernest. *A History of English Utilitarianism*. London: Swan Sonnenschein, 1902. Reprinted, New York: Macmillan, 1962.
Albonico, C. G. *La teoria dei sentimenti morali di Adam Smith*. Mantova: Mondivi, 1920.
Anschutz, R. P. *The Philosophy of J. S. Mill*. Oxford: Clarendon Press 1953.
Aqvist, Lennart. *The Moral Philosophy of Richard Price*. Copenhagen Munksgaard, 1960.
Austin, John. *The Province of Jurisprudence Determined*. London, 1832 Ed. H. L. A. Hart. London: Weidenfeld & Nicolson, 1954.
Bagolini, L. *La simpatia nella morale e nel diritto: aspetti del pensiero d Adamo Smith*. Bologna: Zuffi, 1952.
Bain, Alexander. *Mental and Moral Science*. London: Longmans, 1868
———. *The Emotions and the Will*. New York: Appleton, 1888.
Barnes, W. H. F. "Richard Prince: A Neglected Eighteenth-Century Moralist," *Philosophy*, XVII (1942), 159–73.
Baumgardt, David. *Bentham and the Ethics of Today*. Princeton, N.J. Princeton University Press, 1952.
Beattie, James. *Dissertations Moral and Critical*. London, 1783.
———. *Elements of Moral Science*. 2 vols. Edinburgh, 1790–93.
Beck, L. W. (ed.). *18th-Century Philosophy*. New York: Free Press, 196(
Bentham, Jeremy. *Works*, ed. John Bowring. 11 vols. Edinburgh: Tait, 1838 43. Reprinted, New York: Russell & Russell, 1964.
———. *An Introduction to the Principles of Morals and Legislation*, Londo 1780. Ed. by W. Harrison. Oxford: Blackwell, 1948.
———. *Deontology: Or, the Science of Morality*. Arranged and edited fro the MS of J. Bentham by John Bowring. London: Longmans, 183
Bentham, Jeremy, and Mill, J. S. *Utilitarians*. Garden City, N.Y.: Doubleda 1961.
Broiles, R. D. *The Moral Philosophy of David Hume*. The Hague: Nijho 1964.
Brown, Thomas. *Lectures on the Philosophy of the Human Mind*. 4 vo Edinburgh, 1820.
———. *Lectures on Ethics*. London, 1856.
Burke, Edmund. *Works*. 6 vols. London: Oxford University Press, 192
———. *A Philosophical Inquiry into the Origin of Our Ideas on th Sublime and Beautiful*. London, 1756. Ed. J. T. Boulton. New Yor Columbia University Press, 1958.
———. *Philosophy of Edmund Burke*, ed. L. I. Bredvold and R. G. Ro Ann Arbor: University of Michigan Press, 1961.

Castell, Alburey. *Mill's Logic of the Moral Sciences. A Study of the Impact of Newtonism.* Chicago: University of Chicago Dissertation, 1936.

Coleridge, Samuel Taylor. *Philosophical Lectures.* London, 1818. Ed. Kathleen Coburn. New York: Philosophical Library, 1949.

———. *Aids to Reflection.* London: Bohn, 1825.

Cua, A. S. *Reason and Virtue: A Study in the Ethics of Richard Price.* Athens, Ohio: Ohio University Press, 1966.

Douglas, Charles. *The Ethics of J. S. Mill.* London: Blackwood, 1897.

Ferguson, Adam. *Institutes of Moral Philosophy.* Edinburgh, 1772.

———. *Principles of Moral and Political Science.* Edinburgh, 1792.

Fulton, R. B. *Adam Smith Speaks to Our Times: A Study of His Ethical Ideas.* Boston: Christopher Publishing House, 1963.

Gizycki, Georg von. *Die Ethik David Humes in ihrer geschichtlichen Stellung.* Breslau: Koehler, 1878.

Glathe, A. B. *Hume's Theory of the Passions and of Morals.* Berkeley, Calif.: University of California Press, 1950.

Godwin, William. *Inquiry concerning Political Justice and Its Influence on Morals and Happiness.* London, 1793.

Guyau, J. M. *La morale anglaise contemporaine.* Paris: Alcan, 1900.

Halévy, Elie. *The Growth of Philosophical Radicalism.* Trans. M. Morris. London: Faber & Faber, 1928.

Hamilton, Sir William. *Discussions on Philosophy and Literature.* London-Edinburgh, 1852. (Includes the *Essay on Moral Philosophy.*)

Havard, W. C. *Henry Sidgwick and Later Utilitarian Political Philosophy.* Gainesville, Fla.: University of Florida Press, 1959.

Hedenius, Ingemor. *Studies in Hume's Ethics.* Uppsala: Almqvist & Wiksell, 1937.

Hume, David. *Philosophical Works,* ed. T. H. Green and T. H. Grose. 4 vols. London: Longmans, Green, 1874–75.

———. *A Treatise of Human Nature,* London, 1739. Ed. L. A. Selby-Bigge, Oxford: Clarendon Press, 1888, 1951.

———. *An Enquiry concerning Human Understanding.* London, 1748. Ed. (with the *Principles of Morals*) L. A. Selby-Bigge. Oxford: Clarendon Press, 1902, 1951.

———. *An Enquiry concerning the Principles of Morals.* London, 1751. Ed. C. W. Hendel. New York: Library of Liberal Arts, 1957.

———. *Hume's Ethical Writings,* ed. Alasdair MacIntyre. New York: Macmillan, 1965.

———. *Hume's Moral and Political Philosophy,* ed. Henry Aiken. New York: Hafner, 1948.

———. *Hume Selections,* ed. C. W. Hendel. New York: Scribner's, 1927.

Kidd, Rachel M. *Reason and Conduct in Hume's Treatise.* London: G. Cumberlege, 1946.

Mentani, G. *La Morale della simpatia, saggio sopra l'etica di Adamo Smith.* Genova: Formiggini, 1914.

McCosh, James. *The Scottish Philosophy, Biographical, Expository, Critical.* London, 1875.

MacCunn, John. *Six Radical Thinkers: Bentham, J. S. Mill, Cobden, Carlyle, Mazzini, Green.* London, 1907. Reprinted, New York: Russell & Russell, 1964.

MacNabb, D. G. *David Hume: His Theory of Knowledge and Morality.* London: Hutchinson, 1951.

Mill, James. *Analysis of the Human Mind.* London, 1820.

Mill, John Stuart. *Collected Works.* Toronto: University of Toronto Press, 1965 ff. (3 vols. published by 1966).

———. *System of Logic,* London, 1843; of which Bk. VI is *On the Logic of the Moral Sciences,* ed. H. M. Magid. New York: Bobbs-Merrill, 1965.

———. *Utilitarianism,* London, 1863. Ed. O. Piest. Indianapolis: Library of Liberal Arts, 1957. Ed. Mary Warnock, New York: Meridian, 1962.

Monro, D. H. *Godwin's Moral Philosophy, an Interpretation.* London: Allen & Unwin, 1953.

Newman, John Henry. *Works.* 40 vols. London: Longmans, Green, 1874–1921. Some reprinted, Longmans, 1945 ff.

———. *An Essay in Aid of a Grammar of Assent,* ed. C. F. Harrold London: Longmans, 1947; New York: Doubleday Image, 1955.

———. *Philosophical Readings in Cardinal Newman.* Chicago: Regnery 1961.

———. *The Essential Newman,* ed. V. F. Blehl. New York: Mentor 1963.

Paley, William. *Works.* 8 vols. London, 1805–08.

———. *The Principles of Moral and Political Philosophy.* London, 1785

———. *Natural Theology: Selections,* ed. F. Ferré. New York: Librar of Liberal Arts, 1960.

Parkin, Charles. *The Moral Basis of Burke's Political Thought.* New York Cambridge University Press, 1957.

Passmore, J. A. *A Hundred Years of British Philosophy.* London: Duck worth, 1957.

Plamenatz, John. *The English Utilitarians.* Oxford: Blackwell, 1944.

———. *Mill's Utilitarianism Reprinted with a Study of the English Uti itarians.* Oxford: Blackwell, 1949.

Price, Richard. *A Review of the Principal Questions in Morals.* London 1758. Ed. D. D. Raphael. Oxford: Clarendon Press, 1948.

Reid, Thomas. *An Essay on Quantity . . . Applied to Virtue and Meri* Edinburgh: Philosophical Transactions, 1948.

———. *An Inquiry into the Human Mind on the Principles of Commo Sense.* Edinburgh, 1764.

———. *Essays on the Active Powers of Man.* Edinburgh, 1788.

Schneewind, J. B. "First Principles and Common Sense Morality in Sidgwick Ethics," *Archiv für Geschichte der Philosophie,* XLV (1963), 137–5

Schneider, H. W. *Smith's Moral and Political Philosophy.* New York Hafner, 1948.

Sidgwick, Henry. *The Methods of Ethics.* London: Macmillan, 1874. R printed, New York: Dover, 1966.

———. *Practical Ethics.* London: Macmillan, 1898.

nith, Adam. *Collected Works.* 5 vols. Edinburgh, 1811–12.
——. *Theory of Moral Sentiments.* Edinburgh, 1759.
——. *The Wealth of Nations.* Edinburgh, 1776. 2 vols. New York: Dutton, 1924.
anlis, P. J. *Edmund Burke and the Natural Law.* Ann Arbor: University of Michigan Press, 1958, 1965.
ephen, Leslie. *History of English Thought in the Eighteenth Century.* London: Duckworth, 1876. Reprinted, New York: Harcourt, 1902.
——. *The English Utilitarians.* 3 vols. London: Duckworth, 1900. Reprinted, London: London School of Economics, 1950.
ewart, Dugald. *Outlines of Moral Philosophy.* Edinburgh, 1793. With notes by J. McCosh. London, 1863.
——. *Dissertation Exhibiting the Progress of Metaphysical, Ethical and Political Philosophy.* London: Supplement to *Encyclopaedia Britannica,* in Two Parts, 1815 and 1821.
——. *Philosophy of the Active and Moral Powers of Man.* 2 vols. Edinburgh-Boston, 1828.
abey, W. C. (ed.). *Ethical Theory from Hobbes to Kant.* New York: Philosophical Library, 1961.
ylor, W. L. *Francis Hutcheson and David Hume as Predecessors of Adam Smith.* Durham, N.C.: Duke University Press, 1965.
ard, James. "John Stuart Mill's Science of Ethology," *Ethics,* I (1890), 46–59.
hateley, Richard. *Paley's Moral Philosophy: With Annotations.* London: Parker, 1859.
illey, Basil. *The Eighteenth Century Background.* New York: Norton, 1940.
——. *Nineteenth Century Studies.* New York: Columbia University Press, 1949.

CHAPTER XI

en, H. D. (ed.). *The Age of Ideology.* New York: Mentor, 1956.
th, Karl, *Protestant Thought from Rousseau to Ritschl.* New York: Harper & Row, 1959.
ch, Victor. *L'Individualisme anarchiste: Max Stirner.* Paris: Alcan, 1904.
eke, Friedrich E. *Grundlinien des natürlichen Systems der praktischen Philosophie.* Berlin, 1837. Chap. 3 trans. by B. Rand as "The Natural System of Morals" in *Classical Moralists,* pp. 626–46.
z, R. E. *Die deutsche Romantik.* Leipzig: Reclam, 1937.
ner, H. J. *Schleiermachers christliche Sittenlehre.* Berlin: De Gruyter, 964.
hier, Emile. *Histoire de la philosophie allemande.* Paris: Michel, 1933.
en, H. *Ethik des reinen Willens.* Aufl. 2. Berlin: Cassirer, 1921.
pleston, F. *Arthur Schopenhauer: Philosopher of Pessimism.* London: urns, Oates, 1946.

Eucken, R. *The Value and Meaning of Life.* Trans. W. R. B. Gibso
London: Black, 1909.

Fichte, Johann Gottlieb. *Grundlage des Naturrechts.* Jena, 1796. Tran
by A. E. Kroeger, as *The Science of Rights.* Philadelphia: Lippincot
1869.

——. *Die Bestimmung des Menschen.* Berlin, 1800. Trans. by W. Smi
as *The Vocation of Man* in *Popular Works of J. G. Fichte.* Londo
Trübner, 1889. Ed. with Introduction by R. M. Chisholm. New Yor
Liberal Arts Press, 1956.

——. *Reden an die deutsche Nation.* Berlin, 1807–08. Trans. by R.
Jones and G. H. Turnbull as *Addresses to the German Nation.* Chicag
Open Court, 1922.

Friedrich, Carl J. *The Philosophy of Hegel.* New York: Scribner's, 195

Fries, Jakob F. *Rechtslehre.* Berlin, 1804.

——. *Ethik,* Berlin, 1818.

——. *Psychischen Anthropologie.* Berlin, 1821.

Gardiner, P. *Schopenhauer.* Baltimore: Penguin, 1963.

Gurvitch, Georges. *Fichtes System der konkreten Ethik.* Tübingen: Mo
1924.

Hartmann, J. B. (ed.). *Philosophy of Recent Times. I: Readings in Ni
teenth-Century Philosophy.* New York: McGraw-Hill, 1967.

Hartmann, Nicolai. *Die Philosophie des deutschen Idealismus.* 2 vols. Berl
Leipzig: De Gruyter, 1923–29.

Hegel, Georg W. F. *Sämmtliche Werke* (kritische Ausgabe), hrsg. G. Lass
u. J. Hoffmeister. Leipzig-Hamburg: Meiner, 1905 ff.

——. *Hegels theologische Jugendschriften,* hrsg. H. Nohl. Tübingen: Mo
1907. Partly trans. by T. M. Knox as *Early Theological Writings.* C
cago: University of Chicago Press, 1948.

——. *Die Phänomenologie des Geistes.* Berlin, 1807. Trans. by J. Baillie
The Phenomenology of Mind. London: Macmillan, 1931.

——. *Grundlinien der Philosophie des Rechts.* Berlin, 1821. Trans.
J. M. Sterrett as *The Ethics of Hegel: Selections from the Philosophy
Right.* Boston: Ginn, 1893. Trans. by T. M. Knox as *The Philosophy
Right.* Oxford: Clarendon Press, 1942, 1953. Also trans. by S. W. Dy
London: Bell, 1896.

——. *System der Sittlichkeit.* Berlin, 1893.

——. *Ueber die Differenz des Fichteschen und Schellingschen Syste
Jena, 1801.

Herbart, Johann Friedrich. *Sämmtliche Werke,* ed. G. Hartenstein. 12 v
Leipzig, 1850–52.

——. *Allgemeine praktische Philosophie.* Jena, 1808.

——. *Lehrbuch zur Psychologie.* Berlin, 1816. Trans. by Margaret
Smith as *A Textbook in Psychology.* New York: Appleton, 1891.

Jankélévitch, Vladimir. *L'Odysée de la conscience dams la dernière
losophie de Schelling.* Paris: Alcan, 1933.

Jodl, Friedrich. *Geschichte der Ethik in der neueren Philosophie.* Stuttg
Berlin: Frommann, 1912.

ones, W. T. *Contemporary German Thought.* 2 vols. New York: Macmillan, 1931.

kelley, M. *Kant's Ethics and Schopenhauer's Criticism.* London: Swan-Sonnenschein, 1910.

kojève, Alexandre. *Introduction à la lecture de Hegel.* Paris: Gallimard, 1947.

Kropotkin, Peter. *Ethics: Origin and Development.* Trans. L. S. Friedland and J. R. Piroshnikoff. New York: Dial Press, 1924, 1936.

Lévy-Bruhl, Lucien. *L'Allemagne depuis Leibniz. Essai sur le développement de la conscience nationale en Allemagne, 1700–1848.* Paris: Hachette, 1890.

Lotze, Rudolf Hermann. *Mikrokosmos.* 2 vols. Leipzig, 1856–64. Trans. by E. Hamilton and E. E. C. Jones, as *Microcosmus.* 2 vols. New York: Scribner's, 1887.

MacIntyre, Alasdair (ed.). *Nineteenth-Century Philosophy: Hegel to Nietzsche.* New York: Free Press, 1967.

Mazzei, V. *Il pensiero etico-politica di Friedrich Schelling.* Roma: Sestante, 1938.

Moore, V. F. *Ethical Aspects of Lotze's Metaphysics.* Ithaca, N.Y.: Cornell University Press, 1901.

Nelson, Leonard. *System of Ethics.* Trans. Norbert Guterman. New Haven: Yale University Press, 1956.

Peperzak, A. T. *Le jeune Hegel et la vision morale du monde.* Ten Haag: Nijhoff, 1960.

Pringle-Pattison, A. Seth. *The Development from Kant to Hegel.* 2nd ed. New York: Stechert, 1924.

Raich, M. *Fichte, seine Ethik und seine Stellung zum Problem des Individualismus.* Tübingen: Mohr, 1905.

Reyburn, H. A. *The Ethical Theory of Hegel: A Study of the Philosophy of Right.* Oxford: Clarendon Press, 1921.

Schelling, Friedrich W. J. *Philosophische Untersuchungen über das Wesen der menschlichen Freiheit.* Tübingen, 1809. Trans. by J. Gutman as *Of Human Freedom.* Chicago: Open Court, 1936.

——. *Methode des akademischen Studiums.* Tübingen, 1803. Trans. by E. S. Morgan as *On University Studies.* Athens, Ohio: Ohio University Press, 1966.

——. *Die Zeitalter.* München, 1811. Trans. by F. de W. Bolman as *The Ages of the World.* New York: Columbia University Press, 1942.

Schleiermacher, Friedrich D. E. *Grundlinien einer Kritik der bisherigen Sittenlehre.* Berlin, 1803.

Schopenhauer, Arthur. *Sämmtliche Werke,* hrsg. P. Deussen. 13 vols. München: Piper, 1911–42.

——. *Die Welt als Willie und Vorstellung.* Dresden, 1819. Trans. by R. B. Haldane and J. Kemp as *The World as Will and Idea.* 2 vols. London: Kegan Paul, Trench, 1883–86. Reprinted, New York: Doubleday, 1961.

——. *Die beiden Grundprobleme der Ethik.* Frankfurt, 1841; Leipzig, 1881. Essay I trans. by K. Kolenda as *Essay on the Freedom of the Will.* New York: Liberal Arts Press, 1960. Essay II trans. by A. B. Bullock as

The Basis of Morality. New York: Macmillan, 1903. Also trans. by E. F. J. Payne. New York: Library of Liberal Arts, 1965.
Sterrett, J. M. "The Ethics of Hegel," *Ethics,* II (1892), 176–201.
Stirner, Max. *Der Einzige und sein Eigentum.* Berlin, 1845.
Wahl, Jean. *La conscience malheureuse dans la philosophie de Hegel.* Paris: Aubier, 1951.
Werkmeister, W. H. *Theories of Ethics.* Lincoln, Neb.: Johnsen, 1961.
Wundt, Wilhelm M. *Ethik.* Leipzig, 1886. Trans. by E. B. Titchener *et al.* as *Ethics.* 3 vols. New York: Macmillan, 1897–1901.
Zimmern, Helen. *Arthur Schopenhauer, His Life and His Philosophy.* London: Allen & Unwin, 1876; New York: Scribner's, 1932 (chap. 12)

CHAPTER XII

Alcorta, J. I. "La filosofia etica esencialista-existencialista de Lavelle y Le Senne," *Espiritu,* III (1959), 35–40; V (1961), 20–27.
Baruzzi, Jean (ed.). *Philosophes et savants français du XXᵉ siècle.* Tome III: "Le problème moral." Paris: Alcan, 1926.
Benrubi, Isaak. *Contemporary Thought of France.* Trans. E. B. Dicker New York: Knopf, 1926.
Bergson, Henri. *Oeuvres,* texts annotés par André Robinet. Paris: Presse: Universitaires, 1959 ff.
————. *Extraits e Lucrèce.* Paris: Alcan, 1884.
————. *Essai sur les données immédiates de la conscience.* Paris: Alcan, 1889 Trans. by F. L. Pogson as *Time and Free Will: An Essay on the Immediate Data of Consciousness.* New York: Macmillan, 1950.
————. *Les deux sources de la morale et de la religion.* Paris: Alcan, 1932 Trans. by R. A. Audra and C. Brereton as *The Two Sources of Moralit and Religion.* New York: Holt, 1935. Reprinted, New York: Doubleda Anchor, 1954.
————. *Bergson: Choix de textes,* éd. par R. Gillouin. Paris: Alcan, 1928
————. *Selections from Bergson,* ed. H. A. Larrabee. New York: Appleton Century-Crofts, 1949.
Bochenski, I. M. *Contemporary European Philosophy.* Trans. D. Nichol and K. Aschenbrenner. Berkeley-Los Angeles: University of Californi Press, 1965.
Boutroux, Émile. "The Individual Conscience and the Law," *Ethics,* XXVI (1917), 317–31.
————. "Liberty of Conscience," *Ethics,* XXVIII (1918), 59–72.
————. *Morale et religion.* Paris: Flammarion, 1925.
Bruno, J. F. *Rosmini's Contribution to Ethical Philosophy.* New Yor Science Press, 1916.
Brunschvicg, Léon. *Introduction à la vie de l'esprit.* Paris: Alcan, 190c
————. *La connaissance de soi.* Paris: Alcan, 1931.
————. *La philosophie de l'esprit.* Paris: Presses Universitaires, 1949.
Burnier, André. *La pensée de Charles Secrétan et le problème du fondemer*

métaphysique des jugements de valeur moraux. Neuchâtel: La Baconnière, 1934.
arrel, F. "The Morals of Guyau," *Ethics*, XV (1905), 457–69.
aturelli, Alberto. *La filosofía en Argentina actual*. Córdoba, Argentina: Universidad Nacional de Córdoba, 1962.
opleston, F. *Bergson on Morality*. New York: Oxford University Press, 1957.
ousin, Victor. *Oeuvres complètes*. 22 vols. Paris: Ladrange, 1846–47.
———. *Du vrai, du beau, et du bien*. Paris, 1837. Trans. by O. W. Wight as *The True, the Beautiful, and the Good*. New York: Appleton, 1854.
———. *Cours d'histoire de la philosophie morale au XVIIIe siècle*. Paris: Hachette, 1839–40.
arlu, A. "La morale de Renouvier," *Revue de Métaphysique et de la Morale*, XII (1904), 1–18.
ehove, J. *La théorie bergsonienne de la morale et de la religion*. Lille: Editions de l'Université, 1933.
urber, Marvin (ed.). *L'Activité philosophique en France et aux Etats-Unis*. 2 vols. Paris: Presses Universitaires, 1950. Also in English: *Philosophic Thought in France and the United States*. Buffalo, N.Y.: University of Buffalo, 1950.
errater Mora, José. "The Philosophy of Xavier Zubiri," in *European Philosophy Today*, ed. George Kline. Chicago: Quadrangle Books, 1965. Pp. 15–29.
oucher, Louis. *La Philosophie catholique en France*. Paris: Vrin, 1955.
ouillée, Alfred. *Critique des systèmes de morale contemporaines*. Paris: Baillière, 1899.
———. *La morale, l'art et la religion d'après Guyau*. Paris: Alcan, 1897, 1923.
———. "The Ethics of Nietzsche and Guyau," *Ethics*, XIII (1903), 13–27.
anquiz, J. A. "Personalism in Latin-American Philosophy," *Memorias del XIII Congreso Internacional de Filosofía*, IX (Mexico City, 1964), 571–83.
ioberti, Vicenzo. *Del buono*. Bruxelles: Méline, 1848. Ediz. 2ª, Firenze: Le Monnier, 1853.
———. *Della protologia*. 2 vols. Torino-Paris, 1857. Ed. G. Balsamo-Crivelli. Torino: Paravia, 1924.
———. *Cours de Philosophie*, ed. M. Battistini e Giovanni Calo. Milano: Fratelli Bocca, 1947.
———. *Gioberti (Antologia)*, ed. G. Saitta. Milano: Garzanti, 1952.
uy, Alain. *Les philosophes espagnols d'hier et d'aujourd'hui*. Toulouse-Paris: Editions Privats, 1956.
uyau, Jean-Marie. *Esquisse d'une morale sans obligation ni sanction*. Paris: Alcan, 1885. Trans. by Gertrude Kapteyn as *Sketch of Morality Independent of Obligation or Sanction*. London, 1898.
———. *L'Irreligion d'avenir*. Paris: Alcan, 1887. Trans. as *The Non-Religion of the Future*. New York: Holt, 1897.
———. *La morale anglaise contemporaine*. Paris: Alcan, 1900.
allie, Philip. *Maine de Biran: Reformer of Empiricism*. Cambridge: Harvard University Press, 1959.
omenaje a Xavier Zubiri. Madrid: Editorial Nacional, 1953.

Jankélévitch, Vladimir. *La mauvaise conscience*. Paris: Alcan, 1933.
———. *Le mal*. Paris: Arthaud, 1947.
———. *Traité des vertus*. Paris: Bordas, 1949.
———. *Le pur et l'impur*. Paris: Flammarion, 1960.
Jouffroy, Théodore. *Mélanges philosophiques*. Paris: Joubert, 1842. "De l'éclecticisme en morale," pp. 273–79.
———. *Cours de droit naturel*. Paris, 1834–35.
Korn, Alejandro. *La Libertad Creadora*. La Plata, Argentina: Troquel, 1922
———. *Axiologia*. La Plata, Argentina: Troquel, 1930.
Lavelle, Louis. *La conscience de soi*. Paris: Grasset, 1933.
———. *L'Erreur de Narcisse*, Paris: Grasset, 1939.
———. *La philosophie française entre les deux guerres*. Paris: Aubier, 1942
———. *Quatre Saints*. Paris: Michel, 1951. Trans. by D. O'Sullivan as *The Meaning of Holiness*. London: Downside, 1954.
———. *Conduite à l'égard d'autrui*. Paris: Michel, 1957.
Le Senne, René. *Le devoir*. Paris: Presses Universitaires, 1930.
———. *Obstacle et valeur*. Paris: Aubier, 1934.
———. *Traité de morale générale*. Paris: Presses Universitaires, 1942, 1961
———. *Traité de caractérologie*. Paris: Presses Universitaires, 1945.
———. "De la 'Philosophie de l'esprit,'" in *L'Activité philosophique*, ed. M Farber. II, 113–31.
Lowde, James. *Moral Essays: wherein Some of Mr. Lock's and Mons Malebranch's Opinions Are Briefly Examined*. London, 1699.
Maine de Biran, Marie François Pierre Gonthier. *Oeuvres*, ed. Pierre Tis serand. 14 vols. Paris: Alcan et Presses Universitaires, 1920–49.
———. *Les rapports du physique et du moral de l'homme* (written in 1820) Paris, 1834. In *Oeuvres*, Tome XIII.
———. *Oeuvres choisies de Maine de Biran*, éd. par Henri Gouhier. Paris Aubier, 1942.
Malebranche, Nicolas. *Oeuvres complètes*. 20 vols. dir. par A. Robine Paris: Vrin, 1950 ff.
———. *Traité de morale*. Cologne, 1683. Ed. Henri Joly. Paris, 188: 3me éd. Paris: Vrin, 1953. Trans. by James Shipton as *A Treatise c Morality*. 1699. Chap. 1 reprinted in Rand, *Classical Moralists*. Pp. 286–9:
———. *Dialogues on Metaphysics and Religion*. Trans. Morris Ginsberg. Ne York: Macmillan, 1923.
Maritain, J. "Sur l'éthique bergsonienne," *Revue de métaphysique et de morale*, LXIV (1959), 141–60. In English in *Moral Philosophy*. P 418–47.
Marquinez, A. German. *En torno a Zubiri*. Madrid: Studium, 1965.
Piersol, Wesley. *La Valeur dan la philosophie de Louis Lavelle*. Pari Vitte, 1959.
Renan, J. Ernest. *L'Avenir de la science*. Paris, 1890. Trans. by A. I Vandam and C. B. Pitman as *The Future of Science*. London: Chapma and Hall, 1891.
———. *La Réforme intellectuelle et morale*, ed. P. E. Charvet. Cambridg Eng.: University Press, 1950.

——. *Philosophical Dialogues and Fragments.* Trans. Râs Bihârî Mukhargî. London: Trubner, 1883.

Renouvier, Charles Bernard. *Science de la morale.* 2 vols. Paris: Alcan, 1869, 1908.

——. *Le Personnalisme.* Paris: Alcan, 1903.

Revue Internationale de Philosophie (Bruxelles). Numéro consacré à la 'Philosophie de l'Esprit,' n. 5 (15 oct. 1939).

Rolland, E. *La finalité morale dans le bergsonisme.* Paris: Beauchesne, 1937.

Rome, Beatrice. *The Philosophy of Malebranche.* Chicago: Regnery, 1964.

Romero, Francisco. *Filosofía de la Persona.* Buenos Aires: Losada, 1938.

——. *Theory of Man.* Trans. W. F. Cooper. Berkeley, Calif.: University of California Press, 1964.

Rosmini, Antonio Serbati. *Opere complete.* 28 vols. Milano: Fratelli Bocca, 1934 ff.

——. *Principi della scienza morale.* Milano: Pogliani, 1831. In *Opere complete,* Vols. XXII–XXIII.

——. *Trattato della conscienza morale.* Milano: Pogliani, 1839.

——. *Antonio Rosmini: Anthologie philosophique,* éd. par G. Pusineri *et al.* Lyon: Vitte, 1954.

Sait, U. M. *The Ethical Implications of Bergson's Philosophy.* New York: Columbia University Press, 1914.

Sanabria, José. *El ser y el valor en la filosofía de Louis Lavelle.* Mexico: Universidad Nacional, 1963.

Sanchez Reulet, Anibal. *Contemporary Latin-American Philosophy.* Trans. W. R. Trask. Albuquerque, N.M.: University of New Mexico Press, 1954.

Sciacca, M. F. *La filosofia morale di Antonio Rosmini.* Roma: Perrella, 1938.

——. *Il secolo XX: Storia della filosofia italiana.* 2 vols. Milano: Fratelli Bocca, 1947.

——. *Philosophical Trends in the Contemporary World.* Notre Dame, Ind.: University of Notre Dame Press, 1965.

——. *Etica e Moral.* São Paulo, Brazil: Instituto Brasilerio de Filosofia, 1952.

——. *Ragione etica e intelligenza morale.* Córdoba, Argentina: Universidad Nacional, 1953.

Secrétan, Charles. *La philosophie de la liberté.* 2 vols. Paris: Hachette, 1849, 1879.

——. *Le principe de la morale.* Paris: Hachette, 1884.

Smith, Colin. *Contemporary French Philosophy.* London: Methuen, 1964.

Taine, Hippolyte. *L'Intelligence.* 2 vols. Paris, 1870, 1906. Trans. by T. D. Haye as *On Intelligence.* New York: Holt & Williams, 1872.

——. *Philosophie de l'art.* Paris, 1882. Published as *Philosophy of Art.* London: Baillière, 1865.

Truman, N. E. *Maine de Biran's Philosophy of Will.* Ithaca, N.Y.: Cornell University Press, 1964.

Vasconcelos, José. *Ethica.* Madrid: Aguilar, 1932.

——. *Historia del pensamiento filosófico.* Mexico, D.F.: Universidad Nacional, 1937.

Verga, Leonardo. *La filosofia morale de Malebranche*. Milano: Vita
Pensiero, 1964.
Vidari, Giovanni. *Rosmini e Spencer: studio espositivo-critico di filosofi*
morale. Milano: Hoepli, 1899.
Yoles, Francisca, *et al*. *El pensamiento de M. F. Sciacca: Homenaje* (1908-
1958). Buenos Aires, Argentina: Troquel, 1959.
Zubiri, Xavier. *Naturaleza, Historia, Dios*. Madrid: Editorial Nacional, 1944
————. "Socrates and Greek Wisdom," *Thomist*, VII (1944), 40–45.
————. "El hombre, realidad personal," *Revista de Occidente*, I (1963)
5–29.
————. *Sobre la esencia*. Madrid: Editorial Nacional, 1962.

CHAPTER XIII

Aiken, H. D. (ed.). *The Age of Ideology*. New York: Mentor, 1956
Antolin, Viktor. "La Moral Communista," *Revista de Filosofia*, LV (1955)
565–74. English digest in *Philosophy Today*, I (1957), 106–8.
Ash, William. *Marxism and Moral Concepts*. New York: Monthly Review
Press, 1964.
Banchetti, S. *Il significato morale dell'estetica vichiana*. Milano: Marzorat
1957.
Bausola, Adriano. *Etica e Politica nel pensiero di Benedetto Croce*. Milano
Vita e Pensiero, 1966.
Bax, E. B. *The Ethics of Socialism*. London: Swann, Sonnenschein, 190:
Bazard and Enfantin. *The Doctrine of Saint-Simon, an Exposition*. Tran
George C. Iggers. Boston: Beacon Press, 1958.
Berdyaev, Nikolai. *Smisl Istorii*. Berlin: Obelisk, 1923. Trans. by Georg
Reavey as *The Meaning of History*. New York: Scribner's, 1936.
————. *Freedom and the Spirit*. Trans. O. F. Clarke. London: Bles, 193
————. *Solitude and Society*. Trans. G. Reavey. New York: Scribner's, 193
————. *The Destiny of Man*. Trans. N. Duddington. London: Bles, 194
Reprinted New York: Harper Torchbooks, 1960.
————. *Dialectique existentielle du divin et de l'humain*. Paris: Janin, 194
————. *Christian Existentialism: a Berdyaev Synthesis*, ed. D. A. Lowri
New York: Harper Torchbooks, 1962.
Berlin, Isaiah. *Historical Inevitability*. New York: Oxford University Pres
1955.
Blakeley, T. J. *Soviet Philosophy*. Dordrecht: Reidel, 1964.
Bloch, Ernst. *Das Prinzip Hoffnung*. 2 vols. Frankfurt-am-Main, 195
————. "Man and Citizen according to Marx," in *Socialist Humanism*, e
Erich Fromm. New York: Doubleday, 1965. Pp. 200–06.
Bochenski, I. M. *Contemporary European Philosophy*. Berkeley: University
California Press, 1965.
Bourgin, Hubert. *Fourier, Contribution à l'étude du socialisme frança*
Paris: Bellais, 1905.
Bourke, V. J. "The Philosophical Antecedents of German National S
cialism," *Thought*, XIV (1939), 225–42.

Calian, C. S. The Significance of Eschatology in the Thoughts of Nicolas Berdyaev. Leiden: Brill, 1965.
Caponigri, A. R. Time and Idea. The Theory of History in J. B. Vico. London: Routledge, Kegan Paul, 1953.
Chamberlain, Houston Stewart. Die Grundlagen des neunzehnten Jahrhunderts. 2 Bde. München, 1899. Trans. by J. Lees as The Foundations of the Nineteenth Century. New York: Lane, 1912, 1914.
Collingwood, Robin George. The Idea of History. Oxford: Clarendon Press, 1946.
————. Autobiography. Oxford: Clarendon Press, 1939.
Comte, Auguste. Cours de philosophie positive. 6 vols. Paris: Société Positiviste, 1830–42. Abridged trans. by Harriet Martineau. The Positive Philosophy of Auguste Comte. 3 vols. London: Bohn, 1853.
————. Discours sur l'ensemble du positivisme. Paris: Mathias, 1848. Trans. by J. H. Bridges as A General View of Positivism. London: Routledge, 1910; Stanford: Academic Reprints, 1953.
————. Catéchisme positiviste. Paris, n.d. Reprinted Paris: Garnier, 1909. Trans. by R. Congreve as The Cathechism of Positive Religion. London, 1858.
————. Oeuvres choisies d'Auguste Comte, éd. par Henri Gouhier. Paris: Aubier, 1943.
Condorcet, Antoine-Nicolas de. Oeuvres, éd. par F. Arago. 12 vols. Paris, 1847–49.
————. Esquisse d'un tableau historique des progrès de l'esprit humain. Paris, 1794. Trans. by June Barraclough as The Progress of the Human Mind. New York: Noonday Press, 1955.
Cornu, Auguste. The Origins of Marxian Thought. Springfield, Ill.: Thomas, 1957.
Croce, Benedetto. Filosofia della pratica: Economica ed Etica. Bari: Laterza, 1909. Trans. by Douglas Ainslie as Philosophy of the Practical: Economic and Ethic. New York: Macmillan, 1913.
————. Cultura e vita morale. Bari: Laterza, 1914.
————. Frammenti di etica. Bari: Laterza, 1922. Trans. by Arthur Livingston as The Conduct of Life. New York: Harcourt, Brace, 1924.
————. Etica e Politica, Bari: Laterza, 1931. Trans. by S. J. Castiglione as Politics and Morals. New York: Philosophical Library, 1945.
————. My Philosophy, and Other Essays on the Moral and Political Problems of Our Time. Selected by Raymond Klibansky and trans. by E. F. Carritt. London: Allen & Unwin, 1951.
Cerna, R. C. Filosofia juridica de Benedetto Croce. São Paulo, Brasil: Instituto Brasileiro de Filosofia, 1956.
Deploige, Simon. The Conflict Between Ethics and Sociology. Trans. C. C. Miltner. St. Louis: Herder, 1938.
Deschamps, Léger-Marie. La voix de la raison. Bruxelles, 1770.
————. Le vrai système, ou le mot de l'énigme métaphysique et moral, ed. Jean Thomas et Franco Venturi. Paris: Alcan, 1939.
Dupré, Louis. The Philosophical Foundations of Marxism. New York: Harcourt, Brace & World, 1966.

Durkheim, Emile. *Sociologie et philosophie*. Paris: Alcan, 1924. Trans. by D. F. Pocock as *Sociology and Philosophy*. Glencoe, Ill.: Free Press, 1953.

———. *L'Education morale*. Paris: Alcan, 1925.

———. *Emile Durkheim: Selections from His Work*, ed. by George Simpson. New York: Crowell, 1963.

Edie, J. M., *et al. Russian Philosophy*. 3 vols. Chicago: Quadrangle Books, 1965.

Engels, Friedrich. *Anti-Dühring*. Berlin, 1878. Trans. by Emile Burns as *Herr Eugen Dühring's Revolution in Science*. New York: International Publishers, 1934, 1939.

Evans, Valmai B. "The Ethics of Giovanni Gentile," *Ethics*, XXXIX (1929), 205–17.

———. "The Ethics of Croce," *Ethics*, XLIV (1934), 54–64.

Forti, Edgar. "La Méthode scientifique en morale et en psychologie suivant l'oeuvre de Frédéric Rauh," *Revue de métaphysique et de morale*, XLI (1934), 13–24.

Fourier, François M. C. *Théorie des quatre mouvements*. 2 vols. Leipzig Lyon: Pelzin, 1808.

———. *Le nouveau monde industriel et sociétaire*. 2 vols. Paris: Bossange 1829–30.

Fromm, Erich. *Marx's Concept of Man*. New York: Ungar, 1961.

Garaudy, Roger. *Le communisme et la morale*. Paris: Editions Sociales, 1945

Gentile, Giovanni. *Opere complete*. Firenze: Sansoni, 1938 ff.

———. *L'Atto del pensare come atto puro*. Bari: Laterza, 1912. Trans. by H. W. Carr as *The Theory of the Mind as Pure Act*. New York: Macmillan, 1922.

———. *Discorsi di religione. III: Il problema morale*. Ed. 4. Firenze: Sansoni, 1957.

Ginsberg, Morris. "Ethical Relativity and Political Theory," *British Journa of Sociology*, II (1951), 1–17.

———. *Essays in Sociology and Social Philosophy*, Vol. I: *On the Diversit of Morals*, 1956; Vol. II, *Reason and Unreason in Society*, 1960. London Heinemann.

———. *On Justice in Society*. Ithaca, N.Y.: Cornell University Press, 1965

Gobineau, Arthur de. *Essai sur l'inégalité des races humaines*. 4 vols. Paris 1853–55. Book I trans. by A. Collins as *The Inequality of Human Races* New York: Holt, 1915.

Gumplowicz, Ludwig. *Der Rassenkampf*. Innsbruck: Wagner, 1905; Auf 2, 1927.

———. *Geschichte der Staatstheorien*. Innsbruck: Wagner, 1883.

Harris, H. S. *The Social Philosophy of Giovanni Gentile*. Champaign, Ill. University of Illinois Press, 1960.

Hook, Sidney, *From Hegel to Marx*. New York: Reynal & Hitchcock, 1936

Kamenenka, Eugen. *The Ethical Foundations of Marxism*. London: Routledge, Kegan Paul, 1962.

Kautsky, Karl. *Ethics and the Materialist Conception of History*. Tran J. B. Askew. Chicago: Kerr, 1906, 1918.

Kline, G. L. (ed.). *European Philosophy Today*. Chicago: Quadrangle Books, 1965.
———. "Socialist Legality and Communist Ethics," *Natural Law Forum*, VIII (1963), 21–34.
Lagarde, Paul Anton de. *Deutsche Schriften*. 2 Bde. Göttingen, 1878–81.
Lenin, Vladimir Ilyich Ulyanov. *Collected Works*. Trans. Clemens Dutt *et al.* Moscow: Foreign Languages Institute, 1960 ff. (26 vols. by 1965).
———. *Materialism and Empirio-Criticism*. New York: International Publishers, 1927.
———. *Philosophical Notebooks* (1914–16), in *Collected Works*, Vol. 38.
Lévy-Bruhl, Lucien. *L'Idée de responsabilité*. Paris: Alcan, 1885.
———. *La philosophie d'Auguste Comte*. Paris: Alcan, 1900.
———. *La morale et la science des moeurs*. Paris: Alcan, 1903. Trans. by Elizabeth Lee as *Ethics and Moral Science*. London: Constable, 1905.
Lopatin, L. M. "The Philosophy of Vladimir Solovyev," trans. by A. Bakshy, in *Mind*, XXV (1916), 425–60.
Lubac, Henri de. *The Drama of Atheist Humanism*. Trans. Edith M. Riley. New York: Sheed & Ward, 1950.
Lukacs, Georg. *Geschichte und Klassenbewusstsein*. Berlin: Malik-Verlag, 1923.
———. *Existentialisme ou Marxisme?* Paris: Nagel, 1948.
McGovern, W. M. *From Luther to Hitler*. New York: Houghton, 1941.
Mankiewicz, H. *La conception nationalsocialiste du sens de la vie et du monde*. Lyon: Université de Lyon, 1937.
Marx, Karl. *Zur Kritik der Hegelschen Rechtsphilosophie*. Berlin, 1843.
———. *Karl Marx: Early Writings*, ed. T. B. Bottomore. New York: McGraw-Hill, 1964.
Marx, Karl, and Engels, F. *Historisch-kritische Gesamtausgabe*, hrsg. D. Rjazanow und V. Adoratsky. Frankfurt-am-Main, 1927 ff.
———. *The Communist Manifesto*. London-Brussels, 1848.
———. *Das Kapital*. 3 vols. Berlin, 1867–94. Trans. as *Capital, The Communist Manifesto, and Other Writings*, ed. Max Eastman. New York: Random House, 1932.
Merleau-Ponty, Maurice. *Les aventures de la dialectique*. Paris: Gallimard, 1955.
Meyer, H. *Houston S. Chamberlain als völkischer Denker*. Berlin: Hoheneichen, 1939.
Meyerhoff, Hans (ed.). *The Philosophy of History in Our Time, An Anthology*. Garden City, N.Y.: Doubleday Anchor, 1959.
Popper, K. R. *The Open Society and Its Enemies*. 2 vols. London: Routledge, Kegan Paul, 1945. Vol. II, chap. 8: "Marx's Ethics."
Rauh, Frédéric. *Essai sur le fondement métaphysique de la morale*. Paris, 1890; Paris: Alcan, 1903.
———. *L'Experience morale*. Paris: Alcan, 1903.
———. *Etudes de morale*. Paris: Alcan, 1911.
Romanelli, Patrick. *Croce versus Gentile*. New York: Macmillan, 1947.
Rosenberg, Alfred. *Der Mythus des 20 Jahrhunderts*. München: Hoheneichen, 1938.

Rubel, M. *Pages choisies pour une Ethique socialiste.* Paris: Rivière, 1948.

Rühle, Jürgen. "The Philosopher of Hope: Ernst Bloch," in *Revisionism: Essays on the History of Marxist Ideas,* ed. L. Labedz. London–New York: Praeger, 1962. Pp. 166–78.

Sade, Donatien de. *Les Infortunes de la vertu.* Paris, 1787.

———. *Histoire de Juliette.* Paris, 1790.

Saint-Simon, Claude Henri de. *Oeuvres.* 6 vols. Paris: Anthropos, 1966 ff.

———. *La Société européenne. Paris,* 1814.

———. *Le Système industriel.* Paris, 1821.

Sartre, Jean-Paul. *Critique de la raison dialectique.* Tome I. Paris: Gallimard, 1960.

Seillière, E. *Le Comte de Gobineau et l'Arianisme historique.* Paris: Nourrit, 1903.

———. *Houston Stewart Chamberlain.* Paris: Renaissance du Livre, 1917.

Selsam, Howard. *Socialism and Ethics.* New York: International Publishers, 1943.

Shestov, Léon. *L'Idée de bien chez Tolstoi et Nietzsche.* Paris: Schiffrin, 1925.

———. *Kierkegaard et la philosophie existentielle.* Trad. par T. Rageot et Boris De Schloezer. Paris: Schiffrin, 1936.

Smith, T. V. "The Ethics of Fascism," *Ethics,* XLVI (1936), 151–77

Solovyev, Vladimir. *The Justification of the Good.* Trans. Natalie Duddington. London: Constable, 1918.

———. *The Meaning of Love.* Trans. Janet Marshall. New York: Scribner's 1947.

———. *A Solovyov Anthology,* ed. S. L. Frank. New York: Scribner's, 1950

Stalin, Joseph (Iosif V. Dzhugashvili). *Leninism.* New York: International Publishers, 1942.

———. *Dialectical and Historical Materialism, id.,* 1940.

———. *Marxism and Linguistics. id.,* 1951

Tansill, C. C. "Racial Theories in Germany from Herder to Hitler," *Thought,* XV (1940), 453–68.

Titarenko, Boldyrev, *et al. O Kommunisticheskoi Morali.* Moscow: Academy of Sciences, 1951.

Tucker, R. C. *Philosophy and Myth in Karl Marx.* New York: Cambridge University Press, 1961.

Vico, Giambattista. *Opere.* 8 vols. Bari: Laterza, 1914–41.

———. *De universi juris uno principio et fine uno.* Napoli, 1720.

———. *Scienza Nuova.* Napoli, 1725. ed. 2ᵃ, 1744 (in *Opere,* Vols. III–IV. Trans. by T. C. Bergin and M. H. Fisch as *The New Science (Giambattista Vico.* Ithaca, N.Y.: Cornell University Press, 1948.

Voinea, Serban. *La Morale et le socialisme.* Gand: La Flamme, 195

Westermarck, Edward. *The Origin and Development of the Moral Idea* 2 vols. London: Macmillan, 1906.

Wetter, Gustav. *Dialectical Materialism: a Historical and Systematic Surve of Philosophy in the Soviet Union.* Trans. Peter Heath, New York Praeger, 1958.

Zenkovsky, V. V. A History of Russian Philosophy. Trans. G. L. Kline. New York: Columbia University Press, 1953.
Zis, A. Y. "Moral burzhuaznaya i moral kommunisticheskaya," Pod Znamenem Marksizma, VI (1939), 72 ff.
Zitta, Victor. Georg Lukacs' Marxism: Alienation, Dialectics, Revolution. The Hague: Nijhoff, 1964.

CHAPTER XIV

Allers, Rudolf. Das Werden der sittlichen Person. Freiburg im Breisgau: Herder, 1929. Trans. by E. B. Strauss as The Psychology of Character. New York: Sheed & Ward, 1930.
———. "Ethics and Anthropology," New Scholasticism, XXIV (1950), 237–62.
———. "Reflections on Co-operation and Communication," Proceedings of the American Catholic Philosophical Association, XXXIV (1960), 13–27.
———. The Philosophical Work of Rudolf Allers: A Selection, ed. J. A. Mann. Washington, D.C.: Georgetown University Press, 1965.
Blau, J. L. Men and Movements in American Philosophy. New York: Prentice-Hall, 1952.
Borzaga, Reynold. Contemporary Philosophy. Milwaukee: Bruce, 1966.
Brentano, Franz C. Psychologie vom empirischen Standpunkte. 3 Bde. Leipzig: Meiner, 1874.
———. Vom Ursprung sittliches Erkenntnis. Leipzig: Meiner, 1884. Trans. by Cecil Hague as The Origin of the Knowledge of Right and Wrong. Westminster: Constable, 1902.
———. Grundlegung und Aufbau der Ethik, hrsg. Franziska Mayer-Hillebrand. Berne: Francke, 1952.
Breton, Stanislas. "Le problème de la liberté dans l'éthique de Nicolai Hartmann," Revue Thomiste, XLIX (1949), 310–35.
Brightman, Edgar S. Religious Values. New York: Abingdon Press, 1925.
———. Moral Laws. New York: Abingdon Press, 1933.
———. Person and Reality, ed. P. A. Bertocci et al. New York: Ronald Press, 1958.
Brock, Werner. An Introduction to Contemporary German Philosophy. London–New York: Cambridge University Press, 1935.
Collins, James. "The Moral Philosophy of Max Scheler," Encyclopedia of Morals (1956). Pp. 517–24.
Dupuy, Maurice. La philosophie de Max Scheler. Son Evolution et son unité. 2 vols. Paris: Presses Universitaires, 1959.
Eaton, H. O. The Austrian Philosophy of Values. Norman, Okla.: University of Oklahoma Press, 1930.
———. "The Content of Axiological Ethics," Ethics, XLII (1932), 132–47; XLIII (1933), 20–36, 253–68.
Ehrenfels, Christian von. "The Ethical Theory of Value," Ethics, VI (1896), 371–84.
———. System der Werttheorie. 2 Bde. Leipzig, 1897–1918.

Eklund, H. *Evangelisches und Katholisches in Max Schelers Ethik.* Lund: Uppsala University, 1932.

Finance, Joseph de. *Existence et liberté.* Paris: Vitte, 1955.

———. *Ethica Generalis.* Roma: Universitas Gregoriana, 1959.

———. *Essai sur l'âgir humain.* Rome: Université Grégorienne, 1962.

Findlay, J. N. *Meinong's Theory of Objects.* London: Oxford University Press, 1933.

Frings, Manfred. *Max Scheler.* Pittsburgh: Duquesne University Press, 1965

Gibson, W. R. Boyce. "The Ethics of Nicolai Hartmann," *Australasian Journal of Psychology and Philosophy,* XI (1933), 12–28; XII (1934) 33–61; XIII (1935), 1–23.

Groos, Reinhold. *Die Prinzipien der Ethik Nicolai Hartmanns.* München Kaiser, 1932.

Gurvitch, Georges. *Morale théorique et science des moeurs,* Paris: Alcan 1937.

———. *Les tendances actuelles de la philosophie allemande.* Paris: Vrin, 1949

Hartmann, Nicolai. *Ethik.* 3 Bde. Berlin: De Gruyter, 1926. Trans. by Stanton Coit as *Ethics.* London: Allen & Unwin, 1932.

Hessen, Johannes. *Max Scheler: eine kritische Einführung in seine Philosophie.* Essen: Chamier, 1948.

———. *Ethik: Grundzüge einer personalistischen Wertethik.* Leiden: Brill 1954.

———. *Religionsphilosophie.* 2 Bde. München-Basel: Reinhardt, 1955.

Hildebrand, Dietrich von. "Max Scheler als Ethiker," *Hochland,* XXI (1924) 626–37.

———. "Die Rolle des 'objektiven Gutes für die Person' innerhalb des Sittlichen," in *Philosophia Perennis,* ed. F. J. von Rintelen. Regensburg Habbel, 1930. Pp. 975–95.

———. *Sittliche Grundhaltungen.* Mainz: M. Grünewald, 1933. Trans. a *Fundamental Moral Attitudes.* New York: Longmans, 1950.

———. *Christian Ethics.* New York: David McKay, 1952.

———. *True Morality and Its Counterfeits.* New York: David McKay 1955.

Johnson, O. A. *Ethics. Selections from Classical and Contemporary Writers* New York: Holt, Rinehart, 1965.

Lauer, Quentin. "The Phenomenological Ethics of Max Scheler," *International Philosophical Quarterly,* I (1961), 273–300.

———. *The Triumph of Subjectivity.* New York: Fordham University Pres 1958.

Lepley, Ray (ed.). *The Language of Value.* New York: Columbia Universit Press, 1957.

Lewis, Clarence Irving. *An Analysis of Knowledge and Valuation.* La Salle Ill.: Open Court, 1946.

———. *The Ground and Nature of the Right.* New York: Columbia University Press, 1955.

Margolius, Hans. *Die Ethik Franz Brentanos.* Berlin: Levy, 1929.

Mayer, P. E. *Der Objektivität der Werterkenntnis bei Nicolai Hartmann* Meisenheim: Hain, 1952.

Meinong, Alexius. *Psychologisch-ethische Untersuchungen zur Wert-Theorie.* Graz: Leuschner u. Lubensky, 1894.
——. *Zur Grundlegung der allgemeinen Werttheorie.* Graz: Leuschner u. Lubensky, 1923.
Melden, A. I. (ed.). *Ethical Theories. A Book of Readings.* New York: Prentice-Hall, 1950.
Messer, A. *Deutsche Wertphilosophie der Gegenwart.* Leipzig: Reinicke, 1926.
Most, O. *Die Ethik Franz Brentanos und ihre geschichtlichen Grundlagen.* Berlin: Mittler, 1931.
Muirhead, J. H. (ed.). *Contemporary British Philosophy.* 2 vols. New York: Macmillan, 1931.
Parker, DeWitt H. *Human Values. An Interpretation of Ethics Based on a Study of Values.* New York: Harper, 1931. Reprinted, Ann Arbor, Mich.: Wahr, 1944.
Pepper, S. C. "A Brief History of General Theory of Value," *History of Philosophical Systems,* ed. V. Ferm. New York: Philosophical Library, 1950. Pp. 493–503.
Perry, Ralph Barton. *General Theory of Value.* Cambridge: Harvard University Press, 1926.
Polin, Raymond. *La création des valeurs.* Paris: Presses Universitaires, 1944.
——. *La compréhension des valeurs, id.,* 1945.
——. *Du laid, du mal, du faux, id.,* 1948.
——. "La Philosophie des valeurs en France," in *L'Activité Philosophique,* II (1950), 216–32.
Reck, Andrew. "The Value-Centric Philosophy of W. M. Urban," in *Recent American Philosophy.* New York: Pantheon, 1964. Pp. 154–80.
Rintelen, F. J. von. *Der Wertgedanke in der europäischen Geistesentwicklung.* Mainz: Matthias-Grünewald, 1939–40.
Scheler, Max. *Gesammelte Werke,* hrsg. Maria Scheler. Berne: Francke, 1954 ff.
——. *Beiträge zur Feststellung der Beziehungen zwischen den logischen und ethischen Prinzipien.* Jena: Universitäts Dissertation, 1899.
——. *Ueber Ressentiment und moralisches Werturteil.* Leipzig: Engelmann, 1912. Trans. by W. W. Holdheim as *Ressentiment.* Glencoe, Ill.: Free Press, 1961.
——. *Der Formalismus in der Ethik und die materiale Wertethik,* in *Jahrbuch für Philosophie und phänomenologische Forschung.* Halle, 1913–16.
——. *Vom Ewigen im Menschen.* Berlin: Neue Geist Verlag, 1921. Trans. by B. Noble as *On the Eternal in Man.* New York: Harper, 1960.
——. *Wesen und Formen der Sympathie.* Berlin: Neue Geist Verlag, 1921; Frankfurt: Schulte-Bulmke, 1948. Trans. by Peter Heath as *The Nature of Sympathy.* New Haven: Yale University Press, 1954.
——. *Die Stellung des Menschen im Kosmos.* Berlin: Neue Geist Verlag, 1928. Trans. as *Man's Place in Nature.* Boston: Beacon Press, 1961.
Schlick, Moritz. *Fragen der Ethik.* Wien: Springer, 1930. Trans. by David Rynin as *Problems of Ethics.* New York: Prentice-Hall, 1939.

————. *Gesammelte Aufsaetze, 1926–1936.* Wien: Springer, 1938.
Schutz, Alfred. "Max Scheler's Epistemology and Ethics," *Review of Metaphysics,* XI (1957–58).
Schwarz, B. V. (ed.). *The Human Person and the World of Values: a Tribute to Dietrich von Hildebrand.* New York: Fordham University Press, 1960.
Shaw, C. G. "The Theory of Value and Its Place in the History of Ethics," *Ethics,* XI (1901), 306–20.
Shein, Louis. *A Critique of Nicolai Hartmann's Ethics.* Toronto: University of Toronto Dissertation, 1946.
Sorley, W. S. *The Moral Life and Moral Worth.* Cambridge, Eng.: University Press, 1911.
————. *Moral Values and the Idea of God, id.,* 1918.
————. "Value and Reality," *Contemporary British Philosophy,* II (1925), 245–67.
Spaemann, Robert. "Courants philosophiques dans l'Allemagne d'aujourd'hui," *Archives de Philosophie,* XXI (1958), 274–97.
Stern, Alfred. *La Philosophie des valeurs en Allemagne.* Paris: Alcan, 1933.
Störring, Gustav. *Die moderne ethische Wertphilosophie.* Leipzig: Engelmann, 1935.
Urban, Wilbur M. *Valuation. Its Nature and Laws.* New York: Macmillan, 1909.
————. *The Intelligible World—Metaphysics and Value.* London: Allen & Unwin, 1929.
————. *Fundamentals of Ethics.* New York: Holt, 1930.
Walraff, Charles. *Max Scheler's Theory of Moral Obligation.* Berkeley, Calif.: University of California Press, 1939.
Ward, Leo R. *Philosophy of Value.* New York: Macmillan, 1930.
————. *Values and Reality.* New York: Sheed & Ward, 1935.
————. *Ethics and the Social Sciences.* Notre Dame, Ind.: University of Notre Dame Press, 1959.
————. *Ethics.* New York: Harper, 1965.
Werkmeister, William H. "Ethics and Value Theory," *Proceedings XI International Congress of Philosophy,* X (Brussels, 1953), 119–23.
————. *Theories of Ethics: A Study in Moral Obligation,* Lincoln, Neb.: Johnsen, 1961.
Wittmann, Michael. *Die moderne Wertethik.* Dusseldorf: Schwann, 1940.

CHAPTER XV

Adams, G. P., and Montague, W. P. (eds.). *Contemporary American Philosophy.* 2 vols. New York: Macmillan, 1930.
Adler, Felix. *Life and Destiny.* New York: McClure, Phillips, 1905.
————. *An Ethical Philosophy of Life.* New York: Appleton, 1918.
Barrett, W., and Aiken, H. D. (eds.). *Philosophy in the Twentieth Century* 2 vols. New York: Random House, 1962.
Beck, Lewis White. "A Neglected Aspect of Butler's Ethics," *Sophia,* V (1937), 11–15.

———. "The Formal Properties of Ethical Wholes," *Journal of Philosophy*, XXXVIII (1941), 160–68.

———. "Apodictic Imperatives," *Kant-Studien*, XLIX (1957), 7–24.

Blanshard, Brand. *The Impasse in Ethics*. Berkeley: University of California Press, 1945.

——— *Reason and Goodness*. New York: Macmillan, 1961.

Bosanquet, Bernard. *Psychology of the Moral Self*. London: Macmillan, 1897.

———. *The Principle of Individuality and Value*. London: Macmillan, 1912.

———. *The Value and Destiny of the Individual*. London: Macmillan, 1913.

———. *Some Suggestions in Ethics*. London: Macmillan, 1918.

Bradley, Francis Herbert. *Ethical Studies*. London: King, 1876. 2nd ed., Oxford: Clarendon Press, 1927. Reprinted, New York: Oxford University Press, 1962.

Braithwaite, R. B. *Theory of Games as a Tool for the Moral Philosopher*. Cambridge: University Press, 1955, 1963.

Brandt, R. B. *Ethical Theory*. Englewood Cliffs, N.J.: Prentice-Hall, 1959.

Brogan, A. P. "A Study in Statistical Ethics," *Ethics*, XXXIII (1923), 119–34.

———. "Ethics as Method," *Ethics*, XXXVI (1926), 263–70.

Buchanan, J. M., and Tullock, G. *The Calculus of Consent*. Ann Arbor, Mich.: University of Michigan Press, 1962.

Carritt, E. F. *The Theory of Morals: an Introduction to Ethical Philosophy*. London: Oxford University Press, 1928.

———. *Morals and Politics*, London: Oxford University Press, 1935.

———. *An Ambiguity of the Word Good*. London: Oxford University Press, 1937.

Chubb, Percival. *On the Religious Frontier: From an Outpost of Ethical Religion*. New York: Macmillan, 1931.

Clark, Henry. *The Ethical Mysticism of Albert Schweitzer*. Boston: Beacon Press, 1962. (Includes two essays by Schweitzer: "The Ethic of Self-Perfection," pp. 38–52; and "Reverence for Life," pp. 99–105.)

Cornett, R. A. "Individualism in the Ethics of Elijah Jordan," *Ethics*, LXVI (1956), 61–66.

Cotton, J. H. *Royce on the Human Self*. Cambridge: Harvard University Press, 1954.

Davidson, D., and Suppes, P. *Decision Making*, Stanford, Calif.: Stanford University Press, 1957.

Dewey, R. E., et al. (eds.). *Problems of Ethics*. New York: Macmillan, 1961.

Diggs, B. J. "Rules and Utilitarianism," *American Philosophical Quarterly*, I (1964), 32–44.

Ekman, Rosalind (ed.). *Readings in the Problems of Ethics*. New York: Scribner's, 1965.

Ewing, A. C. *The Definition of Good*. New York: Macmillan, 1946.

———. *Ethics*, London: English Universities Press, 1960.

Frankena, W. K. *Ethics*. Englewood Cliffs, N.J.: Prentice-Hall, 1963.

Fuss, Peter. The Moral Philosophy of Josiah Royce. Cambridge: Harvard University Press, 1965.
Green, Thomas Hill. Works. 3 vols. Oxford: Clarendon Press, 1885–88.
——. Prolegomena to Ethics. Oxford: Clarendon Press, 1883.
——. Principles of Political Obligation. Oxford: Clarendon Press, 1895.
Harrod, R. F. "Utilitarianism Revised," Mind, XLV (1936), 137–56.
Hocking, W. E. Human Nature and Its Remaking. New Haven: Yale University Press, 1918, 1932.
——. Types of Philosophy. New York: Scribner's, 1929, 1959.
Johnson, O. A. Rightness and Goodness, A Study in Contemporary Ethical Theory. The Hague: Nijhoff, 1959.
Jordan, Elijah. The Good Life. Chicago: University of Chicago Press, 1949.
Joseph, H. W. B. Some Problems in Ethics. Oxford: Clarendon Press, 1931.
Kant, Immanuel. Kant: Critique of Practical Reason and Other Writings in Moral Philosophy, ed. and trans. L. W. Beck. Chicago: University of Chicago Press, 1949.
Kiernan, Thomas (ed.). A Treasury of Albert Schweitzer. New York: Philosophical Library, 1965.
Lamont, W. D. An Introduction to Green's Moral Philosophy. London: Allen & Unwin, 1934.
Lyons, David. Forms and Limits of Utilitarianism. London: Oxford University Press, 1965.
Mack, R. D. "Individualism and Individuality in the Ethics of Elijah Jordan," Ethics, LXVII (1957), 139–42.
McCloskey, H. J. "An Examination of Restricted Utilitarianism," Philosophical Review, LXVI (1957), 466–85.
McGlynn, J. V., and Toner, J. J. Modern Ethical Theories. Milwaukee: Bruce, 1962.
Martineau, James. Types of Ethical Theory. 2 vols. Oxford: Clarendon Press, 1886–91.
Mises, Ludwig von. Human Action. New Haven: Yale University Press, 1949.
Muirhead, J. H. Elements of Ethics. London: John Murray, 1892, 1910.
——. The Platonic Tradition in Anglo-Saxon Philosophy. London: Macmillan, 1931.
Munitz, M. K. The Moral Philosophy of Santayana. New York: Humanities Press, 1957.
Neumann, J. von. "Zur Theorie der Gesellschaftspiele," Mathematische Annalen, C (1928), 295–320.
Neumann, J. von, and Morgenstern. O. Theory of Games and Economic Behavior. Princeton, N.J.: Princeton University Press, 1947.
Passmore, John. A Hundred Years of Philosophy. London: Duckworth, 1957.
Paton, H. J. The Good Will, a Study in the Coherence Theory of Goodness. London: Allen & Unwin, 1927.
——. The Categorical Imperative: a Study in Kant's Moral Philosophy. London: Hutchinson's Library, 1946.
——. The Moral Law; or, Kant's Groundwork of the Metaphysic of Morals. Trans. with analysis and notes. New York: Barnes & Noble, 1950.

Patterson, C. H. *Moral Standards*. New York: Ronald Press, 1957.
Prichard, H. A. *Duty and Interest*. Oxford: Clarendon Press, 1928.
———. *Moral Obligation*. Oxford: Clarendon Press, 1949.
———. "Does Moral Philosophy Rest on a Mistake?" *Mind*, XXI (1912), 487–99.
Rashdall, Hastings. "A Critique of Self-Realization," in *The Theory of Good and Evil*. Oxford: Clarendon Press, 1907. Reprinted in Dewey, R. E. *Problems of Ethics* (1961), pp. 257–60.
Rawls, John. "Two Concepts of Rules," *Philosophical Review*, LXIV (1955), 3–32.
Ross, W. D. *The Right and the Good*. Oxford: Clarendon Press, 1930.
———. *Foundations of Ethics*. Oxford: Clarendon Press, 1939.
Royce, Josiah. *The Religious Aspect of Philosophy*. Boston: Houghton Mifflin, 1885.
———. *The World and the Individual*. 2 vols. New York: Macmillan, 1900–01.
———. *Studies of Good and Evil*. New York: Appleton, 1902.
———. *The Philosophy of Loyalty*. New York: Macmillan, 1908, 1924.
———. *The Hope of the Great Community*. New York: Macmillan, 1916.
———. *Fugitive Essays*. Cambridge: Harvard University Press, 1920.
Santayana, George. *Works*. 15 vols. New York: Scribner's, 1936–40.
———. *The Life of Reason*. 5 vols. New York: Scribner's, 1905–06.
———. *Skepticism and Animal Faith*, New York: Scribner's, 1923.
———. *Realms of Being*. 4 vols. New York: Scribner's, 1940, 1942.
Schweitzer, Albert. *Kultur und Ethik*. Leipzig: Barth, 1922. Trans. by John Naish as *Civilization and Ethics*. New York: Macmillan, 1923. Reprinted 1962.
———. *Aus meinen Leben und Denken*. Leipzig: Barth, 1931. Trans. as *Out of My Life and Thought*. New York: Holt, 1933.
———. *The Philosophy of Civilization*. Trans. C. T. Campion. New York: Macmillan, 1949. Reprinted 1964.
———. *The Teaching of Reverence for Life*. London: Peter Owen, 1964.
Segerstedt, T. T. *Value and Reality in Bradley's Philosophy*. Lund: Gleerup, 1934.
Shubik, Martin (ed.). *Game Theory and Related Approaches to Social Behavior*. New York: Wiley, 1964.
Sidgwick, Henry. *Lectures on the Ethics of T. H. Green, Mr. Herbert Spencer and J. Martineau*. London: Macmillan, 1902.
Singer, M. G. "Moral Rules and Principles," in A. I. Melden (ed.), *Essays in Moral Philosophy*. Seattle: University of Washington Press, 1958.
———. *Generalization in Ethics*. New York: Knopf, 1961.
Smart, J. J. C. "Extreme and Restricted Utilitarianism," *Philosophical Quarterly*, VI (1956), 344–54.
———. *An Outline of a System of Utilitarian Ethics*. Melbourne: Melbourne University Press, 1961.
Stace, Walter T. *The Concept of Morals*. New York: Macmillan, 1937. Reprinted 1962.
———. *Mysticism and Philosophy*. New York: Macmillan, 1961.

Taylor, A. E. "Self-Realization—A Criticism," *Ethics*, VI (1896), 356–71.
———. *The Problem of Conduct*. London: Macmillan, 1901.
———. *The Faith of a Moralist*. London: Macmillan, 1930.
Thompson, George. "Game Theory and 'Social Value' Ethics," *Ethics*, LXXV (1965), 36–39.
Urmson, J. O. "The Interpretation of the Moral Philosophy of J. S. Mill," *Philosophical Quarterly*, III (1953), 33–39.
Warnock, Mary. *Ethics Since 1900*. London: Oxford University Press, 1960.
Whitman, M. J. "Forms and Limits of Utilitarianism," *Ethics*, LXXVI (1966), 309–17.
———. *The Public Interest*. New York: Wiley, 1966.
Wolff, R. P. "Reflections on Game Theory and the Nature of Value," *Ethics*, LXXII (1962), 171–79.
Wright, H. W. *Self-Realization. An Outline of Ethics*. New York: Holt, 1913, 1924, 1940.
———. *The Moral Standards of Democracy*. New York: Appleton, 1925.

CHAPTER XVI

Adams, E. M. *Ethical Naturalism and the Modern World-View*. Chapel Hill, N.C.: University of North Carolina Press, 1960.
Aiken, H. D. *Reason and Conduct*. New York: Knopf, 1962.
Allers, Rudolf. "Ethics and Anthropology," *New Scholasticism*, XXIV (1950), 237–62. Reprinted in *Philosophical Work of Rudolf Allers* (1965), pp. 94–110.
Baruk, H. *Psychiatrie morale expérimentale, individuelle et sociale*. Paris: Presses Universitaires, 1950.
Bausola, Adriano. *L'Etica di John Dewey*. Milano: Vita e Pensiero, 1960.
Blewett, J. E. *The Origins and Early Mutations of John Dewey's Ethical Theory (1884–1904)*. St. Louis, Mo.: St. Louis University Dissertation, 1959.
———. (ed.). *John Dewey: His Thought and Influence*. New York: Fordham University Press, 1960.
Brennan, B. P. *The Ethics of William James*. New York: Bookman Associates, 1961.
Cuénot, Claude. "La morale et l'homme selon Pierre Teilhard de Chardin," in *Morale chrétienne et morale marxiste*. Paris-Genève: La Palatine, 1960. Pp. 117–47.
Cunningham, R. L. "The Direction of Contemporary Ethics," *New Scholasticism*, XXXIX (1965), 330–48.
Dennes, William R. *Some Dilemmas of Naturalism*. New York: Columbia University Press, 1960.
Dewey, John. *Collected Works* (20 vols. to be published). Carbondale, Ill.: Southern Illinois University Press, 1966 ff.
———. *The Ethics of Democracy*. New York: Andrews, 1888.
———. *Outlines of a Critical Theory of Ethics*. Ann Arbor, Mich.: Register Publ., 1891.

——. *The Study of Ethics*. Ann Arbor, Mich.: Wahr, 1894.
——. *Logical Conditions of a Scientific Treatment of Morality*. Chicago: University of Chicago Press, 1903.
——. *Ethics*. New York: Columbia University Press, 1908.
——. *Moral Principles in Education*. Boston: Houghton Mifflin, 1909.
——. *Reconstruction in Philosophy*. New York: Holt, 1920.
——. *Human Nature and Conduct*. New York: Holt, 1922.
——. *The Quest for Certainty*. New York: Minton, Balch, 1929.
——. *A Common Faith*. New Haven: Yale University Press, 1934.
——. *Theory of Valuation*. (*International Encyclopedia of Unified Science*, II, 4.) Chicago: University of Chicago Press, 1939.
Dewey, John, and Tufts, J. H. *Ethics*. New York: Holt, 1908, 1932, 1960.
——. *Theory of the Moral Life* (Part II of this *Ethics*), ed. Arnold Isenberg. New York: Holt, Rinehart & Winston, 1960.
Dougherty, Jude. "Recent Developments in Naturalistic Ethics," *Proceedings, American Catholic Philosophical Association*, XXXIII (1959), 97–108.
Dubois, J. *Spencer et le principe de la morale*. Paris, 1899.
Edel, Abraham. "Some Trends in American Naturalistic Ethics," *Philosophic Thought in France and the U.S.* (1950). Pp. 589–611.
——. *Ethical Judgment: the Use of Science in Ethics*. Glencoe, Ill.: Free Press, 1955.
——. *Method in Ethical Theory*. New York: Bobbs-Merrill, 1963.
Edel, Abraham and May. *Anthropology and Ethics*. Springfield, Ill.: Thomas, 1959.
Edwards, Paul. *The Logic of Moral Discourse*. Glencoe, Ill.: Free Press, 1955.
Edwards, Paul, and Pap, Arthur (eds.). *A Modern Introduction to Philosophy*. Glencoe, Ill.: Free Press, 1965.
Feuer, L. S. *Psychoanalysis and Ethics*. Springfield, Ill.: Thomas, 1955.
Flugel, J. C. *Man, Morals and Society: A Psychoanalytical Study*. London: Duckworth, 1945.
Foot, Philippa R. "Moral Arguments," *Mind*, LXVII (1958), 502–13.
Frankena, W. K. "The Naturalistic Fallacy," *Mind*, XLVIII (1939), 464–77.
Freud, Sigmund. *Standard Edition of the Complete Psychological Works*, ed. James Strachey. 24 vols. New York: Norton, 1953.
——. *Vorlesungen zur Einführung in die Psychoanalyse*. Wien, 1916–17. Trans. by Joan Riviere as *Introductory Lectures on Psychoanalysis*. London: Hogarth, 1922.
——. *Civilization and Its Discontents*. Trans. J. Riviere. London: Hogarth, 1949; New York: Doubleday Anchor, 1958.
——. *Beyond the Pleasure Principle*. Trans. J. Strachey. New York: Liveright, 1922, 1950.
——. *Basic Writings of Sigmund Freud*, ed. A. A. Brill. New York: Random House, 1938.
Fromm, Erich. *Escape from Freedom*. New York: Rinehart, 1941.
——. *Psychoanalysis and Religion*. New Haven: Yale University Press, 1950.

——. *Man for Himself. An Inquiry into the Psychology of Ethics*. New York: Rinehart, 1947.
——. *Socialist Humanism: An International Symposium*. New York: Double day, 1965.
Fuchs, Joseph. *Lex Naturae: Zur Theologie des Naturrechts*. Düsseldorf Schwann, 1955. Trans. as *The Natural Law. A Theological Investigation* New York: Sheed & Ward, 1964.
Giddings, F. H. "The Heart of Mr. Spencer's Ethics," *Ethics*, XIV (1904) 496–99.
Glass, Bentley. *Science and Ethical Values*. Chapel Hill, N.C.: University of North Carolina Press, 1965.
Hamburg, C. H. "Fromm's 'Scientific' Ethics of Human Nature," in *Studie in Ethics*. (Tulane Studies, VI.) New Orleans, La.: Tulane University Press, 1957.
Handy, Rollo. "The Naturalistic Reduction of Ethics to Science," *Journa of Philosophy*, LIII (1956), 829–35.
Harding, A. L. (ed.). *Origins of the Natural Law Tradition*. Dallas, Tex. Southern Methodist University Press, 1954.
Hartmann, Heinz. *Psychoanalysis and Moral Values*. New York: Interna tional Universities Press, 1960.
Hartshorne, Charles. *The Divine Relativity*. New Haven: Yale University Press, 1948.
Hawkins, D. J. B. *Nature as the Ethical Norm*. London: Aquinas Society 1951.
Holmes, Samuel J. *The Trend of the Race*. New York: Harcourt, Brace, 1921
——. *Life and Morals*. New York: Macmillan, 1948.
Holt, E. B. *The Freudian Wish and Its Place in Ethics*. New York: Hol 1915.
Hook, Sidney. "The Ethical Theory of John Dewey," in *Quest for Being* New York: St. Martin's Press, 1934. Pp. 49–70.
——. "The Desirable and Emotive in Dewey's Ethics," in *John Dewey Philosopher of Science and Freedom*. New York: Dial Press, 1950.
Huxley, Julian. *Evolutionary Ethics*. (Romanes Lecture, 1943.) London Oxford University Press, 1943. Reprinted in *Touchstone for Ethics*. Ne York: Harper, 1947.
——. *Evolution in Action*. New York: Harper, 1953.
Huxley, Thomas H. *Man's Place in Nature*. London, 1863.
——. *Evolution and Ethics*. (Romanes Lecture, 1893.) London, 1893. R printed in *Touchstone for Ethics* (see Julian Huxley, above).
James, William. "The Moral Philosopher and the Moral Life," *Ethics*, (1891), 330–54. Reprinted in *Essays on Faith and Morals*, ed. R. Perry. New York: Meridian, 1962.
——. *The Will to Believe, and Other Essays*. New York: Longmans, 189
——. *Talks to Teachers on Psychology: and to Students on Some of Life Ideals*. New York: Longmans, 1899, 1939.
Klemke, E. D. "Vivas on 'Naturalism' and 'Axiological Realism,'" *Revie of Metaphysics*, XII (1958), 310–21.

Krikorian, Y. H. (ed.). *Naturalism and the Human Spirit*. New York: Columbia University Press, 1944.

Kurtz, P. W. "Naturalistic Ethics and the Open Question," *Journal of Philosophy*, LII (1955), 113-28.

———. "Decision Making and Ethical Naturalism," *Journal of Philosophy*, LVIII (1961), 693-94.

Lamont, Corliss. *The Illusion of Immortality*. New York: Philosophical Library, 1935.

———. *Humanism as a Philosophy*. New York: Philosophical Library, 1949.

Leclerq, Jacques. *Du droit naturel à la sociologie*. 2 vols. Paris: Spes, 1960.

———. "Natural Law the Unknown," *Natural Law Forum*, VII (1962), 1-15.

Macbeath, Alexander. *The Relationship of Primitive Morality and Religion*. London: Macmillan, 1949.

———. *Experiments in Living*. London: Macmillan, 1952.

Margolis, Joseph. *Psychotherapy and Morality*. New York: Random House, 1966.

———. (ed.). *Contemporary Ethical Theory*. New York: Random House, 1966.

Maritain, Jacques. *Science et sagesse: suivi d'éclaircissements sur la philosophie morale*. Paris: Labergerie, 1935. Trans. by Bernard Wall as *Science and Wisdom*. New York: Scribner's, 1940.

———. *Les droits de l'homme et la loi naturelle*. New York: Maison Française, 1942. Trans. by Doris C. Anson as *The Rights of Man and the Natural Law*. New York: Scribner's, 1942.

———. *Neuf Leçons sur les notions premières de la philosophie morale*. Paris: Téqui, 1951.

———. *La philosophie morale*. Paris: Gallimard, 1960. Trans. by Joseph Evans et al. as *Moral Philosophy*. New York: Scribner's, 1964.

Mead, Margaret. "Some Anthropological Considerations concerning Natural Law," *Natural Law Forum*, VI (1961), 51-64.

Messner, Johannes. *Das Naturrecht: Handbuch der Gesellschaftsethik*. Innsbruck: Tyrolia Verlag, 1950. Trans. by J. J. Doherty as *Social Ethics, Natural Law in the Modern World*. St. Louis: Herder, 1949, 1965.

———. *Kulturethik, mit Grundlegung durch Prinzipienethik und Personalichkeitsethik*. Innsbruck: Tyrolia Verlag, 1954.

———. *Ethics and Facts*. St. Louis: Herder, 1952.

———. "The Postwar Natural Law Revival and Its Outcome," *Natural Law Forum*, IV (1959), 101-05.

Minkiel, S. J. *The General Ethics of John Dewey in the Light of Thomism*. Rome: Angelicum, 1959.

Monist, The (Summer, 1963). Special issue on "Ethics and Anthropology." (Articles by M. and A. Edel, A. C. Garnett, Paul Taylor, John Ladd, and David Bidney.)

Nielsen, Kai. "Examination of the Thomistic Theory of the Natural Law," *Natural Law Forum*, IV (1959), 44-71.

Nodier, Charles. *Les deux sources consciente et inconsciente de la vie morale*. 2me éd. Neuchâtel: La Baconnière, 1947.

Otto, Max. *Science and the Moral Life*. New York: Mentor, 1949.
———. "Humanism," in *American Philosophy*, ed. R. B. Winn. New York: Philosophical Library, 1955. Pp. 172–82.
Pepper, Stephen C. *The Sources of Value*. Berkeley, Calif.: University of California Press, 1958.
———. *Ethics*. New York: Appleton-Century-Crofts, 1960.
Perry, Ralph Barton. *The Moral Economy*. New York: Scribner's, 1909.
———. "The Question of Moral Obligation," *Ethics*, XXI (1911), 282–98.
———. *General Theory of Value*. Cambridge: Harvard University Press, 1926.
Prall, D. W. *Naturalism and Norms*. Berkeley, Calif.: University of California Press, 1925.
Quillian, W. F. "Evolution and Moral Theory in America," in *Evolutionary Thought in America*, ed. S. Persons. New Haven: Yale University Press, 1950. Pp. 398–419.
Ramirez, J. M. "De philosophia morali christiana. Responsio quaedam responsionibus 'completis et adaequatis' Domini Jacobi Maritain," *Divus Thomas* (Fribourg), XIV (1936), 87–122.
Rice, Philip Blair. "Objectivity in Value Judgments," *Journal of Philosophy*. XL (1943), 132–41.
———. "Public and Private Factors in Valuation," *Ethics*, LIV (1944), 41–52.
———. *On the Knowledge of Good and Evil*. New York: Random House, 1955.
Rieff, Philip. *Freud: The Mind of the Moralist*. Garden City, N.Y.: Doubleday Anchor, 1961.
———. "Freudian Ethics and the Idea of Reason," *Ethics*, LXVII (1957), 169–83.
Romanell, Patrick. *Toward a Critical Naturalism*. New York: Macmillan, 1958.
Roth, R. J. *John Dewey and Self-Realization*. Englewood Cliffs, N.J.: Prentice-Hall, 1963.
Sartre, Jean-Paul. *L'Existentialisme est un humanisme*. Paris: Nagel, 1947. Trans. by B. Frechtman as *Existentialism*. New York: Philosophical Library, 1947. Also trans. by P. Mairet. London: Methuen, 1962.
Shelton, H. S. "Spencer as an Ethical Teacher," *Ethics*, XX (1910), 424–37.
Simon, Yves. *The Tradition of Natural Law*, ed. V. Kuic. New York: Fordham University Press, 1965.
Spencer, Herbert. *On Moral and Physical Education*. London, 1861.
———. *The Principles of Ethics*. 2 vols. London–New York: Appleton, 1879–92.
———. *Data of Ethics* (first part of the foregoing). New York: Hurst, 1923.
Stuart, H. W. "Dewey's Ethical Theory," in *The Philosophy of John Dewey*, ed. P. A. Schilpp. Chicago: Northwestern University Press, 1939.
Teilhard de Chardin, Pierre. *Oeuvres*. Paris: Editions du Seuil, 1956 ff
———. *Le phénomène humain*, in *Oeuvres*. Tome I, 1956. Trans. b Bernard Wall as *The Phenomenon of Man*. New York: Harper, 1959
———. *Le Milieu divin*, in *Oeuvres*. Tome IV, 1957. Trans. by B. Wall *et al*

as *Le Milieu Divin*. London: Collins, 1960. Reprinted New York: Harper, 1960, 1965.
'resmontant, Claude. *Pierre Teilhard de Chardin: His Thought*. Baltimore: Helicon Press, 1959.
'ivas, Eliseo. "Julian Huxley's Evolutionary Ethics," *Ethics*, LVIII (1948), 275–84.
———. *The Moral Life and the Ethical Life*. Chicago: University of Chicago Press, 1950.
———. "Animadversions on Naturalistic Ethics," *Ethics*, LVI (1946), 157–79.
Vhitehead, Alfred North. *Science and the Modern World*. New York: Macmillan, 1925.
———. *Process and Reality*. New York: Macmillan, 1929.
———. *Adventures of Ideas*. New York: Macmillan, 1933.
———. *Modes of Thought*. New York: Macmillan, 1938.
Vild, John. "Natural Law and Modern Ethical Theories," *Ethics*, LXIII (1953), 1–13.
———. *Introduction to Realistic Philosophy*. New York: Harper, 1948.
Villiams, Gardner. *Humanistic Ethics*. New York: Philosophical Library, 1951.

CHAPTER XVII

belson, Raziel (ed.). *Ethics and Metaethics*. New York: St. Martin's Press, 1963.
iken, Lillian W. *Bertrand Russell's Philosophy of Morals*. New York. Humanities Press, 1963.
yer, Alfred J. *Language, Truth and Logic*. London: Gollancz, 1936. Reprinted New York: Dover, 1946.
———. "On the Analysis of Moral Judgments," *Horizon* (London), 1949. Reprinted in *Philosophical Essays*. New York: St. Martin's Press, 1954.
———. *Logical Positivism*. New York: Free Press, 1959.
———. *The Concept of a Person and Other Essays*. London: Macmillan, 1963.
iier, Kurt. "Doing My Duty," *Philosophy*, XXVII (1952), 253–60.
———. "Good Reasons," *Philosophical Studies*, IV (1953), 1–15.
———. "Proving a Moral Judgment," *Philosophical Studies*, IV (1953), 33–44.
———. *The Meaning of Life*. Canberra: University College, 1957.
———. *The Moral Point of View*. Ithaca, N.Y.: Cornell University Press, 1958.
nkley, L. J. *Contemporary Ethical Theories*. New York: Philosophical Library, 1961.
ack, Max. "Some Questions about Emotive Meaning," *Philosophical Review*, LVII (1948), 111–26.
andt, R. B. "The Emotive Theory of Ethics," *Philosophical Review*, LIX (1960), 305–18.
———. (ed.). *Value and Obligation. Systematic Reading in Ethics*. New York: Harcourt, Brace & World, 1961.

Broad, C. D. "Is Goodness a Name of a Simple Non-natural Quality?" *Proc., Aristotelian Society*, XXXIV (1933–34), 249–68.

——. "Certain Features of Moore's Ethical Doctrines," in P. A. Schilpp *The Philosophy of G. E. Moore*. Evanston, Ill.: Northwestern University Press, 1942.

——. "G. E. Moore's Latest Published Views on Ethics," *Mind*, LXX (1961).

Carnap, Rudolf. *Philosophy and Logical Syntax*. London: Routledge, Kegar Paul, 1936.

——. "Empiricism, Semantics and Ontology," in *Semantics and the Philos ophy of Language*, ed. L. Linsky. Urbana, Ill.: University of Illinois Press 1952. Pp. 209–12.

Castañeda, H. N., and Nakhnikian, George (eds.). *Morality and the Lan guage of Conduct*. Detroit: Wayne State University Press, 1963.

Charlesworth, M. J. *Philosophy and Linguistic Analysis*. Pittsburgh: Du quesne University Press, 1959.

Copleston, F. *Contemporary Philosophy*. Westminster, Md.: Newman Press 1956.

Ellis, Frank. "Analytic-Positivist Thought," in Mann-Kreyche, *Approaches t Morality* (1966). Pp. 434–557.

Ewing, A. C. "Recent Developments in British Ethical Thought," in *Britis Philosophy in the Mid-Century*, ed. C. A. Mace. London: Macmillar 1957. Pp. 65–95.

——. *Second Thoughts in Moral Philosophy*. New York: Macmillan, 1959

Falk, W. D. "Goading and Guiding," *Mind*, LXII (1953), 145–71.

Frankena, W. K. "Moral Philosophy at Mid-Century," *Philosophical Review* LX (1951), 44–55.

Hägerström, Axel. *Inquiries into the Nature of Laws and Morals*, ed. K Olivecrona. Trans. C. D. Broad. Stockholm: Almqvist & Wiksell, 193

——. *Philosophy and Religion*, ed. R. T. Sandin. New York: Humaniti Press, 1964.

Hall, E. W. "Stevenson on Disagreement in Attitude, *Ethics*, LVIII (1948 51–56.

——. "Practical Reason(s) and Ethics," *Mind*, LXIV (1955), 319–32.

Hampshire, Stuart. "Fallacies in Moral Philosophy," *Mind*, LVIII (1949 466–82.

——. *Thought and Action*. London: Chatto & Windus, 1959.

——. (ed.). *The Age of Reason*. New York: Mentor, 1956.

Hampshire, Stuart, and Hart, H. L. A. "Decision, Intention, and Certainty *Mind*, LXVII (1958), 1–12.

Hancock, Roger. "The Refutation of Naturalism in Moore and Hare *Journal of Philosophy*, LVII (1960), 326–34.

Hare, Richard M. *The Language of Morals*. Oxford: Clarendon Press, 195

——. "Universalizability," *Proceedings, Aristotelian Society*, LV (1954–55 295–312.

——. *Freedom and Reason*. Oxford: Clarendon Press, 1963.

Iare, Richard M., and Gardiner, P. M. "Pain and Evil," *Proceedings, Aristotelian Society*, Suppl. XXXVIII (1964), 91–124.

Iospers, John. *An Introduction to Philosophical Analysis*. New York: Prentice-Hall, 1953.

oad, C. E. M. *A Critique of Logical Positivism*. Chicago: University of Chicago Press, 1950.

Cerner, G. C. *The Revolution in Ethical Theory*. New York: Oxford University Press, 1966.

aird, John. *Recent Philosophy*. London: Butterworth, 1936.

awler, Ronald. "The Nature of Analytic Ethics," *Proceedings, American Catholic Philosophical Association*, XXXIV (1960), 151–57.

ewis, H. D. (ed.). *Contemporary British Philosophy*. London: Allen & Unwin, 1957.

Logical Positivism and Ethics," symposium in *Proceedings, Aristotelian Society*, Suppl. XXII (London, 1948).

IcCloskey, H. J. "Nowell-Smith's Ethics," *Australasian Journal of Psychology and Philosophy*, XXXIX (1961).

Iehta, Ved. *Fly and the Fly Bottle. Encounters with British Intellectuals*. Boston: Little, Brown, 1963.

Iilne, A. J. M. *The Social Philosophy of English Idealism*. London: Allen & Unwin, 1962.

Ioore, Asher. "Emotivism: Theory and Practice," *Journal of Philosophy*, LV (1958).

Ioore, G. E. *Principia Ethica*. Cambridge, Eng.: University Press, 1903. Reprinted New York: Cambridge University Press, 1959.

———. *Ethics*. London: Home University Library, 1912. Reprinted New York: Cambridge University Press, 1949.

———. "The Nature of Moral Philosophy," in *Philosophical Studies*. London: Kegan Paul, 1922. Pp. 310–29.

———. *Philosophical Papers*. New York: Macmillan, 1959.

Iunitz, M. K. (ed.). *A Modern Introduction to Ethics*. New York: Free Press, 1958.

ewsom, G. E. *The New Morality*. New York: Scribner's, 1933.

owell-Smith, Patrick H. "Free Will and Moral Responsibility," *Mind*, LVII (1948), 45–61.

———. *Ethics*. London-Baltimore: Penguin, 1954. Reprinted New York: Philosophical Library, 1958.

———. "Determinists and Libertarians," *Mind*, LXII (1954), 317–37.

———. "Psycho-analysis and Moral Language," *The Rationalist Annual*, (1954). Reprinted in Edwards-Pap, *Modern Introduction to Philosophy* (1965). Pp. 86–93.

———. "Choosing, Deciding and Doing," *Analysis*, XVIII (1958), 63–69.

———. "Contextual Implication and Ethical Theory," *Proceedings, Aristotelian Society*, Suppl. XXXVI (1962), 1–18.

fstad, Harald. "Objectivity of Norms and Value-Judgments according to Recent Scandinavian Philosophy," *Philosophy and Phenomenological Research*, XII (1951–52), 42–68.

Oldenquist, Andrew (ed.). *Readings in Moral Philosophy*. Boston: Houghton Mifflin, 1964.

Rawls, John. "Outline of a Decision Procedure for Ethics," *Philosophical Review*, LX (1951), 177–97.

———. "Two Concepts of Rules," *Philosophical Review*, LXIV (1955), 3–32.

———. "Justice as Fairness," *Philosophical Review*, LXVII (1958), 164–94.

———. "The Sense of Justice," *Philosophical Review*, LXXII (1963), 281–305.

Rhees, Rush. "Some Developments in Wittgenstein's Views of Ethics," *Philosophical Review*, LXXIV (1965), 17–26.

Ross, Alf. *On Law and Justice*. Berkeley–Los Angeles: University of California Press, 1959.

Russell, Bertrand. "A Free Man's Worship," in *Mysticism and Logic*. New York: Norton, 1929. Pp. 46–57. Reprinted New York: Doubleday, 1957

———. *Marriage and Morals*. New York: Norton, 1929.

———. *Religion and Science*. London: Oxford University Press, 1935.

———. "The Elements of Ethics," in Sellars and Hospers, *Readings in Ethical Theory* (1952). Pp. 1–17.

———. *Human Society in Ethics and Politics*. London: Allen & Unwin, 1955

Stapledon, Olaf. "Mr. Bertrand Russell's Ethical Beliefs," *Ethics*, XXXVI (1927), 390–402.

Stevenson, Charles L. "The Emotive Meaning of Ethical Terms," *Mind* XLVI (1937), 10–31.

———. "Ethical Judgments and Avoidability," *Mind*, XLVII (1938), 45–67

———. "Persuasive Definitions," *Mind*, XLVII (1938) 331–50.

———. *Ethics and Language*. New Haven: Yale University Press, 1944.

———. "The Emotive Conception of Ethics and Its Cognitive Implications," *Philosophical Review*, LIX (1950). Reprinted in *Facts and Values Studies in Ethical Analysis*. New Haven: Yale University Press, 1963 Pp. 55–70.

Strawson, Peter F. "Ethical Intuitionism," *Philosophy*, XXIV (1949), 347 57.

———. *Individuals*. Oxford: Clarendon Press, 1959.

———. "Social Morality and Individual Ideals," *Philosophy*, XXXVI (1961) 1–17.

Stroll, Avrum. *The Emotive Theory of Ethics*. Berkeley, Calif.: Universit of California Press, 1954.

Taylor, P. W. *Normative Discourse*. Englewood Cliffs, N.J.: Prentice-Hal 1961.

———. (ed.). *The Moral Judgment: Readings in Contemporary Meta-Ethic* New York: Free Press, 1966.

Toulmin, Stephen E. "Knowledge of Right and Wrong," *Proceeding Aristotelian Society*, LI (1950–51).

———. *An Examination of the Place of Reason in Ethics*. London: Cam bridge University Press, 1950.

———. "Principles of Morality," *Philosophy*, XXXI (1956), 142–53.

———. "The Emotive Theory of Ethics," a symposium in *Proceedings, Ari totelian Society*, Suppl. XXII (1948), 76–140.

nson, James O. "On Grading," *Mind*, LIX (1950), 145–69.

———. *Philosophical Analysis: Its Development between the Two Wars.* Oxford: Clarendon Press, 1956.

atch, H. B. "Non-Cognitivism in Ethics," *Ethics*, LXXVI (1966), 102–6.

aismann, F. *The Principles of Linguistic Philosophy.* London: Macmillan, 1965.

eitz, Morris (ed.). *20th-Century Philosophy: The Analytic Tradition.* New York: Free Press, 1966.

nite, A. R. G. E. *Moore: A Critical Exposition.* Oxford: Clarendon Press, 1958.

aite, Morton (ed.). *Age of Analysis.* New York: Mentor, 1955.

———. *Toward Reunion in Philosophy.* Cambridge: Harvard University Press, 956.

lliams, Bernard, and Montefiore, Alan (eds.). *British Analytical Philosophy.* New York: Humanities Press, 1966.

ttgenstein, Ludwig. "Logisch-philosophische Abhandlung," *Annalen der Naturphilosophie* (Leipzig, 1921). Reprinted as *Tractatus Logico-Philosophicus* (German and English). London: Routledge, Kegan Paul, 1922. New Trans. by D. F. Pearson and B. F. McGuiness. New York: Humanities Press, 1958.

———. *Philosophical Investigations.* Trans. G. E. M. Anscombe. Oxford: Blackwell, 1953.

———. *The Blue and Brown Books.* Foreword by Rush Rhees. Oxford: Blackwell, 1958.

———. *Wittgenstein Notebooks, 1914–1916,* ed. and trans. G. E. M. Anscombe. New York: Harper, 1961.

———. *Philosophische Bemerkungen,* ed. Rush Rhees. New York: Barnes & Noble, 1965.

———. "Lecture on Ethics," plus "Notes on Talks with Wittgenstein," edited y Friedrich Waismann, *Philosophical Review*, LXXIV (1965), 3–12, 2–16.

lter, Allan. "The Unspeakable Philosophy of the Late Wittgenstein," *Proceedings, American Catholic Philosophical Association*, XXX (1960), 58–93.

CHAPTER XVIII

la, Manuel. *La etica de la situación y Thomas Steinbüchel.* Madrid: Consejo Superior de Investigaciones Científicas, 1963.

ntis, Felix. "Social and Political Ideas of José Ortega y Gasset," *New Scholasticism*, XXXIX (1965), 467–90.

guren, J. L. L. *La etica de Ortega.* Madrid: Taurus Ediciones, 1958.

ett, William. *Irrational Man. A Study in Existential Philosophy.* Garden City, N.Y.: Doubleday, 1958, 1962.

h, Karl. *The Word of God and the Word of Man.* Boston: Pilgrim Press, 1928.

————. *The Doctrine of the Word of God.* Trans. G. T. Thomson. New York: Scribner's, 1936.

————. *Protestant Thought from Rousseau to Ritschl.* New York: Harper 1959.

Beauvoir, Simone de. *Pour une morale de l'ambiguité.* Paris: Gallimard 1946. Trans. by Bernard Frechtman as *The Ethics of Ambiguity.* New York: Philosophical Library, 1948.

Beis, R. H. "Atheistic Existentialist Ethics: a Critique," *The Modern Schoolman,* XLII (1965), 153–77.

Benn, A. W. "The Morals of an Immoralist—Friedrich Nietzsche," *Ethics* (1909), 1–13, 192–203.

Bonhoeffer, Dietrich. *Letters and Papers from Prison,* ed. E. Bethge. Tran Reginald Fuller. New York: Macmillan, 1962.

————. *Ethics,* ed. E. Bethge. Trans. Neville Smith. New York: Macmillan 1965.

Borzaga, R. *Contemporary Philosophy. Phenomenological and Existenti Currents.* Milwaukee: Bruce, 1966.

Brisebois, Edmond. "Le Sartrisme et le problème moral," *Nouvelle Revue Théologique,* LXXIV (1952), 30–48, 124–45.

Brunner, Emil. *Justice and the Social Order.* Trans. M. Hottinger. New York: Harper, 1945.

————. *The Divine Imperative.* Trans. Olive Wyon. Philadelphia: Westminster Press, 1947.

Buber, Martin. *Ich und Du.* Berlin, 1923. Trans. by R. G. Smith as *I an Thou,* New York: Scribner's, 1958, 1960.

————. *Good and Evil. Two Interpretations.* New York: Scribner's, 1953.

————. *The Writings of Martin Buber,* ed. Will Herberg. Cleveland: Worl 1956.

Camus, Albert. *Le mythe de Sisyphe.* Paris: Gallimard, 1942. Trans. Justin O'Brien as *The Myth of Sisyphus and Other Essays.* New Yor Knopf, 1955.

————. *L'Homme révolté.* Paris: Gallimard, 1951. Trans. by Anthony Bow as *The Rebel: an Essay on Man in Revolt.* New York: Knopf, 1954, 196

Cassem, N. H. "The Way to Wisdom: A Biodoctrinal Study of Friedri Nietzsche," *The Modern Schoolman,* XXXIX (1962), 335–58.

Collins, James. "Three Kierkegaardian Problems: II, The Ethical Vie and Its Limits," *New Scholasticism,* XXIII (1949), 3–37.

————. "Freedom as Atheistic Heroism," *Giornale di Metafisica,* IV (1949 573–80.

————. *The Existentialists: A Critical Study.* Chicago: Regnery, 1959.

Copleston, F. C. *Friedrich Nietzsche: Philosopher of Culture.* Londo Burns, Oates, 1942.

Diamond, M. L. *Martin Buber: Jewish Existentialist.* New York: Oxfo University Press, 1960.

Dondeyne, Albert. *Contemporary European Thought and Christian Fai* Pittsburgh: Duquesne University Press, 1958.

Dostoyevsky, Feodor M. *Works.* 13 vols. Trans. Constance Garnett. Londo Macmillan, 1949–50.

———. *Notes from Underground* (1864). Trans. C. Garnett. New York: Macmillan, 1949. Excerpted in Walter Kaufmann. *Existentialism*. Pp. 52–82.

Ferrater Mora, José. *Ortega y Gasset*. New Haven: Yale University Press, 1957.

———. *Unamuno: A Philosophy of Tragedy*. Trans. Philip Silver. Berkeley, Calif.: University of California Press, 1962.

———. *Philosophy Today: Conflicting Tendencies in Contemporary Thought*. Berkeley: University of California Press, 1962.

Fletcher, Joseph. *Situation Ethics*. Philadelphia: Westminster Press, 1966.

Friedman, Maurice. *Martin Buber: The Life of Dialogue*. Chicago: University of Chicago Press, 1955. Chap. 21: "Ethics."

Fuchs, Joseph. "Situation Ethics and Theology," *Theology Digest*, II (1954), 25–30.

———. *Situation und Entscheidung, Grandfragen christlicher Situationsethik*. Frankfurt: Carolusdruckerei, 1952.

Fullat, Octavio. *La moral atea de Albert Camus*. Barcelona: Pubul, 1963.

Garnett, A. C. "Phenomenological Ethics and Self-Realization," *Ethics*, LIII (1943), 159–72.

Greene, N. N. *Jean-Paul Sartre: The Existentialist Ethic*. Ann Arbor, Mich.: University of Michigan Press, 1960.

Grisebach, Eberhard. *Gegenwart: eine kritische Ethik*. Halle: Niemeyer, 1928.

Gusdorf, Georges. *Traité de l'existence morale*. Paris: Colin, 1949.

Hartmann, Klaus. *Sartres Sozialphilosophie*. Berlin: De Gruyter, 1966.

Henry, C. F. H. *Christian Personal Ethics*. Grand Rapids, Mich.: Eerdmans, 1957.

Hildebrand, Dietrich von. *True Morality and Its Counterfeits*. New York: McKay, 1955.

Hochberg, Herbert. "Albert Camus and the Ethics of Absurdity," *Ethics*, LXXV (1965), 87–102.

Holmer, P. L. "Kierkegaard and Ethical Theory," *Ethics*, LXIII (1953), 157–70.

Huertas-Jourda, José. *The Existentialism of Miguel de Unamuno*. Gainesville, Fla.: University of Florida Press, 1963.

Husserl, Edmund. *Ideen zu einer reinen Phänomenologie und phänomenologischen Philosophie*, in *Jahrbuch für Philosophie* (Halle: Niemeyer), Vol. I, 1913. Ed. W. Biemel. Ten Haag: Nijhoff, 1950. Trans. by W. R. Boyce Gibson as *Ideas: General Introduction to Pure Phenomenology*. London: Macmillan, 1931.

Jeanson, Francis. *Le Problème moral et la pensée de Sartre*. Paris: Editions du Myrte, 1947.

Jolivet, Régis. "La morale de l'ambiguité," *Revue Thomiste*, XLIX (1949), 278–85.

Kaufmann, Walter (ed.). *Existentialism from Dostoevsky to Sartre*. New York: Meridian, 1957.

Kierkegaard, Søren. *Samlede Vaerker*, ed. A. B. Brachmann. 20 vols. J. L. Heiberg & H. O. Lange. Copenhagen: Gyldendalske Boghandel, 1903–06.

———. *Either/Or: a Fragment of Life*, 2 vols. (1843). Trans. by D. F. and

Lillian Swenson of Vol. I, *The Aesthetic Life*. Trans. by Walter Lowri of Vol. II, *The Ethical Life*. Princeton, N.J.: Princeton University Pres 1944.

————. *Fear and Trembling* (1843). Trans. W. Lowrie. Princeton, 1941; wit *Sickness unto Death*, New York: Doubleday Anchor, 1954.

————. *Philosophical Fragments* (1844). Trans. D. F. Swenson. Princeto 1936; New York: Harper, 1938.

————. *The Concept of Dread* (1844). Trans. W. Lowrie, Princeton, 194

————. *Stages of Life's Way*. Trans. W. Lowrie. Princeton, 1940.

————. *Concluding Unscientific Postscript* (1846). Trans. D. F. Swenson an W. Lowrie. Princeton, 1941.

————. *Christian Discourses* (1848). Trans. W. Lowrie. New York: Oxfor University Press, 1939.

————. *The Sickness unto Death* (1849). Trans. W. Lowrie. Princeton, 195

————. *Purity of Heart Is To Will One Thing*. Trans. D. V. Steere. Ne York: Harper, 1938, 1956.

————. *A Kierkegaard Anthology*, ed. R. A. Bretall. Princeton, N.J.: Princeto University Press, 1946.

Laing, R. D., and Cooper, D. G. *Reason and Violence. A Decade of Sartre Philosophy*. New York: Humanities Press, 1964.

Lauer, Quentin. *The Triumph of Subjectivity*. New York: Fordham U versity Press, 1958.

Lawrence, Nathaniel, and O'Connor, D. D. (eds.). *Readings in Existenti Phenomenology*. Englewood Cliffs, N.J.: Prentice-Hall, 1967.

Lehman, Paul. *Ethics in a Christian Context*. New York: Harper & Ro 1963.

Lindbeck, G. A. "Natural Law in the Thought of Paul Tillich," *Natural La Forum*, VII (1962), 84–96.

McInerny, Ralph. "Ethics and Persuasion: Kierkegaard's Existential Dial tic," *The Modern Schoolman*, XXXIV (1956), 219–39.

Mandelbaum, Maurice. *The Phenomenology of Moral Experience*. Glenc Ill.: Free Press, 1955.

————. "On the Use of Moral Principles," *Journal of Philosophy*, LIII (1956 662–70.

————. "Determinism and Moral Responsibility," *Ethics*, LXX (196 204–16.

Marcel, Gabriel. *Etre et avoir*. Paris: Aubier, 1935. Trans. by Kathar Farrer as *Being and Having*. Boston: Beacon, 1951.

————. *Homo viator*. Paris: Aubier, 1944. Trans. by Emma Craufurd *Homo Viator*. Chicago: Regnery, 1951.

————. *The Mystery of Being* (Gifford Lectures, 1949–50.) 2 vols. Lond Harvill Press, 1951; Chicago: Regnery, 1951.

————. *L'Homme problématique*. Paris: Aubier, 1955.

————. *The Philosophy of Existence*. Trans. Manya Harari. London: Har Press, 1948.

Marty, Martin E. (ed.). *The Place of Bonhoeffer.* New York: Association Press, 1962.

Mehl, Roger, et al. *Le problème de la morale chrétienne.* Paris: Presses Universitaires, 1948.

Minnema, T. *The Social Ethics of Reinhold Niebuhr.* Grand Rapids, Mich.: Eerdmans, 1959.

Morgan, G. A. *What Nietzsche Means.* Cambridge: Harvard University Press, 1941.

Mortimer, R. C. *Christian Ethics.* London: Hutchinson, 1950.

Nabert, Jean. *Eléments pour une éthique.* Paris: Presses Universitaires, 1943.

———. *Essai sur le mal.* Paris: Presses Universitaires, 1955.

Niebuhr, H. Richard. *Kingdom of God in America.* New York: Harper, 1937.

Niebuhr, Reinhold. *An Independent Christian Ethics.* New York: Harper, 1935.

———. *Moral Man and Immoral Society.* New York: Scribner's, 1949.

———. *The Nature and Destiny of Man.* (Gifford Lectures, 1941–43.) 2 vols. New York: Scribner's, 1941–43.

Nietzsche, Friedrich W. *Nietzsches Werke und Briefe: Historischekritische Gesamtausgabe,* hrsg. von C. A. Emge. München: Beck, 1933 ff.

———. *The Complete Works,* ed. Oscar Levy. 18 vols. London: Allen & Unwin, 1923–24.

———. *Die Geburt der Tragödie* (1872). Trans. by Francis Golffing as *The Birth of Tragedy.* New York: Doubleday, 1956.

———. *Jenseits von Gut und Böse* (1886). Trans. by Helen Zimmern as *Beyond Good and Evil.* In *The Philosophy of Nietzsche.* New York: Random House, 1954.

———. *Zur Genealogie der Moral* (1887). Trans. by H. B. Samuel as *Toward a Genealogy of Morals.* In *The Philosophy of Nietzsche.* New York: Random House, 1954.

———. *The Philosophy of Nietzsche,* ed. W. H. Wright. New York: Scribner's, 1937.

———. *The Portable Nietzsche,* ed. W. Kaufmann. New York: Viking, 1954.

Ortega y Gasset, José. *Obras completas.* Madrid: Editorial Aguilar, 1947 ff.

———. *La rebelión de la masas.* Madrid: Aguilar, 1930. In *Obras,* IV, 113–313. Trans. as *The Revolt of the Masses.* New York: Norton, 1956.

———. *El hombre y la gente.* Madrid: Aguilar, 1958. In *Obras,* VI, 13–167. Trans. by W. R. Trask as *Man and People.* New York: Norton, 1957.

Pigou, A. C. "The Ethics of Nietzsche," *Ethics,* XVIII (1908), 343–55.

Poppi, Antonino. "The Background of Situation Ethics," *Philosophy Today,* I (1957), 266–77.

Rahner, Karl. "On the Question of a Formal Existential Ethics," in *Theological Investigations.* Trans. K. H. Kruger. Baltimore: Helicon, 1963. Pp. 421–31.

Ramsey, Paul. *Basic Christian Ethics.* New York: Scribner's, 1952.

———. *Nine Modern Moralists.* Englewood Cliffs, N.J.: Prentice-Hall, 1962.

Rau, Catherine. "The Ethical Theory of J. P. Sartre," *Journal of Philosophy*, XLVI (1949), 536–45.

Rauche, G. A. *The Philosophy of Actuality*. Fort Hare, Republic of South Africa: Fort Hare University Press, 1964. (A complete English analysis of the ethics of Eberhard Grisebach.)

Robinson, John A. *Honest to God*. Philadelphia: Westminster Press, 1963.

———. *Christian Morals Today*. Philadelphia: Westminster Press, 1964.

Roth, Alois. *Edmund Husserls ethische Untersuchungen*. (Phaenomenologica, 7.) Ten Haag: Nijhoff, 1960.

Sartre, Jean-Paul. *Esquisse d'une théorie des émotions*. Paris: Hermann, 1939. Trans. by Bernard Frechtman as *Outline of a Theory of the Emotions*. New York: Philosophical Library, 1948. Trans. by P. Mairet as *Sketch for a Theory of the Emotions*. London: Methuen, 1962.

———. *L'Etre et le néant: essai d'ontologie phénoménologique*. Paris: Gallimard, 1943. Trans. by Hazel Barnes as *Being and Nothingness*. New York Philosophical Library, 1956.

———. *L'Existentialisme est un humanisme*. Paris: Nagel, 1946. Trans. by P Mairet as *Existentialism and Humanism*. London: Methuen, 1948.

———. *Saint Genet: comédien et martyr*. Paris: Gallimard, 1952. Trans. by B. Frechtman as *Saint Genet, Actor and Martyr*. London: Allen & Unwin, 1964.

———. *Critique de la raison dialectique*. Vol. I. Paris: Gallimard, 1960

Sittler, Joseph. *The Structure of Christian Ethics*. Baton Rouge: Louisiana State University Press, 1958.

Smith, Colin. *Contemporary French Philosophy*. London: Methuen, 1964

Spiegelberg, Herbert. *The Phenomenological Movement*. 2 vols. The Hague Nijhoff, 1960.

Stavrides, Ria. "French Existentialism and Moral Philosophy," in *Encyclopedia of Morals*, ed. V. Ferm. New York: Philosophical Library, 1956 Pp. 163–71.

Stern, A. "Nietzsche et le doute méthodologique en morale," *Revue Philosophique de la France et de l'Etranger*, CXXXIX (1949), 48–59.

Thibon, G. "Friedrich Nietzsche, analyste de la causalité matérielle e psychologie et en morale," *Revue Thomiste*, XL (1935), 3–36.

Thomas, G. F. *Christian Ethics and Moral Philosophy*. New York: Scribner's 1955.

Tillich, Paul. *Systematic Theology*. 3 vols. Chicago: University of Chicago Press, 1951–63.

———. *The Courage to Be*. New Haven: Yale University Press, 195 1959.

———. *Love, Power, and Justice*. New York: Oxford University Press 1960.

———. *Morality and Beyond*. New York: Harper & Row, 1963.

Unamuno y Jugo, Miguel de. *Obras completas*. Madrid: Editorial Aguila 1951 ff.

———. *Del sentimiento tragico de la vida*. 2 vols. Madrid: Aguilar, 191 1945. Trans. by J. E. C. Fitch as *The Tragic Sense of Life*. New York Dover, 1954.

Villaseñor, J. S. *Ortega y Gasset, Existentialist.* Trans. J. Small. Chicago: Regnery, 1949.
Virasoro, Rafael. *Existencialismo y moral.* Santa Fe, Argentina: Libreria Castellvi, 1957.
Wahl, Jean. *Existence humaine et transcendence.* Neuchâtel: La Baconnière, 1944.
————. *A Short History of Existentialism.* Trans. F. Williams and S. Maron. New York: Philosophical Library, 1949, 1962.
Wild, John. *The Challenge of Existentialism.* Bloomington, Ind.: Indiana University Press, 1955.
————. *Human Freedom and Social Order: An Essay in Christian Philosophy.* Durham, N.C.: Duke University Press, 1959.
————. *Existence and the World of Freedom.* Englewood Cliffs, N.J.: Prentice-Hall, 1963.
Williams, Martha. "Gabriel Marcel's Notion of Value," *The Modern Schoolman,* XXXVII (1959), 29–38.
Wolff, Edgar. *L'Individualisme radical fondé sur la caractérologie. Pour un renouveau des idées de Nietzsche.* Paris: Bordas, 1955.
Wolff, P. (ed.). *Christliche Philosophie in Deutschland 1920 bis 1945.* Regensburg: Habbel, 1949.

Index

Abelard. *See* Peter Abelard
Abubacer (Ibn-Tufail), 80–81
Abulfaragius, 73
Achillini, Alexander, 119
'Act" and "rule" utilitarianism, 258, 260–61
Adams, E. M., 278
Adler, Felix, 254
Addresses to the German Nation, 190
Advancement of Learning, 131–32
Against Celsus, 50
Ages of the World, 198
Ailly, Pierre d', 136
Aklaq-i Jalali (Jalal's Ethics), 86
Al-Ameri, 76
Albanenses, 62
Albert the Great, 31, 87, 95–97
Albigensians, 62
Albo, Joseph, 72–73
Albrecht von Eyb, 107
Alciphron, 143, 145
Al-Dimishqi, abu-Uthman, 76
Alexander of Hales, 94
Alexandria, Egypt, 41, 49, 50
Al-Farabi, 70, 74–76
Algazel (Ghazzali, Al-), 43, 73, 78–79, 82, 85
Alienation, 225, 226
Allers, Rudolf, 247
l-Razi, Mohammed ibn-Zakariya, 74
Ambiguities (Patrologia Graeca), 51
Ambrose, Bishop of Milan, 47, 53, 54, 91
Analogy of Religion, 146
Analysis Aristotelica ex Euclide restituta, 126
Analysis of Knowledge and Valuation, 246
Analysis of the Phenomena of the Human Mind, 183–84
Analytic ethics, 279–94
Anaxagoras, 12, 13
Andreas Capellanus, 88
Andreas de Novo Castro, 136
Andronicus, 30, 62
Annals of the Parish, 175
Année Sociologique, L', 228
Anniceras, 17

Anselm of Canterbury, St., 53, 60, 61, 63–64, 100, 102
Anthony of Parma, 31
Anti-Dühring, 225
Antipater, 35
Anti-Semitism (racism). *See under* Jews (Judaism)
Antisthenes, 16
Antoninus of Florence, 106–7
Apathy (*apatheia*), 16, 33, 35
Apology (Plato), 15, 17
Appeal from the New to the Old Whigs, 181–82
Appearance and Reality, 251
Aquinas. *See* Thomas Aquinas
Arabs, 31, 43, 47. *See also* Moslems
Archytas of Tarentum, 12
Areopagiticum, 50–51
Aretino, 119
Aretus, 35
Arriaga, Rodrigo de, 152
Aristippus of Cyrene, 17
Aristo, 35
Aristophanes, 14
Aristotle (Aristotelianism), 11–14, 17, 23–31, 35, 41, 42, 47, 57, 61, 87, 100, 258, British ethics and, 132, 136; Elyot and, 118; Francis Bacon and, 132; ideal forms, 89–90; Maimonides and, 69, 70; medieval thought and, 95–96, 102; modern theory and, 185, 291; Moslems and, 74–77, 80–86 *passim*; *Nichomachean Ethics* (*See Nicomachean Ethics*); Plato and, 24, 27, 89–90; Protestants and, 125; and Renaissance, 112–14, 119–24; 17th and 18th century rationalism and, 152; teleological eudaimonism, 23–31
Aspasius, 31
Astrologers, Maimonides on, 72
Ataraxia, 12
Athambië, 12
Athens, 14, 16, 17, 23, 33
Atoms, 38
Augustine, St., 16, 36, 43, 47, 51, 54–57, 60, 63–64, 91, 93, 101, 137; Renais-

sance and, 129; spiritistic ethics and, 203, 204
Austin, John, 184–85, 187, 286
Austria, axiology in, 237–39, 244, 245
Austrian Philosophy of Values, 244
Autobiography of Benjamin Franklin, 145
Avempace, 80
Averroës, 81–82, 86
Averroism, Latin, 99–100
Avicebrón (ibn-Gabirol), 43, 68, 86
Avicenna, 43, 70, 77–78, 86, 93; and mystical love, 88
Axiological ethics, 237–48
Axiology, 215
Ayer, Alfred J., 286, 288–89

Baader, Franz von, 127, 198
Bacon, Francis, 92, 131–32
Bacon, Roger. *See* Roger Bacon
Bad Conscience, 213
Bahya ibn Pakuda, 69
Baier, Kurt, 292
Bain, Alexander, 188, 250
Baldwin, William, 118
Balguy, John, 149
Bar-Hebraeus, 73, 79
Bardaisan of Edessa, 48–49
Barrett, William, 258
Bartholomew of Messina, 88
Baruk, H., 274
Basis of Natural Right, 190
Baumgarten, Alexander G., 166, 167
Beattie, James, 181
Beauvoir, Simone de, 305–6
Beck, Lewis W., 258
Being and Having, 302
Being and Nothingness, 304
Bellarmine, Robert, St., 121
Beneke, Friedrich E., 197
Bentham, Jeremy, 175, 182–84, 187, 188, 249, 260
Berdyaev, Nikolai, 227–28
Bergson, Henri, 211–12, 214, 215, 271
Berkeley, George, 143, 145–46
Bernard of Clairvaux, 61–62
Bessarion, Cardinal, 112
Beyond Good and Evil, 297
Beyond Realism and Idealism, 244–45
Bible, 47, 48, 50, 63, 65–67, 69 (*See also* specific Books); and Jewish ethics, 65–67, 68, 69
Birth of Tragedy, 297
Blackstone, Sir William, 182–83
Blanquerna, 101–2
Blanshard, Brand, 88, 258
Bloch, Ernst, 226
Blondel, Maurice, 185
Boethius, 53, 57–59
Boethius of Dacia, 100
Bohme (Behmen), Jakob, 126
Boke Named the Governour, The, 118
Bolingbroke, Henry St. John, 144
Bonaventure, St., 94–95
Bondage of the Will, 125
Bonhoeffer, Dietrich, 301
Book of Dispositions, 80

Book of Doctrines and Beliefs, 67
Book of the Dove, 73
Book on Felicity, 100
Book of the Laws of Countries, 48–4?
Book on Pleasure, 114
Bosanquet, Bernard, 252
Bourget, Paul, 209
Boutroux, Émile, 210–11
Bowring, John, 182
Bradley, Francis H., 250, 251–52, 27?
Braithwaite, R. B., 259
Bramhall, John, 135, 137
Brentano, Franz C., 238, 244, 266, 295
Brief Disquisition of the Law of Nature 135–36
Brightman, Edgar S., 246
Brisbane, Albert, 222
British. *See* Great Britain and the Englis?
Brook Farm, Mass., 222
Broad, C. D., 289
Brothers Karamazov, The, 298
Brown, Thomas, 181
Browne, Sir Thomas, 135
Brownson, Orestes, 203, 222
Bruni, Leonardo, 119
Brunner, Emil, 47–48
Bruno, Giordano, 115, 116, 129
Brunschvicq, Léon, 212–13
Buber, Martin, 299
Bucer (or Butzer), Martin, 125
Buffier, Claude, 180
Burgersdijck, Francis, 124
Burgundio of Pisa, 51–52
Burke, Edmund, 181–82, 184
Burleigh, Walter, 87, 91
Butler, Joseph, 146–47

Cabal of the Horse Pegasus, 115
Cajetan (Cardinal Tommaso de Vio) 11?
Callicles, 14, 136
Calvin, John, 126, 127
Cambridge University, 136; analytic eth? ics, 280–85; Platonism, 116–19, 13? 43
Campanella, Tommaso, 116
Campbell, Archibald, 147
Camus, Albert, 128, 299, 306
Capital (Marx), 224
Carnap, Rudolf, 285, 288
Cartesian Ethics, 156
Cartesianism, 157, 159, 180, 203, 204
Catechism of Positive Religion, 222
Catharism, 62–63
Catharsis, 42, 43
Catholics and Catholicism, 227; and a? iological ethics, 247–48; and existe? tialism, 301–2; and naturalism, 27? 74; and modern theories, 185, 214–1? 223, 227, 302; scholasticism, 120–2? 17th and 18th century rationalis? ethics, 160, 166; and spiritistic ethi? 214, 215
Cato Uticensis, 36
Cave, Plato's allegory of the, 20
Chamberlain, Houston S., 233–34
Chapman, George, 129–30

Characteristics (Shaftesbury), 140
Charmides, 18
Charron, Pierre, 128
Christian Discussions, 204
Christian Ethics (Hildebrand), 248
Christian Morals (Browne), 135
Christian Morals Today, 301
"Christian philosophy" movement, 212
"Christian Socratism," 62
Christianity, 35, 36, 49–53 (*See also* specific denominations); existential ethics, 296, 299, 300–1; Latin Church writers, 53–64; medieval thought, 47–64, 65, 86–108; and modern theories, 196, 296, 299, 300–1; and Neoplatonism, 40, 44, 54; Renaissance humanism, 112–15; 17th and 18th century rationalism, 151–66ff.; societal ethics, 227, 228; spiritistic ethics, 227, 228
Chrysippus of Soli, 33, 35
Chubb, Percival, 254
Church Council of Florence, 112
Cicero, 31, 35, 36, 54, 62
City of God, 54, 57
City of the Sun, 116
Civilization and Ethics, 257
Civilization and Its Discontents, 266
Clarke, John, 142
Clarke, Samuel, 141–42, 189, 250
Claudius Galen. *See* Galen
Cleanthes, 33, 34–35
Clement IV, Pope (Guido Fulcodi), 92
Clement of Alexandria, 49–50
Clouds, The, 14
Clough, Arthur Hugh, 189
Code of the Law of Peoples, 161
Cohen, Hermann, 201
Coit, Stanton, 254
Coleridge, Samuel Taylor, 184
Collingwood, R. G., 232
Commentaria in libros Sententiarum, 96
Commentaries on the Laws of England, 182–83
Commentary on the Second Part of the Summa Theologiae, 120
Common Faith, 275–76
Communia Naturalium, 93
Communism, 223–28. *See also* Marx and Marxism
Communist Manifesto, 224
Comte, Auguste, 93, 186, 222–23, 249
Concept of Dread, 296
Concept of Morals, 257–58
Concerning the Fundamental Principle of Virtue or Morality, 141
Concerning the Infinite, 129
Concluding Unscientific Postscript, 296
Concorenses, 62
Condemnation of 219 Propositions, 100
Condillac, Étienne Bonnot de, 145, 205, 206
Condorcet, Antoine Nicholas de, 186, 220–21
Conduct in Regard to Others, 215
Confessions (Augustine), 54, 55
Consciousness of Self, 215

Considérant, Victor, 222
Consolation of Philosophy, 53, 58
Contemporary British Philosophy, 243
Contemporary ethics, 237–308
Contra Faustum, 56
Corpus Dionysiacum, 50–51
Courage, 18, 19, 22, 76, 98
Courage to Be, The, 299
Course in Philosophy, 222
Course of Positive Philosophy, 222
Cousin, Victor, 81, 203, 206–7, 208
Crates, 35
Crates of Thebes, 16–17
Creative Evolution, 211
Creative Liberty, 215
Crime and Punishment, 298–99
Critique de la raison dialectique, 304, 305
Critique of Practical Reason, 167, 168, 170, 252
Critique of Pure Reason, 167–68, 170
Crito, 15, 17
Croce, Benedetto, 219, 230–31
Crusius, Christian A., 167
Cudworth, Ralph, 129, 136–38, 141, 177, 250
Culverwel, Nathanael, 136
Cumberland, Richard, 138, 176
Cursus Conimbricensis, 121
Cynics, 16–17
Cyrenaics, 17, 38

Dana, Charles A., 222
Dante Alighieri, 102
Darwin, Charles, 250, 264
Daub, Karl, 196
Dawson, Miles, 15
De amore, 88
De amore divino, 119
De Anima (Aristotle), 24, 25, 29, 75, 82
De Anima (Avicenna), 77
De Anima (Suárez), 121, 124
De bona fortuna, 88
Decalogue (Ten Commandments), 48, 50, 65–67
Decisive Treatise, 81–82
De cive, 132
De corpore (*On Body*), 133
De divisione naturae, 59
De fide orthodoxa (*On the True Faith*), 51
De finibus, 30, 36
Definition of Good, The, 285–86
De Hebdomadibus, 58
De homine (*On Man*), 133
De imperio, 151, 152–53
De Isaac et anima, 54
Deism (Deists), 140ff.
De l'Homme, 183
Deliverance from Error, 78
Democritus of Abdera, 12–13
Dennes, William R., 276
Deontology, 182
Descartes, René, 143, 154–60, 180, 203, 204, 249; existentialism and, 296;

spiritistic ethics and, 203, 204, 205, 212
Deschamps, Dom Léger-Marie, 220
Destiny of Man, 228
Deuteronomy, Book of, 65, 66
De veritate, 130
De Virtutibus et vitiis, 76
De vita beata, 155
De voluptate, 114, 128
Dewey, John, 237, 246, 267–69, 275–76, 277, 287
Dialogue between a Conservative and a Reformer, 221
Dialogue on Truth, 60
Dialogues on Metaphysics, 204
Diderot, Denis, 120, 140, 144–45
Diogenes Laërtius, 17
Diogenes of Seleucia, 35
Diogenes of Sinope, 16
Dionysius the Areopagite, 43
Dionysius the Pseudo-Areopagite, 50–51
Disciple, The, 209
Discourse on the Arts and Sciences, 165
Discourse on the General View of Positivism, 222
Discourse of Liberty and Necessity, A, 137
Discourse on Method, 154–55
Discourse on Natural Religion, 141–42
Discourses (Diatribai), 36, 37
Disputations on the Highest Good, 156
Dissertation upon the Nature of Virtue, A, 146, 147
Divine Comedy, 102
Divine Institutes, 54
Divine Milieu, 271
Doctrine of Right, 196
Dogs (dogness), 24
Dominicans, 87, 95, 102, 120
Dostoyevsky, Feodor, 298–99
Duns Scotus, John, 94, 103–4, 105, 106, 120
Durkheim, Émile, 228–29
Duties of the Heart, 69
Duty (Le Senne), 214
DuVair, Guillaume, 129

Early Theological Writings, 192–93
Eastern Church, 227
Eaton, Howard O., 244
Eckhart, Meister Johannes. *See* Johannes Eckhart, Meister
Edel, Abraham, 277
Edwards, Paul, 278, 293
Egoism, ethical, 131ff.
Ehrenfels, Christian von, 239, 244
Either/Or, 296
Elean-Eretrian group, 16
Elementa philosophiae moralis, 126
Elements of First Practical Philosophy, 166
Elements of Law, 132
Eléments pour une éthique, 303
Elements of Theology, 44
Elizabeth of Bohemia, Princess, 154, 155
Elyot, Sir Thomas, 115, 118
Emmanuel College, Cambridge, 136

Emotional Presentation, 239
Emotivism, 285, 286, 287, 289
Empiricism, 139
Enarrationes in Psalmos, 56
Enchiridion (Augustine), 54
Enchiridion (Epictetus), 36–37, 129
Enchiridion Ethicum, 137–38
Engels, Friedrich, 225–26
England. *See* Great Britain and the English
Enneads (the "Nines"), 41–44, 114
Enquiry concerning Human Understanding, 177, 178–79
Enquiry into Goodness, 293
Enquiry into the Origin of the Human Appetites and Affections, 149–50
Enquiry into the Original of Moral Virtue, 147
Enquiry (as title). *See also* Inquiry . . . (etc.)
Enumeration of the Sciences, 74
Epictetus, 33, 36–37, 129, 132
Epicurus and Epicureanism, 12, 17, 32, 38–40, 42, 49, 54, 114; in the Renaissance, 128–29
Epistola, 56–57
Equity (*epieikeia*), 28
Er, Tale of, 22
Erasmus, Desiderius, 125
Erigena, John Scottus, 53, 59–60
Erkenne dich selbst, 127
Error of Narcissus, 215
Escape from Freedom, 274
Essai sur le Mérite et la Vertu, 140
Essais de Théodicée, 163
Essay concerning Human Understanding, 139–40
Essay on Man, 144
Essay on the Nature and Conduct of the Passions, 147, 148–49
Essays (F. Bacon), 131
Essays (Montaigne), 127–28
Essays, Moral and Political, 177, 179
Essays on the Law of Nature, 138–39
Essays on the Principles of Morality and Natural Religion, 147
Essays on Sociology and Social philosophy, 232
Eternal Gospel, 63
Ethica (Geulinex), 156
Ethica nova (New Ethics), 87
Ethica vetus (Old Ethics), 87
Ethical Characters, 30
Ethical culture movement, 254
Ethical Disputations, 156
Ethical Judgment, 277
Ethical Reason and Moral Intelligence, 217
Ethical Relativity, 229
Ethical Studies, 251
Ethics (Bonhoeffer), 301
Ethics (Dewey and Tufts), 268
Ethics (Fries), 196
Ethics . . . (Garnett), 258
Ethica (Geulincx), 156
Ethics (Hartmann), 241–43

Ethics . . . (Hessen), 247
Ethics (Moore), 281
Ethics (Nowell-Smith), 289–91
Ethics (Pepper), 272
Ethics (Peter Abelard), 61
Ethics (Spinoza), 157–60, 162
Ethics (Vasconcelos), 216
Ethics (Ward), 248
Ethics (Wundt), 201
Ethics and Language, 287
Ethics and the Materialist Conception of History, 226
Ethics and Moral Science, 229
Ethics and Morality, 217
Ethics of Ambiguity, 305–6
Ethikon, 73, 79
Etika, 265
Eucken, Rudolf, 201
Euclid of Megara, 16
Eudaimonism: definitions, translations, 26, 33, 70; early Greek, 12–23; teleological (Aristotle), 24–31; Thomism, 99
Eudemian Ethics, 17, 24, 27, 30, 31, 88
Eudemus, 23
Europe: contemporary ethics, 237–308 passim; rationalistic ethics (17th and 18th centuries), 151–71
Eustratios, Bishop of Nicaea, 31
Euthydemus, 18
Euthyphro, 18
Evolution and Ethics, 265
Evolutionary ethics, 264, 270
Evolutionary Ethics, 270
Ewing, Alfred Cyril, 285–86
Examination of the Place of Reason in Ethics, 293
Examination of Sir William Hamilton's Philosophy, 184
Existential ethics, 295–308
Exodus, Book of, 65
Experiments in Living, 271
Expulsion of the Triumphant Beast, 115

Fable of the Bees, 142–43
Facts and Values . . . , 287
Fada 'il al-Nafs, 76
Faith of a Moralist, 252
Fathers of the Church, 47–53
Fear and Trembling, 296
Feigl, Herbert, 288
Ferguson, Adam, 181
Ferrier, James, 184
Feuerbach, Ludwig, 196, 224
Fichte, Johann Gottlieb, 190–92, 193, 200, 201, 209
Ficino, Marsilio, 114, 119
FitzGerald, Edward, 79
Flavius Arrianus, 36
Flowers of St. Francis, 88
Fons Vitae, 68
Foot, Philippa R., 277–78
Formation in Ethics . . . , 239
Förster-Nietzsche, Elisabeth, 297
Fortescue, Sir John, 106
Foundation of Moral Goodness, 149
Foundation of Morality . . . , 142

Foundations of Ethics, 253
Foundations of the Metaphysic of Morals, 167, 168–70
Foundations of the Nineteenth Century, 233–34
Foundations of Psychology, 205
Fountain of Life, 68
Four Saints, 215
Foure Hymnes, 118–19
Fourier, François Marie Charles, 221–22, 223
Fourteenth-century ethics, 103ff.
Fox, George, 81
Fragment on Government, 182, 183
France, 62, 127–28; axiology in, 248; Deism, 144–45; existential ethics, 303–6; 17th and 18th century rationalism, 154, 164–66; societal ethics, 220–22, 227–29, 232–33; spiritistic ethics, 203–17
Francis of Assisi, St., 88–89
Franciscans, 63, 87, 88, 92–95, 100, 105
Franco-Latin spiritistic ethics, 203–17
Frank, Philipp, 288
Franklin, Benjamin, 145
Freedom and Reason, 292–93
Freedom of the Will, 199–200
Freud (Sigmund) and Freudianism, 238, 265–67, 268, 275
Friars Minor, Order of, 88, 94
Friendship, 39, 40
Fries, Jakob Friedrich, 196
Fromm, Erich, 274–75
Fundamental Moral Attitudes, 248
Fundamental Principles of the Torah, 70

Gabriel Biel, 106
Galen, 30–31
Galt, John, 175
Games theory, 258–60
Garnett, A. C., 258
Gassendi, Pierre, 129, 136
Gauthier of Chatillon, 62
Gay, John, 141
Gegenwart: eine kritische Ethik, 301
Gemistus Pletho, 112
Genealogy of Morals, 298
General Theory of Value, 270
General View of Positivism, 223
"General will," 165–66, 169
Generalization in Ethics, 261
Genesis, Book of, 89
Genesis and Structure of Society, 231
Gentile, Giovanni, 230, 231
Georgios Scholarios, 112
Gerardus de Borgo San Domino, 63
Gerardus Odonis, 88
Gerdil, Sigismond Cardinal, 166
German Writings, 233
Germany: axiology, 237–39, 244, 247; Deism, 144; idealism, 190–202, 206; Marxism, 226; 17th and 18th century rationalism, 153, 156, 160–62, 164, 166, 167–71; situation ethics, 301; societal ethics, 226, 232
Gersonides (Levi ben Gerson), 72

Gesetz and Sittengesetz . . . , 299
Geulincx, Arnold, 156
Gianfrancesco, 115
Giles of Rome, 31, 87, 100
Gilson, Étienne, 212
Ginsberg, Morris, 232
Gioberti, Vincenzo, 203, 207, 208–9
Giornale di Metafisica, 217
Gobineau, Count Arthur de, 232–33
God: in analytic ethics, 285; in Augustine, 55–57; in Boethius, 59; in British ethics, 136–37, 144; in Christian ethics, 47–48, 50, 51, 53, 55–61, 63; in Erigena, 59; in Jewish ethics, 48, 65–69; in Middle Ages, 99, 104–6, 108, 151–52, 153, 158, 159, 162, 163, 165, 167; in modern theories, 182, 189, 193, 305; and Peter Abelard, 61; Renaissance and, 113, 115; right reason and, 89; in spiritistic ethics, 204–9, 212–14; in stoicism, 33–34, 36
Gödel, Kurt, 288
Godwin, William 184
Good and Evil, 299
Good Life, The, 256–57
Good reasons ethics, 280–94
Gorgias, 18, 22
Gorgias the Sophist, 16
Gouhier, Henri, 205
Governance of the Solitary, 80
Grammar of Assent, 185
Great Britain and the English, 131ff.; Aristotelianism, 120; analysis ethics, 279–94; egoism, 131ff.; naturalism, 264, 271, 277–78; Platonism, 116–19, 136–43; societal ethics, 232, 233, 234; stoicism, 129–30; utilitarian and subjectivist ethics, 175–89, 249–53, 257, 258; value ethics, 243
Greek Christian writers, 49–53
Greek (Hellenistic) ethics, 11–22, 23–31ff., 90
Green, Thomas Hill, 250–51, 279
Gregorius Abu al-Faraj, 73
Gregory I (the Great), Pope, 59
Gregory of Nyssa, St., 50
Gregory of Rimini, 123
Gregory of Valencia, 152
Grisebach, Eberhard, 301
Grote, John, 184
Grotius, Hugo, 151–53, 163
Guide for the Perplexed, 67, 69–70
Guido Fulcodi (later Pope Clement IV), 92
Gumplowicz, Ludwig, 233
Gusdorf, Georges, 302
Guyau, Marie Jean, 209–10
Gyges, 21

Hägerstrom, Axel, 289
Halevi, Judah, 68–69
Hamilton, Sir William, 184
Hampshire, Stuart, 291–92
Hare, R. M., 259, 292–93
Hartley, David, 149–50
Hartmann, Eduard von, 198

Hartmann, Nicolai, 241–43, 246, 276, 29
Hartshorne, Charles, 270
Hasdai ben Abraham Crescar, 72
Hawthorne, Nathaniel, 222
Hayy ibn Yaqzan, 78, 81
Hecker, Thomas, 222
Hedonism, 17, 30, 38, 84
Heereboord, Andriaan, 124
Hegel, G. W. F., 192–96, 209, 223, 224 230, 231; existentialism and, 295–96 297, 302
Hēgemonikon, 35–36, 37
Hegesias, 17
Helvétius, Claude Adrian, 120, 183
Henning, Leopold von, 196
Henry VIII, 117
Henry de Bracton, 106
Henry of Ghent, 101, 104, 122
Heraclitus, 12
Herbart, Johann Friedrich, 196–97
Herbert of Cherbury, 130, 143
Hermannus Alemannus, 87
Hermes Tresmegistos, 41
Heroic Frenzies, 115
Hexaëmeron, 89
Hildebert of Tours, 62
Hildebrand, Dietrich von, 247–48
Hillel ben Samuel, 72
Hippias of Elis, 14
Hippias Minor, 18
Hippolytus, 49
Histoire de Juliette, 220
Historical Sketch of the Progress of th Human Mind, 186
History of Ethics (Sidgwick), 188–89
Hitler, Adolf, 192, 232, 301
Hobbes, Thomas, 117, 118, 143, 160, 16 189, 250; ethical egoism of, 131–3 141–42, 146, 153
Hocking, William Ernest, 256
Holbach, Baron d', 120
Holland, 151–52, 157
Holmes, Samuel Jackson, 270
Homenaje a Xavier Zubiri, 216
Homer, 219
Homme problématique, L', 302
Homo Viator, 302
Hooker, Richard, 107–8, 116
Honest to God, 301
Hope of the Great Community, 254, 255
How to Do Things with Words, 286
Human Nature and Conduct, 268
Human Nature and Its Remaking, 256
Human Person and the World of Valu 248
Human Values, 246
Humanism, 13–14, 275, 276; Renaissan 111–24ff.
Humanism as a Philosophy, 276
Humanisme et Terreur, 306
Humanity and Duty, 245
Hume, David, 176–80, 181, 279–80
Husserl, Edmund, 249, 295, 299
Hutcheson, Francis, 147–49, 250
Huxley, Julian, 270, 271
Huxley, Thomas Henry, 265

I and Thou, 299
Iamblichus, 11, 44
Ibn-Bajjah (Avempace), 80
Ibn-Gabirol (Avicebrón). *See* Avicebrón
(ibn-Gabirol)
Ibn-Haylan, Yuhanna, 74
Ibn-Hazm, 80
Ibn-Ishaq, Hunaïn, 73, 76
Ibn-Tufail, 80–81
Idea philosophiae moralis, 124
Ideal forms, 15, 20, 24, 89–90
Idealism, 203, 254ff.; Germany (modern),
190–202, 206
*Ideas: General Introduction to Pure Phe-
nomenology,* 299
Idiot, The, 298
Ignatius of Loyola, 121
Ihya al-Ulum, 73, 78, 79
Immortality: in Aristotle, 25; in Averroes,
82; in Epicurus, 39; in Gregory of
Nyssa, 50; in Plato, 17–18, 22
Immortality of the Soul, 119
Independent Christian Ethics, 300
Individual and His Unique Quality, 200
Inequality of Human Races, 233
Inquiry (as title). *See also Enquiry . . .*
(etc.)
Inquiry concerning Political Justice, 184
*Inquiry concerning the Principles of Mor-
als,* 176
Inquiry concerning Virtue, 140, 141
*Inquiry into the Dictinctness of the Prin-
ciples of Natural Theology and Mor-
als,* 167
*Inquiry into the Human Mind on the
Principles of Common Sense,* 181
*Inquiries into the Nature of Law and
Morals,* 289
*Inquiry into the Original of Our Ideas
of Beauty and Virtue,* 147–48
Intelligible World, The, 244
International Journal of Ethics, 252
*Introduction to the Jurisprudence of Hol-
land,* 151–52
Introduction to Moral Instruction, 119
*Introduction to the Principles of Morals
and Legislation,* 182
Introduction to Stoic Philosophy, 129
Intuitionism, ethical, 175–89, 285, 286, 289,
290
Irrational Man, 258
Islam. *See* Moslems
Italy and the Italians, 62; Aristotelianism,
119–20; Epicureanism, 128–29; Plato-
nism, 112–16; Renaissance, 111–30; so-
cietal ethics, 218–19, 230–32; spiritistic
ethics, 203, 207–9, 215, 217

Jalal al-Din Muhammad ibn-Asad Dawani,
86
James, William, 254, 267
Jankélévitch, Vladimir, 213
Jansenism, 156
Jean Buridan, 88
Jerome, St., 91
Jesuits, 120–24

Jews (Judaism), 43, 47, 48, 233–34, 298;
anti-Semitism, 233–34, 298; contempo-
rary ethics, 299; medieval ethics, 65–
73, 86
Joachim of Flora, 63
Joad, C. E. M., 288
Johannes Eckhart, Meister, 43, 102
John Baconthorpe, 88
John Damascene, St., 47, 51–53
John Duns Scotus. *See* Duns Scotus, John
John of La Rochelle, 94
Jordan, Elijah, 256–57
Jouffroy, Théodore, 207
Judah Halevi, 68–69
Justice, 19–20, 22, 76, 98, 99, 101, 162;
in Aristotle, 28
Justification of the Good, 227

Kalam, the, 74
Kames, Henry Home, Lord, 147
Kant, Immanuel, 60, 79, 100, 102, 161,
165–71, 190, 193, 201, 231; Coleridge
and, 184; existential ethics and, 299,
305; Fries and, 196; Price and, 180;
Scheler and, 240; Schopenhauer and,
199, 200; and self-realization ethics,
249, 250, 252, 254, 258, 261; spirit-
istic ethics and, 205, 212, 215, 216
Kautsky, Karl, 226
Keckermann, Bartholomaeus, 126
Kierkegaard, Søren, 16, 227, 296–97, 303
Kindi, al-, 74, 75
King, William, Archbishop of Dublin, 141
*King and the Education of the King,
The,* 121
Kingdom of God in America, 301
Kleine Schriften, 201
Knutzen, Martin, 166
Kolakowski, Leszek, 227
Koran, 73–74, 79, 84
Korn, Alejandro, 215 16
Kropotkin, P. A., 265

Laches, 18
Lactantius, 53–54
Lagarde, Paul Anton de, 233
Lamont, Corliss, 276
Lange, Joachim, 166–67
Language, Truth, and Logic, 288–89
Language analysis, 279–94
Language of Morals, 292–93
La Ramée, Pierre, 226
Latest Decalogue, 189
Lavelle, Louis, 215, 248
Law, Edmund, 141
Law, 12, 63, 96ff., 108 (*See also* Natural
law); Aristotle on, 29; Augustine on,
56; Judaism and, 66, 67, 69, 70;
rationalistic ethics and (17th and 18th
centuries), 151ff.; stoicism and, 34
Law of Nature and of Nations, 153, 154
Laws, (Plato) 19, 22, 74
Laws of Nature (Cumberland), 138
Leclercq, Jacques, 274
Lectura in libros Ethicorum Aristotelis, 96
Lectures on Ethics (Kant), 167

Lectures on the Ethics (Albert the Great), 96
Lectures on the Summa of Theology, 121
Leibniz, Gottfried Wilhelm von, 115, 126, 143, 153, 160–64, 201
Lenin, V. I., 226
Leonardo Bruni d'Arezzo, 88
Leonardo da Vinci, 111–12
Le Senne, René, 214–15, 248
Letter on Apostasy, 71–72
Letter on Astrology, 69, 72
Letter on the Study of History, 144
Letters (Pseudo-Dionysius), 51
Letters and Moral Essays, 36
Leviathan . . . , 132–33, 135, 136
Leviathan Drawn Out with a Hook, 135
Leviticus, Book of, 67
Lévy-Bruhl, Lucien, 229
Lewis, C. I., 246
Lex talionis, 66
Libellus de beata vita, 126
Liber de Bona Fortuna, 31
Liber Sexus Naturalium, 77
Life of Jesus, 192–93
Life of Reason . . . , 256
Life of the Spirit, 201
Light of Nature Pursued, 150
"Limiting" and "non-limiting" opposites, 12
Lipsius, Justus (Lips, Joest), 129
Locke, John, 138–39, 141, 143, 145, 149, 150, 154, 162, 166
Logic of Moral Discourse, 278
Logic of the Moral Sciences, 186–87
Lollard movement, 107
Lombard, Peter. *See* Peter Lombard
Loquentes, 74
Lotze, Rudolf Hermann, 207, 254
Love: in England, 118; in medieval thought, 88–89, 101; in modern theories, 193; in Renaissance, 113, 114
Love, Power, and Justice, 299
Lucretius, 39–40, 129
Lukacs, Georg, 226–27
Lull, Ramón. *See* Ramón Lull
Luther, Martin, 125, 127

Macbeath, Alexander, 271
McCosh, James, 181
Mach, Ernst, 226
Machiavelli, Niccolò, 127, 231
McLuhan, Marshall, 283
Macrobius, 43, 62
Magna Moralia, 24, 31, 88
Maimon, Salomon, 171
Maimonides (Moses ben Maimon), 67, 69–72, 86
Maine de Biran, 205–6, 207, 212
Malebranche, Father Nicolas, 204–5, 249
Man for Himself, 274–75
Mandelbaum, Maurice, 306–7
Mandeville, Bernard, 142–43
Manichaeism, 62, 63
Marcel, Gabriel, 214, 273, 302, 303
Marcus Aurelius, 33, 37–38
Marheineke, P. K., 196
Mariana, Juan de, 121

Maritain, Jacques, 212, 272–73, 274, 280
Marius Victorinus, 43
Martin of Dumio, Bishop of Braga, 59
Martineau, Harriet, 222
Martineau, James, 185–86, 249–50
Marx and Marxism, 196, 223–28, 274, 305
Materialism, 224–28, 305
Mathematics and ethics, 11–12, 20, 153, 259–60
Matthew, Gospel of, 48
Matthew of Aquasparta, 94
Maurus, Sylvester, 121
Maximus the Confessor, 43
Maximus of Scythopolis, 51
Medici, Cosimo de', 112
Medieval and patristic theories, 47–64, 65–86, 87–108
Meditations (Descartes), 154, 296
Meditations (Marcus Aurelius), 37
Megarics, 16
Meinong, Alexius, 238–39, 244
Meister Eckhart. *See* Johannes Eckhart, Meister
Melanchthon, Philip, 125–26
Memorabilia (Xenophon), 14
Mendemus of Eretria, 16
Mental and Moral Science, 188
Merleau-Ponty, Maurice, 306
Messner, Johannes, 273–74
Metaphysical Disputations, 122
Metaphysical Principles of Christian Morality, 166
Metaphysics (Aristotle), 24
Metaphysics (Lotze), 201
Metaphysics of Morals, 167
Metempsychosis, 11
Method in Ethical Theory, 277
Methods of Ethics, 188–89
Mexico, 216
Michael of Ephesius, 31
Microcosmus, 201
"Middle Stoicism," 35
Milhamot Adonai, 72
Mill, James, 183–84, 186
Mill, John Stuart, 124, 175, 182–89 *passim*, 250, 260
Mind (Stevenson), 287
Miscellanies (*Stromata*), 49
Mishneh Torah (the Code), 69, 70–71
Miskawaihi, Ahmed ibn-Muhammad-ibn Yaqub, 73, 76–77, 85
Modern Theory of Ethics, 265
Mohammed, Prophet, 73, 76
Monads, 161, 209
Montaigne, Michel de, 127–28
Montesquieu, Charles Louis de Secondat, baron de, 164–65
Moore, G. E., 189, 253, 263, 271, 277–85 *passim*, 289, 295
Moral Experience, 229
Moral Life and the Ethical Life, 276
Moral Life and Moral Worth, 243
Moral Man and Immoral Society, 300
Moral Obligation, 253
Moral Philosopher (Morgan), 144

Moral Philosophy (Maritain), 273
Moral Philosophy (Wolff), 164
Moral Philosophy of Antonio Rosmini, 217
Moral Philosophy of the Good-in-itself and the Useful Good, 62
Moral Philosophy in the Eighteenth Century, 206
Moral Philosophy of the Stoics, 129
Moral Point of View, 292
Moral Science, 209
Moral Values and the Idea of God, 243
Moralists (Shaftesbury), 140
Morality of Self-Interest, 275
More, Henry, 137–38
More, Thomas, 115, 117–18
Morgan, Thomas, 144
Morgenstern, O., 259
Moses, 48
Moslems (Islam; Mohammedans), 31, 43, 47, 65, 70, 73–86
Muirhead, J. H., 252
Munk, Solomon, 68
Musonius Rufus, 36
Mussolini, Benito, 230
Mutual Aid . . . , 265
Mystery of Being, 302
Mystical Theology, 51
Myth of Sisyphus, 306
Myth of the Twentieth Century, 234

Nabert, Jean, 303
Najat (*Salvation*), 77
Nasir ad-Din Tusi, 82–86
Nasirean Ethics, The, 82–86
Natural law, 29, 35, 71, 106 (*See also* Law); Aristotle on, 29; British ethical egoism, 133–36, 138; *jus naturale* as, 96–97; modern theories, 182–83, 184–85; rationalistic ethics (17th and 18th centuries), 151ff.; Suárez and, 123–24
Natural System of Practical Philosophy, 197
Naturalism, 263–78, 286, 302
Nature, History and God, 216
Nature and Destiny of Man, 300
Nature of Sympathy, 239
Naville, Pierre, 305
Nazism, 192, 232, 233–34
Nelson, Leonard, 196
Nemesius, Bishop, 52
Neoclassicism, 112–24, 127–30
Neoplatonism, 32, 40–44, 50, 51, 54
Neumann, J. von, 259
New Atlantis, 131
New Essays in Anthropology, 205
New Science, 219
New World of Industry and Society, 221
Newman, John Henry, 185
Nicholas of Cusa, 43, 112–14, 127
Nicomachean Ethics, 24–31, 47, 57, 61, 73, 80, 81, 85, 87–88, 91, 96, 106; Renaissance and, 119, 121; 13th-century commentaries on, 100
Nicomachus, 23, 24
Niebuhr, H. Richard, 300–1
Niebuhr, Reinhold, 300, 301

Nietzsche, Friedrich, 215, 297–98
Nifo, Agostino, 119
Nine Lectures . . . (Maritain), 273
Noemata, 137, 138
Non-Religion of the Future, 210
Notebooks (Leonardo), 111–12
Notes from the Underground, 298
Notion of Responsibility, 229
Notulae, 31
Nouveaux essais sur l'entendement humain, 162
Nouveaux mélanges philosophiques, 207
Nowell-Smith, P. H., 289–91

Observations on Man, 150
Obstacle and Value, 214, 215
Ockham (Ockhamism). See William of Ockham
Ogden, C. K., 287
Olivi, Peter John, 101–1
Olson, Robert G., 275–76
Omar Khayyam, 79–80
On Authority in Matters of Religion, 144
On the Basis of Morality, 200
On the Celestial Hierarchy, 51
On Cheerfulness, 12
On Divine Love, 114
On the Divine Names, 51
On Duty, 33
On the Ecclesiastical Hierarchy, 51
On Ecclesiastical Power, 100
On Eudaimonia, 30
On First Principles, 50
On Free Choice, 114
On the Function of the Clergy, 54
On the Good (Gioberti), 208
On the Good (Plato), 17
Oh Human Freedom, 198
On Human Nature, 33
On the Infinite, Universe and Worlds, 115
On Intelligence, 209
On Justice, 23
On the Knowledge of Good and Evil, 276–77
On the Knowledge of Self, 212
On Law and Justice, 289
On the Law of War, 120
On Laws, 122
On the Laws and Customs of England, 106
On Learned Ignorance, 113
On the Life and Moral Teachings of Epicurus, 129
On Living in Accord with Nature, 33
On Logical and Ethical Principles, 239
On Love, 88
On the Merits of the Laws of England, 106
On Moral Customs, 30–31
On Nature, 38
On the Nature of Man, 52
On the Nature of Things, 39, 129
On the Necessity of Loving God, 61–62
On Order, 56
On the Origin of Ethical Knowledge, 238
On the Origin of Evil, 141

On the Passions, 30
On the Peace of Faith, 113–14
On the Rights of War and Peace, 151
On Seeking and Causing Happiness, 76
On the Soul (John of La Rochelle), 94
On the Soul (Tertullian), 53
On the Spirit and the Letter, 56
On the Trinity, 54, 55
On Truth, 130
On the Union between the Intellect and Man, 80
On University Studies, 197–98
On Virtues and Vices, 24
On the Vision of God, 113
On Wisdom (Charron), 128
On Wisdom (Leibniz), 161
Opera Omnia, 121
Opposites, theory of, 11–12
Opus Majus (Greater Work), 93
Opus Postumum, 167
Or Adonai, 72
Oration on the Dignity of Man, 111, 114
Ordinatio (Duns Scotus), 103–4
Ordinatio (William of Ockham), 105
Origen, 50
Origin and Development of the Moral Ideas, 229
Origin of Species, 264
Ortega y Gasset, José, 303
Outline of a System of Utilitarian Ethics, 260–61
Outline of a Theory of the Emotions, 304
Outlines of a Critique of the Doctrine of Morals up to the Present, 192
Outlines of the Philosophy of Epicurus, 130
Oxford Collection of Moral Writings, 62
Oxford University, 286–92, 293

Paley, William, 182, 250
Panaetius of Rhodes, 35
Parerga and Paralipomena, 198, 200
Paris, University of, 87, 94, 99–100
Parker, DeWitt H., 246–47
Passions of the Soul, 154, 155, 156, 158
Passive Obedience, 146
Paton, H. J., 258
Patristic and medievel theories, 47–64, 65–86, 87–108
Paulsen, Friedrich, 201
Pecock, Reginald. See Reginald Pecock
Pepper, Stephen C., 271–72
Peripatetic school, 30
Perry, Ralph Barton, 237, 242, 245, 270, 287
Persaeus, 35
Peter Abelard, 53, 61, 63–64, 102, 206
Peter Lombard, 95, 96, 103, 105
Pfänder, Alexander, 299
Phänomenologie des Wollens, 299
Phaedo, 15, 17, 22, 42
Phaedrus, 19, 22, 42
Phenomenological ethics, 299–308
Phenomenology of Mind, 193–95
Phenomenology of Moral Experience, 306

Phenomenon of Man, 270–71
Philebus, 19
Philo Judaeus, 40, 66
Philosophia rationalis, 124
Philosophical Analysis, 286
Philosophical Commentaries, 145
Philosophical Dictionary, 144
Philosophical Ethics, 166
Philosophical Fragments, 302
Philosophical Inquiry into the Origin of Our Ideas, 181
Philosophical Investigations on the Essence of Human Freedom, 198
Philosophical Lectures, 184
Philosophical Papers, 286
Philosophical Proof of the Truth of the Christian Religion, 166
Philosophical Rudiments, 135
Philosophical Thoughts on the Sciences, 144–45
Philosophie des deutschen Idealismus, 24
Philosophie de la volonté, 306
Philosophie de l'esprit, 212–13
Philosophumena, 49
Philosophy of the Active and Moral Powers of Man, 181
Philosophy of Freedom, 207
Philosophy of G. E. Moore, 282
Philosophy of History, 193, 195–96, 23
Philosophy and Logical Syntax, 285
Philosophy of Loyalty, 254, 255
Philosophy of the Person, 216
Philosophy of the Practical, 230
Philosophy of Right, 193, 194, 196, 22
Philosophy of Value, 248
Physico-Theology, 144
Pico della Mirandola, Giovanni, 111, 114, 15
Pindar, 14
Plato (Platonic ethics; Platonism), 13–15, 17–23, 35, 41, 42, 49, 57, 62, 6, 256; Aristotle and, 24, 27, 89–90; Cambridge, 116–19, 136–43; in England, 116–19, 136–43; Freud and, 26, and ideal forms, 89; in Italy, 112–16, Maimonides and, 70; Moslems and, 74, 76, 84
Platonic Theology, 114
Plotinus, 40, 41–44, 50, 51, 54, 114
Plutarch, 12
Plutarch of Chaeronea, 40, 41
Polin, Raymond, 248
Political Treatise, 157, 160
Politics (Aristotle), 24, 86, 119
Polus, 136
Pomponazzi, Pietro, 119–20
Pope, Alexander, 144
Porphyry, 11, 41, 73
Portugal, 120
Poseidonius, 35, 52
Practical Philosophy, 196–97
Price, Richard, 149, 250
Prichard, H. A., 253, 306
Primary Science (Protologia), 208
Prince, The, 127

Principes de la nature et de la Grâce, 163
Principia Ethica, 280–81, 282
Principia Mathematica, 269, 279, 283
Principien der Ethik im historischer Entwicklung, 196
Principle of Individuality and Value, 252
Principle of Morality, 207
Principles of Ethics, 264
Principles of Human Knowledge, 145
Principles of Moral and Political Philosophy, 182
Principles of Morals, 184
Principles of Philosophy, 154, 157
Prize Essays, 198
Problem of Conduct, 252
Problems concerning Providence, 44
Problems of Ethics, 245–46
Proclus, 32, 44, 51
Prolegomena to Ethics, 250–51
Protagoras, 13, 17, 136
Protagoras, 13, 18
Protestants and Protestantism, 153, 160, 164; reform ethics, 125–30
Protrepticus, 23
Providence and Fate, 44
Proverbs, Book of, 66
Province of Jurisprudence Determined, 184
Przywara, Erich, 185
Pseudo-Alexander of Aphrodiasis, 31
Pseudo-Dionysius, 51
Pseudo-Heliodorus, 31
Psychology of Character, 247
Psychology from the Empirical Standpoint, 238
Pufendorf, Samuel von, 126, 152, 153–54
Purity of Heart Is to Will One Thing, 296
Pyrrho, 128
Pythagoras (of Samos) and the Pythagoreans, 11–12, 30

Quest for Certainty, 268

Ramirez, J. M., 273
Ramón Lull, 101–2
Rashdall, Hasting, 252
Rational Man . . . , 258
Rationalism (rationality; reason), 12, 33–35, 37, 40, 50; British ethics and, 136ff.; existential ethics and, 303; Judaic, 67–68, 69, 71; middle ages, 90–108; Moslem, 74; right reason theories, 87ff., 103–8ff., 137ff., 152ff.; 17th and 18th century European, 151–71; spiritistic ethics and, 204ff.
Rauh, Frédéric, 229
Rawls, John, 293
Razi, Mohammed ibn-Zakariya, al-, 74
Reason. *See* Rationalism (rationality; reason)
Reason and Goodness, 258
Reason and Religion, 213
Rebel: an Essay on Man in Revolt, The, 306
Reconstruction in Philosophy, 268

Reflections on the Common Concept of Justice, 162
Reflections on the Revolution in France, 184
Reformation (Protestant) ethics, 125–30
Reginald Pecock, 107
Reid, Thomas, 180–81, 207
Relations between the Physical and the Moral in Man, 205
Religio Medici, 135
Religion of the Gentiles, 130
Religion of Nature Delineated, 143–44
Religion and Science, 283
Religious Aspect of Philosophy 254
Renaissance ethics, 111–30; Aristotelianism, 119–24; neoclassicism, 127–28; Platonism, 111–19
Renan, Ernest, 209
Renouvier, Charles, 209
Reportatio, 105
Republic, 14, 17, 18–22 49, 74, 84, 117, 118
Review of the Principal Questions in Morals, 179–80
Rewards of the Soul, 72
Rhetoric (Aristotle), 24
Rice, Philip Blair, 276–77
Richards, I. A., 287
Rickert, Heinrich, 244
Ricoeur, Paul, 306
Right and the Good, 253
Right reason theories, 87ff., 103–8ff., 137ff., 152ff.
Rintelen, Fritz von, 247
Risalat, 78–79
Robert Grosseteste, 31, 87, 91–92
Robinson, John A., 301
Roger Bacon, 92–95
Roman Catholicism. *See* Catholics and Catholicism
Romanell, Patrick, 277
Romans, ethical theories of, 33, 35–39, 43, 44
Romans, Epistle to the, 48
Romero, Francisco, 216
Rosenberg, Alfred, 234
Rosmini, Antonio, 207–8
Ross, Alexander, 135
Ross, Alf, 289
Ross, W. D., 31, 253, 290, 306
Rousseau, Jean Jacques, 165–66, 169
Royce, Josiah, 254–55, 256
Rubáiyat, 79
Rüdiger, Johann Andreas, 166–67
Rules for the Direction of the Mind, 154
Rules of a Christian Lyfe, 115
Russell, Bertrand, 269, 275–76, 279, 282–83
Russia. *See* U.S.S.R.

Saadia ben Joseph al-Fayyumi, 67–68, 69
Sade, Marquis de, 220
Saint Genet, 304
Saint-Simon, Count Claude Henri de, 221
Salter, W. M., 254

Sanchez, Franciscus, 128
Sane Society, 275
Santayana, George, 255–56
Sartre, Jean-Paul, 302, 304–5, 306
Scheler, Max, 239–41, 242, 243, 247, 295, 299, 306
Schelling, Friedrich W. J. von, 193, 197–98, 254
Schleiermacher, Friedrich, 192
Schlick, Moritz, 245–46, 283, 285, 288
Scholasticism, 58, 59, 77, 99, 112, 119 (*See also* specific individuals); Catholic, 120–24; Protestants and, 120–24; 17th and 18th century rationalism and, 152–53
Schopenhauer, Arthur, 198–200, 254
Schweitzer, Albert, 257
Sciacca, M. F., 208, 217
Science and Wisdom, 272
Scienza Nuova, 230
Scotland, 180, 181, 206
Scotus Erigena, 43
Search for Truth, 204
Second Thoughts in Moral Philosophy, 286
Sécrétan, Charles, 207
Sefer ha-ikkarim, 72–73
Sefer ha-Kuzari, 68
Self-Realization, 257
Self-realization ethics, 249ff.
Seneca, 12, 59, 93, 132; and stoic ethics, 33, 36, 129, 155, 163
Sens et non-sens, 306
Sentences (Peter Lombard), 95, 96, 103, 105
Sermon on the Mount, 48
Sermons (Joseph Butler), 146
Sextus Empiricus, 13–14
Shaftesbury, Anthony Ashley Cooper, Lord, 140–41, 142, 144, 145, 250
Shestov (or Chestov), Léon, 227
Shifa (*Book of Healing*), 77
Short Treatise, 157
Sickness unto Death, 296
Sidgwick, Henry, 175, 176–77, 188–89, 271
Siger de Brabant, 31, 100
Simmel, Georg, 303
Singer, Marcus G., 261
"Situation ethics," 301
Skepticism, 127–28
Sketch of a Historical Table on the Progress of the Human Mind, 220–21
Sketch of Morality . . . , 210
Smart, J. J. C., 260–61
Smith, Adam, 180
Sobre la essencia, 216–17
Social Contract, 165–66
Societal ethics in Europe, 218–34
Society of Jesus, 120–24
Sociology, 222–23, 228
Socrates, 13, 14–18, 21
Soloviev, Vladimir, 227
Some Dilemmas of Naturalism, 276
Somnium Scipionis, 43
Sophists, 13–14, 17
Sorley, William R., 243

Soul, 17, 19, 22, 50, 94; in Aristotle, 25, 26; in Augustine, 55–56; in modern theory, 196–97; in Moslem ethics, 76, 77; in Neoplatonism, 40–44, 51–52; in Renaissance, 114; in St. Anselm, 60; in spiritistic ethics, 205, 206
Source of Knowledge, 51–52
Sources of Value, 271–72
Spain, 120, 122, 152; existential ethics, 302; spiritistic ethics, 203, 215
Sparshott, F. E., 293
Spencer, Herbert, 250, 264
Spenser, Edmund, 118–19
Sphaerus, 35
Spiegelberg, Herbert, 299
Spinoza, Benedict de, 115, 143, 157–60, 162–63, 249
Spirit of Christianity, 193
Spirit of the Laws, 164
Spiritistic ethics, 203–17
Stace, Walter T., 257–58
Stalin, Joseph, 226
Stapleden, Olaf, 265
Statesman, 19
Stevenson, Charles L., 282, 286–88
Stewart, Dugald, 180, 181
Stilpo, 16
Stirner, Max, 200–1
Stoicism, 16–17, 32–39, 41, 42, 63 (*See also* specific individuals); neo-stoicism, 129–30; rational view, 90–91; Renaissance, 129–30; 17th and 18th century, 163
Strauss, David F., 196
Strawson, Peter F., 292
Studies of Good and Evil, 254
Suárez, Francis, 93, 121–24, 217
Subjectivist (intuitionist) ethics, 175–89, 285, 289, 290
Subsistence of Evil, 44
Subyektivizm i individualizm, 228
Summa de creaturis, 96
Summa Fratris Alexandri, 94
Summa Theologiae, 96
Switzerland, 207
Symposium, 18, 22, 42
Synderesis, defined, 91, 96
Syrian ethical scholars, 73
System of Ethics, (Fichte), 190
System of Ethics (Hegel), 193
System of Ethics (Keckermann), 126
System of Logic, 186
System of Moral Philosophy, 147, 149
System of Value Theory, 239
Systematic Theology, 299–300

Tahafut al-Falasifa, 78
Tahdhib al-Akhlaq (*Correction of the Dispositions*), 73, 76, 77, 85
Taine, Hippolyte, 209
Taylor, A. E., 252–53
Teachings of the Moral Philosophers, 62
Teilhard de Chardin, Pierre, 270–71
Teleological eudaimonism, 23–31
Tempier, Etienne, Bishop of Paris, 81, 88, 100

en Commandments, 48, 50, 65–67
eodoro Gaza, 112
ertullian, 53
hat Nothing Is Known, 128
heaetetus, 42
heodorus the Atheist, 17
heological-Political Treatise (Spinoza), 157, 160
heophrastus, 30
heories of Ethics, 247
heory of Games . . . , 259
heory of Good and Evil, 252
heory of the Moral Life, 268
heory of Moral Sentiments, 180
heory of Objects, 238–39
heory of Valuation, 237, 269
homas Aquinas (and Thomism), 31, 52, 87, 90, 94–95, 96, 97–99, 102, 106–7; Maritain and, 272, 273; modern theories and, 181, 203; Renaissance ethics and, 120, 121, 122, 124; 17th and 18th century rationalism and, 152, 164
homasius, Christian, 153–54, 164
hought and Action, 292
hrasymachus of Chalcedon, 14, 162
hree Truths, 128
hus Spake Zarathustra, 297
llich, Paul, 299–300
obit, Book of, 66
oulmin, Stephen E., 293
oward a Critical Naturalism, 277
oward a Genealogy of Morals, 297
ractatus Logico-Philosophicus, 283–84
ractus de natura boni, 96
ragic Sense of Life, 303
raité de l'existence morale, 302
raité des premières vérités, 180
raité des sensations, 145
reatise concerning Eternal and Immutable Morality, 136–37
reatise on Free Choice, 125
reatise on General Morality, 214
reatise on Human Nature, 176–79
reatise of the Laws of Nature, 176
reatise on the Love of God, 204
reatise on Morality, 204
reatise on the Virtues, 213
rue, the Beautiful, and the Good, The, 206
rue Intellectual System of the Universe, 136
rue Morality and Its Counterfeits, 248
rue System, 220
ucker, Abraham, 150
ufts, J. H., 267
wain, Mark, 308
wo Basic Problems of Ethics, 18
wo Books of Constancy, 129
wo Sources of Morality and Religion, 211–12, 271
wo Treatises of Civil Government, 139
ypes of Ethical Theory, 185, 249
yrrell, Sir James, 135–36

Unamuno, Miguel de, 303
United States: analytic ethics, 286–88, 289, 292, 293; Deism, 145; existential ethics, 300–1, 306–7; modern theories, 181, 203; naturalistic ethics, 264, 271, 276; personalism, 203; self-realization ethics, 254–58; societal ethics, 222; value ethics, 243–44, 246–48
Universal Practical Philosophy, 163–64
Urban, Wilbur M., 237, 244–45
U.S.S.R., 226–28
Urmson, James O., 286
Utilitarianism, 175–89, 249–63, 286
Utilitarianism (Mill), 186, 187–88
Utopia (More), 117–18

Valla, Laurentius, 114, 128
Value and Destiny of the Individual, 252
Value and Meaning of Life, 201
Values (value ethics), axiology as study of, 237–48
Vanini, Lucilio, 120
Varro, M. Terentius, 36
Vasconcelos, José, 216
Vásquez, Gabriel, 123, 152
Veatch, Henry B., 31, 258
Vico, Giambattista, 219, 221, 230
Virgil, 132
Vivas, Eliseo, 276, 277
Vitoria, Francisco de, 120
Vocation of Man, 190
Voice of Reason, 220
Voltaire (François Marie Arouet), 144

Wagner, Eva, 233
Waismann, Friedrich, 285
Ward, Leo R., 248
Warnock, Mary, 288
Wealth of Nations, 180
Weigel, Erhard, 126, 153
Weigel, Valentine, 126–27
Werkmaister, William H., 247
Westermarck, Edward, 229, 232
Whately, Richard, 185
Whitehead, Alfred North, 269–70, 279
Wieman, Henry Nelson, 270
Will to Power, 297
William of Conches, 62
William of Moerbeke, 44
William of Ockham, 84, 122, 123, 136, 153
Windelband, Wilhelm, 244
Wisdom, John, 283
Witherspoon, John, 181
Wittgenstein, Ludwig, 283–85
Wolff, Christian von, 163–64, 166, 167
Wollaston, William, 143–44
World and the Individual, 254
World as Will and Idea, 198–99
Wright, Henry W., 257
Wundt, Wilhelm, 201

Xenophon, 14

Yahweh, 65, 66
Yahya ibn-Adi, 73

Zabarella, Giacomo, 119
Zaraguëta, Juan, 216
Zeno the Stoic, 16, 33, 35, 132

Zeus, 34
Zimara, Marcantonio, 119
Zubiri, Xavier, 216–17

4/15 DATE DUE